Maritime Decarbonization

Mikael Lind • Wolfgang Lehmacher •
Robert Ward
Editors

Maritime Decarbonization

Practical Tools, Case Studies and Decarbonization Enablers

Springer

Editors
Mikael Lind
Research Institutes of Sweden (RISE)
Chalmers University of Technology
Gothenburg, Sweden

Wolfgang Lehmacher
Independent Supply Chain Expert
Hong Kong, China

Robert Ward
Pymble, NSW, Australia

ISBN 978-3-031-39935-0 ISBN 978-3-031-39936-7 (eBook)
https://doi.org/10.1007/978-3-031-39936-7

This Springer imprint is published by the registered company Springer Nature Switzerland AG
The registered company address is: Gewerbestrasse 11, 6330 Cham, Switzerland

Paper in this product is recyclable.

"This book is an important step in implementing maritime decarbonization at scale. The book explains clear methods and principles on how to tackle the task ahead, together with providing a number of useful case studies, allowing the reader to see how methods and concepts are being brought to life. An informative must-read for those confronting the decarbonization of the maritime sector."
—Bo Cerup-Simonsen, *CEO, Mærsk Mc-Kinney Møller Center for Zero Carbon Shipping*

"The decarbonization of the global maritime transport system needs to proceed with urgency while being mindful of its importance to the global economy. This requires a holistic approach that addresses the challenges from many different angles, based on collaboration and learning from each other. This book—Maritime Decarbonization—provides an impressive foundation of perspectives and viewpoints to move the mission forward."
—Kirsi Tikka, *Board Director*

"Today, this book has inspired me with the knowledge that the era of decarbonization—zero-emissions in the global maritime sector—is not far away, and a country or enterprise leading the journey will have disruptive competitive edge. The world will finally enter into an era of zero-emission through evolving technologies. Whether you're a maritime administrator, entrepreneur, researcher, or about to start to learn about decarbonization, you must read this reference book on supply chain decarbonization."
—Sunbae Hong, *Director, Ministry of Ocean and Fishery, South Korea*

Foreword

The publication of this book on Maritime Decarbonization comes at a time when the maritime industry is at the beginning of one of its most significant transitions in history. The energy which currently powers the maritime industry is based on fossil hydrocarbons derived from oil and gas deposits, whose use is associated with approximately 3% of global anthropogenic greenhouse gas emissions.

The climate impact from shipping is caused by a number of different greenhouse gases (GHG), of which carbon dioxide, methane and nitrous oxide are the most prominent, but also from aerosols, most prominently the emission of black carbon soot, which can affect the Earth's albedo, in particular on the earth's remaining glaciers. The most durable climate effect comes from the carbon dioxide emissions, which are very much representative of the long-term climate impact from fossil fuels, and have helped to coin the term Maritime Decarbonization.

The continued use of fossil fuels, starting with coal and continuing with Liquefied Natural Gas (LNG), Liquefied Petroleum Gas (LPG) and fossil methanol in the maritime sector, is incompatible with keeping the climate of this planet within the targets agreed by the Paris Agreement, and the strategy of the International Maritime Organization (IMO) regulating them. Regulations for reducing GHG emissions in terms of technical and operational measures are already in place and in their combination with the Initial IMO GHG Strategy and 2023 IMO GHG Strategy, mean that the maritime industry is expecting drastic GHG reductions towards net-zero emissions in the decades ahead.

The awareness of this imminent change is absolutely unprecedented, and stakeholders in the industry are thus asking themselves how best to approach this monumental challenge of reorganising the energy supply of the maritime industry. In many cases the questions are extremely complex, straddling on the topics of environment, society and economics, and they include an enormous amount of technological complexity, which inherently lines the pathways that decision makers need to consider and from which they define the optimum decarbonization strategies for the future. Sometimes solutions are opposing in their nature, with digitalisation and artificial intelligence providing the potential for optimisation and energy savings, but at the same time also starting to develop into a significant energy consumer in their own right, with computing power emerging as a major energy consumer.

The solutions thus need to take a holistic perspective and analyse the implications in depth. This is why this book with expert analysis and commentary from numerous maritime experts is of dire need, and comes at exactly the right time. Its contribution is a step-by-step recipe to finding solutions to the question of how to approach decarbonization. The book defines four steps to decarbonization: Scenario thinking, Adopting a value chain focus, Identifying the key enablers, and Collaborative partnerships. Part I of the book defines the potential scope and current status in decarbonization, to set the scene, while Part II introduces the concept of the four-steps to decarbonization to the reader, which is illustrated and fleshed-out in Part III. Part IV identifies and discusses the critical success factors, while Part V provides case studies to demonstrate how this may be implemented. The conclusions leave no doubt that successful Maritime Decarbonization requires the combination of an ambitious target and a timely response.

This book is a must for anyone looking for a practical and holistic approach to embarking on the journey of maritime decarbonization.

World Maritime University, Malmö, Sweden

Cleopatra Doumbia-Henry

Preface

> We will move to a low- carbon world because nature will force us, or because policy will guide us. If we wait until nature forces us, the cost will be astronomical. Christiana Figueres, former Executive Secretary of the UN Framework Convention on Climate Change (UNFCCC)

Whether guided by policy or forced by nature, the maritime industry is under pressure to become a more sustainable sector through decarbonization. Decarbonization is an effort that transcends beyond a single actor and even the industry itself as achieving the Paris climate agreement goals and the International Maritime Organization (IMO) ambitions to decarbonize the maritime industry requires activating enablers across clusters of interdependent value chains in a coordinated way. While this seems to be complex there are some very focused measures actors can launch now. Assisting people to act now is a core goal of this book. The book, created with the help of 73 contributors, aims at helping stakeholders in the maritime ecosystem to make aligned decisions that support and accelerate the decarbonization effort and make the maritime industry a valuable contributor to a zero greenhouse gas (GHG) emission economy and society.

The aim of this book on Maritime Decarbonization is to inform as a way of encouraging the necessary productive discourse on decarbonization in the sector. Achieving zero-carbon in shipping requires the involvement of a broad range of actors and stakeholders including marine fuel and technology providers, ship and engine manufacturers, asset owners and operators, ports, shipowners, charterers and shipping lines, and also policymakers, governmental and non-governmental organisations (NGO) and international organisations (IO). Last, but not least, are the beneficial cargo owners (BCO)—those that buy the services delivered by the maritime transport system. The BCOs are increasingly signalling and exerting demand for sustainable shipping products and practices. Shipping is global with a range of business models that will require different solutions to decarbonize. These solutions are fleshed out in this book.

This edition of Maritime Decarbonization is grounded in the work initiated by the Finnish think tank Nordic West Office in 2022. The initiative resulted in the Practical

Playbook for Maritime Decarbonisation.[1] At the time, 20 stakeholders of a *Coalition of the Willing*, kicked off the process by defining three maritime transition scenarios. Later in the process, the interrelated value chain concept emerged within which 37 decarbonization enablers were posited. The experts concluded that there is no 'silver bullet' in maritime decarbonization and that collaboration is key to achieving set ambitions. Also, the ambitions agreed for today will not suffice, and intermediate targets are needed to ensure a more systematic and incremental process. The Nordic West Office initiative inspired us and created the momentum that resulted in continuous work on decarbonization and this book. Many that participated in the Nordic West Office work have also contributed to this book. We are also grateful to Kirsi Tikka, Board Member Ardmore Shipping, Pacific Basin Shipping, Foreship, and Jan Hoffmann, UNCTAD who have reviewed the book and provided valuable input and feedback.

As decarbonization concerns us all, the target audience for this book is broad. We are writing for everyone interested in the topic of decarbonization. The book should particularly help decisionmakers and project managers that are or will face decarbonization demands, inquiries and challenges. Also, policymakers and consumers can benefit from this book. In fact, anyone that wishes to obtain or extend their knowledge on how to decarbonize a difficult sector like shipping. We even think that this book can inspire people involved in decarbonization in other industries, sectors, and fields. We wish everyone an enjoyable and insightful read of this collection of essays.

[1] Lehmacher W., Lind M. (2022) Practical Playbook for Maritime Decarbonisation—Value chain-based pathways towards zero-emission shipping, Nordic West Office (nordicwestoffice.com/maritime)

Sandra Haraldson, RISE

Gothenburg, Sweden
Hong Kong, China
Pymble, NSW, Australia

Mikael Lind
Wolfgang Lehmacher
Robert Ward

About This Book

Baseline and Perspectives

The last 50 years of globalisation have more than tripled seaborne trade, and the movement of goods is about 70% of all shipping. This rise is due to China's emergence as the world's manufacturing hub and the increase in supply chain independency. The global tonnages of container ships increased about five-fold during the period (Smil, 2022). Globalisation has more than doubled CO_2 emissions during the last five decades, from 14.9 billion metric tons in 1970 to 34.81 billion in 2020.[2] Two major frameworks for reducing these emissions are discussed in chapter "Broadening the Scope of Decarbonization in the Maritime Sector" (McKinnon, 2023), namely Avoid-Shift-Improve (ASI) and Activity-Shift-Intensity-Fuel (ASIF). By advocating reducing the demand for transport, shifting to lower carbon transport modes, and improving energy efficiency, they reinforce the focus on raising capital productivity, which should be the ultimate goal of all businesses (Watson, 2020). Because shipping is the most energy-efficient form of transportation, it dominates the movement of goods and accounts for about 3% of global emissions. Consequently, the shipping industry is a significant target for decarbonization, and the multiple current policy options are explicitly identified in chapter. "Decarbonizing the Maritime Industry: Current Environmental Targets and Potential Outcomes" (Raza & Singh, 2023). Future policies must be based on evaluating the current status, and chapter "The Extent of Decarbonization in the Global Shipping Fleet" (Pålsson & Rydbergh, 2023) analyses data from various authoritative sources to estimate the penetration rate of decarbonization oriented innovations.

[2] https://www.statista.com/statistics/264699/worldwide-co2-emissions/

A Step-by-Step Concept for Decarbonizing Shipping

Decarbonizing shipping is a massive global endeavour that requires the successful completion of many large projects by all the major stakeholders. However, most large projects fail (Flyvbjerg & Gardner, 2023), and the world and the shipping industry cannot afford such costly failures both from environmental and capital productivity perspectives. The probability of success can be increased by iterative planning and learning before scaling up for implementation. Consequently, a four-step approach is advocated in chapter "Four Steps to Decarbonization", namely: scenario analysis, value chain mapping, enabler prioritisation, and partnership selection (Lind et al., 2023a–c). Subsequent chapters elaborate on these phases. Extensive exploration and simulation of alternatives can reduce the risk of failure and raise the likelihood of finishing on time and on budget (Flyvbjerg & Gardner, 2023). As explained in chapter "Scenario Thinking and Its Place in Maritime Decarbonization", scenarios are a handy planning tool for identifying critical uncertainties and establishing priorities (Bentham, 2023b). There is a need to investigate deeply the implications for supply chains as they are the vital links of global trade and shipping operations, as the Covid-19 pandemic convincingly demonstrated. Chapter "Adopting a Value Chain Focus to Tackle Decarbonization" (Petersen & Renken, 2023) deals with the interdependencies between marine fuel supply, shipbuilding, and maritime operational value chains, requiring a successful co-evolution of decarbonization actions. This chain-wide coordination requires applying the decarbonization enablers to facilitate the transition, as outlined in chapter "Identifying the Key Decarbonization Enablers" (Tikka & Esau, 2023b). Chapter "Decarbonizing International Shipping Through Collaborative Partnerships" concludes the second section with a report on the three leading solutions to decarbonization: markets, operational and technological measures, and alternative fuels (Kuttan, 2023).

Bringing the Four Step-Concept to Life

'The devil is in the details' is an oft quoted saying. Completed specifications are essential to handling the devilish task of completing a large technology project on time, on budget, and fulfilling all requirements. Business process modelling (BPM) (Recker et al., 2009) can generate the level of detail necessary to thwart Lucifer. Ideally, these models should be shared across the shipping sector so that the evolvement of effective practices accelerates decarbonization by giving life to the four steps. The collaboration and digitalisation for economic and societal capital creation (cdes) model is another tool for planning the transition. Rather than the decomposition approach of BPM, chapter "How to Get Started: CDES—A New Paradigm for Tackling Decarbonization Projects" (Lind & Lehmacher, 2023) promotes a systems perspective. It argues that decarbonization requires two major inputs, collaboration and digitalization, to produce dual economic and social capital outputs. Chapter "Scenario Thinking: To Build Business Advantages That Accelerate Decarbonization" (Bentham, 2023a) extends the discussion of holistic thinking to discuss its technical and social dimensions by addressing insight generating and executive action. Every value chain consists of various independent actors from different industries, and chapter "How a Value Chain Approach Plays out in Maritime Decarbonization" (Renken & Petersen, 2023) emphasises the four-step process in terms of supply-chain interdependencies. Decarbonization enablers are phase dependent, and their usefulness for a step varies with their maturity, availability, and greenhouse gas (GHG) reduction potential, as explained in chapter "How to Assess Decarbonization Enablers" (Tikka & Esau, 2023a). Partnerships are the glue of a self-organizing ecosystem of which the maritime sector is arguably the leading exemplar (Watson et al., 2020). Thus, mass decarbonization is dependent on many effective partnerships across the industry. Chapter "Effective Partnerships to Support Maritime Decarbonization" (Lind et al., 2023a–c) provides advice on collaborating and aligning actions to create a state change in the maritime sector through decarbonization. Achieving such a transition is challenging as it requires significant reinvention of the ecosystem.

Some Critical Success Factors for Fast and Global Decarbonization

Critical success factors (CSFs) are the three to five essential goals that a project or organisation must achieve to claim success (Rockart, 1982). These factors must be surfaced and agreed upon at the start of a project. Progress towards them must be evaluated continually to ensure ultimate success. A CSF for today's world is knowledge capital, a symbiotic relationship between human and organisational capital (Safadi & Watson, 2023). Humans use software and data (organisational capital) to plan voyages, operate ships, and handle cargo. Without appropriately skilled human capital, there is no shipping industry. This human capital must be reskilled and equipped with new software to operate and manage a decarbonized industry. Chapter "Ensuring Seafarers Are at the Heart of Decarbonization Action" (Platten et al., 2023) explains how seafarers are a CSF in the decarbonization transition. Regulations (organisational capital) are a CSF for the maritime industry because they ensure the playing field is level. For example, fuel mandates ensure some shippers do not gain a cost advantage by using dirty fossil fuels. The importance of such global mandates is covered in chapter "Securing Global Alignment in Regulations Related to Decarbonization" (Tikka & Esau, 2023c). Transaction cost economics (Williamson, 1979) conceives an organisation as a nexus of contracts. Chapter "Decarbonize Shipping or Decarbonize International Maritime Trade: The Present Contractual Framework and the Need for a New Contractual Architecture" (Zografakis et al., 2023) applies this perspective in highlighting the complexity of contracts in international maritime trade, which is exacerbated by its self-organising nature and the multiplicity of regulating authorities. Innovation is a CSF for most countries and organisations. A robust nationally funded basic research program creates seed ideas for commercialisation through applied science. Both forms of research will be required to make the decarbonization state change, as argued in chapter “Engaging the Global Research Communities in Maritime Decarbonization” (Manderbacka & Forsström, 2023). Building circular economies is a global CSF for sustainability advocated in chapter “The Implications of Circular Supply Chains and the EU Digital Product Passport in Maritime Decarbonization” (Jensen et al., 2023). Decarbonization has stimulated thinking about how to reduce the excesses of the current global economy by designing products and services for maximum reuse and minimal waste. Financing the circular economy is one of several state changes requiring additional funding because they need new equipment and training investment. Existing ships that cannot meet the latest environmental standards will decline in value rapidly to become stranded assets. Chapter “Sustainable Finance in the Maritime Sector” (Biermans et al., 2023) details the risks and financial costs facing the shipping industry.

Case Studies: Selected Maritime Decarbonization Initiatives

Leaders frequently learn vicariously by studying the experience of others with similar problems or projects (Bandura, 1977). Case studies are an established method of transferring knowledge between those with firsthand experience and those about to experience a similar challenge. This section has five case studies that can illuminate the path to success. Chapter “Actions Being Taken by Key Segments to Meet the Decarbonization Targets” (Kosmala, 2023) reports on actions taken by essential ecosystem actors. It particularly emphasises the need for an integrated range of initiatives. It is a sectorial change to green shipping and more than adopting green ships. Chapter “Maritime Decarbonization: Actions by Cargo Owners—The Shippers’ Perspective” (Evans & Macnab, 2023) documents cases undertaken with the support of members of F&L, the European Freight and Logistics Leaders’ Forum. It reports that effective collaboration has enabled cargo owners to be key change agents by driving ocean carriers to adopt sustainable logistic practices. Chapter “Practical Decarbonization Action Being Taken by the Shipping Companies” (Manderbacka & Tapaninen, 2023) switches attention from cargo owners to ship owners and charterers. It reports applicable knowledge gleaned from the experiences of early movers in this stakeholder group. Managers need data to make informed decisions, and a Carbon Emissions Index (CEI), as detailed in chapter “Identifying the Best Low-Emission Carriers” (Sand et al., 2023) can guide cargo owners and shippers in selecting low-emission service providers. A detailed case study of the UK’s Port of Plymouth in chapter “Actions by Ports to Support Green Maritime Operations: A Real Case Study—The Port of Plymouth, UK” (Karamperidis et al., 2023) documents five key lessons worthy of consideration by port managers. As major energy consumers and suppliers, ports must re-orient their energy supply around renewably generated electricity. The need to envision their new roles as energy hubs and transport nodes is comprehensively covered in chapter "Towards Ports as Energy Nodes: Strengthening Micro Energy Systems" (Lind et al., 2023a–c). Ports and shipyards are often near cities and thus contribute to urban emissions. As a critical player in the shipping ecosystem, they must not be ignored, and chapter "Decarbonization in Shipyard Cities: A Holistic Approach to Sustainability Assessment" (Vakili, 2023) broadly assesses sustainability with respect to shipyards. Shifting to new fuels, such as hydrogen, requires a coordinated effort by marine engineering, bunkering, and green fuel production. Chapter "Ship Engine, Equipment and Fuel Options for Decarbonization" (Natali & Rego, 2023) details the interdependencies for this set of interrelated R&D challenges. Chapter "Decarbonization Action by Energy Companies" (Esau & Bentham, 2023) reports the three essential lessons distilled from the experiences of two first movers in LNG (liquified natural gas) bunkering. Information systems are critical to efficient operations and essential support tools for changing a sustainable shipping state. Chapter "Decarbonization Support from Digital Solutions Providers" (Pakkanen & Vettor, 2023) reports on some digital tools and metrics for supporting this vital shift. A case for biofuels as an alternative to fossil fuels is developed in chapter "The In-House Production of Biofuel by Shipping Companies: A Case Study" (Hytti et al., 2023). It discusses the issues associated with their adoption by a Finnish shipping company. Sustainability requires a shift from burning fossil fuels to electricity generation technology, such as wind turbines and solar panels. A reliable supply of biofuels will be essential for their adoption. Chapter "Establishing Green Corridors to Accelerate the Use of Alternative Fuels" (Svendsen et al., 2023) introduces the notion of green shipping corridors that ensure shippers operating exclusively in these passageways have a dependable supply of alternative fuels. Chapter "The Getting to Zero Coalition Story" (Asmussen et al., 2023) reports shipping's decarbonization voyage since 2016, when the risks associated with a lack of industry leadership were recognised at a Danish Maritime Forum. The resulting Getting to Zero Coalition saw the need for combining collaborative leadership and systems thinking if the shipping industry were to attain carbon neutrality on its terms.

Concluding Remarks: Calling for a Holistic and Inclusive Approach

Systems thinking (Checkland, 1981; Churchman, 1968; Forrester, 1961) is arguably the most crucial skill for today's leaders. Decision-makers operate in a world of systems within systems within systems. Systems interact continually as the capital creation system evolves, and all systems must co-evolve to persist. Major state changes, such as transitioning to a sustainable society, perturb many systems.

Thus, it is appropriate that this book concludes with a high-level view of the voyage ahead. Chapter "Highlights of the Book: A Menu of Possible Actions for Decarbonization Today and Tomorrow" (Lehmacher et al., 2023a, b) lists recommendations and identifies numerous system-thinking actions that shipping executives should practice to participate in changing the state of the world to zero carbon emissions. An optimistic rallying cry, chapter "The Destination: A Vision of a Climate Neutral Future", for a climate neutral maritime sector concludes the book (Lehmacher et al., 2023a, b). It identifies the actions and attitudes necessary to achieve this ambitious and essential goal. The shipping industry's equivalent of a Manhattan project[3] is a major global challenge. Fittingly, the final chapter identifies the many obstacles this Odyssean voyage must overcome and contains the positive note that a zero GHG emissions maritime industry can be achieved.

Melbourne, Australia Richard T. Watson

References

Asmussen, M., Krantz, R., & Sidenvall Jegou, I. (2023). The getting to zero coalition story. In M. Lind, W. Lehmacher, & R. Ward (Eds.), *Maritime decarbonization – Practical Tools, Case Studies and Decarbonization Enablers*. Springer.

Bandura, A. (1977). *Social learning theory*. Prentice Hall.

Bentham, J. B. (2023a). Scenario thinking – To build business advantages that accelerate decarbonization. In M. Lind, W. Lehmacher, & R. Ward (Eds.), *Maritime decarbonization – Practical Tools, Case Studies and Decarbonization Enablers*. Springer.

Bentham, J. B. (2023b). Scenario thinking and its place in maritime decarbonization. In M. Lind, W. Lehmacher, & R. Ward (Eds.), *Maritime decarbonization – Practical Tools, Case Studies and Decarbonization Enablers*. Springer.

Biermans, M. L., Bulthuis, W., Holl, T., & van Overbeeke, B. (2023). Sustainable finance in the maritime sector. In M. Lind, W. Lehmacher, & R. Ward (Eds.), *Maritime decarbonization – Practical Tools, Case Studies and Decarbonization Enablers*. Springer.

Checkland, P. (1981). *Systems thinking, systems practice*. Wiley.

Churchman, C. W. (1968). *The systems approach*. Dell.

Esau, S., & Bentham, J. B. (2023). Decarbonization action by energy companies. In M. Lind, W. Lehmacher, & R. Ward (Eds.), *Maritime decarbonization – Practical Tools, Case Studies and Decarbonization Enablers*. Springer.

Evans, P., & Macnab, A. (2023). Maritime decarbonization – Actions by cargo owners – The shippers' perspective. In M. Lind, W. Lehmacher, & R. Ward (Eds.), *Maritime decarbonization – Practical Tools, Case Studies and Decarbonization Enablers*. Springer.

[3]https://en.wikipedia.org/wiki/Manhattan_Project

Flyvbjerg, B., & Gardner, D. (2023). *How big things get done*. Currency Press.

Forrester, J. W. (1961). *Industrial dynamics*. M.I.T. Press.

Hytti, M., Rautanen, P., Saari, J., Suuronen, M., & Walls, R. (2023). The in-house production of biofuel by shipping companies – A case study. In M. Lind, W. Lehmacher, & R. Ward (Eds.), *Maritime decarbonization – Practical Tools, Case Studies and Decarbonization Enablers*. Springer.

Jensen, H. H., Sornn-Friese, H., Jensen, S. F., & Aurisano, N. (2023). The implications of circular supply chains and the EU digital product passport in maritime decarbonization In M. Lind, W. Lehmacher, & R. Ward (Eds.), *Maritime decarbonization – Practical Tools, Case Studies and Decarbonization Enablers*. Springer.

Karamperidis, S., Okumus, D., Uzun, D., Gunbeyaz, S. A., & Turan, O. (2023). Actions by ports to support green maritime operations – A real case study: The Port of Plymouth, UK. In M. Lind, W. Lehmacher, & R. Ward (Eds.), *Maritime decarbonization – Practical Tools, Case Studies and Decarbonization Enablers*. Springer.

Kosmala, K. (2023). Actions being taken by key segments to meet the decarbonization targets. In M. Lind, W. Lehmacher, & R. Ward (Eds.), *Maritime decarbonization – Practical Tools, Case Studies and Decarbonization Enablers*. Springer.

Kuttan, S. (2023). Decarbonizing international shipping through collaborative partnerships. In M. Lind, W. Lehmacher, & R. Ward (Eds.), *Maritime decarbonization – Practical Tools, Case Studies and Decarbonization Enablers*. Springer.

Lehmacher, W., Lind, M., Allwright, G., Bentham, J., Cummins, D., Nottebom, T., Svendsen, J. B., Tikka, K., & Tremerie, L. D. (2023a). Highlights of the book – A menu of possible actions for decarbonization today and tomorrow. In M. Lind, W. Lehmacher, & R. Ward (Eds.), *Maritime decarbonization – Practical Tools, Case Studies and Decarbonization Enablers*. Springer.

Lehmacher, W., Lind, M., Jensen, L., & Tremiere, L. d. (2023b). The destination – A vision of a climate neutral future In M. Lind, W. Lehmacher, & R. Ward (Eds.), *Maritime decarbonization – Practical Tools, Case Studies and Decarbonization Enablers*. Springer.

Lind, M., & Lehmacher, W. (2023). How to get started: CDES – A new paradigm for tackling decarbonization projects. In M. Lind, W. Lehmacher, & R. Ward (Eds.), *Maritime decarbonization – Practical Tools, Case Studies and Decarbonization Enablers*. Springer.

Lind, M., Lehmacher, W., Bentham, J. B., Kuttan, S., Tikka, K., & Watson, R. T. (2023a). Four steps to decarbonization In M. Lind, W. Lehmacher, & R. Ward (Eds.), *Maritime decarbonization – Practical Tools, Case Studies and Decarbonization Enablers*. Springer.

Lind, M., Lehmacher, W., Sanjay Kuttan, Carson-Jackson, J., Cummins, D., van Gogh, M., & Rydbergh, T. (2023b). Effective partnerships to support maritime decarbonization. In M. Lind, W. Lehmacher, & R. Ward (Eds.), *Maritime decarbonization – Practical Tools, Case Studies and Decarbonization Enablers*. Springer.

Lind, M., Sandra Haraldson, Wolfgang Lehmacher, Raza, Z., Forsström, E., Astner, L., Bentham, J. B., Fu, X., Suroto, J., & Zuesongdam, P. (2023c). Towards ports as energy nodes: Strengthening micro energy systems. In M. Lind, W. Lehmacher, & R. Ward (Eds.), *Maritime decarbonization – Practical Tools, Case Studies and Decarbonization Enablers*. Springer.

Manderbacka, T., & Forsström, E. (2023). Engaging the global research communities in maritime decarbonization. In M. Lind, W. Lehmacher, & R. Ward (Eds.), *Maritime decarbonization – Practical Tools, Case Studies and Decarbonization Enablers*. Springer.

Manderbacka, T., & Tapaninen, U. (2023). Practical decarbonization action being taken by the shipping companies. In M. Lind, W. Lehmacher, & R. Ward (Eds.), *Maritime decarbonization – Practical Tools, Case Studies and Decarbonization Enablers*. Springer.

McKinnon, A. (2023). Broadening the scope the decarbonisation in the maritime sector. In M. Lind, W. Lehmacher, & R. Ward (Eds.), *Maritime decarbonization – Practical Tools, Case Studies and Decarbonization Enablers*. Springer.

Natali, M., & Rego, R. (2023). Ship engine, equipment and fuel options for decarbonization. In M. Lind, W. Lehmacher, & R. Ward (Eds.), *Maritime decarbonization – Practical Tools, Case Studies and Decarbonization Enablers*. Springer.

Pakkanen, P., & Vettor, R. (2023). Decarbonization support from digital solutions providers. In M. Lind, W. Lehmacher, & R. Ward (Eds.), *Maritime decarbonization – Practical Tools, Case Studies and Decarbonization Enablers*. Springer.

Pålsson, C., & Rydbergh, T. (2023). The extent of decarbonization in the global shipping fleet. In M. Lind, W. Lehmacher, & R. Ward (Eds.), *Maritime decarbonization – Practical Tools, Case Studies and Decarbonization Enablers*. Springer.

Petersen, M., & Renken, K. (2023). Adopting a value chain focus to tackle decarbonization. In M. Lind, W. Lehmacher, & R. Ward (Eds.), *Maritime decarbonization – Practical Tools, Case Studies and Decarbonization Enablers*. Springer.

Platten, G., Selwyn, M., Vicente, H., & Cotton, S. (2023). Ensuring seafarers are at the heart of decarbonization action. In M. Lind, W. Lehmacher, & R. Ward (Eds.), *Maritime decarbonization – Practical Tools, Case Studies and Decarbonization Enablers*. Springer.

Raza, Z., & Singh, S. (2023). Decarbonizing the maritime industry – Current environmental targets and potential outcomes. In M. Lind, W. Lehmacher, & R. Ward (Eds.), *Maritime decarbonization – Practical Tools, Case Studies and Decarbonization Enablers*. Springer.

Recker, J., Rosemann, M., Indulska, M., & Green, P. (2009). Business process modeling – A comparative analysis. *Journal of the Association for Information Systems*. https://doi.org/10.17705/1jais.00193

Renken, K., & Petersen, M. (2023). How a value chain approach plays out in maritime decarbonization. In M. Lind, W. Lehmacher, & R. Ward (Eds.), *Maritime decarbonization – Practical Tools, Case Studies and Decarbonization Enablers*. Springer.

Rockart, J. F. (1982). The changing role of the information systems executive: A critical success factors perspective. *Sloan Management Review*, *24*(1), 3–13.

Safadi, H., & Watson, R. T. (2023). Knowledge monopolies and the innovation divide: A governance perspective. *Information and Organization*, *33*(2). https://doi.org/10.1016/j.infoandorg.2023.100466

Sand, P., Stausbøll, E., Goldman, D., & Rydbergh, T. (2023). Identifying the best low-emission carriers. In M. Lind, W. Lehmacher, & R. Ward (Eds.), *Maritime decarbonization – Practical Tools, Case Studies and Decarbonization Enablers*. Springer.

Smil, V. (2022). *How the world really works: The science behind how we got here and where we're going* (First United States ed.). Viking.

Svendsen, J. B., Petit, E., Selwyn, M., & Bjerregaard, A. K. (2023). Establishing green corridors to accelerate the use of alternative fuels. In M. Lind, W. Lehmacher, & R. Ward (Eds.), *Maritime decarbonization – Practical Tools, Case Studies and Decarbonization Enablers*. Springer.

Tikka, K., & Esau, S. (2023a). How to assess decarbonization enablers. In M. Lind, W. Lehmacher, & R. Ward (Eds.), *Maritime decarbonization – Practical Tools, Case Studies and Decarbonization Enablers*. Springer.

Tikka, K., & Esau, S. (2023b). Identifying the key decarbonization enablers. In M. Lind, W. Lehmacher, & R. Ward (Eds.), *Maritime decarbonization – Practical Tools, Case Studies and Decarbonization Enablers*. Springer.

Tikka, K., & Esau, S. (2023c). Securing global alignment in regulations related to decarbonization. In M. Lind, W. Lehmacher, & R. Ward (Eds.), *Maritime decarbonization – Practical Tools, Case Studies and Decarbonization Enablers*. Springer.

Vakili, S. (2023). Decarbonization in shipyard cities – A holistic approach to sustainability assessment. In M. Lind, W. Lehmacher, & R. Ward (Eds.), *Maritime decarbonization – Practical Tools, Case Studies and Decarbonization Enablers*. Springer.

Watson, R. T. (2020). *Capital, systems and objects: The foundation and future of organizations*. Springer.

Watson, R. T., Lind, M., Delmeire, N., & Liesa, F. (2020). Shipping: A self-organising ecosystem. In *Maritime informatics* (pp. 13–32). Springer.

Williamson, O. E. (1979). Transaction-cost economics: The governance of contractual relations. *Journal of Law and Economics*, *22*(2), 233–261.

Zografakis, H., Henderson, N., Green, A. R., Mace-Kokota, D., & Turner, J. M. (2023). Decarbonise shipping or decarbonise international maritime trade? The present contractual framework and the need for a new contractual architecture. In M. Lind, W. Lehmacher, & R. Ward (Eds.), *Maritime decarbonization – Practical Tools, Case Studies and Decarbonization Enablers*. Springer.

Contents

Editors and Contributors

About the Editors

Mikael Lind has been appointed by Chalmers University of Technology (M2) as the world's first professor in maritime informatics. He is also a Senior Strategic Research Advisor at Research Institutes of Sweden (RISE). He has initiated and headed a substantial part of several open innovation initiatives related to information and communication technologies for the sustainable transport of people and goods, including the recently globally launched Virtual Watch Tower (VWT) initiative (www.virtualwatchtower.org). He is substantially engaged in exploring the opportunity of maritime informatics and recently also maritime decarbonization as applied research fields. Lind serves as an expert for the World Economic Forum, Europe's Digital Transport Logistic Forum (DTLF) and UN/CEFACT. He is well published in the maritime and logistics professional press and has by his initiative on the first two books on Maritime Informatics together with numerous trade press articles become a recognised thought leader in maritime informatics. He is based in Gothenburg, a major Scandinavian shipping centre that hosts a significant number of companies that offer information services to the maritime sector. Lind and Lehmacher co-authored the Practical Playbook for Maritime Decarbonisation[4] in 2022 which was followed by a series of articles in maritime trade press.

Wolfgang Lehmacher is a board member, executive adviser, and business angel, partner at Anchor Group and advisor at Topan AG. He is a global thought leader and practitioner in supply chain and logistics with a bias towards sustainability, advising clients across the globe in innovation, expansion and optimisation initiatives. Previously, Director, Head of Supply Chain and Transport Industries for the World

[4]Lehmacher W., Lind M. (2022) Practical Playbook for Maritime Decarbonisation—Value chain-based pathways towards zero-emission shipping, Nordic West Office (nordicwestoffice.com/maritime)

Economic Forum, in New York and Geneva, Partner and Managing Director, China and India, at strategy firm CVA, Hong Kong, and President and CEO of GeoPost Intercontinental, the global expansion and investment vehicle of France's La Poste. Prior to La Poste, he was Head of Eastern European and Mediterranean Regions, and Country General Manager Switzerland at TNT. He is member of the advisory board of The Logistics and Supply Chain Management Society, Singapore, Ambassador of the European Freight and Logistics Leaders Forum, Brussels, Advisor of Global:SF, San Francisco, and founding member of the Logistikweisen, a logistics expert committee under the patronage of the German Federal Ministry BMDV, and NEXST, a think tank initiated by Reefknot, Singapore. Lehmacher is a prolific writer, and frequent public speaker, and FT, Forbes, Fortune, BI and Nikkei contributor and (co-)author of numerous books, including "Disrupting Logistics—Startups, Technologies, and Investors Building Future Supply Chains" and "Circular Economy—Seventh Industrial Revolution: The path to more sustainability through Circular Economy". Lehmacher and Lind co-authored the Practical Playbook for Maritime Decarbonisation[5] in 2022.

Robert Ward was the Secretary-General of the International Hydrographic Organization (IHO) before his retirement in 2017. Prior to that he was the Deputy Hydrographer of Australia. For more than 20 years, he represented Australia and subsequently the IHO, at the highest international levels where he played an influential role in the development and implementation of the global digital data exchange standards for nautical charting services that now also underpin the IMO's e-Navigation concept of a maritime digital information environment. Ward was also the co-editor, together with Lind, among others, of two reference books on maritime informatics.

Contributors

Gavin Allwright International Windship Association (IWSA), London, UK

Mette Asmussen World Economic Forum, Geneva, Switzerland

Linda Astner Port of Gävle, Gävle, Sweden

Nicolò Aurisano A.P. Moller Maersk A/S, Copenhagen, Denmark

Jeremy B. Bentham World Energy Council, London, UK
Scenarios Team, Shell International, The Hague, The Netherlands
Mission Possible Partnership, Washington, DC, USA

[5]Lehmacher W., Lind M. (2022) Practical Playbook for Maritime Decarbonisation—Value chain-based pathways towards zero-emission shipping, Nordic West Office (nordicwestoffice.com/maritime)

Boston Consulting Group, Amsterdam, The Netherlands
Transformative Scenarios B.V., The Hague, The Netherlands

Maarten L. Biermans PROW Capital, Amsterdam, The Netherlands

Anne Katrine Bjerregaard Mærsk Mc-Kinney Møller Center for Zero Carbon Shipping, Copenhagen, Denmark

Willem Bulthuis Corporate Ventures Advisory GmbH, Inning am Ammersee, Frankfurt, Germany

Jillian Carson-Jackson JCJ Consulting, Canberra, ACT, Australia

Stephen Cotton International Transport Workers' Federation (ITF), London, UK

David Cummins Blue Sky Maritime Coalition, Houston, TX, USA

Steve Esau SEA-LNG, Oxford, UK

Philip Evans The European Freight & Logistics Leaders' Forum, Brussels, Belgium

Ellinor Forsström Research Institutes of Sweden (RISE), Lund, Sweden

Xiuju Fu Institute of High Performance Computing, A*STAR, Singapore, Singapore

Dayna Goldman Xeneta, Oslo, Norway

Sefer Anil Gunbeyaz University of Strathclyde, Glasgow, UK

Sandra Haraldson Research Institutes of Sweden (RISE), Gothenburg, Sweden

Neil Henderson Gard AS, Arendal, Norway

Tobias Holl PROW Capital, Amsterdam, The Netherlands

Mia Hytti Meriaura Ltd, Turku, Finland

Ingrid Sidenvall Jegou Global Maritime Forum, Copenhagen, Denmark

Henrik Hvid Jensen DXC Technology Denmark, Copenhagen, Denmark

Lars Jensen Vespucci Maritime, Copenhagen, Denmark

Steffen Foldager Jensen Aalborg University, Aalborg, Denmark

Stavros Karamperidis University of Plymouth, Plymouth, UK

Kris Kosmala Marine Digital, Lübeck, Germany

Randall Krantz Global Maritime Forum, Copenhagen, Denmark

Sanjay Kuttan Global Centre for Maritime Decarbonisation, Singapore, Singapore

Wolfgang Lehmacher Independent Supply Chain Expert, Hong Kong, China

Mikael Lind Research Institutes of Sweden (RISE), Gothenburg, Sweden
Chalmers University of Technology, Gothenburg, Sweden

Dora Mace-Kokota Stephenson Harwood LLP, London, UK

Audrey Macnab The European Freight & Logistics Leaders' Forum, Brussels, Belgium

Teemu Manderbacka VTT Technical Research Centre of Finland, Espoo, Finland

Alan McKinnon Kuehne Logistics University, Hamburg, Germany

Matteo Natali Wärtsilä Marine Power, Trieste, Italy

Theo Notteboom Ghent University, University of Antwerp and Antwerp Maritime Academy, Ghent, Belgium

Dogancan Okumus University of Strathclyde, Glasgow, UK

Pekka Pakkanen NAPA, Helsinki, Finland

Christopher Pålsson Maritime-Insight, Gothenburg, Sweden

Moritz Petersen Kühne Logistics University, Hamburg, Germany

Elizabeth Petit The Sustainable Shipping Initiative Limited, Hartley Wintney, UK

Guy Platten International Chamber of Shipping (ICS), London, UK

Petri Rautanen Järnros Oy, Salo, Finland

Zeeshan Raza Research Institutes of Sweden (RISE), Gothenburg, Sweden

Rui Rego Wärtsilä Marine Power, Asker, Norway

Katharina Renken Hapag-Lloyd AG, Hamburg, Germany

Andrew Rigden Green Stephenson Harwood LLP, Hong Kong, China

Torbjörn Rydbergh Marine Benchmark, Gothenburg, Sweden

Jessica Saari Meriaura Ltd, Turku, Finland

Peter Sand Xeneta, Copenhagen, Denmark

Martha Selwyn United Nations Global Compact, New York, NY, USA

Sukhjit Singh University of Gibraltar, Europa Point, Gibraltar

Henrik Sornn-Friese Copenhagen Business School, Frederiksberg, Denmark

Emily Stausbøll Xeneta, Copenhagen, Denmark

Jimmy Suroto PSA International Pte Ltd, Singapore, Singapore

Minna Suuronen Meriaura Ltd, Turku, Finland

Johan Byskov Svendsen Mærsk Mc-Kinney Møller Center for Zero Carbon Shipping, Copenhagen, Denmark

Ulla Tapaninen Tallinn University of Technology, Tallinn, Estonia

Kirsi Tikka Board Member Ardmore Shipping, Pembroke, Bermuda
Board Member Pacific Basin Shipping, Hong Kong, Hong Kong SAR
Board Member Foreship, Helsinki, Finland

Louise De Tremerie European Parliament, Brussels, Belgium

Osman Turan University of Strathclyde, Glasgow, UK

James M. Turner KC Quadrant Chambers, London, UK

Dogancan Uzun Lloyd's Register, London, UK

Seyedvahid Vakili Maritime Energy Management Department of World Maritime University, Malmö, Sweden
Research Fellow, University of Southampton, Southampton, UK

Margi van Gogh World Economic Forum, Geneva, Switzerland

Boris van Overbeeke MJ Hudson, Amsterdam, The Netherlands

Roberto Vettor NAPA, Helsinki, Finland

Helio Vicente International Chamber of Shipping (ICS), London, UK

Riinu Walls Meriaura Ltd, Turku, Finland

Richard T. Watson Digital Frontier Partners, Melbourne, Australia

Haris Zografakis Stephenson Harwood LLP, London, UK

Phanthian Zuesongdam Hamburg Port Authority, Hamburg, Germany

Abbreviations

AER	Annual efficiency ratio
AIS	Automatic identification system
BCO	Beneficial cargo owner
BM	Business model
CCI	Consumer confidence index
CCS	Carbon capture and storage
CII	(IMO) Carbon intensity indicator
CFD	Computational fluid dynamics
CO_2	Carbon dioxide
CO_2e	Carbon dioxide equivalent
CS	Corporate sustainability
CSR	Corporate social responsibility
DCS	(IMO) Data collection system
DCSA	Digital container shipping association
DIMT	Decarbonization of international maritime trade
DWT	Deadweight tonnage
EEDI	(IMO) Energy efficiency design index
EEOI	(IMO) Energy efficiency operational indicator
EEXI	(IMO) Energy efficiency existing ship index
EPL	Engine power limitation
ESG	Environmental, social and governance (themes)
ESI	Environmental shipping index
ETA	Estimated time of arrival
ETS	(EU) Emissions trading system
EC	European Commission
EU	European Union
EV	Electric vehicle
FAME	Fatty acid methyl ester
CGMD	Global Centre for maritime decarbonisation
GHG	Greenhouse gases

GSC	Green shipping corridor
GT	Gross tonnage
HFO	Heavy fuel oil
HVO	Hydrotreated vegetable oil
ICE	Internal combustion engine
ICS	International chamber of shipping
IEA	International Energy Agency
IMO	International Maritime Organization
IMT	International maritime trade
IRL	Investment readiness level
IT	Information technology
ITF	International Transport Workers' Federation
JiT	Just-in-time (arrival)
LCA	Life cycle assessment
LDCs	Least developed countries
LNG	Liquified natural gas
LPG	Liquified petroleum gas
MARPOL	(IMO) Convention on the prevention of pollution from ships
MBM	Market-based measures
MCDM	Multi-criteria decision making
MEPC	(IMO) Marine Environment Protection Committee
MHE	Material handling equipment
MGO	Marine gasoil
MMMFCZCS	Mærsk McKinney Møller Center for Zero Carbon Shipping
MRV	(EU) Monitoring reporting and verification
NOx	Nitrogen oxides
OECD	Organisation for economic and co-operation and development
OEM	Original equipment manufacturer
P2X	Power-to-X
PPP	Public-private partnerships
PTI	Power take-in
PTO	Power take-off
R&D	Research and development
RFNBO	Renewable fuels of non-biological origin
RPM	Revolutions per minute
SBM	Sustainable business model
SCR	Selective catalytic reduction
SEEMP	Ship energy efficiency management plan
SFTW	Sail fast—then wait
SIDS	Small Island Developing States
SOFC	Solid oxide fuel cell
SOx	Sulphur oxides
STCW	(IMO) International convention on standards of training, certification and watchkeeping for seafarers

STH	Sustainable technology hub
SWOT	Strengths, weaknesses, opportunities, threat (analysis)
TEN-T	Trans-European transport network
TRL	Technology readiness level
TTW	Tank-to-wake
UCO	Used cooking oil
UNCTAD	United Nations conference on trade and development
UNFCCC	United Nations framework convention on climate change
USD	US dollars
VA	Virtual arrival
VLCC	Very large crude carrier (ship)
VLSFO	Very low sulphur fuel oil
WTW	Well-to-wake
ZEV	Zero emission vessel
ZEWT	Zero emission waterborne transportation

Part I
Outlining Baseline and Perspectives

Broadening the Scope of Decarbonization in the Maritime Sector

Alan McKinnon

Target Audience

This chapter should be of interest to people involved directly and indirectly in global efforts to reduce carbon emissions from maritime supply chains to a small fraction of their current level. This includes those conducting research on the subject, managing shipping and related businesses, financing the transition to low carbon vessels and infrastructure and formulating public policy on the decarbonization of maritime logistics.

Key Takeaway Message

This chapter considers how the scoping of maritime decarbonization can be broadened to enable a more holistic assessment of the related opportunities and challenges.

Introduction

Much research and discussion on the decarbonization of international shipping currently focuses on vessels and energy. This is hardly surprising. The International Maritime Organization (IMO) fourth Greenhouse Gas (GHG) Study predicted that almost two-thirds of carbon reductions in the maritime sector by 2050 will come from the switch to alternative fuels (IMO, 2020). Nor is there any dispute that it will

A. McKinnon (✉)
Kuehne Logistics University, Hamburg, Germany
e-mail: alan.mckinnon@the-klu.org

M. Lind et al. (eds.), *Maritime Decarbonization*,
https://doi.org/10.1007/978-3-031-39936-7_1

ultimately require the use of very low carbon fuels to achieve net zero shipping. There are two respects, however, in which this pre-occupation with the 'defossilisation' of maritime energy appears to be based on too narrow a view of the subject. First, it under-estimates the carbon-reducing potential of a range of other measures that can be applied more quickly and cheaply to reduce the amount of fossil fuel that will eventually need to be replaced. Second, it is 'voyage-focussed' and fails to consider options for decarbonizing the whole maritime supply chain, comprising ports and hinterland logistics as well as shipping operations.

It is important to recognise the full spectrum of carbon-reducing initiatives and avoid over-reliance on a few much-debated and -researched options.

Classificatory Frameworks

The decarbonization of all forms of transport will be achieved by the application of many mutually-reinforcing measures rather than a few 'silver bullets'. To assess the potential carbon impact of these measures systematically it is helpful to group them into several categories. Various classificatory schemes are now widely used for this purpose. The most commonly referenced is the Avoid-Shift-Improve (ASI) framework, distinguishing measures that reduce the demand for transport, shift it to lower carbon modes and improve their carbon efficiency. The Activity-Shift-Intensity-Fuel (ASIF) taxonomy (Schipper & Marie, 1999), adopted by the Intergovernmental Panel on Climate Change (IPCC) (Sims et al., 2014), uses different words for two of the three categories and introduces a separate one for the switch to alternative fuels. The so-called 'five decarbonization lever' framework distinguishes capacity utilisation from energy efficiency in the improve / intensity category, as each can be separately influenced by technology, business practice and public policy (McKinnon, 2018). All three frameworks are illustrated in Fig. 1.

The '5-lever' decarbonization framework has been used by the European Technology Platform for Logistics (ALICE, 2019) to road-map the decarbonization of European logistics, and by other organisations, though mainly for land-based logistics. The next five sections of this chapter discuss the possible role of the five levers in assessing carbon reduction opportunities across the maritime supply chain.

Growth in Demand for Maritime Transport

The first decarbonization lever is freight transport demand. According to the International Transport Forum of the Organisation for Economic Co-operation and Development (OECD) (ITF, 2019), there could be a three-fold increase in the amount of freight movement by sea, measured in tonne-kms, between 2015 and 2050. Future growth in the demand for international shipping of this magnitude would clearly impede its decarbonization. Some advocates of 'de-growth' as an

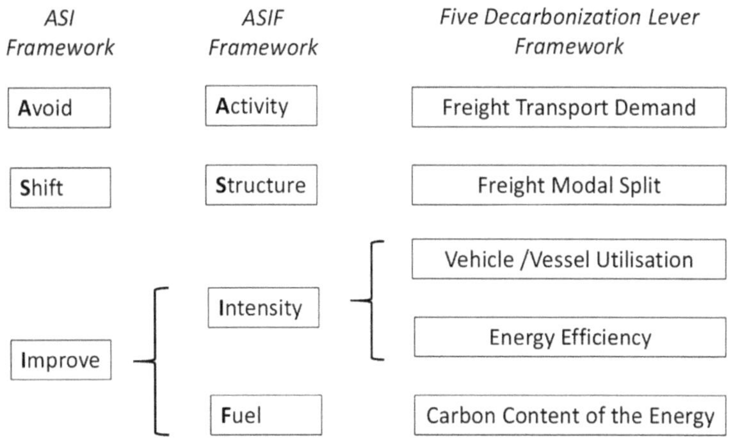

Fig. 1 Inter-relationship between decarbonization frameworks for logistics. Source: McKinnon (2018)

environmental strategy contend that predicted levels of economic and trade growth, which will underpin future increases in maritime freight volumes, are incompatible with carbon-reduction commitments (Hickel, 2020). There are no serious proposals, however, to curb the growth of international trade for environmental reasons. Around 57% of global gross domestic product (GDP) is traded internationally; over three-quarters of this trade is in physical goods that need to be transported and over 80% of this transport is by sea (World Bank, 2023; UNCTAD, 2022a, b). Analysis (Shapiro, 2016) has shown that the economic benefits of international trade substantially exceed the monetary value of CO_2 emissions from that trade even when these emissions are assigned a relatively high carbon price. Measurement of the embodied CO_2 in traded products also indicates that a substantial amount of international trade actually helps to decarbonize the global economy, where production-related emissions are lower in the exporting country than in the importing one (Cristea et al., 2013; Le Moigne & Ossa, 2021). Where this is the case, carbon emissions from international shipping are often small relative to the emission differential between exporting and importing countries.

The future growth in trade and shipping volumes may be constrained by other factors. In recent years, supply chain disruptions caused directly and indirectly by the Covid pandemic, geopolitical developments and extreme weather events have caused companies to review their global production and sourcing strategies and attach greater importance to resilience. There is much talk of de-globalisation, re-localisation, reshoring and near-shoring as strategies for de-risking supply chains, all of which might moderate the upward trend in maritime traffic and, if widely-implemented, even reverse it. Although motivated primarily by a desire to make supply chains more robust, the strategies could also make them more environmentally-sustainable. Anecdotal evidence is accumulating to show that

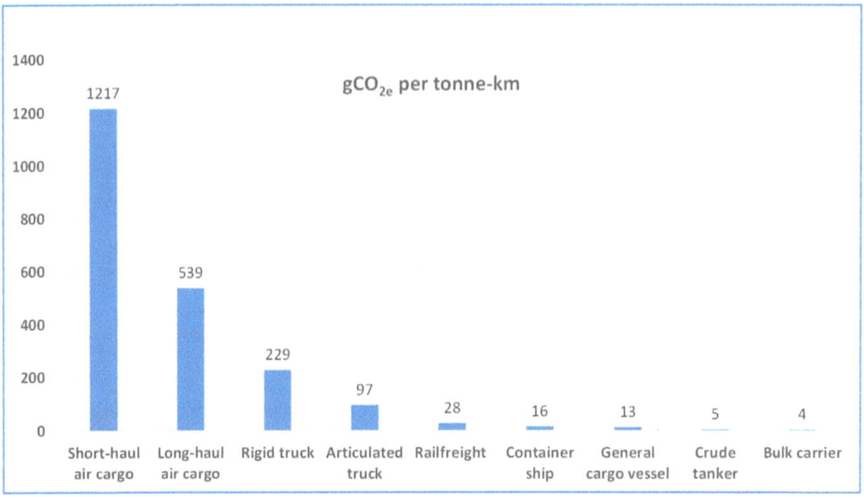

Fig. 2 Variations in the average carbon intensity of freight transport modes (UK government data). Data source: DBEIS and DEFRA (2022)

some large manufacturers and retailers are shortening their global supply lines and large container shipping lines are beginning to notice the effects of this reconfiguration of supply chains on traffic levels. On the basis of available data, however, it is difficult to predict the likely extent of this trend. There is, nevertheless, a widening expectation that international trade will become more regionalised, effectively reducing the amount of maritime freight movement (measured in tonne-kms) per billion dollars of world trade.

More predictable is the likely effect on the maritime sector of the long-term phase-out of fossil fuel, which represents around 40% of sea freight (UNCTAD, 2022b). The decline in oil, gas and coal traffic will, however, be partly offset by growth in the movement by sea of materials required to build a new renewable energy infrastructure and to climate-proof the built environment, as well as renewable fuels and sequestered CO_2 for underground storage or use. So, efforts to deal with the climate crisis may themselves generate substantial volumes of maritime traffic.

Taking a broader maritime supply chain perspective on this first decarbonization lever, what is the potential for rationalising the landward movement of sea freight to cut carbon emissions? This would involve reducing hinterland distances between ports and inland points of origin and destination. Although these distances are typically short relative to deep-sea distances, the carbon intensity of hinterland transport is much higher, particularly if it is by road. Figure 2 shows this.

The channelling of sea freight through smaller numbers of hub ports, partly as a result of increasing vessel size, has extended the average length of hinterland movements, though this trend has been partly mitigated by maritime feeder services serving ‘second-tier’ ports closer to the inland origins and destinations. Port-centric logistics has also been advocated as a means of reducing container movement across hinterlands (Monios & Wilmsmeier, 2012; McKinnon, 2013). While there is undoubtedly potential to lessen the landward movement of sea freight, carbon emissions from the hinterland leg of door-to-door maritime shipments are likely to be more sensitive to the choice of transport mode than to the distances travelled. This leads us to the second of the decarbonization levers—freight modal split.

Choice of Freight Transport Mode

Public policy makers have traditionally seen shifting the movement of freight to cleaner, lower-carbon transport modes as the main way of reducing its environmental impact. This is understandable given the wide variations in the carbon intensity of freight transport modes, as seen in Fig. 2. As shipping is the most carbon-efficient mode for the transportation of most commodities, it may actually become the recipient of freight transferred from other higher carbon modes, particularly air cargo, as businesses strive to decarbonize their global supply chains. This would then inflate the demand for shipping services and counteract the influence of the first lever—freight transport demand. Any displacement of freight from air to sea is likely to be limited, though, as the maritime and air cargo markets are considered to be fairly discrete given the wide differences in their speed, reliability, cost and commodity mix.

In the hinterland, modal shift is a much more pertinent issue and there it can yield significant carbon reductions. In the UK, for example, moving goods by rail rather than by articulated trucks on average cuts carbon emissions per tonne-km by 71% (DBEIS and DEFRA, 2022). Numerous studies have examined the modal choice decision in the hinterland (e.g. Blauwens et al., 2006; Meers et al., 2017), most of it related to the movement of containerised freight. Length of haul, reflecting the geographical extent of the hinterland relative to the port, service frequency and port connectivity to rail and inland waterway networks are key determinants of mode choice. In the continental-scale hinterland of US ports, rail is the dominant mode, using the double-stacking of containers on many routes to secure an overwhelming cost advantage. In Europe, the concept of synchromodality was initially promoted by the port of Rotterdam as a means of shifting container traffic from road to rail and waterborne services by minimising delays at modal interchange points (Zhang & Pel, 2016). The radial development of intermodal corridors from major ports, such as the Betuwe route from Rotterdam to Germany, has also helped rail to capture a higher share of the hinterland freight market. In many hinterland areas 'dry ports' have been developed as inland intermodal terminals usually with a direct rail connection to the port and often becoming nodes to which other logistical activities gravitate. Through their impact on freight modal split, they can significantly reduce hinterland emissions (Bergqvist et al., 2015).

Increasing Capacity Utilisation

The third lever is vessel and vehicle utilisation. There is chronic under-utilisation of freight-carrying capacity across all transport modes. Raising load factors consolidates freight movement in fewer trips and voyages, cutting the distances travelled, fuel consumed and CO_2 emitted. This is generally portrayed as an example of 'low hanging fruit' in the decarbonization of freight transport as it saves money as well as carbon emissions. In addition to having a low, or in many cases negative, carbon mitigation cost, efforts to improve loading can be applied in the short to medium term. This contrasts with the transition to low carbon energy in the maritime sector which will be a slow process given the long replacement cycle for vessels and the time required to transform the marine energy supply system. Pulling this decarbonization lever requires changes to business practice, market dynamics and operational procedures rather than new technology, fleet renewal and high capital investment. Implementing these changes, however, still presents major challenges, particularly in the maritime sector.

We must first clarify what aspects of capacity utilisation influence the carbon intensity of a shipping operation. It is affected mainly by the proportion of the deadweight (in other words, the maximum weight-based carrying capacity) that is actually used. This is normally very high in the case of bulk tankers, shipping dense products such as iron ore, oil or grain. It is lower for container vessels transporting lighter manufactured and food products and repositioning empty boxes. In road, rail and air cargo systems, loading the vehicle below its maximum weight lightens it and thereby reduces energy consumption and emissions. Under-loaded ships, on the other hand, must take on ballast water to maintain stability and 'trim'. This typically represents around 25–30% of a vessel's deadweight and involves moving roughly 10 billion tonnes of water annually in ships (ClearSeas, 2021). The consolidation of maritime cargo on fewer sailings would replace some of this ballast water with freight, thus improving the energy- and carbon-efficiency of shipping.

Measuring the utilisation of container ships is more complicated. It can be expressed as the proportion of available slots on a vessel that are occupied by containers. Some shipping lines only count loaded, revenue-earning containers in this calculation, and exclude empty ones, which can account, on average, for around a quarter of the total. The utilisation of laden containers can vary widely by weight and volume. Their loading is generally the responsibility of the shipper exporting the consignment, rather than the shipping line. Very little data is available on the average loading of containers, making it difficult to judge by how much it could be increased. A survey of exporters' and importers' assessment of container fill rates suggested that utilisation by weight and volume was fairly high though could be significantly raised (McKinnon, 2014). A 2018 US survey found that, on average, inbound containers were around 65% full (Anon, 2021). There are examples of company initiatives that have significantly increased average container fill, motivated mainly by a desire to cut transport costs but also yield carbon savings. The 8- to 10-fold increase in container shipping rates during the Covid pandemic period gave shippers a strong financial incentive to improve container utilisation. It is not known to what extent this will lead to a longer-term upswing in container fill rates.

The main focus of research on capacity utilisation in the container trades has been on the repositioning of empty containers. This is both costly and carbon intensive. Sanders et al. (2015) estimated that globally it cost $15–20 billion per annum and that the related CO_2 emissions could be reduced by 6 million tonnes annually. These figures are so high mainly because of pronounced imbalances in containerised traffic flows on major trade routes. These imbalances can be expressed as the ratio of the number of loaded containers moving in opposite directions on particular trade lanes. In 2021, the ratios for the TransPacific, Asia-Europe and TransAtlantic routes were respectively 3.4:1, 2.4:1 and 1.9:1 (UNCTAD, 2021). These imbalances are even greater for particular types and sizes of container. Numerous studies and modelling exercises, recently reviewed by Abdelshafie et al. (2022), have explored ways of optimising the repositioning of empty containers. In recent years, online container exchanges have improved the matching of container demand and supply, helping to reduce the average distance empty containers move. Also, several companies are now marketing foldable containers that can be collapsed, stacked and transported by land and sea in units of four or five, saving around 75% of the space. It has been estimated that this can save 'up to 0.4 tonnes of CO_2 per forty-foot equivalent container annually when deployed in a round-trip liner service in the same network' (Goh, 2019).

Inefficiency in the repositioning of empty containers also carries a heavy carbon penalty in hinterland transport mainly as a result of their circuitous routeing. Following unloading (or 'de-stuffing') at an import location, an empty container is often routed via a port or distant inland terminal to an export location to be reloaded. This is largely attributable to the refusal of shipping lines to share container capacity, tight demurrage conditions and a lack of stakeholder co-operation and IT support (Acciaro & McKinnon, 2015). To address the first of these constraints, attempts have been made to 'de-brand' containers and create a common pool of 'grey boxes'. The grey box concept, however, remains unpopular with shipping lines, even among those in alliances, leaving the potential hinterland emission savings that it might offer unexploited.

Improving Energy Efficiency

Energy efficiency is the fourth decarbonization lever. The options for cutting energy consumption per nautical mile have been extensively reviewed and their implementation strongly promoted by regulation and market forces. A broad distinction can be made between technical and operational measures, the former relating both to the initial design of the vessel and any subsequent retrofitting with fuel-saving devices. The IMO's Fourth GHG Study (IMO, 2020) assessed the abatement potential and cost of 23 'energy saving technologies' and one operational measure, a speed reduction of 10% relative to a 2018 baseline. Other research, reviewed by Bouman et al. (2017), has examined the carbon impact of a broader range of operational initiatives, including weather routing, improved management of vessel trim and the adjustment of vessel speed to synchronise with port access and operations—so called Just-in-Time arrival. Of the measures analysed by the IMO study, speed reduction offered the largest CO_2 abatement potential by 2030. During the Covid pandemic period when container shipping suffered severe capacity constraints, average container vessel speed increased by around 5–6%, though this was considered a temporary response to very unusual market conditions (Miller, 2021).

The IMO's fuel economy standard for new vessels, its Energy Efficiency Design Index (EEDI), has now been in place for a decade and although criticised on various grounds (Barreiro et al., 2022) has made a significant contribution to maritime decarbonization. The lengthy ship replacement cycle inevitably makes this a long-term, incremental contribution. The IMO's Ship Energy Efficiency Management Plan (SEEMP) programme launched around the same time has encouraged the adoption of a range of short-to-medium term energy efficiency improvements in existing as well as new vessels. In an effort to accelerate the decline in the carbon intensity of shipping, the IMO is extending its fuel economy standard to existing vessels with its Energy Efficiency eXisting ship Index (EEXI) program and introducing Carbon Intensity Index (CII) ratings (IMO, 2021). It is hoped that these measures will help the IMO achieve its target of reducing the average carbon intensity of international shipping by 40% between 2008 and 2030, supplementing the 22% reduction achieved between 2008 and 2018 mainly by slow steaming (IMO, 2020). According to Rutherford et al. (2020), however, the EEXI provisions are likely to make only a marginal contribution of between 0.7% and 1.3% to reductions in the average carbon intensity of oil tankers, bulk carriers and container ships by 2030. This they attribute to 'the continuing prevalence of slow steaming, whereby most ships are being operated at engine loads that would be unaffected by the technical efficiency standard that the EEXI sets'.

Switching to Low Carbon Energy

As noted at the beginning of this chapter, this is the decarbonization lever that is attracting the greatest attention and the only one which, in the longer term, will allow the shipping industry to achieve carbon neutrality. Replacing the 300 million tonnes of fossil fuel currently burned by the maritime sector with renewable energy will be transformational (Jacoby, 2022). This energy conversion is examined in detail elsewhere in this book and so only some of the key issues will be raised here, relating to the future sustainable fuel mix, mechanisms for promoting its adoption and the wider implications for ports and hinterland transport.

After much research and debate, the longer-term choice of low carbon energy for shipping comes down to two synthetic fuels, e-methanol and e-ammonia, both reliant on the cost-effective production at scale of green hydrogen electrolysed from water by low/zero carbon electricity. Given their differing strengths and weaknesses and varying projections of their future cost trends, it is difficult to forecast the 2050 split between these fuels. The International Renewable Energy Agency (IRENA) reckons that 'renewable ammonia will be the backbone of decarbonization' in the shipping sector, accounting for 43% of its energy mix by 2050 (IRENA, 2021). Although e-methanol is much less toxic, requires much less engine modification and can be more easily transported and stored, its reliance on captured CO_2 as a key ingredient ties its future availability and cost to that of CO_2 removal technologies which are currently at a very early stage in their development (Oeko Institute, 2023). Whichever of these e-fuels ultimately dominates, wind assisted ship propulsion (WASP) can provide a low-carbon energy supplement for much of the maritime fleet (Chou et al., 2021). One study has suggested that by 2030 between 3700 and 10,700 bulk carriers and tankers could be equipped with wind propulsion systems, cutting maritime emissions by between 3.5 and 7.5 million tonnes of CO_2 annually (Nelissen et al., 2016).

For the foreseeable future, the transitioning of shipping from fossil to renewable energy will be seriously constrained by the high cost and limited availability of low-carbon alternatives. Increasing numbers of shippers, particularly those with Science-Based Target commitments to make their global value chains net zero by 2040 or earlier, are expressing a willingness to pay premium rates for the use of sustainable fuel (Jameson et al., 2022). Until the volumes of such fuel are hugely increased and a global bunkering network is created to distribute them, it will be virtually impossible to ensure that 'green' shippers' consignments are moved on vessels burning the right proportions of renewable energy. Wide application of the 'mass balance' principle will be required in the maritime sector to allow these shippers to claim carbon credits for the purchase of lower-carbon fuel somewhere in a carrier's network. Such 'book and claim' schemes are strongly advocated by the Global Maritime Forum and Getting to Zero Coalition (2023) as a 'valuable mechanism to advance the uptake of zero- and near-zero-emission fuels' in maritime supply chains.

Ports account for only around 2% of shipping emissions (Merk, 2014) and an even smaller share of global maritime supply chain emissions. These figures, however, give a misleading impression of the future contribution of ports to the defossilisation of marine energy (Alamoush et al., 2022). Ports will have a critical role to play in this process, in several respects.

First, ports will have to develop the capability and capacity to store and supply vast quantities of the new low-carbon fuels. It is estimated that 87% of the 1.4 to1.9 trillion-dollar investment that will be required to switch shipping to low carbon fuel will be on 'land-based infrastructure and production facilities', many of them in or around ports (Krantz et al., 2020).

Second, ports can assist the decarbonization of vessels while in port by giving them access to low-carbon electricity. Between 50% and 60% of total carbon emissions from a port can come from the engines of ships docked there or moored nearby. Using 'cold ironing' technology to power them with onshore electricity while in port can substantially reduce these emissions, the scale of the reduction being dependent on the carbon intensity of the electricity.

Third, ports can help to reduce their carbon intensity by micro-generating renewable electricity locally with solar panels, wind turbines and, where water currents are sufficiently strong, hydro-turbines (Iris & Lam, 2019). Finally, they can switch a whole range of port operations from fossil fuel to renewable energy. The port of Hamburg, for example, is hoping to achieve carbon neutrality by 2040 with the help of 'hydrogen-driven' technologies.

In the hinterland, the shift to renewable energy is already well underway in many countries with trucks running on biodiesel blends of 7% or more and electrified rail freight operations benefiting from the gradual decarbonization of the electricity grid. The use of biofuels in the road freight sector is seen as a transitional phase in a decarbonization process that will ultimately rely on green electricity to reach carbon neutrality. Just as there is uncertainty about the future low-carbon energy mix in shipping, so too is there disagreement about the future dependence on batteries, hydrogen and overhead cabling as the means of distributing low-carbon electricity to trucks, something that will vary by country (ITF, 2023). To ensure that the hinterland movement of maritime traffic takes full advantage of these energy-related decarbonization trends, ports will also need to develop battery-charging and hydrogen-refuelling capabilities and be connected to electrified rail and highway networks.

Closing Summary

This chapter has provided a broad overview of the options for decarbonizing maritime supply chains. It has presented the transition to renewable energy as one of five decarbonization levers, all of which may need to be pulled fairly aggressively to achieve 'net zero' by 2050. It has also advocated the adoption of a supply chain rather than a port-to-port perspective on maritime decarbonization. This takes account of interactions between carbon reduction efforts on the marine and landward sides of the chain and recognises that shippers are coming under increasing regulatory and consumer pressure to decarbonize their entire supply chains and not just their use of particular transport modes. Extending the scope of the analysis in this way can open up new opportunities for cutting emissions by, among other things, the redesign of freight networks, the procurement of maritime services and the scheduling of logistics operations.

Public intervention, mainly in the form of regulatory and market-based measures, is intensifying, but needs to be more carefully co-ordinated at global, continental and national levels to maximise its impact on maritime emission levels. High levels of public ownership in the port and rail freight sectors also involves governments directly in this decarbonization process. Most of the responsibility for achieving ambitious carbon reduction targets will, nevertheless, rest with the private sector which, in this case, comprises shipping lines, shippers, ports, logistics providers, freight forwarders, land-based carriers, energy suppliers and financial institutions. Full decarbonization of the maritime supply chain will require this broad range of enterprises to prioritise carbon mitigation and be prepared to work much more collaboratively to achieve it. This will entail fundamental changes to business practices as well as a physical transformation of transport and energy systems.

There is no question that this physical transformation, using the fifth lever in the framework to reduce the carbon content of energy used by vessels, ports and hinterland transport modes, will be by far the most critical. The IMO and IRENA estimate that just under two-thirds of the reduction in CO_2 emissions from shipping by 2050 will come from the switch to renewable energy (IMO, 2020; IRENA, 2021). That still leaves around a third of the decarbonization dependent on other measures. IRENA's 1.5 °C maximum global temperature rise scenario suggests that 20% will accrue from improved energy efficiency (lever 4) and 17% from 'reduced demand' (lever 1). Although no reference is made in its analysis to a possible increase in the utilisation of vessel capacity (lever 3), this could also make a significant contribution. In assessing carbon mitigation through levers 1, 3 and 4, and through lever 2 in the case of hinterland transport, it is important not simply to measure their likely share of total emission reductions between now and 2050, but also to consider the time-scales over which they can influence emission levels. Given the pressing need for deep reductions in carbon emissions over the next decade, greater priority should be given to those initiatives, both technical and operational, that can be deployed quickly, often with relatively low carbon mitigation costs.

References

Abdelshafie, A., Salah, M., Kramberger, T., & Dragan, D. (2022). Repositioning and optimal re-allocation of empty containers: A review of methods, models, and applications. *Sustainability, 14*(11). https://doi.org/10.3390/su14116655

Acciaro, M., & McKinnon, A. C. (2015). Carbon emissions from container shipping: An analysis of new empirical evidence. *International Journal of Transport Economics, 42*(2), 211–228.

Alamoush, A. S., Ölçer, A. I., & Ballini, F. (2022). Ports' role in shipping decarbonisation: A common port incentive scheme for shipping greenhouse gas emissions reduction. *Cleaner Logistics and Supply Chain, 3*, 100021. https://doi.org/10.1016/j.clscn.2021.100021

ALICE. (2019). *A framework and process for the development of a roadmap towards zero emissions logistics 2050*. C. Brussels.

Anon. (2021) *The challenge of freight container utilisation and why it matters*. Retrieved from https://www.supplychainsecrets.com/the-challenge-of-freight-container-utilisation-and-why-it-matters/

Barreiro, J., Zaragoza, S., & Diaz-Casas, V. (2022). Review of ship energy efficiency. *Ocean Engineering, 257*, 111594. https://doi.org/10.1016/j.oceaneng.2022.111594

Bergqvist, R., Macharis, C., Meers, D., & Woxenius, J. (2015). Making hinterland transport more sustainable a multi actor multi criteria analysis. *Research in Transportation Business and Management, 14*, 80–89. https://doi.org/10.1016/j.rtbm.2014.10.009

Blauwens, G., Vandaele, N., Van de Voorde, E., Vernimmen, B., & Witlox, F. (2006). Towards a modal shift in freight transport? A business logistics analysis of some policy measures. *Transport Reviews, 26*(2), 239–251. https://doi.org/10.1080/01441640500335565

Bouman, E. A., Lindstad, E., Rialland, A. I., & Strømman, A. H. (2017). State-of-the-art technologies, measures, and potential for reducing GHG emissions from shipping - A review, transportation research part D. *Transport and Environment, 52*, 408–421. https://doi.org/10.1016/j.trd.2017.03.022
Chou, T., Kosmas, V., Acciaro, M., & Renken, K. (2021). A comeback of wind power in shipping: An economic and operational review on the wind-assisted ship propulsion technology. *Sustainability, 13*(4). https://doi.org/10.3390/su13041880
ClearSeas. (2021). *Ballast water management: Stopping the spread of invasive species by ships.* Retrieved from https://clearseas.org/en/blog/ballast-water-management-stopping-the-spread-of-invasive-species-by-ships/
Cristea, A., Hummels, D., Puzzello, L., & Avetisyan, M. (2013). Trade and the greenhouse gas emissions from international freight transport. *Journal of Environmental Economics and Management, 65*(1), 153–173. https://doi.org/10.1016/j.jeem.2012.06.002
DBEIS and DEFRA (2022). UK government GHG conversion factors for company reporting. Department of Business, Energy and Industrial Strategy and Department of the Environment, Food and Rural Affairs. .
Global Maritime Forum & Getting to Zero Coalition (2023). Joint statement in support of book and claim chain of custody approaches to accelerate shipping decarbonisation. https://bit.ly/3DJLYMn
Goh, S. H. (2019). The impact of foldable ocean containers on back haul shippers and carbon emissions. *Transportation Research Part D: Transport and Environment, 67*, 514–527. https://doi.org/10.1016/j.trd.2019.01.003
Hickel, J. (2020). *Less is more: How degrowth will save the world.* Random House.
IMO. (2020). *Reduction of GHG emissions from ships. Fourth IMO GHG Study 2020 - Final report.* International Maritime Organisation. Retrieved from https://wwwcdn.imo.org/localresources/en/OurWork/Environment/Documents/Fourth%20IMO%20GHG%20Study%202020%20-%20Full%20report%20and%20annexes.pdf
IMO (2021). Energy efficiency measures international maritime organisation. Retrieved from https://www.imo.org/en/OurWork/Environment/Pages/Technical-and-Operational-Measures.aspx
IRENA. (2021). *A pathway to decarbonise the shipping sector by 2050.* International Renewable Energy Agency.
Iris, Ç., & Lam, J. S. L. (2019). A review of energy efficiency in ports: Operational strategies, technologies and energy management systems. *Renewable and Sustainable Energy Reviews, 112*, 170–182. https://doi.org/10.1016/j.rser.2019.04.069
ITF. (2019). *International transport forum. Transport outlook 2019.* OECD.
ITF. (2023). *Decarbonising Europe's trucks: How to minimise cost uncertainty.* International Transport Forum. OECD.
Jacoby, M. (2022). The shipping industry looks for green fuels. *Chemical and Engineering News, 100*(8) Retrieved from https://cen.acs.org/environment/greenhouse-gases/shipping-industry-looks-green-fuels/100/i8
Jameson, P. et al. (2022). Customers' willingness to pay can turn the tide towards decarbonized shipping. Boston Consulting Group. https://bit.ly/3Yhp48n
Krantz, R., Søgaard, K., & Smith, T. (2020). The scale of investment needed to decarbonize international shipping. *Global Maritime Forum.* Retrieved from https://www.globalmaritimeforum.org/news/the-scale-of-investment-needed-to-decarbonize-international-shipping
Le Moigne, M., & Ossa, R. (2021). *Buy green not local: How international trade can help save our planet.* Kühne Center for Sustainable Globalization, University of Zurich. Retrieved from https://www.kuehnecenter.uzh.ch/impact_series/2021_04_28-03-21-buy_green_not_local.html
McKinnon, A. C. (2013). Decarbonising the deep-sea container supply chain: The possible contribution of port-centric logistics. In *Paper presented to the 13th world conference on transport research.* Retrieved from https://bit.ly/44sZNef

McKinnon, A. C. (2014). The possible influence of the shipper on carbon emissions from deep-sea container supply chains: An empirical analysis. *Maritime Economics and Logistics, 16*(1), 1–19. https://doi.org/10.1057/mel.2013.25

McKinnon, A. C. (2018). *Decarbonizing logistics: Distributing goods in a low carbon world.* Kogan Page.

Meers, D., Macharis, C., Vermeiren, T., & van Lier, T. (2017). Modal choice preferences in short-distance hinterland container transport. *Research in Transportation Business and Management, 23*, 46–53. https://doi.org/10.1016/j.rtbm.2017.02.011

Merk, O. (2014). *Shipping emissions from ports*. OECD/International Transport Forum.

Miller, G. (2021, July 16). *Full steam ahead: Why container ships are racing across the Pacific.* Freight Waves. Retrieved from https://www.freightwaves.com/news/full-steam-ahead-why-container-ships-are-racing-across-the-pacific

Monios, J., & Wilmsmeier, G. (2012). Port-centric logistics, dry ports and offshore logistics hubs: Strategies to overcome double peripherality? *Maritime Policy and Management, 39*(2), 207–226. https://doi.org/10.1080/03088839.2011.650720

Nelissen, D., Traut, M., Köhler, J., Mao, W., Faber, J., & Ahdour, S. (2016). *Study on the analysis of market potentials and market barriers for wind propulsion technologies for ships*. CE Delft.

Oeko Institute (2023). Methanol as a marine fuel: Advantages and limitations. .

Rutherford, D., Mao, X., & Comer, B. (2020). Potential CO_2 reductions under the energy efficiency existing ship index. In *Working paper 2020-27. International Council for Clean Transportation.*

Sanders, U., Kloppsteck, L., Roeloff, C., Schlingmeier, J., & Riedl, J. (2015). *Think outside your boxes: Solving the global container-repositioning puzzle*. Boston Consulting Group. Retrieved from https://www.bcg.com/publications/2015/transportation-travel-logistics-think-outside-your-boxes-solving-global-container-repositioning-puzzle

Schipper, L., & Marie, C. (1999). *Transport and CO_2 emissions*. World Bank.

Shapiro, J. S. (2016). Trade costs, CO_2, and the environment. *American Economic Journal: Economic Policy, 8*(4), 220–254. https://doi.org/10.1257/pol.20150168

Sims, R., et al. (2014). Transport in climate change 2014: Mitigation of climate change. In *Contribution of working group III to the fifth assessment report of the intergovernmental panel on climate change*. Cambridge University Press.

UNCTAD. (2021). *Review of maritime transport 2021.*

UNCTAD. (2022a). *Key statistics and trends in international trade 2021.*

UNCTAD. (2022b). *Review of maritime transport 2022.*

World Bank. (2023). *Trade as % of GDP*. Retrieved https://data.worldbank.org/indicator/NE.TRD.GNFS.ZS

Zhang, M., & Pel, A. J. (2016). Synchromodal hinterland freight transport: Model study for the port of Rotterdam. *Journal of Transport Geography, 52*, 1–10. https://doi.org/10.1016/j.jtrangeo.2016.02.007

Decarbonizing the Maritime Industry: Current Environmental Targets and Potential Outcomes

Zeshan Raza and Sukhjit Singh

Target Audience

This chapter is aimed at policymakers, industry leaders, researchers, and other professionals involved in the maritime industry and in climate change mitigation. Policymakers can benefit from this chapter by gaining insight into the current regulatory frameworks and initiatives for maritime decarbonization and identifying areas where further policy action may be needed. Industry leaders can benefit from understanding the latest developments in the area of maritime decarbonization, as well as the potential impact of regulatory measures on their operations. Researchers can use this chapter to gain a comprehensive understanding of the current state of maritime decarbonization and identify areas where further research is needed. Overall, this chapter is intended to help stakeholders involved in maritime decarbonization by providing a guide to the key drivers, challenges, and opportunities for decarbonization.

Key Takeaway Messages

- To combat climate change and help meet the target agreed at the 21st UN Climate Change Conference (COP21) in Paris in 2015 to limit the global temperature increase to no more than 1.5 °C, the maritime industry should take immediate and

Z. Raza (✉)
Research Institutes of Sweden (RISE), Gothenburg, Sweden
e-mail: zeeshan.raza@ri.se

S. Singh
University of Gibraltar, Europa Point, Gibraltar
e-mail: sukhjit.singh@unigib.edu.gi

M. Lind et al. (eds.), *Maritime Decarbonization*,
https://doi.org/10.1007/978-3-031-39936-7_2

collective action to reduce its emissions. This entails achieving several goals such as decreasing emissions by 45% by 2030 relative to 2010 levels, restricting the consumption of fossil fuels by the worldwide fleet from 12.6 Exajoules annually (equivalent to roughly 300 million tonnes of fossil fuels) to 150 million tonnes or 6 EJ (6×10^{18} J) by 2030, attaining net-zero emissions by 2050, and enhancing the onboard energy efficiency. To do this, shipowners and operators should set ambitious decarbonization targets, prioritise transparency, and use clear and comparable environmental, social, and governance reporting.

Introduction

- While regional measures and initiatives are important, a global approach is necessary to address greenhouse gas emissions from international shipping by both developed and emerging economies.
- As a consequence of stringent environmental regulations developing countries, particularly Small Island Developing States and least-developed countries, may experience a greater decline in gross domestic product and import/export flows compared to developed coastal States. To support vulnerable countries in their efforts to mitigate and adapt to climate change, a portion of the revenues generated by the levy or Market Basket Measures should be allocated for this purpose, with the remainder going towards Research and Development and administrative costs.
- To achieve successful decarbonization in the maritime industry, it is necessary for regulatory, policy, financial bodies, and customers to de-risk the investments and activities of first movers. All stakeholders should support initiatives that drive collective decarbonization, share costs, benefits, and risks, such as green corridors. Policymakers at regional, national, and local levels should develop roadmaps that encourage dedicated investments in green energy and fuel infrastructure, as well as engineering capacity to build these facilities.
- The International Maritime Organization should provide clear enforcement mechanisms, tighten compliance levels, and find regulatory solutions to ensure shared responsibility among all parties that influence vessel emissions.
- Collaboration across value chains is crucial. Ports being central transport nodes and energy hubs should work with parties decarbonizing other value chains to ensure the right fuel is available for its intended use, in the right quantity, at the right time, and at the right price. Alternative fuel producers, ports, and vessel owners should work together to prove technologies, demonstrate business concepts, and share challenges and opportunities.

As one of the most expensive and difficult sectors to decarbonize, the shipping industry is facing increasing pressure from shareholders, regulators, customers, and other stakeholders to decarbonize at a rate that aligns with the needs of our addressing the issue of a warming planet. The European Union (EU), International Maritime Organization (IMO), and individual countries are implementing stricter carbon emission regulations, and customers and clients are seeking decarbonized shipping to meet their Scope 3 decarbonization targets. Scope 3 emissions are the result of activities from assets not owned or controlled by a reporting organisation, but that the organisation indirectly affects in its value chain. Lenders are also striving to decarbonize their lending portfolios, while environmental groups and civil-society organizations are advocating for decarbonization more vigorously than ever before (Almasi et al., 2022). Research by the Boston Consulting Group (BCG) (BCG, 2022) shows that the vast majority of shipping customers are prepared to pay a premium for carbon-neutral shipping, and the willingness to pay is growing fast. Yet the amount of the premium that they will accept remains insufficient to achieve net zero carbon emissions by 2050 as emphasised by BCG (2022).

The Shipping Industry's Carbon Footprint

It would not be an understatement to say that the global shipping industry is what makes international trade possible. The sector is responsible for more than 80 percent of all goods transportation. Shipping remains by far the most energy-efficient form of freight transport, producing 20–25 g of carbon dioxide (CO_2) per ton-kilometre, compared to up to 600 g for aviation and between 50 and 150 g for road-based transport. If we measure CO_2 emissions from *well-to-wake*—that is, emissions from crude-oil extraction, refining into fuel oil, and consumption in the vessel—the sector accounts for about 3% of total global emissions (MMMC, 2021). While *tank-to-wake* is the metric more commonly used in the industry, a well-to-wake figure gives a more comprehensive and realistic measure of the industry's carbon footprint. Three segments, bulk carriers, tankers, and container ships are responsible for around 65% of the shipping industry CO_2 output. While these three categories make up around 90% of shipping volumes and contribute the most in terms of absolute emission volumes, it is worth noting that these large ships tend to be more energy efficient and less carbon intensive than smaller vessels. Still, these segments remain a critical target when planning decarbonization pathways (MMMC, 2021; Psaraftis & Kontovas, 2020).

Global shipping's CO_2 emissions posted a year-on-year gain of 4.9% in 2021. The rise in emissions over 2021 represents *an inconvenient truth* for the maritime industry as reported by Bockmann (2022). Longer tonne-mile trades, higher sailing speeds for some vessel types and increased port congestion pushed emissions higher.

Greenhouse Gas Targets of the IMO

As concerns about climate change and its impacts have grown, the IMO, the United Nations' (UN) specialised agency for the regulation of international shipping, has set environmental targets to decarbonize the maritime industry and mitigate its impact on the planet.

On July 7th, 2023 the 80th session of the IMO's Marine Environment Protection Committee (MEPC 80) approved a revised GHG Strategy, aiming to substantially reduce greenhouse gas emissions from international shipping. The newly adopted targets are ambitious, aiming for a 30% emission reduction by 2030, an 80% reduction by 2040 (compared to 2008 levels), and ultimately achieving net-zero emissions by 2050. It marks a considerable shift from the IMO's initial stance in 2015, which opposed emissions limits, to introducing targets in 2018 to halve emissions by 2050, and now aligning with the Paris Agreement. While the new "Net Zero" targets are a step in the right direction, there are criticisms that they lack specificity, using vague terms like "by or around 2050." Moreover, the absence of binding intermediate targets and the reliance on "indicative checkpoints" are seen as inadequate for a global and fragmented industry like shipping. To drive action across the board, financial incentives or coercive regulations are needed not only for major players but also for smaller owners (Jameson, 2023). Apart from targets, the IMO's mention of "mid-term measures," anticipated to take effect by 2027, is encouraging. These measures include carbon pricing and fuel standards. However, these ideas are not novel and have been discussed before. The lack of necessary details and clarity concerning financial incentives hinders investments in fuel production plants and clean technology development. This uncertainty also affects investment decisions for vessels and green technologies, as assumptions and scenarios continue to drive industry choices. To achieve these targets, the IMO has identified several potential measures, including technical, operational, and market-based measures. Technical measures involve improving ship design and technology, including more energy-efficient engines, propulsion systems, and hull designs. Operational measures focus on optimising ship operations, including slow steaming, improved maintenance, and voyage planning. The IMO has proposed multiple policy measures to limit GHG emissions from ships. These measures include:

- An Energy Efficiency Design Index (EEDI)—This sets energy efficiency standards for new ships based on their size, type, and other factors.
- Ship Energy Efficiency Management Plans (SEEMP)—This requires ships to have a plan in place to improve their energy efficiency and reduce their GHG emissions.
- A Data Collection System (DCS)—This requires ships to collect and report their fuel consumption, distance travelled, and other relevant data to the IMO.
- A Carbon Intensity Indicator (CII)—This sets mandatory carbon intensity targets for existing ships, which are based on their size and type.
- Market-Based Measures (MBMs)—these include policy measures such as a carbon tax, a cap-and-trade system, or a fuel levy, which can incentivise the shipping industry to reduce its GHG emissions.

While the outcome of MEPC80 represents progress, it falls short of adequately addressing the shipping industry's challenges. Comparing it to initiatives like the EU's FuelEU Maritime, Renewable Energy Directive (RED), and ETS reveals missed opportunities for more significant action. The lack of clarity and uncertainties persist, impeding investments and transformative actions. Ship owners, operators, and the broader ecosystem continue to face uncertainty, impacting their respective supply chains and hindering investment in critical areas like fuel supply, vessel orders, and technological research and development (Jameson, 2023).

Current Status of Maritime GHG Emissions

As a result of the IMO's increasingly more stringent regulatory framework some progress has been made in shipping and the first vessels operating on zero-carbon fuels have been deployed. Technology and operating practices have led to improvements in energy efficiency. After decades of growing international trade, the 2008 global financial crisis triggered a reduction in trade growth, which resulted in a temporary shrinking of carbon emissions for about a year. After the recession, the industry managed to achieve substantial business growth while keeping emissions to a minimum through a variety of means. For example, slow steaming—the practice of deliberately slowing down to reduce fuel consumption—helped reduce emission intensity per ton-mile by 13% between 2008 and 2012 and almost to the extent where the industry managed to decouple business growth and emissions for the decade between 2010 and 2020 (MMMC, 2021).

The results of the fourth IMO GHG study (IMO, 2020) show that the overall total maritime GHG emissions, both international and domestic, including CO_2, methane, and nitrogen oxides (NOx), as expressed in CO_2 equivalent emissions (CO_2e), increased from 977 million tonnes in 2012 to 1076 million tonnes in 2018. This was a 9.6% increase. Roughly 98% of the emissions were CO_2 emissions. According to the Initial IMO GHG Strategy (2018), GHG emissions by 2050 need to be at least 50% lower than they were in 2008, which is considered as the base year.

According to the fourth IMO GHG study, the industry has achieved a 29% reduction (from 15.16 g CO_2/t/nm in 2008 to 10.7 g CO_2/t/nm in 2018) (IMO, 2020). As noted by Psaraftis and Kontovas (2020), the voyage-based efficiency operational indicator (EEOI) data reveals that containerships and bulk carriers had achieved a reduction of around 35%, and bulk carriers a remarkable reduction of 60%. On the other hand, LNG tankers showed an increase of 7%. If the annual efficiency ratio (AER) is used as a proxy for carbon intensity, international shipping has achieved a 21% reduction as part of the 40% reduction target of 2030. Note that these carbon intensity metrics make more sense if viewed at a global (or even sectoral) fleet level rather than at an individual ship level, due to the number of uncertain factors that may impact the environmental performance of any individual ship.

In 2021, roughly 54,000 cargo and passenger vessels that voyaged across the oceans were under the ownership of approximately 15,200 companies. The categorization of these 54,000 vessels as 'cargo and passenger vessels' was determined through AIS matching and the calculation of CO_2 values was also based on AIS data. It is important to note that these figures specifically apply to those with higher CO_2 emission levels; smaller vessels with lower CO_2 levels were not included in the count. The 22 largest companies (being 0.15% of the total) owned 3355 ships (about 6.2%). These ships emitted 20% of the total CO_2 emissions. 964 companies (about 6.34%) owned 24,907 ships (about 46.1%) and emitted 80% of the CO_2 emissions. The situation with ports is similar. Out of the 5578 ports that serve the merchant fleet, only 26 (less than 0.5%) were host to 20% of CO_2 emissions from moored cargo and

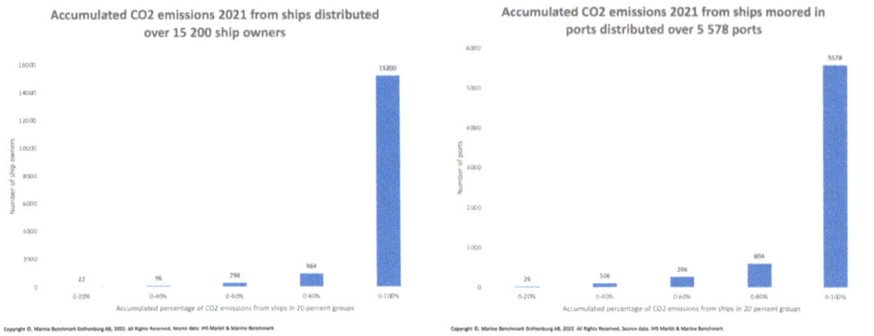

Fig. 1 Accumulated CO_2 emission from cargo and passenger vessels at anchor or berthed during 2021, grouped by number of ship owners and ports (Lind et al., 2022)

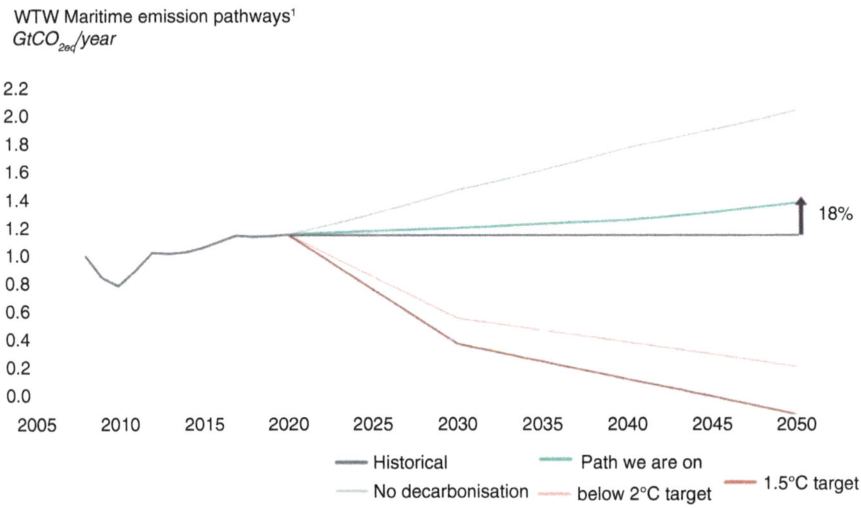

Fig. 2 Maritime emission pathways (MMMC, 2021)

passenger ships. This is shown in Fig. 1. The 747 million tonnes of CO_2 emitted by the merchant fleet include 47 million tonnes (about 6.3%) generated during while at anchor or berthed (Lind et al., 2022).

Potential Outcomes from Current Progress

While sporadic disruptions to global trade may occur, overall trade is expected to continue to grow until 2050, potentially leading to an increase in emissions, especially in East Asia. Despite the emergence of more environmentally conscious shippers who may switch from air freight to seaborne delivery, it is apparent that the current rate of adoption of cleaner fuel sources and energy-efficient ship technologies may not be enough to offset demand growth. In order to achieve its carbon neutral goals by 2050, the shipping industry must overcome several obstacles. Depending on the progress of other industries in reducing their environmental impact, shipping could account for between 5% and 8% of global CO_2 emissions by 2050, up from 3% in 2019 (MMMC, 2021; Kersing & Stone, 2022).

Although progress has been made in the shipping industry over the past decade, there is concern that the current trajectory may result in an increase in CO_2 emissions by 2050. Given the likely rates of improvement in ship efficiency, and the declining costs of alternative fuel technologies, it is expected that the industry's CO_2 emissions will still climb by around 18% until 2050—a significant slowdown over recent years but still not enough to reach carbon zero. This prediction can be seen in Fig. 2.

At present, the industry is significantly short of aligning with the trajectory outlined in the Paris Agreement of limiting the global temperature increase to 1.5 °C. According to a report by the Maersk Centre for Zero Carbon Shipping (MMMC, 2022), the shipping industry, both internationally and domestically, consumes approximately 12.6 EJ of energy annually, equivalent to roughly 300 million tonnes of fossil fuels, resulting in approximately 1.2 $GtCO_2e$ emissions from a well-to-wake (WTW) perspective. To achieve a 45% reduction in emissions by 2030 compared to 2010 levels, the shipping industry must restrict consumption of fossil fuels to approximately 6 EJ, which represents a significant reduction in the total energy demand of the global fleet.

To achieve the net-zero shipping emissions targets set by the IMO, EU, and several countries such as Japan, the United Kingdom, and the United States, the shipping sector needs to adopt comprehensive zero-emission programs within the next decade. However, this is a daunting task as ships have a long operating life of 20–25 years. While the necessary technologies to achieve zero-emission shipping exist, their deployment needs to be at a greater scale, speed, and lower cost. Zero-emission fuels are considerably more expensive than conventional fuels, increasing the total cost of vessel ownership by 40–60% depending on the shipping route (Joerss et al., 2021). Retrofitting systems in existing ships requires significant investment which is currently not supported by any major growth in charter rates or subsidies.

The lack of clarity on the future pathway also creates a challenge. Currently, within the maritime industry it is not clear which decarbonization approach to pursue. Electrification or hydrogen fuel may be appropriate for short-haul vessels, while deep-sea vessels may require green ammonia, methanol, or other low-carbon fuel options with higher energy density may be worth exploring or considering as potential solutions to address the decarbonization challenge. The problem arises because in such circumstances shipping companies opt not to invest in cleaner ships due to the lack of appropriate fuels, while clean-fuel providers do not invest in clean maritime fuels due to insufficient demand, resulting in a 'chicken and egg' situation.

Despite efforts to improve energy efficiency and adopt alternative fuels, the growing demand for maritime transportation, especially in emerging economies, may offset the emissions reductions achieved through technological and operational measures. The slow pace of technological innovation and the lack of regulatory frameworks may also hinder the industry's progress towards decarbonization. Therefore, there is the potential outcome that the maritime industry may not achieve the IMO's target of reducing total annual GHG emissions by at least 50% by 2050 compared to 2008 levels.

The Need to Strengthen Policy Measures

So far, policy measures have been the main drivers in advancing maritime decarbonization, but given the current challenges, targets need to be carefully designed and implemented to be effective. Effective policy measures require collaboration between governments, industry stakeholders, and other relevant parties to ensure that they are both practical and impactful. Research suggests that the decarbonization of shipping requires regulatory measures including market-based measures (MBMs) which could incentivise the development of alternative fuels and other energy saving technologies that are currently non-viable, plus they could produce short-term benefits as well, by encouraging slower speeds and thus reduced emissions. Putting it more simply, so long as fossil fuels are cheap, shipping companies will use them. MBMs would be a mechanism to internalise the external costs of GHG emissions and apply a polluter pays principle. However, due to implications involved in introducing MBMs, so far there has not been much progress on these within the IMO agenda (Psaraftis & Kontovas, 2020). In recent discussions at the IMO, it has been agreed by a significant majority that MBMs are needed as part of a comprehensive package of measures for the effective regulation of GHG emissions from international shipping. However, there is no consensus on the proposal, and it is still unclear how and when this discussion will continue at the IMO.

The lack of unanimity over MBMs may be due to United Nations Conference on Trade and Development (UNCTAD) studies that indicates that there is a major caveat: Irrespective of the exact combination of technical, operational, and market-based measures taken; the cost of shipping will increase. Higher costs will initially be borne by industry, before being passed on to end consumers. In developed economies, these costs may be relatively easy to bear, representing a small share of total shipping costs. However, developing countries, including, Small Island Developing States (SIDS) and Least Developed Countries (LDCs), may see their already disproportionately high shipping costs increase, exacerbating cost of living crises—beyond the current inflationary pressures arising from the Covid pandemic, geopolitical tensions, and crop failures due to climate change. Developing coastal countries, including SIDS and LDCs, are likely to experience a bigger decline in their gross domestic product (GDP) as well as import and export flows, when compared with developed coastal countries. Therefore, it is important that a part of the revenues raised by any levy or MBM measures should be allocated to support climate change mitigation and adaptation efforts in vulnerable countries with the remaining funds allocated for Research and Development and the administrative costs of the measures (UNCTAD, 2021; Shaw & Beukelaer, 2022).

Maritime decarbonization initiatives have been gaining momentum worldwide, with efforts being made in developed, developing and emerging economies to reduce CO_2 emissions in the maritime industry. However, research shows that some countries and regions have made tremendous progress in their efforts and initiatives related to green shipping while other countries are lagging behind. Europe, for instance, has been at the forefront of global efforts to combat climate change, and the maritime industry is no exception. The EU has set ambitious targets for reducing GHG emissions from the maritime sector, aligning with its overall goal under the European Green Deal of becoming carbon-neutral by 2050. The EU's regulatory frameworks, such as its Monitoring, Reporting, and Verification (MRV) regulation and the forthcoming EU Emissions Trading System (ETS) for shipping, aims to incentivise emission reductions and provide a regulatory framework for monitoring and reporting emissions. The EU has also established its Green Deal for Shipping initiative, which aims to accelerate the deployment of sustainable and innovative technologies in the maritime industry, including zero-emission vessels, alternative fuels, and smart and efficient port operations (EC, 2023). To this end, seaports are integral hubs of maritime supply chains and contribute to socio-economic development for communities and to decarbonize the shipping industry by providing alternative fuels and optimising port operations through digitalization. Research by Hossain and others (Hossain et al., 2021) reveals that EU ports have made greater progress in adopting sustainability initiatives while ports in North America and the Asia Pacific region are lagging behind in their efforts. This suggests that although regional efforts are important in the decarbonization of the shipping sector, a more robust and global approach is a prerequisite to clean the shipping sector.

Achieving the maritime industry's ambitious decarbonization objectives requires that we look at both, the larger and the smaller players. The economies of scale generated by the partnerships of larger companies may also have a positive impact on the smaller actors. The larger player-led decarbonization partnerships should find ways to include the smaller companies.

The global cooperation to tackle shipping emissions is difficult to achieve because of the diversity in institutional frameworks and arrangements for environmental and marine pollution that involve many different agendas, strategies, ambitions, and goals (industry, States, non-States, and global and regional organisations). In this respect, improving multilateral cooperation and technical assistance among countries is crucial (Wan et al., 2018). This is because many developing countries lack the resources (economic and organisational) and the technical capacity to fully participate in international Conventions and implement the obligations and regulations effectively.

As customers worldwide become increasingly aware of the environmental consequences of their consumption habits, they may pressure their governments to enforce stricter sustainability regulations. Additionally, investors are increasingly making sustainability-related demands of the companies they invest in. Shipping companies that do not take proactive measures to reduce their emissions may face negative consequences, including a diminished public perception of the industry. Furthermore, if they fail to take action, they could risk losing financial support as investors and banks direct their resources towards other more progressive industries—which, ironically, may have a smaller and therefore less significant carbon footprint to tackle than maritime.

If climate change continues to escalate, it is probable that there will be a surge in extreme weather conditions, including severe maritime weather that could lead to greater losses of ships and cargoes. Additionally, increasing sea levels pose a threat to port and terminal infrastructure. If global temperatures rise beyond 2 °C, as indicated by the Intergovernmental Panel on Climate Change, operators may be forced to allocate more funds towards adaptation measures. To ensure that the shipping industry can continue to facilitate global connectivity, which has been a critical driver of the world economy for centuries, it is vital to pursue the carbon-free targets that will enable the industry to prosper well into the twenty-first century.

The Way Forward

Facilitating maritime decarbonization requires a multi-faceted approach that addresses various aspects of the industry.

For the decarbonization of the maritime industry to happen, a quantum leap is needed in energy saving technologies and alternative fuels. To facilitate the adoption of clean energy technologies, there must be an adequate infrastructure to support them. This includes building the necessary charging and refuelling infrastructure for electric and hydrogen-powered vessels, as well as the infrastructure to support renewable energy sources. Governments and financial institutions have a major role in facilitating this transition by providing financing and incentives to stakeholders that are working towards decarbonization.

Despite continuing progress, such a quantum leap will not happen by itself, rather, it requires the proper incentives to do so. A price on carbon is one such incentive and a large share of the funds generated through a levy or carbon pricing should then be invested in greening the sector, R&D, and innovative projects, as well as climate mitigation. Furthermore, an unprecedented level of collaboration across industry and the maritime ecosystem is needed to reach the speed and scale of GHG reductions required to move out of the danger zone. Collaboration across value chains is crucial. Ports being central transport nodes and energy hubs must work with parties decarbonizing other value chains to ensure the right fuel is available for its intended use, in the right quantity, at the right time, and at the right price. Alternative fuel producers, ports, and vessel owners must work together to prove technologies, demonstrate business concepts, and share challenges and opportunities.

References

Almasi, S., Joerss, M., Kersing, A., Stone, M., Weber, B., & Zampelas A. (2022) *Destination zero: An action plan for shipping CEOs*. Retrieved from https://www.mckinsey.com/industries/travel-logistics-and-infrastructure/our-insights/destination-zero-an-action-plan-for-shipping-ceos

BCG. (2022). *Customers' willingness to pay can turn the tide toward decarbonized shipping*. Retrieved from https://www.bcg.com/publications/2022/customers-willingness-to-pay-to-decarbonize-shipping

Bockmann, M. W. (2022). *Shipping emissions rise 4.9% in 2021*. Retrieved from https://lloydslist.maritimeintelligence.informa.com/LL1139627/Shipping-emissions-rise-49-in2021#:~:text=In%202021%2C%20833m%20tonnes%20of,3%25%20of%20the%20world's%20emissions

EC. (2023). *Reducing emissions from the shipping sector*. European Commission. Retrieved from https://climate.ec.europa.eu/eu-action/transport-emissions/reducing-emissions-shipping-sector_en

Hossain, T., Adams, M., & Walker, T. R. (2021). Role of sustainability in global seaports. *Ocean & Coastal Management, 202*, 105435. Retrieved from https://doi.org/10.1016/j.ocecoaman.2020.105435.

IMO. (2018). *Initial IMO strategy on reduction of GHG emissions from ships*. IMO Resolution MEPC.304(72); International Maritime Organization (IMO). Retrieved from https://wwwcdn.imo.org/localresources/en/KnowledgeCentre/IndexofIMOResolutions/MEPCDocuments/MEPC.304(72).pdf

IMO. (2020). *Fourth IMO GHG study 2020*. International Maritime Organization (IMO).

Jameson, P.J. (2023). MEPC80 - This is not the end but it is, perhaps, the end of the beginning, https://www.linkedin.com/pulse/mepc80-end-perhaps-beginning-peter-jonathan-jameson%3FtrackingId=RfUMHth5RO2GBTd3yO3YBw%253D%253D/?trackingId=RfUMHth5RO2GBTd3yO3YBw%3D%3D

Joerss, M., Kersing, A., Kramer, A., Mohr, D., & Stone, M. (2021). *Green corridors: A lane for zero-carbon shipping*. Retrieved from https://www.mckinsey.com/capabilities/sustainability/our-insights/green-corridors-a-lane-for-zero-carbon-shipping

Kersing, A., & Stone, M. (2022) *Charting global shipping's path to zero carbon*. Retrieved from https://www.mckinsey.com/industries/travel-logistics-and-infrastructure/our-insights/charting-global-shippings-path-to-zero-carbon

Lind, M., Lehmacher, W., Tremerie, L. D., Dubielzig, F., Ellinor, F., Holthus, P., Morgante, A., Singh, S., & Tenenbaum, L. (2022). *Enablers for decarbonizing the maritime industry: Playbook part 4*. Retrieved from https://maritime-executive.com/editorials/partnering-towards-zero-emissions-shipping-playbook-part-4

MMMC. (2021). *Sailing toward carbon zero? Taking stock of maritime transportation's climate impact*. Mærsk Mc-Kinney Møller Center for Zero Carbon Shipping. Retrieved from https://cms.zerocarbonshipping.com/media/uploads/documents/MMMCZCS_Sailing_towards_zero_ver_1.0.pdf

MMMC. (2022). *Maritime decarbonization strategy 2022: A decade of change*. Retrieved from https://cms.zerocarbonshipping.com/media/uploads/publications/Maritime-Decarbonization-Strategy-2022.pdf

Psaraftis, H. N., & Kontovas, C. A. (2020). Decarbonization of maritime transport: Is there light at the end of the tunnel? *Sustainability, 13*(1), 237. https://doi.org/10.3390/su13010237

Shaw, A., & Beukelaer, C. D. 2022 *Why should we talk about a 'just and equitable' transition for shipping?* Retrieved from https://unctad.org/news/why-should-we-talk-about-just-and-equitable-transition-shipping

UNCTAD. (2021). *Assessment of the impact of the IMO short-term GHG reduction measure on states*. Retrieved from https://unctad.org/system/files/official-document/dtltlb2021d2_en.pdf

Wan, Z., et al. (2018). Decarbonizing the international shipping industry: Solutions and policy recommendations. *Marine Pollution Bulletin, 126*, 428–435. https://doi.org/10.1016/j.marpolbul.2017.11.064

The Extent of Decarbonization in the Global Shipping Fleet

Christopher Pålsson and Torbjörn Rydbergh

Target Audience

The information provided in this chapter is important for several maritime trade stakeholders:

Policy makers need to understand the scope of the current maritime trade, the main services provided and the basic fleet structures.

Marine equipment manufacturers have a particular interest in understanding the volume and type of new business to plan for, as well as the size of the market for retrofitting equipment. Many types of equipment relate to the energy efficiency and the propulsion of ships.

Cargo owners are looking at the environmental performance of their supply chains and therefore need to understand the current status and what to realistically expect in the future.

Many **ship owners** look at where the main drive of development is going to ensure they are well positioned to meet the future with right type of capacity and service. Updates about the uptake of new fuels and propulsion solutions help their investment decision processes.

Researchers need to understand the scope and potential use for their research findings. If they for instance find solutions that only are applicable on newbuilds of a specific vessel type with a certain type of engine, then it is of interest to get a perspective on the expected development within this specific market segment.

C. Pålsson (✉)
Maritime-Insight, Gothenburg, Sweden
e-mail: chris@maritime-insight.com

T. Rydbergh
Marine Benchmark, Gothenburg, Sweden
e-mail: torbjorn.rydbergh@marinebenchmark.com

M. Lind et al. (eds.), *Maritime Decarbonization*,
https://doi.org/10.1007/978-3-031-39936-7_3

Key Takeaway Messages

This chapter looks at the size and nature of the global fleet over the last two decades and more. It also identifies the extent of decarbonization in the ships that comprise the global fleet today and provides predictions for the likely changes of the fleet over the next five years.

The chapter is based on international trade data derived from several sources including Eurostat, The United Nations, The Organisation for Economic Co-operation and Development (OECD) and national statistics from various countries. These data have been analysed by the authors as part of maritime-insight and Marine Benchmark.

The world fleet is reviewed to gain a basic understanding of the scope and speed of change. In other words, how many of the ships currently trading are due for replacement in the near future and how many could be expected to be trading several decades more. This is relevant because it has an immediate impact on how quickly new propulsion solutions will penetrate the world fleet. A slow penetration means that retrofit and operational solutions of the current fleet is relatively more important than if the pace of change is fast.

Demand for Transport

Economic Growth

As shown in Fig. 1, over the longer term, even serious disruptions such as the Covid pandemic and a war in Europe are not expected to leave more than short-term dent on the development trajectory (IMF. 2023). This is not to downplay the seriousness of such events, but it is important to put recent developments into a historical perspective.

Trade

Figure 2 shows that a significant share of global trade (in metric tonnes), calculated as 79% by the authors (MI-tdb, 2023 [1]), is carried by sea. Liquid and dry bulk cargoes dominate. Containerised cargo has followed a strong growth trend for decades and has been part of this share. Containerised cargo slowed during the extreme freight rate peaks in 2021 and 2022, but is expected to regain momentum now that rates have normalised.

[1]Vessel data sourced from E.A. Gibson Shipbrokers, ShipPax Information and maritime-insight records.

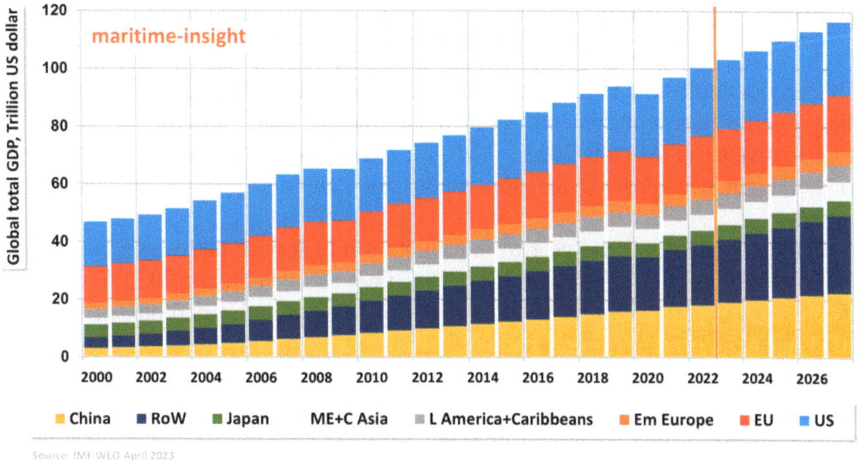

Fig. 1 Historical global GDP development and next five-year prediction, $Tn

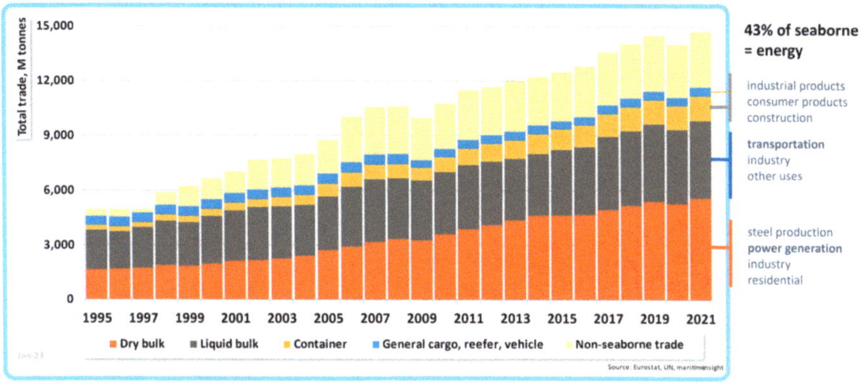

Fig. 2 Volume and means of transport for global trade 1995–2021

About 43% of all current cargoes relate to energy, according to calculations by maritime-insight. The majority of these cargoes are fossil fuels, such as crude oil, refined oil, gas and coal. This means that measures taken to address climate issues likely will seriously impact the demand for seaborne transport as we know it today. The net impact on shipping depends on a combination of many factors, and in particular what will be the requirements to transport the new sources of energy.

Global Fleet Figures

This section looks first at the age profile of the current world fleet to give an idea of the scope for fleet replacements. Then, a summary of expected new ship orders for the next five years (MI-fdb, 2023 [2]), (MI-sff, 2023). This is where new ship additions to the world fleet provide the opportunity for new ship designs and propulsion systems.

Figures 3 and 4 use the year of introduction into service and vessel category to show the age profile of ships in the global fleet as of February 2023. Ships built before 1970 are included in the total for 1969. The global orderbook in February 2023 has been used to present known new ship deliveries.

Figure 3 records the total number of ships in each category.

Figure 4 records the deadweight tonnage (dwt) of vessels in each category.

The age profile by number of ships (Fig. 3) and the age profile by tonnage (Fig. 4) of the world fleet shows that ships in the world fleet are relatively young (average age 16 years) and there are 13,973 ships that were delivered in 2000 or earlier. These ships, which are now more than 20 years old, and make up 26% of the current fleet, are all possibilities for disposal in the next five years. However, as Fig. 4 indicates these 13,973 vessels account for 161 M dwt or only 7% of the total fleet tonnage, given that more modern ships have become increasingly larger.

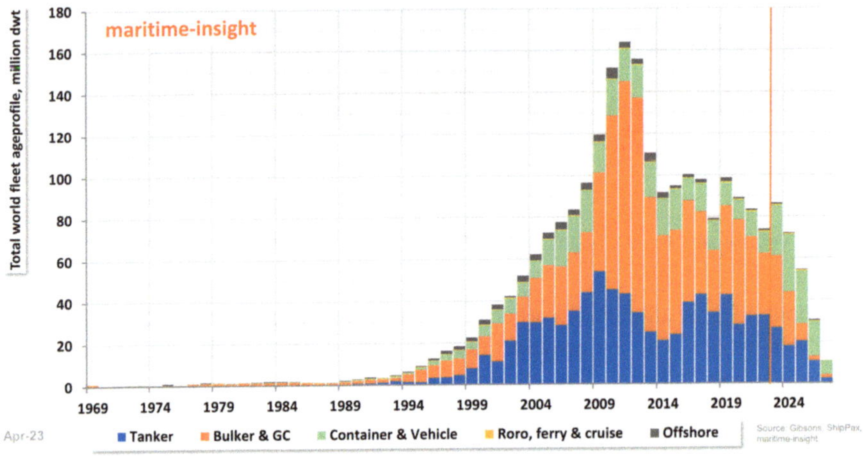

Fig. 3 World fleet age profile by number of ships in each category

[2] Vessel data sourced from E.A. Gibson Shipbrokers, ShipPax Information and maritime-insight records.

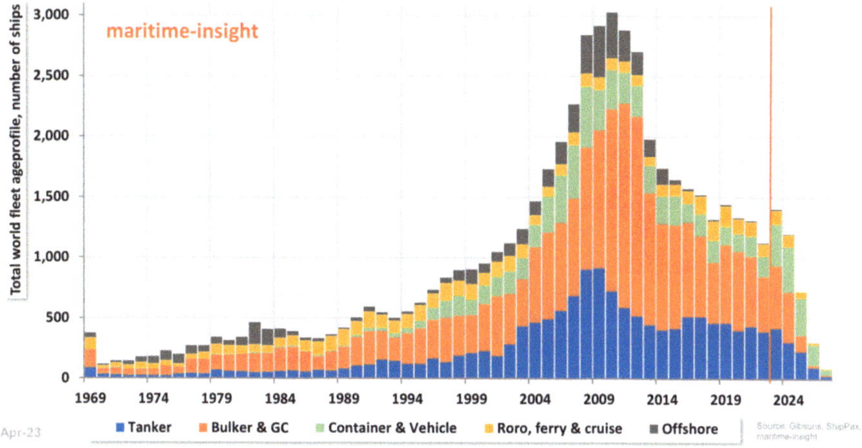

Fig. 4 World fleet age profile by dwt in each category

Shipbuilding

Figure 5 shows the percentage share of shipbuilding (in dwt) for the major shipbuilding nations.

The countries holding the number-one shipbuilding position has changed over time. The authors have three decades of experience talking to marine equipment industry leaders. Many of these leaders started their careers in the European shipbuilding industry in the early 1970s and have experienced first-hand how the business has moved to shipbuilding clusters in Asia.

Since 1950 the main driver of change in market share has been lower production costs. In most cases, the changes have coincided with the lower-cost nations developing and expanding their industrial bases. Shipbuilding has also been seen as a strategically important industry in several countries—Japan began this in the 1950s, South Korea in the late 1980s and China in the 2000s. There is nothing that indicates that these big three nations in shipbuilding output will be replaced within the next 10 years. China will most likely hold around 50% of the output or more.

The shipping market in general has moved towards ever larger ships. This has meant that the average yard output in dwt has been the same or higher even if fewer ships have been built. Larger ships also mean that the cost for steel makes up a bigger share of the total ship price since both the hulls and engines are steel dense. The quest from shipowners to pay as little as possible for the asset has, together with the scaling up of ship size, boosted Chinese builders' competitiveness, since China's steel industry has grown remarkably over the past 20+ years and now dominates the world market for price competitive steel. Prior to China, both Japan and South Korea ramped up steel production as their shipbuilding industries expanded.

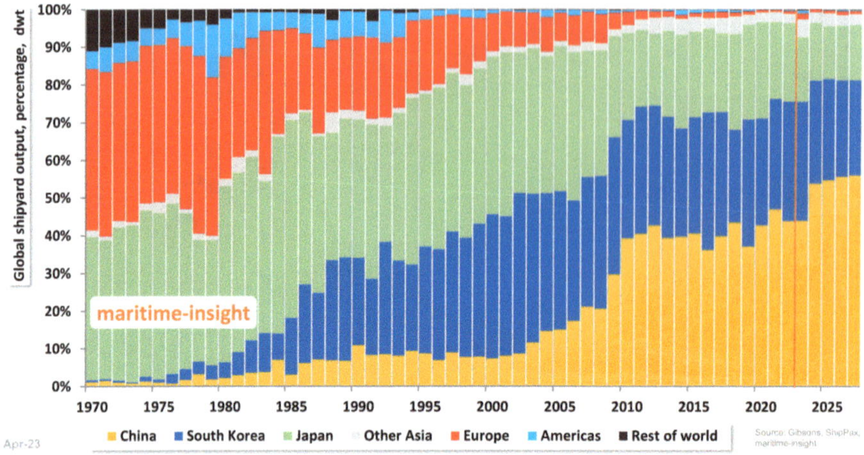

Fig. 5 Share of deliveries to the world fleet 1970 to 2027

The World Orderbook

The following six graphs provide data about the world orderbook in February 2023. The world orderbook is a dataset that contains information about the ships on order from all the world's shipyards. This information is included to provide a factual snapshot of what is in the shipbuilding pipeline over the next few years.

The data may be missing a few orders, but most of the larger ships are included. The time a ship is in the orderbook varies—it is in the orderbook from when it is ordered to when it is delivered or cancelled. The most complex ships, such as large cruise ships or LNG carriers, typically are in the orderbook longer than, for example, small general cargo vessels. Another factor to take into account is the ordering of a series of ships, in which case the first ship delivery could be years before the last, even though they are ordered at the same time. The delivery period for a large order for several complex vessels such as LNG carriers could span a number of years. The time in the orderbook will also be longer if yards are fully booked.

Figure 6 shows the number, type and region of building for ships on the world orderbook in February 2023.

Most orders (1013) are for container vessels and many of these large ships have long delivery times and will remain in the orderbook for a long time since they form part of a larger series of purchases. The next most numerous orders are for dry bulk carriers, where delivery times will be shorter. The third largest volume of orders is for the (unprecedented) 375 LNG carriers that will also remain in the orderbook for some time. These vessels are complex constructions, the series are long and they are being built at busy shipyards.

Figure 7 shows the ships on order presented according to main type and, dwt and the region of building. In total the orderbook stands at 243 M dwt.

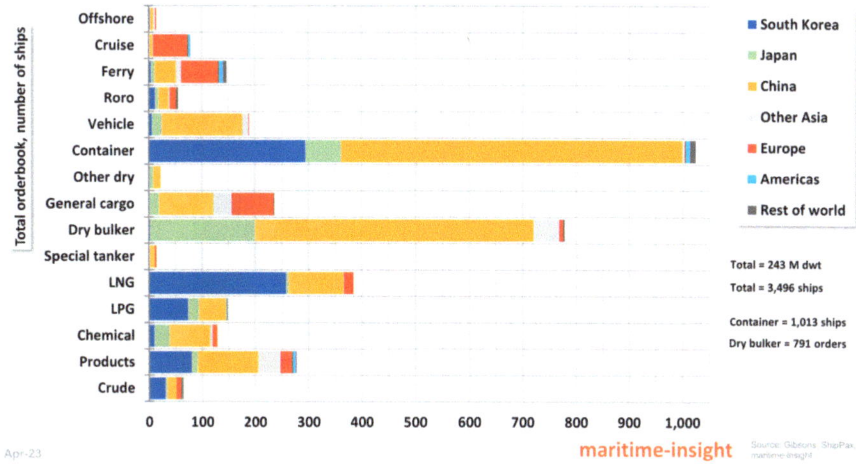

Fig. 6 Ships on order by type, number of ships and location

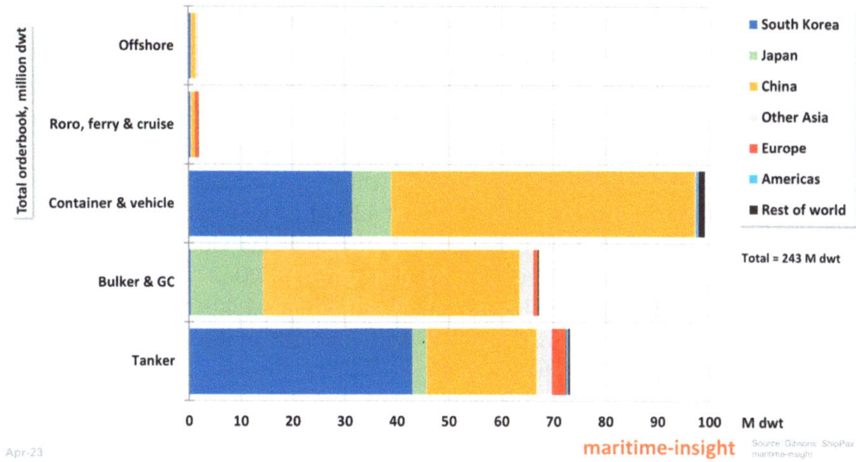

Fig. 7 Ships on order by main type, dwt and region of building

Container and vehicle carriers make up the largest volume in the orderbook due to the 95 M dwt for container carriers on order, ahead of tankers at 75 M dwt. Dry bulker and general cargo carriers together total 69 M dwt in the orderbook. This last group of ships will likely be delivered faster than the first two. At 239 M dwt, the three groups of ships together represent 98% of the dwt capacity in the orderbook.

53% of the current orders or 128 M dwt are to be built in China. South Korea has 31% of the current orders or 76 M dwt and Japan 10% with 25 M dwt.

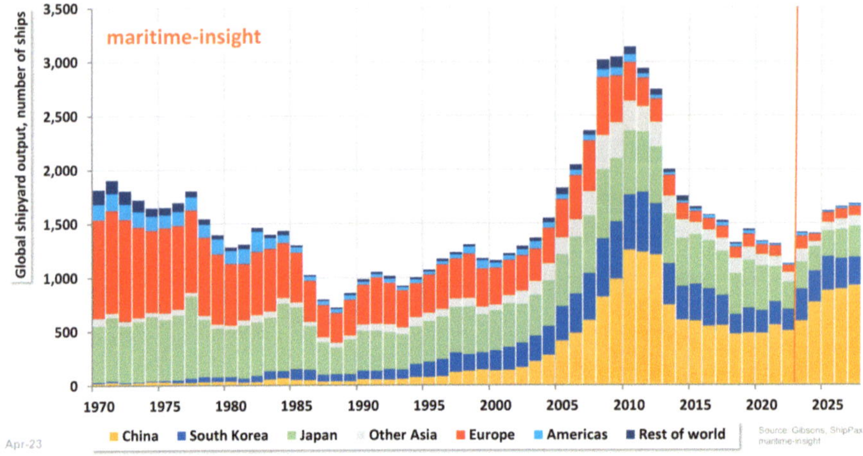

Fig. 8 Deliveries to the world fleet, number of ships, country/region

Figure 8 shows the number of ships delivered, from 1970 until 2022 and forecast deliveries until 2027. The deliveries are a good measure of where the main shipbuilding output is happening and how it has developed over time. Up to now, South Korean builders generally have had a higher degree of technological sophistication in ship construction than China. South Korea's high share of the LNG tanker orderbook is a reflection of this. Over the years, Chinese builders' capabilities have improved quite rapidly and this process will likely continue.

The total deliveries in 2018–2022 stood at 429 M dwt, spread over 6632 ships. This is an average of 86 M dwt per year, noting that the Covid pandemic held deliveries back. China delivered 182 M dwt in 2018–2022. While China was seriously impacted by the Covid pandemic it still provided 42% of the total deliveries. South Korea came in second with 127 M dwt or 30% of the total. Japan had the third largest output at 102 M dwt or 24%.

Figure 9 shows the volume of ships (M dwt) and type in the orderbook each year from 1990 and a forecast for the next five years until 2027, as well as the percentage of that volume in relation to the global fleet.

The forecast for 2023–2027 indicates total deliveries of 485 M dwt, spread over 7609 ships, or an average of 97 M dwt per year. China is forecast to deliver 267 M dwt, 47% more than in the previous five years and 55% of total deliveries. South Korea is forecast to deliver 117 M dwt, 24% of the total, down by 8%; Japan is forecast to deliver 79 M dwt or 16%, which is a 22% decrease over the last 5 years.

Figure 10 shows the number of new vessels ordered each year since 1990. New ship orders add to the orderbook, while new ship deliveries make the orderbook smaller. The net between new orders and deliveries is the orderbook development over time as illustrated in Fig. 9.

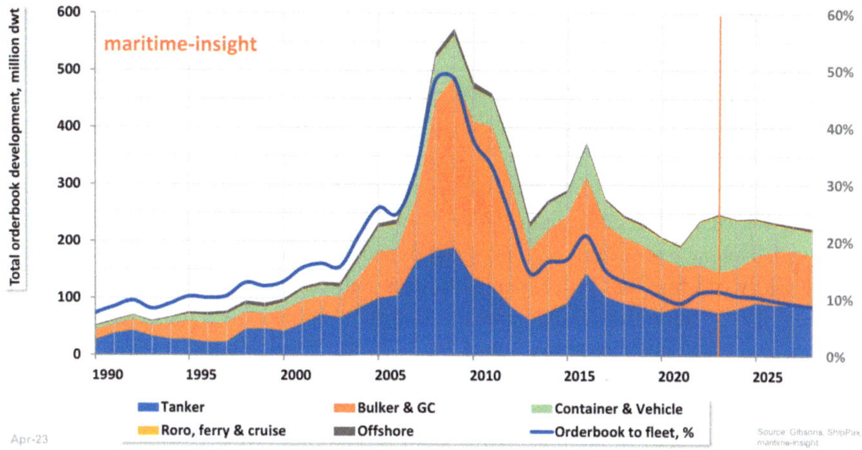

Fig. 9 Total orderbook at year-end, M dwt, and the percentage of the total fleet (blue line)

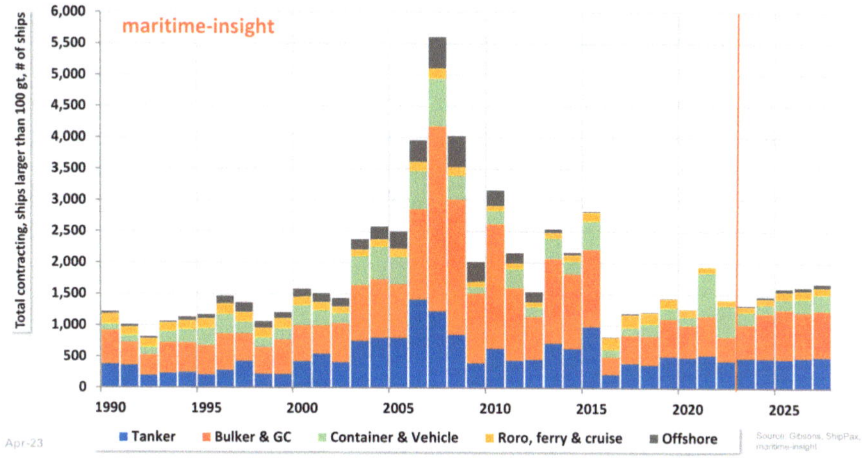

Fig. 10 Number of new contracts for ships since 1990 and predictions for 2023–2025

Between 2018 and 2022 the number of new orders was 7251 with most being bulker and general cargo vessels at 2595 ahead of tankers with 2332 and 1675 container and vehicle carriers.

The maritime-insight forecast for 2023–2027 indicates 7632 ships will be ordered (a 5% increase). The largest increase in orders is forecast for dry bulkers and general cargo vessels which are forecast to increase to 3555 (a 37% increase). New orders for tankers will be the same as the previous five years, but the orders for container and vehicle carriers are forecast to drop by 43% to 953.

Removals

The analysis of ship removals undertaken by maritime-insight is based on when a ship is permanently removed from the maritime transportation market. Some ships are removed by being converted, or are sunk or lost, or are permanently laid-up, but the most common removal by far, is by scrapping.

Ship removals are often matched by new ship orders as capacity needs to be replaced. The pace at which old tonnage is expected to be phased out gives an idea of how rapidly old fuel and propulsion solutions will be replaced by newer ones.

Since 1990 China, India, Pakistan and Bangladesh have been the countries where most tonnage has been scrapped, but China left the ship disposal market in 2018.

When a ship is broken up, the breaker normally disposes of everything. Steel is generally the most financially attractive commodity in a ship. Steel from ships can either be reused as is or as input to the steel production process. The latter uses far less energy than producing steel from iron ore, which makes it environmentally and financially attractive. Between 2007 and 2013 there was significant increase in tonnage that was removed from one market and converted to another. Most were large crude tankers that were converted to floating production and storage (FPSO) vessels. At the time, these conversions were more financially attractive to ship owners than scrapping.

Figure 11 shows the total tonnage of ships removed (scrapping or conversion) since 1990, arranged by vessel type and the country used for the scrapping or conversion. Tonnage, but not the location for removal, is provided for the prediction years 2023 to 2027. Since 2018, when China left the shipbreaking market, Bangladesh has scrapped almost 50% of the total of removed dwt. India and

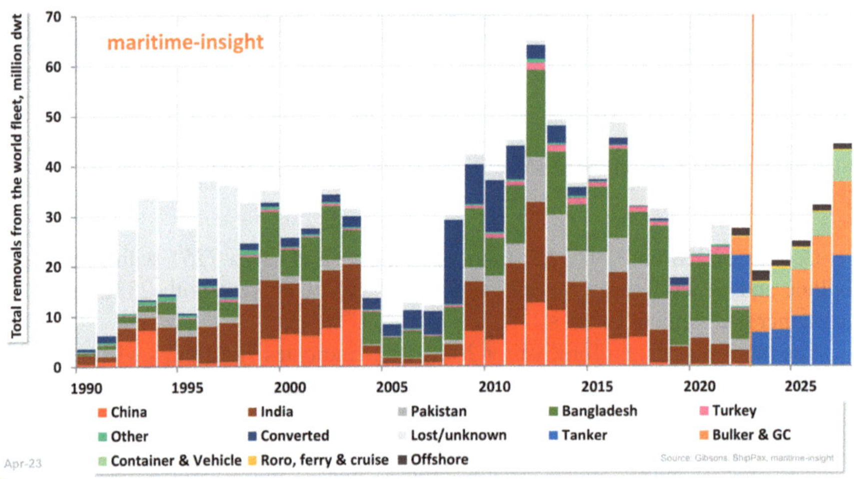

Fig. 11 Ship tonnage removed each year, arranged by dwt and country

Pakistan have captured around 20% each of scrapped tonnage. Turkey held around 5% of the market and is the only country outside Asia of significant size.

The data used to create Fig. 11 indicates that 2022 was expected to end with 20 M dwt of removals. However, there is often a lag in reporting from the smaller disposal sites, so this estimate may change slightly when additional data becomes available. The forecast is for a decrease from 28 M dwt removed in 2021.

Between 2018 to 2022 removals accounted for 125 M dwt or an average of 25 M dwt each year. 53 M dwt of tankers were removed and 47 M dwt of dry bulkers and general cargo ships. 10 M dwt of container and vehicle carriers also left the market.

Between 2023 and 2027 removals are forecast to be 163 M dwt or an average of 32.7 M dwt per year.

Most tonnage will be removed in the tankers sector with 70 M dwt, ahead of dry bulker and general cargo carriers with 64 M dwt. 20.5 M dwt of container and vehicle carriers will also be removed. The forecast includes an increase at the end of the period, mostly due to larger tankers passing 24 years of age.

Figure 12 shows the number of ships removed (scrapping or conversion) since 1990, arranged by vessel type and the country used for the scrapping or conversion. Total numbers, but not the location for removal, is provided for the prediction years 2023 to 2027. Currently, India breaks up approximately as many ships as Bangladesh, around 200 per year, but the ships are smaller in size. Pakistan breaks less than 100 ships yearly, as does Turkey, but the latter breaks up smaller ships.

Between 2018 and 2022 ship removals stood at 4181 ships (average 836 per year). Of these 1309 were dry bulkers and general cargo ships and 1276 were tankers. Notably, 729 came from the offshore fleet. Offshore here refers to the offshore petroleum industry and includes vessel types such as drilling, production, construction, Anchor Handling Tug Supply (AHTS), and platform supply vessels

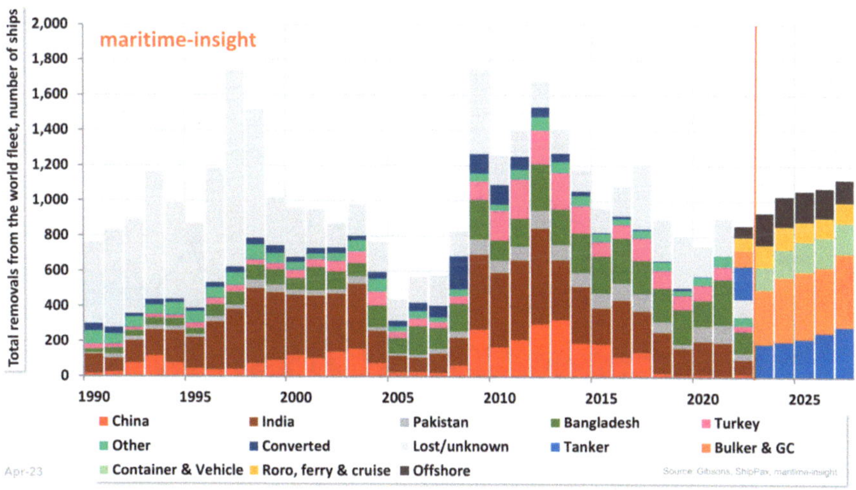

Fig. 12 Ship removals per year arranged by type and by region

(PSV). From 2023 to 2027 the forecast for removals is 5478 ships. This increase of 1096 ships is mainly related to the many smaller and older ships in the global fleet. 2211 ships are forecast to come from the dry bulker and general cargo fleet and 1256 from the tanker fleet. 757 offshore vessels are expected to be removed.

Size of the Global Fleet

Studying the way that the global fleet has evolved can provide insight into how the fleet may grow or contract in the near future. The size of the future fleet and how it evolves, directly affects how many ships, what tonnage and what propulsion systems will be required.

In February 2023 the global fleet stood at 54,142 ships with a combined volume of 2198 M dwt (Figs. 13 and 14). This includes commercial vessels involved in international trade of 100 gross tonnage and above. Service type vessels, like tugs, dredgers and workboats are not included. The fleet grew by 304 M dwt between 2018 and 2022, or 16%. In the same period, the tanker and the container and vehicle segments grew fastest at 18% growth; the dry bulk and general cargo segment grew most by volume with 144 M dwt, corresponding to 16% growth.

The forecast for fleet growth between 2023 and 2027 is for an addition of 321 M dwt. This corresponds to 15% or 2.8% compound annual growth rate (cagr) The blue line in Fig. 13 shows the total annual growth rate. The container and vehicle carrier fleet will grow by 99 M dwt (31%). Most dwt will be added to the dry bulker and general cargo fleet with 147 M dwt—a fleet growth of 14%. 77 M dwt is expected to be added to the tanker fleet giving a fleet growth of 10%, which is historically low.

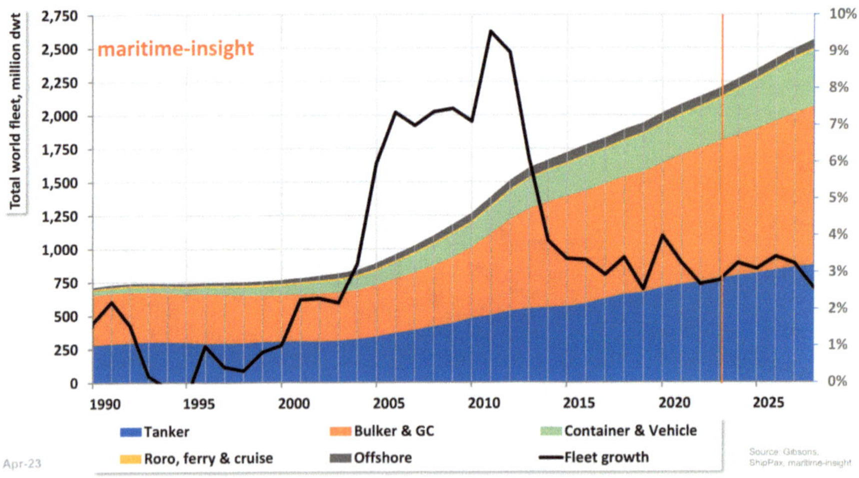

Fig. 13 Global fleet development by volume (dwt) and vessel type

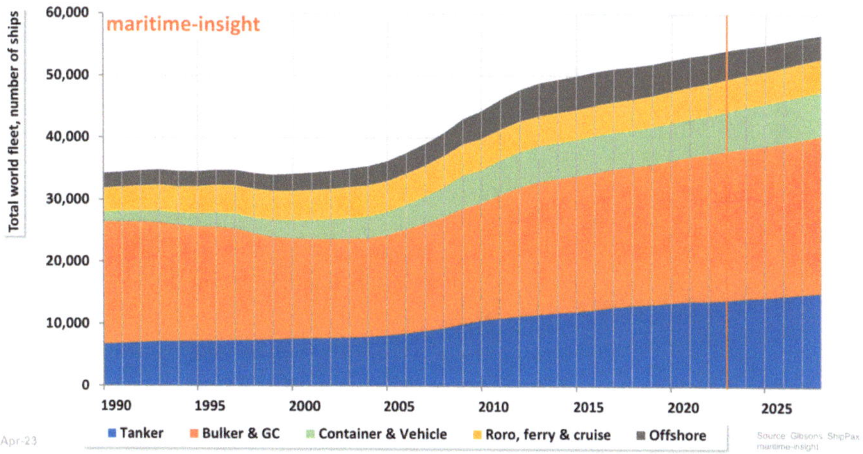

Fig. 14 Number of ships in the global fleet

Between 2018 and 2022 the global fleet grew by 2451 ships, with dry bulker and general cargo carriers growing the most with 1587 additional ships.

The forecast for the period 2023 to 2027 indicates a lower fleet growth, being 1932 ships, mostly highlighting the removal of many smaller ships. Nevertheless, the container and vehicle and the dry bulker and general cargo fleets are forecast to increase by 980 ships each, which means a 16% growth for the former and 4% for the latter. The tanker fleet will grow by 725 ships or 5%.

Table 1 shows the key figures for the global fleet in April 2023.

The Extent of Low- or No-Carbon Ship Propulsion and Fuels in the Global Fleet

The number of solutions on how best to fuel and propel a ship increases by the day. Conventional fossil fuels still dominate, but the more environmentally-friendly options are receiving ever increasing attention and exposure. This is particularly so because of the introduction of ever more stringent carbon-emission restrictions being placed on shipping. According to the current data, the most chosen alternatives to conventional low sulphur fuel oils, gasoil or diesel are LNG (for dual-fuel engines) and high sulphur fuel oil with scrubbers. It should be noted that the latter does not reduce CO_2 emissions but some preliminary tests with added alkali have shown positive results.

Blending conventional fuels with an increasing share of bio-fuels, electrofuels (e-fuels), being alternative drop-in or substitute fuels made using green power

Table 1 Key figures for the global fleet—April 2023

miTYPE			Fleet		Averages					
April-23	miSUBTYPE/SIZE	Unit	1000 cap	Nc	Size	New buildings	removals	age	20 years + 1000 cap	% of fleet
Crude	200′+ dwt	dwt	271,267	883	307,211	311,778	298,455	10.1	25,166	9%
	120′–200′dwt	dwt	100,293	640	156,709	157,656	148,260	10.4	9895	10%
	60′–120′dwt	dwt	71,838	670	107,222	113,557	99,627	13.2	7170	10%
	10′–60′dwt	dwt	399	10	39,934	21,500	47,629	6.3	–	0%
	–10′dwt	dwt	8	2	3824	6613	–	7.5	–	0%
Crude		dwt	443,806	2205	201	208,614	164,930	11.1	42,231	10%
Products	60′+ dwt	dwt	87,599	904	96,901	162,903	88,701	10.8	4669	5%
	20′–60′dwt	dwt	102,156	2240	45,605	56,226	40,252	11.9	8842	9%
	10′–20′dwt	dwt	4159	282	14,749	17,939	16,068	15.4	1017	24%
	–10′dwt	dwt	10,579	2469	4285	5631	2806	21.7	3839	36%
Products		dwt	204,493	5895	35	67,082	21,178	16.0	18,367	9%
Chemical	20′+ dwt	dwt	20,489	596	34,377	42,194	33,960	10.7	2694	13%
	10′–20′dwt	dwt	16,777	1089	15,406	17,102	14,945	13.3	2250	13%
	–10′dwt	dwt	8047	1567	5135	6544	4862	18.8	2652	33%
Chemical		dwt	45,313	3252	14	22,597	10,252	15.5	7597	17%
LPG	50′ + m^3	m^3	31,260	386	80,986	107,783	72,711	9.6	3604	12%
	–50′m^3	m^3	11,186	1205	9283	20,945	7309	17.8	2274	20%
LPG		m^3	42,446	1591	27	64,364	12,695	15.8	5878	14%
LNG	200′ + m^3	m^3	10,139	45	225,309	216,667	–	13.5	–	0%
	–200′m^3	m^3	94,554	659	143,481	187,093	113,760	10.0	9652	10%
LNG		m^3	104,693	704	149	187,913	113,760	10.2	9652	9%
Special tanker		dwt	2540	361	7036	17,484	7055	17.9	480	19%
Dry bulker	200′+ dwt	dwt	172,503	698	247,139	259,370	264,124	6.7	234	0%
	100′–200′dwt	dwt	213,963	1258	170,082	175,012	159,772	10.8	6618	3%
	60′–100′dwt	dwt	326,614	4320	75,605	90,889	71,880	9.2	31,170	10%

	35′–60′dwt	dwt	178,879	3654	48,954	50,367	43,778	12.0	22,671	13%
	10′–35′dwt	dwt	57,911	2129	27,201	24,552	24,291	16.3	14,839	26%
	–10′dwt	dwt	3327	634	5248	6217	4748	28.5	1990	60%
Dry bulker		dwt	953,197	12,693	75	105,222	73,453	12.2	77,521	8%
General cargo	10′+ dwt	dwt	29,645	1549	19,138	34,748	21,810	13.3	5783	20%
	–10′dwt	dwt	33,426	8833	3784	5156	3547	16.7	14,551	44%
General cargo		dwt	63,071	10,382	6	11,875	7003	16.2	20,335	32%
Other dry	Reefer	dwt	4196	692	6064	8691	6474	29.2	3376	80%
	Special	dwt	7122	343	20,765	37,740	17,784	15.0	1124	16%
Other dry		dwt	11,319	1035	11	30,309	9080	24.5	4500	40%
Container	>Panamax	teu	3834	193	19,864	27,994	0	5.0	–	0%
	10′teu –Panamax	teu	6318	491	12,868	17,518	0	6.6	–	0%
	5′–10′teu	teu	7418	1016	7301	10,071	5638	14.0	837	11%
	3′–5′teu	teu	3324	811	4099	5023	4155	13.9	471	14%
	2′–3′teu	teu	2143	797	2688	3206	2478	13.5	546	25%
	1′–2′teu	teu	1913	1332	1436	2019	1581	13.2	436	23%
	–1′teu	teu	548	871	629	642	826	19.7	211	38%
Container		teu	25,497	5511	5	9921	2582	13.6	2501	10%
Vehicle	4′+ ceu	ceu	3667	596	6154	8922	5182	13.7	528	14%
	–4′ceu	ceu	620	251	2469	3124	1920	17.2	150	24%
Vehicle		ceu	4287	847	5	8471	3965	14.8	678	16%
Roro	2000+ lm	lm	897	239	3755	6055	3269	13.1	183	20%
	–lm 1999	lm	494	488	1013	1425	983	26.2	309	62%
Roro		lm	1392	727	2	3987	1269	21.9	492	35%
Ferry	Ropax, 2000+ lm	pax	201	192	1048	1369	773	15.5	69	34%
	Ropax, –1999 lm	pax	1124	1482	759	614	786	24.3	732	65%
	Pax only, 1kgt+	pax	116	197	589	866	773	20.1	49	42%

(continued)

Table 1 (continued)

miTYPE April-23	miSUBTYPE/SIZE	Unit	Fleet		Averages					
			1000 cap	No	Size	New buildings removals age			20 years + 1000 cap % of fleet	
	Pax only, 25kn+	pax	438	1922	228	334	219	25.0	269	61%
	Pax only, <25kn	pax	38	122	315	749	458	22.3	19	49%
Ferry		pax	1918	3915	0	631	595	23.9	1137	59%
Cruise	1000+ berths	berths	739	223	3313	4742	1938	14.7	173	23%
	–999 berths	berths	95	362	263	464	337	19.0	47	49%
Cruise		berths	834	585	1	2458	803	17.4	220	26%
Offshore	Drilling	dwt	2922	99	29,515	39,747	26,246	19.8	260	9%
	Production	dwt	53,147	334	159,123	187,397	159,361	16.2	14,429	27%
	Construction	dwt	2678	294	9110	876	7490	23.6	829	31%
	AHT/S	dwt	3291	2049	1606	2597	1595	22.9	987	30%
	PSV	dwt	4915	1826	2692	4716	1942	22.2	1323	27%
Offshore		dwt	66,953	4602	15	124,456	19,254	22.1	17,827	27%
	Total	*dwt*	*2,209,343*	*54,305*	*40,684*	*79,759*	*34,193*	*15.9*	*240,218*	*11%*

sources, or other types of fuel is one way to meet the tightening regulations. Another way is to switch entirely to another fuel, such as ammonia or hydrogen.

Some fuels can be seen to significantly reduce CO_2 emissions in so called tank-to-wake (TTW) assessments, which only consider what comes out of a ship's engine exhaust. However, well-to-wake (WTW) assessments look at the emissions for the entire supply chain of the fuels, from a fuel's production right through to the engine exhaust. The outcome from a WTW assessment can be quite different to a TTW assessment. An example of this is hydrogen which has zero CO_2 emissions in a TTW assessment, but in a WTW assessment the production and distribution of the hydrogen fuel determines whether it is actually a green, low-carbon solution or a higher polluting grey-carbon solution.

Irrespective of the chosen propulsion fuel there are several other ways to reduce a ship's energy consumption and therefore make it greener. Hull design impacts on the water resistance and therefore energy consumption. Hull drag resistance can be reduced with air bubbles or air cushions below the hull of the ship. Rudders and propeller design can also be altered to reduce fuel consumption. Various shipboard equipment can be made more efficient. Heat recovery can also add to the improvement.

The use of various kinds of wind assisted propulsion is yet another energy-saving feature that in favourable conditions can significantly reduce the fuel needed for propulsion.

Nuclear powered ships also have potential but are not currently considered to be a particularly attractive option due, amongst other things, to environmental sensitivities, and the cost and availability of appropriate commercial systems.

In all cases, ship owners are looking for a financially and logistically justifiable low- or no-carbon solution.

maritime-insight's forecasts have considered the various solutions' lowest resistance and highest attractiveness for each market segment (MI-fpf. 2023). This means for each option/solution:

- Challenge. The existence and height of technological, knowledge and logistic barriers.
- Total annual cost for a vessel, engine, fuel system, and the fuel.
- Certainty. How much uncertainty is there around a specific solution in terms of the ability to overcome the challenges and the future fuel price levels and the gap to other fuels. Higher uncertainty means a higher barrier.
- Adaptability. How flexible or future-proof is the solution based on what we know or have today.
- Sustainability. How green is the solution. Here it is a challenge between WTW and TTW. A TTW assessment that is accepted today stands the risk of turning *grey* in the future if the WTW assessment is declared to be *grey*.
- Longevity. Is the solution for the near-term or the longer term.

In addition, each solution is not equally applicable to all vessel types, vessel sizes or voyage length. Battery-powered very large crude carriers (VLCCs) are most unlikely.

The maritime-insight forecasts build on findings in published work from SINTEF Ocean, Chief Scientist Elizabeth Lindstad, DNV-Det Norske Veritas, BV-Bureau Veritas, ABS-American Bureau of Shipping, and LR-Lloyd's Register.

In maritime-insight's view, the most common alternative fuel is and will continue to be LNG. LNG is still a fossil fuel, but the CO_2 emissions are lower than other fossil fuels. There are also other environmental benefits from using LNG compared with fuel oils, such as much lower or no emission of soot. A significant share of the recent orders for larger container carriers has been for LNG dual-fuel engines. This fuel is an attractive option for most other vessel types too, and particularly so for LNG tankers.

e-LNG and e-diesel both release very low CO_2 emissions. However, the energy used in the production of these fuels is relatively high which means overall energy consumption will be high, and so will the price of the fuels. At this stage, we do not see e-LNG and e-diesel as strong contenders to fuel the future fleet.

Methanol and ammonia have received a lot of attention in recent years. Sometimes they are presented as shipping's future fuel. Both fuels still come with a great deal of uncertainty about availability and future prices. The physical handling of ammonia is quite challenging and should not be overlooked.

Green ammonia has almost zero CO_2 emissions and e-methanol can be carbon neutral, but neither of them is currently widely available. Grey-methanol and grey-ammonia are both produced mainly using natural gas which makes their environmental performance poor in any WTW assessment. In any case, they are not yet widely available either.

The long-term availability of and prices for renewable electricity determines the price gap not only between conventional fuels, but also between the e-fuels like e-LNG, e-diesel, e-methanol, and e-ammonia.

Electric and battery powered ships are generally smaller and sail on shorter voyages between locations where a proper shore-based charging infrastructure can be established.

A rapidly increasing share of new LPG tanker orders will be LPG-fuelled. LPG as a ship fuel has some potential. Nitrogen oxides (NO_x) and sulphur oxides (SO_x) emissions are 13–18% lower than those from heavy fuel oil (HFO) as are CO_2 emissions. However, the fuel is less energy dense, meaning that fuel tank space must be three times larger than for HFO.

LPG is already widely used by many industries. This means that there will be greater competition for LPG fuel supplies, unlike for HFO. The LPG bunkering infrastructure for ships is so far largely limited to LPG tanker terminals.

We expect LPG to become a more established ship fuel for LPG tankers, and to a more limited extent also for other vessel types.

Full-scale feasibility tests of ship-based carbon capture are being carried out in several projects, not least within the EU-backed EverLoNG [3] project which has strong industry support. The EverLoNG project is demonstrating carbon capture in

[3] https://everlongccus.eu/

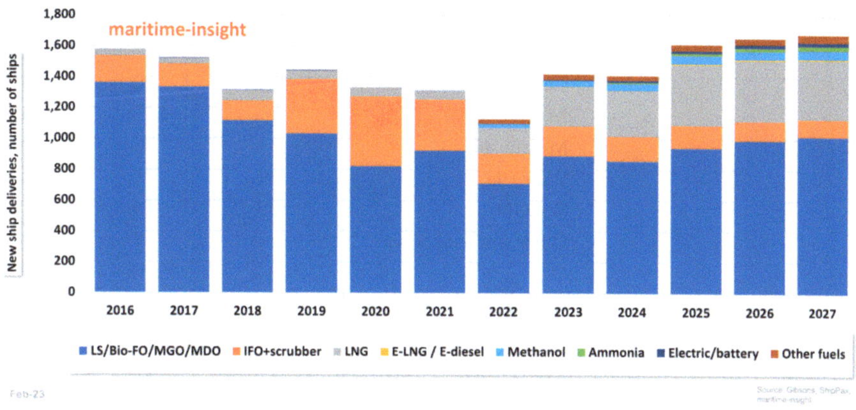

Fig. 15 New ship deliveries by type of fuel, number of ships

LNG-fuelled ships. maritime-insight observes that much of the carbon capture technology exists, but the economic barriers are still too high. A financially justifiable carbon capture solution could still provide a partial reprieve for fossil fuels.

Figure 15 shows the type of fuel being used in new ships delivered since 2016. It is presented as the number of ships for each main fuel/propulsion solution. The blue area represents conventional carbon-based oil fuel engines that run on various kinds of petroleum products with the gradual inclusion of blending with suitable bio-diesels. The share has been and will continue to be significant in the near future.

The orange/brown area indicates ships with conventional oil engines that also are equipped with scrubbers for the reduction of SO_x emissions.

As mentioned above, the most common alternative fuel to fossil-fuel oil has in recent years been LNG. This is expected to continue to be so for several years to come as it is now an established and reliable interim option with few uncertainties and therefore an easy choice for ship operators to make.

Within the next five years, all the other options will have only a limited uptake. Among them methanol is the one that seems to be attracting most interest across vessel types and lengths of haul.

It should be noted that Fig. 15 only considers the number of ships—there is no distinction between small and large ships.

Table 2 provides a summary of the leading providers of ships' engines in the current world fleet organised by main vessel type. There are several engine design brands that historically are linked to MAN Energy Systems. MAN is the largest engine provider overall. Whilst MAN provides engines of most types and sizes, their main foothold is in the provision of large, low speed two-stroke engines. These engines are typically installed on large container carriers, bulk carriers and tankers.

Wärtsilä had a position here as well before the two-stroke business was acquired by WinGD some years back.

In smaller vessels there are more four-stroke engines and also medium to high-speed engines. Caterpillar is, for instance, strong in the high-speed end of the engine

Table 2 Total fleet by main type and engine design group

Bulker & GC Engine design group	Ships	dwt	kW
Caterpillar	7%	1%	3%
MAN	49%	83%	73%
Mitsubishi	5%	4%	5%
Wa rtsila	6%	7%	8%
WinGD	0%	1%	1%
Other (incl unknown)	32%	4%	10%
	100%	100%	100%
Container & vehicle			
Engine design group	Ships	dwt	kW
Caterpillar	5%	1%	1%
MAN	70%	76%	75%
Mitsubishi	5%	2%	2%
Wartsila	14%	15%	17%
WinGD	3%	5%	3%
Other (incl unknown)	4%	1%	1%
	100%	100%	100%
Tanker Engine design group	Ships	dwt	kW
Caterpillar	5%	1%	2%
MAN	54%	76%	68%
Mitsubishi	6%	3%	5%
Wartsila	7%	13%	13%
WinGD	2%	3%	4%
Other (incl unknown)	26%	4%	9%
	100%	100%	100%
Roro, ferry & cruise			
Engine design group	Ships	dwt	kW
Caterpillar	9%	9%	7%
MAN	10%	31%	18%
Mitsubishi	2%	5%	2%
Wartsila	8%	21%	17%
WinGD	0%	0%	0%
Other (incl unknown)	72%	34%	55%
	100%	100%	100%

market. Medium to high-speed engines are quite common in passenger vessels. There is quite a large number of engine providers of smaller medium and high-speed engines.

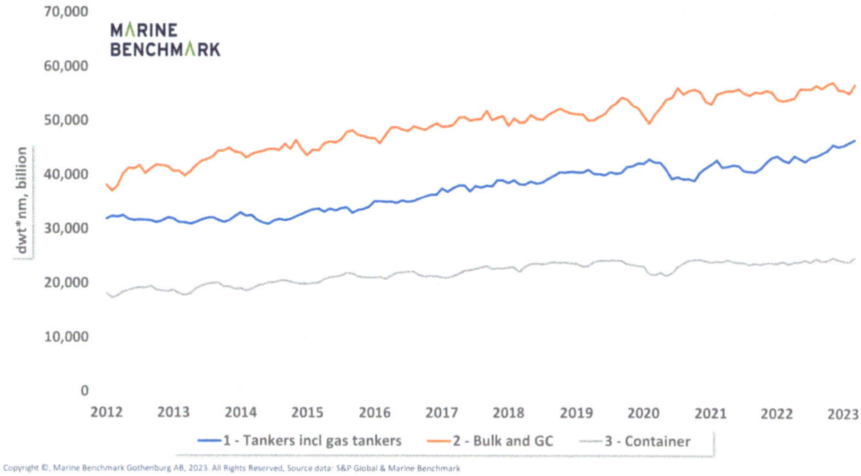

Fig. 16 Fleet dwt*nm, annualised, billion, monthly

Vessel Employment

Figure 16, provided by Marine Benchmark, [4] shows global fleet employment monthly since January 2012, expressed as vessel dwt multiplied by the distance sailed (in nautical miles), for tankers, bulk carriers (including general cargo carriers), and container carriers.

Using this metric, the employment level has followed an increasing trend throughout the period. For tankers the total increase is 43%, for bulkers and general cargo 46% and for container carriers 34%. However, it should be noted that the size of the fleets has increased at even greater rates during the same period, particularly for container carriers.

This indicates that the vessels have sailed slightly shorter distances, which could be a reflection of slower speed steaming, lower relative employment, changes in trading patterns, or combinations of all three.

Vessel employment is an important factor to bring in when trying to understand the future requirements for fuels and propulsion systems.

Vessel Speed

Figure 17, provided by Marine Benchmark, shows average global fleet vessel speed for tankers, bulk carriers and general cargo vessels, and container carriers. These are

[4] https://www.marinebenchmark.com/solutions/

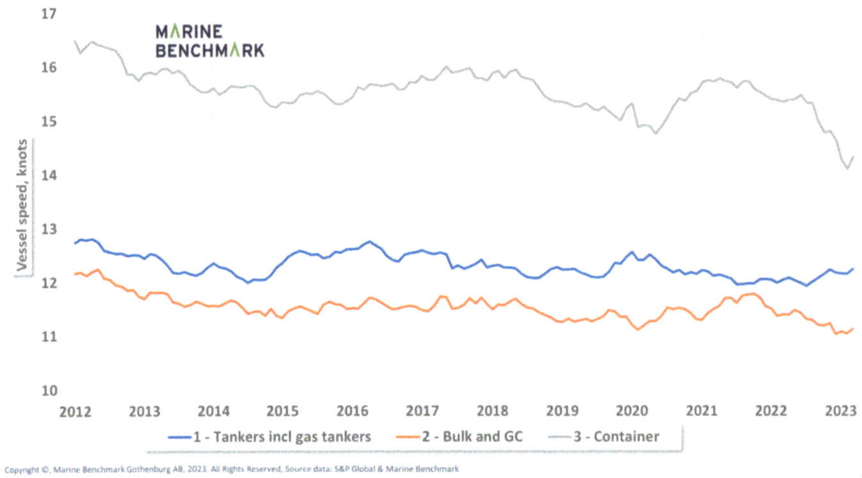

Fig. 17 Vessel speed, knots

based on vessels' steaming speed, which is taken as the average speed when the ships are sailing faster than 6 knots. The data are normalised using the dwt to give larger vessels a higher impact on the average. Large vessels have larger engines, consume more energy, and sail longer distances, but they also transport more cargo. For this reason, it provides a better view of 'who does what'.

It can be seen that the average speed has come down for all three vessel type groups, where the most marked change is for container carriers.

The average speed of the container carriers is also a reflection of the container shipping market from the beginning of the Covid pandemic to spring 2023. The speed fell in the early days of the pandemic, but picked up when activity returned. When freight rates increased sharply, speed increased further. When freight rates fell, speed declined rapidly.

CO_2 Emissions

Figure 18, provided by Marine Benchmark, shows that CO_2 emissions from tankers, bulk and general cargo carriers and container carriers in the global fleet have increased from around 560 million tonnes in the beginning of 2012 to almost 680 million tonnes in the beginning of 2023.

The calculations take into account the factors shown above as well as the relevant characteristics of each individual vessel and their automatic identification system (AIS)-derived employment activity. They also reflect the use of different kinds of fuel and propulsion systems to the extent that this is known.

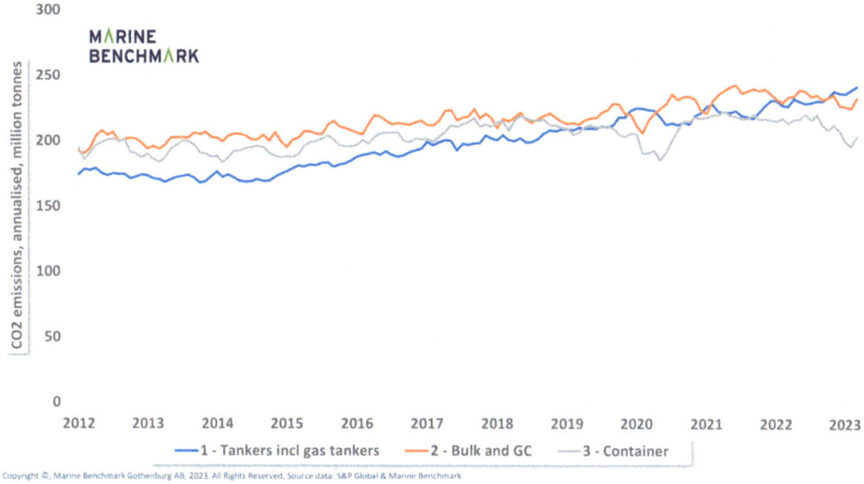

Fig. 18 Annualised CO_2 emissions, by month, million tonnes

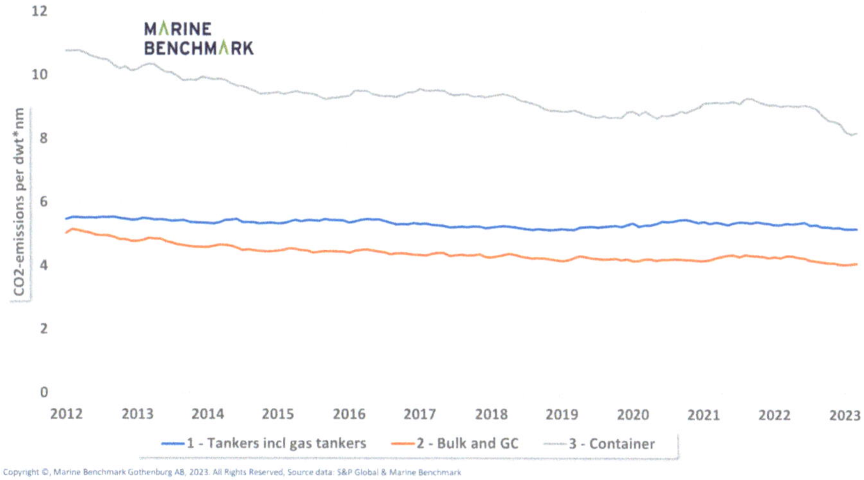

Fig. 19 CO_2 emissions per dwt*nm, by month

In Fig. 19, Marine Benchmark has compared energy efficiency over time, by dividing the CO_2 emissions values by dwt*nm.

The emission calculations have declined for all three vessel type groups over the period. Most significant is the decline for the container carriers.

Closing Summary

A sixty-year perspective on total shipbuilding output clearly shows how the shipbuilding business first moved from Europe to Japan, then to South Korea, and now China has taken pole position.

The orderbook in spring 2023 for the construction of new ships is dominated by large container carriers, tankers and bulk carriers, most of which are to be built in China and South Korea. South Korea has most of the orders for the construction of complex high-value liquified natural gas (LNG) fuelled tankers.

The ratio between the size of the orderbook and the size of the fleet gives an idea of the forward cover. Whilst the total fleet ratio hovers around a historically low level of 10%, it is much higher for LNG tankers, container carriers, cruise ships and liquified petroleum gas (LPG) carriers.

The Chinese orderbook is dominated by container and bulk carriers, South Korea's by container carriers and tankers, while Japan's orderbook is mostly full of bulkers. European builders still dominate the construction of high-end cruise ships.

Since China left the ship scrapping market three to four years ago, most ships are dismantled in Bangladesh, India, Pakistan and Turkey.

The long-term outlook for ship scrapping is one of increasing numbers. Between 2023 and 2027 the forecast for removals stands at 5478 ships which is 1096 ships more than in the previous five years. Initially removals will mainly be the many smaller and older ships in the global fleet.

A mounting challenge will be to recycle all these ships in a sustainable way, according to standards and processes in support of so-called green recycling.

The current status on the use of fossil fuels in the world fleet is that they dominate completely; also in the current orderbook. The main alternative to heavy fuel oil is LNG which has better environmental performance but is still a fossil fuel which emits CO_2.

The number of methanol fuelled ships has increased quickly in recent times, but from a very low level. There are still only a few ammonia fuelled ships on order. The point at which non-fossil fuels replace fossil-based oil as the main propulsion fuel is still a number of years away.

References

IMF. (2023). *World Economic Outlook, January 2023 International Monetary Fund.* Retrieved from https://www.imf.org/en/Publications/WEO

MI-fdb. (2023). *maritime-insight fleet database, maritime-insight, 2023.* Vessel data sourced from E.A. Gibson Shipbrokers, ShipPax Information and maritime-insight records. Retrieved from https://maritime-insight.com/

MI-fpf. (2023). *maritime-insight fuel and propulsion forecasts (part of shipbuilding and fleet forecasts). Maritime-insight, 2023.* Retrieved from https://maritime-insight.com/

MI-sff. (2023). *maritime-insight shipbuilding and fleet forecast, maritime-insight, 2023*. Retrieved from https://maritime-insight.com/

MI-tdb. (2023). *maritime-insight trade database, 2023. Maritime-insight*. International trade data derived from Eurostat, United Nations, OECD and National Statistics. Retrieved from https://maritime-insight.com/

Part II
A Step-by-Step Concept for Decarbonizing Shipping

Four Steps to Decarbonization

Mikael Lind, Wolfgang Lehmacher, Jeremy B. Bentham, Sanjay Kuttan, Kirsi Tikka, and Richard T. Watson

M. Lind (✉)
Research Institutes of Sweden (RISE), Gothenburg, Sweden

Chalmers University of Technology, Gothenburg, Sweden
e-mail: mikael@realsearchers.com

W. Lehmacher
Independent Supply Chain Expert, Hong Kong, China
e-mail: w.lehmacher@gmail.com

J. B. Bentham
World Energy Council, London, UK

Scenarios Team, Shell International, The Hague, The Netherlands

Mission Possible Partnership, Washington, DC, USA

Boston Consulting Group, Amsterdam, The Netherlands

Transformative Scenarios B.V., The Hague, The Netherlands
e-mail: jbentham@live.com

S. Kuttan
Global Centre for Maritime Decarbonisation, Singapore, Singapore
e-mail: sckuttan@gcformd.org

K. Tikka
Board Member Ardmore Shipping, Pembroke, Bermuda

Board Member Pacific Basin Shipping, Hong Kong, Hong Kong SAR

Board Member Foreship, Helsinki, Finland
e-mail: kktikka@outlook.com

R. T. Watson
Digital Frontier Partners, Melbourne, Australia
e-mail: rick.watson@digitalfrontierpartners.com

M. Lind et al. (eds.), *Maritime Decarbonization*,
https://doi.org/10.1007/978-3-031-39936-7_4

Target Audience

This chapter should particularly interest board members, sustainability managers, and project managers who wish to develop a holistic decarbonization programme. This chapter covers:

Key Takeaway Messages

- The four foundational concepts for climate action collapsed into a '4-step process' that drives strategies, business cases, execution plans, and decision-making-are: *scenario analysis* (context) (Lind et al., 2022a), *value chain mapping* (scope) (Lind et al., 2022b), *enabler prioritisation* (focus) (Lind et al., 2022c), and *partnership selection* (synergies) (Lind et al., 2022d).
- Although there is a natural sequence, the four steps support each other in an iterative symbiotic co-development. In combination, the four steps represent the 4-step path to structured decarbonizing actions.
- Recommendations to guide stakeholders in their decarbonization efforts.
- Adopting the 4-step process to structured decarbonizing actions will help companies and governments drive their decarbonization efforts more effectively and efficiently.

A Process of Four Foundational Concepts for Climate Action

Everyone who delves into maritime decarbonization quickly realises that removing greenhouse gas (GHG) emissions swiftly at scale requires a structured, systematic approach. Four foundational concepts for climate action collapsed into a '4-step process' to provide a framework for comprehensive climate action. The four steps drive strategies, business cases, execution plans, and decision-making. These steps are *scenario analysis* (context) (Lind et al., 2022a), *value chain mapping* (scope) (Lind et al., 2022b), *enabler prioritization* (focus) (Lind et al., 2022c), and *partnership selection* (synergies) (Lind et al., 2022d). Although there is a natural sequence, the four steps support each other in an iterative symbiotic co-development. In combination, the four steps represent the 4-step path to structured decarbonizing actions (Fig. 1).

Strategies, business cases, execution plans, and 'go/no-go' decisions leading to the implementation of decarbonization roadmaps are also critical to close the cycle from intent to impact. While these management processes are usually specific to a company or country and are well covered generically in the literature, the 4-step path specific to decarbonization is less documented. This chapter focuses on this 4-step path to structured decarbonizing actions (4-step process).

What are the four steps in detail, and what recommendations can be provided to those who wish to compile a comprehensive climate action programme?

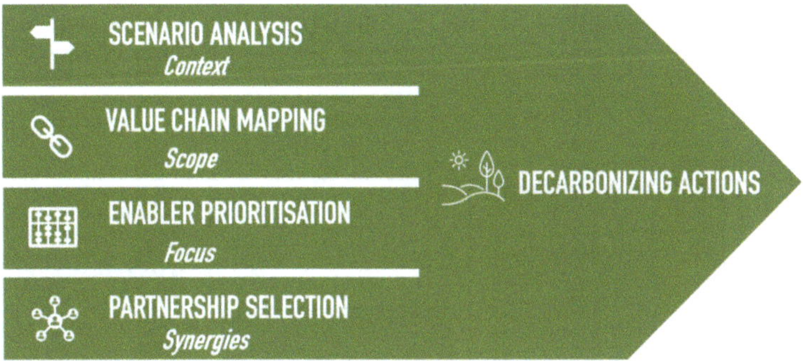

Fig. 1 4-step path to structured decarbonizing actions

Step 1: Scenario Analysis: Understanding the Boundaries

Scenarios offer plausible alternative views of how the macro-environment might develop in the long term. Scenarios are not strategies but probable alternative environments, which strategies might have to factor in to remain robust. Scenarios define boundaries that shape pathways towards different futures. Following a focused study (Lehmacher & Lind, 2022), we developed three maritime-themed transition scenarios: **Swells** place economic recovery first, **Storms** where local or regional interests are put first, and **Clear Sky,** where competing interests and stakeholder alignments primarily drive global maritime decarbonization. Figure 2 depicts anticipated major tipping points that will decarbonize shipping within the three abovementioned maritime transition scenarios.

These structured imagined scenarios are not outlooks cast in stone but are for stress testing the ways forward. They are a planning tool to adjust and refine a course of action to create the desired zero emissions future. Decarbonization begins with outlining probable futures to help define strategies that work in each or most of these futures and to point towards actions that may generate alternative outcomes that meet aspirations more closely.

Recommendations for future work:

- Build or review scenarios to shape or stress-test decarbonization strategies.
- Push boundaries of limiting scenarios, for example, through pioneering actions or urging IMO Member States' governments to support the proposed 'zero by 2050′ plan.
- Approach decarbonization through roadmaps with detailed annual targets.

Step 2: Value Chain Mapping: Scoping the Effort

A value chain (VC) is a step-by-step business process that moves a product or service from idea to reality (Kaplinsky & Morris, 2001). Every step along the chain should add value. The value-creating activities are generally accompanied by energy

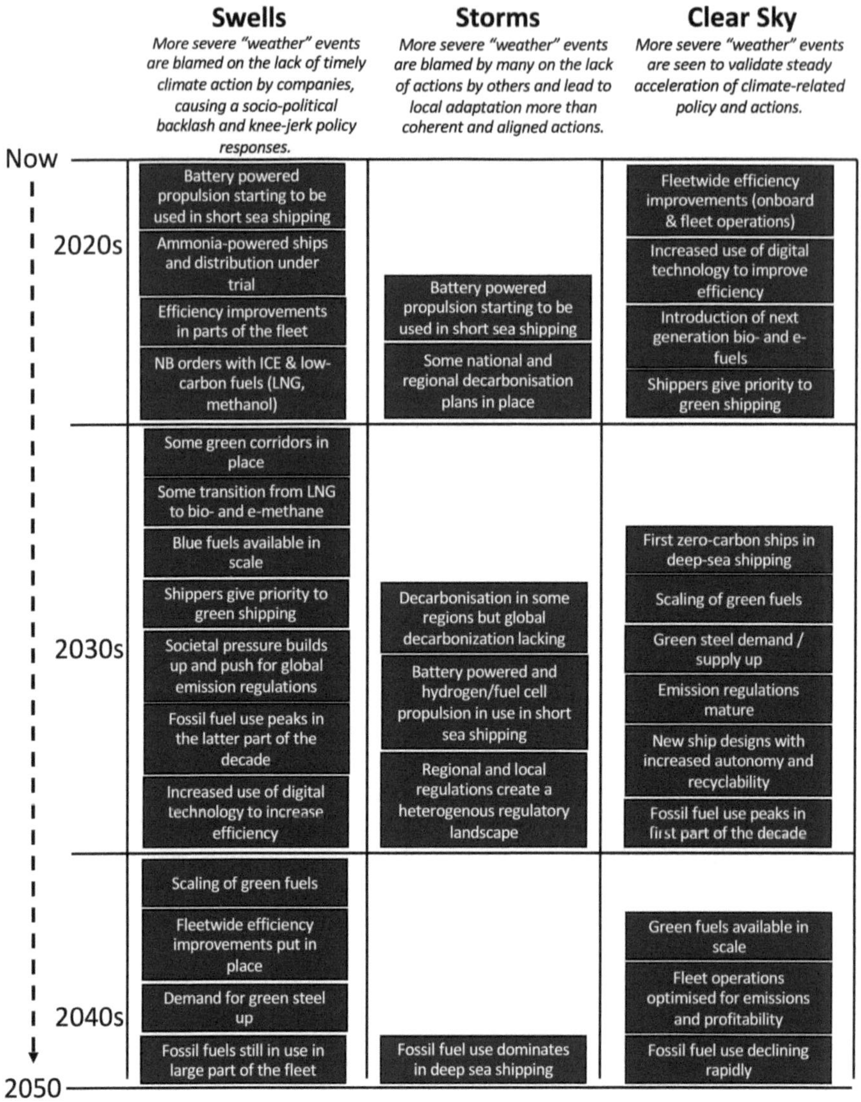

Fig. 2 Major tipping point moments identified in decarbonizing shipping (Lind et al., 2022a)

consumption resulting in GHG emissions. Hence there is a critical need to analyse VCs in detail to drive decarbonization profitably across the maritime sector and the general economy.

Three interdependent maritime VCs are critical to decarbonizing shipping: Marine fuel, Shipbuilding, and Maritime operational value chains.

A detailed analysis of the split of emissions in each VC empowers companies to reduce GHG emissions in a focused and systematic way, irrespective of the VCs in which they are engaged. Such an analysis is, unfortunately, not available currently and should be the object of additional research. The following inset box, however, indicates that significant attention to decarbonization is required for each VC. Despite the variances in impact between VCs, each actor must drive decarbonization with maximum effort to ensure the industry implements the 2023 IMO GHG Strategy. This requires commercial incentives as well as effective regulation.

Emissions from the three key Maritime VCs?

Overall, various estimates ascribe about 2.5–3% of global emissions to the maritime sector but these, for example, exclude indirect maritime-related activities such as the emissions generated by vessel manufacturing and ship steel production. While we are not aware of a detailed analysis of total emissions specifically related to each VC, the proxy analysis described below indicates that all three VCs are important, although possibly to different extents.

To operate, build or move anything requires energy and incurs financial costs. In the maritime industry, most energy used is currently derived from fossil fuels with resulting GHG emissions, so there should be a loose relation between financial measures of activity and emissions as both are driven by the amount of activity undertaken.

Consider a marine bunker of 229 million tons, a VLSFO (Very low sulphur fuel oil) bunkering price of USD 813 (9 August 2022), and a hypothetical levy of USD 100 per ton of carbon with 3.15 tons of CO_2, the commercial value of the Marine fuel VC based on its total annual expenditure can be estimated at approximately USD 250 billion, without factoring in the potentially higher costs and investments in alternative fuels. The shipbuilding VC can be valued at USD 115 billion, based on the contract value for new orders placed in 2021. Estimating an annual commercial turnover of the Operational VC is challenging. As a proxy, the asset value of the world fleet, according to UNCTAD's Review of Maritime Transport 2022, stands at USD 1.4 trillion.

Hence, the larger share of emissions may be generated by the Operational VC, followed by the Marine fuel VC, and then Shipbuilding VCs. The Operational VC is where the bulk of fossil fuels are burned in the direct conduct of maritime activities, but this rough analysis also highlights that it would be wrong to neglect the impact of the other VCs.

Effective decarbonization requires thinking about systems within systems. The cluster of maritime VCs is embedded in a decarbonization ecosystem that consists of several adjacent clusters of VCs (Fig. 3).

The public and private sectors need to address new challenges and opportunities in this broader context of the maritime decarbonization ecosystem. This brings about further questions. With whom does shipping compete for sustainable alternative fuels, and what does this mean for developing such fuels and decarbonizing the

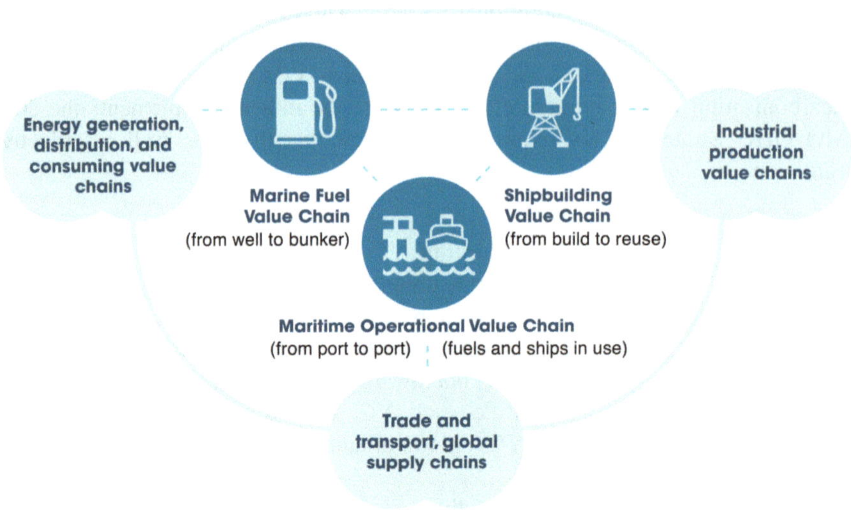

Fig. 3 Interdependencies, tensions, and synergies between related value chains (Lehmacher & Lind, 2022)

maritime industry? What factors influence the costs of building sustainable ships and their adoption price? How can the actors along the Maritime operational VC be motivated to align and reduce their carbon footprint? What global trade and ecosystem dynamics must be factored into the decarbonization calculus? Decarbonization will remain slow until the global community has found answers to these questions, considers the greater ecosystem, aligns across the landscape of actors, and develops appropriate and effective commercial incentives.

Decision-makers in the public and private sectors need to reflect on the value chains they are engaged in and how these VCs are clustered from a decarbonization and ecosystem perspective. They then should identify the stakeholders along those chains and build decarbonization partnerships with them. This is the scope of the decarbonization action.

Recommendations for future work:

- Map clusters of value chains relevant to maritime decarbonization.
- Identify relevant stakeholders in each value chain.
- Explore mechanisms and opportunities to activate the commercial engine to align and accelerate decarbonization actions.

Step 3: Enabler Prioritisation: Decide on Areas of Focus for Action

This step aims at identifying, assessing, and prioritizing relevant perceived decarbonization enablers. To reduce GHG emissions to minimal levels, the shipping industry can leverage various enablers (Lind et al., 2022c) positioned across the cluster of interconnected maritime value chains of Marine fuel, Shipbuilding, and Maritime operations (Lind et al., 2022e). Each industry should be responsible for activating enablers within its sectorial scope. However, enablers are interdependent across an ecosystem. Hence, prioritizing enablers requires a broader understanding of interrelated drivers' readiness, availability, and affordability. Some enablers are specific to only one value chain, while others cut across two or all three. Figure 4 shows a set of selected enablers with their position associated with the three interdependent maritime VCs and the cross-cutting role of some of these enablers.

There is no one-size-fits-all solution to decarbonization, but multiple ways should be explored to reduce emissions. Today, we need to bundle several enablers to achieve significant results. Even if some enablers have limited direct individual impact, the collective and synergistic impact can be significant.

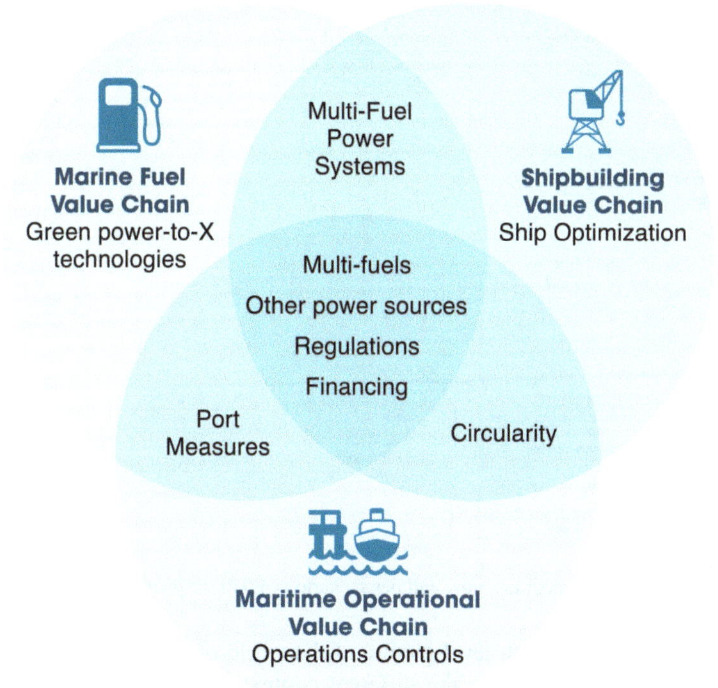

Fig. 4 Examples of enablers related to the three interdependent decarbonization value chains (Lehmacher & Lind, 2022)

Category	Now	Swells (2030)	Storms (2030)	Clear Sky (2030)
Multifuels	Biodiesel LNG	Biodiesel LNG	Biodiesel LNG	Biodiesel Green methanol
Other power sources	---	---	Green electricity	Green electricity
Regulations	MBM EEDI CII/EEXI	Gradual reduction of GHG content in fuel MBM CII/EEXI EEDI	CII/EEXI EEDI	Gradual reduction of GHG content in fuel CII/EEXI EEDI MBM Raw materials regulations
Financing	Green Bonds	Green innovation/R&D funds	Green innovation/R&D funds	Incentives for green fuel production Incentives for green shipbuilding Green innovation/ R&D funds
Multi-fuel Power systems	---	Multi-fuel ICE engines / onboard storages	---	Batteries powered motors Fuel cell technology Multi-fuel ICE engines / onboard storages
Circularity	---	---	---	Battery processes and management
Port measures	---	On-shore power supply Fuel storage/fuelling equipment for sustainable alternative fuels + incentives	On-shore power supply Fuel storage/fuelling equipment for sustainable alternative fuels + incentives	On-shore power supply Fuel storage/fuelling equipment for sustainable alternative fuels + incentives
Green power-to-X technologies	---	---	---	---
Ship optimisation	Hydrodynamics Ship size optimisation	Hydrodynamics Ship size optimisation	Hydrodynamics	Wind support Fleet renewal Ship size optimisation Hydrodynamics
Operations controls	Speed optimisation Advanced weather routing	Slot management Speed optimisation Advanced weather routing GHG emissions calculations	Slot management Speed optimisation Advanced weather routing	JIT Port calls Slot management GHG emissions calculations Speed optimisation Advanced weather routing

■ Usable within limits ■ Usable at scale

Fig. 5 Usable perceived enablers now and per scenario in 2030 (refined from Lind et al., 2022c)

Figure 5 provides a high-level picture of the world of maritime decarbonization now and in 2030, considering the different contextual developments in the three maritime transition scenarios—Swells, Storms, and Clear Sky. The table shows *usable decarbonization enablers at scale*, which are ready, available, and affordable, and *enablers that are usable within limits*. Usable at scale is assumed when an enabler's readiness, availability, and financial viability are assessed as 3 or 4 (medium to high). Usable within limits is assumed when an enabler's readiness and financial viability are assessed at 3 or 4, but the availability scores below 3 (2 = medium/low, 1 = low, or 0 = no availability).

As the public sector remains reluctant—probably rightly so—to prescribe a direction, the private sector is in the driver's seat. Private sector players can push the boundaries of limiting scenarios or even current global realities to go beyond the respective contextualised constraints. The public sector remains essential as it has the authority to implement acceptable, transparent, and predictable policies impacting fiscal, financing and pricing mechanisms, such as a levy on high-carbon marine fuels and subsidies for low-carbon solutions. Such funds can, for example, finance retrofitting ships and decarbonization infrastructure developments. The Covid-caused supply chain crunch (Hoffmann, 2022) has shown that a shortage of shipping supply capacity leads to extreme surges in freight rates, with a strong bearing on food security, inflation, and global value chains. Also, the energy transition can lead to shortages. Therefore, we should provide a stable multilateral framework to prevent these shortages from occurring in the coming decades. Furthermore, governments should direct funding towards investment in port upgrades, energy generation and distribution, and fleet renewal.

In deliberations among diverse stakeholders, multiplicity has emerged as a critical component of decarbonization in shipping: multi-fuels, multi-fuel ship engines, and more digital operational models are core to manoeuvring the multi-layered landscape of the maritime industry and the volatile nature of our world. Flexibility includes upgradable ship engines and ships, and the possibility to retrofit ships emerges as a considerable risk mitigator in the decarbonization effort.

Public and private sector decision-makers need to understand the enablers concerning their applicability and implications on operations. In some instances, the knowledge is already available but needs to be established in other instances. Knowledge-building can be achieved through individual efforts. Additional research is required, commissioned by public and private sector stakeholders.

Recommendations for future work:

- Identify relevant enablers across interrelated value chains to achieve company, industry, and ecosystem ambitions and goals.
- Prioritise relevant enablers based on readiness, availability, and affordability.
- Assess your ability to execute and identify gaps that need to be closed for enabler activation.

Step 4: Partnership Selection: Join Forces

One player can activate some enablers, but collaboration between multiple actors is required to activate the entire range. Collaboration can also help to align, accelerate, or intensify efforts. Hence, partnerships are critical to driving decarbonization across

Table 1 Contemporary partnerships populated in the Maritime Decarbonization Matrix (Lind et al., 2022d)

		Form of partnership		
		A: Vertical	**B**: Horizontal	**C**: Diagonal
Focus of partnership	**1**: Primarily participating companies benefit	**A1** CMA CGM biofuel trial Singapore[a] Hapag-Lloyd and DHL Global Forwarding collaboration on advanced biofuels[b]; BHP and NYK decarbonization partnership[c] MSC Shell partnership[d]	**B1** Tankers International VLCC Pool[e]	**C1** Project Sabre Consortium[f]
	2: Industry also benefits	**A2** Maersk green methanol partnership[g] CMA CGM/ TotalEnergies ship-to-ship LNG bunkering with the goal to establish a Mediterranean maritime LNG hub at Marseille-Fos Port[h] End-to-end shipboard carbon capture[i]	**B2** Digital standards (as one area of focus) in container shipping (Digital Container Shipping Association (DCSA))[j] International Association of Ports and Harbours (IAPH) with emphasis on climate and energy as one of many focuses[k]	**C2** Getting to Zero Coalition (Global Maritime Forum/ World Economic Forum)[l] The Global Centre for Maritime Decarbonisation (GCMD)[m] Mærsk Mc-Kinney Møller Center for Zero Carbon Shipping[n] Blue Sky Maritime Coalition[o] PIONEERS[p]; MAGPIE[q]; Maritime Just Transition Task Force[r]
	3: Ecosystem, also other industries and areas benefit	**A3** Maersk/Egypt green energy partnership[s]	**B3** None identified as yet	**C3** Mission Possible Partnership[t] First Movers Coalition[u] Renewable and Low-Carbon Fuels Value Chain Industrial Alliance[v] Mission Innovation[w] Climate Group's Steel Zero initiative[x]

(continued)

Table 1 (continued)

	Form of partnership		
	A: Vertical	**B**: Horizontal	**C**: Diagonal

[a]https://www.offshore-energy.biz/cma-cgm-launches-biofuel-trial-for-up-to-32-ships/
[b]https://trans.info/dhl-hapaglloyd-biofuels-295768
[c]https://www.nyk.com/english/news/2022/20220609_01.html
[d]https://www.dcvelocity.com/articles/51626-msc-shell-partner-to-decarbonize-global-shipping-industry
[e]https://tankersinternational.com/
[f]https://www.ship-technology.com/news/project-sabre-ammonia-bunker-vessel/
[g]https://www.powerengineeringint.com/emissions-environment/orsted-and-maersk-sign-landmark-green-fuels-agreement/
[h]https://www.cma-cgm.com/news/4083/cma-cgm-and-totalenergies-launch-port-of-marseille-fos-first-ship-to-containership-lng-bunkering-operation
[i]https://www.ogci.com/gcmd-ogci-and-stena-bulk-initiate-project-to-demonstrate-end-to-end-shipboard-carbon-capture-at-scale/amp/
[j]http://www.dcsa.org/
[k]http://www.iaphworldports.org/
[l]https://www.globalmaritimeforum.org/
[m]http://www.gcformd.org/
[n]https://www.zerocarbonshipping.com/fuel-pathways/
[o]https://www.bluesky-maritime.org/
[p]https://pioneers-ports.eu/about-us-2/
[q]https://www.magpie-ports.eu/magpie-project/
[r]https://unglobalcompact.org/take-action/think-labs/just-transition/about
[s]https://www.maersk.com/news/articles/2022/03/28/maersk-explores-new-ways-to-accelerate-green-fuel-production
[t]https://missionpossiblepartnership.org/
[u]https://www.weforum.org/first-movers-coalition
[v]https://transport.ec.europa.eu/transport-themes/clean-transport-urban-transport/alternative-fuels-sustainable-mobility-europe/renewable-and-low-carbon-fuels-value-chain-industrial-alliance_en
[w]http://mission-innovation.net/
[x]https://www.theclimategroup.org/steelzero

the larger ecosystem. Making partnerships work effectively requires strategies grounded in a profound knowledge of what collaborations need and the available collaboration options.

Making partnerships work requires a collaborative culture alongside the ability to compete effectively in the market. Partnership management will be critical to driving the maritime industry towards a zero-emissions future.

But what about the different types of collaboration? The Maritime Decarbonization Partnerships Matrix shown in Table 1 (Lind & Lehmacher, 2022) summarises partnerships along two dimensions; first, the *form of the partnership* (vertical, horizontal, and diagonal), and second, the *focus of the partnership* and who primarily benefits (company, industry, ecosystem).

Partnerships among VCs that exclude competitors are categorised as ‘vertical’. Partnerships fall in the ‘horizontal’ category where only peers are involved, and collaborations that consist of both vertical and horizontal alignment are considered ‘diagonal’. Diagonal partnerships also contain overarching initiatives with (some) focus on the maritime sector. All three forms can and should ideally include governments, international organisations (IOs), intergovernmental organisations (IGOs), and non-governmental organisations (NGOs). A collaboration that primarily impacts the companies involved falls into 'primarily company benefits'. A partnership that helps the entire industry, for example, through building a maritime bunkering hub falls into 'industry also benefits'; and an alliance that impacts multiple industries, like establishing a hub for renewable energy, which many industries can use, falls into 'ecosystem, also other industries and areas benefit'.

Diagonal partnerships that directly benefit the maritime industry and the broader decarbonization ecosystem (matrix cell C2 in Table 1) are paramount to avoid misaligning decarbonization actions.

Further discussion about the information in The Maritime Decarbonization Partnerships Matrix is in Chap. "Effective Partnerships to Support Maritime Decarbonization".

Reaching or exceeding the 2023 IMO GHG Strategy, the EU ambitions, and the Paris Climate Agreement goals requires a holistic and inclusive approach. Whilst the holistic dimension is reasonably reflected in the current partnership landscape, inclusiveness is lagging. The matrix is well populated with acknowledged partnerships, though generally, they consist of major players. Although the actions of current partnerships can have indirect positive impacts, including those of smaller and minor actors, often called the 'long-tail' and usually struggling more than larger companies with adopting decarbonization measures, should have merit. Effective decarbonization needs to involve everyone in a VC.

Public and private sector actors should understand the spread and dynamics of the evolving partnering landscape and engage where needed and appropriate. Based on what enablers they require to activate, actors can benefit from selecting specific partnerships to align, close gaps, accelerate, and intensify their decarbonization efforts.

Recommendations for future work:

- Select partnerships to gradually establish a portfolio of collaborations to align and cover unmet needs/capabilities at the company and possibly at the industry and ecosystem level.
- Ensure sufficient partnership management capabilities are developed across the organisation or accessible through partnerships.
- Establish cross-value chain coordination, for example, along zero-emissions corridors and areas.

The Merits of the 4-Step Process

Adopting the 4-step process to structured decarbonizing actions will help companies and governments drive their decarbonization efforts more effectively and efficiently. The '4-step path to structured decarbonizing action provides a critical foundation in addressing the challenges head-on for this large hard-to-abate transport sub-sector.

References

Hoffmann, J. (2022). *The end of the 2020-2022 supply chain crisis, and what we need to learn for the next one(s), 10/12-2022*. LinkedIn. Accessed from https://www.linkedin.com/pulse/end-2020-2022-supply-chain-crisis-what-we-need-learn-next-hoffmann/?trackingId=HQf42Q1PR5qL%2FSrXR2qBsA%3D%3D

Kaplinsky, R., & Morris, M. (2001). *A handbook for value chain research*. Institute of Development Studies, University of Sussex.

Lehmacher, W., & Lind, M. (2022). *Value chain-based pathways towards zero-emission shipping - A practical playbook*. Nordic West Office. Accessed from www.nordicwestoffice.com/maritime

Lind, M., & Lehmacher, W. (2022). *Positioning partnerships in shipping decarbonization, Article No. 92 [UNCTAD Transport and Trade Facilitation Newsletter N°95 – Third Quarter 2022]*. Accessed from https://unctad.org/news/positioning-partnerships-shipping-decarbonization

Lind, M., Lehmacher, W., Bentham, J., Tikka, K., Thomas, W., Notteboom, T., Fries, S., & Penttilä, R. (2022a). *Three maritime transition scenarios: Decarbonization playbook Part 1, 4/7-2022, The Maritime Executive*. Accessed from https://www.maritime-executive.com/editorials/three-maritime-transition-scenarios-decarbonization-playbook-part-1

Lind, M., Lehmacher, W., Doepel, T., Heinimaa, J., Hoffmann, J., Laurilehto, M., Lebmeier, M., Petersen, M., Rytkölä, I., Saari, J., Singh, S., Walls, R., & Watson, R. T. (2022b). *The benefits of a clusters of value chains perspective in decarbonizing shipping: Decarbonization playbook Part 2, 22/8-2022, The Maritime Executive*. Accessed from https://maritime-executive.com/editorials/the-three-maritime-value-chains-decarbonization-playbook-part-2

Lind, M., Lehmacher, W., De Tremerie, L., Dubielzig, F., Forsström, E., Holthus, P., Morgante, A., Singh, S., & Tenenbaum, L. (2022c). *Enablers for decarbonizing the maritime industry: Decarbonization Playbook Part 3, 25/9-2022, The Maritime Executive*. Accessed from https://www.maritime-executive.com/editorials/enablers-for-decarbonizing-the-maritime-industry-part-3

Lind, M., Lehmacher, W., Kuttan, S., Carson-Jackson, J., Cummins, D., van Gogh, M., & Rydbergh, T. (2022d). *Partnering towards zero emissions shipping: Playbook Part 4, 4/11-2022, The Maritime Executive*. Accessed from https://www.maritime-executive.com/editorials/partnering-towards-zero-emissions-shipping-playbook-part-4

Lind, M., Lehmacher, W., Åhlén Björk, S., Haraldson, S., Pålsson, C., Penttilä, R., Tikka, K., & Watson, R. T. (2022e). *Decarbonizing the maritime sector: Mobilizing coordinated action in the industry using an ecosystems approach, Article No. 89 [UNCTAD Transport and Trade Facilitation Newsletter N°94 - Second Quarter 2022]*. Accessed from https://unctad.org/news/decarbonizing-maritime-sector-mobilizing-coordinated-action-industry-using-ecosystems-approach

Scenario Thinking and Its Place in Maritime Decarbonization

Jeremy B. Bentham

Target Audience

This chapter has been written for those seeking an understanding of the value of scenario thinking in strategic decision-making associated with decarbonization. It is especially relevant to those that have leadership roles in ensuring sustainability in the private sector and for policy makers.

Key Takeaway Messages

The chapter highlights:

- Scenario thinking as a means for grappling with uncertainty.
- Scenarios as the learning tool that help us see beyond the horizon of our inevitably limited personal experiences and current circumstances.
- Scenario thinking as a foundation for prioritisation.
- Summarised maritime scenarios—building on three previously published broad scenarios

J. B. Bentham (✉)
World Energy Council, London, UK

Scenarios Team, Shell International, The Hague, The Netherlands

Mission Possible Partnership, Washington, DC, USA

Boston Consulting Group, Amsterdam, The Netherlands

Transformative Scenarios B.V., The Hague, The Netherlands
e-mail: jbentham@live.com

M. Lind et al. (eds.), *Maritime Decarbonization*,
https://doi.org/10.1007/978-3-031-39936-7_5

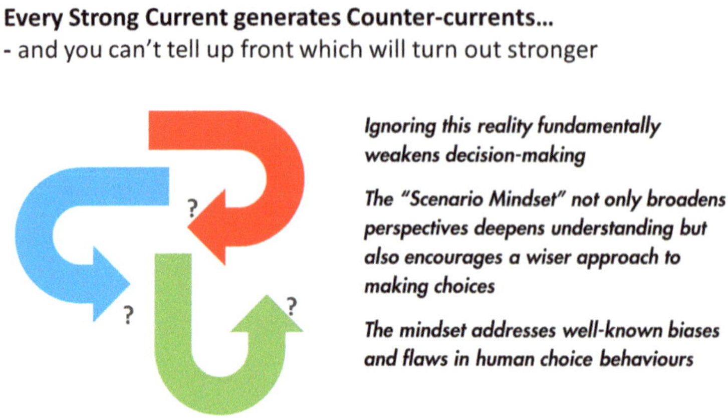

Fig. 1 A fundamental insight into future developments

Grappling with Uncertainties

Powerful currents are shaping our society and economy, indeed our whole world. These drive radical uncertainties and widespread instability. Of course, in the past there has obviously also been great turbulence as well. However, never have there been so many people on the planet, in so many cities, with so much material resource, information and opinion churning so quickly around the globe, such rapid growth in environmental pressures, and so much availability of technological power. We are in a particularly unusual era of volatility and transition.

Every strong current also generates counter currents, and you can rarely tell in advance which of these will prove to be the stronger (Fig. 1). Therefore, there are inevitably multiple different plausible pathways for our future. Much of this is beyond our direct control, and even our own actions can affect the future in ways that may surprise us. This may be awkward for governments and politicians, who try to project an aura of certainty and control, but closing our eyes to this fundamental truth is a recipe for impoverished decision-making. We ignore this essential feature of reality at our peril.

However, while not predictable, neither is the future completely random. There are constraints imposed by, for example, physical laws and biology, and features of society that remain relatively stationary like birth and death rates, human biases, or the time it takes to build major public infrastructures. It is, therefore, possible to explore plausible futures in a systematic way to identify both critical uncertainties and relatively settled trends. This is the art of building scenarios.

Possibly even more significant, is the scenario mindset that appreciates the importance of this.

Scenarios and Scenario Thinking

Scenarios are the learning tool that helps us to see beyond the horizon of our personal experiences and current circumstances, to help us grapple with perspectives and insights from others, and to help us become better prepared for surprises. The default human behavioural approach to considering future possibilities is to make simple forecasts that extrapolate current circumstances or patterns experienced in the past. This reflects the human bias described by behavioural economist Daniel Kahneman as '*What you see is all there is* (WYSIATI)' (Kahneman, 2011). Slightly more sophisticated default approaches may consider sensitivities anchored around a so-called 'most likely' outlook or try to construct so-called 'expectation cases' around assumed possibilities.

These approaches may be sufficient for simple cases over short timeframes when many factors may remain relatively stationary, but completely fail to address the fundamental realities highlighted above. Most important factors do not remain stationary (which also undermines the basis for estimating probabilities from historical evidence), and future human choices are intrinsically unpredictable.

In contrast, scenarios and the scenario mentality encourage stepping beyond WYSIATI, exploring plausible futures more thoroughly, and learning deeply from those explorations. They also help address another default human bias identified by Kahneman—predominantly 'thinking fast' and generally neglecting the more difficult reflective process of 'thinking slow'. The scenario mindset helps redress the balance between jumping to conclusions and reflective exploration. That is why the arrows in the last icon in Fig. 2 point forwards *and* backwards—we construct scenarios, and we also learn from them.

At their best, 'scenario snapshots' can generate a broad range of fresh insights which can then be focused into a smaller number of 'scenario pathways' through

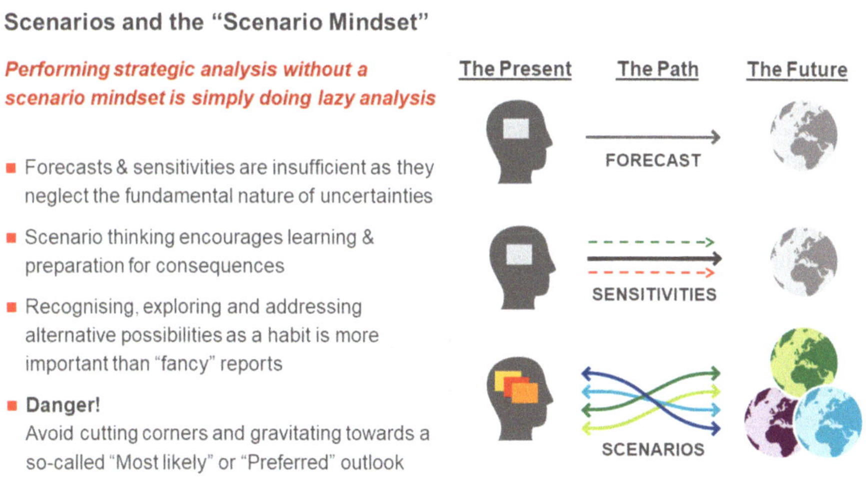

Fig. 2 Contrasting ways of viewing future possibilities

which their essence can be more effectively communicated. These can starkly illuminate the fundamental differences between routes through the future landscape, for example, just how quickly or slowly key developments may progress in decarbonizing the maritime industry.

There is a 'technical' craft in developing scenarios which involves interweaving disparate insights from multiple disciplines such as macro-economics, (geo)-politics, technology, industry/market analysis, sociology, and business studies. This is the 'visible' craft, but it is relatively meaningless unless the key insights are brought to life in the minds and actions of key decision-makers. This is a more subtle 'social' craft and is addressed further in a later 'How to' chapter of this book.

There are different approaches to the 'technical' craft, but well-known approaches are described in the book 'The Art of the Long View' by Peter Schwartz (Schwartz, 1991) and 'Scenarios: An Explorer's Guide' published by Shell (Davis & Bentham, 2008).

Maritime Scenarios

But scenarios are only a means to an end, and that end is making wiser choices. Scenarios, therefore, need to embody the particular critical uncertainties and settled trends that are relevant for the types of choices that *you* need to consider in *your* particular circumstances.

One approach can be to take well-formulated broad scenarios that already incorporate many of the currents and pressures requiring attention and then customise these with the additional specific details of the industrial sector or investment opportunity you need to focus on. This was the approach taken in an exercise conducted in early 2022 (Lehmacher & Lind, 2022) in which Maritime Scenarios were developed based on the published Shell Energy Transformation Scenarios (Bentham and Shell Scenario Team, 2021) as a broader starting point.

The three Shell Energy Transformation Scenarios, as shown in Fig. 3, explore different approaches to building resilience in the face of recent and current crises such as the Covid Pandemic and the Russia-Ukraine conflict. The scenarios are entitled *Waves,* with wealth prioritised first; *Islands* with security prioritised first; and *Sky 1.5* with health/well-being prioritised first.

While most parties will obviously be seeking all three of these positive objectives of wealth, security and well-being, particular circumstances and choices will lead to different emphases. This prioritisation affects where decarbonization is placed on the socio-political agenda.

Only in Sky 1.5 is the decarbonization effort a continuous high priority, with its focus on well-being, learning from experience and from others, and reforming institutions whose weaknesses have been exposed through recent crises. In Islands, with its focus on autonomy and self-sufficiency, decarbonization mainly happens when it fits into the local parameters, such as, the local energy supply. In Waves, with its initial focus on short-term economic growth, decarbonization initially

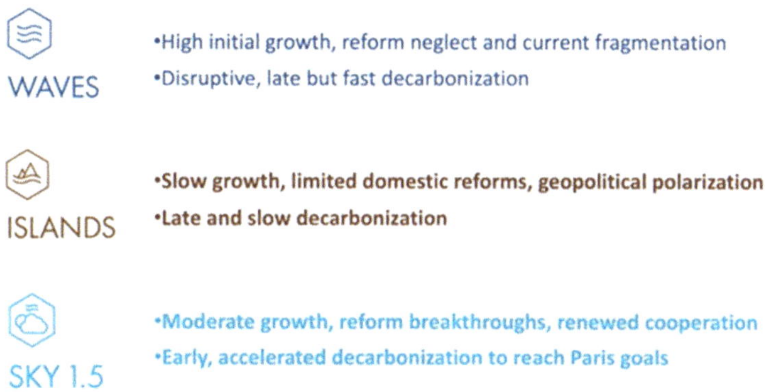

Fig. 3 The Shell Energy Transformation Scenarios

happens only when financially viable in the short-term without targeted policy support or effective alignments between stakeholders (globally) to open new opportunities. Subsequent backlashes, as in Waves, however, occur eventually when extreme weather events are blamed on previous lack of action, leading to knee-jerk regulation driving rapid but disruptive decarbonization.

From these outlooks, and other credible scenarios, we can learn technically what is required for global decarbonization in the coming decades. The major uncertainties are in the *pace* of change, which is driven by human behaviours and socio-political priorities. The *nature* of the changes required, however, is much clearer. Five main core technical areas are highlighted:

- Energy efficiency. This is not just about individual energy end-use applications like lighting or passenger cars but mainly about integrating infrastructures far more effectively like power, heat, waste, and water, and different modes of transport.
- Power generation from Renewables.
- Electrification of the economy. Increasing from 20% of total energy consumption currently to 60%, so power generation from renewables can grow to have much more impact on the whole system.
- Substitution of fossil-based liquid and gaseous fuels in sectors that are hard to electrify. These sectors (like heavy transport and heavy industry) still require energy-dense, portable, thermal, molecular fuels, but with progressive shifts from fossil oil to biofuels and natural gas to hydrogen-based alternatives.
- Carbon removals. Mopping up emissions both through technical approaches like CCS (carbon capture and storage) and nature-based approaches like re-forestation.

Three maritime-themed transition scenarios were developed from these starting points by a diverse group of maritime industry specialists (Lehmacher & Lind, 2022). *Swells* has economic recovery placed first, *Storms* has local or regional interests placed first, and *Clear Sky*, has growing environmental awareness,

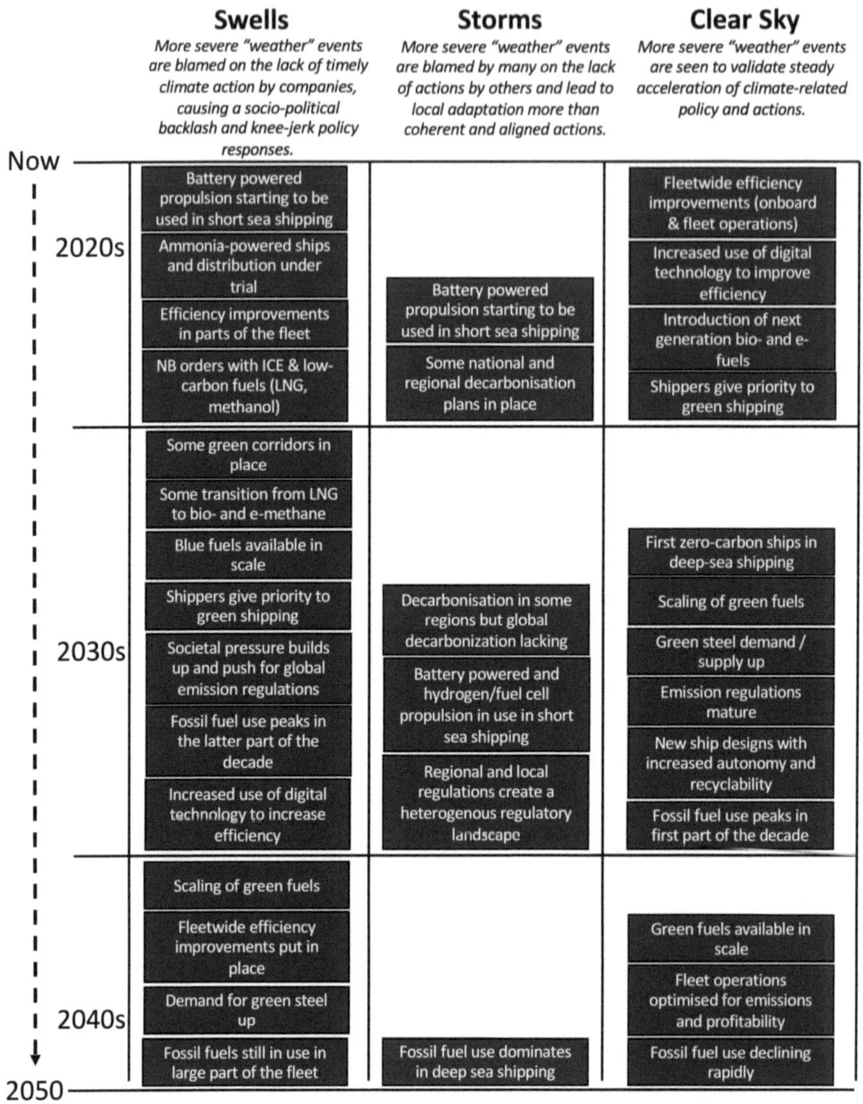

Fig. 4 Features of maritime transition scenarios (Lind et al., 2022)

competing interests and stakeholder alignments primarily driving global maritime decarbonization. Figure 4 (Lind et al., 2022) depicts the anticipated major tipping points in decarbonizing shipping under the three abovementioned maritime transition scenarios.

Concluding Remarks

One fundamental discovery of this scenario study on the decarbonization of shipping, conducted in the first half of 2022, has been that NONE of the specific maritime pathways envisaged by the consulted experts will bring the maritime industry anywhere close to even the 2018 IMO (International Maritime Organization) ambitions, which have actually now been strengthened even further in 2023.

Quoting from the published report on Maritime Scenarios (Lind et al., 2022):

> All developed scenario pathways show that we don't get anywhere near the 2018 IMO decarbonization ambitions, and yet indicate the potential competitive and commercial advantages from acceleration.

This is very concerning, and is driven by the hard-to-abate nature and fragmentation of many aspects of the maritime ecosystem. As and when such a worrying insight becomes increasingly apparent to regulators and stakeholders around the world, there is the real danger of a series of economically damaging knee-jerk reactions, such as ill-informed policy steps or enforced shifts in transport modes (a 'supercharged' *Swells* scenario).

However, the good news is that these structured imagined scenarios are not outlooks cast in stone but are a means for stress-testing different ways forward and learning about what approaches are more or less effective. They are a planning tool that can help us to adjust and refine our courses of action to create the desired zero-emissions future. Effective decarbonization going forwards from now begins with outlining such plausible futures to define strategies that can be robust in each of the future outlooks and can also point towards actions that may generate alternative outcomes that meet aspirations more closely.

Such approaches are the focus of other chapters in this book, which incorporate the lessons from this scenario exercise.

References

Bentham, J., & Shell Scenario Team. (2021). *Shell energy transformation scenarios*. Retrieved from Shell Scenarios www.shell.com/scenarios, https://www.shell.com/energy-and-innovation/the-energy-future/scenarios/the-energy-transformation-scenarios.html

Davis, G., & Bentham, J. (2008). *Scenarios: An explorer's guide*. Retrieved from Shell Scenarios www.shell.com/scenarios, https://www.shell.com/energy-and-innovation/the-energy-future/scenarios/new-lenses-on-the-future/earlier-scenarios.html

Kahneman, D. (2011). *Thinking, fast and slow*. Farrar, Straus and Giroux.

Lehmacher, W., & Lind, M. (2022). *Practical playbook for maritime decarbonisation*. Retrieved from Nordic West Office. https://www.nordicwestoffice.com/maritime

Lind, M., Lemacher, W., Bentham, J., Kuttan, S., Tikka, K., & Watson, R. T. (2022) *Four steps towards maritime decarbonizing actions: Playbook part 5, 11/12-2022, The Maritime Executive*. Retrieved from https://www.maritime-executive.com/editorials/four-steps-towards-maritime-decarbonising-actions-playbook-part-5

Schwartz, P. (1991). *The art of the long view*. Random House.

Adopting a Value Chain Focus to Tackle Decarbonization

Moritz Petersen and Katharina Renken

Target Audience

This chapter is written for those responsible for preparing a decarbonization roadmap or driving a decarbonization project. This will include top-level leaders, project and product managers, and government officials involved in decarbonization programs and initiatives.

Key Takeaway Messages

The chapter identifies:

- value chain thinking as a management approach, based on a broad understanding of the various activities and processes involved in creating value for a company's products or services;
- the three interrelated value chains from the maritime ecosystem that are playing a critical role in decarbonizing shipping: marine fuel, shipbuilding, and maritime operational value chains;
- decarbonization as a joint undertaking of multiple intertwined value chains;
- the need for the entire cluster of chains to be decarbonized chain by chain and sector by sector, ideally in parallel, to avoid gaps and bottlenecks;

M. Petersen (✉)
Kühne Logistics University, Hamburg, Germany
e-mail: moritz.petersen@the-klu.org

K. Renken
Hapag-Lloyd AG, Hamburg, Germany
e-mail: Katharina.Renken@hlag.com

M. Lind et al. (eds.), *Maritime Decarbonization*,
https://doi.org/10.1007/978-3-031-39936-7_6

- broader interdependencies and new opportunities driving the need to expand the thinking about decarbonizing shipping beyond the cluster of the three maritime value chains to a larger decarbonization ecosystem that also includes adjacent clusters of value chains; and
- the significant decarbonization potential expected from optimising international trade patterns, driving down the demand for international shipping in the first place.

Introduction to Value Chain Thinking

Value chain thinking is a management approach that emphasises the importance of understanding the various activities and processes involved in creating value for a company's products or services (Porter, 1985). It involves analysing each step of the value chain, from the raw materials and resources used to create a product to the marketing and distribution of that product to customers. Thus, a value chain describes the full range of activities needed to bring a product or service from idea to reality (Kaplinsky & Morris, 2001). Every step along the chain should add value. The value creation is generally accompanied by greenhouse gases (GHG) emissions from energy production and consumption, among other sustainability issues. Contemporary value creation is usually not concentrated in one company but distributed throughout extensive global supply networks. Thus, efforts to drive sustainability cannot stop at the focal company's border (Villena & Gioia, 2020). Also in the maritime sector, taking a value chain perspective is critical to understanding and assessing decarbonization enablers and building partnerships beyond industry borders (Lehmacher & Lind, 2022).

Value Chains in the Maritime Ecosystem

Three interrelated value chains from the maritime ecosystem are playing a critical role in decarbonizing shipping (see Fig. 1): the marine fuel, shipbuilding, and maritime operational value chains. The marine fuel value chain takes care of the extraction, production and distribution of different fuel types from the well to the bunker. The shipbuilding value chain covers all activities around ships' construction and manufacturing, extending to a ship's end of life. Finally, the maritime operational value chain uses the products of the other two value chains to provide a transportation service for freight and/or passengers from one port to the next. All three value chains jointly respond to specific local, regional, and/or global shipping demands.

The three maritime value chains are highly interdependent. Thus, achieving decarbonization efficiently means aligning supply and demand across this cluster of chains. For example, the marine fuel value chain needs to supply sufficient

Fig. 1 Interdependent value chains in the maritime ecosystem (Lehmacher & Lind, 2022, p. 23)

alternative (green) fuel at suitable refuelling locations to match the demands of alternative fuel. This requires information sharing, collaboration, and synchronisation of the development of each value chain, as well as an understanding of the characteristics and technological requirements of different business models. For example, powering short-sea shipping might be technologically feasible with clean electricity, whereas ocean voyages may need green methanol or ammonia. However, as described in the following chapter, the decarbonization enablers known today extend far beyond the type of fuel used. Jointly pursuing them remains a challenge as, throughout the logistics industry at large, meaningful collaboration to cut GHG emissions is still lacking (McKinnon & Petersen, 2021). However, the cluster of critical maritime value chains needs to be approached holistically and simultaneously from a carbon calculation, design, planning, financing, management and policymaking perspective. The entire cluster of chains needs to be decarbonized chain by chain and sector by sector, ideally in parallel, to avoid gaps and bottlenecks. It is often the gaps across the chains that discourage more substantial commitments to decarbonization (Lehmacher & Lind, 2022).

The Marine Fuel Value Chain

The marine fuel value chain refers to producing, storing, shipping and distributing fuel for use in the maritime industry. It starts with extracting crude oil, refined into various types of marine fuel, including diesel, gas oil and heavy fuel oil. The fuel is then transported to storage terminals and shipped to ports worldwide, where it is distributed to ships and other marine vessels. It is a complex system that involves multiple players, including fuel producers, refiners, traders and distributors. The marine fuel value chain produces roughly 300 million tons of fossil fuel oil per year (Mærsk Mc-Kinney Møller Center for Zero Carbon Shipping, 2022).

The availability of alternative fuels like hydrogen, ammonia, methanol or biofuels is essential for greener shipping (Foretich et al., 2021). This is also the case for other modes of transport like road or air transportation: almost all vehicles today are powered by some form of petroleum-derived fuel that will need to be replaced (McKinnon, 2018). The suppliers of today's fuels are production and processing technology providers, energy companies using these technologies, and carriers transporting these fuels to locations where they are needed. The green energy transition shifts dependencies from fossil fuel producers to renewable energy providers as the feedstocks shift from petroleum towards green electricity, biomass or biowaste. This may reduce the importance of some regions of the world but will also bring new opportunities to other locations with possible shifts in geopolitical power as new feedstocks are likely available throughout the globe. Market structures will also shift. Whereas the current marine fuel market can be considered global in nature, prices for alternative fuel tend to vary much more between locations as the price build-up differs substantially from location to location. Around 10% of the end-user price for today's marine fuels stems from distribution and storage, whereas the costs are significantly higher for alternative fuels. Thus, we can expect that the current (somewhat predictable) global fuel market will become more fragmented. This development is also driven by the emergence of green corridors, which are shipping routes between two or more ports that are shifting towards enabling vessels to sail on alternative fuels (Mærsk Mc-Kinney Møller Center for Zero Carbon Shipping and McKinsey & Company, 2022). Considering the volume of marine bunker, today's bunkering prices, and a hypothetical levy of $100 per ton of CO_2 emitted, an estimate of the commercial value of the marine fuel value chain based on its total annual expenditure is approximately USD 250 billion, without factoring in the potentially higher costs and investment in alternative fuels (Lind et al., 2022a).

The Shipbuilding Value Chain

The shipbuilding value chain refers to the various stages involved in ship design, construction and maintenance. It includes all activities from sourcing raw materials and components to delivering finished vessels to customers. The shipbuilding value chain can be valued at USD 115 billion, based on the contract value for new orders placed in 2021 (Lind et al., 2022a). It typically starts with the design and engineering of a ship. This involves creating detailed plans and specifications for the vessel, including its size, shape and intended use. Once the design is complete, the shipbuilding process begins, with the vessel's construction taking place in a shipyard. During construction, a wide range of materials and components are sourced and assembled to create the ship. This includes steel plates for the hull, engines and propulsion systems, electrical and electronic systems, and various other mechanical and structural components together with appropriate accommodation and other amenities and is tested to ensure it meets all safety and performance standards. Once construction is complete, the ship is delivered to the customer and may undergo further maintenance and repairs as needed. At the end of its life, the recycling of a ship is the final step of the shipbuilding value chain and is concerned with recovering the materials and resources. Ultimately, this can, for example, lower the demand for iron ore mining and reduces energy use in the steelmaking process (Jensen et al., 2021). However, the ships' recycling phase still poses significant environmental and social challenges. In 2009, the Hong Kong International Convention for the Safe and Environmentally Sound Recycling of Ships was negotiated. 63 country delegates attended the conference. However, by early 2023, only 19 States with a combined 29.32% of the gross tonnage of the world's merchant shipping fleet had ratified the Convention. 40% is needed for the Convention to enter in to force, while the combined maximum annual ship recycling volume of those States must constitute not less than 3 per cent of their combined merchant shipping tonnage during the preceding 10 years. (IMO, 2022).

The shipbuilding and marine fuel value chains are interdependent, such that the respective shareholders need to share their long-term investment and development plans to ensure alignment of supply and demand. So far, the answers to three questions determine the shipbuilding process:

- How much capacity for cargo/passengers is needed (determining ship size)?
- Where and how fast should the ship travel (determining engine size, required fuel tank capacity, manoeuvrability and safety measures)?
- How energy efficient should the ship be (determining hydrodynamically efficient hull and propulsion designs)?

In the future, the following questions will also be equally important:

- What fuel and quantity will be used? (the answer will impact tanks, fuel feeding systems, engines, and freight capacity); and
- how many technologies shall a vessel be ready for, to allow for an easy switch if needed? (the answer will impact initial investment and maintenance of the vessel and may potentially reduce the vessel's cargo capacity through extra hardware).

More energy-efficient newbuilds and retrofits will be needed to reduce GHG emissions from the existing and future shipping fleet. What ships and engines will be built and used sustainably largely depends upon the assessment of what fuels will or can be available and their costs. Predicting what is needed and what will be suitable is not easy. With the average age of all ships in the world merchant fleet being just over 20 years (UNCTAD, 2022), every prediction is a long-term gamble. Shipowners need information from fuel suppliers on what will be available, in what quantities, and where and at what prices across the globe. The industry must acknowledge and work with the fact that making accurate predictions for the lifecycle of a ship has become very difficult as energy sources available for use will most likely change over time. 60% of the newbuild orders placed in 2022 are for dual-fuel vessels (UNCTAD, 2022).

The Maritime Operational Value Chain

The maritime operational value chain refers to the activities and processes involved in operating ships and other marine vessels, including management, cargo handling and voyage execution. It plays a crucial role in global trade and transportation, ensuring the efficient and reliable movement of goods and people. The maritime operational value chain involves a wide range of players including ship owners and operators, cargo owners and different service providers.

The maritime operational value chain includes fuelling, provisioning, and cargo and passenger handling. Bunker locations, fuel prices and weather conditions impact routing and operational efficiency. It is widely accepted that there is plenty of room for efficiency improvement along this value chain. Steaming speed is an important factor; synchronisation along the chain is critical. Technology, such as digital berth alignment platforms to optimise ships' arrivals and berth usage, provide solutions to improve fluidity, minimise waiting times, and thus reduce costs and GHG emissions. Optimising the number of ship types in a fleet can reduce fuel consumption per transported unit. However, the significant number of companies with only a few ships may face limits when trying to optimise ship and fleet size. Exploring multiple ways of optimisation is necessary rather than waiting for the marine fuel value chain to provide sufficient amounts of alternative fuels. At the same time, market-based measures (MBMs) should help to expand the fuel value chain and support the acquisition of ships with cleaner technologies and the phasing out older, less efficient vessels after their lifespan (Lagouvardou et al., 2020). Simply put, there are three key performance indicators to watch to reduce GHG emissions along the ship's operational value chain:

- the utilisation rate of the space dedicated to cargo and/or passengers;
- economies of scale (for example, use larger units to transport more cargo/passengers at once, where possible without lowering the utilisation rate); and
- speed (operating a ship at optimal design-speed).

As an example, a study by the International Council of Clean Transportation (ICCT) found that bulk carriers travel about 56% of the time in ballast globally, with a small or no payload. Thus, minimising ballast voyages is crucial to reducing overall bunker consumption. Horizontal partnerships could help to increase ship utilisation through a shared pool of ships, and potential consolidation of the industry may be conducive as well. Virtual arrivals can lead to better synchronisation and minimise bunker consumption but it needs a firm commitment from ports and charterers to make it work. Some cargo could be switched from bulker ships to container ships, making use of a fixed schedule and route instead of an individually planned voyage. This has occurred recently with goods such as lumber on lesser utilised voyages across the world. However, all these solutions inevitably have trade-offs. For example, slower, more fuel-efficient steaming with longer travel times means more ships are needed to move the same amount of cargo, and more ships means more GHG emissions. A holistic approach is required to make optimal decisions across clusters of value chains while in a competitive market. Estimating an annual commercial turnover of the operational value chain with its different segments is difficult. The asset value of the world fleet stands at USD 1.4 trillion (UNCTAD, 2022). Hence, the most commercial value is likely concentrated in the operational value chain. However, the numbers given for the three value chains are hard to compare and should be interpreted carefully.

Value Chain Focus as a Key to Effective Decarbonization in Shipping

Today, the maritime industry burns the type of fuel that hardly anybody else demands. In the future, the sector will compete for feedstock of alternative fuels with other industries that also require low-carbon solutions to decarbonize their operations (Foretich et al., 2021). Biomass, for example, is currently being explored as feedstock fuel for all transport modes. Also, increased competition for the same feedstocks will likely raise prices until supply can expand to meet demand, thus creating challenges for many industries to reduce GHG emissions in the short to medium term. But synergies may also emerge. For example, short-sea ships and trucks can both run on biodiesel. This may raise capital productivity of bunkering and fuelling infrastructure at seaports. Electric vehicles like trucks or passenger cars might recharge onboard ferries using the ship's electrical system. These new opportunities drive the need to expand the thinking about decarbonizing shipping beyond the cluster of the three maritime value chains to a larger decarbonization ecosystem

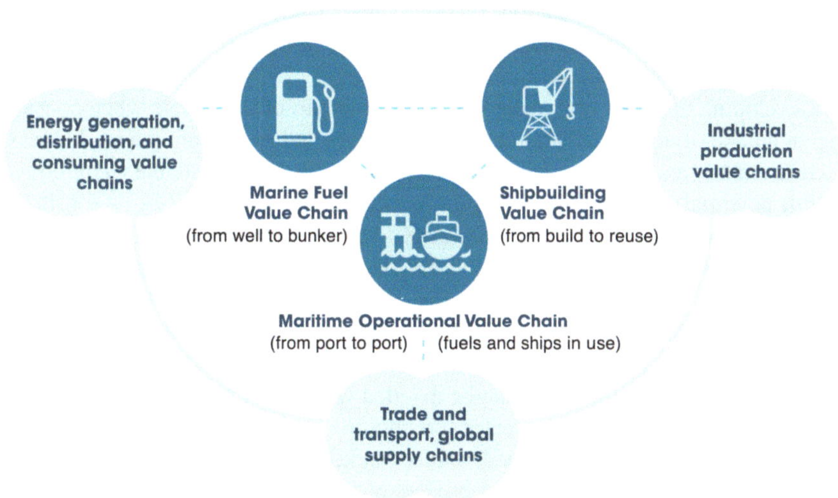

Fig. 2 Interdependencies, tensions, and synergies between related value chains (Lehmacher & Lind, 2022, p. 38)

that consists of adjacent clusters of value chains (see Fig. 2). Taking it one step further, a significant decarbonization potential is expected from optimising international trade patterns, driving down the demand for international shipping in the first place (Wang et al., 2021).

However, in the context of the broader ecosystem, a range of new challenges needs to be addressed by the public and private sectors. Issues to consider are, for example:

- Who is shipping competing with for green fuels, and what does this mean for decarbonizing the maritime industry and prioritizing fuel development?
- What factors influence the costs of building green ships and their price and adoption?
- How can carriers be motivated to reduce their carbon footprint?
- What global trade and system dynamics need to be factored into the decarbonization calculus?

While some of these questions and processes are difficult to predict, some development is already underway. Maersk recently declared a significant cost reduction when ordering its latest green technology-ready ship compared to a conventional vessel. Sourcing costs have decreased from 10–15% in additional charges in 2021 to 8–12% in 2022. Shipping analyst Lars Jensen commented on this development with a positive outlook for the industry, stating,

> The more green ships that are ordered, the more we will see the added cost compared to conventional ships decrease. This can lead to a positive spiral in terms of capital expenditure on green ships, with more green ships leading to lower prices, which leads to more green ships (Holmstad, 2022).

Likewise, Hapag-Lloyd and others are ordering their new, large container ships with new technology-ready installations on board in an attempt to be future-proof regarding diverse acceleration technologies. Additionally, long-gone propulsion technologies are getting re-visited, such as wind (Chou et al., 2021).

Developing and applying technologies are one part of the puzzle when considering an uptake of decarbonization efforts. Processes and people are others. Processes need to change and to be digitalised to employ the new and available technology to its full potential. One factor is to optimise sea voyages. The just-in-time principle must find its way into the shipping industry to avoid idle time and, thus, waste. The berth alignment process between the global fleet and terminal operators is a focus of recent research activities. This follows the informed assumption that waiting time to enter terminals creates unnecessary GHG emissions. Further, a ship not traveling at an optimum speed between terminals generates additional bunker costs and increased GHG emissions. This can be avoided with the synchronised and seamless provision of berth space. With greater certainty in obtaining a berth on arrival, a ship can proceed at a fuel-efficient speed, reduce bunker costs and GHG emissions (dcsa, 2021). Lately, to further support the process of aligned port visits, slot management has been introduced as a process for ships and ports to match the time window for their port visits with the available infrastructure (Lind et al., 2022b).

The weakest point in this scenario may be the people. While there is a global move towards decarbonization, especially with the younger generation, changing processes and training personnel on new equipment, technologies, software and data definitions is a challenging task - especially in a very traditional industry such as shipping. More research is needed on this aspect and suitable methods must be developed to create a positive impact throughout and with the existing and new-joining workforce.

As emphasised in this chapter, decarbonization should be seen as a joint undertaking of multiple intertwined value chains. Only with this broad perspective can the available decarbonization enablers be assessed holistically and implemented in the timescale that society is increasingly demanding.

References

Chou, T., Kosmas, V., Acciaro, M., & Renken, K. (2021). A comeback of wind power in shipping: An economic and operational review on the wind-assisted ship propulsion technology. *Sustainability, 13*, 1880. https://doi.org/10.3390/su13041880

dcsa. (2021). *JIT port call data definitions 1.1*. Digital Container Shipping Association.

Foretich, A., Zaimes, G. G., Hawkins, T. R., & Newes, E. (2021). Challenges and opportunities for alternative fuels in the maritime sector. *Maritime Transport Research Journal Research, 2*, 100033. https://doi.org/10.1016/j.martra.2021.100033

Holmstad, D. (2022). *Cost of Maersk's new methanol ships drops*. ShippingWatch.

IMO. (2022). *Status of IMO treaties: Comprehensive information on the status of multilateral conventions and instruments in respect of which the International Maritime Organization or its Secretary-General performs depositary or other functions.*

Jensen, H. H., Andersen, M. M., Dao, A., Lind, M., Pandey, V., Bapuji, G., Petersen, M., Hobson, B., Lehmacher, W., & Turos, A. (2021). Digitalisation in a maritime circular economy. In M. Lind, M. Michaelides, R. Ward, & R. T. Watson (Eds.), *Maritime informatics: Additional perspectives and applications, progress in IS* (pp. 17–37). Springer. https://doi.org/10.1007/978-3-030-72785-7_2

Kaplinsky, R., & Morris, M. (2001). *A handbook for value chain research*. Institute of Development Studies, University of Sussex.

Lagouvardou, S., Psaraftis, H. N., & Zis, T. (2020). A literature survey on market-based measures for the decarbonization of shipping. *Sustainability, 12*, 3953. https://doi.org/10.3390/su12103953

Lehmacher, W., & Lind, M. (2022). *Practical playbook for maritime decarbonisation - Value chain-based pathways towards zero-emission shipping*. Nordic West Office.

Lind, M., Lehmacher, W., Doepel, T., Heinimaa, J., Hoffmann, J., Laurilehto, M., Lebmeier, M., Petersen, M., Rytkölä, I., Saari, J., Singh, S., Walls, R., & Watson, R. T. (2022a). *The benefits of a clusters of value chains perspective in decarbonising shipping: Decarbonisation playbook part 2* (p. 9). The Maritime Executive.

Lind, M., Lehmacher, W., Hoffmann, J., Jensen, L., Notteboom, T., Rydbergh, T., Sand, P., Haraldson, S., White, R., Becha, H., & Berglund, P. (2022b). An expanded JIT approach: Improving synchronization across maritime global value chains. *Maritime Technology*, 60–65.

Mærsk Mc-Kinney Møller Center for Zero Carbon Shipping. (2022). *Maritime Decarbonization strategy 2022: A decade of change*. Mærsk Mc-Kinney Møller Center for Zero Carbon Shipping.

Mærsk Mc-Kinney Møller Center for Zero Carbon Shipping, McKinsey & Company. (2022). *Green corridors: Feasibility phase blueprint*. Mærsk Mc-Kinney Møller Center for Zero Carbon Shipping.
McKinnon, A. (2018). *Decarbonizing logistics: Distributing goods in a low carbon world* (1st ed.). Kogan Page.
McKinnon, A., & Petersen, M. (2021). *Measuring Industry's temperature: An environmental progress report on European logistics*. Center for Sustainable Logistics and Supply Chains at Kühne Logistics University.
Porter, M. E. (1985). *Competitive advantage: Creating and sustaining superior performance*. Free Press.
UNCTAD. (2022). *Review of maritime transport 2022: Navigating stormy waters*. United Nations Publications.
Villena, V. H., & Gioia, D. A. (2020). A more sustainable supply chain. *Harvard Business Review*.
Wang, X.-T., Liu, H., Lv, Z.-F., Deng, F.-Y., Xu, H.-L., Qi, L.-J., Shi, M.-S., Zhao, J.-C., Zheng, S.-X., Man, H.-Y., & He, K.-B. (2021). Trade-linked shipping CO_2 emissions. *Nature Climate Change, 11*, 945–951. https://doi.org/10.1038/s41558-021-01176-6

Identifying the Key Decarbonization Enablers

Kirsi Tikka and Steve Esau

Target Audience

This chapter should be of interest to board members and company executives who are overseeing company/organisation sustainability strategies and wish to gain an overall understanding of decarbonization enablers for the maritime industry.

It is also written for sustainability managers and managers of decarbonization projects in all parts of the maritime industry to help identify relevant enablers in the decarbonization process.

Key Takeaway Messages

The chapter emphasises:

- There are multiple decarbonization enablers, including technology, practices, zero-carbon fuels, and policies and regulations that are relevant for a specific player and project.
- The enablers need to be activated as appropriate for each case and developed in a coordinated fashion.

K. Tikka (✉)
Board Member Ardmore Shipping, Pembroke, Bermuda

Board Member Pacific Basin Shipping, Hong Kong, Hong Kong SAR

Board Member Foreship, Helsinki, Finland
e-mail: kktikka@outlook.com

S. Esau
SEA-LNG, Oxford, UK
e-mail: steve.esau@sea-lng.org

M. Lind et al. (eds.), *Maritime Decarbonization*,
https://doi.org/10.1007/978-3-031-39936-7_7

- Enablers are not only to be found in one value chain but also in adjacent value chains within and beyond the maritime industry.
- Individual actors cannot decarbonize alone but need to group and collaborate with other actors within and beyond the maritime industry.
- The goal of collaboration is to align on the relevant enablers and on their specifics; for example, the volume of green fuel needed over time to be estimated in a plan.
- As business and evolution are dynamic, collaboration and planning need to be a continuous process.

Introduction

Moving towards the current and future global decarbonization targets set by the International Maritime Organization (IMO) requires the adoption of multiple enablers with varying greenhouse gas (GHG) reduction impact and different levels of required investment (see IMO Resolution MEPC.304(72), 2018 and Chap. 15). This introduction sets out the range of enablers from regulations to zero-carbon fuels.

Figure 1 illustrates the transition towards the decarbonization targets, and the increasing investment needed in the process.

The enablers can be categorised within the three value chains: the Marine Fuel Value Chain, the Maritime Operational Value Chain, and the Shipbuilding Value Chain. Some of the enablers contribute to only one, whereas others have contributions to two or all the value chains. Figure 2 illustrates a set of selected enablers with their position in the three value chains as well as the cross-cutting nature of some of the enablers.

The understanding of the enormity of the challenge to decarbonize maritime transport has made it clear that the shipping industry cannot achieve this alone.

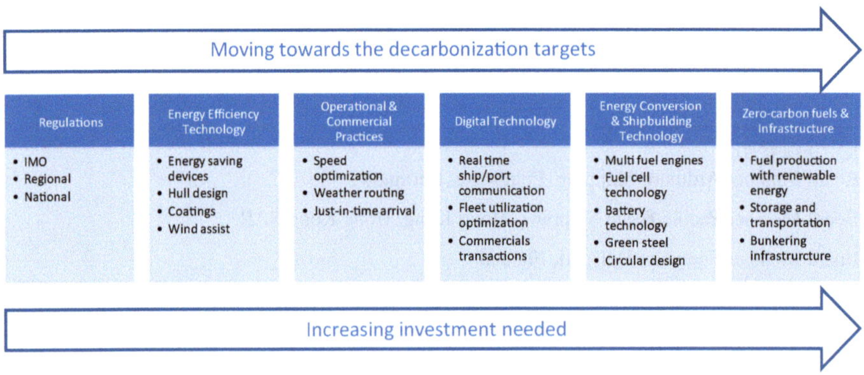

Fig. 1 Enablers for moving towards the decarbonization targets

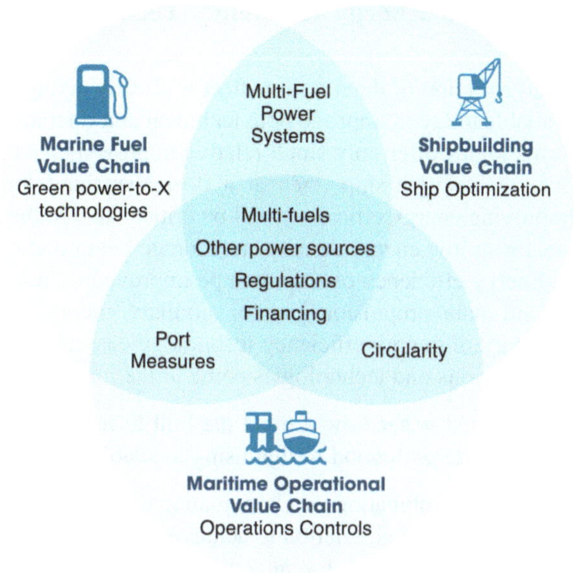

Fig. 2 Examples of enablers related to the three interdependent decarbonization value chains. Source: Lehmacher and Lind (2022)

We need ship operators, ports, cargo owners, charterers, energy providers, and financial institutions to collaborate towards the common goal.

Many industry initiatives and public-private partnerships (PPPs) have been formed to address the challenge and to bring key stakeholders to the same table. The Clydebank declaration for Green Shipping Corridors (COP26, 2022) is an example of an initiative to engage actors of all value chains to deliver low- or zero-carbon maritime transportation in selected maritime transportation routes.

Green Shipping Corridors, the establishment of specific trade routes between major port hubs where zero-emission solutions are supported, require the co-operation of the entire supply chain ecosystem including governments, cities, ports, energy suppliers, shippers, shipping companies, and service companies. If successfully implemented, they will contribute to decarbonization and provide demonstration projects for creating similar corridors in other parts of the world.

Green Shipping Corridors

Signatories to the Clydebank Declaration at COP26 in November 2021 agreed to support the establishment of green shipping corridors—zero emission maritime routes between 2 (or more) ports.

According to the 17 November 2022 Progress Report on Green Shipping Corridors by the Getting to Zero Coalition (GZC) and Global Maritime Forum (GMF), 21 initiatives have emerged around the world since the signing of the Clydebank Declaration. More than 110 stakeholders from across the value chain are engaged in these initiatives including a significant level of public-private collaboration. (GZC and GMF, 2022).

Shipboard Energy Efficiency Technologies

A large section of the maritime fleet is already taking advantage of the technologies available today to improve both technical and operational efficiency. Many of these technologies offer only small relative improvements but these benefits can add up, first for a single ship, then at a fleet level, and finally across the global fleet. Improving energy efficiency will be critical also in the transition to net zero-carbon fuels with low energy density and storage being particular challenges.

Energy efficiency of ships can be improved by reducing the power requirements for the main propulsion and for auxiliary energy generators. The following is a summary of energy efficiency technology categories available today. New innovative solutions and technologies come to the market continuously.

- Improved water flow around the hull to reduce the wave making and frictional resistance with good design using available technology tools, including:
  - The combination of Computational Fluid Dynamics (CFD) analyses, model testing and simulation to achieve good hull form,
  - designing ships for an operational profile rather than for a single design condition to improve performance in realistic operational conditions,
  - use advanced anti-fouling systems, and
  - air bubble technology.
- Energy saving devices (for example, propeller boss cap fins, ducts) installed to improve flow to the propeller and to reduce energy losses aft of the propeller.
- Advanced rudder designs to improve the course control and manoeuvrability efficiency.
- Technology tools to maximise propulsion efficiency and minimise energy losses, including:
  - pairing the engine and propeller for optimum efficiency (for example, lower RPM (revolutions per minute) engines to allow larger propellers),
  - electronically controlled engines,
  - waste heat recovery, and
  - shaft generators.
- Wind-assist technologies to reduce the propulsion power requirement include sails and rotors.
- Auxiliary energy demand can be reduced for example, by using LED lighting and Variable Frequency Drive pumps.

Energy savings depend on many variables such as the vessel type, routes, weather conditions, and operational practices, but potential savings are typically relatively small, less than 10%. Many of the tools provide additive savings, but in some cases, especially for some energy saving devices, the effects can be deductive and good engineering design is important. Although the individual savings are small in percentages a combination of measures can offer significant overall fuel and emission savings.

Operational and Commercial Practices

Operational measures and logistics offer another dimension where efficiency improvements can be achieved. Some of these measures can be implemented onboard the vessel, others involve multiple stakeholders and commercial arrangements.

- Maintenance practices to prevent loss of performance.
  - Hull and propeller cleaning frequency to minimise fouling.
- Trim and draft optimisation for best fuel efficiency.
- Energy management onboard.
- Voyage optimisation, including:
  - weather routing to take advantage of favourable weather conditions and currents,
  - speed optimisation to operate at lower speeds when practicable and significantly reduce fuel consumption, and
  - operate Just-in-Time arrivals to avoid waiting times at ports and terminals and enable speed optimisation.
- Improved fleet utilisation to minimise ballast voyages, by addressing:
  - triangulation, to combine loaded voyages and minimise the length of the ballast leg, and
  - backhaul cargoes to avoid ballast legs.
- Efficient port operations to avoid port congestion, including:
  - efficient loading/discharging and bunkering operations, and
  - streamlined ship, port, and land transportation connectivity.

According to the *Mærsk Mc-Kinney Møller Center* for Zero Carbon Shipping (MMKMCZCS, 2022) the vessel and fleet specific operational energy efficiency measures offer energy efficiency gains up to 15%. Adding energy efficiency measures across the Maritime Operational Value Chain has a significant energy saving potential.

Digital Technology

Technology tools for real time data sharing and communications can be implemented to eliminate bottlenecks in the logistics chain. Just-in-time arrival is a concept that strives for improved efficiency, but port congestion and long waiting times are frequently the reality, even with the progress made by various stakeholders. Ports and terminals are improving their operational efficiencies, and ship operators and charterers are co-operating to achieve optimum ship speeds to reduce waiting times. However, the institutions governing the commercial arrangements have developed for centuries and even with good intentions are not easy to adapt to achieve optimal efficiency.

Just In Time Arrival

The principle of Just In Time (JIT) Arrival is simple; the speed of the ship is adjusted for arrival in port when the berth, fairway, and required services such as tugs are available to avoid waiting time at anchorage. By reducing speed to avoid waiting times the vessel fuel consumption and consequently the emissions are reduced. At the same time the port efficiency is improved. Operationally this can be easily achieved with current technology, but it also involves commercial transactions that allow charterers to request adjustments to the vessel speed and arrival time, and agreements on profit sharing from the reduced fuel cost. The practice has been implemented on case-by-case basis by ship operators and charterers, but for a wider adoption of JIT requires a connected system across the entire supply chain of ports, shippers, charterers, and operators. To facilitate the changes needed Just in Time Arrival Guide (2020, JIT Guide) was published by Global Industry Alliance to support low carbon shipping (Low Carbon GIA). The Low Carbon GIA operates under the framework of the IMO-Norway GreenVoyage2050 Project.

Digital technology is a key for many of the energy efficiency measures discussed already. It provides software tools for design and maintenance, weather routing, energy management, data analytics to transform operational data into information, and commercial platforms and satellite communications for value chain optimisation. Onboard automation, and eventually autonomy, allows more efficient operations.

Although digital technology and automation is already widely used in the maritime industry, it is expected to have a greater impact in maritime decarbonization in the future. However, cybersecurity is a concern and hacks on the digital systems could hinder progress.

Zero-Carbon Fuels and Technology

A lot can be achieved by improving the efficiency of ships, operations, and logistics, but full decarbonization requires breakthrough technologies and zero-carbon fuels.

Unfortunately, today there is no obvious winner among alternative fuel options, and no easy solutions. Production of zero-carbon fuels requires renewable energy, zero-carbon or carbon-neutral feedstocks, infrastructure to transport and store fuels, bunkering facilities, onboard storage and fuel systems, and energy conversion technology. Major capital investment is required for:

- large scale renewable energy production;
- electrolysis to produce the hydrogen building block for renewable, synthetic fuels;
- fuel production, storage, and transportation;
- bunkering infrastructure;
- technology development and manufacture at each step of the process;
- development of quality and safety standards; and
- training of personnel at each step of the process.

We are faced with a chicken-and-egg situation where investment in alternative fuels production and the required infrastructure will follow expected demand, but it is unclear which fuels will be adopted by the industry. This is where early movers are important in piloting and eventually creating demand. The early movers are willing to take the risk of early adoption to gain a competitive edge with clients looking to reduce their carbon footprint when moving their goods and materials.

Since the worldwide availability of zero-carbon fuels is still several years or even decades away, the focus is on the transition from the current use of fossil fuels to low-carbon and eventually zero-carbon fuels, and the alternative fuel pathways to produce these zero-carbon fuels.

The transition focuses on the use of multi-fuel engines that currently burn fossil fuels but offer an option in the future to burn zero-carbon fuels, or the use of biofuel and fuel oil blends, and in the case of liquefied natural gas (LNG), biomethane and LNG blends, that can be burnt in the existing internal combustion engines without modifications (drop-in fuels).

Biofuels and biomethane do have carbon emissions, but the fuel is considered carbon neutral when the carbon emitted equals the carbon needed to produce the biomass used as feedstock. Since the fuel quantity required by shipping and other industries is large, questions remain about the availability of biofuel and biomethane for shipping. There are also concerns about the sustainability of the production of these fuels. It should not use food, fibre, or fodder sources as feedstock, and it should not change land use from the production of food.

Short-sea and inland waterway shipping have more alternatives than deep sea voyages, even today. Batteries to store electricity or fuel cell technology with hydrogen as fuel are viable alternatives if frequent charging or refuelling opportunities are available.

When considering the fuel pathways, it is important to differentiate between well-to-wake (WTW) and tank-to-wake (TTW) emissions. WTW assessments consider the GHG emissions from the fuel production to the end use onboard a vessel, whereas TTW accounts only for the emission from the onboard use of the fuel. If the TTW assessment is used the fuel choice will not account for the full GHG impact.

The low- and zero-carbon fuels considered today include:

- electro-fuels (e-fuels) produced with renewable electricity and electrolysis of water to produce hydrogen:
  - e-hydrogen,
  - e-ammonia,
  - e-methane,
  - e-methanol, and
  - e-diesel;
- blue fuels produced from fossil feedstock combined with carbon capture and storage:
  - blue hydrogen, and
  - blue ammonia;
- biofuels produced from sustainable biomass and biowaste:
  - bio-methane,
  - bio-methanol,
  - bio-oils (biofuel).

    (MMKMCZCS, 2022, 2023)

Nuclear power has been used on military vessels and on icebreakers for a long time and its use to power commercial vessels has recently gained interest with the latest technology developments improving safety and reducing waste. Nuclear power could be used to produce zero-carbon fuels, charge batteries, or as power plants onboard vessels. However, the safety and security concerns make the use of nuclear power for shipping unlikely in the short term.

Energy Conversion and Shipbuilding Technology

At present, worldwide shipping is powered predominantly by internal combustion engines (ICEs) burning mainly fossil fuel oil. A small percentage of the world fleet, mostly LNG carriers, burn LNG in multi fuel engines Multi fuel engines are engines that can burn more than one type of fuel. These engines are typically dual fuel engines capable of burning fuel oil and an alternative such as LNG or methanol. Multi-fuel LNG engines are been adopted increasingly by other vessel types. According to SEA-LNG, a multi-sector industry coalition established to demonstrate

LNG'S benefits as a viable marine fuel, 17% percent of the order book (excluding LNG carriers), in terms of deadweight tonnage, at the end of 2022 specified multi fuel LNG engines. Multi fuel engine designs are currently available also for burning methanol and ethane. Ammonia multi fuel engine is under development.

The multi fuel ICE and biofuel blends in single fuel ICE are the only options available today for long haul shipping to reduce emissions that provide optionality for transition from fossil fuels to low or zero carbon fuels.

Zero carbon fuels, excluding nuclear, have a lower energy density than hydrocarbon fuels. This means that the focus on the fleet's operational and technical energy efficiency is important. The efficiency of the energy conversion from the fuel to powering the onboard systems is significant.

Fuel cell and battery technology offer alternatives to ICEs but with the current state of the art they are not feasible for long-haul shipping and further technology development is needed.

Wind has powered ships for centuries and is a freely available energy source. Wind-assist solutions are being piloted on some ship types, and full wind propulsion on a few ships carrying high-value cargoes. Wind has a significant role in decarbonization as a source of renewable energy needed to produce zero-carbon fuels.

Carbon capture is one of the tools for the maritime decarbonization strategy, but its role is still to be defined. Carbon capture will be needed to produce zero-carbon fuels, but whether it will be used onboard ships depends on technology development. It will also require new infrastructure at ports to enable safe sequestration and usage of the CO_2 captured onboard.

Ships built today should incorporate the available technology for maximum energy efficiency. However, full maritime decarbonization requires retrofitting and renewal of the fleet to burn zero-carbon fuels. Shipbuilding requires large amounts of energy to produce steel and other materials and to construct ships. Ships are designed typically for a 25-year life although many operate safely beyond that. When ships are scrapped some materials are recycled but there is also a lot of waste. By applying circular economy principles this waste can be significantly reduced.

Maritime decarbonization requires green steel produced with zero carbon emissions, and circular economy designs to enable reuse of the materials when ships reach end of life.

Policies and Regulations

Although industry and market driven efforts are necessary for progress, an effective global regulatory framework could accelerate the worldwide adoption of all the decarbonization enablers available today.

Global regulations play a critical role for the global fleet to improve energy efficiency and transition to low and zero carbon fuels. The IMO has a unique role and mandate to regulate ships globally. The short-term measures adopted by the IMO to address the fleet's technical and operational fuel efficiency is a start, but more is required from the global regulatory framework. The IMO revised its 2018 ambitions in July 2023 to align better with the 2015 Paris Climate Accords and the 1.5 °C temperature rise cap, and agreed on further development of mid-term and long-term measures which should keep shipping on the pathway to these targets. No one disagrees on the need for regulatory certainty, but consensus at the IMO requires political acceptance of the proposed measures by its Member States. This can lead to slow progress and compromise outcomes. Since GHG regulations will have a major impact on both the developed and developing countries they must be accepted as equitable for all to reach consensus at the IMO.

Regulatory development at the IMO as well as at the regional and national levels, are discussed in more detail in Chap. "Securing Global Alignment in Regulations Related to Decarbonization" of this book (Tikka & Esau, 2023).

Financing and Incentives

Market based measures (MBMs), such as the fuel levy proposed at the IMO or the EU Emission Trading Scheme (ETS), are needed to accelerate and expand the adoption of low- and zero-carbon fuels beyond the early movers.

Even without MBMs in place shipping can expect higher fuel costs. In the past shipping has been burning fuel that no other industry uses, but going forward, shipping will compete with other industries for supplies of the new fuels. Therefore, it is critical that the shipping energy demand is considered in global energy production projections and infrastructure planning. Ports will have a key role in providing bunkering infrastructure, battery charging stations, and shore-power supply as alternatives for ships alongside. National policies will be important for both energy availability and fuel infrastructure development.

Closing Remarks

In summary, there is a range of maritime decarbonization enablers. Many are already available. Some need additional measures to encourage their uptake. Those involved in the decarbonization journey should consider whether they can act in the following areas:

- Initiate pilot projects on energy efficiency technologies.
- Find joint ventures/partnerships in new ship design and new fuel projects.
- Participate in green corridor developments.
- Join organisations sharing information on decarbonization enablers. For example, the Getting to Zero Coalition (GMF, 2023), The Global Center for Maritime Decarbonization (GCMD, 2023), *Mærsk Mc-Kinney Møller Center* for Zero Carbon Shipping (MMKMCZCS, 2023, Blue Sky Maritime Coalition (Blue Sky, 2023)

References

Blue Sky. (2023). *Blue Sky Maritime Coalition*. Accessed from https://www.bluesky-maritime.org

GCMD. (2023). *The Global Centre for Maritime Decarbonization (GCMD)*. Accessed from https://www.gcformd.org

GMF. (2023). *Getting to zero coalition, Global Maritime Forum*. Accessed from https://www.globalmaritimeforum.org

COP26. (2022). *Clydebank declaration for green shipping corridors*. Accessed from https://www.gov.uk/government/publications/cop-26-clydebank-declaration-for-green-shipping-corridors/cop-26-clydebank-declaration-for-green-shipping-corridors

GZC and GMF. (2022). *Annual progress report on green shipping corridors*. Accessed from https://cms.globalmaritimeforum.org/wp-content/uploads/2022/11/The-2022-Annual-Progress-Report-on-Green-Shipping-Corridors.pdf

JIT Guide. (2020). *Just in time arrival guide – Barriers and potential solutions*. Accessed from https://wwwcdn.imo.org/localresources/en/OurWork/PartnershipsProjects/Documents/GIA-just-in-time-hires.pdf

Lehmacher, W., & Lind, M. (2022). *Value chain-based pathways towards zero-emission shipping - A practical playbook*. Nordic West Office. Accessed from www.nordicwestoffice.com/maritime

MEPC.304 (72). (2018). *IMO resolution on policies and practices related to the reduction of greenhouse gas emissions from ships*. Accessed from https://wwwcdn.imo.org/localresources/en/OurWork/Environment/Documents/Resolution%20MEPC.304%2872%29_E.pdf

MMKMCZCS. (2022). *Maritime decarbonization strategy 2022*. Mærsk Mc-Kinney Møller Center for Zero Carbon Shipping. Accessed from https://www.zerocarbonshipping.com/publications/maritime-decarbonization-strategy/

MMKMCZCS. (2023). *Mærsk Mc-Kinney Møller Center for Zero Carbon Shipping*. Accessed from https://www.zerocarbonshipping.com/

Tikka, K., & Esau, S. (2023). Securing global alignment in regulations related to decarbonization. In M. Lind, W. Lehmacher, & R. Ward (Eds.), *Maritime decarbonization: Practical tools, case studies and decarbonization enablers*. Springer.

Decarbonizing International Shipping Through Collaborative Partnerships

Sanjay Kuttan

Target Audience

This chapter has been written to provide information about successful contemporary partnerships and collaboration to help decarbonize international shipping. It is especially relevant for those in leadership positions, both in the private and the public sector, that have responsibility for ensuring that maritime transportation becomes increasingly sustainable and decarbonized and meets the increasingly stringent climate change targets that are being set by governments and demanded by the public.

Key Takeaway Messages

This chapter highlights:

- The challenges of decarbonization
- The importance of understanding the different types of partnerships that can exist
- Some practical contemporary examples of partnerships and collaboration that are addressing decarbonization

S. Kuttan (✉)
Global Centre for Maritime Decarbonisation, Singapore, Singapore
e-mail: sckuttan@gcformd.org

M. Lind et al. (eds.), *Maritime Decarbonization*,
https://doi.org/10.1007/978-3-031-39936-7_8

The Decarbonization Solution Space

There are numerous reports from the world's classification societies, technology consultants, and think tanks detailing various maritime decarbonization solutions, their feasibility and their short comings.

What is important to note is that the principal solutions can be considered under three main categories:

- market-based mechanisms,
- operational and technological measures, and
- use of alternative low/zero carbon fuels.

A sample of potential practical measures for shipping to reduce greenhouse gas (GHG) emissions is shown in Table 1 (Wang & Lutsey, 2013). Their relative adoption rates as of 2023 are based on a Global Centre for Maritime Decarbonisation (GCMD) internal assessment.

Table 1 Decarbonization measures

Efficiency approaches	GHG reduction measures	GHG emission reduction potential (%)	Relative adoption
Operational	Weather routing	1–4%	Common
	Autopilot upgrade	1–3%	Emerging
	Speed reduction	10–30%	Common
Auxiliary power	Efficient pumps, fans and lighting	0–1%	Common
	Solar panels	0–3%	Low
Aerodynamics	Air lubrication	5–15%	Low but emerging
	Wind engine/power	3–12%	Low but emerging
	Kite	2–10%	Low
Thrust efficiency	Propeller polishing	3–8%	Common
	Propeller upgrade	1–3%	Common
	Propeller/rudder upgrade	2–6%	Common
Engine efficiency	Waste heat recovery	6–8%	Emerging
	Engine controls	0–1%	Emerging
	Engine speed derating	10–30%	Emerging
Hydrodynamics	Hull cleaning	1–10%	Common
	Advance Hull coating	1–5%	Emerging
	Water flow optimisation	1–4%	Via new builds

Market Based Mechanisms

In the grand scheme of things, all our efforts must reduce GHG emissions into the environment. To that end we need to distinguish between 'carbon' accounting and 'carbon' accountability. 'Carbon' accounting converges with carbon accountability when accurate life cycle assessment (LCA) is applied to our decarbonization solutions. Data transparency and accuracy will be key pre-conditions to ensure that LCA are evaluated properly and accepted by the authorities and industry.

LCA is not a simple task, when accuracy is important. Nevertheless, the lack of absolute accuracy should not hold us back from pursuing a solution. Calculations based on less well-defined data can still serve as a signpost that we are heading in the right direction. Mother Nature is more forgiving with our efforts, and we should agree that 'great should not be the enemy of good'. However, the tax office or policy makers, may well insist on accuracy when dealing with policies i.e., carbon tax and carbon credit mechanisms, to avoid disputes between the beneficiaries and the payer.

It should also be remembered that market-based mechanisms i.e., carbon tax, carbon credit mechanisms, only address the vessel's carbon footprint from an accounting perspective by providing incentives to decarbonize. They do not have a direct impact on the absolute emissions reduction effort for the maritime sector per se. Nevertheless, they have an important part to play if the pricing and carbon accounting methodology is right, this to drive the correct behaviour with respect to decarbonisation of ship owners, operators and charterers.

Technological and Operational Measures

Technological and operational measures in Table 1 are important to pave the way towards lowering the energy and/or carbon footprint of vessels. These efficiency measures will continue to be relevant across the lifetime of the vessel, as it will reduce energy cost from the onset, and reduce the use of green alternative fuels in the near future, where these fuels are expected to be more costly, less ubiquitous and have a lower volumetric energy density.

There is also the opportunity to lower the carbon footprint of shipping with shipboard carbon capture technologies, whilst waiting for the time-investment dependent scaling of alternative fuels. This is one potentially effective short- and medium-term technological solution to reduce the carbon footprint of vessels burning fossil fuels. Whilst many challenges still exist in ensuring the captured carbon dioxide (CO_2) does not re-enter the atmosphere, multiple stakeholders across the solution space are working to try to address these challenges which include the shipboard capture systems, off-loading the captured CO_2, aggregation, transportation, utilisation, and carbon sequestration. In addition, policy, legal and liability challenges associated with the handling and disposition of the captured CO_2 are still open issues requiring collective action. The captured carbon dioxide today is considered a waste, hence new business models will need to consider the service provisions of handling the waste which includes sequestration and when the waste becomes a valuable feedstock for the utilisation pathways.

The adoption of all the technical solutions still faces many considerations, that include some or all of the following:

- technology readiness
- operational readiness
- policy coherency
- infrastructure readiness
- interoperability standards
- harmonised standards
- green financing
- commercial viability
- manpower capabilities
- availability and accessibility
- health and Safety
- environmental impact
- insurability
- accounting standards
- performance guarantees

Several other chapters in this book, particularly this chapter and Chaps. “Maritime Decarbonization: Actions by Cargo Owners—The Shippers’ Perspective” and “Actions by Ports to Support Green Maritime Operations: A Real Case Study—The Port of Plymouth, UK”, among others, discuss in more detail the various technological and operational options being considered.

Alternative Fuels

Alternative fuels offer a big decarbonization lever but are not without associated challenges. Properties such as toxicity, flammability, corrosivity and it’s physical nature (boiling point, storage temperatures, etc) must be respected and managed with technological, procedural and policy guidelines. This is required to ensure the health and safety of workers, reliability of assets, as well as the protection of the environment.

The challenges associated with the deployment of alternative fuels can be grouped into seven pillars of considerations, which are shown in Table 2

When considering initiatives related to alternative fuels, it is important to look at the full life cycle across their supply and value chains to make sure that all the different stakeholders fully appreciate and address the issues highlighted in Table 1. Every aspect that thwarts progress is a reason to consider a collaborative project that has a clear problem statement defined with expected outcomes. Identification of the stakeholders responsible for finding the solutions must envisage all forms of

Table 2 The seven pillars of considerations

Fuel properties	Fuel supply	Infrastructure	Standards	Commercial terms	Compliance	Manpower
Volumetric energy density	Ubiquitous production	New	Handling	Price premium	Sectorial and geographical regulations	Readiness
			Custody transfer			
Hazardous materials classification	Availability of supply chain assets	Existing	Testing	Insurance	Data management with increased digitalisation	Competency

Source: Global Centre of Maritime Decarbonisation (GCMD)

collaboration—upstream of the project, within the project and downstream of the project across the supply chain. This is key to ensuring that there are no gaps, and all the barriers are being addressed. This approach also helps identify the key areas to monitor, which might include:

- Production management
  - availability and accessibility of feedstocks
  - quantity of feedstock and products
  - quality of feedstock and products
  - harmonised standards, operating guidelines, and safety procedures
  - production technology
  - production waste stream management
  - manpower capabilities
  - economics of feedstock and products
  - carbon footprint of feedstock and products
  - storage of feedstocks and products
  - policy coherency
- Distribution management
  - storage and distribution infrastructure of products
  - environmental, Health and Safety of transporting products
  - harmonised standards, operating guidelines, and safety procedures
  - manpower capabilities
  - economics of distribution
  - carbon footprint of distribution
  - policy coherency
- Utilisation management
  - technology readiness
  - harmonised standards, operating guidelines, and safety procedures
  - utilisation waste stream management
  - manpower capabilities
  - economics of utilisation
  - carbon footprint of utilisation
  - policy coherency

Understanding Partnerships

A maritime decarbonization matrix framework about partnerships in shipping decarbonization has recently been elaborated (Lind & Lehmacher, 2022). The framework depicts partnerships and their relationships as a two-dimensional matrix; one axis being the type of collaboration or *form of partnership* (vertical, horizontal, and diagonal), and the second axis is the *focus of partnership* looking at the beneficiaries, that is, whether companies benefit, or also industry benefits, or also other industries, the ecosystem benefits. The framework and these partnership relationships are explained and discussed in detail in Chap. "Effective Partnerships to Support Maritime Decarbonization".

The composition of a collaboration is the main criteria for allocating the 'form of partnership' in the table, while the beneficiaries of a collaboration determine where a collaboration sits under 'focus of partnership'.

The focus of partnership for a collaboration that primarily impacts the companies involved falls under 'company benefits'. A partnership that helps the entire industry, for example through building a maritime bunkering hub would be placed under 'industry also benefits'; and an alliance that impacts multiple industries, like establishing a hub for renewable energy which can be used by many industries would be placed under 'ecosystem, also other industries and areas benefit'.

Partnerships without competitors would be placed in the 'vertical' category. Where only peers are involved, partnerships are considered as belonging to the 'horizontal' category. Collaborations that consist of vertical and horizontal alignment are considered to belong to the 'diagonal' category. Diagonal partnerships also reflect overarching initiatives with (some) focus on the maritime sector. All three forms of collaboration can and should ideally include governments, international organisations (IOs), intergovernmental organisations (IGOs), and/or non-governmental organisations (NGOs).

Vertical partnerships that are built along the value chains, downstream, upstream, or a combination of both, are often initiated and driven by one single (stronger) player in the chain such as a larger shipping company. As an example, this type of collaboration could be used to ensure that there is a sufficient supply of green methanol for ships upstream in the transportation chain which would allow a shipping company to offer downstream forwarders cleaner transport solutions enabling them to respond to such demand. This could result in vertical arms-length partnerships that result in vertical integration where a shipping company acquires an energy provider.

Horizontal partnerships are built between peers, for example, among wet bulk carriers that aim to achieve higher asset productivity, and with that they reduce GHG emissions, costs, and delays. Horizontal alliances are usually harder to find as they require specific circumstances, for example, overcoming common exigencies or seeking mutual benefits, and may need to comply with different legislative requirements. Such partnerships may be constrained by anti-competition laws which adds another level of complexity, albeit surmountable.

Diagonal partnerships cut across different stakeholder groups, horizontally and vertically, and usually require a neutral actor, like an IO, NGO or IGO, to make them work. Often, multiple neutral partners are involved. They can initiate multi-stakeholder partnerships by bringing together, for instance, shipping companies, energy providers, financial institutions, and governments. A good example is the Getting to Zero Coalition that is working to commercialise and scale zero-emission ships operating both along deep-sea trade routes and on shortsea passages through engagement with stakeholders across the maritime value chain. Diagonal partnerships can bring all relevant actors to the table to work together to identify efficient technologies or find new business models that fit with and accelerate alternative fuel uptakes. The Mærsk McKinney Møller Center for Zero Carbon Shipping (MMMFCZCS) is another example.

Table 3 illustrates the maritime decarbonization matrix framework. It has been populated with examples of contemporary partnerships.

Table 3 shows several examples of vertical collaborations focusing on decarbonizing individual value chains producing primarily benefits for the companies involved, including the CMA CGM biofuel trial in Singapore. These would be placed at A1 in the framework matrix. The partnership between AP Møller-Mærsk and renewable energy firm Ørsted on a new Power-to-X facility in USA to produce zero emission maritime fuels is an example of a vertical collaboration creating value for the maritime industry that sits in the matrix at A2. An example of a vertical partnership with impact on ecosystem level sitting at A3 is the Mærsk/Egypt green energy partnership that supports the Egyptian government to position Egypt as a global hub for renewable energy.

An example of a horizontal partnership focussed on a single maritime value chain that sits in the matrix at B1 is the Tankers International VLCC Pool that is bringing together peers in a joint pool of resources of wet bulk vessels. Examples of horizontal partnerships benefitting the maritime industry sitting in position B2 in the matrix are the Digital Container Shipping Association (DCSA) created by major container shipping lines to develop standards to increase the fluidity and efficiency of the sector and thus reduce GHG emissions, costs, and delays, and the International Association of Ports and Harbors (IAPH) with their initiatives on decarbonizing their industry. No industry-driven or overarching horizontal partnerships also focussing on the ecosystem that might be placed at matrix position B3 have been identified yet.

However different levels have emerged with the Project Sabre Consortium, focussing primarily on company benefits through the ammonia bunker supply chain is an example of a diagonal partnership that can be placed in the matrix at C1. There are several diverse diagonal initiatives focused on the decarbonization of the maritime industry that can be placed in position C2. These are the GCMD in Singapore, the Blue Sky Maritime Coalition, and the Global Maritime Forum, with the Getting to Zero Coalition pursued in collaboration with the World Economic Forum. This last collaboration brings together more than 150 companies within the maritime, energy, infrastructure and finance sectors, supported by key governments and intergovernmental organisations to prepare a roadmap containing the necessary steps from developing and testing solutions and enabling environments to getting ready for roll-out. Finally, the Mission Possible Partnership, the Renewable and Low-Carbon Fuels Value Chain Industrial Alliance, Mission Innovation, and the Horizon 2020 maritime/port decarbonization initiatives PIONEERS and MAGPIE are diagonal partnerships that focus on the ecosystems and belong in position C3 in the matrix.

Table 3 The maritime decarbonization matrix populated with examples of contemporary partnerships (Lind et al., 2022)

		Form of partnership		
		A: Vertical	**B**: Horizontal	**C**: Diagonal
Focus of partnership	**1**: Primarily participating companies benefit	**A1** CMA CGM biofuel trial Singapore Hapag-Lloyd and DHL Global Forwarding collaboration on advanced biofuels; BHP and NYK decarbonization partnership MSC Shell partnership	**B1** Tankers International VLCC Pool	**C1** Project Sabre Consortium
	2: Industry also benefits	**A2** Maersk green methanol partnership CMA CGM/TotalEnergies ship-to-ship LNG bunkering with the goal to establish a Mediterranean maritime LNG hub at Marseille-Fos Port End-to-end shipboard carbon capture	**B2** Digital standards (as one area of focus) in container shipping (Digital Container Shipping Association (DCSA)) International Association of Ports and Harbours (IAPH) with emphasis on climate and energy as one of many focuses	**C2** Getting to Zero Coalition (Global Maritime Forum/ World Economic Forum) The Global Centre for Maritime Decarbonisation (GCMD) Mærsk Mc-Kinney Møller Center for Zero Carbon Shipping Blue Sky Maritime Coalition PIONEERS; MAGPIE
	3: Ecosystem, also other industries and areas benefit	**A3** Maersk/Egypt green energy partnership	**B3** None identified as yet	**C3** Mission Possible Partnership First Movers Coalition Renewable and Low-Carbon Fuels Value Chain Industrial Alliance Mission Innovation Climate Group's Steel Zero initiative

Designing Pilot Projects

Projects are usually defined by clear objectives specifically addressing problem statements. This is no different for decarbonization related projects within the shipping industry. It is also usually true that projects are scoped to stay within budgetary and time constraints. However, to accelerate the adoption of solutions along the decarbonization pathways, a bolder approach is required that embraces the complexity of multiple stakeholders' engagement to address barriers or gaps to adoption. This approach is founded on collaborative partnership, to drive not only the success of the pilot projects and but also to increase the possibility of adoption at pace and scale. Pilot projects must be designed and executed in a way to ensure institutional "stickiness" for sustained impact beyond the pilot.

Therefore, when designing pilot projects, the 10 keys steps set out below can serve as guideline to ensure the pilot will deliver the desired outcomes with project partners fully aligned and engaged.

Step 1	Clearly articulate the desired outcome of the pilot – *What do we want to achieve and by when?*
Step 2	Identify all practical considerations in executing the pilot – *How would you operationalise the solution after the project?*
Strep 3	List potential stakeholders responsible for identified considerations in step 2 – *Who will be involved to ensure the pathway to operationalisation is clear?*
Step 4	List challenges faced by each stakeholder identified in step 3 – *What are the challenges faced by each stakeholder in executing their role when fully operational?*
Step 5	Deconstruct each challenge in step 4, to identify gaps, bottlenecks, or barriers – *Gap analysis of the challenges—what does the current and future situation looks like?*
Step 6	Develop solution hypotheses for each gap, bottleneck, or barrier – *What are the potential solutions to address the gaps?*
Step 7	Test and refine solution hypotheses with identified stakeholders – *Does the proposed solution make sense and if not how to improve?*
Step 8	Develop pilot project execution plan, to include – *What to do?* – *How to do?* – *Who to do?* – *When to do?*
Step 9	Engage potential project partners with pilot proposal and clear roles, responsibilities, and expectations (cost and time) of involvement – *Avoid observers where possible, as active involvement is key to success (except for Policy makers or Regulators)* – *Respect confidentiality of information* – *Ensure clear engagement plan with all stakeholders* – *Declare all background intellectual property (IP) rights and identify potential foreground IP rights*
Step 10	Finalise project details and letters of collaboration between project owner and project partners

GCMD Projects and Partnership Case Studies[1]

The Global Centre for Maritime Decarbonisation (GCMD) was established on 1st August 2021 as a non-profit organisation. It was an initiative of the Maritime and Port Authority of Singapore (MPA) to continue to consolidate Singapore's position as an international maritime hub following the recommendation to the Singapore government by the International Advisory Panel on Maritime Decarbonization (IAP) convened a year earlier by the Singapore Maritime Foundation. The IAP identified nine pathways to maritime decarbonization, including policy options to accelerate the transition and ways in which Maritime Singapore can support the industry's decarbonization.

The IAP was co-chaired by the Chairman of the Singapore Maritime Foundation, together with the Chairman of the Board and Governing Council of the Singapore Maritime Institute. It comprised 28 other leaders from maritime and related organisations, including shipping associations, shipping companies, port operators, energy companies, engine makers, shipyards, insurance, and finance players, as well as academia.

The IAP envisioned Maritime Singapore supporting decarbonization of the maritime industry to meet or exceed the International Maritime Organization's (IMO) decarbonization goals for 2030 and 2050 by:

- shaping GHG measures to ensure that actions have a real and lasting positive impact.
- setting standards for operational, technical and safety factors
- piloting innovations in the technical, operational, and digital sphere
- building selective infrastructure to support these innovations
- deploying incentives at national, regional, or global level, combined with private capital initiatives, to implement solutions for vessel efficiency and new fuels; and
- connecting global stakeholders to share knowledge and implement actions.

To achieve this vision, the IAP recommended focusing on four strategic objectives:

- harmonise standards
- implement new solutions
- finance projects
- collaborate with partners

These four strategic objectives were then elaborated:

- Harmonise Standards
  - Shape common metrics for carbon accounting
  - Set standards for new technologies and solutions

[1]Extracts from public information and GCMD internal papers by GCMD team consisting of Dr. Prapisala Thepsithar, Mr. Lau Wei Jie and Mr. Koh Eng Kiong.

- Implement New Solutions
  - Pilot trials and deploy solutions
  - Build flexible ship capabilities and relevant infrastructure
- Finance Projects
  - Develop green financing mechanisms
  - Develop mechanisms that could support carbon pricing
  - Act as custodian for and deploy R&D funds and grants
- Collaborate with Partners
  - Multiply local, regional and global collaboration across stakeholders
  - Set up a decarbonization centre

The founding partners of the GCMD that joined the IAP's vision include, BW Group, the DNV Foundation, BHP, Eastern Pacific Shipping, Ocean Network Express, and Sembcorp Marine (renamed to Seatrium in 2023). Each pledged ten million Singapore dollars over a period of five years with the MPA matching the cumulative pledged sum dollar for dollar. Since then, bp, Hapag-Llyod and NYK have joined the founding partners as strategic partners and another 15 companies as corporate partners. In addition to the corporate partnership, more than 80 project level collaborative partnerships have been established across GCMD initiated projects. This has been achieved within 2 years.

Through these partnerships the management team of the GCMD have continued to engage them to help enable greater impact and achieve the four strategic objectives embedded within its mission statement.

Project partnership is defined specifically by the projects that the GCMD established where invited the partners join based on the project specific roles, responsibilities, and expectations. In reference to Table 3 above, GCMD led projects could be potential candidates as examples of B3, which has not been officially identified when the paper was published.

The GCMD driven projects are conceived based on the philosophy of addressing barriers, bottlenecks, and gaps to the adoption of decarbonization solutions in as a holistic manner as possible and is not based on picking winners in the race to establish decarbonization solutions. In a nutshell, the GCMD is agnostic to solutions albeit prioritisation of limited resources would imply it cannot do everything and needs to sequence projects carefully.

The GCMD also made some strategic choices to focus on higher technological readiness solutions that are also low on the commercial readiness index and where it can address operational readiness of the associated decarbonization ecosystem when pertinent.

Partnership Case Study 1: Ammonia Bunkering Safety Study

In 2018, the IMO adopted an initial GHG reduction strategy with the ambition of reducing the total annual GHG emissions from international shipping by at least 50% by 2050 compared to 2008 (Note in 2023 at the MEPC 80, these targets have been recently updated to a more ambitious one with net zero GHG emission by around 2050). To meet this target, an accelerated transition to low-/zero-carbon fuels and technologies is necessary. Among the various alternative fuels, green ammonia is favourably considered by worldwide experts as a zero-carbon fuel that can be implemented for international shipping. Produced with renewable electricity, ammonia can potentially be produced at scale without implications on agricultural land use. However, there remains supply-chain related gaps that need to be addressed before green ammonia can be used by the maritime industry, namely: global production capacity and supply, bunkering standards, and procedures (including safety, operations & environment), bunkering infrastructure, availability of ammonia-fuelled vessels and the overall impact to the marine environment.

At any time, there are around a thousand vessels in the port of Singapore undertaking activities, such as bunkering, cargo operations and crew change. To optimise port stay, ships may be conducting more than one service at the same time, supported by 1600 Singapore harbour craft. Given a high concentration of such activities in Singapore waters, and the proximity of such activities to a population dense city state, a stringent level of safety standards is essential for bunkering operations. A successful trial of ammonia as a marine fuel in the port of Singapore sets a high bar and instils confidence that bunkering of this alternative fuel can be carried out in other seaports around the world.

While there are many initiatives undertaken by the industry to make ammonia-fuelled vessels a reality, starting with designs for different vessel types (for example, container ships[2,3] tankers,[4] bulk carriers[5]) and the development of two[6]- to four-

---

[2]Lloyd's Register, *Industry project to design ammonia-fuelled 23 k ULCS concept*, 03 December 2019. [Online]. Available: https://www.lr.org/en/latest-news/aip-ammonia-fuelled-ulcs/. [Accessed 23 Sep 2021].

[3]American Bureau of Shipping (ABS), *ABS, MAN & SDARI Join Forces to Develop Ammonia-Fueled Feeder Vessel*, 5 December 2019. [Online]. Available: https://ww2.eagle.org/en/news/press-room/abs-man-sdari-develop-ammonia-fueled-feeder-vessel.html. [Accessed 23 Sep 2021].

[4]*The Castor Initiative*, 24 February 2021 [Online]. Available: https://www.lr.org/en/latest-news/unveiling-the-castor-initiative/. [Accessed 23 Sep 2021].

[5]MLIT's ammonia eco-ship design based on an 80,000DWT class bulk carrier. March 2020 [Online]. Available. https://www.ammoniaenergy.org/articles/maritime-ammonia-ready-for-demonstration/#:~:text=In%20Norway%2C%20Color%20Fantasy%2C%20the,deep%20sea%20vessel"%20by%202025. [Accessed 23 Sep 2021].

[6]MAN Energy Solutions, https://man-es.com/discover/two-stroke-ammonia-engine [Accessed 23 Sep 2021].

stroke[7] ammonia combustion engines, the majority of current efforts centre around ship technologies, followed by fuel production and bunkering.[8] In Singapore, studies have been commissioned to address aspects of ammonia bunkering (for example, Ammonia bunker safety study).[9] This study builds upon the knowledge developed thus far to establish the basis for a regulatory testing ground for piloting and demonstrating ammonia bunkering in Singapore.

The study partners were selected by the GCMD with specific roles to help enable ammonia bunkering in general and to facilitate the successful delivery of the study. The partners are shown in Table 4.

To engage more stakeholders to get better alignment around the study outcomes GCMD called for an Industry Consultation and Alignment Panel (iCAP) to provide input to the recommendations of the study before the report was finalised and presented to the regulators. More than 130 industry partners across the broader maritime ecosystem had joined the iCAP by the end of the study.

The GCMD also worked closely with MPA and other government agencies to set up a working group that facilitated the consultation process to develop new technical references and standards.

It is expected that proving the operability of ammonia bunkering by developing safety and operational envelopes will have a ripple effect up and down the value chain in terms of future investments to ensure scalability of green ammonia production, storage, and transportation for the maritime sector and potentially other adjacent sectors, for example, agriculture and power generation.

Partnership Case Study 2: Quality, Quantity and GHG Abatement Assurance Framework for Drop-in Fuels

The IMO Marine Environment Protection Committee (MEPC) adopted an Initial strategy on The Reduction of Greenhouse Gas Emissions from Ships in April 2018 to reduce total annual GHG emissions by at least 50% by 2050 relative to 2008 levels (Note in 2023 at the MEPC 80, these targets have been recently updated to a more ambitious one with net zero GHG emission by around 2050). In support of this ambition, new measures, such as implementing an Energy Efficiency Existing Ship Index (EEXI) was adopted with a Carbon Intensity Indicator (CII) rolled out subsequently at the beginning of 2023.

---

[7] Wärtsilä, https://www.wartsila.com/media/news/30-06-2020-world-s-first-full-scale-ammonia-engine-test%2D%2Dan-important-step-towards-carbon-free-shipping-2737809 [Accessed 23 Sep 2021].

[8] Global Maritime Forum for GTZ, *Mapping of Zero Emission Pilots and Demonstration Projects*, 2nd edition, March 2021.

[9] MESD, ABS & ASTI, *Ammonia as a marine fuel in Singapore - Supply Chain, Bunker Safety, and Potential Issues*, Jan 2021. https://www.manifoldtimes.com/news/abs-and-partners-to-collaborate-on-a-study-of-ammonia-as-bunker-fuel-in-singapore/. [Accessed 28 Sep 2021].

Table 4 Study partners and roles in bunkering supply chain

Study partners	Roles in the bunkering supply chain
Port terminal operators • Jurong Port • PSA	• Operates regulated waterfront facilities which may carry out simultaneous operations (SIMOPS) in the vicinity of ship-to-ship bunkering operations • Facilitates the use of terminal's berth for truck-to-ship bunkering operations
Fuel storage terminal operators • Vopak Terminals • Advario	• Operates current and possible low-carbon fuel storage terminals • Offloads marine fuels to bunker vessel for subsequent bunkering operations • Provides marine fuel to truck to carry out truck-to-ship bunkering operations
Bunker fuel supplier and barge owners • Pavilion Energy • Hong Lam • Fratelli Cosulich • Kenoil	• Supplies bunker fuels to marine vessels via truck-to-ship or ship-to-ship bunkering operations, loading marine fuel from fuel storage terminals • Owns bunker barges
Shipowners or operators • Navigator gas/BW • EPS • ONE • PIL • MOL • NYK • Asiatic Lloyd	• Owns or operates vessels
Shipyards and vessel design • Sembcorp marine (Seatrium as of 2023) • Keppel • Seatech solutions	• Provides principles/guidelines that govern the design and construction of new bunker barges and receiving vessels
Metrology National Metrology Centre	• Provide expert opinion on the acceptable practices for quantity and quality verification during custody transfer
Fuel testing service provider • Viswa lab • VPS	• Provides testing services for the bunkering community

To comply with forthcoming regulations, ships will need to adopt environmentally benign alternative energy sources. As an interim measure, the use of so-called drop-in fuels—synthetic and completely interchangeable substitutes for conventional petroleum-derived fuels. This represents a fundamental shift in sourcing energy and feedstock to produce alternative fuels with low- or zero-carbon intensity (such as green methanol, ammonia, and hydrogen). It is anticipated that the transition from fossil fuels to green fuels will take place over the next few decades, necessitating the production of green fuels to scale up to meet the energy demand of the maritime industry. During this transition, alternative lower-carbon fuels derived from fossil fuels and renewable sources (for example, liquified natural gas (LNG), bio-LNG and synthetic LNG) can be expected to be introduced into the supply chain. In the specific case of LNG, its greener counterparts have the same chemical makeup, but they command a higher cost and deliver a lower GHG footprint. To justify their premium, their greater GHG emissions reduction impact needs to be verified. Furthermore, to ensure there is no value erosion of the premium green fuel through cheating, transparency across the supply chain will be needed to preserve the integrity of any green fuel blends both in terms of quality and quantity.

Currently, there is no commonly accepted robust framework that addresses stakeholder concerns around quality, quantity, GHG emissions abatement and traceability of green fuels, or one that establishes and protects the value of a green premium.

To address this, the GCMD proposed to undertake a project to establish a framework to provide assurance for drop-in green fuels, based on the actual procurement and use of blended fuels for commercial voyages. The project outcomes are intended to build trust in the current supply chain of marine fuels and help stakeholders better cope with the complexities of deploying future green fuels.

The proposed project aims to accelerate the adoption of drop-in green fuels by the shipping sector through the establishment of an assurance framework spanning the supply chain, based on operational data. The assurance framework comprises concepts, principles, technologies, processes, methodology, and best practices to measure and help verify the quantity, quality, GHG emissions abatement and traceability of green fuels. With an assurance framework in place, end-users will be able to realise the genuine benefits of using drop-in green fuels from a well-to-wake perspective and, ultimately, justify the green premium.

The pilot project focuses on biofuels as its first drop-in green fuel candidate, as it illustrates the benefits of reducing GHG emissions with minimal changes to the existing distribution infrastructure, shipboard technologies, and operational norms of ships.[10] Biodiesel (Fatty Acid Methyl Ester (FAME)) and hydrotreated vegetable oil (HVO) have been demonstrated to be compatible with existing ship and bunkering infrastructure with minimal modifications to engines required. To complement the future availability of biofuels, the project will also trial crude algae oil (CAO) produced from third and/or fourth generation feedstocks.[11] The learnings from these biofuels' trials will be used to develop and demonstrate an assurance framework, which can be adapted later for the dropping in of other green fuels, for example., bio-LNG, e-methanol, and green ammonia, into their non-green fuel versions.

In recent years, there have been many ship trials with biofuels[12] (including biodiesel and HVO). However, these projects have focused on the onboard application of biofuels blended with marine fuel oils (either distillates or residual fuels) to

[10] Due to similar energy content of liquid biofuels (FAME, HVO and SVO) and fuel oils.

[11] Referring to algae, microalgae and genetically modified microalgae.

[12] From publicly available information.

understand operational issues of fuel handling and to evaluate engine performance during sea trials, as well as to assess CO_2 emissions reduction.

Despite the learnings from the numerous sea trials, biodiesel and HVO have yet to be adopted widely. The GCMD, in consultation with stakeholders in the bunker supply chain identified the following bottlenecks, which need to be overcome for wider adoption of biofuels:

- Integrity and visibility of the biofuels supply chain, particularly traceability of the authenticity of drop-in biofuels to ensure GHG accounting of sustainable biofuels.
- Robust quantity and quality assurance for biofuels throughout the supply chain.
- Transparent GHG accounting to justify the green premium and its accompanying cost-benefit analysis.
- Understanding of how adoption of drop-in biofuels complies with upcoming regional and global regulations.
- Awareness of global supply availability for sustainable biofuels.

The project is conceived principally to ensure that the shipping routes, scheduling at ports of call, purchase and supply of fuels will be conducted as business-as-usual and on normal commercial terms, except for the purchase of CAO. The use of tracer injection, physical 'lock and seal' systems, supply chain sampling, stability studies, detection test and analytics, will be transparent to the on-going ship operations albeit the results will be shared through the project management framework. Working closely with the fuel purchasers, shipping routes and bunkering ports were established, around which the work plans were organised. Noting the potential shifts in delivery dates of the bunker fuel, close coordination between the GCMD team and all the partners was paramount to ensure each project partner was able to fulfil their roles effectively. In total 5 supply chains covering Europe and Asia are being trialled (Note: US route is being pursued), with a project partnership comprising of 14 shipping companies as fuel purchasers, 4 fuel suppliers, 3 international laboratories for quality assurance, 3 tracer related companies to validate traceability and blend quantity, 1 engine OEM and 1 thought partner for GHG abatement analytics. More details available on the GCMD website. The assurance framework will be articulated based on the data, insights and experience coming out from the project and shared publicly for all to consider using.

Closing Remarks

To decarbonize the shipping industry at pace and scale to meet the very challenging targets of the UN Paris Climate Change Agreement and of the IMO, collaboration is needed not only across economic sectoral ecosystems but also within the maritime ecosystem even where competition exists between parties.

The quality of relationships between organisations and people to make any form of partnership work is paramount. That quality is driven by having a shared aspiration, and decarbonization is the aspiration that will drive the convergence of purpose.

Collaboration is about working with others to produce something together and achieve shared goals. Our shared goal is to curtail the advancement of climate change which is an existential threat by decarbonizing sources of man-made carbon emissions.

Collaborative partnerships must be the new mantra where agreements and actions are made by consenting organisations to share resources to accomplish a mutual goal. Collaborative partnerships rely on participation by at least two parties who agree to share resources, such as finances, knowledge, and people.

References

Lind, M., & Lehmacher, W. (2022). *Positioning partnerships in shipping decarbonization, article no. 92 [UNCTAD transport and trade facilitation newsletter N°95 - third quarter 2022].* Accessed from https://unctad.org/news/positioning-partnerships-shipping-decarbonization

Lind, M., Lehmacher, W., Kuttan, S., Carson-Jackson, J., Cummins, D., van Gogh, M., & Rydbergh, T. (2022). *Partnering towards zero emissions shipping: Playbook part 4, 4/11-2022, The Maritime Executive*. Accessed from https://www.maritime-executive.com/editorials/partnering-towards-zero-emissions-shipping-playbook-part-4

Wang, H., & Lutsey, N. P. (2013, July). *Long-term potential for increased shipping efficiency through the adoption of industry leading practices*. ResearchGate - GCMD analysis.

Part III
Bringing the Four-Step Concept to Life

How to Get Started: CDES—A New Paradigm for Tackling Decarbonization Projects

Mikael Lind and Wolfgang Lehmacher

Target Audience

This chapter is intended primarily for executives, senior sponsors, leaders and managers of decarbonization projects, and in particular, leaders that are working in companies seeking to launch or are in the process of launching a decarbonization programme.

Key Takeaway Messages

The chapter highlights:

- The importance of applying a holistic and balanced approach to decarbonization, bringing to the discussion the idea of circularity, which can support the transition to a no/low greenhouse (GHG) emission economy.
- The value of the **c**ollaboration and **d**igitalisation for **e**conomic and **s**ocietal capital creation (cdes) model.
- The power of the paradigm of balanced development.
- The potential role of cdes in the world of shipping and its importance for decarbonization.

M. Lind (✉)
Research Institutes of Sweden (RISE), Gothenburg, Sweden

Chalmers University of Technology, Gothenburg, Sweden
e-mail: mikael@realsearchers.com

W. Lehmacher
Independent Supply Chain Expert, Hong Kong, China
e-mail: w.lehmacher@gmail.com

M. Lind et al. (eds.), *Maritime Decarbonization*,
https://doi.org/10.1007/978-3-031-39936-7_9

Decarbonizing maritime supply chains starts with applying a holistic lens and approach. It is about focussing on critical, diverse and balanced outcomes. One formula that reflects this idea is the cdes model.

Decarbonization of supply chains requires end-to-end and cradle-to-cradle thinking and digitalisation and collaboration. Decarbonizing shipping is about working together towards an economy in which greenhouse gas (GHG) emissions and waste/excess material are avoided and products and materials are used to the maximum extent possible. This is empowered by digitalisation and creates and increases economic and societal capital. In its final stage it is about a GHG emissions and waste/excess material-free circular economy. A circular economy of products, meaning the extension of the use of no/low emissions products and the circular economy of materials—the extension of materials beyond the last use cycle of a product, for example a ship Lehmacher and Bödecker (2023). There is also a third circularity loop, the circular economy of biosynthesis—the natural growing and decomposing of materials. Circularity and decarbonization are closely linked as every activity in the economy needs some form of resources and energy. Circularity can support the decarbonization transition as it reduces the need for energy in general. The less resources and energy we need the better for the environment and climate. Achieving a no emissions circular economy requires digital tools and collaboration. Optimising the use of resources and energy is best achieved in a digitalised and collaborative world. In a circular economy the waste/excess material of one sector is the resource of another and in the decarbonization ecosystem the output of one value chain, such as the marine fuel value chain, is the prerequisite for decarbonizing another value chain, for example, the maritime operational value chain.

Collaboration and digitalisation are critical drivers of economic and societal value creation. These drivers need to be mutually reinforcing to generate synergistic gains. Digitalisation promotes collaboration through swift and efficient digital information exchange enabling effective coordination. Simultaneously, digitalisation requires collaboration. Otherwise, digitalisation is destined to fail or produces suboptimal results. We make this dire pronouncement mindful of the reality that seven out of eight digital transformations fail (Wade & Shan, 2020).

In the biological world, many species have symbiotic relationships, mutual dependencies with other species, to increase their ecological fitness. There is a comparable symbiotic relationship between digitalisation and collaboration. Together they provide benefits and neither can exist without the other, because they co-determine economic fitness. Successful partnerships co-evolve their collaboration through cooperative digitalisation to contribute to an emerging era of digital symbiosis. Freedom of association is an important feature of most developed economies. Essentially, any organisation is free to create a partnership with another to fashion a symbiotic relationship. Digitalisation turbocharges the benefits of free association by increasing the ease and gains of collaboration.

Consequently, we assert that all industries need to place greater emphasis on the interrelationship between *collaboration* (**c**) and *digitalisation* (**d**), as this powerful duo impacts *economic* (**e**) and *societal* (**s**) success through enhancing human and social capital and preserving and restoring natural capital. Focusing only on one of both dimensions of each pair, either on collaboration or digitalisation, or on economic or societal value, leads to suboptimal results. A conscious, holistic approach addressing all four components of the **cdes** formula ensures durable wealth and well-being for humanity. A *cdes* mindset can take supply chain management and logistics practices to higher levels of digital symbiosis.

Why the World Needs a cdes Approach?

In particular, the shipping industry has much to gain from a *cdes* approach because, as a self-organising ecosystem (Watson et al., 2021), it exemplifies massive freedom of association. Still, it is blighted by a slow evolution of digital symbiosis. This lag is not surprising as a global self-organising ecosystem faces many hindrances to digital collaboration, such as cultural differences and operations spanning many jurisdictions.

The Earth's natural capital is a mix of renewable (for example, plants) and finite (such as metal and water) resources. Overpopulation and economic growth strain both, and we must respond collectively to the existential threat of global climate change. Actors across the economy and the transport ecosystem need to collectively take responsibility for creating a sustainable economy and transport sector while competition remains intact. An unresolved quest is thus to balance where to compete and where to collaborate. What are the global commons (Stang, 2013) that the actors in the ecosystem should collectively preserve or restore while competing? A question that each actor but also industry and ecosystem should answer. A stable climate should certainly be on that list.

Supply chain networks, the backbone of the global economy, require large-scale collaboration, but they can still be highly fragmented. While industry cooperates to create a dynamic self-organising ecosystem, where freedom of association permits, collaboration for positive change has not demonstrated its full potential. This lack of deep cooperation might cause slow digitalisation, which handicaps coordinated action to address global challenges. Also, decarbonization requires collaboration for both, creating economic opportunity and value, and producing societal safety and health capital.

Our twenty-first-century world needs large-scale deep collaboration to ensure a decent life for everyone, today and tomorrow, safe from global challenges like climate change. Collaboration is conducive to elevating everyone out of poverty, minimising greenhouse gas (GHG) emissions, pollution of the oceans, the destruction of marine life, and global wealth inequities. Trade, greatly facilitated by shipping, is the global grease that enables nations to exploit their natural advantages or find a niche for economic and societal growth. The decarbonization of shipping requires a higher level of alignment between industries and their critical value chains, such as the marine fuel, shipbuilding, and shipping operational value chains

(Lind, Lehmacher, Åhlén Björk, et al., 2022) which can at the required scale only be achieved through close collaboration empowered by digitalisation.

A New Paradigm for Balanced Development

Hardly anyone questions the importance of collaboration and digitalisation for the good of the economy generally and the shipping sector specifically. Neither would anyone deny that there are significant obstacles hindering a highly collaborative and digitalised world. We have the choice to collaborate and structure the outcomes or risk replicating in the digital space the current operational fragmentation and challenges.

Collaboration (**c**) powered by large-scale digitalisation (**d**), in combination **cd**, might be the path towards a better balance between economic and societal goals. Advancing collaboration vertically along supply chains, horizontally between peers, and diagonally across the broader ecosystem requires a shift in mindset and behaviour to subvert today's predominantly competitive attitude. We need a cooperative approach to solve the dominating problems of common interest, such as climate change. We need those who direct the levers of change to realise that in today's highly complex world, with a population approaching ten billion, little is achievable without broad goal alignment facilitated by collaboration and digitalisation.

The combination of collaboration (**c**) and digitalisation (**d**), we aver, can drive economic (**e**) and societal (**s**) advances, as depicted in Fig. 1.

The **cd**-duo provides the opportunity to rebalance our approach by accelerating the growth of economic outputs while more rapidly increasing the quality of human

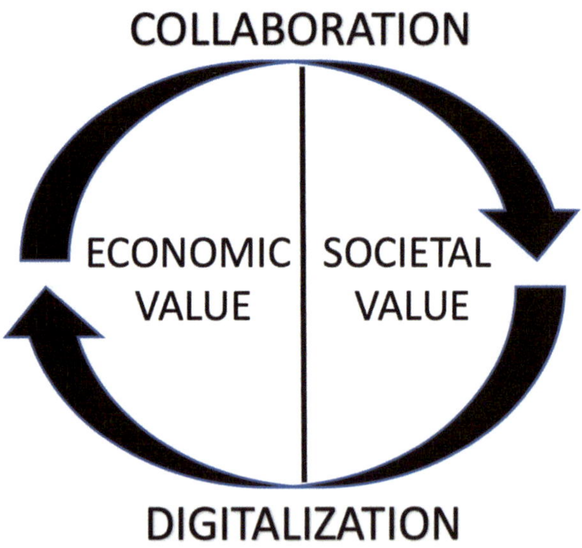

Fig. 1 The cdes model: Rebalancing economic and societal value by the combination of collaboration and digitalisation (Lind, Lehmacher, & Watson, 2022)

and social capital and preserving and restoring natural capital. The outputs ***e*** and ***s*** stand for a broad range of benefits.

Both pairs **cd** and **es** are interrelated. They can be deployed and generated in isolation. Still, the most effective way to drive balanced capital creation is through combining collaboration and digitalisation strategies to drive business models that simultaneously address economic and societal value capital creation. The **cdes** model is a general guideline for public and private sector actors in their quest to deal with today's significant challenges.

Every organisation is in the business of capital creation[1]. But the targeted output is not always economic capital. For example, universities enhance human capital, and service clubs, like Rotary, create social capital. Creating economic capital, the goal of most businesses requires a recipe that blends economic, human, symbolic, social, organisational, and natural capital. The winners are those organisations with a recipe that generates the highest level of productivity within their competitive sphere. A pure short-term focus on profits that neglects a balanced broader stakeholder view can jolt the share price but inflict long-term damage.[2]

Translating cdes into the World of Shipping

The new ***cdes*** paradigm, with its emphasis on digital data sharing, supports the implementation of virtual watch towers (Lind, Lehmacher, Haraldson, et al., 2022) to provide situational awareness of vital assets such as cargo in transit. Collaborative planning and action across multiple *watch towers* in the global supply chain network can facilitate **es**-outputs, such as supply chain resilience and safety as illustrated in Fig. 2.

Beyond that, the digitally assisted networked approach yields higher delivery reliability and reduced transport induced GHG emissions. In the typical transport chain, the many independent operators own data that could be relevant to partners for planning and forecasting processes. A virtual watch tower can gather 'public data,' such as the traffic flows of different transport modes and 'private data' from network participants to fashion a shared situational awareness among a chain's participants. When aggregated and analysed at a network level, these data can improve the accuracy of arrival time forecasting and predict potential congestion hotspots. A higher level of shared situational awareness can also increase safety across the supply chain.

The Clydebank declaration made at the 26th UN Climate Conference (COP26) emphasises the creation of national, regional, and international green corridors (Lehmacher & Lind, 2021). Their establishment will require collaboration across marine fuel supply, shipbuilding, and maritime operations value chains.

[1]For a comprehensive coverage of capital creation, see Watson (2020)

[2]For a detailed analysis of the consequences of myopic profit maximization, see Gelles (2022)

Fig. 2 Networks of collaborating virtual watch towers generating economic and societal value (Lind, Lehmacher, Haraldson, et al., 2022) (illustration: Sandra Haraldson)

Uncoordinated transitions between modes at transport hubs are typically less energy efficient. Ideally, green corridors and networks cover an entire supply chain, and coordinated digitalisation should be used to extend gradually tendrils to all non-green lanes.

Complex Systems Increase the Need for Data Generation and Sharing

Complexity often results in actions in one cluster of value chains impacting other clusters. Bottlenecks in the renewable energy sector will cause that multi-fuel engines in cleaner ships continue to run on fossil fuel. These transitive or domino effects require a higher level of data sharing to ensure sufficient alignment across related chains to enable effective collaboration to resolve unanticipated interactions and reduce GHG emissions.

A Navigational Matrix for Effective Partnerships

Navigating the diverse landscape of challenges that collaborators face requires that stakeholders engage in different forms of digital symbiosis or persisting partnerships, as exemplified in Table 1. The complexity of any option is determined by the scope of the relationship, from actors along a chain to an industry-impacting collaboration to the breadth of an ecosystem, and the degree of integration, from vertical in a chain or horizontal between peers to diagonal across all key partners.

A canvas of possible partnerships cannot tell the whole story. Most of the members of existing partnerships are the more prominent industry players who are generally adept at increasing their productivity because of their managerial depth and financial resources. Overall industry productivity gains, however, require a balanced and inclusive approach to ensure that the long tail of small participants operating along chains and across industries and ecosystems can benefit from enhanced digitalisation and collaboration. This necessitates a change in the way partnerships are operated and data are shared, so that thousands of ports and tens of thousands of ships have the chance to prosper as members of an efficient and no/low-emissions global shipping industry that has extensively implemented maritime informatics principles (Lind et al., 2021).

Table 1 Generic partnership framework

			Creation of joint efficiencies for ...		
High		Ecosystem	Partners in a cross-industry value chain	Peers in cross-industry value chains	Partners and peers in cross-industry value chains
	Degree of scope and complexity	Industry	Partners in an industry value chain	Peers in industry value chains	Partners and peers in industry value chains
Low		Chain	Partners in a company value chain	Peers in parallel company value chains	Partners and peers in company value chains
			Vertical	Horizontal	Diagonal
			Degree of integration and complexity		
			Low		High

Based on The Maritime Decarbonization Partnerships Matrix as depicted in Lind and Lehmacher (2022)

Pivoting to a More Balanced Future

The world needs a new paradigm to deal with the global challenges of the twenty-first century. Companies that follow the **cdes** approach will fare better than those that do not. They have higher chances to mobilise capital and find partners and talent. They know how to align. The **cdes** model, focusing on collaboration and digitalisation for balanced economic and societal value creation, is intended to guide industry action in the field of decarbonization and beyond. While currently, it might be a voluntary business model shift, new regulations, particularly in Europe and North America, will make this new way of thinking and operating a prerequisite for economic survival. Therefore, it is good to start now.

References

Gelles, D. (2022). *The man who broke capitalism: how Jack Welch gutted the heartland and crushed the soul of corporate America-and how to undo his legacy*. Simon & Schuster.

Lehmacher, W., & Lind, M. (2021). COP26: 5Zs that changed the world, Part 2—Defining the execution. *LogiSym—the Magazine for Supply Chain Executives*, February 2022, pp. 22–24. https://logisym.org

Lehmacher, W., & Bödecker, J. (2023). Circular Economy – 7. Industrielle Revolution: Der Weg zu mehr Nachhaltigkeit durch Kreislaufwirtschaft. (German Edition), 37–38, Springer Gabler

Lind, M., & Lehmacher, W. (2022). Positioning partnerships in shipping decarbonization, Article No. 92 [UNCTAD Transport and Trade Facilitation Newsletter N°95 – Third Quarter 2022]. https://unctad.org/news/positioning-partnerships-shipping-decarbonization

Lind, M., Lehmacher, W., Åhlén Björk, S., Haraldson, S., Pålsson, C., Penttilä, R., Tikka, K., & Watson, R. T. (2022). Decarbonizing the maritime sector: Mobilizing coordinated action in the industry using an ecosystems approach, Article No. 89 [UNCTAD Transport and Trade Facilitation Newsletter N°94—Second Quarter 2022]. https://unctad.org/news/decarbonizing-maritime-sector-mobilizing-coordinated-action-industry-using-ecosystems-approach

Lind, M., Lehmacher, W., Haraldson, S., Simha, A., Larsson, T., Hagerstrand-Avall, B., Lyrberg, M., Zuesongdham, P., Hurley, S., & Fu, X. (2022). Virtual watch towers for supply chain visibility, 29/3-2022. Smart Maritime Network. https://smartmaritimenetwork.com/2022/03/29/virtual-watch-towers-for-supply-chain-visibility/

Lind, M., Lehmacher, W., & Watson, R. T. (2022). Collaboration and digitalisation for balanced economic and societal capital creation by shipping, Article No. 96. UNCTAD Transport and Trade Facilitation Newsletter N°96—Fourth Quarter 2022. https://unctad.org/news/transport-newsletter-article-no-96-fourth-quarter-2022

Lind, M., Michaelides, M. P., Ward, R., & Watson, R. T. (Eds.). (2021). *Maritime informatics*. Springer.

Stang, G. (2013). Global commons: Between cooperation and competition, Issue 17—April 2013. European Union Institute for Security Studies. https://www.iss.europa.eu/sites/default/files/EUISSFiles/Brief_17.pdf

Wade, M., & Shan, J. (2020). Covid-19 has accelerated digital transformation, but may have made it harder not easier. *MIS Quarterly Executive, 19*(3), 213–220.

Watson, R. T. (2020). *Capital, systems and objects: The foundation and future of organizations*. Springer.

Watson, R. T., Lind, M., Delmeire, N., & Liesa, F. (2021). Shipping: A self-organising ecosystem. In M. Lind, M. Michaelides, R. Ward, & R. T. Watson (Eds.), *Maritime informatics*. Springer.

Scenario Thinking To Build Business Advantages That Accelerate Decarbonization

Jeremy B. Bentham

Target Audience

This chapter has been written for those seeking to understand better how to use scenario thinking in strategic decision-making, with a particular focus on decarbonization efforts. It is especially relevant for leadership in sustainability in the private sector when considering a company's future orientation, and/or policymaking to encourage private sector activity.

Key Takeaway Messages

A previous chapter of this book, 'Scenario Thinking and Its Place in Maritime Decarbonization' focused on the fundamental importance of thinking in terms of alternative plausible scenarios about the future, with an introduction to scenario perspectives and insights for the maritime industry. In this chapter, the focus will turn to driving and using scenario thinking in, and across, organisations.

This chapter highlights:

- A widespread and misleading neglect of scenario thinking in organisations, and how to address this.

J. B. Bentham (✉)
World Energy Council, London, UK

Scenarios Team, Shell International, The Hague, The Netherlands

Mission Possible Partnership, Washington, DC, USA

Boston Consulting Group, Amsterdam, The Netherlands

Transformative Scenarios B.V., The Hague, The Netherlands
e-mail: jbentham@live.com

M. Lind et al. (eds.), *Maritime Decarbonization*,
https://doi.org/10.1007/978-3-031-39936-7_10

- A 'learning journey' approach to scenario and strategy development.
- Better balancing of risks and opportunities for different choices through considering different scenarios.
- The pace of change in deploying new technologies as the primary critical uncertainty facing decisions on decarbonization and energy transitions.
- Utilising explosive take-off growth as a driver for competitive advantage, and the frequently underestimated value of being a forerunner.

The Two Crafts of Scenario Thinking, and the Learning Journey

As noted briefly in chapter 'Scenario Thinking and Its Place in Maritime Decarbonization', there are two 'crafts' in scenario thinking—the 'technical' craft of generating innovative scenario content that interweaves perspectives and brings out fresh insights, and the 'social' craft that brings those insights to life in the minds and actions of decision-makers. These are illustrated in Fig. 1.

The importance and practice of the second craft is often neglected by organisations as it is less tangible or visible than the first craft and is typically context-specific for particular organisations. This is the reason why enterprises are regularly disappointed by scenario exercises when they engage external specialist consultants to generate scenarios and are left at the end with glossy reports (reflecting the first craft)

Fig. 1 The two crafts necessary for effective scenario approaches

that sit on shelves but have little lasting impact. It is not widely appreciated that as much, if not more, attention is required to practicing the second 'social' craft as the first.

At the outset, there is both good news and bad news in terms of people's willingness to engage with a scenario mindset. The good news is that most people are increasingly recognising that there are radical uncertainties ahead and that their default approaches to considering future developments in terms of forecasts, sensitivities and probabilities may be insufficient (and indeed misleading). There is growing appreciation that more attention should be given to plausible but significantly different alternative outlooks, such as the Energy Transformation and Maritime scenarios outlined in chapter 'Scenario Thinking and Its Place in Maritime Decarbonization' of this book. More detail can be found in Bentham and Shell Scenarios Team (2021) and Lehmacher and Lind (2022).

The bad news is that human biases still drive people towards the short-cuts of 'thinking fast' rather than performing the harder work of 'thinking slow' required for the scenario mindset (Kahneman, 2011). In addition, the act of 'bringing insights to life in the mind' is a learning/teaching process that many senior leaders automatically resist. Most say, of course, that they are always 'open to learn' as this is a required mantra for leaders these days. But most simply hate to feel 'taught'—after all, their success and seniority is built upon what they already know and have done effectively for years! So, a good part of the second craft is creating circumstances for leaders to learn for themselves.

This, then, also exposes a psychological challenge for the scenario practitioner. To result in effective organisational action, new insights need to be both coherent and shared. At the outset, however, they emerge as fragmented and recognised only by an individual or small team. The default behaviour of practitioners is then to work endlessly on refining and underpinning the insights until they are more-or-less fully coherent, and then finally trying to 'sell' them to their senior stakeholders. People are very reluctant to risk 'losing face' by presenting 'half-baked' ideas to their seniors and being publicly challenged by them. The problem with this approach, however, is that it is rarely successful. As illustrated in the diagram in Fig. 2, people resist being 'sold' ideas that come at them out of the blue.

Instead, a more subtle process needs to be adopted, as illustrated in Fig. 3. The insights need to be refined only to the point that they can first be shared tentatively even though they are 'half-formed'. Then, in the process of sharing and challenge and improvement, the insights not only become more refined but also a growing number of people already take psychological ownership of the outcome because of their involvement in the refining process. This can be uncomfortable for the practitioner as initial failings may be exposed and their 'personal brilliance' obscured, but the outcome is generally much more effective.

Planning and managing this 'S-curve' (shown in red in Fig. 3) is at the heart of 'Craft 2' and requires sensitivity to the culture and norms of an organisation as well as an understanding of the broader agendas and concerns of the senior leaders who need to be engaged. In fact, the S-curve represents a weaving together of both the scenario crafts. Initially, the first technical/analytical craft enables the generation of

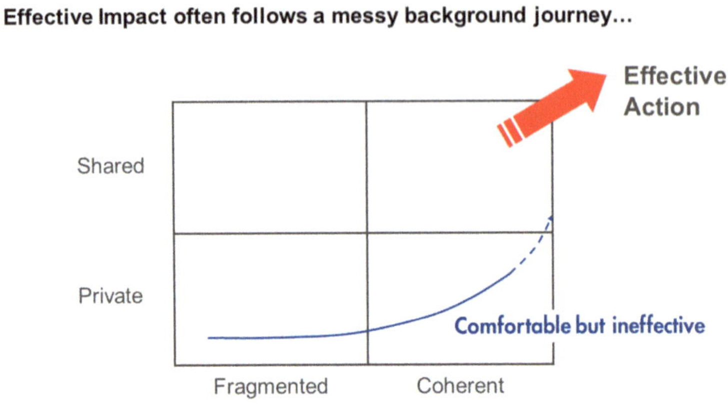

Fig. 2 A common but flawed approach to supporting strategic action

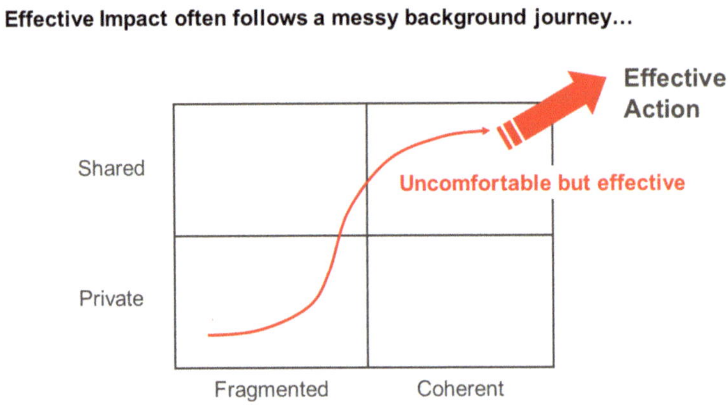

Fig. 3 A more successful approach to supporting strategic action

content that is at least sufficiently coherent to be shared without outright rejection. Then the social craft must be deployed for the sharing, learning and co-refinement aspects of the journey. Finally, the analytical craft is required towards the end of the S-curve to ensure full coherence, with care being taken to avoid premature actions being taken based on ideas that were already well socialised but not yet well-tested or coherent, as the author has seen on more than one occasion!

To help people on the 'learning journey' requires insight into where their minds and concerns are from the outset. You need to meet people 'where they are' with what is already of interest to them. You can then provide circumstances that expand their horizons and encourage them well beyond their initial perspectives. As the great John Maynard Keynes has noted '*The difficulty lies not so much in developing new ideas as in escaping from old ones*' (Keynes, 1936), and as a former head of

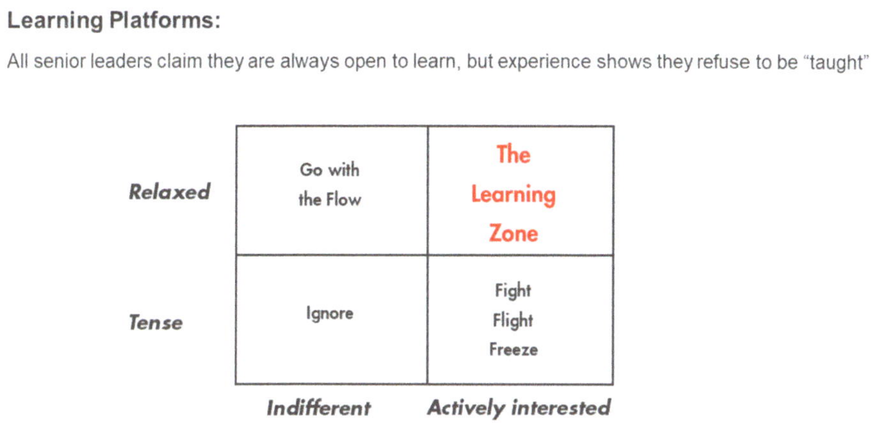

Fig. 4 Circumstances more and less conducive to learning

planning in Shell, the global group of energy and petrochemical companies, has asserted, 'The ability to learn faster than competitors may be the only sustainable competitive advantage' (de Geus, 1997).

Insights into practical pedagogy can be helpful in this regard. When faced with new circumstances, people may be in a relaxed or tense state. They may also either be indifferent towards, or actively interested in, the material in which they are being immersed. Only if people are *both* relaxed and actively interested do they enter the open-minded and engaged state in which effective learning and mindset change can take place.

In other circumstances, other mental modes come to the fore. This can be, for example, unhelpful knee-jerk stress responses if individuals in stressful situations need to deal with issues that they know to be important. Figure 4 illustrates the various combinations. This dynamic is discussed in more detail in Goethem, (2018).

Part of Craft 2, therefore, is designing informal, relaxed opportunities for strategic conversations, for example, through individual one-to-one chats or over dinner or in informal workshops, as much as in the formal meetings or presentations that are the normal mode of senior-level engagements. This requires a good sense of the culture of the relevant organisation(s) to understand how to balance necessary informality with being sufficiently 'business-like' that stakeholders appreciate the seriousness of what is being addressed.

Interweaving Scenario Thinking with Strategic Choices

Depending on the particular circumstances being addressed, this S-curve process may need to be accomplished over a matter of days or weeks, such as when responding to a crisis or assessing an investment of limited significance, or it may

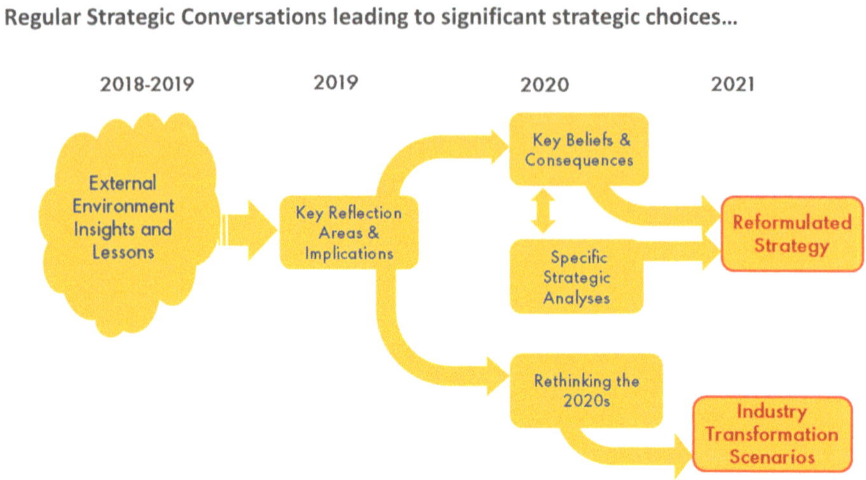

Fig. 5 Example—interwoven strategy and scenario development

extend over more than a year if it involves significantly redirecting the focus of a whole organisation or group of organisations.

An example of the latter is illustrated in Fig. 5, which summarises how scenario work and strategic conversations with the C-Suite (those executives playing a senior strategic role within an organisation) and the Board of a major multinational company were interweaved over several years, leading to a major step-change in the strategy of the company. This culminated in announcements to investors in early 2021, just preceded by the publication of a broader suite of industry scenarios that would help investors better understand the choices being made by the company in the light of the critical uncertainties and settled trends seen ahead.

While the tangible outcomes of the S-curve became visible in 2021, the origins of the process began with Craft 1 work in 2018/19 followed by Craft 2 work in 2019/20 and then final Craft 1 attention in 2020/21.

In this case, a particularly powerful component in the Craft 2 approach involved individual and group discussion with senior stakeholders around key beliefs and their consequences. These conversations focused on the critical uncertainties and the relatively settled trends that scenario-like work was uncovering or illuminating and, crucially, what the company should start, stop, or continue doing as a result of each key belief. Beginning with a 'strawman' overview that underpinned initial individual conversations between senior stakeholders and scenario practitioners, this enabled both alignments and differences of opinion on actions to be brought forward. This helped guide subsequent engagements and analyses towards confirming and generating further alignments, refining the 'consequential beliefs', and ultimately re-directing company strategies.

This interweaving of scenario and strategy attention is a key to using the scenario mindset in enhancing the choices being made by organisations, and in cementing the

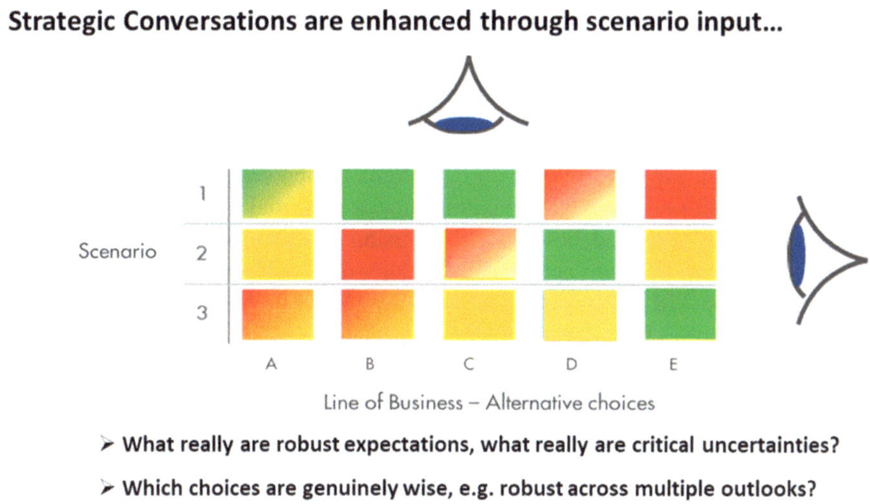

Fig. 6 Strategic conversations are enhanced through scenario input

importance of using that mindset in organisations. Most people already appreciate the central importance of 'strategy' in organisations. When staff also see that scenario thinking impacts, and deepens, strategic thinking, then this helps considerably in driving that scenario mindset more widely. In this way, scenario thinking can become embedded deeply in the DNA of organisations. This scenario-thinking DNA can be seen in companies like Shell and in governments like that of Singapore, both of which have used scenarios to help grapple with radical uncertainties over decades, and continue to do so (Ong & Public Service Division, Singapore, n.d.; Wilkinson & Kupers, 2014).

The interweaving needs to be conducted in an effective way, requiring the 'social' craft referred to earlier, but the principle is actually straightforward, as illustrated in Fig. 6. The interplay of options and scenarios sharpens the understanding of the resilience and attractiveness of different choices.

In examining this matrix of possibilities, some guidance in balancing potential risks and rewards can be helpful. Intuitively, people seek to avoid choices that might have large downsides, and they also try not to miss out on opportunities that might have large upsides. They are considering potential regrets both ways, and this neutral language of 'regrets' is helpful as it avoids triggering the human biases towards risk-avoidance and anchoring to the status quo that can be activated by over-use of the term 'risk'.

The technical term for using the 'regret' perspective in considering the matrix of possibilities is 'Minimising Maximum Regret (MMR)'. For each scenario, the choice with the most attractive outcome is identified, and then the regret involved in making other choices can be compared to this. Once all the scenarios have been considered in this way, each option has an identified list of potential regrets associated with the full suite of scenarios. Once the biggest potential regret is identified for each option, the choice with the lowest 'biggest regret' is the most responsibly risk/reward balanced.

In contrast, if you were extremely risk-averse, then you might only consider the potential downsides in choices and apply the 'minimise all downsides' (MAD) mentality. Or, if you were willing to be extremely opportunity-seeking, then you might seek to choose simply to 'maximise upside potential' (MUP) irrespective of the downside risks. Instead, however, 'minimising maximum regrets' is a more risk-balanced decision-making approach in addressing a future with considerable uncertainties—MMR being better than being MAD or a MUPpet!!!!).

While the approach may seem overly complicated or 'technical' when spelled out in detail this way, as noted above, it is actually the 'intuitive' approach applied by many people in considering choices in the face of uncertainty. For example, while not explicitly using the term 'MMR', the extremely successful businessman Jeff Bezos has adopted this approach. He has described his method for the early building of the company Amazon in terms of seizing large but uncertain upside opportunities as he saw them while never risking the loss of so much money that the entire enterprise would be jeopardised. He avoided both the 'regret' of missed mega-opportunities and also the 'regret' of bankruptcy; in other words, he minimised his regrets. For an introduction to the Bezos approach see, for example, Dahl (2022).

It is the explicit and deliberate use of well-considered scenarios and the thoughtful application of MMR that both broadens and deepens the 'natural' intuitive approach and enables a collective development and deliberation of choices to be undertaken.

Using Scenario Thinking to Assess Potentially Undervalued Opportunities for Forerunners

In the face of radical uncertainties, as indicated above, individual choices are best considered in the light of the most positive and negative plausible scenarios to be faced. With decarbonization and energy transitions, for example, the general shape of future changes has become relatively clear and the primary uncertainty is actually the pace of change.

As noted earlier in this book, there are particular concerns around decarbonization for the maritime industry. This is partly due to the hard-to-abate nature of many activities that may be difficult to significantly decarbonize before cost-effective alternative fuels become widely available, and partly due to the fragmented nature of the industry.

Hence while transitions in the energy system globally are urgently required, these are not taking place at the necessary pace to meet societal aspirations, particularly in the maritime sector. Nevertheless, in the past, several other transition-related developments have already 'taken off' globally, such as power generation from solar and

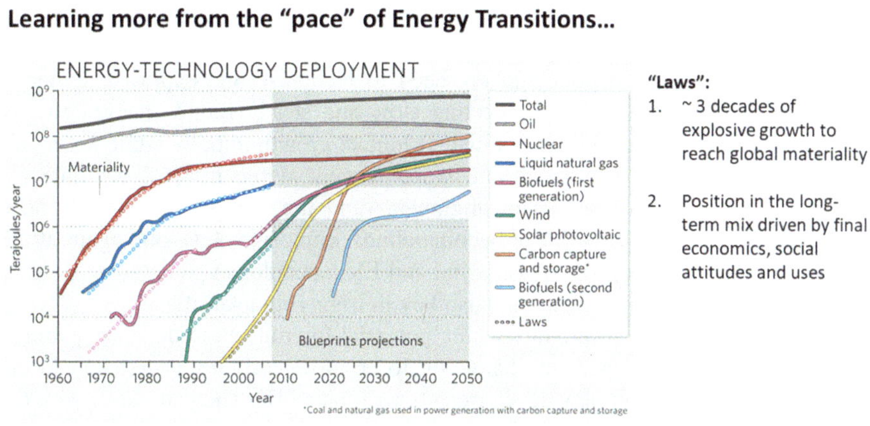

Fig. 7 History and some 2007 projections of energy technology deployment

wind energy, and sales of light-duty electric vehicles. Indeed, it seems a feature of energy-related developments that they take-off very quickly once a turning point has finally been reached, as highlighted in Fig. 7 (Haigh & Kramer, 2009). Because of the sheer scale and diversity of the global economy, decades of significant double-digit annual growth rates are possible before saturation begins to be significant and a longer-term equilibrium mix is approached.

As an additional example, the take-off in the global sales of electric vehicles (EVs) has been even more dramatic, with global growth rates averaging more than 40% p.a. over the past decade (International Energy Agency, 2022). This is particularly interesting because it demonstrates not only high early-stage growth rates but the potential commercial value from being a successful pioneer in such a high-growth market, with the company Tesla having rapidly become the automotive company with far-and-away the highest market-value in the world while others are now playing catch-up in the EV game. With an initial focus on a specific location with a supportive policy environment (California), and a customer segment wealthy enough to pay a premium for an innovative, image-enhancing vehicle (a highly differentiated product), this experience is the poster-child example of the lessons described earlier—the combination of a pioneer, business innovation, smart policy and the emerging alignment of actions from the public-sector, businesses and consumers to drive abrupt growth.

A simple model gives insight into why take-offs are usually very rapid once they come, and hence why companies should anticipate such a dynamic and invest for advantage and/or resilience. It is competitive dynamics that trigger the shift in industry structure behind a take-off, rather than a simplistic interpretation that the new situation will have intrinsically better financial returns than the old situation. Once one business has indicated the potential attractiveness of a new approach, other businesses rush to respond due to 'fear of missing out (FOMO)', particularly if the existing industry equilibrium has already become highly competitive and typical returns have been driven to low levels, as is often the case in mature industries.

More businesses and policymakers need to recognise this explosive dynamic better, and not be misled into expecting slow and steady future changes simply because of the extended time it can take to initiate growth initially while necessary value-chain or policy alignments are being forged. While it may take time for background policy or value-chain alignments and the pioneers to emerge, once they do, then take-off growth can become almost explosive. Just look again at the current global growth rates in solar, wind and EV technologies.

As noted, pioneer businesses are also key in triggering take-offs.

However, the main uncertainty facing potential forerunners in the energy transition arena is the future pace of change or, to be more accurate, uncertainty in the timing of when different new developments will 'take off'. They are faced with the 'too early/too late' investment dilemma. Unfortunately, human and organisational biases steer institutions towards acting late, but scenarios can help decision-makers recognise that acting early ('too soon') may bring only mild economic disappointment at worst but, at best, can lay the foundation for significant company or domestic industrial competitive advantage for years to come. The potential regret of acting late is often considerably greater than the potential regret of acting early.

As explained below, one of the key challenges for many organisations is that they have become 'trapped' by an unhelpful metaphor in the financial assessment of the potential economic value of future opportunities with relatively unfamiliar features. The British statistician George Box has noted that 'All models are wrong, but some are useful', but the corollary of this is that some models are not useful, at least if applied well outside the limited area where their usefulness resides.

The dominant model, or metaphor, for assessing uncertain future financial returns in most companies is that of the corporate bond, particularly because it can easily be represented in the spreadsheets that now dominate analytical approaches. A base-case of cash-flows is assumed, with the 'present value' of future cash-flows discounted by a fixed percentage to account for the risk that the 'bond-payer' may be forced to default. Some sophistication may be added through computing sensitivities or assigning probabilities to different elements of the calculation, but the underlying metaphor for the nature of future uncertainty remains the same—that is, it looks like the risk of holding corporate bonds.

This metaphor may be reasonable in numerous traditional circumstances but, the type of uncertainty highlighted above for energy transition 'take-offs' looks very different. We may be confident that the potentially 'explosive' take-off of particular approaches will occur in the next 5, or 10, or 15, or 20 years, but just do not know when. We may be able to secure long-term competitive advantage if we are a forerunner, but not if we are a later follower, and, indeed our own actions could trigger the take-off. The potential regret of investing to be a forerunner may be poor returns until take-off actually occurs, while the potential regret of waiting may be foregoing significant long-term economic value.

Scenario thinking is essential for grappling with the shape of uncertainty under these circumstances, and the discounted cash-flow model is inadequate, even misleading. In contrast, even a simple model (using MMR) that considers the 'boundary scenarios' of take-off occurring soon or after a delay of several years, combined with a business investing early or later, is already more illuminating. It suggests that it would *already* be economically and commercially sensible for businesses to invest seriously as pioneers in a number of areas that are likely to take-off during the timescale of energy transitions.

A few businesses seem to be attempting this, but not as many, or as aggressively, as the type of commercial competitive perspective developed above should encourage. Of course, not all pioneering activities will succeed over the long-term if competitive strongholds cannot be secured or if it takes forever for take-off to occur. However, the vibrancy of the venture capital markets and the examples of companies like Tesla, Orsted and NextEra Energy indicate what can be achieved.

Concluding Remarks

Who will become the new high-value-generating forerunners in the maritime ecosystem?

Adopting the perspectives outlined here (already anticipating high-growth take-offs, minimising regrets, and recognising the potential long-term competitive advantage of participating in and driving take-off) will not only enhance commercial advantage for fast-moving companies but also drive faster energy transitions overall in a reinforcing cycle. Building competitively advantaged strongholds as a forerunner will bring economic advantage across all the maritime scenarios explored for this book (Lehmacher & Lind, 2022; Lind et al., 2022), albeit with the exact timing of the rewards differing between the outlooks. Potential advantage areas are explored elsewhere in this book, including port ecosystems, flexible shipbuilding, alternative fuel drivetrains, fuel supply, low-carbon premium logistics and taking a lead in forging alignments across relevant activities.

Similar considerations are pertinent for policymakers seeking to develop domestic economic competitive advantage. They should recognise the competitive dynamic in policymaking between different economies. They should then focus on creating significantly favourable conditions to enable, motivate and reward more pioneer businesses in new target energy-transition areas while also encouraging lively competition in areas that have already taken off.

Given the possibility of explosive take-off growth and the economic, job-creation and environmental benefits of this approach occurring within a political cycle, scenario thinking and stimulating take-offs in a targeted and well-designed way can be a sweet spot combining smart policy and smart business with smart politics.

References

Bentham, J., & Shell Scenarios Team. (2021). *Shell energy transformation scenarios*. Retrieved from Shell Scenarios. www.shell.com/scenarios, https://www.shell.com/energy-and-innovation/the-energy-future/scenarios/the-energy-transformation-scenarios.html

Dahl, W. (2022). finance.yahoo.com. Retrieved from jeff-bezos-principle-regret-minimization: https://finance.yahoo.com/news/jeff-bezos-principle-regret-minimization-182553489.html

de Geus, A. (1997). The living company. *Harvard Business Review*.

Goethem, P. v. (2018). *True persuasion*. Business Contact.

Haigh, M., & Kramer, G.-J. (2009). No quick switch to low-carbon energy. *Nature, 462*, 568–569.

International Energy Agency. (2022). *Global sales and sales market-share of electric vehicles 2010-2021*. Retrieved from iea.org/data-and-statistics: https://www.iea.org/data-and-statistics/charts/global-sales-and-sales-market-share-of-electric-cars-2010-2021

Kahneman, D. (2011). *Thinking, fast and slow*. Farrar, Straus and Giroux.

Keynes, J. M. (1936). *The general theory of employment, interest and money (preface)*. Macmillan.

Lehmacher, W., & Lind, M. (2022). *Practical playbook for maritime decarbonisation*. Retrieved from Nordic West Office: https://www.nordicwestoffice.com/maritime

Lind, M., Lehmacher, W., Bentham, J., Tikka, K., Thomas, W., Notteboom, T., Fries, S., & Penttilä, R. (2022). *Three maritime transition scenarios: Decarbonization playbook part 1*. Retrieved from Maritime-Executive.com: https://maritime-executive.com/editorials/three-maritime-transition-scenarios-decarbonization-playbook-part-1

Ong, P., & Public Service Division, Singapore. (n.d.). *Conversations for the future*. Retrieved from https://www.csf.gov.sg/files/media-centre/publications/conversations-for-the-future.pdf

Wilkinson, A., & Kupers, R. (2014). *The essence of scenarios*. Amsterdam University Press.

How a Value Chain Approach Plays Out in Maritime Decarbonization

Katharina Renken and Moritz Petersen

Target Audience

This chapter has been written for those responsible for preparing and realising a decarbonization roadmap or driving a decarbonization project. This will include project or product managers working for a top-level industry leader and government officials involved in decarbonization programs and initiatives.

Key Takeaway Messages

The chapter discusses:

- The leverage of each of the value chains on decarbonizing shipping.
- A step-by-step value chain approach for bringing models of interdependencies to the table.
- Recommendations on what needs to happen within each value chain to empower decarbonization efforts.
- The critical role of ports in identifying interdependencies between the value chains and driving decarbonization efforts.

K. Renken (✉)
Hapag-Lloyd AG, Hamburg, Germany
e-mail: Katharina.Renken@hlag.com

M. Petersen
Kühne Logistics University, Hamburg, Germany
e-mail: Moritz.Petersen@the-klu.org

M. Lind et al. (eds.), *Maritime Decarbonization*,
https://doi.org/10.1007/978-3-031-39936-7_11

Fig. 1 High-level strategy per critical maritime value chain (Lehmacher & Lind, 2022, p. 26)

Introduction

As has been laid out by Petersen and Renken (2023), value chain thinking can be an important enabler of maritime decarbonization. Value chain thinking is a management approach emphasising the importance of understanding the various activities and processes involved in creating value for a company's products or services (Porter, 1985). Thus, a value chain describes the full range of activities needed to bring a product or service from idea to reality (Kaplinsky & Morris, 2001). Contemporary value creation is usually not concentrated in one company but distributed throughout extensive global supply networks. Thus, every value chain consists of various independent actors from different industries. Regarding grand challenges like decarbonizing the economy, multiple value chains and their interrelationships need to be considered. Also in the maritime sector, taking a value chain perspective is critical to understanding and assessing decarbonization enablers and building partnerships beyond industry borders (Lehmacher & Lind, 2022). A holistic approach and broader ecosystem thinking drive emissions-efficient operations (the maritime operational value chain), production of alternative fuels (the marine fuel value chain), and green shipbuilding practices (the shipbuilding value chain) in a coordinated way. The high-level strategies for these three maritime value chains derived from today's state of decarbonization in shipping are (see Fig. 1):

- Ramp-up the alternative (low-carbon and zero-emissions) fuel value chain
- Accelerate the low-carbon shipbuilding value chain and
- Adopt low-carbon and zero-emissions fuels, green ships, and other greenhouse gas (GHG) emissions-reducing measures such as optimised routing and just-in-time arrival in the maritime operational value chain

The three maritime value chains and their approaches to decarbonization are closely interrelated. Thus, when deciding about decarbonization measures, actors within one value chain need to have a good overview of the other two value chains and even clusters of adjacent value chains. Otherwise, reducing carbon emissions within one value chain's boundaries might negatively impact other value chains' prospects of decarbonization. We propose a four-step process for developing such a value chain approach to decarbonizing shipping. First, the structure of the individual value chains and their key stakeholders needs to be understood. Second, the decarbonization leverage of each value chain needs to be determined. Third, ports should be understood as critical nodes to decarbonize shipping. And fourth, the individual value chain strategies must be refined based on the uncovered interdependencies between them. We explain each of the steps in the following and give examples of how to achieve an integrated value chain perspective.

Step 1: Understanding Value Chain Structures and Key Stakeholders

To develop successful decarbonization pathways for the maritime industry, a good understanding of the power structures and key stakeholders of the three value chains and also their adjacent clusters is necessary. Without such a holistic perspective, there is a risk of unilateral optimisation that will not meet the speed of decarbonization that society is increasingly demanding.

When considering the cluster of maritime value chains and the key players, from a ship owners' point of view, beneficial cargo owners (BCOs), the parties that ultimately own the products being shipped, are the most influential part of the ecosystem. BCOs are under increasing pressure from their end customers to decarbonize and will therefore request carriers to implement certain decarbonization measures with the other stakeholders across the maritime cluster of value chains. The BCOs are paying for the transport service the ship owners offer. Thus, the BCOs' requirements can influence how the carriers act in the market and design their product. BCOs come in all sizes, but the larger ones, such as global freight forwarders, are most influential given the large amounts of cargo that they consign daily. The voice of the end-user has more and more weight, finding its way through all layers of the transport service, reaching shipping lines, terminals, and ports.

Effective execution of decarbonization enablers requires a focus on the most influential stakeholders in each value chain. Across the ecosystem beyond the shippers or BCOs, the ship owners/operators/charterers are influential actors. They can drive change because other stakeholders, like fuel providers, shipbuilders, and ports, must react to their decisions and requirements. But each chain also has its own key influencers. In the marine fuel value chain, the energy producers are the powerhouses, and in the shipbuilding value chain, shipbuilders and engine manufacturers are critical for decarbonization. In the maritime operational value chain, charterers, shippers, and shipping companies need to carry the torch. Governments also play an essential role and must be regularly informed by the private sector to ensure that policies and programs support rather than hinder decarbonization efforts.

Step 2: Determining the Leverage of Each Value Chain

As decarbonization efforts are not necessarily self-financing, it is important to focus on those that are the most cost-efficient. As a first step towards assessment, it is necessary to understand the distribution of GHG emissions across the three critical maritime value chains for different types of shipping services. Figure 2 provides a breakdown of the typical lifecycle of carbon dioxide equivalent (CO_2e) emissions for cruise ships, based on data from the Meyer Turku shipyard. As can be seen, most emissions lie within the operational value chain. A fifth of the emissions are emitted during fuel production, and only 5% stem from shipbuilding. While the chart in Fig. 2 relates to cruise ships, numbers of a similar order of magnitude are expected for container ships and ferries.

Figure 3 shows the GHG emissions associated just with the shipbuilding phase. Only 16% arise from the shipyard itself (including employee commuting, business travel and other aspects not directly related to manufacturing). Most of the emissions are associated with the materials, such as steel.

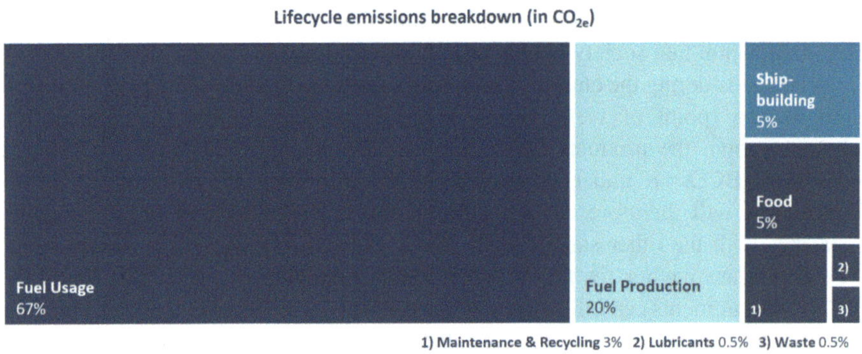

Fig. 2 Breakdown of typical lifecycle CO_2e emissions for cruise ships (based on Lind et al., 2022)

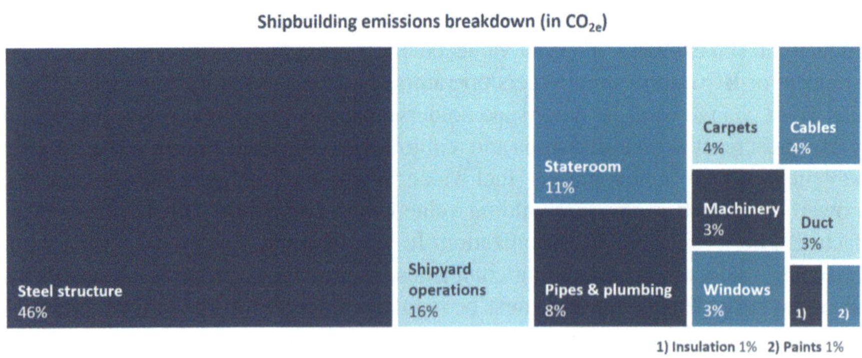

Fig. 3 Breakdown of GHG emissions for building a typical cruise ship (based on Lind et al., 2022)

Such analyses empower companies, irrespective of the value chains that they belong to, to reduce GHG emissions by systematically considering the other parts of the larger ecosystem. Creating visibility and awareness with regard to which sections of the process and to which extent emissions are located supports addressing the source directly. Identifying the most emission-intensive process steps alerts attention and can initiate immediate action.

Some process steps or emission sources are more straightforward to address than others. Focussing on easy-to-implement measures first and thus creating "quick wins" can increase the overall acceptance of emission reduction activities. Despite the variances in impact between maritime value chains, each actor needs to drive decarbonization with maximum effort to ensure that the industry achieves the International Maritime Organization (IMO) 2018 ambitions to cut annual greenhouse gas emissions from international shipping by at least half by 2050—a task deemed possible, at least for the container shipping segment as long as trade volumes do not grow too quickly (Cariou & Lindstad, 2021).

Still, most emissions, costs and economic competitiveness are rooted in the operational value chain and not in processes such as shipbuilding, retrofitting or repurposing. Parties deploying a vessel, whether for cargo or passengers, are the most critical drivers of a green transition in shipping. Even if alternative fuels are available and state-of-the-art shipbuilding processes are in place, the expected increase in costs of each critical maritime value chain during the transition period over the following years or even decades will need to be dealt with by the cargo owners and ultimately be absorbed by consumers, hopefully, eased by effective market-based measures and sustainability policies. However, just like in other areas of freight transportation, some of the solutions to reduce GHG emissions have already been economical for some time (McKinnon & Petersen, 2021).

Step 3: Recognise the Port as a Crucial Node

The port has an important position in interconnected maritime value chains. It helps to keep the chain together, not only physically when the ships visit the terminals but also as an institution mandated by governments. The port is of utmost importance as an information exchange hub for the whole ecosystem. Through the local port authority, the government can release laws and regulations for vessels (Acciaro et al., 2022). Some of the laws and regulations are financial and safety related, but increasingly they relate to sustainability, GHG emissions and the environment. With many ports located in highly populated geographical areas, public pressure is growing to reduce negative environmental impacts on people and nature—while acknowledging the importance of trade and travel. At the same time, governments are offering potential solutions and programs. Some examples are incentivising the availability of alternative fuels in ports and changing regulations for them to be more accessible, installing shore-side power supplies for cargo ships and cruise liners to replace the use of auxiliary engines while alongside, and enforcing slower speeds along coasts and during the port approach phase of a voyage. Recently, a perspective on ports as energy nodes was brought forward (Lind et al., 2023).

Ports can also increase and simplify the data and knowledge exchange between carriers, customers, authorities, and other stakeholders and, thus, lead the way to more synchronised digital value chains (Acciaro et al., 2020). Port arrivals, channel transits, traffic crossings, weather and tide predictions, predicted port stay times and planned sailing times are all inter-related yet currently not fully aligned between all parties. Investments and new digital technologies are as important as innovations and regulations. Additionally, the marine fuel and maritime operational value chains intersect in the port. Therefore, any activities and measures to decarbonize these two value chains must also be aligned with those in the ports. It follows that the decision-makers must have a global understanding of decarbonization activities and local sustainability regulations while aiming at knowledge exchange and close cooperation with port authorities and regulatory institutions. This becomes especially important when deciding on long-term investments for new vessels with a lifespan of 20 years or more (UNCTAD, 2022).

Step 4: Identify Interdependencies and Refine Value Chain Strategies

Based on a better understanding of the relevant value chains, their leverage on decarbonization, and the key stakeholders, interdependencies need to be identified, and each value chain needs to refine its overarching decarbonization strategy. Different services or regulations already existing or on the horizon can drive such an integrative view of the three value chains. Examples of services could be digital services for matching the supply and demand of specific low-carbon fuel types or analytic services for continuous operations improvement (for example, large engine manufacturers now offer services around gathering and analysing performance data of different onboard equipment types). Also, the push towards a more circular economy provides opportunities to untangle interdependencies between the maritime operational and shipbuilding value chain (Jensen et al., 2021).

In some areas of maritime decarbonization, the value chains already overlap in their push to bring new solutions to the market. One prominent example is the large container liner companies that increasingly venture into producing or securing the feedstock for new low-carbon fuels for their next generation of vessels. In another example, two value chains are affected by new regulations around decarbonization, offering opportunities to untangle interdependencies. In June 2021, the IMO adopted the Energy Efficiency Existing Ship Index (EEXI), annual operational carbon intensity indicator (CII) rating and an enhanced Ship Energy Efficiency Management Plan (SEEMP) as short-term measures to reduce GHG emissions and carbon intensity in existing vessels. While EEXI is a measure of the energy efficiency of the technology and design of a ship, CII is a measure of the ship's operational efficiency or how efficiently it is being operated to transport goods and passengers, based on the amount of fuel consumed in a year. This measure will impact all cargo, ferry, and cruise ships above 5000 gross tonnage trading internationally. With these revised measures in force since 2023, existing ships must calculate their EEXI and seek technical means to improve their energy efficiency and establish their annual operational CII and CII rating (from A to E). The rating thresholds will be increasingly stringent towards 2030 in line with initial IMO ambitions. CII will effectively provide a means for charterers to rank ships. These new regulations only increase and renew interest from BCOs and consumers in the emissions produced by the value chains. Achieving the mandatory requirements will create pressure on various clusters of value chains. The associated impacts on other socio-economic aspects will be equally important, further justifying the need for an integrative and holistic approach.

Analysing operational processes holds the potential to identify interdependencies. While ship design plays a significant role in reducing bunker usage and thus minimising emissions on passage, the route itself contains opportunities to bring down emissions, too. While the distances between terminals is fixed, weather and sea conditions including currents and streams can impact the routes taken by ships. Avoiding rough weather may result in a longer travel distance, but an economical sailing speed and the optimal use of winds, tides and currents can still result in lower bunker use and, thus, lower emission discharge.

In recent years, one of the key focus points in container shipping on fixed, long-term schedules, has been just-in-time arrival at terminals (DCSA, 2021). Vessels' arrival at terminals can be interrupted by delays along the sea passage or late departure from the previous terminal. Likewise, terminals can be congested by extended port stay times caused by labour shortages, equipment failures and increased cargo volumes. When free or congested berth capacities are not communicated early, a vessel cannot optimise its passage speed. However, when berth alignment is done reliably in advance and continuously updated, vessel speeds can be adjusted and optimised to meet availabilities (Sung et al., 2022). Further, unproductive times can be reduced by this exchange of information and sea passage execution, making better use of large and expensive plant and equipment, berth space, infrastructure and vessels. However, this requires open and trustful cooperation between terminals and carriers, digital and real-time IT solutions for all involved parties and a process change in most instances. However, the effort should realise rewards: A recent IMO-commissioned study found that on average almost 15% of GHG emissions could be saved (MarineTraffic, 2022).

Closing Remarks

As indicated throughout this chapter and the book, decarbonizing shipping means decarbonizing value chains. Adopting an interdependent value chain-perspective will lead to identifying holistic cluster strategies based on identified gaps, bottlenecks and shortages that result in imbalance and dysfunction across the cluster. Tensions and synergies will become obvious when applying a broader ecosystem view. A focus on clusters of value chains will ensure that the different components are integrated, and developments are aligned. Cross-ecosystem initiatives will create opportunities for economic growth, jobs, cleaner air and mitigate the risks of increased GHGs.

References

Acciaro, M., Renken, K., & El Khadiri, N. (2020). Technological change and logistics development in European ports. In A. Carpenter & R. Lozano (Eds.), *European port cities in transition: Moving towards more sustainable sea transport hubs, strategies for sustainability* (pp. 73–88). Springer. https://doi.org/10.1007/978-3-030-36464-9_5

Acciaro, M., Stemmler, L., Renken, K., & Ahting, J. C. (2022). Regulation and finance in the port sector: Current practices in Germany. In C. Ferrari, H. Haralambides, S. Prete, & A. Tei (Eds.), *Regulation and finance in the port industry: Lessons from worldwide experiences* (Palgrave studies in maritime economics) (pp. 211–235). Springer. https://doi.org/10.1007/978-3-030-83985-7_13

Cariou, P., & Lindstad, E. (2021). Container shipping decarbonization pathways. In B.-W. Ko & D.-W. Song (Eds.), *New maritime business, WMU studies in maritime affairs* (pp. 75–93). Springer. https://doi.org/10.1007/978-3-030-78957-2_5

DCSA. (2021). *JIT port call data definitions 1.1*. Digital Container Shipping Association.

Jensen, H. H., Andersen, M. M., Dao, A., Lind, M., Pandey, V., Bapuji, G., Petersen, M., Hobson, B., Lehmacher, W., & Turos, A. (2021). Digitalisation in a maritime circular economy. In M. Lind, M. Michaelides, R. Ward, & R. T. Watson (Eds.), *Maritime informatics: Additional perspectives and applications, progress in IS* (pp. 17–37). Springer. https://doi.org/10.1007/978-3-030-72785-7_2

Kaplinsky, R., & Morris, M. (2001). *A handbook for value chain research*. Institute of Development Studies, University of Sussex.

Lehmacher, W., & Lind, M. (2022). *Practical playbook for maritime decarbonisation—Value chain-based pathways towards zero-emission shipping*. Nordic West Office.

Lind, M., Haraldson, M., Lehmacher, W., Raza, Z., Forsström, E., Astner, L., Bentham, J., Fu, X., Suroto, J., & Zuesongdham, P. (2023). *Thinking the future energy model nodes of the world—A reflection framework for port development (No. 97)*. UNCTAD Transport and Trade Facilitation Newsletter. UNCTAD.

Lind, M., Lehmacher, W., Doepel, T., Heinimaa, J., Hoffmann, J., Laurilehto, M., Lebmeier, M., Petersen, M., Rytkölä, I., Saari, J., Singh, S., Walls, R., & Watson, R. T. (2022). The benefits of a clusters of value chains perspective in decarbonising shipping: decarbonisation playbook part 2. *The Maritime Executive, 9*.

MarineTraffic. (2022). *Just in time arrival: Emissions reduction potential in global container shipping*. International Maritime Organization.

McKinnon, A., & Petersen, M. (2021). *Measuring industry's temperature: An environmental progress report on European logistics*. Center for Sustainable Logistics and Supply Chains at Kühne Logistics University.

Petersen, M., & Renken, K. (2023). A step-by-step concept for decarbonizing shipping: Value chain focus. In M. Lind, W. Lehmacher, & R. Ward (Eds.), *Maritime decarbonization—Practical Tools, Case Studies and Decarbonization Enablers*. Springer.

Porter, M. E. (1985). *Competitive advantage: Creating and sustaining superior performance*. Free Press.

Sung, I., Zografakis, H., & Nielsen, P. (2022). Multi-lateral ocean voyage optimization for cargo vessels as a decarbonization method. *Transportation Research Part D: Transport and Environment, 110*, 103407. https://doi.org/10.1016/j.trd.2022.103407

UNCTAD. (2022). *Review of maritime transport 2022: Navigating stormy waters*. United Nations.

How to Assess Decarbonization Enablers

Kirsi Tikka and Steve Esau

Target Audience

This chapter should be of interest to board members and company executives who are overseeing company/organisation sustainability strategies and wish to gain general understanding of the assessment of decarbonization enablers. It is also written for sustainability managers and managers of decarbonization projects in all parts of the maritime industry to help them to prioritise and select relevant enablers in the decarbonization process.

Key Takeaway Messages

The chapter emphasises:

- Decarbonization enablers vary in their maturity, availability, and greenhouse gas (GHG) reduction potential, among other criteria, and the selection and prioritisation are important steps in the decarbonization process.
- Different approaches can be used for assessment depending on the objective.

K. Tikka (✉)
Board Member Ardmore Shipping, Pembroke, Bermuda

Board Member Pacific Basin Shipping, Hong Kong, Hong Kong SAR

Board Member Foreship, Helsinki, Finland
e-mail: kktikka@outlook.com

S. Esau
SEA-LNG, Oxford, UK
e-mail: steve.esau@sea-lng.org

M. Lind et al. (eds.), *Maritime Decarbonization*,
https://doi.org/10.1007/978-3-031-39936-7_12

- Combining a scenario approach with scoring criteria is a useful tool in developing and testing decarbonization strategies and plans.
- Low carbon and zero carbon fuels will be critical for maritime decarbonization. Therefore, assessing and tracking the development of fuel pathways should be the focus for stakeholders in the three value chains: *marine fuel*, *maritime operational*, and *shipbuilding value chains*.

Getting to zero carbon shipping is a journey. Decarbonization enablers are selected at various stages of the journey, depending on their maturity, availability, and GHG reduction potential, among many other criteria. An important step in the selection of enablers or a bundle of enablers is their assessment and prioritisation. The approach used depends on the objective of the assessment.

To gain an understanding of the current state of the art of the decarbonization enablers an overall assessment of all enablers is needed. If the objective is to improve the performance of an existing ship or a fleet with currently available decarbonization enablers different criteria is used in the selection process. To decide on technology and fuels for a future ship, design enablers still under development can be included in the assessment. Finally, to find investment opportunities in future low and zero carbon fuels, fuel pathways and transition fuels must be considered.

Available technology and fuels can be assessed quantitively based on available data, but including future enablers, such as e-fuels, requires dynamic criteria in the evaluation. The assessment is largely qualitative which can introduce bias. Therefore, to track decarbonization readiness and the adoption of various enablers it is important to update the assessments periodically.

Assessment of Enablers for Decarbonization Readiness

The *Practical Playbook for Maritime Decarbonization* published in 2022 (Lehmacher & Lind, 2022) lists 37 enablers that range from regulations to new fuels and scores them based on three general criteria:

- Impact on GHG reduction
- Ease of execution
- Acceptance across stakeholders

and on three dynamic factors:

- Readiness of solution
- Availability and
- Financial viability

Three maritime-themed transition scenarios with different decarbonization pathways and outcomes added another dimension to the assessment. The scenarios were termed *Swells*, which places economic recovery first; *Storms*, where local or regional interests are placed first; and *Clear Sky*, where competing interests and stakeholder alignments primarily drive global maritime decarbonization. The enablers were given a score in each scenario for now and for 2030 and based on the scores assessed as *usable decarbonization enablers at scale*, which are ready, available, and affordable, and *enablers that are usable within limits*, which are financially viable but not widely available.

The findings were indicative because of the immaturity of some of the solutions, the uncertainties in the data, and the filters and biases of the data providers/assessors. However, the assessment provided a high-level picture of the world of maritime decarbonization now and in 2030, based on the different pace of development in three scenarios that were developed.

The approach combines scenario methodology with scoring criteria, and it can be used when developing and testing a decarbonization strategy or plan.

Assessment of Enablers Available Today

Enablers available today are mainly energy efficiency technologies or operational measures. If an owner considers an investment to improve the current fleet or a new design, the decision criteria is likely to include:

- Compliance with current and upcoming GHG regulatory requirements and further GHG reduction potential
- Cost/benefit analysis (Payback Period, Internal Rate of Return), where the financial benefit is from fuel savings and
- Improved commercial position, for example, charterers' preference for fuel efficient ships, increased cargo flexibility, better utilisation

The report *Maritime Decarbonization Strategy 2022* (MMMCZCS, 2022) provides an energy efficiency assessment of solutions ready for implementation today. Potential energy efficiency gains from operational measures such as voyage optimisation range from 1 to 10%, and fleet strategies (including utilisation and speed optimisation) from 1 to 15%. Potential gains from technology solutions such as hull and propeller efficiency range from 1 to 8%, engine and systems from 1 to 5%, and wind assisted propulsion from 1 to 8%.

The report provides a comparative assessment of uptake of the measures across bulker, tanker, container, and passenger sectors. Voyage optimisation has the highest uptake across the sectors, and the passenger sector has the highest uptake across all the measures, followed by the container sector.

Overall, the potential energy efficiency gain from operational measures is assessed at 15%.

Adoption of available energy efficiency measures is not only good for emission reduction, but also good business as it lowers fuel consumption and operating expenses. Another driver for the adoption of these measures is regulatory pressure. The new International Maritime Organization (IMO) short term measures, Energy Efficiency Existing Ship Index (EEXI) and Carbon Intensity Indicator (CII), are targeting carbon dioxide (CO_2) emission reductions by driving technical and operational energy efficiency improvements for ships to meet the requirements. The effectiveness of these measures will be reviewed by January 2026 at the latest, using the fuel consumption data collected by the IMO Data Collection System (DCS).

Although the assessment of available technology can be conducted mostly quantitatively, the reduction of fuel consumption and harmful emissions is not easy to measure accurately in the environmental conditions where ships operate. Therefore, the benefit is usually given as a range to account for the uncertainty.

This type of assessment is prepared by technical management for decision making by senior management.

Assessment of Developing Technologies

Technology development for maritime decarbonization includes technology to improve energy efficiency and energy conversion. Regulatory requirements, GHG reduction potential, and commercial considerations are again the drivers for development and adoption.

Energy conversion technology development, on multi-fuel internal combustion engines (ICEs), on batteries, and on fuel cells, is closely associated with expected use of alternative fuels. The technology is reviewed and certified by classification societies to meet the relevant class and statutory regulations, but the assessment of the technology maturity for global shipping is independent of the certification process.

New technology is often tested and assessed in pilot and demonstration projects or trades most suitable for the specific technology. For example, dual fuel engines burning fuel oil and liquefied natural gas (LNG) were first installed on LNG carriers, before the technology matured on other vessel types. The next step is introducing other fuel types and multi-fuel engines. Hydrogen fuel cells and batteries are being piloted on small vessels in inland waterway or coastal service.

Technology is also assessed by its societal and stakeholder acceptance. It is an important criterion for technologies associated with safety hazards, for example, toxicity concerns with ammonia burning ICEs, and radiation concerns with nuclear reactors. Adoption of LNG both as cargo and fuel faced considerable resistance initially because of concerns over leaks and flammability, but good operational experience has eliminated most of these concerns.

Assessment of Fuels and Fuel Pathways

Zero carbon and carbon neutral fuels are needed for maritime decarbonization. However, zero carbon fuels and carbon neutral biofuels are not available today for global shipping.

Alternative fuels being considered today include LNG, methanol, ammonia, hydrogen, and biofuel. LNG is widely available, and the engine technology is mature, but it is a fossil fuel. The feedstock for methanol is mainly LNG and it contains carbon. Engine technology for methanol is available. Ammonia production today uses energy that is not carbon free, although the fuel is carbon free. However, toxicity is a problem for ammonia and to a lesser extent methanol. The engine technology is under development. Hydrogen production today uses energy that is not carbon free. It is difficult to transport and store and for global shipping, fuels which include hydrogen in their molecular structure, such as methanol and ammonia, are considered more likely alternatives either as is or as reformed to hydrogen. Biofuels are not available in required quantities and their feedstock can be controversial as discussed in chapter "Identifying the Key Decarbonization Enablers" on decarbonization enablers.

Fuels available today in larger scale are not zero-carbon from production to consumption onboard ships. The IMO agreed in July 2023 that the levels of ambition in the revised IMO GHG Strategy should take into account the well-to-wake GHG emissions as addressed in the Guidelines on life cycle GHG intensity of marine fuels (LCA Guidelines) (IMO, 2023). This outcome is important for fuel selection and investment in fuel pathways.

The Mærsk Mc-Kinney Møller Center for Zero Carbon Shipping published a report *Creating a Global Fuel Lifecycle Methodology* in January 2023 that includes a qualitative assessment of seven existing fuel lifecycle methodologies (MMMCZCS, 2023). The report recommends WTW methodology supported by a global fuel lifecycle methodology in the IMO regulatory framework. The US National Academies of Sciences, Engineering, and Medicine report *Current Methods for Life Cycle Analyses of Low-Carbon Transportation Fuels in the United States* provides another assessment of methods for estimating life cycle emissions associated with transportation fuels (NASEM, 2022). The report makes several recommendations on further research needs to leverage the available LCA methods.

Publicly available qualitative assessments of alternative fuels provide insight into the current view of alternative fuels and potential pathways.

LNG is currently the alternative fuel of choice due to its availability and lower emissions onboard. However, it is a fossil fuel, and therefore considered a transition fuel. In 2019 SEA-LNG, a multi-sector industry coalition established to demonstrate LNG's benefits as a viable marine fuel, commissioned DNV GL, the assurance and risk management company, to carry out a study to assess the commercial and operational viability of alternative marine fuels and to assesses how they perform compared to LNG (SEA-LNG, 2019). The alternative fuels considered in the study were hydrogen, ammonia, methanol, liquefied petroleum gas (LPG), advanced biodiesel (hydrotreated vegetable oil) and electricity (batteries).

The study assessed the fuels based on:

- Energy density
- Technological maturity
- Local emissions (SOx (sulphur oxides), NOx (nitrogen oxides), PM (particulate matter))
- GHG emissions

- Energy cost
- Capital cost and
- Bunkering availability

Other key parameters considered were:

- Flammability
- Toxicity
- Regulations and guidelines and
- Global production capacity and locations

The study noted the importance of the level of research and development (R&D) efforts, regulatory developments, and economic incentives for the commercial viability of alternative fuels. The study found gaps and large uncertainty in the available data and knowledge.

A report by the International Renewable Energy Agency (IRENA) published in 2021 *A pathway to decarbonize the shipping sector* by 2050 (IRENA, 2021) reviewed the readiness level of shipping fuels. The fuels considered included fuel oil, LNG, advanced liquid biofuels, renewable gaseous fuels, hydrogen, ammonia, and methanol. The categories assessed included:

- Fuel technological readiness
- Engine technological readiness
- Scalability and time to market
- Energy density
- GHG reduction and
- Engine technology

The report concluded that in the short-term advanced biofuels will play a key role in the reduction of CO_2 emissions, and in the medium to long term green hydrogen-based fuels will drive the international shipping decarbonization. By 2050 renewable ammonia could represent up to 43% of the fuel mix, according to the report.

The Maritime Decarbonization Strategy 2022 (MMMCZCS, 2022) considered four alternative pathways: methane, methanol, ammonia, and biofuel/e-diesel. The report assessed the maturity of the pathways to e-fuels, blue fuels (with carbon capture) and biofuels as *mature*, *solutions identified*, or *major challenges*, using the following criteria:

- Feedstock availability
- Fuel production
- Fuel storage, logistics and bunkering
- Onboard energy storage and fuel conversion
- Onboard safety and fuel management
- Vessel emissions and
- Regulation and certification

The alternative pathways were found to be at different stages in maturity with all having barriers across value chains. The interactive maturity map can be found at https://www.zerocarbonshipping.com/fuel-pathways/.

Low carbon and zero carbon fuels will be critical for maritime decarbonization, and the selection of future fuels will impact all three maritime value chains: *marine fuel value chain*, *maritime operational value chain*, and *shipbuilding value chain* (Lehmacher & Lind, 2022). Therefore, assessing and tracking the development of fuel pathways will be the focus for most stakeholders.

Closing Remarks

There is a range of maritime decarbonization enablers available. Those involved in the decarbonization journey must select ones most appropriate for their situation. In doing so, it is recommended that they:

- Use the scenario approach with scoring criteria as a tool for developing and testing decarbonization strategies or plans and
- Support the development and use of well-to-wake methodology for GHG regulations at the IMO

References

IMO. (2023). Lifecycle GHG—Carbon intensity guidelines. https://www.imo.org/en/OurWork/Environment/Pages/Lifecycle-GHG%2D%2D-carbon-intensity-guidelines.aspx

IRENA. (2021). *A pathway to decarbonise the shipping sector by 2050*. International Renewable Energy Agency. https://www.irena.org/publications/2021/Oct/A-Pathway-to-Decarbonise-the-Shipping-Sector-by-2050

Lehmacher, W., & Lind, M. (2022). *Value chain-based pathways towards zero-emission shipping—A practical playbook*. Nordic West Office. www.nordicwestoffice.com/maritime

MMMCZCS. (2022). *Maritime decarbonization strategy 2022*. The Mærsk Mc-Kinney Møller Center for Zero Carbon Shipping (MMMCZCS). https://www.zerocarbonshipping.com/publications/maritime-decarbonization-strategy/

MMMCZCS. (2023). *Creating a global fuel lifecycle methodology*. The Mærsk Mc-Kinney Møller Center for Zero Carbon Shipping (MMMCZCS). https://cms.zerocarbonshipping.com/media/uploads/documents/Creating-a-Global-Fuel-Lifecycle-Methodology.pdf

NASEM (National Academies of Sciences, Engineering, and Medicine). (2022). *Current methods for life cycle analyses of low-carbon transportation fuels in the United States*. The National Academies Press. https://doi.org/10.17226/26402

SEA-LNG. (2019). *Alternative marine fuels study comparison of alternative marine fuels*. SEA \LNG Ltd, DNV GL AS Maritime Environment Advisory, 2019-09-25. https://sea-lng.org/reports/comparison-of-alternative-marine-fuels/

Effective Partnerships to Support Maritime Decarbonization

Mikael Lind, Wolfgang Lehmacher, Sanjay Kuttan, Jillian Carson-Jackson, David Cummins, Margi van Gogh, and Torbjörn Rydbergh

Target Audience

This chapter is for everyone in an organisation that wishes to set up and effectively run a partnership to create economic and societal capital. It is particularly pertinent for those that are working on collaboration initiatives aimed at maritime decarbonization.

M. Lind (✉)
Research Institutes of Sweden (RISE), Gothenburg, Sweden

Chalmers University of Technology, Gothenburg, Sweden
e-mail: mikael@realsearchers.com

W. Lehmacher
Independent Supply Chain Expert, Hong Kong, China
e-mail: w.lehmacher@gmail.com

S. Kuttan
Global Centre for Maritime Decarbonisation, Singapore, Singapore
e-mail: sckuttan@gcformd.org

J. Carson-Jackson
JCJ Consulting, Canberra, ACT, Australia
e-mail: jillian@jcjconsulting.net

D. Cummins
Blue Sky Maritime Coalition, Houston, TX, USA
e-mail: president@bluesky-maritime.org

M. van Gogh
World Economic Forum, Geneva, Switzerland
e-mail: Margi.VanGogh@weforum.org

T. Rydbergh
Marine Benchmark, Gothenburg, Sweden
e-mail: torbjorn.rydbergh@marinebenchmark.com

M. Lind et al. (eds.), *Maritime Decarbonization*,
https://doi.org/10.1007/978-3-031-39936-7_13

Key Takeaway Messages

This chapter can be summarised by the following key points.

- Partnering is a core activity in achieving effective decarbonization
- Setting a clear objective and outlining a business model for decarbonization efforts is an important starting point for ensuring successful collaboration
- The roles, responsibilities, and contributions of each actor in an initiative needs to be clarified so that each entity works together as a piece of the jigsaw puzzle
- Leadership, and leadership style, plays a critical role in managing the dynamics of relations; the more complex a partnership, the more important neutral, impartial leadership becomes—'Leadership through Partnership'
- Partnerships can be vertical, horizontal, and diagonal, and produce benefits for companies, industry, and ecosystems (multiple industries); the most complex are horizontal (also due to competition law) and ecosystem partnerships
- The Maritime Decarbonization Partnerships Matrix, a framework developed in 2022, is well populated
- The long-tail—the large group of smaller players, has potential to achieve set climate goals through, for example, open approaches and digital platforms

Introduction

Effective, large-scale decarbonization of the maritime sector requires alignment and collaboration across the ecosystem. This as evidenced by various partnerships that have already emerged to collectively address maritime decarbonization. The ability to balance multistakeholder interests and build trust through collaborative partnership is the core competence in order to achieve decarbonization of shipping. Therefore, it is important to understand the landscape of collaboration so that an actor is well positioned to set up or join partnerships that are relevant to the state of development of their organisation. By exploring the landscape of the maritime industry and the maritime decarbonization ecosystem we can assess whether the current approach is holistic and sufficiently inclusive to achieve ambitious commitments from industry leaders, and milestones set by the International Maritime Organization (IMO), the European Union (EU), and the Paris Climate Agreement.

The maritime decarbonization ecosystem includes critical value chains. These involve ship owners, ship operators, charterers, marine fuel producers and suppliers, shipbuilders, engine makers, technology providers, port authorities and operators, maritime service providers, and policy makers (Lind, Lehmacher, Åhlén Björk, et al., 2022). Executing initiatives effectively is dependent on keeping the delicate balance between supply and demand, and addressing timeliness, scalability, and readiness. The availability of green steel, for example, will impact shipbuilders' efforts to build greener ships over and above the requirements set by the IMO Energy Efficiency Design Index (EEDI). Engine makers are required to provide assurance for the safe and reliable use of alternative fuels, either in current engines or future engine models, and for new and retrofitted ships. The availability of alternative fuels and the operational and infrastructure readiness, including procedures and training, of the bunkering ecosystem to provide these new fuels is also critical for the decarbonization of shipping. Ensuring optimised operations and verifying the effectiveness of decarbonization solutions requires digital systems with strong communication networks to monitor vessel performance for fuel consumption and greenhouse gas (GHG) accounting. Bringing these components together in a cohesive, aligned manner requires conscious and timely orchestration across the ecosystem.

Coordinating the activities of multiple stakeholders that own and drive decarbonization initiatives is critical. These stakeholders include private and public sector actors, academia, and all levels of governmental organisations (international (IOs), intergovernmental (IGOs), and non-governmental organisations (NGOs)). Roles, responsibilities, and contributions of each actor within an initiative needs to be clarified so that each entity works together as a piece of the jigsaw puzzle. This requires that complex, multistakeholder interests are consciously balanced to enable trust to be built for cohesive action. As an example, where technology and policy gaps exist, the role of research in technology and regulations needs to be aligned with the clearly stated objectives for the overall decarbonization effort. Different stakeholders support decarbonization in different ways. While IOs, IGOs, and NGOs, for example, can initiate and facilitate the interaction between actors, the private sector needs to own and execute deployment of decarbonization solutions. The various stakeholders across the value chain, industry, and ecosystem need to work together to ensure cooperation occurs in a timely manner. Primary (directly involved) and secondary (indirectly involved) actors work together in this orchestra of stakeholders, driven by technical feasibility, financial needs, regulatory compliance, and ownership of intellectual property. The nature of such relationships can range from the simple to the vastly complex. This results in different team, group, chain, industry, and system dynamics and leadership, in order to work well.

Stakeholders Across the Decarbonization Ecosystem

We need a new paradigm with respect to the adoption of business models with innovative technologies to effectively decarbonize the maritime sector. The new paradigm can be dubbed 'Leadership through Partnership'. Collaborative multi-stakeholder efforts are vital to accelerate maritime decarbonization, through sharing risks and ensuring early buy-in to fast-track multilateral financing and adoption. The heterogenous nature of the industry, including the range of vessel types with different designs for specific use cases, creates a complexity for the deployment of low/zero carbon technologies. Therefore, setting clear objectives and outlining business models for decarbonization efforts is an important starting point. The objective will determine the type of ship needed, the amount and type of fuel required, the type and capability of technology to be installed, and the infrastructure and operational requirements, including training.

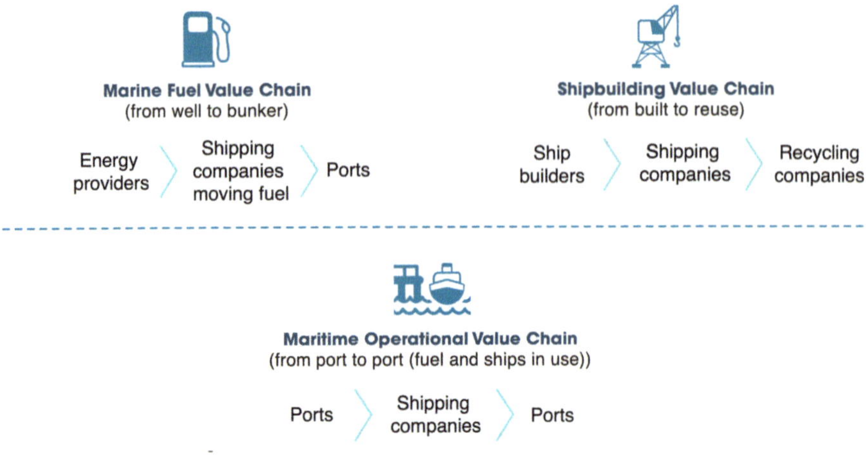

Fig. 1 Key players in the different value chains (Lind, Lehmacher, Kuttan, et al., 2022)

Decarbonization enablers are interdependent and should be scalable. This requires a well-planned and coordinated effort across value chains which needs information exchange and coordinated action, for example based on aligned plans. An effective way to achieve this is through formalised partnerships across the relevant value chains working towards common, collaborative objectives. Decarbonization is achieved through decarbonization enablers. Part of the stakeholders' responsibility is to identify and activate their specific enablers that support specific business models and the adoption of low/zero carbon technology and practices (Lind, Lehmacher, De Tremerie, et al., 2022).

There are key stakeholders with different levels of influence across the cluster of the three critical maritime value chains (Lind, Lehmacher, Doepel, et al., 2022) as well as in adjacent clusters. The three critical maritime value chains and stakeholders are shown in Fig. 1.

As the ecosystem begins to mature the more indirect stakeholders become crucial. These can include banks and financial institutions that provide capital; academia and other areas that drive research and innovation; and workforce development (including education and training). The common vision of the overarching maritime value chain should be that decarbonization is ingrained in the industry, focusing not only on those people directly involved in the industry, but also the communities that live near maritime ports, consumers that ship and use the goods, and the related services that rely on a strong, resilient and sustainable maritime transport system.

When well-orchestrated, such as by a leading or impartial player, or an entity with distributed governance, the different stakeholders or stakeholder groups can work together in a complementary and synergetic fashion. In a diverse collaboration neutral/impartial actors like international organisations are well placed to take on the role of orchestrators. The inclusive and consultative approach adopted by the EU and the IMO is often criticised for being slow due to the need for consensus; but once consensus is reached, implementation can then be achieved quickly. In response to these longer up-front processes, there are individual private and public sector pioneers taking initiative by aligning with selected parties and investing in specific decarbonization enablers to give impetus—aiming to set direction and standards themselves. The balance between these approaches is often through the setting of goal-based, aligned objectives.

Examples of such private sector pioneering is evidenced in the creation of the Digital Container Shipping Association (DCSA)[1] by leading container shipping lines to establish standards, and the investments of pioneers Maersk Line and CMA CGM in methanol-powered ships. Shipping lines are concerned that different standards and inconsistent regulations can cause significant challenges for the industry, shippers, and beneficial cargo owners (BCOs). Regulatory clarity is considered by many experts to be the key for acceleration of decarbonization. Investing in specific enablers can be seen as attempts to establish clarity and a kind of de facto standard.

The Role of Influencers

Accelerating decarbonization requires key influencers to step up to inspire others or initiate collaboration. The most influential actors are those that drive the demand for clean technologies, ships, fuels, and practices. Shipowners, operators, and charterers find themselves under increasing pressure from beneficial cargo owners (BCOs) to reduce their carbon footprint. The BCOs are reacting to national governments that are seeking to meet emission targets by pressuring shipowners, operators, and charterers. When they move, others in the industry usually follow. As an example, ports will begin to store and bunker the alternative fuels their customers, the shipowners, operators, and charterers demand. In this way, the demand signals from BCOs, shipowners, operators, charterers and energy companies influence supply. Of course, the supply side can send signals, too. An example is the engine manufacturer MAN which has developed ammonia powered engines even before fuel stocks could be put in place. This was a strategic decision that sent a supply signal. Key influencers such as the BCOs and MAN, can be instrumental aggregators of demand and preferences for decarbonization from across the ecosystem.

Pioneers and early followers are key influencers. By moving first and fast, companies position themselves as leaders and exemplars. In the context of decarbonization this pushes others to believe that there is a ‘first mover advantage’ to be gained. Those that then follow may be motivated by the idea of an early mover advantage or because they wish to proactively mitigate anticipated compliance requirements or other risks. The momentum created by subsequent followers is critical to reach the tipping point triggering accelerated decarbonization.

The effect of ‘first movers’ and ‘early followers’ has been exemplified by container shipping company CMA CGM. In 2022 it confirmed an order for six

[1] http://www.dcsa.org/

15,000 20-foot (container) equivalent unit (TEU) dual-fuel methanol-powered ships. This was shortly after their peer and competitor Mærsk had announced an order for 12 methanol-powered ships in 2021. Since these ships will use dual fuel engines that can run on both conventional fuel and on low/no carbon fuel, the risk for these purchases is limited. It should be noted that Maersk operates on a 'no waiting' approach with its commercial contracts with major ports. This means it gains priority, which can result in delays for other container vessels, with congestion in ports and associated ancillary emissions. This illustrates the need for a collaborative systems approach, with horizontal collaboration—the coordination of activities to achieve mutual benefits, being required.

While these orders for methanol-powered ships may be an influencer, the current world production of low-carbon methanol is insufficient to power them. The energy sector faces two main production hurdles to overcome—the availability of green hydrogen and the availability of biogenic carbon dioxide. However, it is likely that fuel manufacturers will nevertheless pick up on the demand signal, seeing a business case which motivates them to produce the required quantities of green methanol. Figure 2 illustrates how a range of different stakeholders either exert influence or are influenced with regard to green energy production.

The regulators are important influencers. National, regional, and international regulators can accelerate decarbonization efforts by setting rules or adopting frameworks that guide industry. An example of this is the setting, and the monitoring of progress against ambitious targets and obligations, such as carbon reporting. Furthermore, regulators can support private sector activities with policies and programmes that stimulate investment, capacity building, and innovation in specific areas, for example in the area of green technology. Doing this effectively usually requires structured collaboration and (open) exchange between the public and the private sector. Such collaboration helps to contextualise research projects with specific problem statements from the private sector (the industry) that engages academia and research institutes in a meaningful way.

Positioning Decarbonization Partnerships

Different partnerships have different purposes and fall into distinct categories. This is important for choosing the right form of collaboration an actor wishes to establish or join. A clear understanding of the types of partnerships helps in communication and increases the chances of success. Based on an elaborated framework, The Maritime Decarbonization Partnerships Matrix (Lind & Lehmacher, 2022), acknowledged collaborations can be placed in a matrix with two dimensions or axes. The first dimension considers the type of collaboration or *form of partnership* (vertical, horizontal, and diagonal), and the second dimension is the *focus of partnership*, which looks at the beneficiaries, that is, whether companies benefit, a specified industry benefits, or the ecosystem (multiple industries) benefits. Figure 3 shows the layout of the matrix.

Fig. 2 Power dynamics in the maritime industry, in an energy production and societal context (Lehmacher & Lind, 2022)

We have looked across the maritime industry and identified several different collaborations or partnerships We have then placed them in the matrix, as shown in Fig. 4. The information was drawn from public announcements and websites.

The stakeholder composition of the collaboration (vertical, horizontal, diagonal) was the main criteria for identifying the 'form of partnership' dimension.

Vertical Partnerships of business partners without competitors fall into the 'vertical' category.

Vertical constructs that are built along the value chains, downstream, upstream, or a combination of both, are often initiated and driven by one single (stronger) player in the chain such as a larger shipping company. Taking the example of methanol-powered ships, a shipping line can collaborate with energy providers and ports to

		Form of partnership		
		A Vertical	B Horizontal	C Diagonal
Focus of partnership	1 Primarily participating companies benefit	*A1*	*B1*	*C1*
	2 Industry also benefits	*A2*	*B2*	*C2*
	3 Ecosystem, also other industries and areas benefit	*A3*	*B3*	*C3*

Fig. 3 The Maritime Decarbonization Partnerships Matrix (Lind, Lehmacher, Kuttan, et al., 2022)

implement no/low-carbon fuel distribution hubs which secure the supply of green methanol for ships upstream in the transportation chain. This also allows them to offer downstream forwarders cleaner transport solutions, enabling then them to make the same offer to BCOs which, in turn, helps them to deal with their need to reduce the carbon footprint. Vertical arms-length partnerships sometimes turn into vertical integration where, in the example provided, the shipping company could acquire an energy provider or hub operation.

Horizontal Partnerships where only peers are involved fall in the 'horizontal' category.

Horizontal partnerships are established between peers, for example, among tanker operators that aim to achieve higher fleet/asset productivity, and with that they reduce GHG emissions, costs, and delays. Horizontal alliances are usually harder to find as they require specific circumstances. For example, exigencies or mutual benefits, with a need to comply with different legislative requirements. These partnerships are also governed by anti-competition laws which adds another level of complexity, albeit usually surmountable. Horizontal partnerships tend to focus on the problems/challenges that cannot be solved individually but can be effectively approached through collaboration.

Diagonal Collaborations that consist of both vertical and horizontal elements are considered 'diagonal'. Diagonal partnerships also include overarching initiatives which are in one form or another relevant for the maritime sector. These are launched by other industries, supra-industrial bodies, IOs, IGOs, and NGOs, and governments, or a mixed group.

Focus of partnership	Form of partnership: A: Vertical	B: Horizontal	C: Diagonal
1: Primarily participating companies benefit	A1 CMA CGM biofuel trial Singapore Hapag-Lloyd and DHL Global Forwarding collaboration on advanced biofuels; BHP and NYK decarbonization partnership MSC Shell partnership	B1 Tankers International VLCC Pool	C1 Project Sabre Consortium
2: Industry also benefits	A2 Maersk green methanol partnership CMA CGM / TotalEnergies ship-to-ship LNG bunkering with the goal to establish a Mediterranean maritime LNG hub at Marseille-Fos Port End-to-end shipboard carbon capture	B2 Digital standards (as one area of focus) in container shipping (DCSA) International Association of Ports and Harbours (IAPH) with emphasis on climate and energy as one of many focuses	C2 Getting to Zero Coalition (Global Maritime Forum / World Economic Forum) The Global Centre for Maritime Decarbonisation (GCMD) Mærsk Mc-Kinney Møller Center for Zero Carbon Shipping Blue Sky Maritime Coalition PIONEERS; MAGPIE
3: Ecosystem, also other industries and areas benefit	A3 Maersk / Egypt green energy partnership	B3 None identified as yet	C3 Mission Possible Partnership First Movers Coalition Renewable and Low-Carbon Fuels Value Chain Industrial Alliance Mission Innovation Climate Group's Steel Zero initiative

Fig. 4 Contemporary partnerships populated in the Maritime Decarbonization Partnerships Matrix (Lind, Lehmacher, Bentham, et al., 2022)

Diagonal partnerships cut across different stakeholder groups, horizontally and vertically, and usually require a neutral actor, like an IO, IGO, or NGO to make the collaboration work. Often, multiple neutral/impartial partners are involved. They can initiate multi-stakeholder partnerships by bringing together, for instance, shipping companies, energy providers, financial institutions, and governments. A recent example is the Getting to Zero Coalition[2]—founded in 2019 by the World Economic Forum, Friends of Ocean Action and Global Maritime Forum—engaging stakeholders across the maritime value chain to accelerate zero emission shipping. Partners are actively working facilitate commercialisation and increase the use of zero emission vessels operating along both deep-sea and short-sea trade routes. Diagonal partnerships can bring a variety of relevant actors to the table to work together to identify efficient technologies or find new business models that fit with and accelerate alternative fuel uptakes, like the Mærsk McKinney Møller Center for Zero Carbon Shipping (MMMFCZCS).[3]

All three forms of partnership (vertical, horizontal, diagonal) can, and should, usually include governments, IOs, IGOs, and/or NGOs as this may benefit the group dynamics and outcomes of the partnership.

Identifying the main beneficiaries (companies, industry, ecosystem) determines the 'focus of partnership'.

Companies Benefit A collaboration that primarily impacts the companies involved falls into 'company benefits'.

Entire Industry Benefits A partnership that helps the entire industry, for example through building a maritime bunkering hub falls into 'industry benefits'.

Ecosystem Benefits An alliance that impacts multiple industries, like establishing a hub for renewable energy which can be used by many industries falls into 'ecosystem benefits', which includes other industries and areas.

Figure 4 shows some maritime industry collaborations or partnerships placed in the Maritime Decarbonization Partnerships Matrix.

We identified several examples of vertical collaborations focusing on decarbonizing individual value chains producing primarily benefits for the companies involved (**A1**), such as the CMA CGM biofuel trial in Singapore,[4] the Hapag-Lloyd and DHL Global Forwarding collaboration on advanced biofuels,[5] the BHP and NYK decarbonization partnership,[6] and the MSC Shell partnership.[7] There are also vertical collaborations also creating value for the maritime industry (**A2**), such as the partnership between AP Møller-Mærsk and renewable energy firm Ørsted on a

[2] https://www.globalmaritimeforum.org

[3] https://www.zerocarbonshipping.com

[4] https://www.offshore-energy.biz/cma-cgm-launches-biofuel-trial-for-up-to-32-ships/

[5] https://trans.info/dhl-hapaglloyd-biofuels-295768

[6] https://www.nyk.com/english/news/2022/20220609_01.html

[7] https://www.dcvelocity.com/articles/51626-msc-shell-partner-to-decarbonize-global-shipping-industry

new Power-to-X facility in the United States of America (USA) to produce zero emission maritime fuels,[8] the CMA CGM/TotalEnergies ship-to-ship LNG bunkering with the goal to establish a Mediterranean maritime LNG hub at Marseille-Fos Port, and the end-to-end shipboard carbon capture initiative by the Global Centre for Maritime Decarbonisation (GCMD),[9] the Oil and Gas Climate Initiative (OGCI) and Stena Bulk.[10]

An example of a vertical partnership with impact on ecosystem level (**A3**) is the Mærsk/Egypt green energy partnership [11] that supports the Egyptian government to position Egypt as a global hub for renewable energy.[12]

An example of a horizontal partnership focussed on a single maritime value chain (**B1**) is the Tankers International VLCC Pool bringing together peers in a joint pool of resources of tankers. Examples of horizontal partnerships benefitting the maritime industry (**B2**) are the Digital Container Shipping Association (DCSA)[13] created by major container shipping lines to develop standards to increase the fluidity and efficiency of the sector and thus reduce GHG emissions, costs, and delays, and the International Association of Ports and Harbors (IAPH)[14] with their initiatives on decarbonizing their industry. We have not yet identified an industry-driven or overarching horizontal partnerships that also focusses on the ecosystem (**B3**).

Diagonal partnership on different levels have emerged with the Project Sabre Consortium[15] focussing primarily on company benefits (**C1**) through the ammonia bunker supply chain. There are several diverse diagonal initiatives focused on the decarbonization of the maritime industry (**C2**), such as the Global Centre for Maritime Decarbonisation (GCMD) in Singapore,[16] the Blue Sky Maritime Coalition,[17] the Mærsk Mc-Kinney Møller Center for Zero Carbon Shipping (MMMCFZCS),[18] the PIONEERS consortium addressing the challenges faced by European ports to reduce their environmental impact while remaining competitive and offering added value in a sustainable global trade ecosystem,[19] the MAGPIE

[8] https://www.powerengineeringint.com/emissions-environment/orsted-and-maersk-sign-landmark-green-fuels-agreement/

[9] https://www.cma-cgm.com/news/4083/cma-cgm-and-totalenergies-launch-port-of-marseille-fos-first-ship-to-containership-lng-bunkering-operation

[10] https://www.ogci.com/gcmd-ogci-and-stena-bulk-initiate-project-to-demonstrate-end-to-end-shipboard-carbon-capture-at-scale/amp/

[11] https://tankersinternational.com/

[12] https://www.maersk.com/news/articles/2022/03/28/maersk-explores-new-ways-to-accelerate-green-fuel-production

[13] http://www.dcsa.org/

[14] http://www.iaphworldports.org/

[15] https://www.ship-technology.com/news/project-sabre-ammonia-bunker-vessel/

[16] http://www.gcformd.org/

[17] https://www.bluesky-maritime.org/

[18] https://www.zerocarbonshipping.com/

[19] https://pioneers-ports.eu/about-us-2/

project for smart green ports,[20] and the Global Maritime Forum,[21] Getting to Zero Coalition founded in collaboration with the World Economic Forum and Friends of Ocean Action bringing together 'more than 150 companies across the maritime, energy, infrastructure and finance sectors, supported by key governments and intergovernmental organisations'[22] developing a roadmap highlighting steps from developing and testing solutions, to the enabling environment necessary to enable roll-out and scaling.

Last, but not least, there are also diagonal partnerships that focus on the ecosystems (**C3**), such as the Mission Possible Partnership,[23] the First Movers Coalition,[24] the Renewable and Low-Carbon Fuels Value Chain Industrial Alliance,[25] Mission Innovation,[26] and the Climate Group's SteelZero initiative.[27]

Diagonal partnerships that directly benefit the maritime industry and the broader decarbonization ecosystem are paramount to avoid misalignment of decarbonization actions. Stakeholders, in particular larger actors, can engage in multiple partnerships which may differ in form and/or focus to achieve a variety of objectives.

Engaging Actors Along the Entire Distribution Curve

None of the identified decarbonization partnerships includes the *long-tail* of smaller enterprises. In 2021, about 54,000 cargo and passenger vessels, which excludes the smaller vessels in the world fleet, that travelled the oceans were owned by approximately 15,200 companies. 22 larger players (less than 0.15%) owned 3355 ships (about 6.2%) representing 20% of the CO_2 emissions, and 964 players (about 6.34%) owned 24,907 ships (about 46.1%) representing 80% of the CO_2 emissions. The situation with ports is similar. Out of the 5578 ports that serve the merchant fleet, only 26 (less than 0.5%) is responsible for 20% of CO_2 emissions from moored or berthed cargo and passenger ships, as shown in Fig. 5. The 747 million tonnes of CO_2 emitted by the merchant fleet includes 47 million tonnes (about 6.3%) from vessels in port or waiting in a port area.

Achieving the maritime industry's ambitious decarbonization objectives requires that we look at both the larger and the smaller players. The economies of scale generated by the partnerships of larger companies may also have a positive impact

[20] https://www.magpie-ports.eu/magpie-project/

[21] https://www.globalmaritimeforum.org/

[22] https://www.globalmaritimeforum.org/getting-to-zero-coalition

[23] https://missionpossiblepartnership.org/

[24] https://www.weforum.org/first-movers-coalition

[25] https://transport.ec.europa.eu/transport-themes/clean-transport-urban-transport/alternative-fuels-sustainable-mobility-europe/renewable-and-low-carbon-fuels-value-chain-industrial-alliance_en

[26] http://mission-innovation.net/

[27] https://www.theclimategroup.org/steelzero

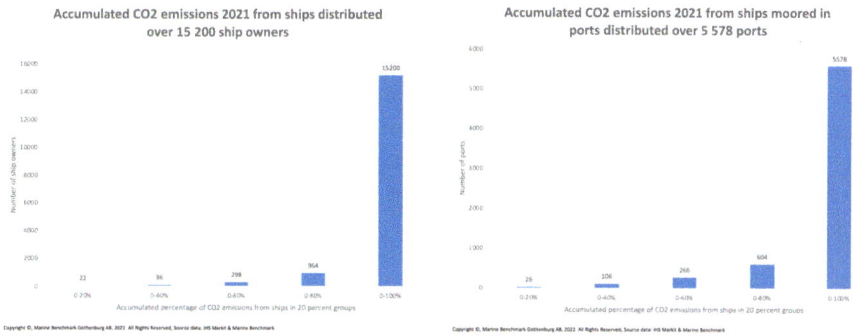

Fig. 5 Accumulated CO_2 emissions in 2021 from cargo and passenger vessels, grouped by number of ship owners and ports (source: Marine Benchmark) (Lind, Lehmacher, Kuttan, et al., 2022)

on the smaller actors. Nevertheless, the larger player-led decarbonization partnerships should find ways to also include the smaller companies. The MMMCFZCS seeks decarbonization solutions and best practices to make them available to all. The MMMCFZCS is also working on a Nordic-Baltic green corridor and on a book & claim system, attractive for smaller players that cannot have or afford to administer their own mass-balancing system, offering green services to customers. The GCMD ideates, curates and finances pilot/demonstration projects that help address complex system level challenges that engages the entire value chain, and that will benefit everyone in the maritime industry.

Curating like-minded players large and small that have clear roles in these projects is important to ensure an effective collaborative effort. Long-tail actors could be further engaged through a digital interface that helps bring smaller companies onto digital partnership platforms at a lower participation cost, thus enabling them to easily provide input and let them, in turn, benefit from the output of other participants. On such platforms, new approaches like open and collaborative innovation can help to complement the current work (Lind et al., 2021). Smaller and larger actors benefit from initiatives like the World Economic Forum's Data for Common Purpose Initiative[28] that engages the private and public sector to build data sharing frameworks. Ultimately, we need to think beyond our current requirements and the current actors to those that are likely to become key actors as the transition to decarbonization matures and becomes the new normal.

[28] https://initiatives.weforum.org/data-for-common-purpose-initiative/home

The Need for a Holistic and Inclusive Approach

We are pleased to acknowledge that the maritime industry has been progressing. Pioneers and influencers have emerged, triggering followership and giving birth to a decarbonization movement in the maritime sector. The immediate goal is to reach the critical mass of stakeholders that support the initiatives that accelerate GHG emissions reductions.

Context Matters

The Playbook (Lehmacher & Lind, 2022), has outlined three maritime transition scenarios using nautical terms as metaphors: *Swells*, where wealth is prioritised first; *Storms*, where autonomy is prioritised first; and *Clear Sky* where well-being is prioritised first (Lind, Lehmacher, Kuttan, et al., 2022). All scenarios are plausible and part of our current reality. Swells reflects the capitalist world that brought us our current wealth but also unwanted consequences; Storms stands for the decoupling between the East and the West; and Clear Sky manifests itself in the many examples of decarbonization initiatives being taken. In all these worlds, each form of partnership has a role to play to drive decarbonization progress.

Vertical partnerships work best in *Swells*, as they follow the spirit of competitive advantage, but will hardly exert the required large-scale impact on industry and the ecosystem. Horizontal partnerships help the industry to prepare for a world of *Storms*; the global shipping industry is well positioned to overcome barriers and avoid multiple standards and inconsistent regulations across the globe provided all players in the industry are aligned. Diagonal partnerships are most compatible with the *Clear Sky* scenario, as the diverse groupings allow for broader industry and ecosystem decarbonization. History has repetitively shown that human attitude and behaviour leans towards a *Swells* world and scenario resulting in late, massive, and expensive responses often preventing the worst 'last minute'. By learning from the lessons of the past we hope that we can avoid the cost and risk of such a pattern this time.

Reaching, or even exceeding the IMO 2023, EU, and Paris Climate Agreement ambitions requires a holistic and inclusive approach. Whilst the holistic angle is reflected in current efforts, inclusivity is lagging. This chapter aims to offer a realistic view that will help the maritime industry refine its collaboration approach by embracing partnerships which also include the smaller players that populate the long-tail of the distribution chain of maritime companies. Establishing your place on The Maritime Decarbonization Partnerships Matrix is an important step in successful maritime decarbonization collaboration supported by clear objectives and roles.

References

Lehmacher, W., & Lind, M. (2022). *Value chain-based pathways towards zero-emission shipping—A practical playbook*. Nordic West Office. www.nordicwestoffice.com/maritime

Lind, M., & Lehmacher, W. (2022). Positioning partnerships in shipping decarbonization, Article No. 92 [UNCTAD Transport and Trade Facilitation Newsletter N°95—Third quarter 2022]. https://unctad.org/news/positioning-partnerships-shipping-decarbonization

Lind, M., Lehmacher, W., Åhlén Björk, S., Haraldson, S., Pålsson, C., Penttilä, R., Tikka, K., & Watson, R. T. (2022). Decarbonizing the maritime sector: Mobilizing coordinated action in the industry using an ecosystems approach, Article No. 89 [UNCTAD Transport and Trade Facilitation Newsletter N°94—Second quarter 2022]. https://unctad.org/news/decarbonizing-maritime-sector-mobilizing-coordinated-action-industry-using-ecosystems-approach

Lind, M., Lehmacher, W., Bentham, J., Tikka, K., Thomas, W., Notteboom, T., Fries, S., & Penttilä, R. (2022) Three maritime transition scenarios: Decarbonization playbook part 1, 4/7-2022. *The Maritime Executive*. https://www.maritime-executive.com/editorials/three-maritime-transition-scenarios-decarbonization-playbook-part-1

Lind, M., Lehmacher, W., De Tremerie, L., Dubielzig, F., Forsström, E., Holthus, P., Morgante, A., Singh, S., & Tenenbaum, L. (2022). Enablers for decarbonising the maritime industry: Decarbonisation playbook part 3, 25/9-2022. *The Maritime Executive*. https://www.maritime-executive.com/editorials/enablers-for-decarbonizing-the-maritime-industry-part-3

Lind, M., Lehmacher, W., Doepel, T., Heinimaa, J., Hoffmann, J., Laurilehto, M., Lebmeier, M., Petersen, M., Rytkölä, I., Saari, J., Singh, S., Walls, R., & Watson, R. T. (2022). The benefits of a clusters of value chains perspective in decarbonising shipping: Decarbonisation playbook part 2, 22/8-2022. *The Maritime Executive*. https://maritime-executive.com/editorials/the-three-maritime-value-chains-decarbonization-playbook-part-2

Lind, M., Lehmacher, W., Knäpper, I., van Gogh, M., Maaouni, T., Benhayoun, J., Ashikhmin, D., Lahmar, H., & Sigal, M. (2021). Collaborative innovation within the maritime sector: the path to grow back better, Article No. 73 [UNCTAD Transport and Trade Facilitation Newsletter N° 89—First Quarter 2021]. https://unctad.org/news/collaborative-innovation-within-maritime-sector-path-grow-back-better

Lind, M., Lehmacher, W., Kuttan, S., Carson-Jackson, J., Cummins, D., van Gogh, M., & Rydbergh, T. (2022). Partnering towards zero emissions shipping: Playbook part 4, 4/11-2022. *The Maritime Executive*. https://www.maritime-executive.com/editorials/partnering-towards-zero-emissions-shipping-playbook-part-4

Part IV
Some Critical Success Factors for Fast and Global Decarbonization

Ensuring Seafarers Are at the Heart of Decarbonization Action

The Maritime Just Transition Task Force Secretariat, Guy Platten, Martha Selwyn, Helio Vicente, and Stephen Cotton

Target Audience

This chapter has been written to highlight the vital importance of ensuring that seafarers are appropriately trained for the changing technologies that are involved in the decarbonization of the maritime industry. This is relevant to all those that are involved in the planning, management or execution of the employment, deployment, education, training, or welfare of seafarers.

Key Takeaway Messages

Key issues discussed in this chapter are:

- The global community is increasingly recognising the imperative of achieving a Just Transition to a green economy.

The Maritime Just Transition Task Force Secretariat

G. Platten · H. Vicente
International Chamber of Shipping (ICS), London, UK
e-mail: Guy.Platten@ics-shipping.org; helio.vicente@ics-shipping.org

M. Selwyn (✉)
United Nations Global Compact, New York, NY, USA
e-mail: selwyn@unglobalcompact.org

S. Cotton
International Transport Workers' Federation (ITF), London, UK
e-mail: cotton_stephen@itf.org.uk

M. Lind et al. (eds.), *Maritime Decarbonization*,
https://doi.org/10.1007/978-3-031-39936-7_14

- Shipping has an opportunity to shift to a decarbonized future in a way that promotes decent work and leaves no one behind. Governments, employers, and seafarers' unions all have a role to play in shipping's Just Transition.
- The Maritime Just Transition Task Force, formed at COP26 to ensure that shipping's response to the climate emergency puts seafarers and communities at the heart of the solution.
- Seafarer training and skills needed to support shipping's decarbonization.
- The 10-point action plan on 'Mapping a Maritime Just Transition for Seafarers'.

Introduction

The world is facing a climate emergency (IPCC, 2022) urgent action is needed to limit global warming to 1.5 °C or we will face disastrous consequences. This is impacting global structures including food security, property, and the transport sector. To limit the devastating impacts of climate change, we need unprecedented collaboration to facilitate rapid moves away from the use of carbon intensive fuels to renewable energy sources. Governments, employers, workers, and all stakeholder groups must work together to create positive change, investing in new fuels, technologies, and infrastructure to enable a green transformation.

According to the International Labour Organization (ILO), a *Just Transition* is a people-centric response to addressing the climate emergency. This means greening the economy in a way that is as fair and inclusive as possible to everyone concerned, promoting decent work opportunities, and leaving no one behind. This entails addressing the climate crisis on multiple socio-economic fronts, to ensure as inclusive a transition as possible, a lens through which actions and strategies can be reviewed to identify opportunities and manage risks. If properly implemented, a Just Transition has the potential to be a driver of sustainable growth and a net creator of quality green jobs, contributing to poverty eradication and social inclusion.

The guiding principles of a Just Transition are established in the ILO's 'Guidelines for a Just Transition towards environmentally sustainable economies and societies for all' (ILO, 2015). These guidelines are the main globally endorsed framework on Just Transition. They reflect the views and perspectives of governments, employers, and workers' organisations and outline principles and potential policy entry-points to promote and manage a Just Transition; and are relevant for all countries and sectors, including shipping. In addition, the Paris Climate Agreement adopted in 2015, in the context of the United Nations Framework Convention on Climate Change (UNFCCC), describes the need to pursue climate and sustainable development goals together and acknowledges *'the imperatives of a just transition of the workforce and the creation of decent work and quality jobs in accordance with nationally defined development priorities'*.

More recently, in the outcomes of the 27th Conference of the Parties to the United Nations Framework Convention on Climate Change (COP27) at Sharm el-Sheikh, Egypt, and in particular, the Implementation Plan, governments 'emphasised that enhanced effective climate action should be implemented in a manner that is just and inclusive while minimizing negative social or economic impacts that may arise from climate action' (UNFCCC, 2022). They also affirmed 'that sustainable and just solutions to the climate crisis must be founded on meaningful and effective social dialogue and participation of all stakeholders' (UNFCCC, 2022).

Alongside governments, employers and workers (including in shipping) also have a role to play. This could entail, for example, ensuring that there is Just Transition planning, as part of wider decarbonization plans. Businesses can also support a just transition through their own policies and strategies (UN Global Compact, 2022). Some companies, including from the energy sector, have also developed Just Transition plans; for example, Scottish energy company SSE plc (SSE, 2020). Stakeholders expected to be impacted by shipping's transition include maritime employers, national governments, communities, suppliers, consumers—and the world's nearly two million seafarers.

What Does a Maritime Just Transition for Seafarers Mean?

Responsible for transporting over 80% of global trade (UNCTAD, 2022) and supplying the world with food, fuel, medicines and goods, the global shipping industry accounts for 3% of global greenhouse gas (GHG) emissions. After a long history of wind, coal, and oil-fuelled ships, a fourth propulsion revolution is now underway to shift away from fossil fuels and transition towards alternative low- and zero-carbon fuels and technologies. This will support the global community in reaching the Paris Agreement goal of limiting global warming to 1.5 °C by the end of the twenty-first century. The global seafaring workforce will be key to powering shipping through a successful transition. Low- and zero-carbon fuels, technologies and ships are expected to introduce new skillsets and training needs for seafarers, requiring a health-and-safety-first approach. A maritime just transition for seafarers, will therefore ensure that those seafarers have the adequate skills, education, training and familiarisation, to operate new technology systems on board and to manage new fuels.

The global shipping sector already has several instruments and initiatives to support a just transition for seafarers. These include the Maritime Labour Convention, 2006 (ILO, 2006) which contains comprehensive provisions for the worldwide protection of the rights of seafarers; establishes a level playing field for countries and shipowners committed to providing decent working and living conditions for seafarers, protecting them from unfair competition from substandard ships.

In addition, the International Maritime Organization (IMO) International Convention on Standards of Training, Certification and Watchkeeping for Seafarers (STCW) provides global minimum standards for training and certification of seafarers, with the objective of promoting safety of life and property at sea and the protection of the marine environment. This global seafarer training framework is now undergoing a comprehensive review.

Recognising that seafarers are key to shipping's decarbonization and considering the unique risks in using some of the fuels being considered for propulsion of ships (such as ammonia and hydrogen), the review of the STCW Convention is a timely development, to assess and discuss the training and skills seafarers will need to support a decarbonized shipping industry. As such, it is crucial that the IMO Maritime Safety Committee (MSC) (overseeing the STCW review) works in synergy with the IMO Marine Environment Protection Committee (MEPC), in the context of the latter's work on the revised greenhouse gas reduction strategy which was adopted in July, 2023.

A recent report by classification society DNV indicated that as many as 800,000 seafarers might require additional training by the mid-2030s to support shipping's transition (DNV, 2022). The revised IMO greenhouse gas strategy will have an impact on the timing and type of training and the scale and speed of investment needed to safely train seafarers.

Seafarer labour-supplying countries in particular, may need support during shipping's transition, as they confront the challenges of keeping pace with the demands of new training standards associated with decarbonization. This might require targeted technical cooperation and capacity building support—with special focus on developing countries, Least Developed Countries (LDCs) and Small Island Developing States (SIDS). International organisations such as the IMO and the ILO are best positioned to provide this.

Maritime Just Transition Task Force

The Maritime Just Transition Task Force is an unprecedented global sectoral initiative dedicated to a Just Transition. It was set up during the 26th Conference of the Parties to the United Nations Framework Convention on Climate Change (COP 26) in Glasgow in 2021. It comprises the International Chamber of Shipping (ICS)—representing shipowners, the International Transport Workers' Federation (ITF)—representing seafarers' unions, and the United Nations Global Compact, the world's largest corporate sustainability initiative; alongside the ILO and the IMO.

The Task Force aims to ensure that shipping's response to climate change puts seafarers and communities at the heart of the solution, by strengthening and coordinating collaboration between governments, industry, workers, and academia for a safe, equitable and human-centred approach to the transition towards a decarbonized shipping industry.

The Task Force is supported by a Global Industry Peer Learning Group, comprising representatives from international organisations, private companies, workers, and academia (including training providers), with Lloyd's Register Foundation currently serving as the primary funder of the project. This international collaborative group serves as a platform for these global partners to engage in strategic and social dialogue around maritime just transition, complementary to shipping's decarbonization agenda and part of the wider international community's transition to a green economy. Representatives from the UN Global Compact, ICS and the ITF—which make up the Task Force Secretariat—facilitate the meetings of the Group.

How Will Maritime Decarbonization Impact the Workforce?

With future alternative fuel technologies, such as renewable e-fuels—including hydrogen, ammonia, and methanol—and biofuels, expected to introduce new training requirements for seafarers, the Task Force Secretariat commissioned a major report from classification society DNV, to:

- Provide insights into seafarer training and the skills needed to support shipping's decarbonization
- Provide an overview of the challenges that training seafarers throughout the transition will entail and
- Explore how best to support seafarers during shipping's transition

The report (DNV, 2022), entitled *Insights into seafarer training and skills needed to support a decarbonized shipping industry*, examined three emission reduction scenarios to estimate the number of seafarers requiring additional training to handle alternative fuels up to 2050. The three scenarios have varying decarbonization trajectories. An estimate was made for each scenario of the number of seafarers that would require additional training to handle alternative fuels up to 2050, together with the timing and type of training required and the future fuel mix. Table 1 shows the key elements and outcomes of the DNV report.

The estimated number of seafarers required in ships using alternative fuel technologies between now and 2050 are tabulated in Table 1 and shown graphically in Fig. 1.

Under all three study scenarios, there is an immediate need to create the appropriate training infrastructure. No matter which fuel or fuels are ultimately favoured, transitioning to a decarbonized shipping industry will require additional training for at least hundreds of thousands of seafarers over the time-period to 2050.

Skills and Competencies for Future Seafarers

Figure 2 summarises the range of seafarer skills and competencies required for the decarbonization of the shipping industry, as identified in the DNV report.

Table 1 Key elements and outcomes

Scenario	Source	Key features	Training implications
Scenario 1 50% reduction in GHG emissions compared to 2008	As set out in the Initial IMO GHG Strategy (2018) modelled in the DNV Maritime Forecast (2021), assessed in DNV (2022)	• Reduce GHG tank-to-wake emissions by at least 50% by 2050 compared to 2008 • GHG reduction trajectory from 2008 levels: 2030: 17%, 2040: 30%, 2050: 67%	310,000 seafarers would require some additional training for alternative fuels and new engines by 2050
Scenario 2 Decarbonization by 2050	Modelled in the DNV Maritime Forecast (2021), assessed in DNV (2022)	• 95% reduction in tank-to-wake GHG from 2008 levels by 2050 • GHG reduction trajectory from 2008 levels: 2030: 17%, 2040: 47%, 2050: 95%	750,000 seafarers would require some additional training by 2050
Scenario 3 Zero carbon by 2050	Modelled by Lloyd's Register and University Maritime Advisory Services (2019) assessed in DNV (2022)	• 100% reduction in well-to-wake GHG from 2008 levels, using Intergovernmental Panel on Climate Change (IPCC) 1.5 (2018) estimates of wider energy system transition • GHG reduction trajectory from 2008 levels: 2030: 33%, 2040: 61%, 2050: 100%	450,000 seafarers would require some kind of additional training by 2030, and 800,000 seafarers by the mid-2030s

Source: DNV (2022)

New Safety Challenges and Skills Needed Against a Backdrop of Existing Training Constraints

The DNV report noted that the introduction of alternative fuel technologies is expected to have a significant impact on maritime operations on board ships and will require seafarers to develop and acquire new skills and competencies to ensure safe and efficient operations in the decades up to 2050 and beyond. The report shed light on some of the safety challenges related to alternative fuels in shipping. These include pressurised storage, low flashpoint fuels, and toxicity. Hydrogen, for example, is substantially more flammable than diesel, while ammonia is toxic to humans and the marine environment.

Except for hydrogen, which was until recently only transported on board ships in packaged form, most of the alternative fuels being considered for shipping are currently carried as bulk marine cargo. The shipping industry is therefore both

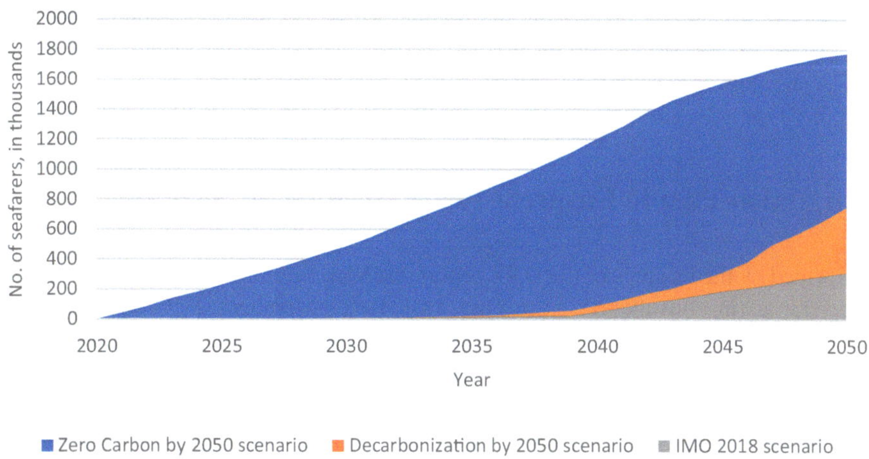

Fig. 1 Estimated number of seafarers in ships using alternative fuel technologies 2020–2050. Source: DNV (2022)

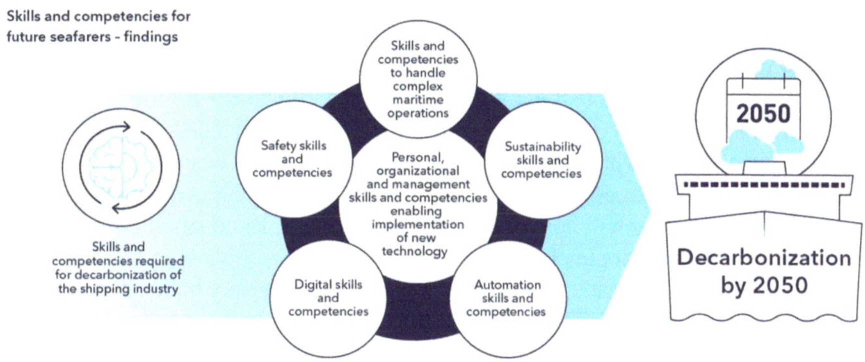

Fig. 2 Seafarer skills and competencies required for the decarbonization of the shipping industry. Source: DNV

knowledgeable and experienced regarding their handling. However, for the sake of their own safety, the environment and local communities, seafarers will need additional training with respect to specific risks associated with using these fuels for propulsion.

This is all happening against the backdrop of existing constraints regarding seafarer training to support shipping's decarbonization. These include:

- The slow pace of regulatory development and lack of clarity surrounding the viability and uptake of alternative fuel options and decarbonization trajectories, which makes investment in seafarer training challenging

- A need to increase investment in training centres and up to date equipment
- A lack of competent trainers and
- A shortage of experienced seafarers

An Action-Plan to Ensure a Just Transition for Seafarers

Informed by the findings of the DNV report, the Maritime Just Transition Task Force Secretariat (in consultation with other Task Force Members, IMO and ILO) has developed a forward looking 10-point-action plan for international organisations, industry, workers and academia (including training providers), setting out concrete recommendations to unlock the seafarer skills needed to support shipping's decarbonization goals. The key action points are summarised and further contextualised in Fig. 3.

Unlocking Consensus on Decarbonization and Ensure Coherence Between Environmental and Skills Policies

The DNV report concluded that a lack of clarity about viability and the uptake of alternative fuel options is making it difficult to plan effectively for the transition of the maritime workforce. To help unlock the investments needed to equip the maritime workforce with essential skills necessary for a decarbonized shipping industry, it is critical to establish global consensus on an ambitious decarbonization goal for shipping. This will help provide the certainty needed to stimulate the uptake of clean energy technologies for shipping and unlock investments in training.

It will be important that a global decarbonization goal or any national action plan pursues a coordinated, joined-up approach with other relevant ministries and bodies—including those responsible for skills and education. In general, coherence between skills and environmental policies remains weak and fragmented in many countries (ILO, 2019). While responsibilities for climate change policies often rest solely with a country's environmental ministry, ensuring a successful and just transition to a green economy which leaves no one behind must involve multiple governmental departments—from transport, labour and education, to energy and trade.

In the context of shipping, this means that now a more ambitious decarbonization trajectory has been agreed in the framework of the IMO's Revised GHG Strategy, national governments at the IMO should react by fast-tracking the development of training standards for alternative fuels. This would in turn ensure that the training infrastructure is in place to safely train enough seafarers by the 2030s (Platten et al., 2023).

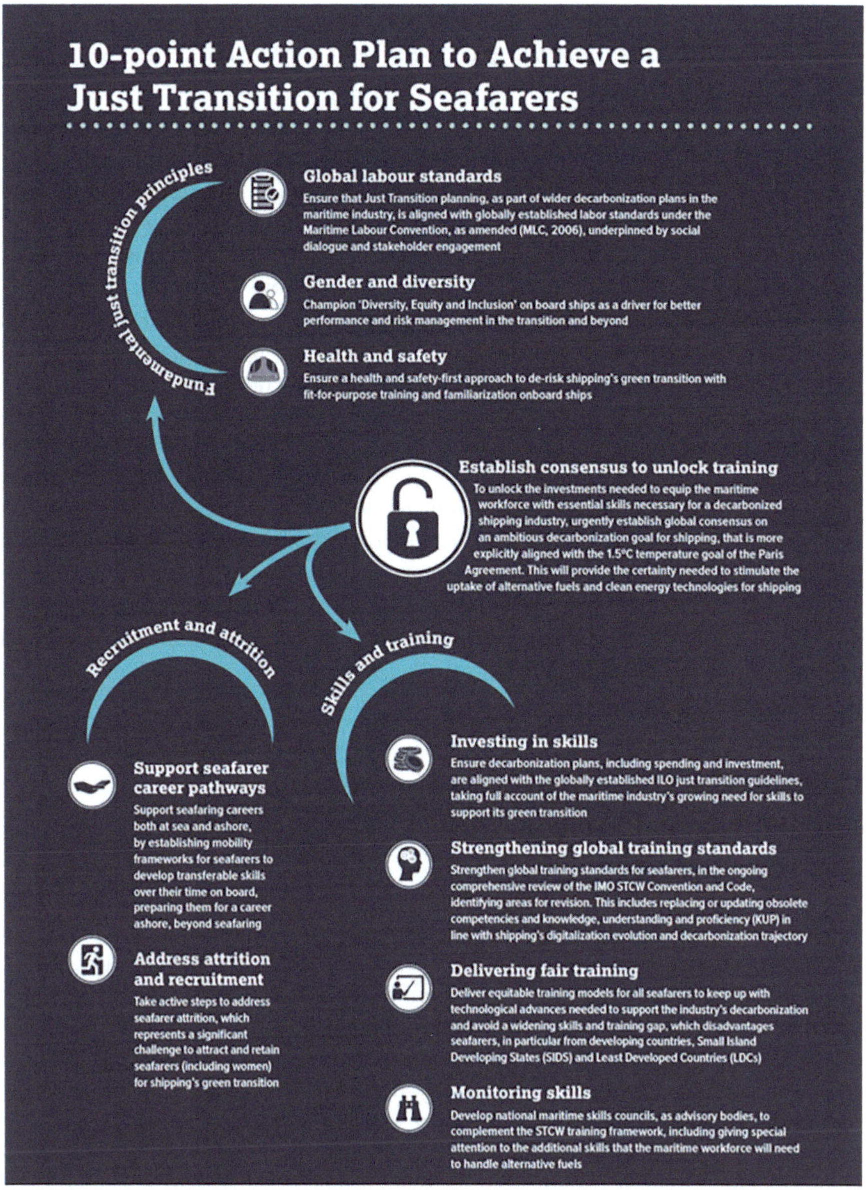

Fig. 3 10-point action plan. Source: Maritime Just Transition Task Force (2022)

Strong Labour Standards, a Robust Health and Safety Approach, and Championing Gender and Diversity

Green jobs are not good jobs by default, they are good by design and must be underpinned by fundamental just transition principles. As such, a just transition to a decarbonized shipping industry should be in accordance with global obligations under the ILO's Maritime Labour Convention, 2006 (ILO, 2006), as well as other international principles defined by the ILO, including the ILO Just Transition guidelines (ILO, 2015) and the ILO Tripartite Declaration of Principles concerning Multinational Enterprises and Social Policy (ILO, 2017). Social dialogue between the shipping industry and the seafarer unions, supported by international organisations and national governments lies at the heart of Just Transition.

As new fuels could represent a significant health and safety risk, a health-and-safety first approach—which also considers mental wellbeing—will be essential to de-risk shipping's transition. Alongside fit-for-purpose training, this also means providing sufficient familiarisation periods on board for seafarers.

The green transition also represents a major opportunity for the sector to diversify the maritime workforce—allowing shipping to draw from a wider talent pool of well-trained individuals. All stakeholders have a role to play to actively promote diversity, equity, and inclusion—including through investment, targeted programmes, and other measures.

Using the Green Transition to Address Recruitment and Attrition, and Support Seafarer Career Pathways

The industry must significantly increase training and recruitment levels to avoid a serious shortage in the years to come. There is already a shortfall in officers and almost 90,000 additional officers will be needed by 2026 (ICS and Bimco, 2021). The Covid-19 pandemic has also had a significant impact on the number of available seafarers. In addition, Ukrainian (4%) and Russian (10.5%) seafarers make up 14.5% of the global seafarer workforce. The numbers of both Ukrainian and Russian seafarers available has been impacted by the conflict between the two nations. Moreover, while the Philippines remains the largest supplier of seafarers globally, and this is not expected to change in the foreseeable future, its share of the global total of nearly 2 million seafarers has declined from around 20% to around 14%.

Against this backdrop, the green economy can present an opportunity to attract new workers into the maritime sector, create new high-quality green maritime jobs and to develop advanced skill-sets. Seafaring is already an important provider of livelihoods in the East Asian region and a source of development and national gross domestic product (GDP). In 2019, 380,000 Filipino seafarers contributed $6.5 billion to the Philippine economy (Romero, 2021). Further countries and talent pools also have opportunities to become world leaders in seafarer training and capitalise on the green shipping jobs of the future. For example, Africa has a strategic opportunity to help provide the world with seafarers, trained with the skills needed for the future, and in turn, support its economic development (UN Global Compact, ITF, and ICS, 2023). Establishing a global centre of excellence for seafarer training in Africa, spearheaded by the African Union, could be an important step towards supporting the continent leverage the opportunities of shipping's green transition.

Some emerging green industries are already leveraging the green transition in their recruitment strategies to attract new talent, for example, the 2023 campaign '1,000 new green jobs', spearheaded by Scottish Power. With decarbonization and digitalisation expected to continue to create shore-based job opportunities, it is vital to provide a holistic landscape of seafarers' potential career pathways. Highlighting career pathway frameworks for seafarers within the shipping industry is an important tool to promote lifelong learning and highlight sector wide employment opportunities, such as the Skills Framework developed by SkillsFuture Singapore, Workforce Singapore, and the Maritime and Port Authority of Singapore.

New Skills and Development of Training Standards for All Seafarers

A Just Transition can be realised through strengthening global training standards at pace, to ensure a level playing field for all seafarers. This is a truly unique aspect of the global shipping industry which has its global training standard—the IMOs STCW Convention—which is currently undergoing a comprehensive review. The review should pay close attention to the relevant skills required at present, as well as those that will be required for seafarers by 2050. Obsolete competencies should be updated or removed to mitigate and manage the training burden on seafarers, and new competencies to reflect skills needed for decarbonization should be included.

As seafarers' future education will increasingly rely on Science, Technology, Engineering, Maths (STEM) skillsets, special attention will need to be placed on strengthening and investing in national education and training frameworks, to support the future generation of seafarers.

Some countries have established green jobs initiatives to foster and support job creation and skills development. Where mechanisms are already in place, such as the Philippine Green Jobs Act 2016, the Task Force recommends that these could be leveraged to support seafarer skills development for shipping's transition, as well as provide fiscal incentives for skills training, which could be made available for maritime training institutions.

Monitoring and anticipating skills needs will also be a critical component to ensure a Just Transition for Seafarers. Establishing tripartite maritime skills councils or similar advisory bodies on seafarer skills and training will be increasingly critical. This will help to ensure that the workforce and training institutions can be advised on the quantity of training needed overall and where it should be based, thereby helping to plug national and regional skills gaps and support the overall decarbonization of the industry by ensuring a competent workforce and avoiding any delays to the implementation of clean technologies.

National governments have an important role to play in supporting the development of national skills councils or similar advisory bodies. In the Philippines—whose seafarers make up 14% of the global seafarer workforce—the government is already taking action to secure their nation's place as a maritime leader of tomorrow through engaging with the Maritime Just Transition Task Force and the newly-established tripartite 'International Advisory Committee on Global Maritime Affairs' (IACGMA), which will contribute to the global competitiveness of Filipino seafarers and prepare them for decarbonization. This includes advising the government on training for green shipping. Global leaders from organisations representing shipowners, seafarers and other maritime employers signed a memorandum of understanding with the Philippines's Department of Migrant Workers in January 2023, to form the IACGMA (ICS, 2023).

This IACGMA collaborative initiative is already yielding positive results for the Philippines maritime workforce, including the recent announcement by the European Commission that it will continue to recognise certificates issued by the Philippines to seafarers, thanks in large part to the efforts of this new partnership (European Commission, 2023). The seafarers' landscape in 2050 will be very different from what it is today, bringing with it new challenges, but also opportunities for collaboration to ensure that the workforce is fully prepared for what lies ahead.

Continued Cooperation Towards Implementation of the 10-Point Action Plan

The Maritime Just Transition Task Force is expected to continue to engage extensively with all stakeholder groups impacted by shipping's decarbonization journey, to shape the global policy agenda of empowering seafarers through the transition, including at the IMO and ILO. Its focus will be on programmes and workstreams which can support the implementation of its 10-point action plan. To achieve this, it has identified three priority areas for which the project parameters are being established:

- Development of a baseline decarbonization training framework for seafarers.
- Development of a comprehensive global recruitment and retention strategy for the maritime industry.
- Development of pilot projects and a blueprint to serve as a template for national-level advisory bodies to advise on training, skills, and other policy areas, as necessary.

The Task Force will also oversee projects and activities to accelerate the development of training programmes and other educational material to support seafarers in the handling of alternative fuels.

References

DNV. (2022). Seafarer training and skills for decarbonized shipping. Retrieved from: https://www.dnv.com/Publications/seafarer-training-and-skills-for-decarbonized-shipping-235124

European Commission. (2023). Maritime transport: Commission continues to recognise Filipino seafarer's certificates. Retrieved from: https://transport.ec.europa.eu/news/maritime-transport-commission-continues-recognise-filipino-seafarers-certificates-2023-03-31_en

ICS. (2023). New advisory committee launched to address major maritime issues impacting Filipino seafarers. Retrieved from: https://www.ics-shipping.org/press-release/new-advisory-committee-launched-to-address-major-maritime-issues-impacting-filipino-seafarers/

ICS and Bimco. (2021). Seafarer Workforce Report, 2021 edition. Retrieved from: https://www.ics-shipping.org/publication/seafarer-workforce-report-2021-edition/

ILO. (2006). Maritime Labour Convention, 2006, as amended (MLC, 2006). Retrieved from: https://www.ilo.org/dyn/normlex/en/f?p=NORMLEXPUB:91:0::NO::P91_INSTRUMENT_ID:312331

ILO. (2015). Guidelines for a just transition towards environmentally sustainable economies and societies for all. Retrieved from: https://www.ilo.org/wcmsp5/groups/public/@ed_emp/@emp_ent/documents/publication/wcms_432859.pdf

ILO. (2017). Tripartite declaration of principles concerning multinational enterprises and social policy. Retrieved from: https://www.ilo.org/wcmsp5/groups/public/%2D%2D-ed_emp/%2D%2D-emp_ent/%2D%2D-multi/documents/publication/wcms_094386.pdf

ILO. (2019). Skills for a greener future: Challenges and enabling factors to achieve a just transition. Retrieved from: https://www.ilo.org/skills/pubs/WCMS_731957/lang%2D%2Den/index.htm

Intergovernmental Panel on Climate Change. (2022). Climate change 2022: Impacts, adaptation and vulnerability. Contribution of Working Group II to the sixth assessment report of the Intergovernmental Panel on Climate Change. Retrieved from: https://www.ipcc.ch/report/ar6/wg2/resources/press/press-release

Maritime Just Transition Task Force. (2022). Mapping a maritime just transition for seafarers. Position paper. Retrieved from: https://www.ics-shipping.org/wp-content/uploads/2022/11/Position-Paper-Mapping-a-Maritime-Just-Transition-for-Seafarers-%E2%80%93-Maritime-Just-Transition-Task-Force-2022-OFFICIAL.pdf

Platten, G., Cotton, S., Henriksen, S., Slingsby, T., & Van Gogh, M. (2023). Why skills development is vital for shipping's green transition. Retrieved from: https://www.weforum.org/agenda/2023/02/why-skills-development-it-vital-for-shipping-s-green-transition/

Romero, P. (2021). Villars laud seafarers as 'sustainers of global economy'. Retrieved from: https://www.philstar.com/headlines/2021/06/28/2108549/villars-laud-seafarers-sustainers-global-economy

SSE. (2020). Supporting a just transition. Retrieved from: https://www.sse.com/media/xtrlsctj/just-transition-strategy-sse-final.pdf

UN Global Compact. (2022). Think Lab business brief on just transition. Retrieved from: https://unglobalcompact.org/take-action/think-labs/just-transition

UN Global Compact, ITF and ICS. (2023). Africa could be green jobs leader as shipping undergoes low carbon revolution. Retrieved from: https://www.itfglobal.org/en/news/africa-could-be-green-jobs-leader-shipping-undergoes-low-carbon-revolution

UNCTAD. (2022). Review of maritime transport 2022. In *United Nations Conference on Trade and Development (UNCTAD)*.

UNFCCC. (2015). Paris Agreement. Retrieved from: https://unfccc.int/sites/default/files/english_paris_agreement.pdf

UNFCCC. (2022). Sharm el-Sheikh Implementation Plan. Retrieved from: https://unfccc.int/sites/default/files/resource/cop27_auv_2_cover%20decision.pdf

Securing Global Alignment in Regulations Related to Decarbonization

Kirsi Tikka and Steve Esau

Target Audience

This chapter should be of particular interest to those wishing to understand the principle legislative measures in place to support the decarbonization of the maritime transportation sector. This could include board members, company executives and sustainability managers who wish to evaluate the impact of maritime regulations on their company's/organisation's strategy for decarbonization.

Key Takeaway Messages

The chapter covers:

- The importance of global regulations for maritime decarbonization.
- The International Maritime Organization (IMO) mandate for regulating international shipping.
- EU policy for climate change impacting shipping.

K. Tikka (✉)
Board Member Ardmore Shipping, Pembroke, Bermuda

Board Member Pacific Basin Shipping, Hong Kong, Hong Kong SAR

Board Member Foreship, Helsinki, Finland
e-mail: kktikka@outlook.com

S. Esau
SEA-LNG, Oxford, UK
e-mail: steve.esau@sea-lng.org

M. Lind et al. (eds.), *Maritime Decarbonization*,
https://doi.org/10.1007/978-3-031-39936-7_15

- The role of national decarbonization plans in maritime decarbonization.
- The current IMO and EU regulatory status and principal regulations covering the decarbonization of international shipping.

The Importance of Global Regulations

Adoption of decarbonization enablers has been led by early movers while others are waiting for regulatory mandates. Consequently, the change in carbon dioxide (CO_2) emissions from shipping is not on track with the Paris Climate Accord target of limiting global warming to 1.5 °C. According to the International Energy Agency (IEA) emissions declined in 2020–2015 levels but grew again by 5% in 2021 (IEA, 2022). The fluctuations can be attributed to the changes in trade volumes and ship speeds rather than decarbonization measures adopted by the maritime industry.

Steady progress on greenhouse gas (GHG) emission reduction is important to reach the targets and to avoid a risk of negative public reaction which could lead to inadequate regulatory decisions and costly solutions. Since the decarbonization enablers available today are mainly efficiency improvements, each providing relatively small emission reductions, action should be taken across the entire fleet to make a significant impact. The world fleet is large, 102,899 commercial ships in 2022 (UNCTADstat), and incremental improvements on individual ships add up.

Effective global regulations play a critical role in achieving steady progress across the global fleet. According to the Mærsk Mc-Kinney Møller Center for Zero Carbon Shipping *Maritime Decarbonization Strategy 2022* (MMMCZCS, 2022), even if the net zero pledges made by shipowners in the tanker, bulk, container, and RoRo/car carrier sectors materialise, they would translate to only a 13% reduction in global emissions.

The shipping industry has demonstrated in the past that with regulatory certainty environmental goals can be reached. Successful past regulatory developments include the introduction of double-hulled tankers, which has contributed to the significant reduction in oil spills from tankers (NASEM, 2022). Regulatory certainty is needed to move the industry forward on the decarbonization journey.

Global regulations can:

- Provide a level playing field
- Accelerate the worldwide adoption of enablers available today and achieve the cumulative benefit from the improved global fleet efficiency
- Introduce financial incentives and economic drivers by assigning a cost to carbon with market-based measures to accelerate and expand the adoption of low-and zero-carbon fuels and
- Support orderly fleet renewal that incorporates new technology and fuels and stop the building of conventional vessels which cannot be converted to zero carbon fuels in the future

The International Maritime Organization: Regulations for International Shipping

The International Maritime Organization (IMO) has a unique role and mandate to regulate global shipping. It is a specialised agency of the United Nations with responsibility for the safety and security of shipping and the prevention of marine and atmospheric pollution by ships. The IMO today has 175 Member States and three Associate Members. Additionally, 66 intergovernmental organisations have observer status, and 88 international non-governmental organisations (NGOs) have consultative status. IMO regulates shipping with Conventions and Protocols (IMO, 2022a).

Within the IMO structure the Marine Environment Protection Committee (MEPC) addresses environmental issues. The 1973 International Convention for the Prevention of Pollution from Ships, (MARPOL), regulates ship-generated marine and atmospheric pollution through its two Protocols of 1978 and 1997, respectively. MARPOL 1978 has been ratified by 161 IMO Member States, covering 98.89% of the world tonnage. MARPOL 1997 has been ratified by 105 Member States, covering 96.81% of the world tonnage. Enforcement of the Convention is the responsibility of the individual member governments of the IMO.

The MARPOL Convention, and its amendments, must be adopted formally by individual Member Governments. The process within MEPC, and more widely in the IMO, is largely based on finding consensus. Since the GHG regulations will have wide-reaching impact on IMO Member States, finding agreement can be challenging as it requires that the regulations be perceived as fair and equitable.

In 2018 the IMO agreed on an initial GHG strategy (MEPC 304(72)) with a goal to cut annual GHG emissions from shipping by at least half by 2050 compared with the emissions in 2008, and to work towards zero GHG emissions as soon as possible. The strategy included an ambition to reduce the international shipping carbon intensity by at least 40% by 2030 and 70% by 2050, compared to 2008. In July 2023, the IMO adopted a revised strategy with an ambition to increase the uptake of zero or near-zero GHG technologies, fuels and/or energy sources to represent at least 5% striving for 10% of the energy used by 2030, and to reach net-zero GHG emissions close to 2050, taking into account different national circumstances. The strategy is supported by indicative checkpoints: 1. to reduce total annual GHG emissions by at least 20%, striving for 30%, by 2030 compared to 2008, 2. to reduce the total annual GHG emissions by at least 70%, striving for 80%, by 2040 compared to 2008. The levels of ambition and indicative checkpoints should take into account well-to-wake GHG emissions.

The Initial GHG Strategy was preceded by energy efficiency regulations for new ships, adopted in July 2011.

Energy Efficiency Design Index (EEDI)

The EEDI regulation sets a minimum energy efficiency level in terms of CO_2 emissions per capacity mile (tonne/mile) for different ship types and sizes. The EEDI value that new ships must meet gets reduced every 5 years starting at 10% in 2013 and reaching 30% reduction from the reference level in 2025. The reference level represents the average efficiency level of ships built between 2000 and 2010. The reference levels were first set for tankers, bulk carriers, gas carriers, general cargo ships, container ships, refrigerated cargo carriers, and combination carriers. In 2014 new ship types were added: LNG carriers, vehicle carriers, ro-ro cargo ships, ro-ro passenger ships and cruise passenger ships with conventional propulsion.

The EEDI formula determines the nominal CO_2 emissions per capacity mile calculated based on the ship's technical parameters, such as main engine and auxiliary power, engine specific fuel consumption, and conversion factors from fuel consumption to CO_2 emissions. The capacity in the formulation depends on the ship type; for example, deadweight tonnage is used for tankers and gross tonnage for passenger ships as the capacity measure. The EEDI formula is specified in IMO Resolution MEPC. 308(73).

The EEDI regulation does not prescribe how to achieve the acceptable efficiency levels. It is designed to encourage development and implementation of energy efficiency technology. The formulation only accounts for the tank-to-wake emissions, which benefits fuels that have lower onboard CO_2 emissions but may have high well-to-tank emissions.

Ship Energy Efficiency Management Plan (SEEMP)

The requirement for a SEEMP for every ship to continually improve its energy efficiency with operational and technical measures, supported by an Energy Efficiency Operational Indicator (EEOI) comprising a combination of the CO_2 emissions for every cargo carried and the distance travelled. While the EEDI is a technical measure applied to new ships the SEEMP is an operational measure applicable to all ships. The regulation mandates that each ship has a plan to improve and monitor energy efficiency performance.

EEOI was introduced as a voluntary tool to monitor the performance of the ship in terms of CO_2 emitted per transport work for a single voyage or several voyages. The CO_2 emissions are calculated based on the fuel consumed multiplied by a conversion factor. The transport work is defined as cargo carried times the distance. Other mandatory measures (DCS and CII) have been adopted since to monitor the efficiency performance, but the EEOI can still be used, and is recommended to be used, to provide data that includes the actual cargo carried in the calculation of transport work.

A Part III has been added to the SEEMP to provide a system for documenting and managing a vessel's operational efficiency over time.

IMO Data Collection System (DCS)

In 2016 the IMO adopted a mandatory requirement for ships to record and report their fuel consumption and a proxy for the transport work, which is based on capacity (not actual cargo) and distance travelled (MEPC.278(70)). The data is reported annually to Flag States who transfer the data to the IMO Ship Fuel Consumption Database. The data collection started in 2019. The DCS supports the mandatory collection of the required data.

In 2018 the IMO agreed on several short-term measures for existing ships, to support the goals of its Initial GHG Strategy. These requirements entered into force in January 2023 and will be reviewed in 2026. The measures included:

Energy Efficiency Existing Ship Index (EEXI)

The EEXI was adopted with the objective to reduce CO_2 emissions from existing ships, especially older ships that do not comply with the EEDI requirements. The EEXI formula is based on the EEDI formula and ships that already have a compliant EEDI value can use it as their EEXI value. The required EEXI values are calculated using the EEDI reference values with reduction factors which vary by ship type and size category. Ships that do not meet the EEXI requirement must take measures to comply by the first periodical survey in 2023. Compliance can be achieved by implementing engine power or shaft power limiters which reduce the maximum available power and effectively reduces the maximum available speed.

Carbon Intensity Indicator (CII)

The CII indicates the operational CO_2 emission intensity of a ship. Starting in 2024, ratings from A to E will be assigned to ships based on their CII value achieved in the previous year. A is the highest rating while D and E ratings are considered non-compliant. Operators of ships rated D for three consecutive years or E for a single year will have to develop a corrective action plan to bring the vessel to compliance by the end of the following year.

The CII reference values used to assign the required CII are based on 2019 data. Ratings are determined based on deviation from the required CII value. The requirements will become stricter over time. The reduction factors for the required CII relative to the 2019 reference values start at 5% in 2023 and then increase by 2% per year until 2026 (MEPC.338(76)). Further reduction levels will be determined after review of the regulation in 2026.

The CII is measured as a combination of CO_2 emissions per capacity (not actual cargo carried) and distance travelled. This approach was selected to align with the data format available in the IMO DCS. It has been criticised because it does not support improved vessel utilisation. Perversely, operating in ballast will provide a better rating than when carrying cargo. The supporters of the measure believe that commercial drivers will push for higher utilisation regardless of the CII rating. The CII regulation also opens a door for potential disputes between ship owners/operators and charterers because of the impact that different trading patterns can have on a ship's rating. Enforcement of the CII is based on developing improvement plans for ships with the two lowest ratings being without penalties as long as improvement plans are prepared and are approved by the Flag State or a Recognised Organisation.

These short-term measures are a significant step in the IMO GHG reduction regulatory development, but they also reveal the shortcomings of regulations that are constrained by the lack of appropriate data and the focus on tank-to-wake emissions rather than well-to-wake emissions and the full fuel lifecycle.

In July 2023 agreed that the basket of mid- and long-term GHG reduction measures should include a fuel standard to provide a gradual transition towards low-carbon and zero-carbon fuels (a technical element), and a GHG emissions pricing mechanism (an economic element). A review of impacts of the proposed measures on IMO Member States, and particularly on Small Island Developing States (SIDS) and least developed countries (LDCs), is included in the IMO work plan.

IMO Resolutions and Guidelines related to energy efficiency of ships can be found at: https://www.imo.org/en/OurWork/Environment/Pages/Index-of-MEPC-Resolutions-and-Guidelines-related-to-MARPOL-Annex-VI.aspx#4.

National Decarbonization Plans for Shipping

In parallel with the IMO's global regulations, national and local policies are important to ensure renewable energy availability for zero carbon fuel production and fuel infrastructure development. Government policies are also needed to optimise the port and ground transportation links with ship operations and to support zero carbon shipping. These national plans are not limited to international shipping, which is the IMO's remit.

The IMO Initial GHG Strategy invites its Member States to develop national action plans with strategies to address GHG emissions from international shipping (IMO, 2022b). By the end of 2022 only seven countries (Finland, India, Japan, Marshall Islands, Norway, Singapore, United Kingdom) had submitted national plans to the IMO.

Other Regions and Geographies: European Union

Many environmental groups and countries are not satisfied with the progress made at the IMO. Finding agreement among the Member States has been challenging and even if an agreement is found the process at the IMO takes years from the time of agreement to the implementation of a regulation. Because of the long regulatory timeframe, environmental groups and some countries have pushed for earlier revision of the Initial GHG Strategy and a decision on the associated measures, but without success. Concern about stricter targets that a revised Strategy could introduce and their impact on less developed countries is one of the reasons put forward as an objection to expediting the revisions.

Although the European Union (EU) Member States support the IMO process, the EU has its own climate change policy and is pushing forward its regulations on decarbonizing shipping both within the EU and in and out of the EU, independent of the IMO. An EU objective is to inspire and pave the way for broader climate action within the IMO. This action is not dissimilar to an earlier regulatory development when the United States passed its Oil Pollution Act (OPA) in 1990 unilaterally requiring double hulls on tankers in US waters. This had a major impact on international oil shipping and led to the IMO subsequently bringing in its own requirements.

EU Policy for Climate Change

The EU climate change policy agenda is set by the European Green Deal. It is a package of policy initiatives, which aims to set the EU on the path to a green transition, with the goal of reaching climate neutrality by 2050. The European Green Deal was launched by the European Commission (EC) in December 2019. The European climate law regulation, which came into force in May 2021, makes the goal of climate neutrality by 2050 a legal obligation for the EU. By adopting it, the EU and its Member States are committed to cutting net greenhouse gas emissions in the EU by at least 55% by 2030 compared to 1990 levels.

The European Green Deal consists of a range of policy initiatives including the *Fit for 55* package. This aims to translate the ambitions of the Green Deal into law and consists of a set of 16 major proposals to revise climate, energy and transport related legislation and put in place new legislative initiatives to align EU laws with the EU's climate goals.

EU Regulations on Decarbonizing Shipping

It is the EC's view that while the recent progress achieved in the IMO is to be welcomed, the proposed measures are insufficient to decarbonize international shipping in line with international climate objectives.

Given this situation, the Commission committed to proposing a basket of EU measures, as part of its Fit for 55 package, to increase the contribution of maritime transport to the EU climate efforts, along with the measures agreed at the global level within the IMO. The basket of measures is made up of several policies, several of which are currently (2023) in the course of revision and upgrading.

EU Emission Trading System (EU ETS)

The goal of the EU ETS, through its extension to shipping, is to reduce GHG emissions from the maritime sector. It is a cornerstone of the EU's policy to combat climate change and is the key market-based mechanism for reducing GHG emissions cost-effectively. It is the world's first major carbon market and remains the biggest, covering around 40% of the EU's GHG emissions. It includes CO_2 emissions from electricity and heat generation and energy-intensive industrial sectors plus commercial aviation and other greenhouse gases such as nitrous oxide (N_2O) and perfluorocarbons from the chemicals and aluminium sectors.

A revision to the EU ETS proposes the inclusion of maritime transport, starting in 2023 with a 3-year phase-in period. In 2025, 40% of emissions reported for 2024 must be covered by emission allowances, by 2026 this increases to 70% reported for 2025, and by 2027, this increases to 100% of reported emissions. The EU ETS will cover 100% of emissions from ships performing intra-EU voyages and from ships at berth in European ports For extra-EU voyages it will include 50% of emissions from ships departing from or arriving at an EU port. Non-CO_2 emissions, such as methane and nitrous oxide, from shipping will also be included in the ETS from 2026 onwards.

The obligation to surrender allowances in the maritime transport sector will gradually be phased-in over the period 2023–2025, with shipping companies having to surrender allowances corresponding to 100% of their verified emissions as of 2026.

The same rules that apply to other sectors covered by the EU ETS will apply to maritime transport regarding auctioning, the transfer, surrender and cancellation of allowances, penalties, and registries. The rules for monitoring, reporting, verification, and accreditation will be based on previous legislation.

With respect to non-compliance—in addition to the general EU ETS rules on penalties, expulsion orders can be issued against ships under the responsibility of a shipping company that has failed to surrender allowances for two or more consecutive reporting periods, with the result that ships under its responsibility can be detained by the Flag EU Member State and denied entry into a port under the jurisdiction of a Member State. Shipping companies are attributed to a Member State for the purposes of administration.

There is a concern that an EU ETS emissions pricing policy focused only on shipboard, or tank-to-wake emissions—rather than on the full fuel lifecycle, well-to-wake emissions—could undermine market incentives to adopt low and zero-carbon fuels.

Methanol, LNG, ammonia, and hydrogen are among the potential alternative fuels for shipping, and all require energy to produce them. This energy can come from fossil fuels (grey) or renewable sources (green). If the EU ETS only considers on-board GHG emissions, then the grey and green fuels used by ships will get the same treatment even though the full climate impact of grey fuels is significantly worse.

FuelEU Maritime

The goal of the FuelEU Maritime legislation is to regulate emissions on the demand side to increase the share of renewable and low-carbon fuels in the fuel mix of maritime transport. FuelEU Maritime is a goal-based regulation designed to accelerate the maritime industry's decarbonization through the adoption of renewable and low-carbon fuels and technologies. It does so through the application of targets for GHG energy intensity reductions from 2025 onwards.

The FuelEU Maritime regulations apply to EU and non-EU ships above 5000 gross tonnage and to all energy used on board in or between EU ports, and to 50% of energy used on voyages where the departure or arrival port is outside the EU.

GHG reduction targets are determined against a reference value reflecting the fleet average GHG intensity of energy used on-board by ships in 2020 and reduced by the following percentages: 2% in 2025, 6% in 2030, 14.5% in 2035, 31% in 2040, 62% in 2045, and 80% in 2050.

GHG emissions are measured on a well-to-wake basis and include emissions from non-CO_2 gases, including methane and nitrous oxide (N2O). Emissions will be monitored on an annual basis using the existing EU's Monitoring Reporting and Verification (MRV) System which has been in place for shipping since 2018.

Significant penalties for non-compliance with the GHG targets are included. The penalty will be calculated on an annual basis using a formula which converts the compliance imbalance in energy terms to a tonne equivalent of Very Low Sulphur Oil (VLSFO) multiplied by 2400 €. Other penalties are defined for non-compliance at berth.

In addition to the GHG energy intensity reduction goals, a target has been proposed of 2% for RFNBO (Renewable Fuels of Non-Biological Origin) usage in maritime transport by 2030.

Critics of FuelEU Maritime, within the EU, suggest that the regulation is not ambitious enough if shipping is to achieve climate neutrality by 2050. They are calling for higher GHG intensity reduction targets, increasing targets for renewable e-fuel use, and rewards for early adopters of these fuels.

Shipping industry stakeholders wish to see requirements placed on Member States to ensure that fuel suppliers in European ports deliver the compliant fuels in sufficient quantities to ships to meet regulatory objectives.

The support of the fuel suppliers is essential to achieving the ambitious regulatory targets called for in the proposed legislation. Thus, it is imperative to introduce robust requirements on Member States under the FuelEU Maritime to ensure that fuel suppliers in European ports deliver compliant fuels to ships in sufficient quantities to meet the regulatory objectives (shared responsibility). In addition, more concrete obligations should be placed on fuel suppliers under the Renewable Energy Directive.

Renewable Energy Directive (RED III)

The goal of RED III is to set out binding, sector-specific targets for renewables in Europe's energy mix, including maritime. RED III will perform two main roles: defining what energy sources are regarded as 'renewable' and setting out binding targets for renewables in Europe's energy mix. In 2018, in the first revision of the Renewable Energy Directive (RED II) the EU set a 32% target for renewable energy in Europe's mix by 2030, up from around 20% currently. In the latest revision, RED III, the Commission proposes to increase the EU-wide renewable energy target for 2030 to 42.5% with specific sectoral targets for manufacturing, heating and cooling, buildings, and transport, including maritime.

For transport, sub-targets are increased in RED III for advanced biofuels and introduced for RFNBOs, with a binding combined sub-target of 5.5% in the share of renewable energies supplied to the transport sector. Member States will have the choice between a binding target of 14.5% reduction of GHG intensity in transport from the use of renewables by 2030, or a binding share of at least 29% of renewables within the final consumption of energy in the transport sector by 2030.

There are concerns from the shipping industry that the requirements on fuel suppliers in RED III should match the requirements placed on shipowners by FuelEU Maritime. This is crucial to ensure that enough alternative marine fuels are made available on the market at an affordable price.

Directive on Deployment of Alternative Fuel Infrastructure (AFIR)

The goal of AFIR is to support the deployment of renewable and low-carbon fuel infrastructure in road and maritime transport. The 2014 Alternative Fuel

Infrastructure Directive (AFID) requires EU Member States to set up long-term national policy frameworks for the development of the market for alternative fuels and the planning of the deployment of relevant alternative fuels infrastructure. It also stipulates requirements for the rollout of alternative fuels infrastructure, including onshore power along the core network of the Trans-European Transport Network (TEN-T) which includes major European ports. The Directive sets common technical specifications for recharging and refuelling stations and for consumer information.

In the Fit for 55 package the revision of AFID, known as AFIR, supports the deployment of infrastructure for renewable and low carbon fuels in road and maritime transport in addition to other alternative fossil fuels such as LNG, CNG and LPG for a transitional phase. The requirement for LNG fuelling infrastructure in core TEN-T ports continues to 2025 and the regulation includes a mandate for containerships and passenger vessels to use onshore power supply while at berth in the main EU ports by 2030.

Energy Taxation Directive

As part of the Fit for 55 package, a revision of the Energy Taxation Directive is proposed. This will end tax exemptions for marine fuels within the EU. LNG would, following a transitional period of 10 years being charged two thirds of the reference tax rate from 2023, be fully taxed as of January 2033. To provide an incentive to their use, sustainable alternative fuels (including sustainable biofuels and biogas, low-carbon fuels, advanced sustainable biofuels and biogas, and RFNBOs) and electricity would have a minimum rate of zero applied for 10 years.

Applicability

The various proposed EU regulations discussed above will apply to European ships above 5000 gross tonnage, which are in principle responsible for 90% of CO_2 emissions from shipping in Europe. The revision to the EU ETS provides the overall market signal for decarbonization; FuelEU Maritime addresses the demand side, RED III addresses the supply side and the revisions to AFIR addresses the enabling infrastructure linking supply to the maritime users.

As of August 2023, the policy proposals are passing through the EU's legislative process where legislation proposed by the EC is reviewed and amended by the European Parliament and Council. Proposals are adopted into law when the Parliament and Council agree on a joint text.

Closing Remarks

Having a sound regulatory framework in place is crucial to providing the industry with the direction it needs to invest in technologies that will advance the decarbonization of the maritime sector and meet the climate change targets. All those involved in the industry have a part to play. Wherever possible, participants should consider:

- Providing input into regulatory development at IMO by engaging directly with the Member Governments, or through NGOs with consultative status at the IMO.
- Providing input to regional regulatory development, such as the EU, by engaging with Governments and NGOs.
- Supporting a well-to-wake approach in emission regulations.
- Supporting the use of actual cargo carried in the formulation of the Carbon Intensity Index.

References

EU 2015/757. https://eur-lex.europa.eu/legal-content/EN/TXT/PDF/?uri=CELEX:32015R0757&from=EL#:~:text=This%20Regulation%20applies%20to%20ships,call%2C%20as%20well%20as%20within

IEA. (2022). IEA international shipping tracking report—September 2022. https://www.iea.org/reports/international-shipping

IMO. (2022a). International Maritime Organization. https://www.imo.org

IMO. (2022b). National action plans 2022. https://www.imo.org/en/ourwork/environment/pages/relevant-national-action-plans-and-strategies.aspx

MEPC 304(72). Initial IMO strategy on reduction of GHG emissions from ships. https://wwwcdn.imo.org/localresources/en/KnowledgeCentre/IndexofIMOResolutions/MEPCDocuments/MEPC.304(72).pdf

MEPC.308(73). https://wwwcdn.imo.org/localresources/en/OurWork/Environment/Documents/Air%20pollution/MEPC.308(73).pdf

MEPC.338(76). https://wwwcdn.imo.org/localresources/en/OurWork/Environment/Documents/Air%20pollution/MEPC.338(76).pdf

MMMCZCS. (2022). Mærsk Mc-Kinney Møller Center for Zero Carbon Shipping (MMMCZCS), Maritime Decarbonization Strategy 2022. https://www.zerocarbonshipping.com/publications/maritime-decarbonization-strategy/

NASEM. (2022). *Oil in the sea IV: Inputs, fates, and effects*. National Academies of Sciences, Engineering, and Medicine. https://nap.nationalacademies.org/catalog/26410/oil-in-the-sea-iv-inputs-fates-and-effects

UNCTADstat. https://unctadstat.unctad.org/wds/ReportFolders/reportFolders.aspx

Decarbonize Shipping or Decarbonize International Maritime Trade: The Present Contractual Framework and the Need for a New Contractual Architecture

Haris Zografakis, Neil Henderson, Andrew Rigden Green, Dora Mace-Kokota, and James M. Turner KC

Key Takeaway Message

The key point in this chapter is that the maritime decarbonization involves much more than just the regulation of ships by the IMO; the contractual framework of international maritime trade is central to achieving the global carbon emission targets, and this requires an appropriate and realistic re-consideration of the contractual architecture of international maritime trade.

The Legal Foundations of International Maritime Trade

International Maritime Trade (IMT) is a complex web of contracts, within a framework of regulations, national laws and international conventions. The International Maritime Organization (IMO) plays an important role in relation to certain aspects of safety, design and operation of ships. IMT includes, but is not limited to, ships and

H. Zografakis (✉) · D. Mace-Kokota
Stephenson Harwood LLP, London, UK
e-mail: Haris.Zografakis@shlegal.com; Dora.Mace-Kokota@shlegal.com

N. Henderson
Gard AS, Arendal, Norway
e-mail: Neil.Henderson@gard.no

A. Rigden Green
Stephenson Harwood LLP, Hong Kong, China
e-mail: Andrew.RigdenGreen@shlegal.com

J. M. Turner KC
Quadrant Chambers, London, UK
e-mail: James.Turner@quadrantchambers.com

M. Lind et al. (eds.), *Maritime Decarbonization*,
https://doi.org/10.1007/978-3-031-39936-7_16

shipping, and it is a mistake to think of the IMO as IMT's 'regulator'. This chapter will focus on elements of IMT that will be critical to its decarbonization, and are largely unrelated to the IMO. As the term 'maritime decarbonization', as generally used, places heavy emphasis on the regulatory aspects of shipping, we have adopted the term "Decarbonization of International Maritime Trade": DIMT.

IMT has been described as '*... the 'perfect' market place ... an economic Jurassic Park where the dinosaurs or classical economics roam free ...*' (Stopford, 2008). From a legal perspective, that free market is the domain of contracts—a largely unregulated network of relationships, where the common denominators are freedom of the high seas, freedom of contract and party autonomy under English law, as the law of choice, with New York, Singapore and Hong Kong law, playing a smaller role.

International regulations set out a minimum framework for ship safety and environmental protection, primarily, but not exclusively, through the IMO. Unlike aviation, where some commercial aspects are regulated through international conventions, there is no equivalent in IMT, where both the commercial operation of cargo ships, as well as the trading of goods, are not regulated by any international body or international convention.

The contractual architecture of maritime trade presents two main features:

- *Fragmentation*: a myriad of contracts, mostly bilateral, underpinned by the English law principle of privity of contract, pursuant to which, a contract binds only the parties to it. Trade associations (such as the Baltic and International Maritime Council (BIMCO), the Grain and Feed Trade Association (GAFTA), and the Federation of Oils, Seeds and Fats Associations (FOSFA)) facilitate trade through the production of contractual templates, which are invariably amended by market participants, exercising their contractual freedom and
- *Continuity*, with successive amendments of contractual templates, some of which date back to the early 1900s.

A relatively small number of international conventions supplement, and often limit, parties' contractual freedom. There is no widely adopted international convention for the purchase and sale of goods carried by sea. Accordingly, the trading of commodities is almost exclusively the domain of contracts. Attempts by the United Nations (UN) to introduce a degree of uniformity have failed, as the UN Convention on Contracts for the International Sale of Goods is routinely excluded from application in commodities trading.

The very significant areas of salvage and marine pollution are the subject of separate international conventions (rather than IMO regulations), and the same approach was adopted by the High Seas Treaty and the Hong Kong International Convention for the Safe and Environmentally Sound Recycling of Ships.

The legislative production of the European Union (EU) resembles that of international conventions, and its decarbonization focus in recent years is having an impact on IMT, with the EU Emissions Trading System (ETS) featuring prominently.

Flag States have jurisdiction over vessels in the high seas, but the approach of offshore shipping registries, which dominate the ocean-going fleet, is laissez-faire, and their influence on IMT is small. The DIMT therefore poses a challenge: Countries that have committed to zero targets for their domestic economy may find it difficult to justify why vessels flying their flag are exempt from such targets.

Port States have jurisdiction over matters within the port and their territorial waters but, traditionally, have not tried to exercise influence beyond that of safety and marine pollution. Some elements of Port State intervention are multilateral: safety standards collectively enforced by the Paris and Tokyo Memoranda of Understanding (MOUs) on Port State Control. DIMT poses a similar challenge to Port States, as with Flag States, if they must reconcile a zero-carbon port with a non-zero-carbon ship using the port. It is possible that multilateral legal structures along the lines of the Paris and Tokyo MOUs will be used to introduce a degree of regional uniformity on matters related to the DIMT.

The above outline offers four lessons for the decarbonization of international maritime trade:

- The IMO is only one of multiple factors that influence the regulatory framework of IMT.
- The plurality and fragmentation of national rules is a feature of IMT.
- Contracts will be key to any measure that has commercial impact, both bilaterally, as well as through consensus contractual documents, either in the shape of templates produced by trade associations or following the model of the York-Antwerp Rules on general average.
- The vehicle of international conventions is likely to become necessary in relation to aspects of the DIMT. However, unless such efforts are compatible with the structure of IMT, international conventions may not be widely ratified, becoming dead letter, in other words, ineffectual.

The Contractual Architecture of International Maritime Trade Through a Decarbonization Lens

Before outlining issues that arise under the main contracts in IMT, we need to address some structural issues that inform our analysis.

Structural Issues

The gigantic scale of the energy transition in IMT will involve not only engineering challenges, but also adaptations to an array of contracts. The common denominator of English law as the law of choice in IMT provides the basis for consistency. However, the contractual challenge is formidable, aggravated by some key structural features of IMT, as follows:

- Corporate entities involved in IMT are registered or domiciled in jurisdictions with opaque corporate structures, and practically non-existent shareholder protection and director accountability. This applies both to so-called open shipping registries, which is the dominant model for ship owning companies, but also to many users of ships (commodities traders, charterers). The absence of legal or societal pressure emanating from their country of incorporation will hinder the DIMT.
- IMT is almost exclusively business-to-business, and, mostly invisible to consumers. However, as 80% of world trade is carried by sea, the carbon footprint of most consumer products includes at least some kilograms of CO_2 from their ocean carriage, or that of the raw materials used for their production. Greenhouse gas emissions (GHG) are divided into three categories for businesses and organisations—Scope 1, Scope 2 and Scope 3.[1] The Scope 3 category includes GHG emissions from the supply chain, with transportation featuring heavily. To the extent that consumer-facing companies come under pressure to reduce their Scope 3 emissions, that pressure will ultimately impact upon IMT. In this sense, developments with no apparent relevance to shipping will cascade down to IMT. Examples from the EU are Carbon Border Adjustment Mechanism (CBAM) and the Green Claims Directive.
- Most contracts for the commercial employment of dry bulk vessels and tankers (chartering) are on a spot contract basis. While this contributes to resilience and competitive pricing, it also encourages short-termism that is not conducive to the investments needed for the required energy transition. It also incentivises operational practices that are carbon-inefficient, such as speed chosen to meet commercial requirements, long ballast voyages, and the practice of 'sail fast, then wait' (SFTW), which will be discussed again later in this chapter.
- Much of commodities' trading is also undertaken on a spot basis, with ships chosen to perform obligations under short-term sale contracts, which are at the root of many of the carbon emission inefficiencies observed in chartering. IMO and EU regulations have raised awareness as to carbon emission efficiency in charterparties (the contract for the commercial employment of vessels), but this has not been extended to commodities trading.
- Regardless of the identity of the party responsible for bunkering (time charterers or voyage chartered owners), most bunkering contracts are on a spot basis. This model will be incompatible with the era of new fuels, which will depend on long-term offtake agreements (agreements where the supplier and the buyer agree on the purchase of large quantities and on a long-term basis).
- Technical management of ships is often outsourced to third party managers, increasing the distance (and removing the contractual link) between the

[1] Scope 1 emissions are 'direct' emissions from a company's operations.

Scope 2 emissions are 'indirect' emissions from the production of the energy that an organisation consumes.

Scope 3 emissions are also indirect emissions and include the emissions from the operations of suppliers of good and services that the company uses.

commercial employment of a vessel by the charterer, and the operational and technical reality of its carbon emission efficiency.

- The web of contracts in maritime trade involves thousands of companies, most of which are small and medium-sized enterprises (SMEs), sometimes short-lived and asset-light, and often lacking the resources necessary to design and implement a decarbonization strategy, including its contractual aspects.
- Ships travel, and are thus exposed to a multitude of jurisdictions, each with its own legal framework, including on matters relating to decarbonization.
- Strings or chains of contracts are common in IMT. It is common for a commodity to be the subject of several sale transactions during its ocean carriage by a vessel that is itself the subject of a chain of charterparties. This amplifies all the above features.

Shipbuilding

Shipbuilding has been estimated to be responsible for about 4% of a ship's lifetime GHG emissions (Chatzinikolaou & Ventikos, 2014). That figure, however, assumes the consumption of fuel oil throughout a vessel's operational life. As shipping transitions to zero-carbon fuels, therefore, the relative contribution of shipbuilding will rise.

Shipbuilding takes the form of a specialist contract for the sale of goods by description. There are no contractual levers in the typical shipbuilding contract which might be adapted to encourage or produce a reduction in GHG emissions. The only incentive for a shipyard to reduce its emissions is a financial one (in that less energy expended on a project will reduce its overheads). Indeed, much of the GHG footprint in the process is already 'locked in' before the construction process starts, in the production of the steel from which the hull and machinery are constructed.

Shipbuilding's contribution to the DIMT is thus limited, as matters stand, to what is built, rather than how it is built. What is built depends in part on the parties' (in practice the buyer's) choices, and in part on regulatory requirements. The only relevant regulatory stipulation, which is invariably reflected in the shipbuilding contract itself, is that a ship's design complies with the EEDI (Energy Efficiency Design Index) regulations in the (IMO) International Convention for the Prevention of Pollution from Ships (MARPOL) Annex VI.

The carbon footprint of a built vessel belongs to the buyer's Scope 3 emissions. It will, over time, become very much in buyers' interests to bear down on the size of that footprint. This will result in a series of warranties and other obligations in shipbuilding contracts that will address both the source of materials (mainly, 'green' steel), and the carbon intensity of the construction process.

The scope for reductions in GHG emissions is not limited to hull form, or other parameters at the time of a vessel's construction. Specialist types of equipment are increasingly being used to reduce carbon intensity (wind propulsion, air lubrication of hulls, etc.). Some of these customisations may form part of newbuild projects, but for now they are seen as retrofits. Considerable contractual complications arise, with regard to the interplay amongst the shipowners, the shipyard and the original equipment manufacturers (OEMs), in relation to warranties, liabilities, the interdependence of equipment, and the benchmarks used to assess emission reductions. Indeed, as many such technologies are relatively new and untested, the prospect for disputes is considerable.

Ship Finance

Financial institutions are increasingly required to justify their investment choices based on environmental risk, which has led to initiatives such as the Poseidon Principles,[2] the Climate Bonds Initiative[3] (which steers investments by rewarding vessels not carrying fossil fuels or that are or in the process of becoming zero-emission) and the Green Shipping Financing/Guarantee Programme[4] (which supports the financing of greener vessels, alongside retrofitting of existing ships).

Ship finance lenders are offering green financings (in which the loan proceeds must be used for a 'green' purpose) and/or sustainability-led financings (in which borrowers are incentivised to improve their sustainability profile through better pricing if they meet pre-determined sustainability performance targets measured against sustainability key performance indicators (KPIs).

Green loans mostly take the form of a green tranche within a wider facility or an up-size facility to finance a particular retrofit, or to cover research and development (R&D) expenses. Facilities for entirely green purposes have been focused on liquified natural gas (LNG)-fuelled vessels but financiers are making more capital available to dual-fuel ships. The focus in this area may change, as there is an ongoing debate on whether vessels that run on fossil fuel deserve the 'green' investment status under the relevant classification in Regulation (EU) 2020/852 of the European Parliament and EU Council (the EU Taxonomy).

Sustainable (*green*) financing is discussed further in chapter "Sustainable Finance in the Maritime Sector" of this book.

Financing ship retrofits presents legal challenges such as the choice of the appropriate security for new equipment (such as, whether the piece of new equipment is an 'appurtenance' of the vessel already 'covered' by the existing ship mortgage or whether it is not an integral part of the vessel therefore requiring new, separate security). In addition, if the original financier is not financing the new equipment, disagreements relating to priority are likely to arise with the new

---

[2] www.poseidonprinciples.org/finance/about/

[3] https://www.climatebonds.net/about/what-we-do

[4] https://www.eib.org/en/projects/pipelines/all/20150334#:~:text=Environmental%20aspects,protection%20including%20Climate%20Action%20initiatives

financier. Intercreditor terms will be necessary to avoid enforcement complications. When a retrofit is financed purely by way of a green loan or tranche, it is currently unusual for financiers to monitor the performance of a retrofit for the rest of the facility period. However, in the future, some financiers may look to introduce pricing penalties if a retrofit does not improve a vessel's performance, in which case it will be crucial to agree on and set out in the finance documentation, the methodology that should be used to demonstrate such improvement.

Sustainability-linked loans are primarily used as working capital or revolving credit facilities and have been more popular amongst liner ship-owning companies. The most common KPI used is the reduction of GHG emissions at a faster rate than the IMO target, by reference to a vessel's Annual Efficiency Ratio (AER).

The Loan Market Association has published principles (the Green Loan Principles and the SSL Principles), best practice guidance and a glossary of terms for both types of loans as well as some template provisions for sustainability-linked loans, which can be adapted to ship finance.

To the extent that the use of decarbonization solutions (be it new fuels or retrofits) becomes part of finance contracts, operational problems will have repercussions under those, too.

On the other side of the energy transition, the number of vessels that will be considered stranded financially is expected to increase significantly, which is likely to lead to defaults under existing financing arrangements.

Commodities Sale and Purchase Contracts and Trade Finance

The obligation to organise transportation (to '*procure an effective contract of carriage*') falls on the buyer or seller, depending on the terms of the sale contract (FOB (free on board) for the buyer or CFR (cost and freight)/CIF (cost, insurance, and freight)/DAP (delivered at place) for the seller). Accordingly, the terms of the sale contract influence the choice of ship, but also operational factors such as laycan, delivery periods, laytime, and demurrage.

There is no regulatory regime that requires the FOB buyer or the CFR/CIF/DAP seller to '*procure a contract of carriage*' that is carbon emission efficient or zero-carbon emission.

As ocean transportation forms part of the Scope 3 carbon emissions applicable to both buyers and sellers of goods, it is apparent that sale contracts will be a key driver in the DIMT. Carbon intensity requirements will become part of commodities sale contracts, which will result in equivalent provisions in charterparties and bills of lading, both of which will be discussed in the next sections of this chapter.

The area of financing of commodities trading (trade finance) has not focused on maritime decarbonization, either in terms of initiatives or in terms of KPIs, as much as ship finance (see the section "Ship Finance" earlier in this chapter). However, carbon emission efficiency requirements in trade finance can set in motion a domino effect starting with sale contracts, through to charterparties and bills of lading.

While not designed to regulate commodities trading, the draft EU Directive on Supply Chain Due Diligence is likely to have an impact on sale contracts. It requires companies of a certain size operating in the EU to report the carbon intensity of their direct and indirect suppliers—including ocean transport providers.

Charterparties

Charterparties (CPs) are contracts for the commercial employment of ships, either on voyage terms (VCP) or for a period of time (TCP). Both types present features that are problematic from the perspective of the DIMT:

- TCPs contain 'speed and fuel consumption' warranties, which determine the speed at which voyages will be performed. While slow steaming and eco-speed clauses do exist, carbon emission efficiency is only slowly being contractually implemented.
- In TCPs, the financial and contractual responsibility for bunkering falls on the time charterer, which gives rise to one of shipping's classic 'split incentives' problems. The owner of a time-chartered vessel has no direct financial interest in energy efficiency measures, and the short-termism encouraged by the spot nature of the trade acts as a disincentive for investments in such measures.
- The shipowner in TCPs is required to follow the charterers' orders for the employment of a ship, unless they are unlawful or illegitimate. With the advent of IMO's Carbon Intensity Index (CII) regulations, the carbon intensity of such orders becomes relevant, and there has been a proliferation of additional clauses attempting to deal with CII. However, it would be difficult to demonstrate that any order, even if it were to negatively impact CII rating, would be unlawful or illegitimate. If shipowners were to take matters into their own hands and slow steam, or divert from the agreed route, this would place them in breach of the charterparty and may invalidate insurance cover or invalidate the limitation protections set out in bills of lading. Frequently vessels are sub-chartered, and the charterer will also look to pass the obligations down the chain. However, the shipowner will have no direct contract with the sub-charterer and there will be difficulties in ensuring compliance down what could be very long chains.
- A voyage charterer does not have the same power to dictate how a ship is operated as a time charterer. However, shipowners are obliged to prosecute voyages with utmost dispatch. Therefore, although the shipowner may be in a better position to ascertain how the ship should operate to maintain its CII rating, if the shipowner were to slow-steam or choose an unconventional route, they may be held liable for wrongful deviation, which is considered to be a repudiation of the contract, with very serious consequences. Further, deviation may be a breach of the shipowner's usual insurance policy.
- In VCPs, shipowners have the financial and contractual responsibility for bunkering, but here there is a different obstacle to achieving carbon emission

efficiency: the notion of demurrage, that is, payment to the shipowner for a vessel's delay in port. This incentivises the practice of 'sail fast, then wait', which is the largest systemic carbon inefficiency in maritime trade. This is discussed again, later in this chapter.
- Appreciation of the importance of charterparties in the DIMT has grown since the establishment of The Sea Cargo Charter in 2020. The introduction of IMO's CII regulations in 2023, and the forthcoming application of the EU ETS have increased awareness of features of charterparties that are inconsistent with carbon emission efficiency. Most of the present effort revolves around piecemeal additional clauses to long-established templates, which were never designed to deal with carbon emission efficiency. This often exacerbates the problems of CII as an imperfect metric. Over time, the focus will shift to the necessity for a new contractual architecture that would be consistent with the DIMT, which will include, but not be limited to charterparties.

Bills of Lading

Whilst charterparties and new fuels have attracted the attention of decarbonization debates both in the context of regulations, as well as in the voluntary space, the importance of Bills of Lading (BLs) in the DIMT is not widely appreciated. BLs often serve the function of a contract of carriage and present several features that can be problematic from the DIMT perspective:

- The paramount obligation of the carrier is to exercise due diligence to provide a seaworthy vessel, which is widely defined, and includes cargoworthiness, matters relating to equipment, crew qualifications and training. At the present state of evolution of maritime law, it does not include any concept of carbon emission efficiency (which could be termed 'greenworthiness'). English law has the flexibility to develop such a notion, as discussed in the section "The Third Pillar", later in this chapter.
- The standard of due diligence is that of a reasonably prudent shipowner, which may not overlap with activities of the so-called *first movers*. The adoption of new technologies and new fuels (and the related issues of training and safety) will raise questions as to whether the 'ambition' of a first mover conflicts with the established notion of due diligence of a prudent shipowner. Any discrepancy may result in breach of the seaworthiness obligation and, thus, liability on the part of the early adopters of decarbonization technologies.
- The obligation of the carrier under a BL to proceed with the utmost despatch to the discharge port (to the extent that safety is not compromised) is not qualified by the need for carbon emission efficiency. Similarly, speed reduction is treated as deviation, which is also a breach of contract. It is apparent that these features of BLs are inconsistent with any notion of operational carbon emission efficiency.

- The proliferation of charterparty clauses related to the IMO's CII regulations, as well as the metrics of the IMO Energy Efficiency Operational Indicator (EEOI) that enables operators to measure the fuel efficiency of a ship in operation and to gauge the effect of any changes in operation, will give rise to disputes as to whether they are effectively incorporated into BLs and as to their effect in that context.
- In the liner trade carriers have wide liberty to tranship the goods. This may result in carbon emission inefficiency and would need to be addressed contractually by cargo shippers and receivers interested in their Scope 3 carbon emissions.

Marine Insurance

The most significant marine insurance decarbonization initiative is the Poseidon Principles for Marine Insurance (PPMI), launched in December 2021. Currently, the PPMI are limited to Hull and Machinery (H&M), not Protection and Indemnity (P&I) insurers. The purpose is to obtain data about the carbon emission efficiency and climate alignment of their respective portfolios. Insurers have stated that they do not currently intend to use the data to determine premia and instead wish to work with clients to assist them decarbonize. However, in the longer term the wider insurance market may move towards carbon emission pricing and marine insurance would likely mirror such a general trend.

New fuels pose considerable insurance challenges: ammonia is highly toxic and poses risks to crew, people in proximity to vessels, and the environment. Methanol is another toxic potential fuel, though less so than ammonia.

Multiple projects are progressing to understand ammonia from a technical perspective, but the necessary legal framework is not yet in place. For instance, the International Convention on Civil Liability for Bunker Oil Pollution Damage (the Bunker Convention) does not cover ammonia. The risks and anticipated liabilities in the event of an incident involving the bunkering and operation of ammonia-fuelled ships will need to be addressed in both H&M and P&I insurance policies, and are likely to have a significant impact on insurance premia.

In addition to new fuels, there will also be a new cargo: ships will transport captured CO_2, requiring new types of insurance cover for cargo loss or for damage caused thereby. This is covered further under "Carbon Capture and Storage" in a later section of this chapter.

Another area in which the DIMT will impact upon marine insurance is the possible expansion of the concept of seaworthiness to include 'greenworthiness', as potential claims by cargo interests against shipowners falling within the expanded scope of P&I insurance might include excessive carbon emissions during the carriage of goods, or limitations placed on the routing of vessels or their access to certain ports. The areas outlined in the earlier sections "Charterparties" and "Bills of Lading" will also become relevant in relation to insuring liabilities thereunder.

Bunkering Contracts

Bunkering contracts resemble sale contracts, with the added complication that the buyer is often not the shipowner (in the case of a TCP). Such contracts are often in a chain, where the seller outsources the actual delivery of bunkers to a physical supplier.

Bunkering sometimes gives rise to quality disputes, often caused by the nature of bunkers as residual fuels of inherently poor quality. The introduction of biofuels and the emergence of dual-fuel ships will add layers of complexity not only to bunkering operations and fuel storage and consumption, but also to bunkering contracts. Four aspects stand out:

- The spot nature of bunkering is incompatible with the need of long-term offtake agreements, where the contract is made for a longer-term supply of fuel.
- The sale of biofuels and zero-carbon fuels introduces the entirely novel issue of their environmental attributes, which can be sold separately to the physical bunkers. The sophistication and complexity of carbon accounting (including, mass balance, and book and claim) is often not matched by a robust contractual architecture, while profound legal questions arise around fitness for purpose and transfer of title in environmental attributes.
- The operational aspects of ammonia bunkering will introduce complexities due to its toxicity. The allocation of responsibility, exclusions of liability and insurance aspects will require a complete rethinking of today's bunkering contracts.
- Pollution from bunkers is covered by the Bunker Convention, which applies to 'oil bunkers', and will require amendment to include non-fossil-fuel marine bunkers. In relation to ammonia, it is possible that an entirely new liability and compensation regime will become necessary, which may, in turn, require a new international convention.

Demolition Contracts

Contracts for demolition or, more optimistically, the recycling of ships focus in the main on prosaic matters such as the handover of the tonnage and compliance with the relevant international conventions: The Basel Convention on the Control of Transboundary Movements of Hazardous Wastes and their Disposal (Basel), which has been in force since 1992; and The Hong Kong International Convention for the Safe and Environmentally Sound Recycling of Ships (HK), which has yet to enter force except as the underpinning to the European Ship Recycling Regulation, and its United Kingdom equivalent.

Neither Basel nor the HKC has anything to say about carbon emissions. Their focus is on the more directly toxic substances used in ship construction. The same is true of the standard form demolition contracts. Over time, there is scope for reducing the carbon footprint of recycling operations. Suitable terms need to be introduced into the standard forms of ship-recycling contract. Four factors will contribute to this:

- The growth in the demolition market, as carbon-inefficient ships end their lives.
- Increasing awareness of the lifecycle emissions of ships consuming zero-carbon fuels, as the emissions from their operations are reduced or disappear.
- Increasing focus on shipowners' Scope 3 emissions, of which demolition forms part.
- Ship recycling has a principal role in producing steel with a lower carbon footprint than steel made from iron ore.

Towage and Salvage, Wreck Removal

While the carbon footprint of port tugs is relatively small, their operations are rather unusual in that they fall within both shipowners' and charterers' Scope 3 emissions. Contractually, port towage is treated as the owners' responsibility in a VCP, and a charterer's responsibility in a TCP. From a Scope 3 carbon emissions perspective, VCPs and TCPs will require 'green towage' provisions.

Salvage tug operations raise the prospect of carbon accounting as part of salvage payments, which would form part of the Scope 3 emissions of all salved interests: owners, charterers, as well as cargo interests.

Wreck removal, which often involves tugs, is the responsibility of insurers, and would form part of their Scope 3 emissions.

Vessel Sale and Purchase

The CII rating of a ship will likely transfer with the transfer from one owner to another. In such circumstances, new warranties and data will be required on ship sale and purchase and modifications will need to be made to the standard ship sale contract forms.

Carbon Capture and Storage

Carbon Capture and Storage (CCS) will have contractual impact in two main areas:

- CCS projects will probably be vertically integrated, similar to the early LNG projects. This may lead to the development of a bespoke contractual architecture that will cover shipment, transportation and discharge of CO_2. At a future point in time, a spot market for CO_2 may develop, which will lead to the need for different types of charterparties and sale contracts.

- As with any cargo carried by sea, there will be shortage claims, which will lead to complex questions as to liability, financial loss (including carbon credits), possible fines for leakage, and P&I insurance. It seems unlikely that there will be contamination issues, as there would be no value of the cargo linked to its quality. At present, CO_2 leakages would not be classified as pollution, but this could change.

Green Shipping Corridors

The Clydebank Declaration for green shipping corridors was launched in 2021 at the 26th UN Climate Change Conference (COP26). Green Shipping Corridors (GSCs) are a shipping route on which zero-carbon emissions ships and other emissions reduction programmes are deployed, and emissions reductions are measured and enabled through public and private actions and policies. COP26 set a target of at least six such routes to be operational by 2025. The Declaration envisages that GSCs will provide '*pockets of predictable demand for zero-carbon fuels at specific ports and accelerate operational learning on zero-carbon fuel production and bunkering*... [and] *encompass the full value chain including vessels, fuels, regulators and finance providers, and secured by demand from customers*'.

The policy considerations were mapped out in associated announcements, but there seems to be very little examination of the legal and contractual issues that GSCs will raise. By way of illustration:

- GSCs assume trade certainty and predictability, combined with the rigidity of dedicated ships. It is perfectly possible to design contracts that meet such requirements, but those will not be compatible with spot trading and spot chartering. The liner trade exhibits some of those characteristics, but the similarities are only superficial, as liner trade does not have a 'full value chain' element, as described earlier.
- The financing of ships plying the GSC routes will be a form of 'green' project finance (as opposed to the traditional shipping model of asset finance), including from the point of view of credit risk and capital regulation. It will need to fall within the eleven categories of 'Green Projects' listed in the Loan Market Association (LMA) Green Loan Principles, with loan agreements and security documents structured accordingly. Loan agreements would need to be linked to guaranteed income from charterparties spanning the entire life of the ship, as well as linked to long-term fuel offtake agreements for bunkers at predictable cost, with pure asset-focused security being of lesser importance in this context. From the perspective of the loan agreements, such contracts would need to exhibit very small tolerance for operational disruption and very limited application for exclusion clauses.
- Commercial employment of the vessels involved in GSCs would need to be through ultra-long-term charterparties with vetted counterparties and zero

counterparty risk. Performance guarantees or bonds will need to be involved. The traditional owner-charterer model may not be fit for purpose, thus dispensing with a charterparty altogether.
- Technical and crewing management of the vessels involved in GSCs cannot be done on the basis of the wide exclusions and limitation of liability of the present management contracts, as failure would be intolerable to the GSCs operational needs. For the same reason as above, the close integration necessary is likely to require that ship management is performed within a joint venture.
- From the perspective of the sale contracts for the commodities carried on board the ships in bulk trade GSCs, both integration and long-term duration will be vital. Ultra-long-term offtake agreements are often linked to equity participation, which will again point towards a type of joint venture model.
- To the extent that GSCs require the construction of zero-carbon ships, their full lifecycle emissions, from steel cutting to demolition, will need to be considered, as their operational emissions will be zero, as noted earlier in this chapter. Accordingly, a high level of predictability and integration with the shipyard and the ship demolition facility are likely to require a new type of contract that combines operations with shipbuilding and demolition.
- Accommodating contractual chains of any type within GSCs will be difficult, as contractual fragmentation will increase the risk of default.
- Domestic or intra-EU GSCs will raise anti-trust questions, for example, State aid, access to market, and to essential facilities. Unless wide-ranging exemptions are secured for the participants, anti-trust challenges will be inevitable. Outside the EU, GSCs may be underpinned by national legislation that would pre-empt such issues, possibly adding a protectionist layer, along the lines of the US Jones Act.

It is apparent from the above outline of the issues that GSCs, as envisaged by the Clydebank Declaration, are not compatible with the present contractual architecture of IMT. In essence, the overall structure is likely to be that of large-scale State-sponsored project finance, coupled with joint ventures handling the full spectrum of the activities that would be vital to the financial, commercial and operational viability of the project: shipbuilding, commercial employment, technical management, fuel offtake and bunkering, cargo offtake, vessel demolition, and recycling. The overall structure might resemble certain projects for gas production and LNG carriage, but with a deeper level of integration across a larger number of participants.

Green Shipping Corridors are discussed further in chapter "The In-House Production of Biofuel by Shipping Companies: A Case Study" of this book.

Sail Fast, then Wait: The Biggest Single Carbon Inefficiency in Maritime Trade

A common thread running through the fragmented world of IMT is that the ocean journeys of cargo ships are not systemically optimised, following the same operational practice since the age of sail: each vessel departs towards its destination at its own optimal speed, without regard for other vessels or for the conditions at the destination: '*Sail Fast, Then Wait*' (SFTW).

SFTW is reinforced by some of the features of the contractual architecture described above: laycan, speed warranties in TCPs, demurrage in VCPs and utmost dispatch in BLs—regardless of the conditions at the port of destination. Viewed from the perspective of supply chains, the contracts for sale and purchase of commodities also contain provisions that encourage SFTW.

Despite progress in weather routing and voyage planning of individual vessels, a systemic solution to SFTW has proved elusive and the two main attempts have been ineffectual:

- The concept of Virtual Arrival (VA) was developed in the early 2010s by the Oil Companies International Marine Forum (OCIMF), but has not gained traction. It is a bilateral contractual mechanism and does not address the wider supply chain. Similarly, it does not address the systemic optimisation problem—the fact that other vessels proceeding to the same port might steam at a higher speed to gain an advantage over those participating in VA.
- Just-in-time (JIT) systems have a systemic optimisation target, and operate outside any bilateral relationship between shipowners and charterers of one ship. However, JiT seeks to optimise port operations, rather than optimise the approaching vessels as a distinct system. By their nature, JiT systems are port-specific and cannot be deployed at the scale necessary for the DIMT.

SFTW is incompatible with the imperative of carbon emission efficiency for the purposes of shipowners' regulatory compliance, as well as with the emissions reduction Scope 3 commitments of users of ships. Beyond the transition, and in the era of zero-carbon fuels, SFTW will be incompatible with energy efficiency, which will be vital due to the much lower energy density of those fuels.

A project that seeks to eradicate SFTW is the Blue Visby Solution (BVS), which takes a systemic approach and deploys a contractual architecture embracing the entire supply chain. It also includes a sharing mechanism inspired by general average (a principle of maritime law whereby all stakeholders in a sea venture proportionately share any losses resulting from a voluntary sacrifice of part of the ship or cargo to save the whole in an emergency), designed to incentivise adoption, which can be reinforced through the ship finance facility documentation.

The Third Pillar

IMT currently rests on two contractual pillars: navigational safety and commercial orders. The former is the exclusive domain of the shipowner, and takes precedence over the latter, which is the domain of the charterer.

Carbon emission efficiency falls within neither of these two pillars, but it is now equally important, and requires a comprehensive and consistent contractual treatment, not merely a patchwork of charterparty clauses. It will be necessary to introduce a contractual framework for decarbonization actions and measures, which will take precedence over commercial orders, but will yield to safety. Such a *Third Pillar* would comprise two elements:

- 'Greenworthiness' with provisions that will discourage operational inefficiencies, while promoting the DIMT through mechanisms including optimised voyages, wind propulsion, retrofits, electricity supplies at port, freight rates dependent on CO_2 emission efficiency, emission warranties that will replace speed and consumption warranties.
- Structures that transcend the fragmented bilateral contractual landscape, which will support solutions that require multilateral collaboration, including off-take of new fuels; carefully designed GCs; systemic optimisation, such as the Blue Visby Solution discussed earlier.

Maritime Decarbonization and Climate Litigation

IMT is a litigious industry, as a consequence of features mentioned earlier, but also due to the risks and uncertainties that are inherent in ocean transportation.

A common narrative in the decarbonization debate is that somehow IMT will abandon its litigious nature, to be replaced by 'collaboration' during the energy transition and, presumably, also in the era of zero-carbon fuels.

An early indication that collaboration is not a panacea came during the industry deliberations in relation to an appropriate clause to deal with the IMO CII regulations. Disagreements and friction were reported in the press, and a proliferation of divergent clauses has emerged.

As is apparent from the above analysis, every aspect of IMT's contractual architecture will be impacted upon by decarbonization. This will lead to contractual disputes across the entire contractual spectrum. For example:

- Operational disputes arising out of IMO/EU regulatory compliance
- Technical disputes, including retrofit performance, bunker disputes, shipbuilding warranties
- Financial disputes, including interpretation of standards, KPI compliance
- Collaboration disputes, including anti-trust, intellectual property, information sharing disputes

- Voluntary Carbon Market disputes regarding projects, the secondary market, offsets, insets, mass balance, book and claim—especially in the context of the absence of regulation and standardisation of carbon accounting and
- Greenwashing disputes, while it is conceivable that the Brussels Convention 1952 on ship arrests will be used strategically in certain jurisdictions, as a means of attracting attention

Many disputes will arise from contracts under English law. In those cases, the English courts will be called upon not only to define key notions (for example, carbon intensity, environmental attributes of biofuels, and zero-carbon fuels), but also expand the boundaries of maritime law, perhaps developing notions such as *greenworthiness* or the *Third Pillar*, mentioned above.

Through the prism of evolution of maritime law, litigation is not only inevitable, but also desirable. In the history of maritime trade, the English courts have been instrumental in defining and expanding notions such as safe ports, unseaworthiness, due diligence, and fitness for purpose, which are indispensable in IMT.

The Future

The following points can be identified as critical to the decarbonization of international maritime trade in the coming years:

- Maritime trade is a web of contractual relationships, which has evolved through a process of gradual adaptation to changing needs, assisted by the flexibility of common (predominantly, English) law and underpinned by the principles of freedom of navigation, freedom of contract and party autonomy. This was achieved within a very light regulatory framework, comprising a small number of international conventions, national laws of Flag States and Port States, supranational legislative production (predominantly, in recent years, from the EU) and IMO regulations. Litigation has played a major role in defining and clarifying notions, and in the process of evolution of maritime law.
- It is conceptually possible to re-design international maritime trade, so that it resembles a regulated industry. However, that will require a wholesale repudiation of the existing contractual architecture, a series of new international conventions, and a new international organisation to regulate commodities trading and port activities, which are hitherto not subject to international uniformity. Even if this process were desirable to the international community and acceptable to market participants, it would take decades to complete and cause considerable dislocation.
- From a legal and contractual perspective, the decarbonization debate that focuses exclusively on policy, the role of the IMO and of governments is misplaced, especially as it does not place sufficient emphasis on the raison d' être of cargo ships: to perform obligations assumed under contracts for the sale of goods.

- The contractual and legal challenges of certain aspects of Green Shipping Corridors are formidable. The ocean transportation of bulk commodities cannot be converted into a series of GSCs without an entirely new contractual paradigm that would encompass the entire life of a vessel, both as a hull (from steel cutting to demolition), but also as the embodiment of a series of contracts—finance, fuel, operations, cargo, and technical management.
- The imperative of carbon emission efficiency (and energy efficiency, in the era of new fuels) is very difficult to achieve within today's fragmented contractual environment. Contractual norms that result in carbon inefficiencies (including, demurrage, speed warranties, utmost despatch, laycans) will need to be reconsidered. It will become increasingly difficult to achieve the necessary efficiencies through the process of additional clauses to existing contractual templates. A complete re-appraisal of charterparties, bills of lading, the carbon element of sale contracts for commodities, as well as finance documents will be necessary. A Third Pillar must emerge, in which a new notion of greenworthiness will complement seaworthiness and navigational safety, and will override commercial expediency. Multilateral structures will need to evolve to deal with the carbon emission dysfunctions of bilateral contracts.
- The cost, limited availability, operational uncertainty, and low energy density of new fuels will require changes to contracts relating to fuel purchase, bunkering, chartering, vessel operations, technical management, and carriage of goods. Zero-carbon fuels cannot simply be 'dropped into' the existing contractual architecture of international maritime trade.
- Ammonia fuels will raise difficult and complex issues regarding liabilities, operational obligations and insurance, and may require not only new IMO regulations, but also amendments to international conventions for environmental protection.
- Environmental attributes of new fuels will require their own contractual regime, especially in the absence of global standards of carbon emissions accounting.
- A drive towards integration and multilateral contracts will raise anti-trust questions, especially when combined with State aid.
- An international convention on maritime decarbonization may represent a more efficient approach (especially with regard to market-based measures) than the present expectation that the IMO or the EU or national governments can address, in a uniform manner, all legal issues relating to maritime decarbonization.

In summary, no maritime decarbonization target can be achieved without an appropriate and realistic re-consideration of the contractual architecture of international maritime trade, rather than simply the regulation of ships by the IMO.

References

Chatzinikolaou, S. D., & Ventikos, N. P. (2014, October). Applications of life cycle assessment in shipping. In *2nd international symposium on naval architecture and maritime, Istanbul, Turkey*.

Stopford, M. (2008). *Maritime economics* (3rd ed.). Taylor and Francis.

Engaging the Global Research Communities in Maritime Decarbonization

Teemu Manderbacka and Ellinor Forsström

Target Audience

This chapter has been written for those seeking knowledge and additional information to guide their efforts within decarbonization projects aimed at various parts of the maritime industry. It may concern both technical and behavioural aspects. Typically, this would be project managers in industry-driven projects as well as decision-makers for dedicating and approving finance for sustainability efforts.

Key Takeaway Messages

In this chapter, emphasis is placed on:

- Different types of research have different roles; applied research is necessary in the latter stages closer to implementation with basic research aimed at more foundational knowledge development.
- Company R&D efforts should be supported by engagement with research institutes.
- There is a need for global research collaboration to cope with the global industry needs.
- Pilot implementations and demonstration are necessary to guide the industry in their efforts towards maritime decarbonization.

T. Manderbacka (✉)
VTT Technical Research Centre of Finland, Espoo, Finland
e-mail: teemu.manderbacka@vtt.fi

E. Forsström
Research Institutes of Sweden (RISE), Lund, Sweden
e-mail: ellinor.forsstrom@ri.se

M. Lind et al. (eds.), *Maritime Decarbonization*,
https://doi.org/10.1007/978-3-031-39936-7_17

- The role of research centres and public investments are crucial to push emerging technologies further up the technology readiness level (TRL) scale.

The Research Communities

As shown in Fig. 1, research communities can be divided roughly into entities performing; basic research (universities), applied research (national research centres or institutes), and research and development for the industry (companies' research units and industry research centres or institutes). This is a rough division and clearly different entities are not limited to only performing the above-mentioned types of research, instead the research by different entities is normally overlapping. Nevertheless, this rough division of the research communities helps us to understand how different research entities are engaged in research driving maritime decarbonization and how their results can be applied.

Types of Research and Related Constraints

Research entities and the type of research they perform vary globally. However, there are several key distinctions. Typically, universities in Europe and Asia operate under specific mandates and requirements from their national governments and are

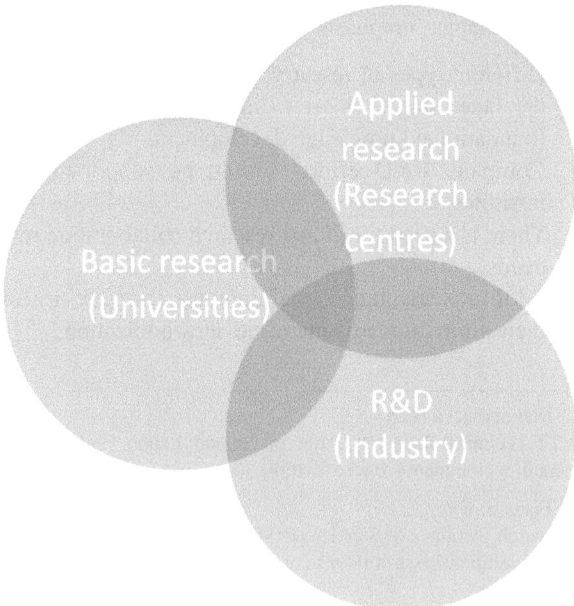

Fig. 1 Rough division of the research communities

tasked to perform research and give education at the highest academic level and serve society. While in the US and UK universities may have more autonomy, the funding mechanisms emphasise scientific quality and impact. These tasks and mechanisms typically require universities to adhere to open research result publication. Although, depending on the national laws under which the universities operate, they can and do, to some extent, perform company specific research, where results are not openly shared. Many research centres are generally either fully or partly owned or controlled by national governments. Thus, they may then be called national research institutes. However, especially the US and UK have extensive networks of universities and private research institutions that operate independently of direct government ownership. In addition, many large companies have introduced research centres or institutes either as their own endeavours or together with other companies, to support their own research and development units. National and private research centres perform both publicly funded research, where the results are also published, and company specific research projects in which case the ownership of the results, the intellectual property rights and any patents can be moved to the ordering company according to previously made agreements. Naturally company specific research centres perform confidential research for the company benefit. An example is Wärtsilä's Sustainable Technology Hub (STH). [1]

The TRL and the time scope for the application of results varies from lower TRL and longer time scope basic research to the highest TRL and shortest time scope to the market ready solutions of industry R&D. Totally new technologies can emerge from fruitful collaboration between these various entities. In optimal cases, advances in basic research are applied to existing technologies and combined in a novel way to satisfy industry needs. Collaboration is the key. The effective exchange of knowledge from research advances together with the identification of industry requirements and any market or business case boundaries to the applied research, can lead to successful innovations.

Research Funding and Demand

The availability of research funding directs the topics. Within the European area, dialogue between the maritime industry and public research funding institutions is coordinated under Waterborne TP [2] (Transportation Platform) the European research and innovation platform for waterborne industries. The European Commission has agreed with Waterborne TP on a co-Partnership Program (cPP) called Zero Emission Waterborne Transportation (ZEWT) under which Horizon Europe research funding calls are announced. Waterborne TP and the ZEWT are significant and successful endeavours of the European maritime community, encompassing many different

[1] https://www.sustainabletechnologyhub.com/

[2] https://waterborne.eu/

actors in the maritime transport sector, ranging from port and ship side stakeholders to inland navigation and from industry to research communities.

In a report (ICS and Ricardo, 2021) published by the International Chamber of Shipping (ICS) towards the end of 2021 it was emphasised that massive scaling up of finance for research and development (R&D) is essential to achieve net-zero carbon emissions by 2050 in the shipping industry. To meet the International Maritime Organization (IMO) emissions targets, thousands of vessels running with zero carbon powertrains will need to be operating by 2030 and most vessels will need to be zero-carbon by 2040. Currently, 95% of the ships in the world fleet run on conventional fuels. Although orders of newbuild vessels operating on alternative fuels are on the rise (38% in 2022 from 28% in 2021 of the newbuild orderbook by tonnage), still more than half of the ordered vessels are set to use conventional fuels. These figures can partly be explained by the fact that more than 60% of the emissions reductions required in 2050 will come from technologies that are not commercially available today. This clearly points to the need for research effort.

The role of research centres and public investments will be crucial to pushing appropriate technologies further up the TRL-scale. The latest figures from the International Energy Agency (IEA) regarding private-sector R&D spending in the maritime domain has fallen from \$2.7 billion in 2017 to \$1.6 billion in 2019 (IEA, 2022). This is much lower than the estimated financial requirement. In the publication from ICS (ICS and Ricardo, 2021) more than 260 example R&D projects are identified and labelled as necessary to overcome key technical and systemic challenges and accelerate the transition to net-zero carbon emissions in shipping. In total, the cost for all these endeavours is estimated to be \$4.4 billion in funding and a majority of the projects identified will take between 1 and 6 years to reach commercialisation. As the lifespan of a ship often falls in the range of 20–30 years the need for research effort and R&D funding is now, in order that industry can meet the emission targets. It is important that government and industry act now to collaborate effectively to push forward and ensure that policies, funding, and incentives are in place to perform the much-needed R&D efforts in shipping.

According to a recent publication by Lloyd's Register (Lloyd's Register, 2022), which keeps track of the TRL, IRL (investment readiness level) and CRL (community readiness level) for alternative fuels for the maritime industry, the top three topics are summarised as 'scaling technology', 'stimulating investments' and 'ensuring sustainability'. In terms of the former, many technologies remain to be scaled-up to a level which could achieve a wider impact in the industry. As an example, if the connected fuel supply technologies are not scaled-up in the nearest future, the fuel will not be available in the volumes needed to supply the growing uptake of zero emission vessels. This includes land-based infrastructure, such as, energy resources, production, and bunkering technologies.

Some examples of areas that need scaling-up to avoid bottlenecks for decarbonization are electrolyser dimensioned for renewable marine fuel production purposes, direct air capture technologies to be scaled-up to produce renewable methanol, demonstrations of carbon capture and storage (CCS) designed for production of natural gas derived fuels and last but not least, bunkering for alternative fuels on a larger scale, in particular ship-to-ship. In all these areas, collaboration between private R&D and research centres providing test and demonstration facilities, play an important part.

When it comes to the topic of 'stimulating investments' the top priorities according to Lloyd's Register includes the formation of regulatory incentives to ensure price competitiveness of zero-carbon fuels and also the need to establish green corridors—specific trade routes between major port hubs where net-zero emission solutions are supported, to demonstrate fuel requirements in specific locations. Especially in the latter case, the combined efforts of applied research, R&D and basic research is crucial, as the realisation of a green corridor for any of the alternative fuels today requires effort at all levels of the TRL-scale.

For the last topic, 'ensuring sustainability', the Lloyd's Register report points out the existing knowledge gap over understanding the long-term sustainability of the fuel choices and the linked technologies that are now being considered. More detailed life cycle assessment (LCA) is needed to study the environmental and socio-economic aspects of the fuel alternatives as informed input to regulatory policies concerning standards for fuel production and usage. This task will most probably fall on the applied research players and universities.

The Need for Pilot Projects and Technology Demonstrators

Substantial R&D effort is still required to make the technologies expected to contribute to the lowering of emissions from shipping by 2050 market ready. The TRL of the most frequently discussed alternative fuels, such as ammonia, hydrogen, methanol (bio or CCS) falls in the range of TRL 4–7. This means that the readiness level is ranging from validated in lab to operational demonstrations and the technologies are ranging from in development to deployment phases. Reaching TRL 9 (proven in an operational environment) still represents a significant leap in maturity and can take from several years to decades, depending on various factors such as availability of funding and level of collaboration. This highlights the need for large scale testing, and validation in the real environment with full-scale pilot demonstrations. This type of system demonstration should address all five dimensions of system innovation (Vinnova, 2022):

- Technology, products, and processes
- Business models and procurement
- Policy and regulations
- Behaviour, culture, and values
- Infrastructure

In a report 'Mapping of Zero Emission Pilots and Demonstration Projects' (Getting to Zero Coalition, 2022), pilot and demonstration projects are described as the key to accelerate the energy transition within the maritime industry. In the same report, a comprehensive screening of current pilot projects is presented and reviewed. The

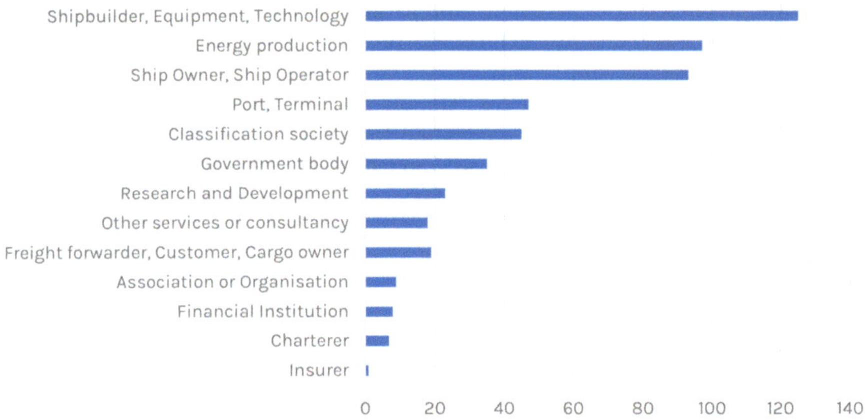

Fig. 2 Pilot and demonstration project participation by different parts of the value chain (source: Getting to Zero Coalition, 2022)

number of pilot and demonstration projects has grown rapidly during 1 year. At the time of publication in March 2022, 203 projects were identified, compared to 106 projects a year earlier.

The acceleration in the number of projects also indicates the industry's increased interest and need to decarbonize. Among the identified projects, 67% of the projects focus primarily on ship technology, 31% on fuel production, and 19% on bunkering and infrastructure. A number of the projects encompass two or all three focus areas. Regarding the nature of the projects, 65% fall under the category 'demonstration in normal operations', 34% represent concept studies and 4% laboratory testing. Most of the projects are at a higher TRL, where the technology is tested in a real and relevant environment.

The consortia structure for the projects is notable. In the report, the importance of initiatives that include representatives from different parts of the value-chain is highlighted, both in terms of succeeding with the establishment of green corridors and for conducting viable demo-projects. As can be seen in Fig. 2, among the different types of stakeholders, the most recurring was 'Shipbuilder/Equipment/Technology', 'Energy production', and 'Ship owner/Ship operator'.

The importance of initiatives that consist of representatives from different parts of the value-chain is also highlighted in Fig. 2. 84% of the projects involve multiple types of stakeholders and 20% of the projects include stakeholders from more than four categories. This indicates an importance and need for collaboration.

Green Corridors

The need for broad industry/stakeholder collaboration becomes even more clear when the concept of green corridors is considered. As stated in University Maritime Advisory Services (UMAS) (2021), in order to achieve the IMO's Initial GHG

Strategy 2030 and 2050 emission targets, at least 5% of the world fleet needs to have adopted carbon neutral fuels by 2030. The percentage is even higher after the 2023 agreement on the IMO GHG Strategy. This requires a rapid scaling-up of both the fuel production and connected infrastructure. Even if over 200 projects regarding alternative fuels for shipping are already underway globally, the actual uptake, as previously described, is still very low.

To accelerate and widen the effects of all demo/pilot activities and create greater impact, green shipping corridors are being seen as the way forward. Green corridors are specific trade routes between major port hubs where net-zero emission solutions are being supported. In a green corridor one or several alternative fuels that can be considered green are available and in use in real traffic and at scale, with all surrounding infrastructure in place covering at least the two terminal ports on the corridor route. The benefit of this concept is that it allows for the multitude of barriers hindering the global uptake of zero-emission fuels, such as technical, practical, organisational, legal, political, and financial issues, to be addressed and resolved on a manageable scale and spread among multiple stakeholders, rather than tackling the issues on a currently uncontrollable global scale in multiple isolated projects and diverse locations. Green corridors allow a whole net-zero emission system to be demonstrated and integrated. By doing this, the multiple benefits for participants can be realised and the beneficial experiences used to encourage further uptake on other routes, thereby eventually achieving an ever-increasing global uptake. Figure 3 shows a number of Public/Private, Industry/Third sector, and Government led Green Corridor initiatives that are underway or planned.

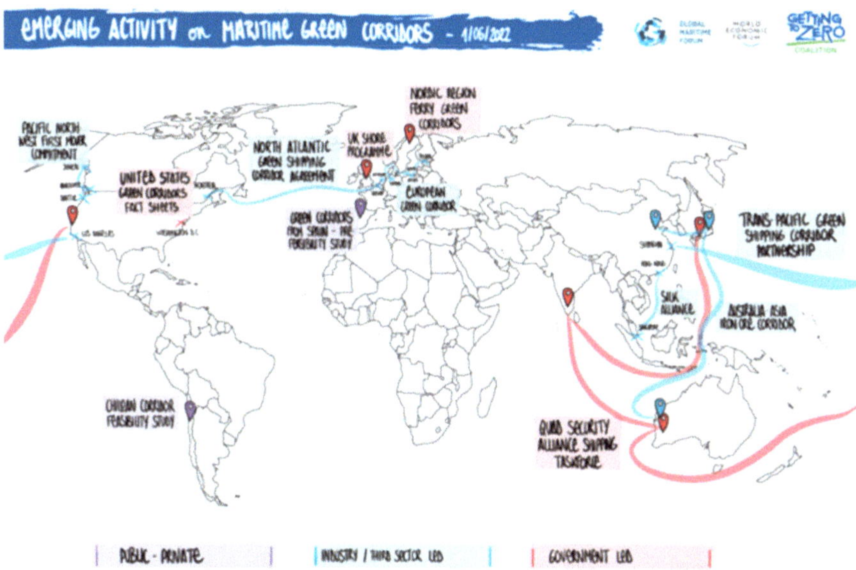

Fig. 3 Emerging activity on Maritime Green Corridors (source: Global Maritime Forum, 2022)

Examples of Maritime Decarbonization Research

The research focus of the various partnership initiatives engaged in decarbonizing the shipping industry varies. The following summaries indicate that range:

- The Global Centre for Maritime Decarbonisation (GCMD) [3] is a non-profit organisation to support the maritime industry in its decarbonization goals. It comprises the Maritime and Port Authority of Singapore (MPA), BHP, BW, DNV Foundation, Eastern Pacific Shipping, Ocean Network Express and Sembcorp Marine.
- The Mærsk Mc-Kinney Møller Center for Zero Carbon Shipping [4] is a non-profit, independent research and development centre. It aims to accelerate the transition towards a net-zero future for the maritime industry by facilitating implementation of new technologies and driving systemic and regulatory change. The centre includes 53 partners consisting of all the stakeholders within the maritime ecosystem.
- The Blue Sky Coalition [5] strives to accelerate the transition of waterborne transportation in Canada and the United States toward net-zero greenhouse gas emissions by accelerating the development of vessels and infrastructure, encouraging innovation in commercial and operational practice, and promoting policies supporting transition to net-zero emissions.
- The Global Maritime Forum (GMF) [6] is a non-profit organisation that brings together stakeholders from across the shipping industry to identify and address challenges related to decarbonization. The GMF brings together decision-makers from across the maritime spectrum to work on initiatives exploring ways to develop solutions for a safe, clean, inclusive, and efficient maritime industry.

In addition to the above partnership initiatives, there are many research groups and initiatives focused on maritime decarbonization within universities and research institutes. These groups are focused on developing technologies and strategies for reducing greenhouse gas emissions from the shipping industry, such as wind-assisted propulsion systems and batteries for ships, alternative net-zero carbon fuels and power sources and carbon capture and storage technologies.

[3] https://www.gcformd.org/
[4] https://www.zerocarbonshipping.com/
[5] https://www.bluesky-maritime.org/
[6] https://www.globalmaritimeforum.org/

Role to the Research Communities in Accelerating Decarbonization

Research communities play an important role in the efforts to decarbonize maritime transport by identifying and developing technologies and strategies that can reduce greenhouse gas emissions from shipping. This can include the development of low-carbon fuels and propulsion technologies, as well as the identification of policies and regulatory measures that can encourage the adoption of these technologies.

Research can also help to inform the public and policymakers about the potential benefits and challenges of transitioning to a low-carbon shipping industry. In this way supporting decarbonization efforts and encouraging the adoption of policies and regulations that support the transition to low-carbon shipping.

In addition, research can help to identify and assess the potential impacts of decarbonization on different stakeholders, including ship owners, cargo owners, and port communities. This can help to ensure that decarbonization efforts are fair and equitable, and that the benefits of decarbonization are shared by all stakeholders.

The role of research in decarbonizing maritime transport is to identify and develop technologies and strategies that can reduce greenhouse gas emissions from the shipping industry, inform the public and policymakers about the potential benefits and challenges of decarbonization, and assess the potential impacts of decarbonization on different stakeholders.

References

Getting to Zero Coalition. (2022). *Mapping of zero emission pilots and demonstration projects* (3rd ed.). https://www.globalmaritimeforum.org/content/2022/03/Mapping-of-zero-emission-pilots-and-demonstration-projects_third-edition.pdf

Global Maritime Forum. (2022). *Discussion paper—Green corridors: Definitions and approaches*. A Discussion paper from the Global Maritime Forum. https://www.globalmaritimeforum.org/content/2022/08/Discussion-paper_Green-Corridors-Definitions-and-Approaches.pdf

ICS and Ricardo. (2021). A zero emission blueprint for shipping. https://www.ics-shipping.org/wp-content/uploads/2021/11/A-zero-emission-blueprint-for-shipping.pdf. Accessed 9 Mar 2023.

IEA. (2022). Global corporate R&D spending of selected sectors, 2007-2019 (last update 26 Oct 2022). https://www.iea.org/data-and-statistics/charts/global-corporate-r-and-d-spending-of-selected-sectors-2007-2019-2

Lloyd's Register. (2022). Zero carbon fuel monitor, July 2022 update. https://www.lr.org/en/marine-shipping/maritime-decarbonisation-hub/zcfm/findings/

University Maritime Advisory Services (UMAS). (2021). A strategy for the transition to zero-emission shipping, 27 Oct 2021. https://www.globalmaritimeforum.org/content/2021/10/A-Strategy-for-the-Transition-to-Zero-Emission-Shipping.pdf

Vinnova. (2022). Vinnova develops system innovation for a sustainable future (last updated 29 June 2022). https://www.vinnova.se/en/m/vinnova-develops-system-innovation-for-a-sustainable-future/

The Implications of Circular Supply Chains and the EU Digital Product Passport in Maritime Decarbonization

Henrik Hvid Jensen, Henrik Sornn-Friese, Steffen Foldager Jensen, and Nicolò Aurisano

Target Audience

This chapter has been written to assist decision makers within the industry and maritime equipment manufacturers on the implications of the circular economy and the European Union proposed Digital Product Passport on the value, manufacture, use, re-use and disposal of materials throughout the maritime transportation value chain.

Key Takeaway Messages

The key points in this chapter are that:

- without a competitive global circular economy, the maritime sector will never be able to reach the global climate and environmental targets;
- circular economy principles should be built into every stage of the maritime equipment life cycle—from design to construction; to operations and recycling;

H. H. Jensen (✉)
DXC Technology Denmark, Copenhagen, Denmark
e-mail: henrikhvid.jensen@dxc.com

H. Sornn-Friese
Copenhagen Business School, Frederiksberg, Denmark
e-mail: hs.si@cbs.dk

S. F. Jensen
Aalborg University, Aalborg, Denmark
e-mail: steffenfj@mp.aau.dk

N. Aurisano
A.P. Moller Maersk A/S, Copenhagen, Denmark
e-mail: nicolo.aurisano@maersk.com

M. Lind et al. (eds.), *Maritime Decarbonization*,
https://doi.org/10.1007/978-3-031-39936-7_18

- the Digital Product Passport is a key to create the digital landscape, data-exchange mechanisms, and transparency needed to close information gaps in maritime circular value chains enabling informed decision-making throughout a product's lifetime;
- reaching the global climate and environmental goals requires collaborations to enable a coherent and competitive maritime circular economy; and
- given the maritime sector's pivotal role in global trade, expediting maritime circularity becomes vital for other industries to achieve their climate and environmental objectives.

The Next Economy: The Circular Economy

Imagine an economy where resources get used, but not used up. Where new business strategies keep products, components, materials, and energy in the system, both during their use and after. And where dangerous, dirty waste is kept to an absolute minimum.

You have just imagined the circular economy.

It is called 'circular' because it is based on the idea of closing the loop of resource use and waste generation, in contrast to a more traditional 'linear' economy in which products are made, used, and then discarded. Recently, the linear economy has been modified somewhat with recycling,[1] which adds some reuse and removes some waste. But, as illustrated in Fig. 1, a truly circular economy goes much further. It creates a virtuous circle around use that includes making, repairing, refurbishing, remanufacturing, reusing, and recycling.

Without a competitive global circular economy, we will never be able to reach the global climate and environmental goals. The current leading sustainability measures in the maritime sector as well as most other industries focus primarily on electrification and alternative fuels, including the July 2023 published International Maritime Organization (IMO) greenhouse gas (GHG) Strategy. However, these two paths together only address 55% of emissions. The remaining 45% comes from producing the cars, clothes, food, equipment, and other products we use every day (Ellen Macarthur Foundation, 2021). The circular economy offers a systematic response to the pending climate and environmental crisis by both reducing emissions and increasing resilience to its effects.

The benefits of a circular economy include (Jensen, 2023a, 2023b):

- Transforming today's 'throwaway economy' by eliminating waste and pollution, and by recirculating resources.
- Simultaneously tackling both climate change and biodiversity loss.
- Separating economic growth from the consumption of natural resources.

---

[1] Recycling includes cascading where resources are first used in their highest-value application, and then passed down through a series of lower-value applications until they reach the end of their useful life.

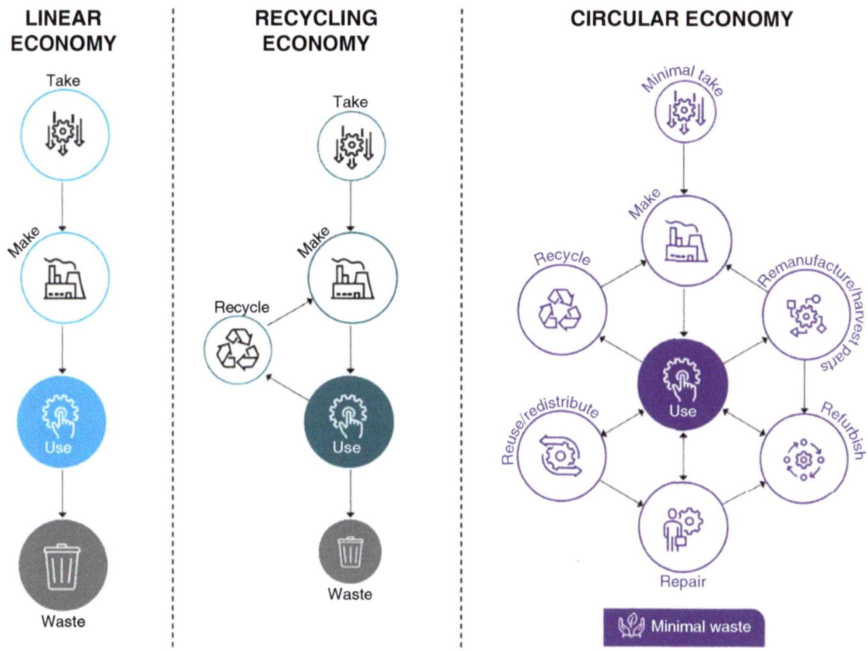

Fig. 1 A truly circular economy creates a virtuous circle around use that includes making, returns, repairs, refurbishing, remanufacturing, reuse and recycling—Source DXC Technology (Jensen, 2023a, 2023b)

- Gains of new jobs, general prosperity, and overall resilience—as well as dramatically lowered GHG emissions, waste, and pollution.
- New business cases that are both sustainable and competitive.

This chapter examines the circular economy transition in the maritime sector, which is a significant consumer of resources (energy and raw materials) and a major contributor to global GHG emissions. A special focus is on the European Union (EU) Digital Product Passport (DPP), which is expected to be a cornerstone in a global circular economy across all industries, including the maritime sector.

The share of shipping in total world trade is substantial, given that around 80% of the goods are carried by ships globally (UNCTAD, 2023). The size of the merchant fleet—and therefore the majority of maritime assets, is directly correlated with world trade volume. More than 100,000 ships sail globally, of which 57% are more than 15 years old (UNCTAD, 2023). International shipping accounts for approximately 3% of global GHG emissions and is considered a hard-to-abate sector. For the full decarbonization of shipping, we need both a clean energy transition at a massive scale, shifting from fossil fuels to renewable energy and low GHG emissions fuels as well as a transition to a competitive maritime circular economy.

The transition to a circular economy will impact all industries, not least being heavy equipment manufacturers, by adopting circular economy thinking, generating economic benefits by creating new business models, reducing costs, and increasing profitability. However, even though circular economy business models, such as remanufacturing, are widespread among sectors that produce capital-intensive and durable goods (including other transportation sectors such as aircraft, aerospace, automotive and rail), they tend to be underdeveloped in the maritime industry (Wahab et al., 2018; Milios et al., 2019; Sornn-Friese et al., 2021).

We believe that study of the circular economy in the maritime sector can provide valuable insights into the unique challenges and opportunities of this industry, and how circular economy principles can be applied to create a more sustainable, efficient, and profitable sector. We also believe that these insights can be applied to other sectors of the economy, helping to accelerate the transition to a more circular and regenerative economic model. For example, the maritime sector is characterised by complex and interconnected supply chains that span multiple industries and geographic regions. Studying the circular economy in this context can thus provide insights into how circular economy principles can be applied across an entire supply chain, from raw material extraction to end-of-life disposal.

However, while the circular economy discussion is advancing quickly in many sectors, and circular economy principles are beginning to appear more commonly in many regulatory frameworks, the application of its principles is still limited in the maritime sector.

The maritime sector is actively responding to the global decarbonization challenge by focusing on a transition towards alternative fuels, renewable energy, and enhancing energy efficiency. This approach is crucial since, for many shipping companies, over 90% of their Scope 1 GHG emissions (those generated directly by the company) are directly linked to fuel consumption (Yiqi Zhang, 2022). It follows that much of the effort of the industry is towards reducing the GHG emissions related to fuel usage. Traditionally, the focus has been on quantifying GHG emissions using a 'tank to wake' system boundary approach, that is, limiting the assessment to the emissions related to onboard fuel combustion. More recently, the industry's focus has been expanded to a 'well to wake' system boundary approach, in other words, covering the GHG emissions over the full life cycle of the fuel. This is shown as the yellow row in Fig. 2.

'Tank to wake' emissions of alternative fuels can provide a distorted view of the climate impacts of those fuels (Carvalho et al., 2023). However, these perspectives alone present an incomplete understanding of the issue. For example, little has been done on reducing and minimising the GHG emissions related to the life cycle of ships—this is the role of the circular economy.

Despite occupying a significant position in the global economy, the maritime industry is currently facing notable gaps in terms of circularity (Okumus et al., 2022). It is essential to recognise that establishing a circular economy within the maritime industry is a fundamental and necessary step towards reaching the sector's climate targets. By embracing circularity, the industry can unlock additional avenues for reducing emissions thereby achieving sustainability goals beyond the scope of fuel usage alone. Additionally, the circular economy offers attractive business

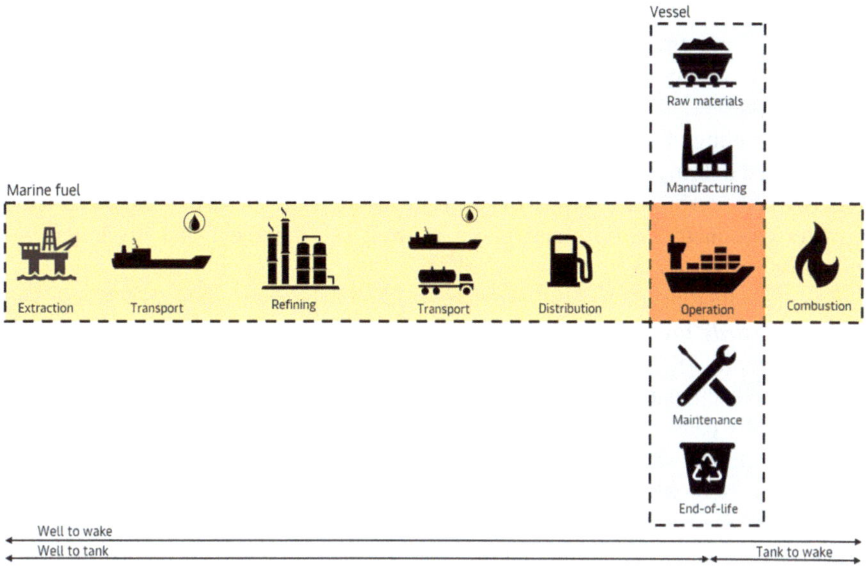

Fig. 2 Example of the life cycle of a marine fuel (yellow row) and its interaction with the life cycle of a vessel (light blue bow). The two life cycles overlap during the operation (use phase). The arrows at the bottom of the figure graphically represent the differences between the 'well to wake', 'well to tank' and 'tank to wake' approaches when assessing the GHG emissions related to marine fuel

models, including how well-implemented circular business models are superior in eight dimensions compared to a linear economy (Jensen, 2023a, 2023b).

The maritime industry is playing a key role in facilitating the movement of materials and waste to enable a global competitive circular economy. It is, therefore, a critical component in realising other industries' circular opportunities.

Logistics will be the engine driving the circular economy. The current operating models of the logistic service providers (LSP) primarily support a linear economy. The circular economy enables an even more important and expanded role for LSPs (Jensen & Clarke, 2023). It is therefore important for any actors within logistics to prepare for the global circular economy and endorse the circular principles to ensure that logistics reduce barriers for any industries' transition to circularity that includes their logistics requirements.

Circularity within Maritime

There are several '*semi-circular business models*' in the existing maritime industry such as sharing equipment in container logistics, chartering, reselling ships, and ship demolition (Jensen et al., 2021). However, there is a significant way to go to enabling a coherent and efficient global circular maritime sector, that is both competitive and environmentally responsible, and has a clear strategy to eliminate waste and ensure products and materials are kept at their highest value for as long a time as possible.

The recycling of ships is widespread in the maritime industry, and the industry is experienced in bringing assets back to the material flow. The principal commododity is steel but many other types of materials (including hydrocarbons, ferrous/non-ferrous metals, wood, and glass) as well as equipment and machinery are available for recycling.[2]

On the other hand, it has been identified '*that current practices in the ship recycling yards prevent the full utilisation of the industry's recycling potential*'(-Okumus et al., 2022). Additionally, recycling is at the end of the circular economy intention to keep materials in use at the highest possible value for as long as possible, as it typically causes a reduction in quality. If the recycling yards have information readily available (which is the purpose of the EU's DPP) and processes implemented to circulate steel while avoiding its contamination, the industry can contribute to (UNEP, 2018) estimation that a circular steel economy would avoid 500 M tons of additional primary steel production by 2050. This corresponds to more than 1 billion tons of CO_2 equivalent (CO_2e) emissions per year.

According to Danish Maritime,[3] a ship can, depending on its type and size, include equipment and components from more than 2000 different suppliers. Ships are complex because they must operate in a harsh ocean environment (which includes corrosion and often-times extreme wave forces) while carrying thousands of tons of cargo, and because a crew both works and lives on board, which places special demands on the working environment (such as ergonomics, safety, security, connectivity, and well-being). Table 1 provides a generalised overview of the main categories of components, equipment and machinery on ships and provides examples of equipment in each category. A large commercial vessel can contain tens of thousands of components, equipment, and machinery.

In addition, compared to cars, trains and planes, ships are built in short series, which means that design and class approval is typically carried out on a case-by-case basis and require sophisticated engineering effort and close interaction with the individual customer. Often, the equipment installed on a ship will be developed during the shipbuilding process (Emblemsvåg, 2014). Shipbuilding can thus be characterised as a complex engineering-to-order (ETO) supply chain (Alfnes et al.,

[2]Ship recycling must comply with relevant international regulation, including the Hong Kong Convention (IMO, 2009) the European Union Ship Recycling Regulation (EU, 2013), the Basel Convention, the Basel Ban Amendment, and the European Waste Shipment Regulation. This may have the implication that certain used equipment on board an end-of-life ship may be considered as waste and hence subject to an export ban.

[3]Danish Maritime is the main industry association for the shipyards and marine supplies industry in Denmark.

Table 1 Equipment on ships. Based on (BALance Technology, 2014)

Main equipment category	Examples
Propulsion and power generation	Diesel engines (two stroke and four stroke); turbines; gears and couplings; propeller; shafts and bearings; electrical engines
Auxiliary power generation	Generator sets; auxiliary boilers
Electrical systems, plants, and cables	Switchboards; control panels; cables; batteries; fuels cells; electric accumulators
Instrumentation, control, and navigation	Consoles; automation systems; alarm/safety systems and components; navigation equipment; radar plants; cargo control; compasses; trim and load indicators; hydraulic or pneumatic control and display systems
Communication and entertainment	Radio equipment; telephones; data processing systems; entertainment systems; audio; video
Lighting	Electric lighting systems for engine and boiler room, electric lighting systems for accommodation, electric lighting systems for decks and cargo holds; electrical heaters; signal lights; radiators
Steering	Steering gear; hydraulic oil systems; rudders; accessories
Special ship operations	Thrusters; special rudders; roll-damping; anti-heeling systems; stabiliser fins and fin-moving machinery; stabiliser tanks and pumps; berthing aid systems
Mooring, deck machinery	Anchor and chains; mechanical brakes; chain stoppers; winches; ropes and fenders; towing systems; accessories (bollards, hawse-pipes, etc.); lube oil systems; deck cleaning machines; hull cleaning machines; common cleaning equipment
Safety, lifesaving, and environmental protection	Boats and lifeboats; davits, cranes and ramps; lifebuoys, rescue nets; lifejackets; thermal protection bags; survival suits; line-throwing appliances; distress signalling equipment, distress rockets; MARPOL equipment (such as oil skimmers, spray booms, chemicals)
General outfitting	Stairs, ladders, catwalk, railing, etc.; emergency doors; side scuttles; windows; skylights; clear view screens
Auxiliary (piping) for engine operation, ship operation, cargo operation, accommodation, and firefighting	Oil separators; air water separators; cooling water pumps; air conditioning cooling compressors; discharge pumps; lube oil pumps; gas generator compressors; fuel pumps; cargo pumps; loose tanks (for lube oil, fresh water, etc.); valves and fittings; tank cleaning hatches, deck washing; swimming pool technology; pressurised air; heaters and coolers; filters; fire hoses; sprinkler noses; water cannons; CO_2

(continued)

Table 1 (continued)

Main equipment category	Examples
	plants, firefighting systems; main engine accessories; special liquid gas equipment
HVAC	Ventilation/air condition systems for accommodation; ventilation fan centrals; air condition central units and distribution boxes; humidity regulation equipment; heat exchangers
Cargo systems	Cargo lifts; roller conveyors; cranes; mechanical shovels; pneumatic plants; cargo shifting boards; deck cranes; grabbing equipment; masts and booms; hatch covers; bow ports (for ro-ro ships); driving ramps; stern and side ports; cargo hold outfitting (locking devices, platforms, pallets, etc.); heavy lifting gear; backhoe equipment; dredge pumps; cable handling equipment; pipe handling equipment; twist locks; tanks (for tankers); fishing gear, fish processing plants, and factories
Accommodation	Walls and wall panels; steps and ladders; staircases; doors and openings; lifts; toilets; shower cabinets; furniture and decoration; shelves and racks; washstands; refrigerators; grills and ovens; boilers and mixers; coffeemakers; dishwashers; clothing washing machines;
Other	Special offshore equipment; special underwater equipment

2021), with 70 to 80% of the final output value of a ship being generated upstream (Gourdon & Steidl, 2019).

In the Circular Economy, many products that have stopped working will be refurbished to like-new or even better-than-new conditions. An important circular opportunity for the maritime sector is the asset lifetime extension, as the maritime industry will then need fewer new materials and consequently reduce its costs and its environmental impact. Cost-benefit analysis has shown that the remanufactured engine acquisition cost is nearly half of the cost of a new engine with similar operating performance and operating cost and finds that most original equipment manufacturers (OEMs) like Wartsila, Caterpillar, Volvo Penta, MTU and Cummins have some kind of take-back strategy and offer some level of remanufacturing options (Okumus et al., 2022).

Refurbishment and remanufacturing can generate new revenue in the maritime industry for both the manufacturer and the processor. And by increasing the service life of a product, remanufacturing can also lower the demand for raw materials and therefore cost.

Alfa Laval and Stena Recycling's 'Re-Made to Matter' program retrieves worn plate heat exchangers with a refund, and recycles and refurbishes them into new and improved heat exchangers (Sornn-Friese et al., 2021). This reduces virgin material extraction and processing, and allows customers to upgrade less energy-efficient plate heat exchangers with state-of-the-art, environmentally friendly products.

Harvested parts can be reused multiple times rather than being discarded or shredded for recycling. Functioning, reusable parts can be taken out of a used product and then rebuilt into another product. Along the way, the processor performs quality assurance and may also enhance or change the component. Using second-hand parts requires warranties that guarantee the same or better performance than new parts.

An overview of circular economy initiatives for the maritime sector is provided in Fig. 3 (Sornn-Friese et al., 2021).

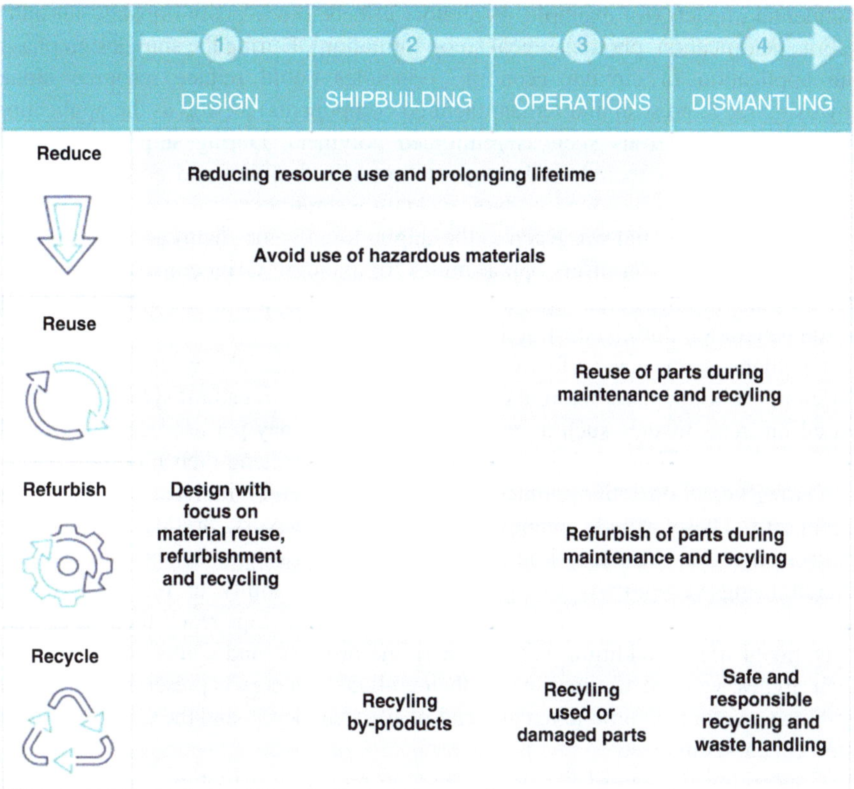

Fig. 3 Overview of circular initiatives in a ships life cycle (Source https://www.sustainableshipping.org/)

Failing to Transform into a Circular Economy Will Make the Maritime Sector's Climate Targets Unachievable

The operation phase is the source of more than 90% of shipping's GHG emissions, primarily from the combustion of fuels. Nevertheless, the sector's current decarbonization focus will shift the emphasis towards emissions from producing the components, the ships themselves, and the recycling of ships. This is because it will increasingly represent a larger share of the maritime sector's emissions (t'Hoff & Hoezen, 2022).

Applying circular economy principles to transform the way goods and materials are produced and used in the maritime sector would offer significant potential to reduce GHG emissions (Ellen Macarthur Foundation, 2021) as well as other environmental impacts (for example, respiratory effects, biodiversity impacts, eutrophication, acidification, photochemical smog formation). During the ship design phase, the application of circular economy principles could reduce resource inputs (by using recycled steel and remanufactured components) as well as the application of composite materials such as reinforced polymers. During ship construction, potential initiatives include reducing resource consumption and emission factors through such things as advanced laser welding techniques.

Eliminating material waste across the shipbuilding value chains and in the design of maritime equipment offers opportunities for avoiding GHG emissions by reducing the amount of material input in products and assets, and in the end, eliminating waste generation during construction.

Circular systems make effective use of renewable materials by encouraging many different economic uses before they are returned safely to natural systems. Service-based business models such as renting, sharing, and pay-per-use can increase the utilisation of maritime products and assets, as well as extend their lifetime.

During vessel operation, numerous interventions can be initiated to fully enable circularity. These include, among others, onboard repairs, drydock, retrofit and refurbishing. For instance, implementing modular designs in shipbuilding and standardising vessel parts can greatly enhance the ability to refurbish, repair, upgrade, and recover components and resources when ships reach the end of their operational life. In addition, keeping maritime products and components in use at their highest value at all times means their embodied energy is preserved for longer, and the need for new production and end-of-life treatment—and the GHG emissions they entail—is reduced.

Concerning the end-of-life phase, through recycling activities, emissions from production and incineration would be avoided by bypassing the need for new material production and using less energy-intensive facilities compared to the production of virgin materials. In this case, some of the hardest-to-abate emissions would be avoided. For steel, recycling is already well established, with a largely electrified process. However, current product design, end-of-life dismantling, and scrap handling processes are polluting and degrade the quality of the steel. Increasing recycling rates would therefore require measures that prevent the downgrading of the steel stock (Önal et al., 2021). For plastics, increasing recycling rates can be enabled by improving uptake and quality. Key measures include improving recyclability, collection, and sorting processes, as well as reducing contamination of recycling streams and exploring the potential of chemical recycling to achieve virgin quality (Aurisano et al., 2021; UNEP, 2023).

The Digital Product Passport in a Maritime Context: Enabling Circularity through Material Traceability and Supply Chain Transparency

The deficiency of high-quality data to support decision-making for the design of industrial circular systems has been known for several years (Geng & Doberstein, 2008) and still poses a dominant challenge to industries today (Sudusinghe & Seuring, 2022). Recently, the challenge has received increasing attention, as the EU proposed its *Ecodesign for Sustainable Products Regulation* as an extension to the *Ecodesign Directive* (European Commission, 2022). Herein, the DPP is being considered as a vital lever to encourage more sustainable production and consumption patterns. This means that companies placing products on the EU market will have to comply with DPP regulations in the coming years, where selected product groups like batteries are required to comply by 2026 and all other covered product groups, including maritime equipment, not later than 2030.

Containing relevant product and supply chain data, DPP is expected to enhance transparency through the continuous exchange of data, thus enabling informed decision-making throughout a product's lifetime (Walden et al., 2021). Detailed DPP data need to be collected across the product life cycle. At the latest, it is required to be created upon market entry of a product into the EU market but could already be created before this. It could be created at any step between raw materials and distribution. The earlier the DPP is created, the easier will be the data collection along the shipbuilding value chain consisting of more than 22,000 OEMs and suppliers (Sornn-Friese et al., 2021). Consequently, the DPP can be the vehicle connecting the shipbuilding value chain to an efficient organism.

Often, collection of supply chain data has proven difficult, as the reconciliation of forward-oriented and reverse supply chains entails new modes of decision-making—on a strategic and operational level, both of which are hampered by uncertainties. A dominant challenge is the fragmented nature of shipbuilding supply chains, particularly at end-of-life. This exacerbates the limited transparency, particularly in cases where ships and maritime equipment often end up at third-party recycling sites far from where they were produced (Okumus et al., 2022).

An example of a complex industry that has managed to collect supply chain data globally is the automotive sector's Industry Material Data System (IMDS). IMDS collects, maintains, analyses, and archives data on all materials used for automobile manufacturing by the majority of the global automotive OEMs. IMDS facilitates meeting the obligations placed on automobile manufacturers, and thus on their suppliers, by national and international standards, laws, and regulations (IMDS, 2023).

While navigating in unfamiliar territory in terms of circulating products at their highest utility, uncertainties are often caused by a prevalent data gap (Serna-Guerrero et al., 2022). Extant dataflows are often configured to support efficient production in a forward-oriented setup, where much data is lost as soon as products leave the factory or shipyard. Consequently, as maritime supply chains increasingly explore circular resource flows, it raises demand for additional data, which cannot be met by current configurations. This is problematic, as companies within the maritime ecosystem might either refrain from exploring value-retention potentials or settle for harvesting the material value through recycling rather than unlocking the functional value through refurbishment, remanufacture, reuse, or repair.

The DPP is expected to close this data gap and support the circulation of products, thus both unlocking the functional and the material value. Doing so requires active participation in operationalising the DPP from the entire supply chain in terms of defining, identifying, providing and utilizing high-quality data.

Contents of the Digital Product Passport

In terms of regulatory compliance, it remains unclear, as to what will be the required contents of the DPP. Indications have been given that regulation will in general define a set of reachable requirements to push the limits of supply chain transparency, yet with flexibility for frontrunners to add more content to the DPP.

Much research is contributing to deciding on the contents of the DPP in aid of transparent and circular supply chains. When transferring and contextualising such knowledge to the maritime sector seven data clusters can be defined, as shown in Table 2.

Use Cases for Digital Product Passports

We see three aggregated areas, in which the DPP can be a valuable asset in a maritime context:

- for sustainable procurement,
- for value-retention throughout product life cycles, and
- for market surveillance.

These areas are not mutually exclusive. Rather, they complement each other, as they are all required at various stages during the product life cycle.

Table 2 List of relevant contents of the DPP in a maritime context. Based on Jensen et al., (2023) with inputs from King et al., (2023) and Götz et al., (2022)

Products and materials	Product identification	Guidelines and manuals	Supply chain and reverse logistics
Material composition Hazardous substances Recycled content Average lifetime expectance Availability of spare parts	Serial and product numbers Manufacturing date Country of origin	Guidelines for non-destructive disassembly Service manuals Product Manuals Waste sorting guideline Installation guidelines Safety instructions	Suppliers of components Customer return channels
Environmental data	**Compliance**	**Usage and maintenance**	
Emissions to air, water, and soil Indicators for climate change Resource consumption (energy, water)	RoHS/REACH Energy Labelling Directive EcoDesign Directive Labour conditions Consumer rights	Running hours and power External environment Service log Repairability score	

Sustainable and Economical Procurement

Recognising the engineered-to-order nature of a ship, enhanced transparency throughout shipbuilding supply chains enables participants to obtain knowledge about product configuration and performance, particularly in terms of environmental matters, as well as performance measures.

By containing data about recycled content, resource consumption, and emissions, the DPP enables customers to select the most sustainable and economical alternative. This holds additional benefits, as it generates an incentive for maritime equipment manufacturers to continuously improve environmental performance to remain competitive. The DPP is further expected to contain upstream data about compliance, both with the regulation on environmental parameters (such as chemical thresholds) and social parameters (such as labour conditions) (King et al., 2023).

Digital Product Passports for Value-Retention throughout Product Life Cycles

As a repository for data, information, and documents, the DPP can provide new confidence in the previous levels of uncertainty that beset operational decision-making for selecting and employing circular value-retention strategies throughout product life cycles. This requires that the DPP can be accessed by a wide range of authorised actors (Berger, 2022).

When service providers assess a potentially defective part, the DPP is deemed a suitable carrier of product identification measures and guidelines for non-destructive disassembly, as provided by product manufacturers, if a product has been designed using strategies such as 'design-for-disassembly' (King et al., 2023).

Product passports could act as a repository for digitised versions of product manuals, service manuals, and installation guidelines. With further access to the average lifetime expectancy of the product and a list of available spare parts, the DPP supports the assessment of appropriate interventions—both in terms of efficiency (reducing downtime) and effectiveness (retaining the functional value). Finally, integrating the service log into the DPP could provide valuable insight into repair histories to benefit service providers as well as manufacturers, while delegating an active role to the former in terms of updating the DPP (Jensen et al., 2023).

Such a service log could also enable decision-making for ship owners or maritime equipment manufacturers if they organise take-back/buy-back programs. As maritime equipment reaches end-of-life and becomes decommissioned, it must be decided what value-retention strategy is most suitable for circulating the product as a whole or selected components at their highest utility. Accessing the service log would provide insight into repair histories to distinguish newly installed components from older ones, as they might qualify for a second life. With a great variety of material routes, in an often-new territory, such decisions must be supported by a wide range of data. Besides the remaining estimated functionality, the DPP could support decisions by carrying data about the environmental footprint, including on a component level to target those with the highest impact.

Selected durable and robust components can be returned to suppliers of maritime equipment for remanufacturing/refurbishment, who would utilise the DPP to obtain valuable use-phase data (for example, through sensors) (Berger et al., 2023). Furthermore, it could provide access to material composition and hazardous substances, which has proven critical, as regulations may differ from the first to the second product life cycle, for examble, by introducing more strict thresholds for certain substances.

Notwithstanding the development of the DPP, the maritime sector has already established a well-functioning recycling infrastructure with a high throughput of worn-out products and materials, where steel is the most significant but also aluminium, copper alloys, lead, nickel, titanium, and zinc are materials normally used in ships that are harvested. This is done by either suppliers of maritime equipment or by third-party recycling companies. However, within recycling loops, there is still potential for improving the quality of materials, thus pursuing a transition from recycling with irreversible losses of material properties to reversible losses, if any at all, and thereby slowing the pace of downcycling materials (Jensen et al., 2023). Similarly there is an untapped potential for harvesting rare-earth materials in the maritime sector, such as cerium (used for ignition in some engine types), terbium (in lighting systems and navigation equipment), and yttrium (used in such things as compressors, radar systems, and turbochargers). Unlocking such strategies for recycling requires access to disassembly guidelines. Combined with data about material composition and hazardous substances, as provided by the DPP, third-party recycling companies can generate clean material fractions, thus enhancing the quality of the material output by preventing contamination from other substances (Jensen et al., 2023).

Digital Product Passports for Market Surveillance

No sector can absolve itself of responsibility for rethinking material flows in favour of a circular economy. Being able to monitor market tendencies in a broader industrial context is a critical constituent of a systemic circular transition for the maritime sector. In aid of this, the DPP can be used by market surveillance authorities to ensure compliance with product regulation, while pursuing a just market competition (Adisorn et al., 2021). Simultaneously, enhanced transparency across shipbuilding supply chains enables such authorities to monitor sustainability and the stage of the circular transition (Berger et al., 2023), e.g., through access to percentages of recycled content, emissions, and resource consumption.

The use of the DPP in the marine sector has significant potential, one example application is mooring ropes. These ropes are essential for securing vessels to docks and other structures, and the average mooring rope weighs about half a tonne. Vessels replace them three to four times a year, yielding over 70,000 tonnes of waste each year from the world fleet (Wilhelmsen, 2023). Mooring ropes are made of plastic, usually a combination of polyethylene, polypropylene, polyester, and various chemical additives. Furthermore, for those ropes discarded at sea, the constant motion of the ropes in the ocean causes the fibres to break down into microplastics, which only exacerbates the plastic pollution issue.

Despite the massive amounts of waste generated by old mooring ropes, few are being recycled. The majority of these ropes are either dumped in the ocean, sent to landfills, or incinerated. However, as textile products made of chemical fibres, mooring ropes are a perfect candidate for the circular economy. DPP can serve as an enabler by providing all the players along the mooring ropes' life cycle with information concerning reusability, possibility of maintenance and presence of substances of concern. Whether these ropes are intended for reuse within or beyond the maritime industry (for such things as towing ropes for small boats and barges or repurposing them for craft and decorative purposes), or if they are destined for mechanical and chemical recycling, having access to such information is important. This transparency and traceability will thus facilitate the transition of mooring ropes from a waste product to a valuable resource in the circular economy.

Specific circular mooring ropes examples are the 'Circular Rope Pilot Project' carried out by Wilhelmsen (Wilhelmsen, 2023) and 'From Rope To Rope' (Plastix, 2021).

Digital Product Passport Challenges and Opportunities

Although details of the DPP are still under development, companies and industries can benefit from starting their preparations now. The realisation of the DPP brings opportunities and challenges for maritime businesses in three ways:

- internal readiness,
- value chain interoperability, traceability and transparency, and
- extracting benefits from the increased transparency

Internal Readiness

Many of the ESG-related investment decisions companies are facing today hold similar requirements as can be expected from the DPP implementation. The investigation of internal IT readiness, understanding where the DPP will require changes, and alignment of DPP plans and ESG-related digital investment are important to avoid repeating activities done for ESG reporting when the DPP must be implemented. It includes the decision of where the DPP should reside, where data that should be shared will be stored, what internal IT systems can benefit from DPP data, and so on, as well as understanding the security measures required for a safe DPP implementation.

Value Chain Interoperability, Traceability, and Transparency

The DPP's consistent digital information sharing enables a new digital capability that creates transparency, traceability, and harmonisation across global shipbuilding value chains.

It is a collaborative effort for the maritime sector to decide how to implement the DPP for maritime equipment and how to securely share sufficient information to improve the circularity of maritime products. The maritime sector must today start initiatives to understand where data are available and where to fill in the gaps.

A coherent and efficient implementation of value chain security, interoperability, and enabling transparency while maintaining confidentiality to ensure the protection of intellectual property rights (IPR) and commercially sensitive information requires shared digital design and will be critical decisions maritime actors need to start taking.

Jensen et al. discuss the need for a shared global digital backbone to accelerate the transformation to a competitive global maritime circular economy and conclude that '*collaborative, focused and responsible digitalisation of the circular economy will be important to accelerate the realisation of its economic and environmental potentials. A shared interoperable digital backbone for the maritime circular economy will add substantially to the digital benefits, accelerate the environmental impacts, and make more circular economy business models attractive*' (Jensen

Table 3 Characteristics of a shared interoperable digital backbone for the maritime circular economy—(Jensen et al., 2021)

Characteristic of a circular economy backbone	Description
Modularity	Every component will work independently as a feature and together with other components to complete the digital backbone for the circular economy
Interoperability	Facilitate a digital ecosystem of many-to-many interoperability to reduce barriers, costs, risks, and resources for participation in global circular economy value chains.
Extendibility	Industries can broaden the generic components according to their specific needs
Differentiation and innovation	The backbone must be designed as an open software platform, allowing innovators and companies worldwide to realise individual value-adding and differentiating but still interoperable applications on top
A global public good	To be globally acceptable the digital backbone must be designed and governed as a global public good. The digital backbone must be politically, commercially, and competitively neutral
Control your data	Sharing of data must be controlled by the owner of the data.

et al., 2021, p. 17). They set out the characteristics of a shared digital backbone for the maritime circular economy in Table 3.

Extracting Knowledge from the Increased Transparency

Where the first two challenges primarily focus on getting data efficiently, securely and timely to the right entity, the third challenge is about using analytics to extract value and knowledge from the data.

A well-implemented DPP in the maritime sector enables transparency and collaboration tools that did not exist before, which gives interesting business and value chain insights and opportunities, including:

- **Environmental visibility** that companies do not have today will enable more environmentally conscious decisions in design, production, and consumption
- **The shared knowledge** and data will enable increased value chain collaboration on a foundation of shared visibility
- **Improved visibility and predictability** in the availability of recycled material, parts, and refurbished equipment, will reduce the risks in relying on circular inputs
- **Enablement of circular decisions** based on the current market situation of the secondhand market, refurbishing, repair cost, recycling value etc.
- **New revenue streams** based on data instead of raw materials and decreasing dependency on raw materials for creating income

- **Effective management** of waste flows and end-of-life treatment, thereby increasing recycling rates and access to recycled materials and products

Conclusion: Embracing the Power of Visibility, Collaboration, and Technology

Without a competitive global circular economy, the maritime sector will never be able to reach the global climate and environmental targets. Circular economy principles should be built into every stage of the maritime equipment life cycle—from design to construction; to operations and recycling.

Adopting circular economy principles can help to increase resource efficiency, reduce waste and emissions, and minimise the environmental impacts of maritime activities. By embracing circularity, the industry can unlock additional avenues for reducing emissions and achieving sustainability goals, beyond the scope of fuel usage alone.

The DPP is a key tool being proposed by the European Commission to create the digital landscape, data-exchange mechanisms, and transparency needed to close information gaps in maritime circular value chains enabling informed decision-making throughout a product's lifetime.

The Maritime implementation of the DPP would enable the availability of data to support sustainable and economical procurement, value-retention throughout product life cycles, circular product design, and market surveillance.

It is a collaborative effort for the maritime sector to decide how to implement the DPP for maritime equipment and how to share sufficient information to improve the circularity of maritime products. Despite some challenges, uncertainties, and a potentially lengthy timelines, it is imperative for companies in the maritime sector to begin preparing for DPP implementation now.

Reaching the global climate and environmental goals requires collaborations to enable a coherent and competitive maritime circular economy. These include harmonising global circular processes as well as the digitalisation of the maritime circular business ecosystem to ensure efficient and secure transparency, predictability, collaboration, and management throughout the global maritime business ecosystem.

The adoption of maritime circularity should not be delayed. By taking immediate action on the shared responsibilities and opportunities, the industry can swiftly reap the economic, climate, and environmental advantages offered by a circular economy. Given the maritime sector's pivotal role in global trade, expediting maritime circularity also becomes vital for other industries to achieve their climate and environmental objectives.

References

Adisorn, T., Tholen, L., & Götz, T. (2021). Towards a digital product passport fit for contributing to a circular economy. *Energies, 14*. https://doi.org/10.3390/en14082289

Alfnes, E., Gosling, J., Naim, M., & Dreyer, H. C. (2021). Exploring systemic factors creating uncertainty in complex engineer-to-order supply chains: Case studies from Norwegian shipbuilding first tier suppliers. *International Journal of Production Ecosystem.*

Aurisano, N., Weber, R., & Fantke, P. (2021). Enabling a circular economy for chemicals in plastics. *Current Opinion in Green and Sustainable Chemistry, 31*, 100513. https://doi.org/10.1016/j.cogsc.2021.100513

BALance Technology, C. (2014). *Competitive position and future opportunities of the European marine supplies industry* (Final Report to Contract N. SI2.630862). Bremen.

Berger, K., Baumgartner, R., Weinzerl, M., Bachler, J., & Schöggl, J.-P. (2023). Factors of digital product passport adoption to enable circular information flows along the battery value chain. *Procedia CIRP, 116*, 528–533. https://doi.org/10.1016/j.procir.2

Berger, K. S.-P. (2022). Digital battery passports to enable circular and sustainable value chains: Conceptualization and use cases. *Journal of Cleaner Production, 353*, 131492. https://doi.org/10.1016/j.jclepro.2022.131492

Carvalho, F., O'Malley, J., Osipova, L., & Pavlenko, N. (2023). *Key issues in LCA methodology for marine fuels*. ICCT - The Internatilnal Council on Clean Transportation.

Ellen Macarthur Foundation. (2021). *Completing the picture - How the circular economy tackles climte change.* Retrieved from https://ellenmacarthurfoundation.org/completing-the-picture

Emblemsvåg, J. (2014). Lean project planning in shipbuilding. *Journal of Ship Production and Design, 30*(2), 79–88.

EU. (2013). *Regulation (EU) No 1257/2013 of the European Parliament and of the Council of 20 November 2013 on ship recycling and amending Regulation (EC) No 1013/2006 and Directive 2009/16/EC Text with EEA relevance*. EU. Retrieved from https://eur-lex.europa.eu/eli/reg/2013/1257/oj

European Commission. (2022). *Communication from the commission to the European Parliament, the Council, the European Economic and Social Committee and the Committee of the Regions – On making sustainable products the norm.*

Geng, Y., & Doberstein, B. (2008). Developing the circular economy in China: Challenges and opportunities for achieving 'leapfrog development'. *International Journal of Sustainable Development and World Ecology, 15*, 231–239. https://doi.org/10.3843/SusDev.15.3

Götz, T., Berg, H., Jansen, M., Adisorn, T., Cembrero, D., Markkanen, S., & Chowdhury, T. (2022). *Digital Product Passport: The ticket to achieving a climate neutral and circular European economy?* Retrieved from https://www.corporateleadersgroup.com/digital-p

Gourdon, K., & Steidl, C. (2019). *Global value chains and the shipbuilding industry* (OECD Science, Technology and Industry Working Papers, No. 2019/08). OECD https://doi.org/10.1787/7e94709a-en.

IMDS. (2023). *IMDS Information pages*. International Material Data System. Retrieved from https://public.mdsystem.com/en/web/imds-public-pages

IMO, I. (2009). Hong Kong international CONVENTION for the safe and environmentally sound recycling of ships, 2009.

Jensen, H. H. (2023a, March 20). *8 ways the circular economy will transform how business is done.* World Economic Forum. Retrieved from https://www.weforum.org/agenda/2023/03/8-ways-the-circular-economy-outperforms-traditional-business-models/

Jensen, H. H. (2023b, 04). *The circular economy: What it is, why it matters now, and how it can help your organisation.* Retrieved from DXC Technology. https://dxc.com/uk/en/cp/intelligence-delivered/perspectives/blogs/the-circular-economy-what-it-is-why-it-matters-now-and-how-it-can-help-your-organisation

Jensen, H. H., Andersen, M. M., Dao, A., Lind, M., Pandey, V., Bapuji, G., & Turos, A. (2021). Digitalisation in a maritime circular economy. In M. Lind, M. Michaelides, R. Ward, & R. T.

Watson (Eds.), *Maritime informatics - additional perspectives and applications* (p. 17). Springer Professionals.

Jensen, H. H., & Clarke, D. (2023, 05). *DXC perspective*. Retrieved from the more circular the economy, the greater the opportunity for logistics providers. https://dxc.com/uk/en/cp/intelligence-delivered/perspectives/blogs/the-more-circular-the-economy-the-greater-the-opportunity-for-logistics-providers

Jensen, S., Kristensen, J., Adamsen, S., Christensen, A., & Waehrens, B. (2023). Digital product passports for a circular economy: Data needs for product life cycle decision-making. *Sustainable Production and Consumption*. https://doi.org/10.1016/j.spc

King, M., Timms, P., & Mountney, S. (2023). Proposed universal definition of a Digital Product Passport Ecosystem (DPPE): Worldviews, discrete capabilities, stakeholder requirements and concerns. *Journal of Cleaner Production, 384*, 135538.

Milios, L., Beqiri, B., Whalen, K. A., & Jelonek, S. H. (2019). Sailing towards a circular economy: Conditions for increased reuse and remanufacturing in the Scandinavian maritime sector. *Journal of Cleaner Production, 225*, 227–235.

Okumus, D., Gunbeyaz, S. A., Kurt, R. E., & Turan, O. (2022). Towards a circular maritime industry: Identifying strategy and technology solutions. *Journal of Cleaner Production, 382*, 134935.

Önal, M., Neşer, G., & Gürsel, K. T. (2021). Environmental impacts of steel ship hulls building and recycling by life cycle assessment (LCA). *Ships and Offshore Structures, 16*(10), 1061–1066.

Plastix. (2021). *From rope to rope - Industry partners close the loop*. Retrieved from https://plastixglobal.com/from-rope-to-rope-industry-partners-close-the-loop/

Serna-Guerrero, R., Ikonen, S., Kallela, O., & Hakanen, E. (2022). Overcoming data gaps for an efficient circular economy: A case study on the battery materials ecosystem. *Journal of Cleaner Production, 374*, 133984. https://doi.org/10.1016/j.jclepro.2022.1339

Sornn-Friese, H., Roth, E., Sofev, P., Kaiser, B., Sinding, K., Vágsheyg, H., et al. (2021). *Creating circular economy clusters for sustainable ship recycling in Denmark*. CBS Maritime.

Sudusinghe, J., & Seuring, S. (2022). Supply chain collaboration and sustainability performance in circular economy: A systematic literature review. *International Journal of Production Economics, 245*, 108402. https://doi.org/10.1016/j.ijpe.2021.108402

t'Hoff, P. V., & Hoezen, D. (2022). *Exploring shipping's transition to a circular economy*. The Sustainable Shipping Initiative (SSI).

UNCTAD. (2023). *Review of maritime transport 2022*. United Nations Conference on Trade and Development.

UNEP. (2023). *Chemicals in plastics: A technical report*. United Nations Environment Programme and Secretariat of the Basel, Rotterdam and Stockholm Conventions. Retrieved from https://www.unep.org/resources/report/chemicals-plastics-technical-report

UNEP. (2018). *Emissions gap report 2018*. United Nations Environment Programme. Retrieved from https://wedocs.unep.org/bitstream/handle/20.500.11822/26895/EGR2018-FullReport-EN.pdf

Wahab, A. D., Blanco-Davi, E., Ariffin, A. K., & Wang, J. (2018). A review on the applicability of remanufacturing in extending the life cycle of marine or offshore components and structures. *Ocean Engineering, 169*, 125–133.

Walden, J., Steinbrecher, A., & Marinkovic, M. (2021). Digital product passports as enabler of the circular economy. *Chemie Ingenieur Technik, 93*, 1717–1727. https://doi.org/10.1002/cite.202100121

Wilhelmsen. (2023). *Circular rope pilot project*. Retrieved from https://www.wilhelmsen.com/ships-service/ropes/the-new-era-of-safer-mooring/circular-rope-pilot/

Yiqi Zhang, Y. C. (2022). Life-cycle energy and environmental emissions of cargo ships. *Industrial Ecology, 26*(6), 2057. https://doi.org/10.1111/jiec.13293

Sustainable Finance in the Maritime Sector

Maarten L. Biermans, Willem Bulthuis, Tobias Holl, and Boris van Overbeeke

Target Audience

This chapter is intended for senior executives, leaders and managers in the maritime industry that are seeking to decarbonize the activities for which they are responsible. The chapter will also be of interest to policy makers in government and other organisations that need to understand the finance pressures, options and opportunities available to industry. This will assist in ensuring that relevant policy and regulations are feasible and much more likely to be achievable.

Key Takeaway Messages

The chapter covers:

- the ways in which the topic of sustainability has entered the financial sector both as an investment theme and (more recently) as an integral part of risk management;
- the various forms of sustainable finance;

M. L. Biermans (✉) · T. Holl
PROW Capital, Amsterdam, The Netherlands
e-mail: maarten.biermans@prow-capital.com; tobias.holl@prow-capital.com

W. Bulthuis
Corporate Ventures Advisory GmbH, Inning am Ammersee, Frankfurt, Germany
e-mail: willem@corporate-ventures.com

B. van Overbeeke
MJ Hudson, Amsterdam, The Netherlands
e-mail: borisvanoverbeeke@gmail.com; boris.vanoverbeeke@mjhudson.com

M. Lind et al. (eds.), *Maritime Decarbonization*,
https://doi.org/10.1007/978-3-031-39936-7_19

- developments in the risk dimension, especially those surrounding the Task Force on Climate-related Financial Disclosures, as this framework will influence the conditions of access to finance in the foreseeable future;
- the recent developments surrounding sustainability as an investable theme, most notably the rise of the integration of Environment, Social and Governance (ESG) in investment strategies as well as the European Union (EU) policies aimed at increasing the transparency of the sustainability related impact of investments;
- sustainable finance (especially on the debt side of finance);
- specific applications of sustainable finance in the maritime sector. Among the examples are the various green bond issuances, sustainability linked loans but also venture (corporate) investment initiatives that have emerged in the maritime space.
- some observations on the way ahead, covering topics such as the impact of the EU Emissions Trading System (ETS), the proposed Maritime Fund and the possible usage of (voluntary) Carbon Credits.
- a closing summary of the main points of the chapter in addition to providing some suggestions for further reading.

Introduction

The maritime sector faces numerous environmental challenges, including pollution from shipping activities, marine ecosystem degradation, and climate change impacts. In particular, the sector is responsible for a significant amount of greenhouse gas emissions, contributing to global warming and ocean acidification. Decarbonization is necessary to mitigate these negative impacts, reduce air pollution, and improve the sustainability of the industry. This includes transitioning to low-carbon fuels and investing in more efficient, eco-friendly technologies.

Financing the decarbonization of shipping will require a combination of both public and private funding sources. Governments and international governmental organisations, being the public sector, can and already do, play an important role in providing financial incentives, such as through providing subsidies, tax credits and other financial incentives, to encourage investment in low-carbon technologies. In addition, these institutions, through new policies can alter conditions in ways that can benefit those companies that are quicker to decarbonize. At the same time, the transition towards a low carbon sector will require a lot of private sector investment, particularly from ship owners and operators. In addition, innovative financing models, such as green bonds and more general sustainable finance can also play a role in financing decarbonization efforts in the maritime sector.

By focusing on finance, this chapter aims to draw attention to one of the key questions in the decarbonization debate: namely, who is going to pay for the transition? This question is especially of importance in an overall low margin business such as shipping. It is even more pressing for the maritime sector, given that as more capital is needed to finance the transition, traditional capital providers such as banks have been reducing their exposure to the sector over the past couple of years (Petrofin Research, 2022; Biermans & Holl, 2023). Various private debt providers have filled (some of) the void left by the traditional banks, but new ways of attracting durable finance will remain a key challenge for the industry at large. As it is with so many current challenges, there is no simple solution and answers will have to come from multiple sources and in a variety of ways. End-users will also have a role to play. There are already examples that some are stepping up to the plate, such as in the case of the companies IKEA and Amazon. These companies have committed to long term shipping contracts with carriers that are using more environmentally friendly ships. While important, such end-user initiatives are not the focus of this chapter. This chapter focusses on the developments surrounding the integration of sustainability in the financing of the maritime sector.

Sustainability as a Topic in the Financial Sector

The integration of sustainability in the world of finance starts with the emergence of responsible investing. While responsible investing has always been part of investing—it is, after all, nothing more than the introduction of non-financial considerations in the investment process—the last thirty years have seen a distinct increase in the level of attention to it, or in *ESG investing*, as it has also come to be known. The acronym ESG stands for Environment, Social and Governance and denotes the various topics that are introduced in the ongoing development and debate on responsible investing.

Responsible investing has its roots in the socially responsible investing (SRI) movement of the 1960s and 1970s. At that time, investors increasingly began to consider the social and environmental impact of their investments apart from their financial returns. The concept evolved over the years, with the introduction of ESG criteria in investment analysis and decision-making. Today, responsible investing has become increasingly mainstream, with investors seeking to align their investments with their values and a growing recognition of the potential risks and opportunities posed by environmental and social factors. The focus is on investing in companies that promote sustainability and responsible business practices while avoiding those that have a negative impact on society and the environment.

Apart from rising intrinsic motivation for SRI and the integration of nonfinancial concerns in capital allocation decisions there are other reasons why responsible investing has increased over the years. It is beyond the scope of this chapter to go in-depth into the history of responsible investing and discuss these initiatives. What can be said is that any such overview would have to cover the origins and workings of the United Nations (UN) backed Principles for Responsible Investment (PRI). The PRI is the UN-backed initiative that aims to promote responsible investing by institutional investors, such as pension funds and asset managers. Launched in 2006, the PRI provides a framework for investors to incorporate ESG factors into their investment decision-making processes. The PRI has spawned a leading global network of investors committed to responsible investment practices. as well as to other institutional initiatives supporting the integration of ESG considerations in capital allocations. Special mention is also warranted for the EU Agenda for Sustainable Growth, not in the least because of the far-reaching consequences this legislative drive is having on the availability and promotion of SRI and sustainable finance (SF). The EU agenda is discussed in more detail later in this chapter.

With the integration of ESG in investment decisions becoming more mainstream, it has in turn caught the ire of those who believe that non-financial considerations have no place in financial markets. Those that propagate this vision seem to overlook that the integration of ESG is not only about highlighting the opportunities for financiers but also about highlighting (previously) overlooked sources of financial risk.

Sustainability as a Risk Factor

In 2015, Mark Carney, then Governor of the Bank of England, gave a speech in the City of London in which he introduced the concept of the 'Tragedy of the Horizon'. Carney argued that climate change poses significant long-term risks to the financial system and that these risks are not being adequately addressed. More importantly, Carney noted that the financial risk models did not have a long enough time horizon to capture and incorporate the long-term risks associated with climate change, such as extreme weather events or sea-level rise. The tragedy is thus that these risks are not captured by traditional risk models and when they finally do become apparent, it will be too late to do anything about them.

In response to the debate on the inadequateness of traditional risk models, the Financial Stability Board (FSB) that was established as an international body in 2009 by the G20 to promote global financial stability and whose members are drawn from national financial authorities and international standard-setting bodies. The FSB then initiated the Task Force on Climate-related Financial Disclosures (TCFD) under the guidance of Mark Carney and now chaired by Michael Bloomberg, the American businessman, politician, philanthropist. The aim of the taskforce was to come up with recommendations that would help (financial) companies disclose their climate-related risks and opportunities.

In 2017 the taskforce published its recommendations (TCFD, 2017). Part of these recommendations was a new approach to assessing the risks associated with climate change. It introduced a distinction between the physical, and the transition risks of climate change. *Physical risks* refer to those risks that are connected to acute or chronic manifestations of climate change, like extreme weather events, floods or droughts. Separate from the physical risks of risks are the *transition risks*, which occur *because of the existence of climate change* but not through the visible effects of the climate itself. This category includes amongst others, changes in consumer behaviour (for example, a butcher's risk of declining revenue when people switch from meat to more plant-based proteins, or an airline's risk of declining clientele when society grows more concerned about climate change) but also—and arguably more important—changes in laws and regulations.

The TCFD's approach to integrating the climate change into risk management has become more influential. It has shown itself to be the model that is currently used by central banks across the globe as the way to integrate climate risks in their oversight mandates. This in turn will have (and already has had) an impact on the way financial—(institutional) investors, insurance companies but also banks—will integrate climate risks in their overall risk models, which will in turn, impact the cost of capital going forward.

TCFD and the Maritime Sector

As more and more financial institutions will be subject to TCFD related reporting this will impact the maritime sector at large. Indeed, the consequences of TCFD for the maritime sector can be labelled as significant, as companies will need to identify and disclose to their capital (whether debt or equity) providers their exposure to climate-related risks, such as extreme weather events, rising sea levels, the impact of lower inland waters and stricter emissions regulations. This requires companies to assess the potential impacts of climate change on their operations, supply chains, and financial performance. In addition, companies may need to make significant investments in low-carbon technologies and infrastructure to reduce their emissions and remain competitive in a decarbonizing world. Overall, TCFD is likely to drive greater attention to climate-related risks and opportunities in the maritime sector from financiers (for example, banks) as well as other capital providers, and thus it is likely to encourage companies to take action to address those risks.

Physical Risks

In 2022, a report was published by the Environmental Defense Fund (Houtven et al., 2022) on the physical risks of climate change. The report focuses on the questions, 'In what ways does climate change impact the shipping and port industries?', as well as 'How large will the economic effects of climate change be on the shipping and port industries if actions are not taken to reduce emissions?' For the former question the report provides an overview of the costs associated with the damage to port infrastructure due to, for instance, hurricanes, but also from disruptions to port operations, vessel incidents at sea, and other occurrences. The overarching conclusion of this research is that climate change impacts such as port adaptation costs to counter projected sea level rise and larger storm surges could cost the shipping industry an additional US$ 25 billion every year by 2100.

Transition Risks

For most companies in the maritime sector the real challenges lie with the transition risks of climate change. The entire industry is subject to environmental regulations (local as well as supranational regulations via the International Maritime Organization (IMO)) with the aim of reducing the negative impact of the sector on the environment. Capital providers will increasingly be looking for assurances that the companies they invest in or those that they finance will be able to meet these ever more stringent requirements down the road. And it is not just about setting minimal standards for the IMO Energy Efficiency Design Index (EEDI) or Energy Efficiency Existing Ship Index (EEXI), nor just about the new Carbon Intensity Indicator (CII) standard setting that is taking place but also the introduction of a price on carbon emissions such as through the inclusion of shipping in EU Emissions Trading System (ETS) (Biermans & van der Klip, 2023).

The point of this brief expose is to accentuate that sustainability is no longer a nice to have but now a very much need to have factor for any enterprise. All of these developments will influence the value of existing ships and the current business models of maritime companies. Unsustainable business activities will hinder a company's ability to attract finance at favourable conditions, if at all.

Sustainability as an Investment Theme

Over the past ten years, the idea that investors should integrate ESG factors in their investment decisions has become firmly rooted and is rapidly becoming the new normal. If not because of pressure from regulators, as discussed in the previous section, then surely because of changes in the preferences of investors, ESG is now part of the standard financial vocabulary. One of the ways, and arguably the first, in which this has materialised is through the emergence of so-called ESG ratings for companies. These ratings signify the extent to which a company is addressing its ESG related challenges. These types of ratings look closely at the type of policies and practices to be found at companies but also outcomes, such as carbon emissions. Although these ratings are, in theory, available to all types of companies, they do tend to be mostly applied to the larger publicly listed companies. This is generally the result of the fact that public equity investors are the main clients of the ESG rating companies, through subscriptions (Biermans and Önal (2022).

One the reasons for the wider usage of ESG data in recent times is the result of active legislation from the European Commission (EC). It can even be argued that what the EC instigated in the financial circles of Europe was very much the cause of the significant recent surge in interest in the rest of the globe.

The European Plan for Financing Sustainable Growth

In 2017, the European Commission found that it needed to mobilise more private capital if it was to achieve the environmental targets for 2030 that it had set for itself. It formed a high-level expert group to look into this particular matter. The findings of the high-level expert group on Sustainable Finance (HLEG on Sustainable Finance, 2018) were subsequently used for the EU's Action Plan for Financing Sustainable Growth. (EU Commission, 2018).

At the heart of this action plan, which was subsequently integrated in the EU's Green Deal and 'Fit-for-55' agenda, is the desire to increase transparency regarding the environmental and social impact of capital flows. In addition, the EU started a project that will help in identifying which activities and/ or assets can be considered 'green' in order to facilitate this needed transparency and to weed out possible *greenwashing*, the activity of organisations that use environmentalism as a marketing tool to appeal to growing concerns about sustainability, without actually making significant efforts to reduce their environmental impact.

DNSH and Minimum Safeguards

The *do no significant harm* (DNSH) principle is a key part of the EU Taxonomy for classifying economic activities that are environmentally sustainable. The DNSH principle is intended to ensure that activities that are classified as environmentally sustainable do not cause significant harm to other environmental objectives.

Under the DNSH principle, economic activities that are classified as environmentally sustainable must not cause significant harm to any of the six environmental objectives identified in the EU Taxonomy:

- climate change mitigation,
- climate change adaptation,
- sustainable use and protection of water and marine resources,
- transition to a circular economy,
- pollution prevention and control, and
- protection and restoration of biodiversity and ecosystems.

In addition, they should not create significant environmental risks, such as pollution or emissions, that may have negative impacts on the environment or human health. Also, they should not undermine the integrity of protected areas or species, including sites that are designated as Natura 2000 sites under EU legislation. Natura sites are a network of protected areas covering Europe's most valuable and threatened species and habitats.

To ensure that economic activities meet the DNSH principle, the EU Taxonomy sets out specific technical screening criteria that must be met for each environmental objective. These criteria take into account scientific evidence, best practices, and existing legislation and standards. In addition, the EU also stipulated that alignment with the Taxonomy should not be at the expense of social standards. The 'Minimum Safeguards' thus ensure that companies engaging in sustainable activities meet certain standards when it comes to human and labour rights, bribery, taxation and fair competition.

EU Regulation 2021/2139 Chapter 6

EU Regulation 2021/2139—Technical screening criteria for determining the conditions under which an economic activity qualifies as contributing substantially to climate change mitigation and for determining whether that economic activity causes no significant harm to any of the other environmental objectives of the EU Taxonomy, goes into great detail to describe when a particular activity/ asset is taxonomy aligned (European Commission, 2021).

The sixth chapter of the Regulation is devoted to transport, with subsections 6.7 to 6.16 directly related to maritime transport. As an example, subsection 6.10 that deals with sea and coastal freight water transport states, amongst other things, that a vessel can be considered taxonomy aligned if it has zero direct (tailpipe) carbon dioxide (CO_2) emissions; or derives at least 25% of its energy from zero direct (tailpipe) CO_2 emission fuels or plug-in power for their normal operation at sea and in ports. These limits, set for hybrid and dual fuel vessels are valid until 31 December 2025. A vessel that has an EEDI that is 10% below the EEDI requirements applicable on 1 April 2022 is aligned. The list goes on. In short, the regulation outlines both how and when a particular activity or asset in the maritime sector can be classified as taxonomy aligned.

Sustainable Finance: The Basics

Sustainable finance refers to financial products, services, and activities that have a positive impact on the environment and/or on societal issues. It encompasses a wide range of financial instruments and practices that support the transition to a more sustainable (and in some cases also a more equitable) society.

The origins of sustainable finance are very much linked to the developments in responsible investment (RI) as outlined in the previous section. Sustainable Finance started out as a way to extend the RI activities already found in the (public) equity side of financial markets to the realm of the debt side. One of the earliest forms of a sustainable finance instrument are the so-called green bonds, which were first issued by the World Bank in 2007. The idea was that organisations could issue publicly traded bonds whereby the capital that was raised would be used for projects with identifiable environmental benefits, such as renewable energy, energy efficiency, and pollution prevention. The issuance of green bonds would thus enable investors to fulfil their sustainably responsible investment mandates with investments in the debt capital markets apart from those in the equity markets.

Although sustainable finance has its roots in the bond market, since then and based on size, the regular (corporate) loan markets has taken the lead. Nowadays there is not a financial product without a Sustainable Finance variant, including derivatives and commercial paper.

There are two elements to any sustainable finance structure that jointly determine its very nature. One element has to do with the *use-of-proceeds*, in other words, with the issue for what the capital can be used. This can be general purpose—without limitations as to what the money can be spent on—or pre-defined and thereby tied to specific items or topics. In the case of a pre-determined use-of-proceeds, the question (and thus second element to the Sustainable Finance structure) has to do with the focus area of the capital deployment: is the money to be used for Environmental, Social (related) issues or a combination of both? This in turn will determine—for the bond market—whether the issuance is a Green Bond, a Social Bond or a Sustainable Bond. For the loan market corresponding names are used.

Green, Social and Sustainable Bonds

A green bond is a type of debt instrument that is issued by an organisation to finance environmentally-friendly projects. These projects can include renewable energy, energy efficiency, clean transportation, and other initiatives that have a positive environmental impact.

The structure of a green bond is similar to that of other types of bonds. It involves the issuance of debt securities by the issuer, which are then purchased by investors. The issuer agrees to make periodic interest payments to the investors, and to repay the principal amount of the bond at maturity.

The key difference between green bonds and other types of bonds is the use of the proceeds. With a green bond, the issuer must use the proceeds from the bond sale specifically for environmentally friendly projects. This is usually outlined in the bond's prospectus and may be verified by a third party such as Sustainalytics (now part of Morningstar) or Cicero (now part of S&P).

One of the interesting, but also challenging, things in the whole field of sustainable finance is that there is no internationally shared definition on when something can be labelled as 'green'. This also means that nothing can stop someone from using the label as they see fit and identifying and labelling any bond as a green bond. In order to address this issue, various initiatives have emerged to provide guidance, the most important being the Green Bond Principles.

The Green Bond Principles

The Green Bond Principles (GBPs) are a set of voluntary guidelines developed by the International Capital Markets Association that provide a framework for issuing and reporting on green bonds. The GBPs were developed by a group of market participants, including investors, issuers, and underwriters, in order to standardise the green bond market and increase transparency.

The GBPs consist of four core components:

- Use of Proceeds: The issuer must specify how the proceeds from the bond sale will be used to finance environmentally-friendly projects.
- Process for Project Evaluation and Selection: The issuer must have a clear and transparent process for identifying and selecting eligible green projects.
- Management of Proceeds: The issuer must have systems in place to manage the proceeds from the bond sale and ensure that they are used for the intended purposes.
- Reporting: The issuer must disclose information about the use of proceeds and the environmental impact of the financed projects on a regular basis.

The GBPs are intended to provide guidance to issuers and investors and to help ensure that green bonds are used to finance projects that have a positive environmental impact. Adherence to the GBPs is voluntary, but many issuers and investors choose to follow them in order to demonstrate their commitment to sustainability. Comparable to the GBPs the Social Bond Principles (SBPs) were developed and also the Sustainability Bond Guidelines (as these refer to bonds that combine the concepts of both GBPs and SBPs they are called guidelines rather than principles).

A final observation for the bond market is warranted. The previously discussed activities of the EU Commission on Sustainable Finance have led to the development of the EU Green Bond Standard or EUGBS. What makes this standard different from the GBPs is that it has some additional requirements for the issuer and for the use-of-proceeds categories. Most importantly, a bond that is issued following the EUGBS needs to ensure that in the deployment of the use-of-proceeds the organisation adheres to social minimums (such as the International Labour Organization (ILO) international core labour standards), commits to external validation and will follow the EU Taxonomy in the identification of the use-of-proceeds.

Before turning to the general-purpose variants of sustainable finance it is important to note that the loan markets have mimicked the developments in the bond market. Through institutions like the Loan Market Association, various guidance documents have been drawn up to help in the structuring of Green and Social loans, with the Green Loan Principles and the Social Loan Principles respectively.

General Purpose Sustainable Finance

There are Sustainable Finance structures whereby the money is not tied to specific uses and can in fact be used to finance all sorts of activities, these are often referred to as *general purpose bonds* or *general-purpose loans*. What makes these structures part of Sustainable Finance lies in the additional demands/ criteria included in the loan or bond documentation. These additional criteria link the structure of the loan or bond to specific ESG or sustainability issues, which is why these types of structures are known as *sustainability-linked*. In short, sustainability-linked loans are a form of corporate lending that is linked to the borrower's sustainability performance. These loans provide financial incentives for companies to meet or exceed sustainability targets, such as reducing greenhouse gas emissions or improving supply chain practices.

The most common incarnation of a sustainability-linked loan will be structured in such a way that when the borrower is successful in achieving the aforementioned key performance indicators (KPIs) it will receive a discount on the margin it has to pay on its loan. Conversely, if the borrower fails to achieve some or all of the KPIs, its margin will increase, and it is thus penalised for failing to achieve the sustainability-linked targets. All in all, these loans are becoming increasingly popular as a way for companies to finance their sustainability initiatives and to align their borrowing with their sustainability goals.

Although the sustainability linked variant of Sustainable Finance originated in the loan market, since then, sustainability linked bonds have also emerged. In the case of bonds, the structure tends to be somewhat different and more one-sided meaning that when a company achieves its goals nothing is altered in relation to the coupon (or interest) a company has to pay. However, when a company fails to achieve its sustainability related KPIs/ targets by a certain date (for instance, at the halfway point of the lifetime of the bond) it will pay a penalty to the bond holders in the form of a higher coupon.

Sustainable Finance as the 'New Normal'

Any assessment of the rise in Sustainable Finance, needs to look not only at the developments in the actual manifestations of Sustainable Finance, but also show how these developments compare with the overall market. Biermans and Holl have reviewed this for the development of the largest shipping (loan) portfolios held by banks. Their analysis shows that where the shipping portfolios increased in absolute terms, these tended to merely follow the overall increase of the assets of the respective banks or in fact decreased as a percentage of them (Biermans & Holl, 2023). The analysis is easier to perform using data from the public markets, especially the bond market due to the regulatory requirements on disclosures.

Figure 1 shows the development of the share of Green, Social, Sustainable and Sustainability-Linked (GSSS) bonds in the total bond market taken from a research paper published by S&P Global Ratings. The research found that between 2018 and 2022 the share of GSSS bonds rose from 4% to 13% and is expected to further increase to as much as 16% in 2023. As overall bond issuance decreased significantly in 2022, due to higher interest rates in an inflationary environment, the share of GSSS bonds has shown great resilience hinting that this is more than just a fad.

The next section will cover, in particular, sustainable finance in the maritime sector.

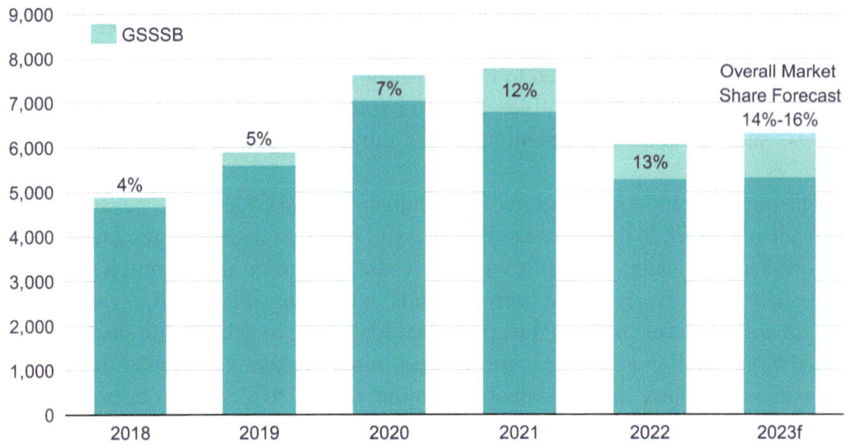

Fig. 1 Development of the GSSS Bonds as % of the overall bond market (2018–2023). Source: Sugrue and Popoola (2023)

Sustainable Finance: Maritime Examples

Although the Maritime sector was not necessarily at the forefront of the advance of sustainable finance, various elements of the sector have embraced it all the same. A number of maritime companies have issued Green and Sustainability linked Bonds and/ or have taken out sustainability-linked loans with many more considering obtaining them.

In the maritime space, sustainable finance has been used to finance a range of projects that promote sustainability. Green bonds have been used to finance the construction of energy-efficient ships and the retrofitting of existing vessels with more sustainable technologies. Sustainability-linked loans (SSL) have also been used to finance the development of sustainable shipping practices, such as the increased use of alternative fuels but mostly about the reduction of CO_2 intensity of operations.The emergence of SLLs has contributed to the spread of more sustainable shipping practices by way of tying the margin of a loan to the achievement of specific targets for specific KPIs (Lloyd's List, 2022) (Orix, 2022). In most cases one (or more) of the key performance indicators (KPIs) underpinning the structure of the loan refer to activities that can be seen as being part of the decarbonization process (Hellenic Shipping News, 2022). GHG-reduction targets, whether nominal or relative (in the form of a reduction of the overall CO2 intensity of the loan recipient company), are more often than not included as a KPI. The loan itself is general purpose and the money can be used for anything the company wants to use it for, but by including KPIs that embody GHG-reduction targets, the loans contribute to the promotion or further development of more sustainable shipping practices.

The Penetration of Sustainable Finance in the Maritime Sector

Using the database of Bloomberg, the financial, software, and data company, it is possible to have an indication of the sustainable finance transactions for Maritime companies. It should be noted that the database does not claim to be complete as it only reports on transactions that have been publicly disclosed. In some cases, privately owned companies opt to not disclose publicly their financial transactions, In such cases, banks and other involved parties are also silenced. With that caveat in mind, the overview in Table 1 below shows the Sustainable Finance transactions for Maritime companies between 2018 and 2022.

The data shows the very large increase in annual capital deployed in the Maritime Sustainable Finance transactions, from slightly above 2 billion USD in 2018 to more than 9.2 billion in 2021. The largest growth has been in the form of sustainability linked loans.

Table 1 shows that during the entire period, sustainable finance transactions were executed to the tune of USD 24.8 billion. One fifth of this amount came in the form of bonds while the remaining 80% were structured as loans. A similar division is to be found when looking at the distribution between use-of-proceeds type of structures (such as, green bonds and loans) and general purpose structures that are sustainability linked. The latter accounts for 81% of all recorded transactions and the remaining 19% is for the former.

Examples of Maritime Sustainable Finance Transactions

For both types of transactions, use-of-proceeds and sustainability-linked, there some general observations to be made as to the underlying environmental objectives deployed in the maritime sector. For most, if not all green bonds and green loans, the proceeds were used to finance new cleaner vessels or retrofit existing ones. Several examples are described in the next sub sections of this chapter.

Table 1 Sustainable finance transactions for the maritime sector (2018–2022)

	2018	2019	2020	2021	2022
Bonds					
Green	$ 0.2b	$ 0.2b	$ 0.4b	$ 1.6b	$ 0.3b
Sustainability		$ 0.2b		$ 0.0b	
Sustainability-linked				$ 1.5b	$ 0.5b
Loans					
Green	$ 0.1b	$ 0.2b	$ 0.0b	$ 1.3b	$ 0.0b
Sustainability-linked	$ 2.0b	$ 0.8b	$ 6.0b	$ 4.8b	$ 4.6b
Total	**$ 2.3b**	**$ 1.4b**	**$ 6.4b**	**$ 9.2b**	**$ 5.5b**

Source: PROW Capital based on data from Bloomberg

In the case of sustainability-linked debt instruments, the most important target used in the structures was for the reduction of the CO_2 intensity of ships, usually defined as carbon (or greenhouse gas (GHG)) emissions per goods transported per nautical mile. This is closely connected with the Poseidon principles, the global framework by which financial institutions can assess the climate alignment of their ship finance portfolios. The Poseidon Principles are discussed later in this chapter.

Green Bonds

In early October 2019 Teekay Shuttle Tankers LLC (Teekay) placed its USD 125 million inaugural green bond. The accompanying documentation indicated that this was to be a Green Bond and the proceeds were to be used to finance the company's E-shuttles—shuttle tankers powered by battery hybrid technology, liquified natural gas (LNG) and condensed volatile organic compounds as an LNG additive. The company had commissioned S&Ps Cicero Shades of Green, an enterprise that provides independent, research-based evaluations of green bond and sustainability financing frameworks to provide a second opinion on its Green Bond framework. Using Cicero's Shades of Green methodology, it designated the Green Bond as *light green*.

When the company went to market to place the bond, investors responded less than enthusiastically. With the title 'Investors balk at green bond from group specialising in oil tankers' the Financial Times reported on the poor market reception for Teekay's bond issue. This particular case has become one of the examples of the limits of sustainable financing as a way to provide capital to companies whose business models may be at odds with overall environmental objectives such as the transportation of fossil fuel.

In 2021 shipping company A.P. Moller—Maersk placed its inaugural 10-year, €500 million green bond to fund the build of its first feeder vessel as well as a series of eight large ocean-going container vessels which will be capable of operating on carbon neutral methanol by 2023 and 2024, respectively. The Bond was assessed by Cicero, which gave it a *medium green* label and the market reception was very positive as exemplified by the many investors that signed up to the bond. The final order book was €3.7bn, which in turn, contributed to the transaction being priced at a coupon of 0.75%, the lowest coupon ever for Maersk.[1]

Sustainability Linked Bonds

In 2021, Odfjell SE, a worldwide shipper of chemicals and other speciality bulk liquids successfully placed shipping's first Sustainability-Linked Bond. The bond,

[1] www.maersk.com/news/articles/2021/11/19/maersk-issues-first-green-bond-to-fund-first-green-methanol-vessels

with a tenor (maturity) of four years and a value of NOK 850 million, created a link between the way the company is financed and its fleet transition plan and its ambition to reduce the carbon intensity of its controlled fleet by 50% by 2030 compared to 2008 levels.[2]

The bond emission by Odfjell was followed by a sustainability linked bond by German international shipping and container transportation company Hapag-Lloyd in April of the same year. Here the terms of the EUR 300 million bond were explicitly linked to Hapag-Lloyd's sustainability target, namely, to significantly reduce the CO_2 intensity of the company's own fleet. With a tenor of seven years, the details of the bond stipulate that 'If the shipping company succeeds in achieving this goal, the bond will continue to have a coupon of 2.5%. However, if Hapag-Lloyd misses the intermediate target, the coupon will rise by 25 basis points for the remaining maturity of the bond—that is, until 2028.'[3]

Loans

Over the last couple of years various green loans have been issued to shipping companies to retrofit their existing fleet with so-called scrubbers, a type of exhaust gas cleaning system that is installed on ships to reduce air pollution emissions, specifically sulphur dioxide (SO_2) and particulate matter (PM). While scrubbers are an effective way to reduce air pollution emissions from ships, it should be noted that there is ongoing debate about the environmental impact of scrubbers, as they produce a waste stream that needs to be treated and disposed of properly. Not every scrubber that was financed by a green loan in the past would still be eligible for such a loan at present. As such, this is a good example of the fact that the nature of sustainability is not static but is developing and becoming more stringent over time.

In 2020 the Hong Kong-based Seaspan Corporation the biggest lessor of container ships in the world, agreed to the sector's first sustainability-linked loan, a term-loan of $200 m with a tenor of six years.[4] A supplementary sustainability opinion was issued by Sustainalytics. In addition, the structure was fully aligned with the Poseidon principles. The sustainability element was based on achieving two key sustainability performance targets related to greenhouse gas emissions. The first target was to reduce the company's greenhouse gas emissions intensity by 2% annually. The second target was to achieve a 25% reduction in greenhouse gas emissions intensity by 2025, compared to a 2018 baseline. If the company is

[2] www.odfjell.com/about/our-stories/odfjell-se-successfully-places-shippings-first-sustainability-linked-bond/

[3] www.hapag-lloyd.com/en/company/about-us/newsletter/2021/04/hapag-lloyd-s%2D%2Dgreen%2D%2Dbond-is-linked-to-sustainability-target-fo0.html

[4] www.seaspancorp.com/press_release/seaspan-announces-closing-of-sustainability-linked-loan-increases-portfolio-financing-program-to-1-8-billion/

successful in achieving these targets, it will receive a discount on the margin of the loan.

Financing Green Innovations in the Maritime Sector

The rapid transformation towards a more sustainable maritime industry requires not only substantial capital investments but also a broad range of breakthrough innovations. Ranging from alternative energy systems to non-polluting anti-fouling hull treatments and waste-water solutions, and smart digital voyage planning and routing tools, there is a plethora of innovative ventures (startups and scale-ups) in this space, with some databases listing over 600. However, such innovations require venture capital funding and risk-taking lead customers, willing to pay a premium for being a leader. Maritime innovation ecosystems nurturing such ventures are developing, although still on a rather small scale compared to other industry sectors.

Accelerator Programs

Accelerator Programs are supporting innovative ventures especially in demonstrating their solution, raising venture capital and securing pilot or lead customers. Examples of such programs are the business-to-business (B2B) maritime accelerator PortXL,[5] founded in 2016 and active in Rotterdam, Antwerp and Singapore, or the new Ashdod Port Accelerator by 500 Global.[6] In Singapore, the Maritime Port Authority (MPA) and the National University of Singapore (NUS) have been working with the PIER71[7] accelerator, supporting 100 ventures and cooperating with over 60 corporations, and their network of venture capital partners.[8]

Venture Capital

Venture Capital firms (VCs) are essential to finance risky ventures in the growth phase and surviving the 'valley of death'—the transition phase between being an early startup and a growth company serving demanding customers. An increasing number of VCs are addressing maritime decarbonization. As in most other industries, these VCs have been mostly focused on rapidly scalable digital solutions, but gradually adding 'hard tech' to their portfolio, especially with a focus on green

[5] portxl.org

[6] 500.co/accelerators/ashdod-port-accelerator.

[7] pier71.sg/

[8] sbr.com.sg/shipping-marine/news/three-new-vcs-boost-mpas-maritime-tech-startup-accelerator-programme

shipping solutions. Examples of maritime-focused VC Funds are the Rotterdam Port Fund,[9] The Dock[10] in Israel, and the Singapore-based Maritime Fund.[11] Other VC Funds are strongly impact-oriented, focusing on preserving the oceans, such as the Blue Ocean fund of Future Planet Capital.[12]

Banks can play a key role at a later stage, in financing the ships that are deploying innovative technologies from ventures. About 30 banks have subscribed to the Poseidon Principles,[13] the global framework for assessing and disclosing the climate alignment of financial institutions' shipping portfolios, to increase the transparency of the climate impact of their investments.[14]

Corporations

Corporations, especially major maritime shipping companies, play an essential role as paying customers for innovative ventures, both by providing an income stream, and by validating the offered solution and providing useful feedback. As large corporations are typically, and understandably, somewhat risk-averse, securing lead customers is often the most challenging hurdle for ventures. Therefore, corporations in some industries, like the automotive sector, have established not only their own accelerators, but also Venture Client organisations, specialising in identifying relevant ventures and supporting them to secure deals with relevant business units in the corporation.

Another approach is to create a Corporate Venture Capital unit, dedicated to investing venture capital into promising ventures, with the aim of learning about their solution and potentially acquiring the venture later. Maersk Growth,[15] for example, is the venture arm of Maersk, founded in 2017 to address especially the digitalisation and decarbonization of supply chains, making about ten venture investments a year. CMA CGM[16] offers a range of services to maritime ventures, so far focused mostly on digital transformation, including identifying corporate venture capital and the services of the Accelerator ZEBOX.

---

[9] www.rotterdamportfund.com

[10] www.thedockinnovation.com/

[11] www.hellenicshippingnews.com/maritime-sector-gets-venture-capital-boost-from-top-asian-fund/

[12] futureplanetcapital.com/news/2022/3/23/future-planet-capital-launches-new-20m-blue-ocean-mandate

[13] www.poseidonprinciples.org/finance/about/

[14] Some ventures become investors and acquirers of innovative technologies themselves, such as the Pacific Green Technologies Group—see www.pacificgreen-group.com/articles/green-shipping-will-be-powerful-lure-investors/

[15] www.maersk.com/growth

[16] www.cmacgm-group.com/en/innovation/digital-startup%20support

Government and Collaborative Funding

Government and collaborative funding are key instruments for capital investment in new vessels and energy infrastructure, deploying emerging innovations at large scale. One of the earliest collaborative efforts was the Sustainable Shipping Initiative,[17] founded in 2010 with companies including Lloyd's Register, BP Shipping, Maersk Line, Gearbulk and ABN Amro. In 2019 The Global Maritime Forum initiated the Getting to Zero Coalition,[18] focusing on decarbonizing international shipping and involving over 200 organisations, including shipping companies such as Hapag-LLoyd, technology suppliers such as Wärtsilä, energy companies such as Shell, and investment funds such as Prow Capital. An example of a collaborative investment effort, since cancelled, was the Global Environment Facility (GEF) Greener Shipping Investment Platform,[19] initiated by the World Bank, Cargill, Maersk and Mitsui. In China, the Sustainable Shipping Innovation & Development Initiative[20] has been launched as collaborative research platform by COSCO Shipping Energy Transportation, Sinopec and others.

The Way Ahead: ETS, Carbon Tax and Carbon Credits

In contrast to the previous sections where the focus has been on what is currently available in terms of financing the decarbonization of shipping, this section will cover two more, albeit interconnected topics that will have a significant influence on the business cases for decarbonization from now on. Both of the topics deal with the pricing of carbon emissions. The first is about the consequences of shipping being brought under emissions trading systems. The second topic covers the potential opportunities for shipping in the voluntary carbon credit market.

EU Emissions Trading System[21]

The EU Emissions Trading System (EU ETS) was established by the European Union and designed as a cap-and-trade system for greenhouse gas emissions. Such a system entails that a cap is set on the total amount of greenhouse gases that can be emitted by covered facilities, and emitters are required to hold allowances—EU

[17] www.sustainableshipping.org/

[18] www.globalmaritimeforum.org/getting-to-zero-coalition

[19] www.thegef.org/projects-operations/projects/10501

[20] www.seatrade-maritime.com/sustainability-green-technology/sustainable-shipping-innovation-development-initiative-launching

[21] This section is based on Biermans and van der Klip (2023).

Allowances (also known as EUAs or permits to emit) equivalent to their emissions. The cap is gradually reduced over time, so as to decrease total emissions. Companies that emit less than their allotted amount can sell or bank their excess allowances, while those that emit more than their allotted amount must purchase additional allowances. This creates a financial incentive for emitters to reduce their emissions.

Since its inception well over a decade ago, the EU ETS has seen various adjustments to its operations. Firstly, the number of industries covered and thus subject to the ETS is on the increase, the addition of shipping bears this out. Secondly, the way the system works is also changing, moving away from a cap-and-trade mechanism towards a system whereby all emissions are subject to ETS. This, in effect, means that the system becomes more comparable to a carbon tax than a cap-and-trade.

For the time being it has been decided that only ships of a certain size will be included in the EU ETS. As it stands, only vessels of 5000GT (gross tonnage) and upwards will be subject to the ETS. It covers vessels performing voyages that transport cargo for commercial purposes (including ballast voyages) or passengers.

Emissions that are considered in scope under the current ETS proposals, are:

- all emissions at a berth in an EU port
- all emissions from vessels performing voyages between EU ports
- half of the emissions of voyages arriving at an EU port from a non-EU port, and
- half of the emissions of voyages departing from an EU port to a non-EU port

The current plan is that shipping emissions will be subject to the ETS incrementally. In 2025 allowances will be required for 40% of all relevant emissions reported for 2024. This percentage will rise by 30% in 2026, meaning that in 2026 allowances would be required for 70% of the emissions reported for 2025. As of 2027, permits for all emissions reported in the previous year will be required. Important to note is that a failure to surrender the required allowances will lead to heavy fines and may even result in banning from EU ports.

The basis for emission reporting is the EU Monitoring, Report and Validate (MRV) template. As of 1 January 2018, ships over 5000 GT loading or unloading cargo or passengers at ports in the European Economic Area (EEA) are required to monitor and report their CO_2 emissions as well as other relevant information.[22]

Depending on the price of EUA's and the volume of emissions the total annual costs of ETS for the shipping industry could be anything between €6.6 billion and €7.3 billion by 2027 (Lalkens & Schiffers, 2022). To an extent, shipowners will be able to pass on the increased costs to their customers, as all vessels will be confronted by the ETS cost at the same time. At the same time, ETS puts a penalty on more polluting vessels and a relative cost benefit for less polluting vessels. The figures provided in these pages indicate that the total ETS cost per vessel, assuming more than 100 sailing days, combined with a daily ETS cost of €10 k, could be more than a million euros per year per vessel.

[22] See Biermans and van der Klip (2023).

The introduction of the ETS in the Maritime industry will have a significant impact on the demand for cleaner vessels and accelerate retrofits on existing ones. This, in combination with operational improvements means that the introduction of ETS will help in speeding up the decarbonization of the sector. (Biermans & van der Klip, 2023).

There are plans to divert some of the income generated by the auctioning of EUAs (the revenue from 20 million emission allowances) to an 'Innovation Fund' to be used for shipping-specific projects. This would constitute a new source of capital for the decarbonization of shipping.[23] At the same time it remains to be seen whether private companies will be able to tap into these funds and if so, if small and medium-sized enterprise (SME) types of businesses will be able do so as well.

Carbon Credits

Apart from the buying of Carbon credits in the EU ETS compliance market, there are other developments taking place in the maritime sector that are also linked to carbon credits but as a voluntary market. In early 2023, the Blue Sky Maritime Coalition (BSMC), an organisation committed to accelerating the transition of waterborne transportation in Canada and the United States toward net-zero greenhouse gas emissions, published a report on accelerating the maritime industry's transition toward net-zero greenhouse gas emissions by leveraging carbon credit markets.[24]

Voluntary carbon credit markets are a type of market where companies, organisations, and individuals can purchase carbon credits to offset their greenhouse gas emissions voluntarily.

Carbon credits represent a unit of carbon dioxide (CO_2) or other greenhouse gas that has been reduced or removed from the atmosphere through a project that has been verified to meet certain standards. For example, a project might involve planting trees, which absorb CO_2 from the atmosphere, or investing in renewable energy projects that displace the use of fossil fuels, such as building and operating vessels on alternative fuels.

Voluntary carbon credit markets differ from compliance carbon markets, which are regulated by government bodies and require companies to offset their emissions to comply with emissions reduction targets or regulations. By contrast, voluntary carbon credit markets are not mandatory, and companies and individuals purchase carbon credits voluntarily to demonstrate their commitment to reducing their carbon footprint.

Voluntary carbon credit markets are typically operated by intermediaries, such as brokers, who connect buyers and sellers of carbon credits. Buyers can choose to

[23] See also Faber et al. (2022)

[24] www.bluesky-maritime.org/post/new-report-expands-on-how-carbon-credit-markets-can-support-maritime-decarbonization

purchase carbon credits from a range of projects that have been verified to meet certain standards, such as the Verified Carbon Standard (VCS) and Gold Standard Carbon Credits.

In their research paper the Blue Sky Maritime Coalition notes that:

> 'Without an industry-specific framework, the maritime sector would participate on an individual company basis; however, existing standards or protocols already provide a pathway for maritime-specific methodologies. Gold Standard has a maritime carbon credit methodology, covering emissions reductions linked to retrofits that improve vessel hydrodynamics and engine performance. Carbon credits have been issued under that methodology, and more projects are underway. Another example of an emerging opportunity is adapting truck stop electric vehicle methodologies (fuel switching) to maritime vessels. Individual companies can continue building investment pathways by developing additional protocols with the standards rating bodies.' (BSMC, 2023, p7)

Although still somewhat in its infancy there are various initiatives (such as CarbonLeap[25]) that are specifically targeting the maritime sector to help maritime parties to enhance the price, value, and status of their decarbonization activities. For some companies the reduction of their emissions may take a bit more time and for those, offsetting their emissions by acquiring the voluntary carbon credits generated by ship owners, based on the operations of their more environmentally friendly vessels.

Closing Remarks

The maritime sector faces various environmental challenges, including pollution, marine ecosystem degradation, and climate change impacts. Decarbonization is crucial to reduce negative consequences and improve the industry's sustainability, requiring a mix of public and private funding sources. This chapter aims to address the question of who will pay for the transition and focuses on integrating sustainability into the financing of the maritime sector.

Sustainability has entered the financial sector as an investment theme and as a risk management aspect. The integration of Environment, Social and Governance factors in investment decisions is becoming mainstream, and the Task Force on Climate-related Financial Disclosures has introduced a new approach to assessing climate-related risks. The Task Force's approach is increasingly influential and impacts the maritime sector by requiring companies to disclose their exposure to climate-related risks.

Over the past decade, integrating Environment, Social and Governance factors into investment decisions has become increasingly important. This shift has been driven by regulatory pressure and investor preferences. During that same period sustainable finance became more prevalent in various financial products.

[25] https://carbonleap.nl/

The maritime sector has increasingly embraced sustainable finance, with various companies issuing green and sustainability-linked bonds and loans. Sustainable finance in the sector has been used for projects promoting sustainability, such as constructing energy-efficient ships and retrofitting existing vessels with eco-friendly technologies. Financing green innovations in the sector requires more venture capital and risk-taking lead-customers.

The EU Emissions Trading System and voluntary carbon credit markets will have a significant impact on the decarbonization of shipping. Shipping will be gradually included in Emissions Trading System, with full inclusion by 2027, leading to annual costs for the industry of between €6.6 billion and €7.3 billion. With this considerable cost increase the Emissions Trading System is expected to accelerate the demand for cleaner vessels and retrofits, speeding up decarbonization in the sector. This development only accentuates the need for ship owners to change their current operations if they want to have access to finance and remain competitive in a rapidly changing market.

References

Biermans, M. L., & Holl, T. (2023). *Ship finance update: An analysis of the petrofin top 40* (PROW Capital incidental white paper series 2023#02). PROW Capital. Retrieved from www.prowcapital.com/assets/files/prowcapital-whitepaper-202302-shipfinance.pdf

Biermans, M. L., & Önal, D. I. (2022). *ESG ratings for the maritime industry: A review* (PROW Capital incidental white paper series 2022#01). PROW Capital. Retrieved from www.prow-capital.com/assets/files/prowcapital-whitepaper-202201-esg-ratings.pdf

Biermans, M. L., & van der Klip, M. (2023). *The financial consequences of bringing shipping under ETS: A preliminary review* (PROW Capital incidental white paper series 2023#01). PROW Capital. Retrieved from www.prow-capital.com/assets/files/prowcapital-whitepaper-202301-ets.pdf

BSMC. (2023, February). Blue Sky Maritime Coalition, maritime decarbonization investments should leverage the carbon credit market to overcome investment hurdles. *Finance, Commercial & Chartering Workstream*. Retrieved from https://www.bluesky-maritime.org/post/new-report-expands-on-how-carbon-credit-markets-can-support-maritime-decarbonization

European Commission. (2018). EU's action plan for financing sustainable growth. Retrieved from https://eur-lex.europa.eu/legal-content/EN/TXT/HTML/?uri=CELEX:52018DC0097

European Commission. (2021). *Commission delegated regulation 2021/2139 Technical screening criteria for determining the conditions under which an economic activity qualifies as contributing substantially to climate change mitigation and for determining whether that economic activity causes no significant harm to any of the other environmental objectives of the EU taxonomy*. Retrieved from. https://eur-lex.europa.eu/legal-content/EN/TXT/PDF/?uri=CELEX:32021R2139#:~:text=Article%201-,The%20technical%20screening%20criteria%20for%20determining%20the%20conditions%20under%20which,down%20in%20Article%209%20of

Faber, J., Meijer, C., Nelissen, D., & van den Toorn, E. (2022). *Fit for 55 and 2030, milestones for maritime shipping: A pathway towards 2050*. CE Delft.

Hellenic Shipping News. (2022). *Wallenius Wilhelmsen releases a sustainability-linked financing framework*. Published February 10, 2022. Available via https://www.hellenicshippingnews.com/wallenius-wilhelmsen-releases-a-sustainability-linked-financing-framework/

HLEG on Sustainable Finance (2018). *Financing a sustainable European economy*. Final report 2018 by the High-Level Expert Group on Sustainable Finance, Secretariat provided by the European Commission; European Commission, Brussels. Retrieved from https://finance.ec.europa.eu/publications/high-level-expert-group-sustainable-finance-hleg_en

Houtven, G., Van, M., Gallaher, J. W., & Decker, E. (2022). *Act now or pay later: The costs of climate inaction for ports and shipping*. EDF & RTI International. Retrieved from www.edf.org/media/shipping-industry-and-ports-susceptible-billions-dollars-damage-disruption-climate-change

Lalkens, P., & Schiffers, M. (2022, December 1). Kogel door de kerk: scheepvaart gaat betalen voor CO_2-uitstoot, Het Financieele Dagblad. Last accessed May 22, 2023, from fd.nl/economie/1459784/kogel-door-de-kerk-scheepvaart-gaat-betalen-voor-co-uitstootlast

Lloyd's List. (2022). *Special report: Shipping finance*. Published August 30, 2022. Available via https://lloydslist.maritimeintelligence.informa.com/special-reports/2022/Shipping-Finance/Report

Orix. (2022). *News release - ORIX begins providing sustainability-linked loans for ship finance*. Published February 17, 2022. Retrieved from https://www.orix.co.jp/grp/en/newsrelease/220217_ORIXE.html

Petrofin Research. (2022). *Key developments and growth in global ship-finance*, September 2022 by Ted Petropoulos, Head, Petrofin Research; Petrofin Research, Athens, Retrieved from www.petrofin.gr

Sugrue, D., & Popoola, B. (2023). *Sustainable bond issuance will return to growth in 2023*. S&P Sustainability Insights | Research, S&P Global Ratings. Retrieved from www.spglobal.com/ratings/en/research/pdf-articles/230207-sustainable-bond-issuance-will-return-to-growth-in-2023-101572346

TCFD. (2017). *Task force on climate-related financial disclosures (2017): Recommendations of the task force on climate-related financial disclosures*. Retrieved from www.fsb-tcfd.org/wp-content/uploads/2017/06/FINAL-2017-TCFD-Report-11052018.pdf

Part V
Case Studies: Selected Maritime Decarbonization Initiatives

Actions Being Taken by Key Segments to Meet the Decarbonization Targets

Kris Kosmala

Target Audience

Who should read this chapter:

- Policy researchers and policy makers working on defining and implementing regulations related to decarbonization efforts in the shipping industry
- Senior managers in charge of decarbonization strategies working for port authorities, marine terminal operators, and ship operators
- Senior information management and technology managers in charge of digital-led transformation projects within ports, terminals and ship operators

Key Takeaway Messages

The aim of this article is to:

- Identify actions actually taking place in the key segments of the maritime shipping industry to meet the decarbonization targets being set by the regulators.
- Identify the implications of the major regulations targeting decarbonization on the behaviours of key actors within the industry.
- Describe some of the digital technologies and how they can impact decarbonization.

K. Kosmala (✉)
Marine Digital, Lübeck, Germany
e-mail: kriskosmala@yahoo.com

M. Lind et al. (eds.), *Maritime Decarbonization*,
https://doi.org/10.1007/978-3-031-39936-7_20

Introduction

When in April 2018 the International Maritime Organization (IMO) adopted its Initial IMO Strategy on Reduction of GHG Emissions from Ships, hardly anybody across the various segments of the shipping industry appreciated the implications of the effort required to achieve industrial scale decarbonization of shipping by 2050. The year 2050, with its 32-year lead-time, seemed to give the industry sufficient time to fully achieve complete decarbonization.

While outsiders tend to think of decarbonization as simply a matter of changing ships to operate on fuel which causes no carbon emissions, the fact is that shipping does not consist of just the ship operators, but a myriad of other supporting and complementary segments, each with distinct business models and their unique decision frames which affect how they can go about implementing such a radical change as decarbonization.

The Shipping Value Chain

The shipping value chain is not a linear process, but a series of loops which cross each other. At each of these crossings, at least two types of businesses representing two distinct segments of the industry need to interact. More often than not, the result of such interaction is a level of friction, with both sides operating to maximise their business and at the same time achieve their own, often very different, decarbonization objectives (ABS, 2021). The complexity of this overlapping and interconnected system is further affected when conflicting regulations apply to each segment without any meaningful coordination.

The interactions between a visiting ship and the services in a port of call is a key scenario that illustrates many of the problems that need to be solved if industry-wide decarbonization is to be achieved. Let us take a port located in a congested metropolitan area that has been regulated to reduce emissions from operations by a date not too far in the future. Obviously, operations in that port interact with the operations of the shipping companies calling at that port, with most ships today burning carbon-based bunker and some liquefied natural gas (LNG). While the decarbonizing of those ships is in the regulatory purview of the International Maritime Organization (IMO), the regulations imposed on a port by the local authority, often owning whole or part of the port, has the potential to set more stringent emissions limits such that existing ships calling on the port are unable to meet.

Bunkering provides another demonstration of the potential conflicts and the need for much greater cooperation, even when low- or no-carbon fuels are available. As has been reported in other chapters in this book, the energy density of low- or no-carbon fuels is up to 3 times less, meaning that ships must fuel more often or carry 3 times more fuel than at present. So, a ship using carbon-neutral fuel will need to replenish her fuel supply in more ports or in larger volumes than before.

The ports in question will need to have an infrastructure in place to fuel ships efficiently and minimise the time a ship spends in port beyond the time necessary to load or to discharge her cargo. The bunkering procedures followed by the port and the ship operator may need to be updated as well. For example, current agreement between the ship operator, the port and the bunker supplier may allow execution of bunkering operations at the same time as cargo was being loaded/discharged. Use of alternative fuels may represent much higher risk of unintended combustion posing different risks to the vessel, the crews and the cargo than those known with bunkering of fossil fuels.

Multiple supply chains operated by parties independent of a port and the ship operator also influence fuelling operations. There is the supply chain of the cargo owner, the supply chain of the port (workforce, equipment, land), the supply chain of the fuel supplier, and the supply chain of the fuel delivery operator. All these unique parties must operate cooperatively for the fuelling interaction between the primary players, the port and the ship operator, to be optimised and efficient. If we have two types of carbon-neutral fuel available for ships visiting a port, then the complexity, from the perspective of the port and the port-related parties, can also easily double.

Ships being refuelled with carbon-neutral fuels is the vision for 2050. Many things and many decisions will occur in the various segments of the shipping industry, as they move along a path from now towards 2050. For each company involved, its path needs to be understood in the context of the IMO's 2050 shipping decarbonization objectives (IMO, 2018) and the Greenhouse Gas Protocol—the global standard for companies and organisations to measure and manage their greenhouse gas (GHG) emissions (GHG Protocol, 2004). The GHG Protocol provides accounting and reporting standards for carbon emissions that occur in the value chain of a company. They include Scope 1, 2 and 3 emissions. Scope 1 emissions are the direct emissions from a company's operations; Scope 2 emissions are those from indirect energy emissions, such as energy purchased by a company; and Scope 3 emissions are all other indirect emissions (not included in Scope 2) that occur in the value chain of a company.

Different Segments, Different Decarbonization Paths

It should be understood that every type of stakeholder in shipping (ship owners, ports, charterers, and others) are likely to focus their decarbonization effort on so-called 'low hanging fruit' within their domain and most will only invest to the extent of meeting their obligations under the existing regulations. This is critical to understanding that cross domain initiatives such as Just-in-Time port call optimisation (IMO, 2022) requiring collaboration between stakeholders in two different domains may be much slower than decarbonization steps that do not rely on tight collaboration between different domains.

The situation in Singapore and California ports provide interesting examples to consider how regulators and operators of maritime assets affect each other.

In the case of Singapore, the Singapore Maritime and Port Authority (MPA) issues regulations to reflect updates to The International Convention for the Prevention of Pollution from Ships (MARPOL). Using MPA's regulatory circulars as the basis, the operator of the Port of Singapore (PSA) has set ambitious targets to reduce Scope 1 and Scope 2 carbon emissions by 50% by 2030 and by 75% by 2040, from 2019 levels (PSA, 2021). However, no hard commitments have been made for Scope 3 emissions. Why? Because as a major bunkering port in South East Asia for all types of fuel, Singapore is visited by fleets of bulk and tanker vessels which may not meet the in-port emissions limits set by PSA.

In the case of California, The California Air Resources Board (CARB) has issued regulations designed to reduce emissions from ocean-going vessels while docked at California's busiest ports (CARB 2014–2023). The intention of the regulator is clearly aimed at reducing air pollution from ships in California ports, but terminals operators, port authorities, and ship owners are free to decide how they comply with the regulations. In the busiest California port, the Port of Long Beach has pledged to slash emissions that worsen air quality across Southern California. However, the terms of terminal concessions with terminal operators have no hard emissions targets placed on the operators. As a result, there has been no significant lowering of emissions from the terminals. The government of the City of Long Beach argues that it is powerless to deliver the pledged air quality improvements since the terminal operators are not bound by the regulations.

These two examples clearly show that independently of actions and behaviours regulated within any two interacting domains, it is only the synchronisation of multiple domains that will guarantee significant and meaningful progress in decarbonizing the maritime ecosystem.

Ship Owners/Operators

The decarbonization path to be followed by ship owners/operators consists of eventually retiring ships burning conventional fossil fuels and acquiring ships burning carbon-neutral fuels. In addition to acquiring suitable ships that will be economically viable, the owners face the huge capital expense of acquiring such ships. At the moment, it seems the tempo for ordering replacement ships will be different for the various segments of owners. There are several factors that influence this, as explained below.

Fuel for Ships

While switching to ships powered 100% by methanol, ammonia or hydrogen is the long-term objective of the shipowners, current orders are being placed predominantly for ships with dual-fuel engines, with LNG being the most popular choice for the secondary fuel (UNCTAD, 2021). There is, of course, an ongoing dispute on harmful emissions from burning LNG, but from the perspective of ship owners needing to place orders right now, LNG is attractive as a transition fuel that avoids the high costs of 100% carbon-neutral fuel powered ships.

LNG dual-fuel engines deliver an estimated 35% reduction in CO_2 emissions and a significant reduction of nitrogen oxides (NOx) and particulate matter from vessel exhausts. The combination of traditional+LNG fuel and voyage optimisation technology will allow ships to maintain a Carbon Intensity Indicator (CII) rating in bands A to C, an attractive outcome to the ship buyer and operator. The CII regulation is a set of reporting measures implemented by the IMO to reduce GHG emissions from commercial ships.

The orders for carbon-neutral fuel vessels are slowly trickling in. In terms of all orders, they represent only a very small percentage of newly ordered vessels, but it is a trickle growing in size. According to Alphaliner, of the 222 vessels ordered in 2022, about 80% will be using LNG as the carbon-neutral fuel and about 13% will be using methanol. Owners of container ships are at the forefront of placing orders for carbon-neutral ships. At the time of writing, the top 10 container carriers have placed orders for methanol-fuelled ships (Moore, 2023) bringing the total on order and in operation to nearly 50 ships.

Owners of bulkers and tankers are moving more slowly, mostly due to the fact that their profit margins are too low to accumulate sufficient capital to place large orders for new ships. While majority of tankers fitted to use carbon-neutral fuel use LNG, uptake of methanol as a carbon-neutral option is increasing. At the time of writing, there are about 25 methanol-fuelled chemical tankers on order and in operation.

Meanwhile, the owners/operators of existing older vessels are guided by several regulations set out by the IMO in The International Convention for the Prevention of Pollution from Ships (MARPOL) Annex VI. The policy instruments under the MARPOL umbrella relevant to ship owners/operators include bans on carrying non-compliant fuel oil, global and regional sulphur caps, and technical standards for engine installations. The technical standards to reduce carbon emissions under MARPOL are focused on ships using conventional fossil fuels. These standards are known as the Energy Efficiency Design Index (EEDI), the Energy Efficiency Existing Ship Index (EEXI), and the CII. The standards are all set to become progressively more stringent over time. This is to ensure that ships either become increasingly less carbon intensive or are withdrawn from service. Calculation and reporting these indicators do not apply to alternative propulsion technologies. This means that owners ordering vessels powered by alternatives such as battery-hybrid propulsion, synthetic fuels, or green methanol do not gain any credit for their investments through the existing regulations.

It has to be noted that there is nothing in the IMO policy toolkit directly targeting economic incentives for the shipping industry to shift to zero emission fuels (Bach & Hansen, 2023).

Engine Power Optimisation

Ship's speed significantly influences the fuel consumption and emissions during a voyage. Thus, owners with vessels which are still economically and operationally sound, are acting to achieve an acceptable level of fleet compliance by implementing technology solutions on their vessels' existing engines, such as engine power limitation or shaft power limitation. The expectation of the owners is that limiting the engine's power combined with finding the optimal speed for sailing using voyage optimisation technology can allow ships to maintain their EEXI and CII ratings for two to three years longer, while also burning less expensive conventional carbon-based fuels. Engine power limitation technologies can improve a ship's CII and can also benefit from digital information management solutions both on the ships and ashore.

The IMO regulations themselves do not stipulate what the various solutions could be. The calculations of EEDI, EEXI and CII are not influenced by the use of software applications by the ship's operator. However, software solutions can make a difference for fuel efficiency and will be used increasingly by owners/operators while the fleet composition is in transition.

Voyage Optimisation

Finding the optimal sailing/service speed for ships can be extremely beneficial to reducing fuel consumption and air emissions (Solem et al., 2015). The digital information management solution is known as voyage optimisation. Voyage optimisation is a software which will increasingly include the use of artificial intelligence. It can be readily adapted to different types of ships sailing varying distances and routes at different speeds and creating different energy demands. For each ship's voyage, the software takes into consideration a vessel's technical specifications, fuel specifications, distance to sail and the predicted weather along the intended route. While the vessel is sailing, the software can make adjustments to the engine controls to limit fuel consumption or provide recommendations for the Master to consider, while preserving a ship's ability to manoeuvre, her integrity and her safety.

The earliest versions of voyage optimisation software offered less flexibility, as they were based on what the vessel reported once per day back to shore in a format known as the 'noon report'. This way of reporting and consequently adjusting operations in the reporting vessel created a significant lag between the time the sailing decisions are taken on the ship and the time the on-shore operations controllers understand the impacts of those decisions on the commercial and operational efficiency of the voyage.

Modern versions of voyage optimisation technology rely on on-board installation of a software controller connected directly to sensors and equipment controls. The data is read from sensors and instruments in real time which offers significantly higher data accuracy and granularity than that collected through the typical noon report process. Progress in artificial intelligence (AI) will continually enhance capability of such on-board voyage optimisation solutions thereby potentially maintaining vessels' positive EEXI and CII ratings for longer.

At present, computing resources consumed by AI require onshore processing of data collected from the ship. The future of ship digitalisation is in the technology known as Edge AI.

Edge AI is the deployment of AI applications on devices at the location of the user at the edge of the network, close to where the data is located, rather than in some centrally located data centre (in the cloud or on premise). Since the internet has near-global reach, the edge of the network can be any location. The connectivity to on-shore vessel operations control is still maintained, but only exceptions/anomalies are exchanged and resolved between the ship application and the application working in a land-based operations centre.

Ports

The decarbonization path for ports is not affected by the regulations issued by the IMO. Instead, ports must comply with the environmental regulations issued by the jurisdiction in which they operate. Those jurisdictions may be the domain of a city or regional government, and in some rare cases, the national government.

What the port may do with regard to decarbonization will differ according to their business and operating models, for example, whether they are landlords on whose land port terminals implement their own decarbonization efforts or they are active operators of the terminals and can scale up decarbonization efforts to encompass both port and terminal operations.

Ports can nevertheless influence ship operators in the uptake of IMO-based decarbonization efforts. The most popular approach today is through offering lower port fees to vessels that generate lower emissions. This approach can be even more powerful, if accompanied by a port's investment in infrastructure supporting value chains for zero-emission fuels, allowing vessels to bunker their preferred carbon-neutral fuel. This is being instigated through the Green Corridors initiative (COP26, 2021) discussed elsewhere in this book.

Cold Ironing

Another significant incentive available to ports is the provision of shore power supply to ships, also known as cold ironing, to prevent emissions originating from onboard power generation based on heavy fuel oil or diesel oil, while the ships are at berth. Ports deciding to invest in on-shore power have to address both the issue of installing the infrastructure and designing an attractive pricing structure for the use of shore electricity by ships. Leading the way are the ports on the Baltic Sea. At the time of writing, there are five ports with shore power, rising to between 9 and

14 ports by 2030. Where there is a supply, the demand follows, as evidenced by major cruise lines offering cruises in the Baltic region. They collectively signed a Memorandum of Understanding which committed the lines to using shore power available at ports in the Baltic Sea, as soon as possible and no later than from January 1, 2024. Significant progress has also been made on the US coast to service cruise ships.

Electrification

Harbour craft such as tugboats, inspection vessels and fuel lighters, are another source of in-port emissions and a natural target for electrification. As many harbour craft are operated by small companies, port authorities will need to consider how to incentivise the transition in addition to issuing appropriate regulations. An example to watch is the port of Singapore, where the MPA has directed that by 2030 all new harbour craft (including pleasure craft) will have to be fully electric, be capable of using pure biodiesel (B100), or be compatible with net-zero fuels such as hydrogen.

Optimisation of Port Operations

Decarbonization gains from electrification, however substantial, are not comparable to the scale of gains obtained through the implementation of computer-assisted optimisation of operations. Consider that there are two key sources of emissions within ports' boundaries. These are generated by vessels waiting at anchorages in expectation of loading/unloading their cargo and the movements of cargo vessels between the port boundary and the berths.

According to studies (Xia et al., 2021), minimising vessel movements between the port boundary and a berth would result in a significant reduction in in-port emissions. It follows that managing the end-to-end process of ships' arrivals and departures with minimal re-planning effort should be the first objective of port decarbonization efforts.

According to current thinking, port's activities begin at the moment when a ship arrives at the port boundary, engages vessel traffic service (VTS) and is directed to the pilot boarding place or proceeds directly to a specific berth, if the vessel is authorised to arrive at/depart from the berth without pilotage assistance. At the other end of the arrival management process is the moment of declaring 'all lines fast' at a berth. In between these two events, various actors (including the ship's master, port traffic controller, pilot, tugboat operator, bunker supply vessel, quay mooring team, and others) act according to the data they have at their disposal or data that was passed to them by another actor. In the majority of the ports, the means of transferring information between any two actors in possession of their own information are inefficient and prone to errors, as they often rely on one-to-one telephone calls, e-mails or printed documents.

Data inconsistencies between any two or more actors are one of the major issues of efficiently managing a vessel's arrival and departure. As many ports see the time wasted to resolve data inconsistencies as having direct impact on increased in-port emissions from ships and craft needed to serve the vessel on arrival, at berth and at departure, their digitalisation efforts aim to establish a data-enabled process of managing vessel's arrival with minimal friction between decisions taken by each actor and minimal human effort.

Digitalising the Port

Ensuring the efficient movement of a vessel around a port requires data from the vessel, port waters and the terminal. Some of this data is static (for example, berth's length) and some is dynamic (such as, wind, wave direction and height). Data provided dynamically can be obtained in real time from surveillance systems and sensors. On the vessel's side, the port needs to have knowledge of a vessel's identity, parameters, payload, and status to know which of the port's service partners are required. On the terminal's side, the port needs to have knowledge of any berth constraints, a schedule of all berthing requirements across multiple time horizons, pier length, and any mooring constraints due to wind, tide or waves. Regarding the port's waters, the port needs to know the weather conditions, movements of all vessels within the channels and basins, safety distances between a ship and other vessels moving/stationary within the port, and any other port-specific constraints.

Processing such diverse and voluminous data into operational insight and awareness is neither cheap, nor easy. The technology solution that encompasses data collection, real time processing and real time operations optimisation is known as digital twinning. A digital twin is a virtual representation of a system that spans its lifecycle, is updated from real-time data, and uses simulation, machine learning and reasoning to help decision making. Digital twinning is not a simulation solution. It is a real time operations decision support solution powered by AI. At the time of writing, just a handful of ports have invested in the operational digital twin technology solutions capable of envisioning and solving operational problems based on the diverse events reported to a port's operations centre.

More ports have invested in partial solutions targeting the optimisation of ship movement scheduling with an objective to increase ports' vessel traffic throughput and improve the safety in ports' access channels and basins. It should be noted that decarbonization was not the primary objective of those projects, even though fewer emissions are the probable side results of such projects. While ports applying advanced information technology to optimise traffic need to be commended for their initiatives, the greatest impact on decarbonization objectives of shipping will come from ports managing vessels' arrivals.

Just in Time Port Call Optimisation

As mentioned earlier, ships' operators will be optimising their voyages so that the CII rating of their ships continues to meet the ever more stringent regulatory requirements. However, any benefits on a ship's CII measure resulting from slower steaming dissipate quickly, if the vessel arrives in port, but the port is not ready to take the vessel. Current experience in ports around the world is that vessels arrive at ports all too often only to find that the berth space they need is not available because another ship is occupying it, their cargo is not available for loading, or no terminal yard space is available to accept their cargo to be discharged. This results in the ship either having to wait at anchor for hours, days, or even weeks, or manoeuvre at very low speeds in the port area while waiting for the availability of a berth.

Solving the problem of managing vessels' arrivals in such a way that they are never forced to anchor and wait for their berth slot in a port is a key stage in the achievement of decarbonization in the shipping industry as a whole (Xia et al., 2021). The implementation of a 'never wait' concept is broadly known as Just in Time Port Call Optimisation (JiT Port Call). The purpose of JiT Port Call is to counteract the current modus operandi of ships' operators responding to ports' policy of handling the ships in order of their arrival at the destination port. The 'first come, first served' operating model, which forces the ships' operators to 'hurry up and wait', rather than steam at lower speeds, needs to change.

While conceptually JiT Port Call is simple to understand, in practice it is incredibly difficult to implement. At the heart of the problem is the existence of multiple planners, each responsible to a different domain. On one side there is the vessel voyage operator who plans the voyage and arrival at a port on behalf of the ship's operator (owner/operator or charterer). Then there is the port planner who plans the allocation of port resources (including pilot, tugboats, access channel, lock, etc.) to manage ship's arrival/departure. Then there is the terminal planner who allocates ship's berthing positions and coordinates quay mooring crews. All functions have their own 'optimal' plans of work, but each can be mutually dependent of the plans of another. This means that as the plans of one planner change, then it can affect the plans of others. The dynamics affecting each actor's planning are impossible to solve by means of informatics. At best, the computation and analytics available today can make each unique planner aware of a developing situation in near real time with the understanding that any decision taken by the planner *ad hoc* will destroy the 'optimal' plan created by the planners of other actors.

Just as the future of vessel voyage optimisation may lie in AI being deployed to the vessel and not solely in shore-based operations centres, JiT Port Call may become possible with the AI being able to run multiple optimisations observing each actor's constraints and operational realities and then make optimal decisions that best satisfy an ideal scenario from each actor's perspective. That level of sophistication is still a distant informatics future, but also an inevitable direction of progress for JiT Port Call.

Terminals

The decarbonization of marine terminals follows another path. Energy consumption and the resulting emissions by the terminals are significant in terminals due to the material handling equipment (MHE) used every day and the necessity to provide near daylight conditions at night to facilitate 24-hour operations. Equipment that relies on green electrical energy is the likely long-term solution.

Upgrading the lighting systems in terminals is one of the 'lowest hanging fruit' in terminal decarbonization. The high-pressure sodium or metal halide lighting currently in use consumes significantly more energy comparing to LED lighting. Additionally, LED lights last about 10 years, while traditional light fixtures need to be replaced about every 2 to 3 years. Thus, upgrading the lighting system not only reduces energy consumption, but also offers significantly lower annual maintenance costs.

The MHE represents both the challenge and the opportunity in decarbonizing terminal operations. The most energy intensive is the quay-to-yard interface involving movement of the cargo between the ship and the quay by yard cranes and the subsequent moving of the cargo about the yard. For obvious reasons, many more moves by equipment are performed within a container yard as compared to a bulk yard.

The majority of container terminals currently use diesel-operated equipment. Electrification of that equipment, including quay cranes, yard horizontal transport equipment, and yard cranes represents the *low hanging fruit* in the decarbonization efforts.

Digitalising the Terminal

The cornerstone information technology at the disposal of a terminal operator is the Terminal Operating System (TOS). A vessel stowage plan is maintained within the TOS and used to plan the loading/discharging order, assignments of quay-side equipment and the workforce required to operate the equipment and supervise the quay and yard operations.

While the TOS may help vessel planners, container terminals frequently use different systems to plan and optimise yard operations, a major source of fossil fuels emissions today However, a terminal's ability to reduce emissions by applying advanced optimisation technology is incredibly difficult. There are simply too many variables considering ship-to-shore moves, quay-to-yard transport, intra-yard moves, and yard-to-gate moves. Current technology cannot handle instantaneous re-optimisation that can be propagated forward to assure 100% of times that there are no negative unintended consequences on delivery of subsequent planned activities and tasks. On hectic days when more equipment units break down, containers lifted are not in the sequence that is indicated on the stow plan, or human injury is reported that temporarily stops the equipment work, pre-arranged optimal plans are invalidated in an instant and KPIs can drop substantially. This makes any emissions reduction gains sporadic and unpredictable. However, it is important to understand that gains.

The existence of unique planning problems requires every terminal to maintain two unique roles: vessel planner and yard planner. Both functions have their own 'optimal' plans of work that are mutually impacted by the other. The reality of the planning is that the first draft of a plan is no longer valid from the moment a vessel is berthed and the operations begin. Equipment breakdowns experienced during the operations force ad hoc decisions to be made by the operations crew on the quay resulting in consequential replanning by the two planners, each of which is affected by the plans of the other, which further compounds the inefficiencies. The result is often a far greater consumption of energy by the equipment moving the cargo between the quay and the yard, as well as, within the yard. Considering that about 8 litres of diesel equivalent are needed to handle a single dry container, solving the issue of data integration and function integration with the help of information technologies would open significant opportunities to decarbonize ports where diesel-operating equipment is in use.

The dynamics of quay operations, regardless of the type of the terminal are very difficult to solve by means of information management solutions. TOS in use today do not have sufficient sophistication to perform real time re-optimisation of plans, as new events on the quay and in the yard become known. The cost of researching and developing optimisation technologies and retrofitting them into the existing TOS fabric is very high and the payback to the developer very uncertain.

Where terminals differ from the port is in the level of robotics and automation that has been developed specifically for each terminal handling specific types of cargo. The existence and implementation of robotic automation on quay cranes, yard cranes and yard equipment which can work autonomously and eventually communicate directly with each other without requiring actions by TOS or human planners. This is happening in no small measure thanks to the work of The Terminal Industry Committee 4.0 (TIC 4.0) which has brought together terminal operators and terminal equipment manufacturers to collaboratively establish formats and protocols for electronic data exchange between the machines and the software.

Just as the future of JiT Port Call optimisation may lie in AI being deployed close to the makers of operational decisions, better terminal optimisation may become possible with the AI being able to run multiple optimisations observing each resource's (quay machine, yard machine, human worker, etc) constraints and the operational realities to make optimal decisions.

Closing Remarks

Moving to a low-carbon shipping value chain is not going to be as easy as imagined. Various segments of shipping, be it the owners, ports, terminals, or charterers will consider designing this process only in the context of their own business models and their own business objectives. This is not a criticism on my part. I am simply conscious of the realities of each type of business touching the shipping value chain.

Shipowners need to be conscious of the fuels that their ships will need to burn in a low carbon future. Their strategy of ordering dual-fuel (MGO + version of carbon-neutral fuel) ships combined with advances in vessel voyage optimisation software technology will carry them through the next 15–20 years during which time the demand and supply of low/zero carbon fuels will form a competitive global market of producers, wholesalers and fuel suppliers in ports.

Ports need to be conscious that clear steps are required toward the better organisation of port and terminal resources to avoid ships arriving at their ports and not being serviced immediately. There will be circumstances when a ship's arrival and departure will have nothing to do with the efficiency and the work organisation of a port. That is understandable, but likely an exception. Not offering the JiT Port Call will slow down decarbonization efforts of ships' operators.

All technology solutions, not just the digital ones, that support the decarbonization of international shipping will continue to advance more rapidly than any stakeholder within any segment of shipping can possibly imagine. Meanwhile, decarbonization for some will only move at the pace of the slowest acting/reacting stakeholder. An ability to understand and adapt to changes with the least possible disruption should be the primary objective of each business related to shipping.

Politics will always be part of shipping and careful consideration needs to be given to the implementation of carbon-accounting principles and regimes varying by geography, economic bloc or specific administrative jurisdiction. Conflicts will undoubtfully arise, but shipping stakeholders would be wise to spend less energy on complaining and more energy on finding and implementing solutions ahead of the curve of political pressures and changes.

A harmonised decarbonization strategy of every segment of shipping would be better than the current patchwork of actions taken by each specific segment of shipping. In the absence of such, stakeholders in each segment need to reach out to their counterparts in other segments and demonstrate that cooperation across the business lines is better for decarbonization than trying to achieve one in the silo.

References

ABS. (2021). *Setting the course to low carbon shipping. view of the value chain*. American Bureau of Shipping.

Bach, H., & Hansen, T. (2023). *IMO off course for decarbonisation of shipping? Three challenges for stricter policy. 2023*. Marine Policy 147. 105379. https://doi.org/10.1016/j.marpol.2022.105379. Available via https://www.researchgate.net/profile/Hanna-Bach/publication/365338928_IMO_off_course_for_decarbonisation_of_shipping_Three_challenges_for_stricter_policy/links/637b519f54eb5f547cf033f4/IMO-off-course-for-decarbonisation-of-shipping-Three-challenges-for-stricter-policy.pdf

CARB. (2023). *Ocean-going vessel at-berth regulation*. California Air Resources Board (CARB), 2014–2023. Available via https://ww2.arb.ca.gov/our-work/programs/ocean-going-vessels-berth-regulation

COP26. (2021). *Clydebank declaration for green shipping corridors*. 26th UN Climate Change Conference. Available via https://www.gov.uk/government/publications/cop-26-clydebank-declaration-for-green-shipping-corridors/cop-26-clydebank-declaration-for-green-shipping-corridors

GHG Protocol. (2004). *The greenhouse gas protocol*. World Resources Institute and World Business Council for Sustainable Development. Available via https://ghgprotocol.org/sites/default/files/standards/ghg-protocol-revised.pdf

IMO. (2018). *Initial IMO strategy on the reduction of greenhouse gas emissions from ships*. Available via https://unfccc.int/sites/default/files/resource/250_IMO%20submission_Talanoa%20Dialogue_April%202018.pdf

IMO. (2022). *IMO Marine Environment Protection Committee 79th session record of proceedings and record of updates to the regulations*. Available via https://www.imo.org/en/MediaCentre/MeetingSummaries/Pages/MEPC-79th-session.aspx

Moore, R. (2023). *Top 20 container carriers: Going for growth – and methanol*. Riviera Maritime Media Ltd. Published April 29, 2023. Available via https://www.rivieramm.com/news-content-hub/news-content-hub/top-20-carriers-going-for-growth%2D%2Dand-methanol-75949

PSA. (2021). *PSA international sustainability report 2021 - Green horizons: Collaborating for change*. Port of Singapore Authority (PSA). Available via https://www.globalpsa.com/sustainability-report/

Solem, S., Fagerholt, K., Erikstad, S. O., et al. (2015). Optimization of diesel electric machinery system configuration in conceptual ship design. *Journal of Marine Science and Technology, 20*(3), 406–416. https://doi.org/10.1007/s00773-015-0307-4

UNCTAD. (2021). *Review of maritime transport 2021*. United Nations Conference on Trade and Development (UNCTAD). Available via https://unctad.org/publication/review-maritime-transport-2021

Xia, Z., Guo, Z., Wang, W., & Jiang, Y. (2021). *Joint optimization of ship scheduling and speed reduction: A new strategy considering high transport efficiency and low carbon of ships in port*. State Key Laboratory of Coastal and Offshore Engineering, Dalian University of Technology. Available via https://www.sciencedirect.com/science/article/abs/pii/S0029801821006521?via%3Dihub

Maritime Decarbonization—Actions by Cargo Owners: The Shippers' Perspective

Philip Evans and Audrey Macnab

Key Takeaway Messages

This chapter sets out the strategies adopted by leading cargo owners and their partners to influence the actions and services provided by the maritime sector. It includes a number of case studies based on interviews[1] with key personnel in prominent cargo owner companies, whose aim is to accelerate decarbonization and offer a more sustainable freight logistics solution.

Target Audience

This chapter aims to provide insight and interest for those who have a role or interest in global supply chains, freight logistics and sustainable growth, and in particular the decarbonization of the maritime trade through the lens of major cargo owners and their partners.

In particular, this chapter is written with the following in mind: logistics managers, procurement and sustainability specialists and all those with management responsibility in freight logistics within global supply chains.

[1]Contributions for this chapter have been provided by Stora Enso (Berit Hägerstrand-Ävall, Vice President, Sea Logistics), Cargill (Jan Dieleman, Business Leader, Ocean Transportation), Electrolux Group (Daniel Cole, Logistics Purchasing Director), Henkel (Istvan Lencz, Director, Global Logistics), DB Schenker (Sophie Drakopoulos, Manager, Strategic Projects & Sustainability), BICEPS Network (Coen Faber, Director), and FrieslandCampina (Walter Vermeer, Head of Logistics Procurement)

P. Evans (✉) · A. Macnab
The European Freight & Logistics Leaders' Forum, Brussels, Belgium
e-mail: philip.evans@europeanfreightleaders.eu; audrey.macnab@europeanfreightleaders.eu

M. Lind et al. (eds.), *Maritime Decarbonization*,
https://doi.org/10.1007/978-3-031-39936-7_21

The chapter should also be of interest to policy makers and academics with interest in the movement of freight and the development of policies related to decarbonization and sustainability regulation.

Introduction

He who pays the piper calls the tune. This much-quoted proverb has historically held little sway in the maritime world with carrier behemoths and their alliances dominating the supply side for containers against a highly fragmented demand side (even large cargo owners each make up less than 1% of the total container volumes) and bulk carriers are often too remote from the consumer. Furthermore, the sector is highly cyclical and subject to external non-controllable but significant variables, distorting the decision-making process and willingness to make the required investment, thus making it complex to analyse the influence that cargo owners may have on the progress of maritime decarbonization.

This chapter is intended to show how the cargo owners or shippers are influencing the actions of the maritime community, in particular the ocean carriers, to accelerate change and incentivise more sustainable logistics solutions. Supply chains continue to develop and geopolitical forces will always throw up roadblocks but the waterways of the world will still be critical to global trade from inland barges to giant container vessels navigating safe passage for commodities, parts and products to keep global trade afloat.

The case studies included in this chapter have been compiled under the auspices of the Freight and Logistics Leaders' Forum (F&L). The purpose of the comments and case studies in the chapter is to demonstrate how leaders in the cargo owner community are driving change and acting in a collaborative way.

F&L is an international network of senior business leaders focused on issues around freight logistics across the supply chain and operates in all industry sectors and transport modes, based across the continent of Europe and globally. Set up as an AISBL and registered in Belgium (established 1994), F&L is a not for profit and non-lobby members' forum (F&L, 2023).

F&L's network encompasses a wide variety of stakeholders and discussions are based on the premise that a variety of inputs and an open mind helps promote positive change. The authors have approached a number of their contacts to learn of their views on maritime decarbonization and the actions they are taking, or propose taking, which they believe will influence the speed of decarbonization.

To exert influence or encourage change there are a number of different strategies being adopted from simple demand aggregation at one end to direct sustainable vessel investment at the other. It is important to note that sustainability must mean both economic as well an environmental sustainability. To prosper businesses must build and sustain a successful model which can incentivise and drive growth and change. We must therefore look at how the traditional competitive model can be updated to show that legal co-operation or collaboration can break the often-perceived conflict between shared knowledge and competitive advantage. How have leaders or sustainability pioneers amongst the cargo owner community made this work? The leaders in the F&L network believe in both necessity and opportunity!

Reasons for the slow pace of change in the decarbonization of the maritime industry are many and are covered elsewhere in this book. Here we focus on evidence that cargo owners have, or plan to have, a guiding hand. That guiding hand can be derived from three broad sources at the cargo owner level:

- a method for aggregating demand;
- an incentivisation to improve efficiency, use new technology or more energy efficient fuels; and
- a changed mindset and identification of opportunities in leadership and business models.

In turn these broad categories create change through:

- exerting leverage through volume, the tendering process and adherence to certain key performance indicators (KPIs),
- creating incentives or mutually beneficial trading relationships where there is upfront support or longer-term volume commitment, and
- an acceptance that leading change will derive benefits through efficiencies, enhanced credibility and preferred product choice.

All these categories or strategic themes are designed to achieve a consistent aim - in the short term to incentivise the demand side for a lower emission solution and in the medium term to build scale embedding change and permanent commercially viable solutions.

In this debate difficulties arise not least due to the highly fragmented demand base, but also because maritime logistics, often outsourced, makes up a small part of so-called scope 3 emissions, usually equating to less than 10% of total emissions. Scope 3 emissions are those from activities not owned or controlled by a reporting organisation, but that the organisation indirectly affects in its value chain.

To be effective any of the available options can only be viable in the short term if the premium the cargo owner believes they might pay for a lower carbon logistics supply chain does not dilute any competitive advantage. The cargo owner will pay if it does not become competitively disadvantageous. If the cargo owner believes a lower carbon option requires investment or is at a higher cost then there must be a balancing pressure, from customers, other stakeholders, regulators, or a derived leadership advantage. There is an inherent conflict between the wish to collaborate with the fear of giving away or undermining a competitive advantage.

Demand Aggregation: Using Customer Pressure to Force Improvement

The first and seemingly most straightforward influence that the cargo owners can exert on decarbonization efforts is that of demand aggregation; in other words, providing 'visibility' of the demands or wishes of customers generally through the process of coordinating and consolidating individual requirements. This turns out to be somewhat complicated. In theory it should be relatively straightforward for cargo owners to build pressure through volume aggregation and therefore demand control, influencing carriers through choice of sailings. The choice would be based on data setting out the emissions for each option and together the collaborative group select the most suitable vessels. The assumption would be that gradually the carriers react and the maritime sector moves forward.

One example is the Boosting Initiatives for Collaborative Emissions reduction with the Power of Shippers or BICEPS network (a non-profit foundation including global shippers) which is a collaboration of procurement and global logistics managers working together to create a sustainable approach in their procurement of ocean freight solutions (BICEPS, 2023). They have developed a rating system to improve the procurement process for members (McNally, 2015) (Bunkerportsnews, 2016). The members use five sustainability criteria for their procurement decisions. They still require service, reliability and a competitive price but also include sustainability as a relevant KPI. Tenders require all BICEPS data to be included in a standardised form in the rating system. The BICEPS network encourages change and supports the scaling up of innovative ideas. As a result of the members combined strategy and other cargo owners' choices, around 20% of outbound containers from Rotterdam now fall under the sustainable procurement process.

In addition, the network is driving innovation. An example, is a collaborative project between shippers (the Dutch Sustainable Growth Coalition with BICEPS members), the carrier Maersk, and Shell that was a successful bio-fuel trial completed in 2019 on the Rotterdam to Shanghai route (Maersk, 2019). This has provided the impulse for bunkering and use of various biofuels, in total equating to more than 10% of bunker fuel at the Port of Rotterdam.

Walter Vermeer, Head of Logistics Procurement at FrieslandCampina, the Dutch multinational dairy cooperative, has said 'Creating demand by the collaboration of shippers is a powerful mechanism to speed up sustainable innovations in shipping and supply chains. The BICEPS network aims to create an effective and impactful development towards decarbonization of shipping'.

The BICEPS example and their members proactive decision-making helps avoid one of the obstacles to the approach where end customers have not yet prioritised reductions in scope 3 emissions. Some customers see scope 3 as a less significant responsibility or have just not yet been able to focus beyond scope 1 (direct emissions) and scope 2 (indirect emissions). It is also clear that some intermediate manufacturers are not being encouraged to lead on decarbonization in the maritime logistics sector because the pressure has yet to come down through the supply chain. BICEPS members have taken that decision into their own hands.

Any initiatives have to overcome the basic barriers of provision and access to consistent accurate data, a common clear message, legal compliance and critically, trust. Any form of collaboration relies on conformity to common agreed standards and working methods or operational procedures, and completion of agreed obligations, whether or not a contractual arrangement is in place. In a marketplace where demand is so fragmented, trust in working together for a common cause can make all the difference.

Logistics service providers have an important role to play in demand aggregation as the conduit to, or the direct supplier of, maritime services. DB Schenker, the global logistics service provider (LSP) which is a significant freight forwarder for the maritime sector, has taken a direct role in decarbonization by committing to the purchase of additional second-generation biofuel for the container vessels that the ocean carriers will use in 2023. In its agreement with the shipping lines, DB Schenker's purchase of 17,000 metric tonnes of marine biofuel now enables it to offer a greener solution to its customers. This is equivalent to around 50,000 standard containers that can be shipped with net-zero CO_2 emissions, depending on how the fuel is used during voyages. By bunkering biofuel but not designating it to a specific vessel for its use or linking it to an individual customer's containers, DB Schenker is satisfying the growing demand for more environmentally friendly shipping and takes on the risk of investing in marine biofuel upfront without a guaranteed buyer for it. The Company over allocates the marine biofuel as its goal is to reach zero emissions. The aim is to find enough customers to share its vision and therefore purchase the biofuels option, but regardless, the biofuel option is now in place; and it is the consequent creation of confidence in demand for alternative fuels in the shipping industry and the aim of scaling up that is so critical.

DB Schenker's displacement of fossil fuels through the direct purchase of biofuels as today's best alternative, should build confidence for others to follow. As usage builds, this form of guaranteed demand should become less necessary with ocean carriers confident that the demand for lower carbon or zero carbon new fuels is here to stay. Until then, it falls upon leaders, whether cargo owners or their partners, to create demand and build confidence. These committed leaders and sponsors of new fuels are, of course, balancing the risk of investment against the inspiration others may draw from involvement. One hopes that in due course, their actions will improve their company's status and credibility and it will enjoy lasting and long-term benefits.

Each year approximately 350,000 metric tons of CO_2 are emitted as a result of the distribution of Electrolux Group goods by sea, air and land transport in Europe, North America, Australia, Egypt, Brazil, Chile and Argentina.

The Electrolux Group has developed its supplier relationships with ocean carriers Maersk Line and CMA-CGM by investing in sustainable fuels improving CO_2 efficiency in ocean logistics by 12% and absolute emissions by 20% in 2022. The agreement with Maersk Line involves using a second-generation biofuel that includes used cooking oil and generates 85% less greenhouse gas emissions compared to traditional bunker fuel. The CMA-CGM agreement uses a cleaner liquid natural gas (LNG) solution based on guarantee of origin biomethane that reduces greenhouse gas emissions by at least 25%.

Electrolux Group is also engaged with the ocean carriers to continue exploring options and development within sustainable fuels, with increasing annual sustainability targets towards the goals of climate neutral transportation by 2030 and zero-net carbon emissions throughout its supply chain by 2050.

Daniel Cole, Logistics Purchasing Director at Electrolux Group has said 'We have very ambitious climate targets here, and I am proud of how these high achieving goals have remained on the agenda in a challenging ocean market. Through strong partnerships we are able to not only ensure we meet short term goals, but also create the roadmap to achieving future commitments.'

Encouraging the Use of Technology and Innovation

Another influence available to the cargo owners to move decarbonization efforts forward involves pushing the use of technology, some form of shared incentivisation, and the mechanism of shared endeavour or risk. This overlaps somewhat with the demand aggregation discussed earlier in this chapter that seeks some form of customer demand-driven commitment to scale up and achieve longer term changes. The result may not be a direct finance-driven decision to adopt a new fuel or an innovation, but rather a longer-term commitment to provide volume and make use of an innovation.

There are many technological innovations that would make a considerable difference in tackling specific company requirements and in changing demand for sustainable maritime delivery. Henkel, the German multinational industrial and consumer goods company, is looking at several opportunities, but a mode shift could bring considerable reductions to the company's emissions. There are technological reasons requiring Henkel to currently use air transport for its products, because of the shorter lead times. Product specifications necessitate shipment using dry ice and rapid delivery. Product changes allowing for longer delivery times and a shift to movement by sea would bring noticeable reductions in scope 3 emissions. There are many efficiencies being pursued to improve delivery times including better container utilisation, shared less-than-container load shipments and where possible ensuring full containers. Henkel is working with external partners, particularly logistics service providers, using data analytics to drive efficiencies. In China, Henkel utilises container building software to optimise space.

Changing the Mindset and Seizing New Opportunities

The theme for the third area where cargo owners can influence the' decarbonization strategy, in a way is an overarching one, covering both demand aggregation and the use of innovation. The difference is that the strategic driver is opportunity as well as necessity. Whilst there is an understanding that decarbonization is a critical necessity for longer term economic and environmental sustainability, there is also the belief that leadership (and perhaps first mover positioning) brings real gains whether through efficiencies, credibility or operational knowledge. Falling behind might be just costly or potentially disastrous as change in the freight logistics sector accelerates.

Stora Enso, a leading provider of renewable products for packaging, biomaterials and wood construction, and one of the largest private forest owners in the world, has taken a holistic approach to its logistics decarbonization journey. The company has set itself the target of reducing scope 1, 2 and 3 GHG emissions by 50% by 2030 from a 2019 baseline (Stora Enso, 2023). Many companies have found that to achieve ambitious targets requires multiple strategies and the use of many innovations. It also necessitates reviewing the end-to-end supply chain journey across land, sea and air for all products. As so much of the success in meeting the targets will be subject to scope 3 reductions, collaboration is critical, and partner buy in to the strategy must be comprehensive. Importantly, both the consistency and availability of measurement tools and data can now enable companies to take meaningful action by measuring against science-based targets.

Stora Enso's roadmap on GHG reductions is taking place in several different ways - operational efficiency, a move to using renewable fuels, exploiting innovation and new technologies, and compliance with policies and regulations. One of the interesting learnings from the company's better than target reductions to date (27% lower against the 2019 baseline for scope 1, 2, and scope 3 emissions), is that significant strategic decisions have been taken as well as many smaller incremental actions that have made a material contribution.

An increasing number of cargo owners are participating in trade associations, partnerships or industry decarbonization initiatives to learn, influence, and accelerate their GHG reduction programmes. For example, Electrolux Group maintains a dialogue within the industry and amongst peers to push the sustainability agenda. Electrolux Group is a member of the U.S. Environmental Protection Agency-led SmartWay and the Smart Freight Centre Clean Cargo initiative with commitments to decrease road and sea transport-related emissions respectively, as well as having joined the Cargo Owners for Zero Emission Vessels (coZEV) initiative together with 18 other companies, the Aspen Institute and climate-leading cargo owners.

In practical terms, in 2022 Electrolux Group secured the commitment from 14 global logistics companies (31% of total logistics spend) to disclose their emissions and set targets through the CDP Supply Chain Program. CDP is a not-for-profit charity that runs a global disclosure system for investors, companies, cities, states and regions to manage their environmental impacts.

Cargill, which trades, processes and distributes agricultural and other commodities, established a benchmark for their carbon emissions in 2017. Cargill's strategic aim is to develop policies which are environmentally sound, applicable in today's markets (digital and agile) and profitable, thus ensuring a sustainable economic model. In 2017 there was an acceptance that the shipping sector was in both the hard-to-abate and slow-to-modernise categories. There was also an acceptance, even as a significant global business, that change would require a collaborative effort. No one company had all the answers and so Cargill had to build external partnerships.

One significant step at the start of Cargill's new journey was to find a way to pool ideas that might bring leverage to the company in solving sustainability issues. Their model was based on technical expertise from DNV the international accredited registrar and classification society and a framework developed by Rainmaking, a leading corporate innovation and venture development firm, enabling the company to understand up-to-date maritime technical developments and roll out a process to assess and select new ideas and entrepreneurial partners to work with. Cargill's understanding that as a major global corporate it did not have all the answers and that it needed to benefit from external innovation and new internal project evaluation methodologies reflected an important change.

Cargill started with 180 ideas but had to be able to filter opportunities and develop business cases for working with each startup where they wished to collaborate. This required a new mindset, building trust and admitting mistakes. It also meant establishing clearly where the bottlenecks occurred and how the company could collaborate with external partners or acquire expertise. For example, in 2020 Cargill developed a strategic partnership with technology company ZeroNorth to use their data expertise, modelling and software to understand and reduce its maritime emissions; in other words, data driven decision making. On technology and new fuels, external partnerships were critical including through The Maersk Mc-Kinney Moller Center for Zero Carbon Shipping, which Cargill joined as a founding partner in 2020. Overall, the critical mindset change was seeing these partnerships or investments as opportunities for growth and efficiencies and not just a cost. Furthermore, these investment decisions were not seen as defensive but rather offensive in the sense that the resulting actions would help reinforce Cargill's leadership position.

These mindset changes had to be complemented by building trust both internally and externally. Part of this came about through greater openness and publishing data with sustainability reports and joining organisations such as the Global Maritime Forum and Getting to Zero Coalition, with the requisite commitments for emission reductions. Such collaborations with the *coalition of the willing* stimulate change.

To make progress it is necessary to accept risk, to be able to understand and evaluate that risk and to set it against the potential solution it may bring about and subsequent financial and other gains. This requires a risk/reward analysis as might be carried out in Cargill's trading business. For external stakeholders that risk must be in some form underwritten. This may mean direct investment or building a case for external support by creating an enabling mechanism, such as longer-term commitment to the use of a service or vessel. Here again we see the generation or support of demand driving change.

An important point made by the Cargill team was to note the regional differences where some of the supply chain was not yet capable of exploiting technical innovation. Some modern ships may not be able to dock at certain ports in East Africa whether due to conflicts, inability to insure or lack of infrastructure. The pace of change will inevitably be different across the world. Everyone is working with the assets currently in the supply chain and whilst there will be some 'low hanging fruit' and efficiency gains, investment decisions made now will only crystallise operational actions in a few years; but signals matter.

It is also worth noting that many companies will look to assess their decarbonization by transport mode through organisational necessity but ultimately will need to make end-to-end progress covering all modes along their complete supply chains. In the same way that we refer to value chains we must also accept the full carbon chain.

The Cargill team started like others by trying to ramp up green fuels along green lanes or corridors (port to port) and, working with other companies, to build scale. Some lanes made logical sense due to volumes and access to biofuels in, for example, Singapore. To really gain proof of concept Cargill and its partners want a significant number of ships and sailings on dedicated routes. Here, to break the cycle of low supply and demand, Cargill has ordered its own methanol fuelled ships for delivery in 2025/2026. The risk is availability of fuel and critically the fuel costs, which it may not be possible to pass on to end customers. Therefore, it would be better for all the new ships to use the same route thus helping to meet the scale and demand requirements. A company, like Cargill, will calculate its downside risk and then take a decision, mitigating that risk as far as possible. The signal is important; if global leaders are prepared to take calculated risks to drive change, then others may follow.

If the pricing and availability of biofuels is uncertain, where does that leave wind power? The payback on investment looks distant, break-even unknown given the variables and any owner needs to avoid a mismatch between the fuel, for example, wind (North Atlantic) and customer base (further south). It will therefore be important to strike a balance between different fuel options, the availability of those fuels and customer requirements. Balance must be struck between utilising all the fuel options to find the right mix for each ship on each route. One answer is to use wind and other new fuels to create hybrid fuelled ships (Cargill, June 2022).

Jan Dieleman from Cargill said 'Beyond acting on today's efficiencies and low hanging fruit to drive decarbonization in the maritime sector, Cargill wants to use its size and leadership as a cargo owner with significant demand for logistics to encourage the acceptance of balanced risk in the use of lower carbon fuels and hybrid fuel options including wind assisted power (WAP); the signal Cargill and its collaborative partners send out is critical to creating the acceptance and scale to create sustainable fuels.'

Two core questions underlie the discussion - will the fuels be available in the long-term and will customers pay the long-term market price? If you believe the answer should be yes, you take a calculated risk knowing the downside or potential write off. This market signal is significant and can drive positive change. Cargill and BAR Technologies are working together on sail options – noting that WAP creates noise and gets noticed!

The logistics sector survives on small margins but takes major investment decisions, such as purchasing several ships at once, highlighting the difference between operational and capital investment decisions. Whether sector mergers and acquisitions and volume chasing investments are more than a reflection of access to cheap capital is a separate question. However, cargo owners purchasing or controlling new ships through long leases, enables them to dictate the specifications and influence the shipbuilding yards. This drives innovation alongside engine manufacturers. Yards have to be persuaded that, given the element of proof of manufacturing capability, they should share some risk. Green finance will not yet fill the risk gap. It is worth mentioning that the difference between public and private companies with specific stakeholder groups and influences may lead to pressures on their criteria for decision making and of course divergent sustainability targets.

Regulators, governments and other external forces or stakeholders and their decrees will play an important part in influencing cargo owners, not least through taxation, environmental incentives or requirements. Decarbonization is moving faster than the sector regulators. The International Maritime Organization (IMO) and some regional regulators have competing stakeholder interests, often leading to the creation of minimum standards rather than aspirational higher targets. Cargo owners therefore must accept there is a price on pollution and fill the gap. A clear preference would be for subsidies and long-term price and policy certainty.

Whether the EU's Emissions Trading System (EU ETS, 2023), import carbon tax or the USA's Inflation Reduction Act will be of greater influence on either the demand or supply side is not for this chapter but in impacting cargo owners, these taxes and subsidies will feed through to the maritime sector. The sector may be global and there will be no global tax soon, but it is impacted by local or regional forces. It cannot ignore them; burning dirty fuel off the shores of Africa is not completely disconnected from the need to satisfy the environmental demands of customers in Europe.

Closing Remarks

We may not yet be at a tipping point on maritime decarbonization but if cargo owners have a concrete option to put to their customers, perhaps tailored to an industrial sector sweet spot, and believe there is a credibility and leadership advantage in doing so, then those waiting for a signal may follow and act. Remove the barriers and, given shipbuilding and infrastructure lead times, it is necessary to think about where you will want to be in three to five years. The 2030 window is closing.

One final anecdote from Cargill. The company used to talk about its original hopes for wind power using a massive kite and the failure of that innovation. When wind was back on the agenda, the Cargill team did their homework, modelling and built a more confident plan. They also recovered the old kite, cut it up and made it into bags with a message - *we will innovate, trial, learn, move on and get better*. These innovations are complex and you will not get it right first time. We need to learn how to create the right diverse collaborative team to solve complex problems.

In conclusion, there does appear to be some evidence that those paying the bills can influence sustainable outcomes but the cause and effect is not always easy to discern and may be the result of the interaction and pressure of multiple stakeholders, including cargo owners, consumers and regulators, as well as the leadership and the vision of individuals and companies focused on accelerating the economic and environmental sustainability of global supply chains.

References

BICEPS. (2023). The biceps network of global shippers who drive decarbonization of ocean shipping with the power of demand. *BICEPS Network*. Retrieved May 28, 2023, from https://bicepsnetwork.org

Bunkerportsnews. (2016, August 25). Launch of BICEPS rating system to stimulate more sustainable ocean shipping. *Bunker Ports News Worldwide*. Accessed May 28, 2023, from http://www.bunkerportsnews.com/News.aspx?ElementId=b99469ab-040e-4ab9-a5a6-a2b1637395c6

Cargill. (2022, June). *Making zero carbon shipping a reality*. Accessed May 28, 2023 from https://www.cargill.com/doc/1432213554081/making-zero-carbon-shipping-a-reality-2022-report.pdf

EU ETS. (2023). *EU emissions trading system*. Retrieved from https://climate.ec.europa.eu/eu-action/eu-emissions-trading-system-eu-ets_en

Maersk. (2019). *Dutch sustainable growth coalition partners with Maersk in world's largest maritime biofuel pilot*. A.P. Møller - Mærsk A/S. Press release published March 22, 2019. Accessed May 28, 2023, from https://www.maersk.com/news/articles/2019/03/22/dutch-sustainable-growth-coalition-partners-with-maersk-in-world-s-largest-maritime-biofuel-pilot

McNally, B. (2015, June 17). *Ahoy! five global shippers collaborate to drive sea freight sustainability*. Accessed May 28, 2023, from https://sustainablebrands.com/read/collaboration-cocreation/ahoy-five-global-shippers-collaborate-to-drive-sea-freight-sustainability

Stora Enso. (2023). *Sustainability targets and key performance indicators*. Retrieved from https://www.storaenso.com/en/sustainability/targets-and-key-performance-indicators

Practical Decarbonization Actions Being Taken by the Shipping Companies

Teemu Manderbacka and Ulla Tapaninen

Target Audience

This chapter has been written, in particular, for shipowners and charterers and provides case studies demonstrating actions that shipping companies can take to drive decarbonization.

Key Takeaway Messages

The chapter emphasises:

- Shipping companies and ports are rapidly preparing for new fuels developed by energy companies and new ship designs are improving energy efficiency.
- There is no silver bullet for decarbonizing vessels; multiple enablers need to be activated.
- Shipping companies join coalitions to learn, align and take collective action.
- The case studies in this chapter are from the North Sea region and cover wind assisted propulsion, energy efficiency improvements, auto mooring, virtual arrival, biofuel, and the logistics chain.

T. Manderbacka (✉)
VTT Technical Research Centre of Finland, Espoo, Finland
e-mail: teemu.manderbacka@vtt.fi

U. Tapaninen
Tallinn University of Technology, Tallinn, Estonia
e-mail: ulla.tapaninen@taltech.ee

M. Lind et al. (eds.), *Maritime Decarbonization*,
https://doi.org/10.1007/978-3-031-39936-7_22

Introduction

Currently, the maritime industry is undergoing a revolution, and it is still difficult to predict what will be the main ways to reduce carbon emissions in the future in shipping. Shipping companies and ports are already rapidly preparing for new fuels developed by energy companies. Simultaneously, ship designs are becoming more and more energy efficient, reducing the required energy and fuel consumption required to propel the vessels.

There are several initiatives to decarbonize shipping, where shipping companies are participating including the Getting to Zero Coalition (GMF, 2023) in partnership with the Global Maritime Forum and the World Economic Forum. This alliance contains more than 200 organisations, where 160 companies, among which the major shipping lines are present. The Coalition aims to make zero emission vessels (ZEVs) commercially viable and scalable by 2030, contributing to full decarbonization by 2050.

Decarbonization commitments in shipping finance also affect the technology and operational choices of the shipping companies. An important example of this influence is the Poseidon principles—that establish a framework for assessing and disclosing the climate alignment of ship finance portfolios. The principles set a benchmark for what it means to be a responsible bank in the maritime sector and provide actionable guidance on how to achieve this. At the end of 2022, 30 financial institutions were signatories to the Poseidon Principles, representing a bank loan portfolio to global shipping of over 70% of the global ship finance portfolio (Poseidon Principles, 2022), and the number is expected to increase. The International Chamber of Shipping (ICS), representing the world's national shipowner associations and over 80% of the world merchant fleet, has taken an initiative by submitting to the IMO its vision on plans for regulatory measures to decarbonize shipping (ICS, 2021). Those include a compulsory R&D fund for zero-carbon technologies, and a carbon levy for shipping.

Practical Actions by Shipping Companies

Presently, there is no 'silver bullet' to achieve the environmental targets that have been set for shipping, but multiple means will be needed to reduce the carbon emissions of vessels. There are numerous papers covering various ways to reduce the carbon emissions of shipping, for example, Bouman et al. (2017), Laasma et al. (2022), Law et al. (2021), Lindstad et al. (2021), Mallouppas and Yfantis (2021), McKinlay et al. (2021), Miola et al. (2011), Serra and Fancello (2020) and Solakivi et al. (2022). Balcombe et al. (2019) provide an overview of various means to decarbonize shipping.

Figure 1 groups the main means to reduce exhaust emissions from ships into three categories:

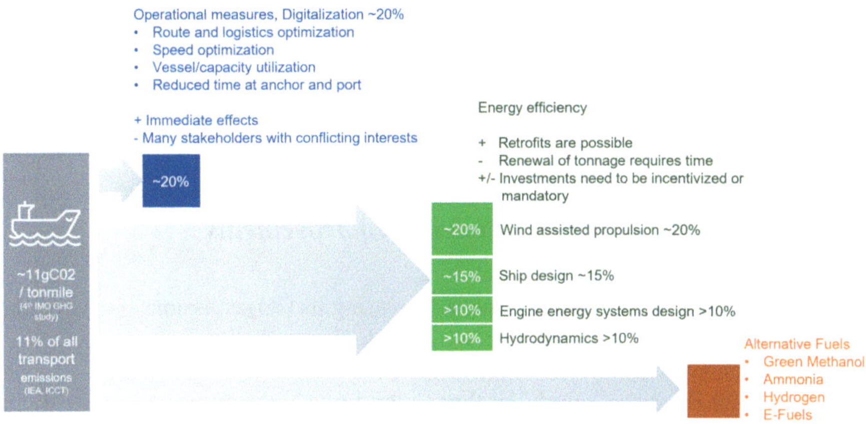

Fig. 1 Means for decarbonizing shipping

- operational measures,
- ship design and technological development, and
- alternative fuels.

Several of the measures shown in Fig. 1 are already feasible for shipping companies to use in their existing operations and fleets today. They are mainly operational measures, such as speed reduction or operational changes. Most of the solutions work by combining digital solutions with traditional shipping.

Practical Examples of Action Taken by Shipping Companies

In the following section, we present cases of wind assisted propulsion, energy efficiency improvements with batteries and air-lubrication, auto-mooring systems, port arrival information system and removing cargo from land to an automatic vessel and use of biofuel. They all have managed to reduce fuel consumption from a few percent up to 25%.

Case: Bore—Wind Assisted Propulsion

Bore Ltd. is a roll-on/roll-off (ro-ro) cargo ship company operating mainly in the North Sea. It has decreased its fuel consumption by adding wind-power to its vessels.

Rotor Sail Solutions are a modernised version of the Flettner rotor—a spinning cylinder which uses the Magnus effect to harness wind power to propel a ship forward, delivering fuel-savings and a reduction in all related emissions.

The rotor sail solution by Norsepower Ltd. was installed on M/S Estraden from Bore Ltd. fleet in 2015. In the first installation over 6% fuel savings were recorded. However, with the use of Flettner rotors it is possible to obtain notable fuel savings of up to 20%.

Case: Finnlines—Energy Efficiency Improvements

Finnlines (part of the Grimaldi group) is decreasing its CO_2 emissions by increasing the size of its vessels, by using new technologies including batteries and with air-lubrication systems.

In 2022–23 Finnlines introduced three hybrid modern ro-ro vessels on its Baltic Sea routes that use several energy saving technologies. The ships are 238 metres long with a cargo capacity of 5800 lane metres. Consequently, the vessels can carry 400 trailers per voyage. Compared with the company's second largest vessels, the cargo carrying capacity of the hybrid newbuilds increases by nearly 40%.

The vessels are designed to be partially operated on battery power. The hybrid solution reduces fuel consumption and enables zero emissions at berth. Noise pollution during port visits also decreases. Battery banks of 5 MWh allow the use of stored electricity while in port. In addition, there are 600m^2 of solar panels to provide electrical power for users onboard.

The vessels are also equipped with air lubrication systems, and exhaust gas cleaning equipment to cut carbon emissions further.

Case: Tallink—Auto-mooring

Tallink operates regular traffic between the port of Helsinki and the port of Tallinn. Its large roll-on/roll-off passenger (ro-pax) vessels have a schedule with only one hour in port then 2 hours at sea. An auto-mooring system reduces the time required for mooring and therefore, the vessels can reduce their speed at sea.

In March 2017, Tallink began using an automatic ship mooring system in West Harbor of the port of Helsinki. The new auto-mooring system significantly speeded up the mooring and unmooring of ships.

The system comprises six MoorMaster units which use vacuum pads to pull the side of the ship towards its berth. The mooring system is controlled remotely from the bridge of the ship, or alternatively from ashore.

The auto-mooring system speeds up the mooring and unmooring of ships, reducing fuel consumption, emissions into the air and noise in the process. The system reduces the time needed in port and allows for slower, more cost-efficient transit speeds—hence, reducing bunker consumption.

The automatic mooring system is the first of its kind to be used in frequent passenger traffic in the Baltic.

Case: ESL Shipping—Virtual Arrival

ESL Shipping, is a leading handy-size Baltic bulk carrier, that has been able to reduce CO_2 emissions by changing the way it manages port arrival information using a Virtual Arrivals process.

The common practice in shipping is for vessels to be scheduled to meet a pre-arranged and agreed arrival time at a port. The agreed time is nominated regardless of whether a berth is likely to be free on arrival or not. A ship then proceeds at a speed to make the nominated arrival time. If the assigned berth is not available on arrival, the vessel must wait outside the port either drifting, circling or waiting at anchor. This increases fuel consumption and pollution. A vessel is rarely informed while it is on passage, even when it becomes known by the destination port that a previously intended berth will be unavailable, and it cannot join a queue until it arrives in the port area. This is often termed 'hurry up and wait' arrivals.

The basic idea of a Virtual Arrival is to reduce congestion and pollution in a port area and minimise fuel usage by enabling vessels to adjust their passage speed when it is known that a berth will not be available on arrival. Regardless of the actual arrival time, the vessel still retains its place in the queue based on its originally agreed arrival time. Virtual Arrival also contains a model to share the savings in the fuel costs between the operator and the cargo owner.

ESL Shipping, steel producer SSAB and the port of Oxelösund started a Virtual Arrival trial on the Luleå-Oxelösund (distance ~500nm) route. Early experience has been positive. The average reduction of CO_2 emissions was 24% during a month of Virtual Arrival operations.

After each ship arrival the value of any fuel savings gained by using Virtual Arrival are shared between the operator and the customer.

Case: Meriaura—Biofuel

One important step towards reducing CO_2 emissions is for shipping companies to start using local low-carbon fuels. One example is Meriaura, a Baltic coastal shipping company.

Meriaura undertook its first bio-oil experiment in 1992 using the tugboat 'Aura'. Since 2007 it has been testing the feasibility of 100% biofuel made from recycled raw materials in long-term tests. The bio-oil is manufactured from recycled oils and by-products of the food industry. As such, the bio-oil production does not compete with land required for agriculture.

Waste-based bio-oil reduces ship CO_2 emissions by up to 96% compared to traditional fossil fuel options. When running also with catalytic converters, nitrogen oxides (NOx) emissions are close to zero and there are no methane emissions unlike in LNG (liquified natural gas) production and combustion. Waste-based bio-oil is the most sustainable fuel solution currently available in maritime transport.

Case: Yara—Changing the Logistics Chain

Moving from land to sea transport can reduce CO_2 emissions. Yara, a world leading fertilizer company, will replace 40,000 diesel-powered truck journeys by introducing an electrically powered, autonomous container vessel.

Yara is a leading global fertilizer company. Currently, many diesel truck journeys are needed to transport products from its Porsgrunn plant to the coastal ports of Brevik and Larvik in Norway, from where products are shipped to customers around the world.

Yara Birkeland will be the world's first fully electric, autonomous container ship to enter into commercial use, with zero emissions. It will carry up to 3200 deadweight tonnage (DWT). With this vessel, Yara will avoid 40,000 diesel-powered truck journeys every year and reduce NOx and CO_2 emissions, improve road safety, reduce road dust formation and traffic noise.

Yara Birkeland was put into commercial operation in the spring of 2022. During its first two years of operation, the vessel will go through a gradual transition towards full autonomous sailing

Recommendations towards the Decarbonization of Ships

According to Tapaninen (2021), there are six important steps how the maritime sector can prepare itself for a carbon-free future. The first four actions are for shipping companies, with another for shippers and one for regulators.

Shipping Companies

- Shipping companies should improve the energy efficiency in their newbuild ships. The service life of a vessel is practically always more than 20 years, sometimes 30 or more. It is therefore very important that the ship designs on the table are as energy efficient as possible. This action has already decreased substantially shipping companies' emissions, for example bulk vessels being built today can use 50% less fuel compared to the ones built 10 years ago (ESL Shipping, 2016).
- Shipping companies should pilot various technical solutions to increase their energy efficiency. These include rotor sails; smart IT- solutions to manage data for maintenance, bunker optimisation and safety; air lubrication systems; use of batteries in ports and fairways; virtual arrivals, etc. There are multiple solutions for the energy efficiency of vessels being developed around the world, and shipping companies should be active to bring them into everyday use. Their

effect might be only a few percent in decreasing carbon emissions, but they are always worth testing and evaluating. It is the total effect that counts.

- Shipping companies should optimise their passage speed and port companies should improve their operational efficiency. One of the most efficient ways to decrease greenhouse gas emissions from vessels is to reduce vessels' speed. With the fastest vessels, a speed reduction of a few knots can decrease emissions by one third. In many cases, the improvement of data operations and cargo handling in ports can save time that can be used at the sea without increasing the total transport time.
- Shipping companies should prepare themselves for new low or zero carbon fuels. We do not exactly know what are the fuels of tomorrow—will it be hydrogen, ammonia, biofuels, methanol, or even electricity? Or all them? Whatever, some of these fuels are now becoming available so shipping companies should increase their understanding of what are the various alternative fuels suitable for their own business models.

Shippers

- Shippers cannot rely solely on the maritime sector changing its operations. Shippers must also re-evaluate their complete transport chains. Are there possibilities to use slower speed vessels instead of high-speed? or use containers instead of trucks? or rail instead of road? or have more cargo transported at the same time? or more precise cargo tracking to give better estimations for the time of arrival? Should there actually be more inventory and not rely on fast just-in-time transport? Finding answers to these questions starts by analysing the needs of the final customer, for example, do they want high speed transport or do they just wish to have their products when needed?

Authorities and Regulators

- Authorities and regulators must introduce rules and support mechanisms and carbon taxes to help the shipping industry move towards carbon-neutrality. It is very important that the rules and mechanisms treat shipping companies in a fair way, so that they really focus on carbon reduction and do not lead to unfair situations in competition.

By following the steps above, there is a way for the shipping sector to achieve carbon neutrality in a balanced way and make the shipping companies even stronger in the future.

References

Balcombe, P., Brierley, J., Lewis, C., Skatvedt, L., Speirs, J., Hawkes, A., & Staffell, I. (2019). How to decarbonise international shipping: Options for fuels, technologies and policies. *Energy Conversion and Management, 182*, 72–88.

Bouman, E. A., Lindstad, E., Rialland, A. I., & Strųmman, A. H. (2017). State-of-the-art technologies, measures, and potential for reducing GHG emissions from shipping—A review. *Transportation Research Part D: Transport and Environment, 52*, 408–421.

ESL Shipping. (2016). *ESL Shipping and Sinotrans & CSC Shippuilding Industry Corporation agree to assign building of LNG-fueled bulk carriers to Sinotrans & CSC Jinling Shipyard*. ESL Shipping news release 27 September 2016. https://www.eslshipping.com/en/news/aspos-esl-shipping-and-sinotrans-csc-shipbuilding-industry-corporation-agree-to-assign-building-of-lng-fueled-bulk-carriers-to-sinotrans-csc-jinling-shipyard

GMF (2023) Getting to Zero Coalition. https://www.globalmaritimeforum.org/getting-to-zero-coalition

ICS. (2021) *Reduction of GHG emissions from ships - Comments on a proposed draft MEPC resolution on zero emission shipping by 2050, and revision of the IMO GHG Strategy, MEPC77/7/22 XX October 2021*. Pre-session public release. https://view.officeapps.live.com/op/view.aspx?src=https%3A%2F%2Fwww.ics-shipping.org%2Fwp-content%2Fuploads%2F2021%2F10%2FCommenting-paper-on-net-zero-target-final-1.docx&wdOrigin=BROWSELINK

Laasma, A., Otsason, R., Tapaninen, U., & Hilmola, O.-P. (2022). Evaluation of alternative fuels for coastal ferries. *Sustainability, 14*, 16841. https://doi.org/10.3390/su142416841

Law, L. C., Foscoli, B., Mastorakos, E., & Evans, S. (2021). A comparison of alternative fuels for shipping in terms of lifecycle energy and cost. *Energies, 14*, 8502.

Lindstad, E., Lagemann, B., Rialland, A., Gamlem, G. M., & Valland, A. (2021). Reduction of maritime GHG emissions and the potential role of E-fuels. *Transportation Research Part D: Transport and Environment, 101*, 103075.

Mallouppas, G., & Yfantis, E. A. (2021). Decarbonization in shipping industry: A review of research, technology development, and innovation proposals. *Journal of Marine Science and Engineering, 9*, 415. https://doi.org/10.3390/jmse9040415

McKinlay, C. J., Turnock, S. R., & Hudson, D. A. (2021). Route tozero emission shipping: Hydrogen, ammonia or methanol? *International Journal of Hydrogen Energy, 46*, 28282–28297.

Miola, A., Marra, M., & Ciuffo, B. (2011). Designing a climate change policy for the international maritime transport sector: Market-based measures and technological options for global and regional policy actions. *Energy Policy, 39*, 5490–5498.

Poseidon Principles. (2022, December). *Annual disclosure report 2022*. www.poseidonprincples.org, https://www.poseidonprinciples.org/finance/wp-content/uploads/2022/12/Poseidon-Principles-Annual-Disclosure-Report-2022.pdf

Serra, P., & Fancello, G. (2020). Towards the IMO's GHG goals: A critical overview of the perspectives and challenges of the main options for decarbonizing international shipping. *Sustainability, 12*, 3220.

Solakivi, T., Paimander, A., & Ojala, L. (2022). Cost competitiveness of alternative maritime fuels in the new regulatory framework. *Transportation Research Part D: Transport and Environment, 113*, 103500.

Tapaninen, U. (2021). Six steps to reach carbon-free shipping. In K. Liuhto (Ed.), *Baltic Rim economies*. Centrum Balticum Foundation. https://sites.utu.fi/bre/six-steps-to-reach-carbon-free-shipping/

Identifying the Best Low-Emission Carriers

Peter Sand, Emily Stausbøll, Dayna Goldman,
and Torbjörn Rydbergh

Target Audience

This chapter has been written to provide a practical understanding of how the CO_2 emissions performance of ships can be monitored using an independent analysis service, thereby enabling shippers, freight forwarders and others to select only those carriers that deliver a proven low emission service operation.

Key Takeaway Messages

The chapter emphasises:

- The recent development of a Carbon Emissions Index (CEI) that allows carriers, freight forwarders and shippers to track, on selected trade routes, the historic development of emissions, the development of a carrier's performance over time, and how a carrier compares with the trade route average and other carriers on the route.
- The CEI is not meant for carbon accounting, but to allow users and carriers to monitor, compare and identify the best performing carriers.

P. Sand (✉) · E. Stausbøll
Xeneta, Copenhagen, Denmark
e-mail: peter.sand@xeneta.com; emily.stausboll@xeneta.com

D. Goldman
Xeneta, Oslo, Norway
e-mail: dayna.goldman@xeneta.com

T. Rydbergh
Marine Benchmark, Gothenburg, Sweden
e-mail: torbjorn.rydbergh@marinebenchmark.com

M. Lind et al. (eds.), *Maritime Decarbonization*,
https://doi.org/10.1007/978-3-031-39936-7_23

- Shippers and freight forwarders can use the CEI data to decarbonize their supply chains.
- Carriers' reputation improves when the aggregation of their fleet data indicates low CEI values.

Introduction

In November 2022, Xeneta, specialists in ocean and air freight rate benchmarking and market analytics and Marine Benchmark (MB), maritime data analysts, jointly launched the Carbon Emissions Index (CEI) for ocean container shipping (Xeneta, 2022; Xeneta, 2023). The CEI is a first-of-its-kind data solution that tracks and compares the carbon emissions of ocean carriers across 13 main global trade routes, with new data published quarterly. It is currently the only factual, timely and independent (zero input from carriers) reference that is based on actual vessels and voyage data.

The CEI is based on the calculated CO_2 emissions per ton of cargo on selected trade routes, indexed to data from the first quarter of 2018 (2018 Q1). As well as showing results per carrier, the CEI can be used to show the development in CO_2 emission rates on each trade route. In this way users can track:

- the historical development of emissions on each trade route,
- the development of a carrier's performance over time,
- how a carrier compares to the trade route average, and
- how a carrier compares to other carriers.
- Furthermore, if you know which service you are on, you can identify the operator and then match that with the index.

How Can the CEI Progress Maritime Decarbonization?

Governments and the general public are increasingly insisting that shipping dramatically reduces its carbon footprint. Under this scenario, carriers, as a key part of the maritime transportation chain, have an important part to play by prioritising decarbonization within their fleet or supplier relations.

Currently, the only carbon emissions data on carriers is obtained from the carriers themselves and is compiled in a way that makes it difficult to compare. This data is not based on real voyage data. Rather than make assumptions for several key variables such as cargo load and speed, the CEI uses ships' automatic identification system (AIS) tracking to source data on what actually occurred during a voyage, including changes in speed, cargo load, number of intermediate ports visits, time steaming, as well at time spent at anchorages. Whether carriers are willing to be transparent about their emissions performance will no longer be a factor—the CEI

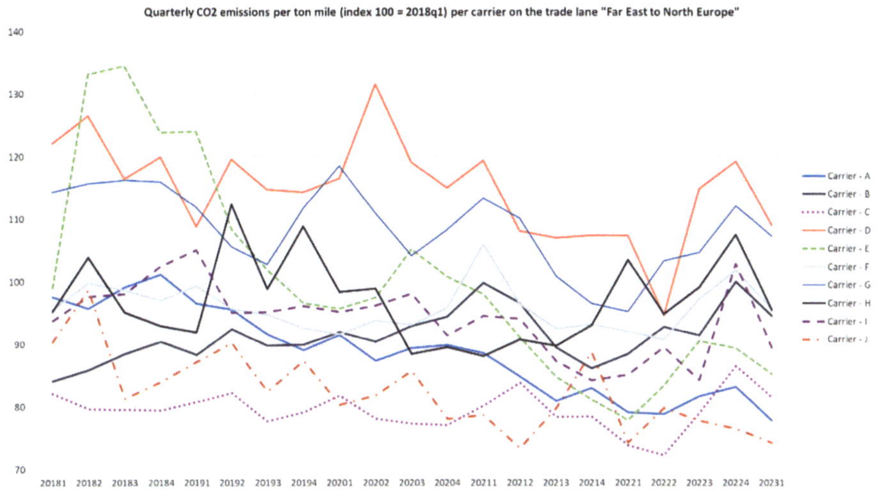

Fig. 1 CEI (average CO_2 emissions per ton of cargo transported) in container ships on the trade route from Far East to Northern Europe for ten major carriers, index

provides access to ships' emissions performance whether the carriers want it to be available or not, and that holds a lot of value for consumers.

With the advent of the CEI, the actual carbon intensity of vessels, calculated from the routes they actually travelled and the cargoes they carried, can become a real discriminator in carrier selection both for shippers and for freight forwarders. This can only encourage carriers to show proven improvement in their carbon emissions, rather than just making claims of improvement.

Figure 1 shows the average carbon dioxide (CO_2) emissions per ton of cargo transported for ten major carriers, anonymised as carriers A to J, for the Far East—Northern Europe trade route.

From 2018 to Q1 2022, the trend for CO_2 emissions per ton of cargo transported was downwards. While an upwards trend was developing in the following three quarters where the carbon intensity grew, the improving trend returned in Q1 2023. The CEI scores of Carriers A-J were all lower, though with large differences between carriers.

In the first quarter of 2023, the average carbon intensity for Carrier-J, for example, was 32 percent lower than that of Carrier-D.

Figure 2 provides three graphs that show average vessel sizes, ages and speeds plotted against each of the ten carrier's CEI for 2018 through to Q1 2022.

The graphs show that deploying larger and younger vessels and slow steaming have helped reduce emissions. Carrier-G attained the largest reduction—increasing its average vessel size by 210 percent, decreasing average age by 86 percent, reducing average speed by 23 percent, and enabling lower-carbon fuel compatibility in 83% of its vessels. In contrast, Carrier-E had the oldest vessels of which none could use alternative fuels (UNCTAD, 2022).

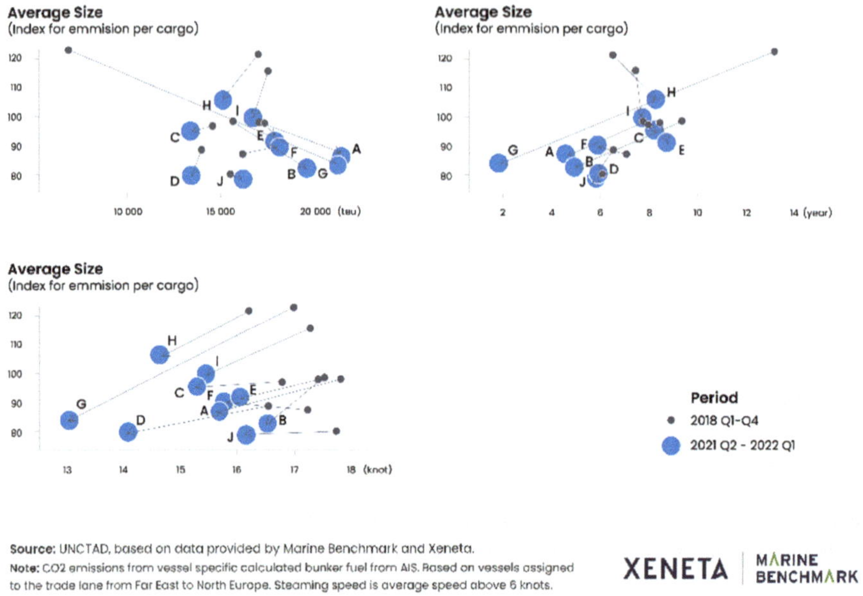

Fig. 2 Carriers' CEI's plotted against their ships' average size, age and speed

Why an Index?

- The Carbon Emissions Index is based on *independent data*, sourced from MB, with no input from carriers.
- It is based on factual data combining vessel specifications with data on every journey carried out to calculate the CO_2 emissions, using real values rather than assumptions on variables such as speed, cargo load and distance travelled.
- It allows for direct comparisons over time and between carriers.
- It is easy to use, with users able to select trade routes and carriers.
- Users of the CEI can identify the greener carriers in their procurement process.

How Is it Done?

AIS Positions

Using AIS data, the company MB tracks vessels, including their current position, speed, direction, draught, and destination, to determine ships' activities, which are then combined with each vessel's specifications, particularly the type of fuel used, to calculate its CO_2 emissions.

Intake

MB then models each vessel's intake of cargo in tons, based on the AIS-derived draught, vessel specifications and a calculated TPC (tonnes per centimetre). Based on this input, MB can also calculate the filling factor, in other words how close is the vessel to being fully loaded.

Fuel Calculation

Fuel consumption and CO_2 is calculated for each vessel at every stage of its journey based on the primary fuel type used by the vessel. This calculation takes many vessel parameters and environmental factors into account.

Voyage Legs

MB monitors around 80,000 areas covering almost all ports/terminals/berths, such that when a vessel arrives in one of these areas (as indicated by AIS data) a data record is made.

A voyage leg is recorded as when a vessel leaves a berth to when it leaves the next berth. A voyage leg includes exit from port, sea passage, any activities during sea passage, waiting times and port time at the next destination port.

Sequential Voyages

Vessels rarely call at only two ports on a journey, so voyage legs are combined to make one sequential voyage between given port pairs. For example, a vessel sailing from Shanghai to Hamburg, might call at Singapore, Jeddah, and Barcelona before arriving in Hamburg.

Outbound and inbound journeys along each trade route are treated separately. This is because fronthaul trade (the direction of a round-trip voyage where most cargo is carried) is usually the most revenue-generating for a carrier with optimised freight capacity. Backhaul trade (moving the same vessel from the destination port back to its origin) is often less profitable because a full load is harder to achieve on backhaul voyages. This means that the resultant CEI's for fronthaul may be different to backhaul.

Once a voyage is completed, the CO_2 per ton of cargo for the whole voyage is then calculated using the CO_2 emissions and transport work per leg. By transport work we mean the tons of cargo carried between individual port pairs as part of the total voyage. This allows for the distance weighted transport work to be taken into account.

What Data Is Included and Excluded?

The fuel calculation is done on a tank-to-wake (TTW) basis; well-to-tank (WTT) emissions are not considered. In other words, the calculations account for the emissions resulting from burning the fuel onboard a ship during a voyage, rather than the total CO_2 emissions resulting from getting the fuel out of the ground and into the ship.

The fuel used to power reefer (refrigerated) containers during sea passages is not included in the calculation of the CEI. This allows for a fairer comparison between carriers, regardless of what share of their cargo is reefer.

The aim of the CEI is to reflect normal day-to-day operations for carriers. Therefore, if there are any individual journeys which show significant variance from usual carrier behaviour, they are excluded as being outliers.

As the CEI is based on cargo weight, and not twenty-foot equivalent unit (TEU) numbers, the weight of empty containers is included in the cargo load of the ships. As more weight carried offers a better result for the CO_2 emitted per ton calculation, carrying an empty container instead of a loaded container might see efficiency fall, but carrying an empty container instead of no container at all improves CEI performance. This correctly reflects the fact that returning empty containers is an essential part of the container shipping model and in shippers' interest and therefore should be included in the index.

Alliances and slot sharing agreements are not considered in the CEI. The results are only calculated for ships operated by the chosen carrier, without considering whether a share of the cargo onboard may have been contracted through another carrier. This is one of the reasons why the CEI is not suitable for carbon accounting. However, the CEI remains a valid measure for prospective customers to identify the best performing carriers even when some of their cargoes are carried on other companies' ships.

What Factors Affect Carrier Carbon Emissions?

While many variables affect carrier performance, some stand out as having a very large influence. These variables are a mixture of the technical specifications of the ships as well as various operational measures.

Vessel Specifications

The size of a ship is the biggest factor in a vessel's CO_2 performance, offering economies of scale because adding capacity requires a proportionally lower increase in fuel consumption. Also, important is engine type, ship age and hull shape.

Other Operational Variables

Important operational variables include the cargo load, ship's speed, distance covered, total time (steaming, manoeuvring, waiting and moored), capacity, filling factor and number of port calls.

Table 1 compares the total carriers' average CEI with the average CEI for Mediterranean Shipping Company (MSC) and Maersk Line on the same route between 2018 and 2023.

It can be seen that the CEI scores indicate that CO_2 emissions for the two carriers have been volatile over the years, and that none of them consistently had proved to be better than the all-carriers average for the route.

General improvements in average CO_2 emissions (a lower CEI score) for carriers can be attributed to improvements in:

- capacity—if the average ship size increases
- sailing speed—if the average speed falls
- filling factor—if the average filling factor increases.

Working against improvements to the score, could be an increase in the total time of each journey; which could go up if ports are congested. The consequential increases in waiting times play a significant part in the amount of ships' CO_2 emissions.

Who Can Benefit from Using the CEI?

Shippers and freight forwarders can use the CEI data to decarbonize their supply chains, carriers can also benefit from this unbiased, reliable aggregation of their fleet data and that of their competitors.

Table 1 Average CEI for trade lane, MSC and Maersk Line

CEI	2018 Q1	2019 Q1	2020 Q1	2021 Q1	2022 Q1	2023 Q1
Trade Route N. Europe to US East Coast	100	98.1	97.5	97.5	84.7	99.7
MSC	109.1	104.1	116.2	82.5	81.4	112.2
Maersk Line	99.9	96.3	103.7	96.0	96.0	110.6

Source: Marine Benchmark, Xeneta

While the CEI has a strong use case today, the full value of this kind of data is yet to be reached, since it is a relatively new development. What is known, is that the more transparency is created within the ocean freight industry, the more conversations will take place between all the players in the industry, and the more advances can then be made to improve efficiencies and the global carbon footprint of ocean freight.

What's Next for the CEI?

Establishing an independent guide that serves as a common and actionable reference point for all buyers and sellers of freight globally is seen as a must have, to pull and push the decarbonization of the container shipping industry—and any other shipping sector.

Dr. Pierre Garreau, CEO & Co-Founder of SeaRoutes, on a webinar with Xeneta in 2020, suggested that giving shippers the possibility to choose and measure accurately the services that reduce their CO_2 footprint is a step in the right direction to reducing emissions from transport.

According to Garreau, shippers and freight forwarders have traditionally based their freight buying and selling decisions on the reliability of carriers' transit times but, in future, they will be insisting on CO_2 emissions data to compare and then choose their carriers.

Together, Marine Benchmark and Xeneta continue to develop the CEI, first by adding to the original 13 trade routes which were monitored. The first expansion was released in May 2023, expanding the usage of the CEI by covering a larger share of shippers' total business in terms of volume and scope. The data within the CEI will also be further developed and used in increasing detail, as customers become more comfortable with reading the index and understanding how to use it.

References

UNCTAD. (2022). *Review of maritime transport 2022 – Navigating stormy waters*. United Nations Conference on Trade and Development (UNCTAD). Available via https://unctad.org/system/files/official-document/rmt2022_en.pdf

Xeneta. (2022). *Xeneta and Marine Benchmark partner to launch Carbon Emissions Index (CEI)*. Xeneta and Marine Benchmark. Available via https://www.xeneta.com/news/xeneta-and-marine-benchmark-partner-to-launch-carbon-emissions-index-cei

Xeneta. (2023). *Carbon Emissions Index. Xeneta and Marine-Benchmark*. Available via https://www.xeneta.com/products/cei

Actions by Ports to Support Green Maritime Operations: A Real Case Study—The Port of Plymouth, UK

Stavros Karamperidis, Dogancan Okumus, Dogancan Uzun, Sefer Anil Gunbeyaz, and Osman Turan

Target Audience

This chapter should be of interest to senior leaders and managers in helping them take the most appropriate and informed actions in support of a carbon-free maritime transportation chain by ensuring the availability of alternative carbon-free fuels and services for shipping.

It should interest those in port organisations and in shipping companies. It aims to enhance knowledge on how ports can make decisions on the quantity and the types of alternative fuels that they will need to provide in the future. Policy makers should be interested in the chapter as a way to obtain knowledge on how ports will determine which carbon-free fuels to provide.

Five Key Take Aways

- Ports can become energy hubs not only for vessels, but also for other modes of transport. However, space may be a big challenge, as alternative fuels require more storage space than fossil-based fuels.

S. Karamperidis (✉)
University of Plymouth, Plymouth, UK
e-mail: stavros.karamperidis@plymouth.ac.uk

D. Okumus · S. A. Gunbeyaz · O. Turan
University of Strathclyde, Glasgow, UK
e-mail: dogancan.okumus@strath.ac.uk; sefer.gunbeyaz@strath.ac.uk; o.turan@strath.ac.uk

D. Uzun
Lloyd's Register, London, UK
e-mail: dogancan.uzun@lr.org

M. Lind et al. (eds.), *Maritime Decarbonization*,
https://doi.org/10.1007/978-3-031-39936-7_24

- Building infrastructure requires time and thorough planning based on a life cycle assessment. Thus, we need to carefully consider the characteristics of the port in terms of traffic and safety, and based on that, to propose alternative fuels.
- Port ownership models could have an impact on decarbonization targets. For example, publicly owned ports could have a larger impact on maritime decarbonization, as governments are obliged to meet the decarbonization targets.
- Ports could act as catalysts in the supply chain and unlock decarbonization in different transport modes that interact with the port by developing suitable infrastructure that supports alternative fuels. To achieve this, they need to work collectively with other stakeholders, including governments, shipping companies, and logistics providers.
- By following the methodology described in this chapter, any port could identify the energy output requirements needed to support visiting ships and port infrastructure. This would then provide them with a basis for determining what alternative fuels and investments may be the most appropriate.

Ports' Essential Role in Maritime Decarbonization

The International Maritime Organization (IMO) has adopted a set of key short-term measures to reduce the carbon intensity of all ships by at least 40% by 2030. These measures are mandatory. Ships must calculate and declare their Energy Efficiency Existing Ship Index (EEXI) and ships over 5000 gross tonnage (GT) must report their annual operational carbon intensity indicator (CII) data and CII rating (IMO, 2022). Recent estimations indicate that shipping may be responsible for 10–15% of global sulphur oxides (SOx) and nitrogen oxides (NOx) emissions and 2–3% of global carbon dioxide (CO_2) emissions; however, if no action is taken, that percentage will increase significantly by 2050 (Zis & Psaraftis, 2019; Bjerkan & Seter, 2019). For shipping to meet the same greenhouse gas (GHG) targets that have been set for countries under the most recent revisions to the UN Framework Convention on Climate Change (UNFCCC), it would have to reduce its CO_2 emissions from approximately 25 g to 4 g of CO_2 per ton-nautical mile (Bouman et al., 2017). At the same time, the demand for sea freight transportation continues to increase due to growing populations and economic developments. If no precautions are taken, shipping emissions could become the second largest source of pollution in the transport section, following land-based emissions (Zhang et al., 2021) (Rahim et al., 2016) (Sun et al., 2020).

Ports are where ships' cargoes are loaded and unloaded. Ships also refuel in some of the ports that they visit—either concurrently with cargo operations or separately but as part of the same port visit. This avoids vessels having to divert from their voyages to refuel, which would add additional costs and time to shipowners. As part of maritime decarbonization efforts, there are moves towards using alternative low- or no-carbon fuels and the use of 'cold ironing', taking shore-based power for ships while ships are in port. However, fuelling with alternative fuels (hydrogen, electricity, etc.) requires more time than for refuelling with traditional fossil-based fuels. In future, ports will need to be able to provide the alternative fuels to ships and ideally, provide them concurrently with loading and unloading operations. Failure to do so will increasingly make a port less attractive for the loading or unloading of vessels, as the ships will have to spend valuable time, perhaps at another location, solely for refuelling. As the alternative fuels, currently under consideration, are all less energy intensive, vessels may also need to refuel more often and add more ports of call, unless they opt for larger fuel storage space onboard. This highlights the potential for more and more ports to act not only as transport nodes but also as energy providers for vessels (Lind et al., 2023).

Trucks and locomotives, currently using fossil-based fuels, often wait in dockside areas and then refuel at intervals—often off-site. As land-based transport moves towards greater electrification and the use of batteries, or uses the same alternative fuels as the ships, waiting time at ports could be used for recharging or replacing electric batteries or for refuelling. In this way, ports of the future will play a key role in supplying energy not only to vessels, but also to the land-based motive power that uses the ports.

Cargo movement through ports will increase in the next few years as green maritime corridors are established throughout the globe. A green maritime corridor is a specific trade route between major port hubs where zero-emission solutions are supported (Getting to Zero Coalition, 2021). An essential driver for green corridors is the modal shift from road and rail to maritime transport, as maritime transport has the lowest environmental footprint/per ton of cargo carried compared to road and rail (IMO, 2009). It can be anticipated that more and more cargo will be channelled through ports. Therefore, the fact that ports could refuel transport modes while they are waiting to load or unload cargo gives them the opportunity to become energy hubs.

Of course, the importance of ports in a new business environment provides opportunities but, at the same time, challenges. The biggest challenge is that ports will need more space for the new alternative, but lower energy intensity, fuels than they currently do for fossil-fuels. In addition, they will be supplying both their traditional customers (ships) and potentially new customers (road and rail). Another challenge, especially for medium and small-size ports, will be to determine which fuels they will be supplying to their customers. If the volume of ships calling at small/medium size ports is low, it may not be economically viable to offer a wide range of the technologically feasible alternative fuels. Considering that each fuel will require a different infrastructure, ports will have to make a choice that may not satisfy all their customers. In the past some ports have taken nearly 20 years to create the infrastructure needed to supply liquified natural gas (LNG) fuel to vessels (Baker, 2021). 20 years may seem like a long time when decarbonization is high on the agenda. However, it is not only the time required to build the infrastructure but also to test it and make sure that it is safe for operations. Usually, that takes time, especially when the alternative fuel is flammable and gaseous, as is the specific case of LNG. Several alternative fuels have similar volatile characteristics that requires the safety aspects to be carefully considered.

To effect changes, ports will need additional investment to create the safe infrastructures that will support maritime decarbonization. It is vital to have a sound understanding of the port, its characteristics, its customers and its future potential, to ensure that investments are both forthcoming and well-spent. Such an analysis should be tackled holistically, considering other energy efficiency practices to increase energy efficiency and reduce emissions. This includes the implementation of berth optimisation (for maritime and land operations) (Arango et al., 2013), and Just in Time (JIT) arrival for all modes interacting with ports (Lind et al., 2023). Those practices were included in our case study of the port of Plymouth, which we discuss in the next parts of this chapter.

Green Bunkering Options

The push is on for maritime transportation to be more energy efficient. Ways of doing this can be divided in to four groups (Bjerkan & Seter, 2019):

- Improved port management and policies (port planning, management of environment and energy, monitoring, concession agreements);
- Green power and fuels at sea and ashore (electrification, wind, solar, wave and tidal energy, methanol and hydrogen, LNG, etc.);
- Voyage optimisation (speed reduction, efficient vessel handling, just-in-time arrival, etc.); and
- Improved technology ashore (trucks and drayage, modal shifts, efficient truck operations, automation and intelligence).

Selecting the most appropriate measures and tools to implement in a port needs comprehensive feasibility studies that consider many parameters including ship call statistics and particulars, energy type and availability, other modes of transport servicing the port, and land and water space availability for new or expanded facilities or storage and port equipment. Studies should involve a life cycle assessment (LCA) analysis. In any analysis, a significant challenge is to take account of the large variety of fuels, their current and likely future availability and the costs involved.

Table 1 provides a snapshot of the costs (based on the fuel), benefits and Technology Readiness Levels (TRL) for some of the greener fuel options potentially available for ships.

The TRLs values used in Table 1 are:

TRL	Description
1	Basic principles observed
2	Technology concept formulated
3	Experimental proof of concept
4	Technology validated in lab
5	Technology validated in relevant environment
6	Technology demonstrated in relevant environment
7	System model or prototype demonstration in an operational environment
8	System complete and qualified
9	Actual system proven in an operational environment

Table 1 Onboard technology/fuel cost, benefits and Technology Readiness Level

Technology/ fuel	Cost	Benefit	TRL
LNG	Varies	• Existing technology • Reduces CO_2 emissions	9
Electrification (cold ironing)	See Table 4	• Existing technology (we have cases in the UK, please see Table 4) • Net-zero	9
Ammonia	$100 M	• Usable in ICE engines with minor adaptation, commercially available in 3–5 years. • More energy dense, less burden on total cost of ownership (TCO) than hydrogen/ammonia • Established global market and logistics infrastructure • Less price uncertainty relative to other fuels (electrolyser technology, electricity prices) • Low SO_2, particulate matter, metal, and polycyclic aromatic hydrocarbon pollution • Less flammable than hydrogen or synfuels. Safe handling expertise already exists	4 to 7
Methanol	$175 M for a 16,000 TEU containership	• Methanol is a fuel that can be stored at ambient temperature without cooling or pressurisation • Currently there is lack as a fuel	5
Hydrogen	$20 M	• Cheaper and less electricity-intensive than ammonia and synfuels • No toxic by-products • Does not require co- firing of another fuel (for ignition engines) • Engines commercially available in 3–5 years	5 to 7
Biofuel	Varies	• Compatible with existing engines/ powertrains • High energy density, low storage volume • High compatibility with existing bunkering infrastructure • No co-firing required in spark ignition engines	8
Batteries	$10 M	• Most efficient use of energy • Battery costs low and still declining. Already cost-effective for short distances • Lower maintenance costs	9
Solid-Oxide fuel cells		• More efficient converter of fuel energy than internal combustion engines (ICE) • Fuel 'agnostic' (can be used with Hydrogen, LNG, Ammonia) • Can save more emissions than cold-ironing • If on the ship, is available in all ports with no requirement for land-side infrastructure and net-work upgrade.	3

Source: Authors

More discussion on the various options under consideration are also covered in other chapters in this book.

From Table 1, it can be seen that most of the green fuel options are not yet ready to be deployed extensively. Electrification is readily available, but is limited to short trips. The other alternative fuel sources still need development—some more than others. That makes the choice of what to invest in all the more difficult for ports, as they cannot know which fuel will be dominant in a few years' time, while at the same time, they are unlikely to have the space or the funding to invest in all the available options. Therefore, the strategy for many seems to be to wait and see. Ironically, such a strategy then makes shipowners hesitant over which fuels to invest in, because they do not know which fuels will be available in ports. So, we end up with a 'chicken and egg' scenario between the ports and the ships over the best path to take for maritime decarbonization. In such a scenario, it may be those ports that are publicly owned ports that take the lead, because many governments are now obliged to put mechanisms in place to reach the decarbonization targets.

Scope of the Analysis of the Port of Plymouth

The authors recently completed an analysis that has estimated the power capacity requirements for the port of Plymouth (UK) and the potential volumes and types of alternative fuels that could be considered for visiting ships and port infrastructure in the future.

The energy analysis relies on representative ships, chosen from historical port visit data, using a similar process to modelling by Rossetti (2016). The four chosen representative categories are:

- Roll-on/Roll-off passenger (Ro-Pax) ferry
- Tanker
- Bulk Carrier
- General Cargo

Data from specific ships visiting the port was then used to represent each category.

Table 2 shows data for each representative ship type visiting the port, using information obtained in 2022 from Marinetraffic,[1] Vesselfinder,[2] and Fleetmon.[3] The particulars of each representative ship are shown in Table 2.

The use of various alternative fuels was modelled for each of the four vessel types to obtain estimates of the energy requirements for the current and three alternative fuels. The fuels used for comparison in the study were:

[1] www.marinetraffic.com

[2] www.vesselfinder.com

[3] www.fleetmon.com

Table 2 Particulars of the selected representative ship types

Ship type	Ro-Pax	Tanker	Bulk Carrier	General Cargo
Ship Size	41,700 GT	7479 DWT	4216 DWT	4497 DWT
Installed Main Engine Power	43,200 kW	3840 kW	1530 kW	1950 kW
Installed Auxiliary Engine Power	7200 kW	900 kW	596 kW	522 kW
Service Speed	27 knots	14.2 knots	11 knots	11 knots
Auxiliary Engine load factor	0.64	0.67	0.22	0.22
Auxiliary Engine specific fuel consumption	184 g/kWh	197 g/kWh	238 g/kWh	238 g/kWh
Main Engine specific fuel consumption	177 g/kWh	178 g/kWh	188.7 g/kWh	188.7 g/kWh
Port calls per year	171	197	30	231
Hoteling hours per call	4.2 hours	24.7 hours	37.9 hours	26 hours
Hoteling hours per year	718.2 hours	4865.9 hours	1137 hours	6006 hours

Source: Authors

- diesel (heavy fuel oil (HFO)),
- hydrogen,
- ammonia,
- and methanol.

The alternative fuels were selected because, in the authors' view, they appear at present to have the highest potential to replace conventional fuel such as HFO.

An estimate and comparison of bunkering fuel requirements was also made, based on the four fuels used in the study.

The port of Plymouth is located on the south coast of Devon, in southern England, near the English Channel's entrance (Latitude 500 22' N, Longitude 040 09'W, inside Plymouth Sound). Plymouth is a coastal city, and the port is right in the middle of the city. Therefore, ships' emissions affect a significant portion of its residents. More than five hundred ships visit the port each year. Onshore power supply (OPS), also known as cold ironing systems, can be extremely useful in mitigating the emissions generated by those vessels.

The port of Plymouth offers services to general cargo ships, Ro-Pax, tankers, and bulk cargo carriers. Currently, bunkering is available only for Ro-Pax vessels.

In the port of Plymouth case study, the authors used Arena Simulation Software by Rockwell Automation (Rockwell Arena, 2022) to model the port and carry out discrete event simulation. The simulation model concentrated on determining the peak power and energy consumption of berthed ships and port activities, such as land operations (trucks) and cargo handling equipment. To achieve that, the authors calculated:

- Cold ironing component: the power and energy capacity required to support the OPS.
- The port's Greenhouse gas (GHG) emissions.

- Bunkering part: the mass and volume of alternative fuels necessary to compensate for ship propulsion energy consumption.

Using their framework, the authors were able to build a solid simulation environment and then estimate the energy needs for the port of Plymouth.

Onshore Power Systems

Onshore power systems (OPS) are seen as an important element is reducing the carbon emissions of ships while alongside. The basic idea behind OPS, also known as cold ironing, is to connect ships to the local electrical grid when they are docked, such that generators or auxiliary engines, consuming fossil fuels, are not required.

A detailed power demand study for the visiting ships and the port infrastructure is a prerequisite for implementing an OPS.

OPS capacity calculations in the study accounted for ships' auxiliary power needs and supporting shore-based infrastructure such as cargo handling equipment and trucks for loading and unloading cargo. Selecting alternative fuels to supply in a port.

The authors continued their analysis, by using the available data to determine and compare the potential alternative-fuel bunkering options for the range of vessels using the port of Plymouth. This comparison took into account the differences in the energy densities and volumes of the different fuels and their impact on storage facilities both ashore and on-board ships.

Key Steps in the Analysis

Based on their work with the port of Plymouth, the authors propose the following key steps should be taken in any future green energy analysis of another port:

- Obtain records of vessels that visit the port over a period. An extended timeline for ships visit data, will provide a better understanding of a port's needs. The authors recommend that an analysis relies on at least three years of data if it is available.
- A database containing the names and type of ships, deadweight tonnage (DWT) and/or gross tonnage (GT) capacity, load condition (laden, in ballast), (IMO number, entry, anchorage, berthing, and departure dates) is essential. Details of installed propulsion and auxiliary power information would be extremely useful. Getting this data from the port's records is best. However, if it is not available, online platforms can supply most of the data needed.
- A field observation study should be carried out to generate process flows for each vessel type and each quay in the port facility. The process flows should comprise truck and other material handling equipment (such as cranes and wheel loaders)

activities as well as ship operation phases, including loading and discharging operations. Analysing the port's previous berth call history should be undertaken concurrently. The data analysis findings and the process flows can then be merged to create a discrete event simulation model (Banks et al., 2014; Robinson et al., 2010).

- Each port operation's process timings and queue lengths (in asset quantity and hours), such as berth waiting times, truck waiting times, and material handling waiting times, can be derived when the overall port operation is simulated using simulation software.
- Next, a statistical analysis can be performed for each ship type to choose a representative ship. In fact, using the DWT distribution for each ship type category, the average ship capacity and a representative ship for the intended ship type can be chosen (Rossetti, 2016).
- Once representative ships for each ship type have been chosen, more information about the ships, such as their main dimensions, main and auxiliary engine power, service speed, fuel consumption (at service speed), tank capacities, previous routes, endurance, port calls per year, and in-port hours per call, can be obtained from various sources, such as port records, shipping companies' websites, and the traffic monitoring sites Marine Traffic, FleetMon, or Vesselfinder.
- The power-consuming components in this process can then be multiplied by the operating periods based on the timings (in hours) acquired from the simulation. The energy demand in kWh and peak power demand in kW can then be determined by considering each component's load factor.
- The fuel consumption and greenhouse gas emissions can be calculated using the power and energy requirements for all steps of the process.
- Bunkering estimates and associated energy consumption can be calculated for the different fuel types, using the sample ships' voyage scenarios.

Findings of the Study

Power Demand

Using the results of the simulations and the representative ships, the authors calculated the required power and energy demands for the port of Plymouth, as shown in Table 3.

According to the authors' calculations (as shown in Table 3), the representative Ro-Pax vessel spent 9.02 hours less time at berth than the bulk carrier. That is logical because roll-on roll-off cargo is easier to move, whereas bulk cargo requires hatches and cranes to load or unload cargo. If we were considering only the time spent at berth, then we might prioritise an investment in cold iron facilities at the dry bulk terminal. However, we must also consider the size of the vessel and the energy needs.

Table 3 Simulation results (for 100 runs)

	The annual number of ship calls (#)			Total time spent in port per ship call (h)			The average time at berth per ship call (h)		
Vessel type	Average	Min. Average	Max. Average	Average	Min. Average	Max. Average	Average	Min. Average	Max. Average
Ro-Pax	171	137	211	5.0	4.7	5.6	4.2	3.8	4.8
Tanker	197	171	222	33.6	29.7	40.7	24.7	23.9	25.7
Bulk Carrier	30	18	40	61.9	49.5	81.0	37.9	30.7	44.7
General Cargo	231	196	275	42.7	35.7	49.9	26.0	23.8	29.1

Source: Authors

Table 4 Power demand and annual energy demand for OPS—according to ship type

Ship type	Power demand for OPS (MW)	Energy demand per ship for OPS (MWh)	Annual energy demand for OPS (MWh) (%Total)
Ro-Pax	4.6 MW	19.35 MWh	3309.5 MWh (46.7%)
Tanker	0.6 MW	14.89 MWh	2934.1 MWh (41.4%)
Bulk Carrier	0.13 MW	4.97 MWh	149.1 MWh (2.1%)
General Cargo	0.12 MW	2.99 MWh	689.7 MWh (9.7%)

Source: Authors

Detailed energy and power requirement calculations were conducted based on the operation timings obtained from the discrete event simulation, representative ship particulars, truck features, and material handling equipment. The port of Plymouth has various berths: Millbay, Victoria and Cattedown. Millbay and Cattedown can serve two vessels simultaneously, whereas Victoria can service only one ship. However, it is important to note that although Millbay has a two-berth capacity, only one berth is used, according to the data. The Millbay port management confirmed this. The peak power and energy demand were calculated by assuming that all berths in the port were occupied simultaneously.

Table 4 shows the power and energy demand per ship type and the annual total energy demand for OPS depending on ship type. The peak power demand was found to be 5.95 MW when berth capacities were taken into account. The peak power demand is when the berth allocation scenario comprises two tankers, one Ro-Pax and one Bulk Carrier berthed simultaneously.

Energy Demand for Trucks

The annual truck energy demand was calculated by considering the truck operations for each ship visit. A truck cycle for each visit of our representative ship types was calculated by dividing the cargo volume for the ship types ships by the cargo capacity of a truck. The port authority provided the truck operational hours for each cycle (TOH) and truck fuel consumption per hour (TFCH). Table 5 tabulates the parameters and values and calculated annual fuel consumption of trucks (AFCT) in a litre (diesel) for each vessel type.

Energy Demand for Material Handling Equipment

The last calculation in the port energy demand assessment was the energy demand of the material handling equipment (MHE) such as cranes and loaders. This was calculated based on data provided by the port authority. Cranes and wheel loaders are the predominant MHEs used in the port's operations. The port authority

Table 5 Truck energy demand calculation

Vessel type	T_{cycle}	TFCH (litre/h)	TOH(hour)	AFCT (litre)
Ro-Pax	2	5.8	1	1984
Tanker	200	6.27	0.25	61,760
Bulk Carrier	150	6.27	0.33	9311
General Cargo	150	6.27	0.33	71,694

Source: Authors, based on calculations from Canbulat (2021)

Table 6 Material handling equipment operating times and fuel consumption rates

Ship type		Bulk Carrier	General Cargo
Per vessel	Crane operation time (h)	19	13
	Av. Crane fuel consumption (L/h)	24	24
	Wheel loader operation time (h)	26.5	18.2
	Av. wheel loader fuel cons (L/h)	20	20
Annual fuel consumption (L)		29,562	156,156

Source: Authors

highlighted that the Ro-Pax and Tanker operations do not involve any MHE use therefore, the energy demand of the MHE was calculated for Bulk Carrier and General Cargo vessel only. Table 6 shows the detailed MHE data provided by the port authority and the calculated annual fuel consumption (AFC) for MHEs.

Ships' Emission Calculations

The calculation of emissions for the representative ships was made based on the total fuel consumption, including auxiliary engines, material handling equipment and trucks. Fuel-to-emission conversion factors or each pollutant were adapted from the Fourth IMO GHG Study (IMO, 2020). Table 7 shows the calculated amount of annual pollutant emissions for each of the representative ship types.

Table 8 shows the percentage of CO_2 emissions distribution induced by ships' auxiliary engines trucks and MHE for each vessel type. The results indicated that the port's dominant source of CO_2 emissions is auxiliary engine-induced CO_2 emissions, with 99.7% for Ro-Pax and 91.9% for Tanker, 52.6% for Bulk Carrier and 46.7% for General Cargo. The percentages of CO_2 emitted due to truck operations are 0.3% for Ro-Pax, 8.1% for Tanker, 11.3% for Bulk Carrier and 16.8% for General Cargo vessels.

Providing an OPS system could cut the CO_2 emissions for Ro-Pax and Tanker by more than 90%, whereas for Bulk Carriers and General Cargo vessels, this would only be by around 50%. Therefore, to achieve net-zero targets, the port would need to acquire battery-powered trucks and electric-powered MHE and provide the infrastructure for charging the trucks.

Table 7 Pollutant emissions in tons for each type of ship at the port during the period 2020–2021

Ship type	Pollutant type (tons/year)									
	CO_2	CH_4	N_2O	NO_X	CO	NMVOC	SO_X	PM	$PM_{2.5}$	BC
Ro-Pax	1957.49	0.0312	0.1105	34.545	1.641	1.475	0.835	0.548	0.505	0.231
Tanker	2015.75	0.0545	0.1333	33.136	3.493	1.816	0.813	0.52	0.48	0.220
Bulk Carrier	216.1	0.0179	0.0248	2.236	1.348	0.355	0.062	0.032	0.294	0.013
General Cargo	1126.17	0.1027	0.1373	10.622	7.787	1.975	0.304	0.148	0.136	0.062
Total	**5315.5**	**0.206**	**0.406**	**80.54**	**14.27**	**5.62**	**2.02**	**1.25**	**1.151**	**0.527**

Source: Authors

Table 8 Percentage of CO_2 emissions distribution among ships' auxiliary engines, trucks and material handling equipment

Emissions source	Ro-Pax	Tanker	Bulk Carrier	General Cargo
Ships' auxiliary engines	99.7%	91.9%	52.6%	46.7%
Trucks	0.3%	8.1%	11.3%	16.8%
MHE	No MHE Operation	No MHE Operation	36.0%	36.5%

Source: Authors

Calculation of Alternative Fuel Volumes (Safety and Storage of Alternative Fuels vs Traditional Fuels)

Fuel volume comparisons were made between conventional diesel (heavy fuel oil (HFO)) and the three alternative fuels in the study, hydrogen, ammonia, and methanol. The methodology given by McKinlay et al. (McKinlay et al., 2021) was followed to calculate the required amount of fuel mass and volume reference to the diesel fuel.

Table 9 compares the physical properties of the alternative fuels and diesel. The efficiency percentage ranges and the upper boundary for efficiencies for the alternative fuels were based on corresponding values in work by McKinlay et al. (2021). It was possible to calculate values for diesel propulsion systems rather than using assumed values.

The figures in Table 9 show that the required volume of fuel for each alternative fuel is larger than for conventional fuel (diesel). This means that more storage tanks would be required at ports and in ships if a move to alternative fuels is to take place.

A weekly bunkering scenario was created for the representative ships, based on average voyage distance. It was assumed that ships return to the port of Plymouth with empty tanks. The weekly distance for the Ro-Pax vessel type was calculated based on historical data obtained from the ferry company. The weekly fuel value calculated from this data was confirmed by the Ro-Pax ferry company. For the other reference ship types, the weekly fuel consumption values were based on the assumption that the port provides a fuel volume equivalent to seven days of the ships' cruising at their service speeds.

Using the weekly voyages, fuel mass and volumes were calculated for each vessel type and each of the four fuels chosen in the study. The results are shown in Table 10.

Table 10 shows that hydrogen is clearly advantageous in terms of mass as it can provide the required energy requirement with less fuel mass than the other fuels. However, hydrogen is much less attractive when the volume required to store the fuels is taken into account. Table 10 shows that the required volume required for hydrogen is around 3.5 times that for diesel. The volumes for methanol and ammonia are about 1.8 times and about 1.5 times, respectively.

Table 9 Comparison of Diesel (HFO), Hydrogen, Ammonia and Methanol fuels

Fuel type	Diesel (HFO)	Hydrogen (Liquid, −252 °C)	Ammonia (−34 °C)	Methanol (15 °C)
Fuel volume per vessel (m^3)	Ro-Pax:295 Tanker:129.5 BulkCarrier:54.7 General Cargo:69.5	Ro-Pax:1114.5 Tanker:491 Bulk Carrier:196 General Cargo:261	Ro-Pax:743.1 Tanker:327.1 Bulk Carrier:130.5 General Cargo:174	Ro-Pax:602 Tanker:265 Bulk Carrier:106 General Cargo:141
Fuel density (kg/m^3)	950 @14.85 °C	71 @ −252 °C	681.9 @ −34 °C	796 @ 15 °C
Fuel mass per vessel (ton)	Ro-Pax:280 Tanker:123 BulkCarrier:52 General Cargo:66	Ro-Pax:79.1 Tanker:34.8 Bulk Carrier:13.9 General Cargo:18.5	Ro-Pax:506.7 Tanker:223.1 Bulk Carrier:89 General Cargo:118.7	Ro-Pax:479.1 Tanker:210.9 Bulk Carrier:84.2 General Cargo:112.2

Source: Authors

Table 10 Weekly bunkering scenarios: fuel mass and volume requirements for Diesel, Hydrogen, Ammonia and Methanol for each vessel type

	Weekly bunkering fuel requirement							
	Diesel		Hydrogen		Ammonia		Methanol	
Ship type	(t)	(m^3)	(t)	(m^3)	(t)	(m^3)	(t)	(m^3)
Ro-Pax	920.8	969.2	260.2	3665	1666.4	2443.7	1575.5	1979.2
Tanker	466	490.5	132	1858.6	845.1	1239.3	799	1003.7
Bulk Carrier	30	31.6	8	112.9	51.4	75.3	48.5	61
General Cargo	293.2	308.6	82.3	1159.5	527.2	773.1	498.4	626.2

Source: Authors

Closing Remarks

Ports have an important part to play in the decarbonization of the different transportation modes that interact with a port by developing suitable infrastructure that both relies on and supplies carbon-free energy. However, this infrastructure will be expensive and not without risk. Before such a transition can take place, ports must consider several aspects—and in particular, what will be the demand for alternative green fuels, and what fuels should or can a port provide.

The fuel or fuels that ports will provide will vary from port to port. Each case should be handled separately, taking the unique characteristics of the port, operation type, ships that are served, geographical conditions, supply around the ports, and routes.

The maritime industry and ports need scientific support to enable informed decision-making. The authors have developed their analysis methodology to consider and compare the various alternative fuel options in relation to a port's particular activities. The model can be extended to include various ship types, and can include different relevant information such as a port's operations flow, port services and equipment, etc., as appropriate. The energy analysis of the port of Plymouth is offered as a model of how some of the questions could be answered in other ports by using the same methodology.

References

Arango, C., et al. (2013). Simulation-optimization models for the dynamic berth allocation problem. *Computer-Aided Civil and Infrastructure Engineering, 28*(10), 769–779.

Baker, C. (2021). *A feasibility study of LNG bunkering in UK ports*. MSc Dissertation,. University of Plymouth.

Banks, J., Carson, J. S., II, Nicol, D. M., & Nelson, B. L. (2014). *Discrete event system simulation*. Pearson Education Limited.

Bjerkan, K. Y., & Seter, H. (2019). Reviewing tools and technologies for sustainable ports: Does research enable decision making in ports? *Transportation Research Part D: Transport and Environment., 72*, 243–260.

Bouman, E. A., Lindstad, E., Rialland, A. I., & Strømman, A. H. (2017). State-of-the-art technologies, measures, and potential for reducing GHG emissions from shipping – A review. *Transportation Research Part D: Transport and Environment., 52*, 408–421.

Canbulat, O. (2021). *Integrated energy efficiency of shipping*. [PhD Thesis]. University of Strathclyde.

Getting to Zero Coalition. (2021). The next wave green corridors. *Getting to Zero Coalition*. Accessed in April 2023, from https://www.globalmaritimeforum.org/content/2021/11/The-Next-Wave-Green-Corridors.pdf

IMO. (2009). *Second IMO GHG study*. International Maritime Organization.

IMO. (2020). *Fourth IMO GHG study*. International Maritime Organization.

IMO. (2022). *Rules on ship carbon intensity and rating system enter into force*. International Maritime Organization. Accessed November 2022, from https://www.imo.org/en/MediaCentre/PressBriefings/pages/CII-and-EEXI-entry-into-force.aspx

Lind, M., Haraldson, S., Lehmacher, W., Raza, Z., Forsström, E., Astner, L., Bentham, J., Fu, X., Suroto, J., & Zuesongdham, P. (2023) *Thinking the future energy model nodes of the world - a reflection framework for port development, Article No. 103* [UNCTAD Transport and Trade Facilitation Newsletter N°97 – First Quarter 2023]. Accessed April 2023, from https://unctad.org/news/transport-newsletter-article-no-103-future-energy-nodes

McKinlay, C. J., Turnock, S. R., & Hudson, D. A. (2021). Route to zero emission shipping: Hydrogen, ammonia or methanol? *International Journal of Hydrogen Energy, 46*, 28282–28297.

Rahim, M. M., Islam, M. T., & Kuruppu, S. (2016). Regulating global shipping corporations' accountability for reducing greenhouse gas emissions in the seas. *Marine Policy, 69*, 159–170.

Robinson, S., Brooks, R., Kotiadis, K., & Van Der Zee, D.-J. (2010). *Conceptual modeling for discrete-event simulation*. CRC Press.

Rockwell Arena. (2022). *Automation R. Arena user guide*. Rockwell Arena.

Rossetti, M. D. (2016). *Simulation modeling and Arena*. John Wiley & Sons.

Sun, Y., Yang, L., & Zheng, J. (2020). Emission control areas: More or fewer? *Transportation Research Part D: Transport and Environment, 84*, 102349.

Zhang, X., Bao, Z., & Ge, Y.-E. (2021). Investigating the determinants of shipowners' emission abatement solutions for newbuilding vessels. *Transportation Research Part D: Transport and Environment., 99*, 102989.

Zis, T., & Psaraftis, H. N. (2019). Operational measures to mitigate and reverse the potential modal shifts due to environmental legislation. *Maritime Policy & Management., 46*, 117–132.

Towards Ports as Energy Nodes: Strengthening Micro Energy Systems

Mikael Lind, Sandra Haraldson, Wolfgang Lehmacher, Zeeshan Raza, Ellinor Forsström, Linda Astner, Jeremy B. Bentham, Xiuju Fu, Jimmy Suroto, and Phanthian Zuesongdam

M. Lind (✉)
Research Institutes of Sweden (RISE), Gothenburg, Sweden

Chalmers University of Technology, Gothenburg, Sweden
e-mail: mikael@realsearchers.com

S. Haraldson · Z. Raza
Research Institutes of Sweden (RISE), Gothenburg, Sweden
e-mail: sandra@realsearchers.com; zeeshan.raza@ri.se

W. Lehmacher
Independent Supply Chain Expert, Hong Kong, China
e-mail: w.lehmacher@gmail.com

E. Forsström
Research Institutes of Sweden (RISE), Lund, Sweden
e-mail: ellinor.forsstrom@ri.se

L. Astner
Port of Gävle, Gävle, Sweden
e-mail: linda.astner@gavlehamn.se

J. B. Bentham
World Energy Council, London, UK

Scenarios Team, Shell International, The Hague, The Netherlands

Mission Possible Partnership, Washington, DC, USA

Boston Consulting Group, Amsterdam, The Netherlands

Transformative Scenarios B.V., The Hague, The Netherlands
e-mail: jbentham@live.com

X. Fu
Institute of High Performance Computing, A*STAR, Singapore, Singapore
e-mail: fuxj@ihpc.a-star.edu.sg

J. Suroto
PSA International Pte Ltd, Singapore, Singapore
e-mail: sjimmy@globalpsa.com

P. Zuesongdam
Hamburg Port Authority, Hamburg, Germany
e-mail: Phanthi-an.Zuesongdham@hpa.hamburg.de

M. Lind et al. (eds.), *Maritime Decarbonization*,
https://doi.org/10.1007/978-3-031-39936-7_25

Target Audience

This chapter has been written for decision-makers, senior executives and project managers involved in the transformation of ports into micro energy hubs supplying both ships and port infrastructure, and surrounding areas such as industrial zones, communities, and cities with power.

Key Takeaway Messages

The chapter highlights:

- Ports are not only a transport and digital node (Lind et al., 2021) but also energy hubs (Lind et al., 2023) in the global energy ecosystem
- A framework for guiding ports on how to fully develop their energy node capabilities and play a role as model energy nodes that will demonstrate and influence the pace of decarbonization locally, regionally, and globally
- Multiple ways that ports can support the decarbonization effort throughout the maritime industry and the global economy
- The importance of collaboration and digitalisation in the process of decarbonizing the economy
- The benefits and rewards players can reap by supporting decarbonization and the energy transition

Introduction

Ports are not only a transport and digital node (Lind et al., 2021) but they are increasingly becoming energy hubs (Lind et al., 2023) in the global energy ecosystem. On average 40% of goods going through ports are energy related (HaskoningDHV, 2022). Industrial clusters are regularly located in and near ports which points to potential synergies and co-creation opportunities. Ports are central nodes for sector coupling and energy system integration (Lind et al., 2022a) as they host and serve multiple industries including oil and gas, shipping, trucking, railways, cruise-tourism, manufacturing, and offshore wind supply.

Energy production and distribution is at the heart of decarbonization. Decarbonization of transport requires all stakeholders to align, even collaborate, and take action, including shippers, transport operators, freight forwarders, ports, vehicle makers, engine manufacturers, energy producers, policy makers, etc. The reduction of greenhouse gas (GHG) emissions requires activating a range of decarbonization enablers across a number of value chains. Ports can play an important role at the intersection of marine fuel, shipbuilding (including ship supplies), and operational value chains (Lind et al., 2022c) in their capacity as energy providers to both seaborne visitors (wet and dry bulk, container, car carriers, etc.) and land-borne means of transport including trucks and trains—but also barges that move cargo within ports and on rivers across the hinterland.

Ports also have a role in synchronisation along the transportation value chain by assisting the fluidity of goods flow by reducing waiting / idle times, costs and carbon emissions. Synchronisation requires data sharing and large-scale end-to-end digitalisation as well as the adoption of all the available and relevant enablers of transport decarbonization (Lind et al., 2022b).

In this chapter we describe a framework based on a larger Swedish study (Bach et al., 2022) that can guide ports on how to develop their energy node capability and play a role as model energy nodes demonstrating and influencing the pace of decarbonization locally, regionally and globally.

Maturity Framework for Ports as Energy Nodes

Figure 1 illustrates a four-level maturity framework for developing a port as an energy node. The framework should not be seen as a one-direction/step-by-step framework but needs to be understood as a self-improving circular system, where

Fig. 1 Maturity framework for a port as an energy node (Lind et al., 2023) (Illustration: Sandra Haraldson)

ports can move back and forth between the levels as well as engaging in several levels simultaneously.

The maturity framework builds upon a port's energy strategy (Level 1), points at the need for proactive actions, taking into account its own operations (Level 2), the provision of sustainable energy to visitors of the port (Level 3), and the port's role as part of the transport ecosystem—which includes to a certain extent, the global energy system (Level 4).

Level 1: Developing an Energy Strategy

Ports need to be proactive if they want to contribute to a sustainable transport ecosystem to capitalise on the opportunities presented by the energy transition. They need to measure and quantify energy efficiency for energy strategy decision-support and effective energy consumption reduction.

Ports can generate new lease earnings or incomes through the sale of energy. Port authorities are therefore advised to start by devising an energy strategy for their own energy needs and for their energy supply capacity in their role as a transport and logistics services provider (first level of the maturity framework depicted in Fig. 1). Such an energy strategy should encompass all port operations and services as a guide for the entire port community including customers who use ports as transport, digital, and energy nodes. This implies that the port authority's energy strategy is not only the compass for port authorities but also influences, to varying degrees, the strategies of the actors that operate within the port and those that visit the port, including terminal operators, shipping companies, inland operators of trucks/trains, as well as Beneficial Cargo Owners (BCOs). All port-related and energy-related investment and partnership decisions should support mutual interest and be aligned with the port authority's overall strategy.

In the process, ports need to consider levels 2 to 4 of the framework, by holding stakeholder dialogues, and initiating collaborations, etc. The energy strategy should be revised and developed continuously.

Level 2: Establishing Sustainable Operations within the Port

At the next level of the framework (Fig. 1), after defining the port authority's energy strategy (level 1), ports should evaluate their current energy needs and emissions from their own assets and operations within the port area and develop measures to reduce the port area's carbon footprint.

One of the measures for ports to improve energy efficiency and make sure that their own needs within the port area are met sustainably is the shift from fossil-fuels to sustainable energy solutions. Electrification with low-carbon electricity for cranes, reach-stackers, prime-movers, tugboats, forklifts, and the port's vehicle fleet contributes to a reduction of the carbon footprint. Many ports install LED and smart lighting in port premises and within the port area. Ports can acquire green electricity from energy companies, and alternatively produce their own renewable energy through investments in solar and wind power. Evidence from Swedish ports suggests that adopting such measures can result in substantial operational expenditure (OPEX) savings next to a number of other benefits including reduced carbon emissions and less noise pollution, also helping ports to contribute to the United Nations sustainable development goals (SDGs).

Most ports are landlords with multiple independent operators, leases and terminals within their port area. By creating or leveraging, together with other stakeholders, collaborative platforms, regulative incentives, and partnerships, port authorities can improve their alignment of decarbonization efforts across multiple fields and supply chains to achieve an effective reduction in carbon emissions. They can, for example, initiate joint roadmaps with terminals, other operators and logistics service providers, establish infrastructure by planning for, and investing in, grid capacity for terminals, and develop shared port processes for efficient traffic management between terminals and actors in the port community.

A critical success factor for creating momentum in collaborating with the often many independent port actors and a high level of port community engagement, is transparency and active dialogue with the port community. This can be achieved by, for example, the digital sharing of updated roadmaps, measures and activities between the actors. Inviting the port actors to co-create a joint vision or joint target picture for the carbon net-zero or climate neutral port is another example of a fruitful tool.

Level 3: Providing Sustainable Energy to Port Visitors

Recently, a growing number of operators of vessels, railways, and heavy vehicles have set ambitious CO_2 reduction targets as part of the need to comply with various regional and global environmental regulations. This requires, among other factors, that carriers will need to optimise their operations by reducing their reliance on fossil fuels by switching to no/low carbon energy sources like green electricity generated from renewable sources.

Increasingly, ports can be expected to supply and facilitate sustainable energy for carriers (seaborne and land borne) operating through their port. To do this they will need to develop appropriate capabilities. Port authorities can, for instance, facilitate the bunkering of alternative fuels (for example, green ammonia, green hydrogen, and green methanol) and offer shore-side green electricity to vessels while berthed. They can also provide charging stations and alternative fuel stations (such as, liquified bio-gas (LBG) and green hydrogen) for heavy freight vehicles transporting goods to and from ports, and electrification of rail with no/low carbon electricity.

Actively engaging in planning of the port area to secure available land for storage and distribution of renewable energy is vital for a port, as there is often competition for land resources in ports. Moreover, besides securing land in the planning process, ports can also take a proactive and leading role in securing the legal permits necessary for handling renewable energy.

Beyond the provision of clean energy, ports can support decarbonization with just-in-time arrivals and slot management practices (Lind et al., 2022d), which can have a significant impact on the level of emissions in the port area, including terminals. These reductions can also be significant in the entire end-to-end cargo flow. An important step towards actively working with the port traffic processes, in order to enable just-in-time arrivals and eco-driving, is digitalizing traffic management and the sharing of digital traffic information. This includes sharing estimated and actual time stamps between port actors and vessels. Working deliberately with the port processes, such as traffic management, has the potential of enabling energy savings and emission reductions in the end-to-end cargo flow that will considerably outnumber the savings that can be reached from measures that only affect emissions within the geographical port area.

Level 4: Involving the Broader Industry in the Energy Transition

Countries and industries across the globe have ambitions to reduce GHG emissions by the middle of this century, triggered by legislation such as the EU Green Deal, the EU energy efficiency improvement target of at least 32.5% for 2030 (EU, 2023a) and the REPowerEU plan (EU, 2023b), which aims to replace Russian natural gas with imported (10 million tons) and locally produced (5 million tons) of renewable hydrogen. Industries will increasingly rely on low to zero carbon fuels. Driven by considerations of long-term domestic industrial competitiveness, these moves by the EU are in parallel with the US Inflation Reduction Act (White House, 2022) and the Chinese 5-Year Plans (ADB, 2021) aimed at stimulating investment in energy transition. The recently adopted 2023 IMO GHG Strategy is just another very recent step forward on this path. These regulatory measures are all driving international competition to meet new requirements and to secure domestic industrial advantages.

Ports can, for example, provide land to energy companies for new renewable energy production sites. Ports can support developments by directly investing or co-investing in energy production facilities. These are all aspects to consider at level 4 in the maturity framework. Large-scale electrification of different industries, including transportation, triggers the need for capacity upgrades for the production and distribution of no/low carbon fuels. Like other industries, the port sector will need to assess and estimate its potential need for such energy sources for their own operations, for visitors/customers, and in relation to the needs of other nearby industries and cities. Moreover, ports need to acknowledge that they will become not only energy nodes, but also energy systems coupled to the larger transport system and the surrounding communities and societies.

Establishing level 4 capabilities can be supported by digital solutions such as digital twins which can take advantage of complex modelling to provide insights into energy demand and enable the testing of alternative scenarios, the optimal siting of energy infrastructure to reduce transmission losses, and the applicability of power transfer within the port area during periods of peak demand. Finally, ports can reconsider the types of cargo they handle, by entering partnerships that envisage terminals for handling goods that enable local regions to transition to a carbon free industry and economy. Ports can also be testbeds or enablers for new technologies such as Carbon Capture and Storage (CCS).

The Role of Ports in Decarbonization

Over recent years, we have seen some of the world's leading ports moving themselves towards becoming key energy hubs. The ports of Antwerp-Bruges (Vandermeiren, 2022), Hamburg (HamburgNews, 2022a), Rotterdam (Rotterdam, 2023), and Singapore (MPA, 2023) are examples of ports that aim to become multi-fuel bunkering hubs to support transport carriers by acquiring, storing, and supplying low and zero-carbon fuels including biofuels, methanol, ammonia, and potentially hydrogen, as well as no/low carbon electricity.

Ports can support and facilitate decarbonization, energy efficiency, and energy transition in multiple ways, including:

- As landlord and investor, ports can optimise spatial planning to ensure that land and basic relevant infrastructure is available to facilitate energy projects (as with Hamburg (HamburgNews, 2022b) and Antwerp-Bruges (Mayor, 2022)), while proactively investing and co-investing in sustainable alternative energy solutions to meet their own energy needs, as well as to support the energy needs of customers, industrial clusters located in the vicinity, and wider society.
- As 'regulators', port authorities can develop and leverage tariffs and incentives to support no/low carbon measures, and upgrade environmental and safety standards to facilitate production, storage, bunkering and transportation of alternative fuels.
- Ports can create (digitally supported) processes that help other stakeholders to become more (energy) efficient, independently of changing to low/zero carbon energy sources. Through efficient processes and appropriate digital/technology applications, ports can help minimise carbon emissions, directly, for example, by the provision of renewable electricity for refrigerated containers and indirectly by ensuring that those containers are plugged in on time so that the contents are not spoiled.
- Ports as 'enablers/collaboration partners' can initiate collaboration, partnerships, and business consortia with a broad spectrum of players involved in the transport and energy ecosystem to align climate goals, predict energy needs, and develop

energy-related projects for production, storage and transportation of low/zero carbon fuels.
- Energy-empowered ports can expand the port community by inviting 'energy' actors and tracking/tracing energy generation/consumption flows through big data intelligence and blockchain technologies, etc.

Such new-style ports can drive new revenue streams and can be instrumental in decarbonizing the maritime industry and the economy at large.

Some Summary Thoughts

The clean energy landscape consists of a plethora of enablers and alternative solutions for substituting high-carbon forms of energy. There are several complementary enablers (Lind et al., 2022b) that can be put in place to decarbonize operations being pursued by the maritime sector. But collaboration with adjacent sectors is a must. Many of the decarbonization enablers that help to decarbonize shipping are also relevant for other transport segments. The different segments across the transport industry affect each other in their strategic planning and investment, and the need to find the most effective distribution of the yet still scarce sources of sustainable energy.

In the above context, this chapter closes with four key messages:

- In the maritime industry's efforts to decarbonize the transport ecosystem, ports can play an essential role by functioning as an intermediary and model node for the transport chain by providing opportunities for the production, storage, and provision of sustainable alternative fuels to visitors—both seaborne and land borne.
- Ports will benefit from responding proactively to stakeholders (particularly, shipowners, operators, visitors, local communities, and the society at large) that demand that ports conduct their operations with the lowest possible level of GHG emissions and provide sustainable alternative fuels and energy to port visitors.
- Ports' investments in becoming model energy nodes require a re-definition of the group of actors that are engaged in port operations, with the need to include also energy actors.
- Cross-value chain collaboration is critical, requiring a port to work with parties that are decarbonizing non-maritime value chains, which is, for example, necessary to ensure that the right fuel is available, for its right use, at the right quantity, at the right time and at the right price.
- Ports should seize the opportunity of not just responding and complying with decarbonization, but take a leadership role with other stakeholders, at the forefront of decarbonization and sustainability solutioning.

The community that must be aligned to decarbonize the maritime industry is huge. Ports can play a model role in aligning supply and demand of sustainable alternative no/low carbon energy sources by strengthening engagement with the energy value chain. This requires that ports enhance their scope of activity by adding energy production, storage, and provision to their business portfolio. With this comes also the need to raise the knowledge and skill-base of the people working in the port and elsewhere across the maritime value chain network. This requires new training programmes with an emphasis on digitalisation to enable new approaches to skilling.

References

ADB. (2021). *The 14th five-year plan of the People's Republic of China—Fostering high-quality development*. https://www.adb.org/publications/14th-five-year-plan-high-quality-development-prc

Bach, A., Forsström, E., Haraldson, S., Holmgren, K., Lind, K., Lind, M., Piehl, H., Raza, Z., & Rydbergh, T. (2022). Hamnen som energinod – ett koncept för hamnens roll i omställningen mot ett hållbart transportsystem. *RISE Rapport, 2022*, 125. http://ri.diva-portal.org/smash/record.jsf?pid=diva2%3A1707500&dswid=-7796

EU. (2023a). *Energy efficiency targets*. European Commission. Retrieved March 27, 2023, from https://energy.ec.europa.eu/topics/energy-efficiency/energy-efficiency-targets-directive-and-rules/energy-efficiency-targets_en

EU. (2023b). *REPowerEU: Affordable, secure and sustainable energy for Europe*. European Commission. Retrieved March 27, 2023, from https://commission.europa.eu/strategy-and-policy/priorities-2019-2024/european-green-deal/repowereu-affordable-secure-and-sustainable-energy-europe_en).

HamburgNews. (2022a). Energy imports - Hamburg to become decarbonising hub. *Hamburg News*. https://www.hamburg-news.hamburg/en/innovation-science/energy-imports-hamburg-become-decarbonising-hub

HamburgNews. (2022b). Senate approves EUR 223 million for key IPCEI hydrogen projects. *Hamburg News*. https://www.hamburg-news.hamburg/en/innovation-science/senate-approves-eur-223-million-key-ipcei-hydrogen-projects

HaskoningDHV. (2022). The new energy landscape: Impact on and implications for European ports, released 31/5 2022, *ROYAL HASKONINGDHV*. https://www.espo.be/media/The%20new%20energy%20landscape.pdf

Lind, M., Haraldson, S., Lehmacher, W., Raza, Z., Forsström, E., Astner, L., Bentham, J., Fu, X., Suroto, J., & Zuesongdham, P. (2023). *Thinking the future energy model nodes of the world - a reflection framework for port development*. Article No. 103 (UNCTAD Transport and Trade Facilitation Newsletter N°97 – First Quarter 2023). https://unctad.org/news/transport-newsletter-article-no-103-future-energy-nodes

Lind, M., Haraldson, S., Lind, K., Lehmacher, W., Svan, M., Renz, M., Gardeitchik, J., Singh, S., & Zuesongdham, P. (2021). *Ports of tomorrow: Measuring digital maturity to empower sustainable port operations and business ecosystems*. Article No. Article No. 82 (UNCTAD Transport and Trade Facilitation Newsletter N°92 - Fourth Quarter 2021). https://unctad.org/news/ports-tomorrow-measuring-digital-maturity-empower-sustainable-port-operations-and-business

Lind, M., Lehmacher, W., Åhlén Björk, S., Haraldson, S., Pålsson, C., Penttilä, R., Tikka, K., & Watson, R. T. (2022a). *Decarbonizing the maritime sector: Mobilizing coordinated action in the industry using an ecosystems approach*. Article No. 89 (UNCTAD Transport and Trade Facilitation Newsletter N°94 - Second Quarter 2022). https://unctad.org/news/decarbonizing-maritime-sector-mobilizing-coordinated-action-industry-using-ecosystems-approach

Lind, M., Lehmacher, W., De Tremerie, L., Dubielzig, F., Forsström, E., Holthus, P., Morgante, A., Singh, S., & Tenenbaum, L. (2022b) Enablers for Decarbonising the Maritime industry:

Decarbonisation Playbook Part 3, 25/9–2022. *The Maritime Executive*. https://www.maritime-executive.com/editorials/enablers-for-decarbonizing-the-maritime-industry-part-3

Lind, M., Lehmacher, W., Doepel, T., Heinimaa, J., Hoffmann, J., Laurilehto, M., Lebmeier, M., Petersen, M., Rytkölä, I., Saari, J., Singh, S., Walls, R., & Watson, R. T. (2022c). The benefits of a clusters of value chains perspective in Decarbonising Shipping: Decarbonisation Playbook Part 2, 22/8–2022. *The Maritime Executive*. https://maritime-executive.com/editorials/the-three-maritime-value-chains-decarbonization-playbook-part-2

Lind, M., Lehmacher, W., Hoffmann, J., Jensen, L., Notteboom, T., Rydbergh, T., Sand, P., Haraldson, S., White, R., Becha, H., & Berglund, P. (2022d). *An expanded JIT approach: Improving synchronization across maritime value chains, Marine Technology*. January 2022, pp. 60–65, The society of Naval Architects & Marine Engineers. https://maritimeinformatics.org/wp-content/uploads/2022/01/An-Expanded-JIT-Approach.pdf

Mayor. (2022). Belgium's new hydrogen strategy puts Antwerp-Bruges at the heart of Europe's energy transit. *The Mayor.eu*. Retrieved March 27, 2023, from https://www.themayor.eu/en/a/view/belgium-s-new-hydrogen-strategy-puts-antwerp-bruges-at-the-heart-of-europe-s-energy-transit-11115

MPA. (2023). Maritime Singapore Decarbonisation Blueprint: Working Towards 2050. *MPA Singapore*. Retrieved March 27, 2023, from https://www.mpa.gov.sg/maritime-singapore/sustainability/maritime-singapore-decarbonisation-blueprint

Rotterdam. (2023). *Hydrogen in Rotterdam, Port of Rotterdam*. Retrieved March 27, 2023, from https://www.portofrotterdam.com/en/port-future/energy-transition/ongoing-projects/hydrogen-rotterdam

Vandermeiren, J. (2022). *How ports can be transformed into energy hubs of the future*. World Economic Forum. https://www.weforum.org/agenda/2022/04/co-creating-change-ports-as-energy-hubs-of-the-future/

White House. (2022). Inflation reduction act guidebook. *White House*. https://www.whitehouse.gov/cleanenergy/inflation-reduction-act-guidebook/

Decarbonization in Shipyard Cities: A Holistic Approach to Sustainability Assessment

Seyedvahid Vakili

Target Audience

This chapter is written for those seeking to understand sustainability and air emissions reduction in various industries. It is particularly relevant to local, regional, and international policymakers, managers, researchers, and investors at various levels in the public and private sectors who drive, design and implement decarbonization in land-based facilities, such as ports and shipyards, and in shipping.

Key Takeaway Messages

This chapter highlights that:

- There is room for improvement in decarbonizing the manufacturing phase of ships through the reduction of air emissions and other measures.
- Based on a limited sample of shipyards, a focus on decarbonization is strongest in developed countries and is progressively weaker in shipyards in developing and least developed countries.

S. Vakili (✉)
Maritime Energy Management Department of World Maritime University, Malmö, Sweden

Research Fellow, University of Southampton, Southampton, UK
e-mail: s.vakili@soton.ac.uk

M. Lind et al. (eds.), *Maritime Decarbonization*,
https://doi.org/10.1007/978-3-031-39936-7_26

Introduction

Although shipping, as the most fuel-efficient mode of transport, contributes to transporting well over 80% of global freight by volume and 70% by value and plays an important role in human well-being (UNCTAD, 2022), it is responsible for 2.9% of global greenhouse gas (GHG) emissions (Joung et al., 2020). The International Maritime Organization (IMO), serving as the governing body overseeing global maritime activities, has formulated an objective of attaining a state of net-zero GHG emissions by approximately 2050. Concurrently, the IMO has introduced interim milestones for the years 2030 and 2040. These interim targets have been established to guide the journey towards achieving net-zero GHG emissions. The initial aim is to curtail total annual emissions by a minimum of 20%, with an aspiration for 30%, by 2030 in comparison to the emissions recorded in 2008. Subsequently, the ambition extends to a reduction of at least 70%, with a striving for 80%, by 2040 relative to the emissions of 2008 (IMO, 2023). To meet the IMO's ambitious goal collaboration among all active stakeholders is crucial. The IMO has considered the role of other active stakeholders, such as the role of ports in decarbonizing the shipping industry. In 2019 the IMO adopted Marine Environment Protection Committee (MEPC) Resolution 323(74) inviting IMO Member States to encourage voluntary cooperation between the shipping sector and ports to help reduce GHG emissions from ship and port interfaces. Studies have been conducted that highlight the importance of decarbonization in ports to improve city sustainability (Ballini et al., 2022; Vakili et al., 2023b). However, there is a lack of study in decarbonization of the shipbuilding industry and the sustainability of shipyard-cities (Vakili et al., 2022d).

As most shipyards are located near large towns or cities, improving energy efficiency and reducing polluting airborne emissions from the ship building industry will contribute to a green shipping life cycle by reducing the negative impacts of shipyards on society, particularly in urban areas and improve sustainability (Vakili et al., 2021b). Vakili et al. (2021a) and Line et al. (2022a, 2022b) emphasise a holistic approach and a cluster approach to the shipbuilding and ship operation value chain for decarbonizing the maritime industry. Meanwhile, Lind et al. (2022c, 2022d) have highlighted the importance of the sustainability and profitability of actions and the need to establish sufficient, transparent and predictable financing and pricing mechanisms. Lind and Lehmacher (2022a, 2022b) and Lehmacher and Lind (2022) have noted that establishing partnerships among stakeholders is critical to strengthening the stakeholders' collaborative competencies and knowledge base.

Many studies have been conducted to improve energy efficiency and promote sustainable shipping; however, the focus has been on the operational life cycle of ships and less attention has been paid to life cycle aspects, particularly the shipbuilding phase (Vakili et al., 2023a).

A Study of Shipyards in Relation to Energy Efficiency, Reducing Air Emissions and Sustainability

This study undertook an investigation of five shipyards, each possessing distinct characteristics. The selected shipyards were in Bangladesh, Italy, and Türkiye.

The aim of the study was to determine whether the size, geographical location and portfolio of those yards have an impact on their business decision making in terms of improving energy efficiency, reducing air emissions, and improving the sustainability of their processes. To evaluate sustainability in the studied shipyards, four sustainability theories were employed.

Corporate Social Responsibility (CSR)—that refers to a company's responsibility to consider the impact of its decisions and activities on society, the environment, and its stakeholders. It involves taking steps to ensure that the company operates in an ethical and sustainable manner.

Stakeholder Theory—that focuses on the idea that a company has obligations to all its stakeholders including shareholders, employees, customers, suppliers, and the community. It requires companies to balance the needs of multiple stakeholders to achieve sustainable business success.

Corporate Sustainability—that involves considering the long-term environmental, social, and economic impact of a company's activities. It requires a company to take a holistic approach to sustainability, considering not only financial performance but also the impact on people and the planet.

Green economics—the branch of economics that focuses on creating sustainable economic growth and development. It incorporates environmental, social, and economic factors into decision-making, promoting the transition to a low-carbon, resource-efficient economy.

The study began with a systematic literature review to design and develop a framework that identify the related disciplines and provided potential strategies within each discipline. The proposed framework contained thirty-seven potential strategies in five disciplines. The five disciplines were:

- human factors
- technology and innovation
- operations
- policy and regulation
- economics.

The disciplines and potential strategies were intended to enable the shipyard decision makers to rank what they considered would be the most effective measures and tools to improve energy efficiency and reduce air emissions from operations in their shipyards (Vakili et al., 2022d).

Table 1 sets out the disciplines and the potential strategies used in the study.

Table 1 Disciplines and potential strategies

Disciplines	Potential strategies
Human factors	Training
	Governance and corporate social responsibility
	Access to skilled workers
	Capacity building
	Awareness raising
	Research and Development
Technology and innovation	Smart and micro grid
	Digitalisation (4th industrial revolution) (Artificial Intelligence, intelligent robot, big data, etc.)
	Renewable energy
	Electrification (battery, fuel cell)
	Carbon capture and storage
	Cleaner fuel and hybridisation (natural gas, hydrogen, methanol, etc.)
	Changing old equipment
	Digital twin
Operations	Resource management
	Lean approach
	Production planning and strategy
	Optimising shipyard design
Economic indicators	Levelised cost of energy
	Lifecycle cost
	Societal cost
	Cost benefit analysis
	Cost of energy
	Environmental impact
	Capital cost (as an economic indicator)
	Maintenance cost
Economic measures and tools	Financial resources
	Market competitiveness
	Incentives regime
	Subsidy regime
	Governmental financial support packages
	Financial resources for R&D
	Capital cost (as a measure and tool)
	Skilled and knowledgeable labour wages
	Pool funds
Policy and Regulations	Environmental regulations (international, regional, national, and local)
	Life cycle orientation
	Green products
	Innovation, sustainability, and competitiveness
	Energy management system (ISO 50001)
	Environmental management systems (ISO 14001)
	Cyber security

(continued)

Table 1 (continued)

Disciplines	Potential strategies
	Circular economy
	Voluntarily agreement.
	Stakeholder policy

Source: Vakili et al. (2022d)

Data Collection Methodology

The study used mixed methods to answer research questions and undertook interviews and focus-group discussions to provide a comparative analysis between the different shipyards.

Interview is a part of case study and comparative analysis (Empson, 2018). It allows the researcher to elicit different kinds of information in more detail and in-depth from various interviewees (Bryman, 2016). A questionnaire was designed in eight different sections in a semi-structured format. The questionnaire for the interview included both qualitative and quantitative measures, which allowed the interviewees to provide both in-depth responses and numerical evaluations of the various aspects of their awareness and the use of the potential strategies. The semi-structured format of the questionnaire enabled the interviewees to explain more about their concerns, beliefs, ideas, and actions regarding the topic (Barriball & While, 1994).

Using focus groups is a technique for interviewing a group of people about a specific topic (Bryman, 2016). In this method, the researcher emphasises discussing the topic in depth, tries to understand how people react to each other, and pays attention to the interaction between people, which distinguishes it from interviews (Grim et al., 2006). In a focus group, people can argue with each other, and criticise and challenge others' perspectives on a topic. This helps the researcher to understand the problems of different perspectives and their reasons for holding certain views (Parker & Tritter, 2006). The results in this method are more qualitative. Its semi-structured format helps the facilitator to control the discussion, and at the same time the group of people can explore their ideas, opinions, and views on the topic (Kitzinger, 1995).

Shipyard Selection

The size, portfolio and geographical location, as well as the economic situation in the host country were taken into consideration when selecting the shipyards. Table 2 provides a breakdown of the shipyards used in the study.

Table 2 List of shipyards used in the case studies

Country	Development state of country	Code	Size of shipyard	Shipyard portfolio
Türkiye	Developing country	S1	Small	Specialised types of offshore vessels, small passenger ships, fishing vessels, aquaculture vessels
Türkiye	Developing country	S2	Medium	Specialised types of offshore vessels, small passenger ships, fishing vessels, aquaculture vessels
Türkiye	Developing country	S3	Large	Any types of oceangoing vessels, offshore specialised vessels, and infrastructure
Bangladesh	Least developed countries	S4	Small	Multipurpose container ships, dry cargo ships, tankers with capacity of 15,000 DWT (passenger vessels, ro-ro ferries, tugs, dredgers, crane boats, survey vessels, fishing vessels and metal ships).
Italy	Developed country	S5	Large	Cruise and passenger vessels, merchant ships, offshore vessels, and Navy ships

Results

To rank the potential strategies within each discipline for each shipyard, multi-criteria decision making (MCDM) methods were used, which were a fuzzy analytical hierarchy process (FAHP) and fuzzy technique for order preference by similarity to ideal solution (FTOPSIS) (Vakili et al., 2021b).[1] The equations and the transdisciplinary approach are discussed more fully in the relevant study reports (Vakili et al., 2021a, 2021b, 2022a, 2022b).

Decision-Making Processes and Ranking of the Disciplines by the Shipyards

Figure 1 shows the ranking by the shipyards of the five disciplines: human factors, technology, operations, policy and regulation, and economics. A focus group at each yard was asked about their priorities (1 = highest, 5 = lowest) among the proposed disciplines. The FAHP method was used to analyse the results.

[1] Multi-Criteria Decision Making (MCDM) methods are used to evaluate complex decision-making problems where multiple criteria are involved. FAHP and FTOPSIS are two of the commonly used MCDM methods in decision making. FAHP considers the subjective opinions of decision makers to determine the weights of the criteria, while FTOP-SIS calculates the relative distance between the decision alternatives and an ideal solution to determine the best alternative (Vakili et al., 2021b).

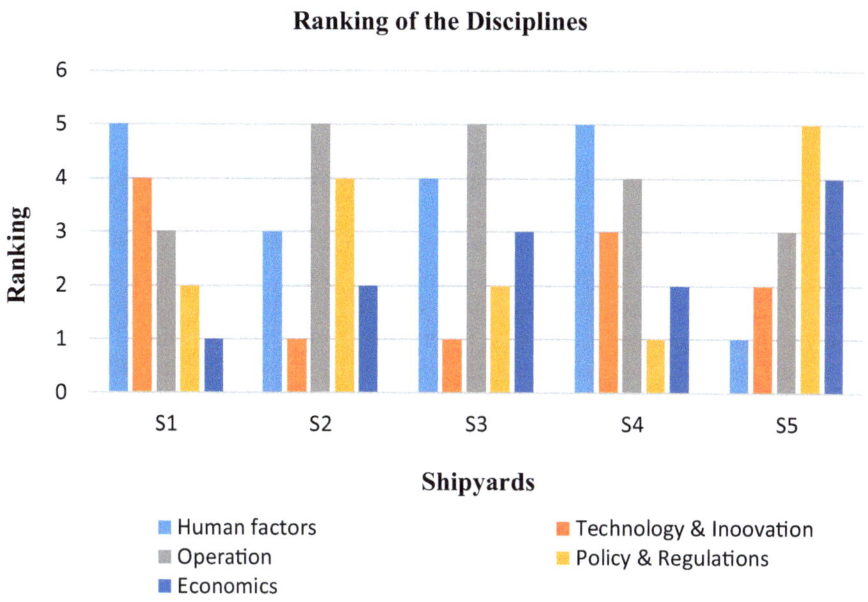

Fig. 1 Ranking of the disciplines

The top three ranking disciplines for shipyard S1 (Türkiye—small sized shipyard) were economics, policy and regulation, and operations. The yard focused more on Business Model than on Sustainable Business Mode[2] in relation to Corporate Sustainability theory of sustainable development and considered the theory of economic growth (Chang et al., 2017) rather than other sustainability factors. The order of ranking of the disciplines indicated a one-dimensional approach rather than a multidimensional approach to decision-making. Compliance with regulations and policies was ranked second. This was the only yard where operations were ranked among the top three disciplines. This could be due to the nature of their activities—repair and conversion—where they are constantly servicing different types and sizes of vessels, for which flexible ways of operating would be important. Moreover, compared to the other shipyards, they use and need a simpler technology and less skilled workers (Hanlon, 2018). As a result, technology and the human factors were ranked fourth and fifth, respectively.

Shipyard S2 (Türkiye—medium sized shipyard), with its production of special vessels, aimed to promote the concept of sustainability within its portfolio. Business Model was the preferred business management model rather than Sustainable

[2]Sustainable Business Model (SBM) is a business approach that focuses on balancing financial, social, and environmental sustainability. It involves considering the long-term impacts of business decisions on all stakeholders and the planet, rather than just maximizing short-term profits. By adopting SBM, companies can increase their competitiveness, reduce their risks and costs, and enhance their brand reputation and customer loyalty.

Business Model. The shipyard reported that it had plans to achieve long-term sustainability along with the green economy theory. Although the gap between different disciplines shows that the shipyard decision makers have a more one-dimensional than multi-dimensional approach to reduce air emissions and improve energy efficiency, this gap was smaller in shipyard S2 (Türkiye—medium sized shipyard) compared to shipyard S1 (Türkiye—small sized shipyard) and shipyard S5 (Italy—large sized shipyard).

Technology, policy and regulation, and economics were the three priority disciplines for shipyard S3 (Türkiye—large sized shipyard). The analysis showed that decision-making focused more on Sustainable Business Model than Business Model and considered the Green Economics theory in the context of its policy. The location of the shipyard forces decision-making to address the European Union (EU) regional regulations, as well as the market trend for green technologies and services. The ranking order of the different disciplines showed that the yard's decision-making has a more multidimensional approach than the other yards.

Policy and regulation, economics, and technology were the top three priorities for shipyard S4 (Bangladesh—small sized shipyard). Interviewees said that the economic pillar in sustainability has the highest priority for them. In addition, they preferred Business Model rather than Sustainable Business Model within their business context. Analysis identified that the yard's decision-making had a more one-dimensional than multi-dimensional approach to reducing air emissions and improving the energy efficiency of their processes.

For shipyard S5 (Italy—large sized shipyard), analysis indicated a multi-dimensional approach to reducing air emissions and improving energy efficiency. It was the only shipyard to consider human factors as the most important discipline, and indeed it was the only shipyard to have a comprehensive annual Corporate Social Responsibility report as part of its activities. Interviewees highlighted that they pay special attention to Sustainable Business Model in the context of corporate sustainability and that they follow the green economic theory as the trend of the market in the EU. 'EU environmental legislation is more homogeneous and stricter in comparison with other parts of the world, which creates a trend for companies in future operations', one of the interviewees pointed out. Shipyard decision-making incorporated its green and clean aspects to enhance its reputation in the market and act as a brand in a competitive market. Although the shipyard was well equipped, the interviewees reported that it needed to adapt to more automation, digitalisation, and new technologies to further increase its competitive advantage in the tough shipyard market.

Ranking by the Shipyards of the Potential Strategies

The different shipyards were asked to preference the 37 potential strategies listed in Table 1 under the five Discipline headings—human factors, technology and innovation, operations, policy and regulations, and economics. They were asked to rank them in relation to improving energy efficiency and the mitigation of air emissions at their shipyards and with respect to the four criteria of safety and security, social cost, air emission, and cost. The weight of each criterion was applied to the analysis to rank the top priorities in each discipline. Then, FTOPSIS was used to rank the potential strategies under each discipline.

Human Factors

The Human Factors discipline covers the relationship between people, technology, tools, environments, and systems and takes into account cognitive, physical, behavioural, physiological, social, developmental, affective and motivational aspects of human performance and plays an important role in the reduction of carbon emissions in maritime transport (Vakili et al., 2022c).

Six potential strategies were proposed to the shipyards for addressing human factors. Figure 2 shows that training was ranked as the most important for shipyards S1 (Türkiye—small sized shipyard), S3 (Türkiye—large sized shipyard) and S4 (Bangladesh—small sized shipyard). Training was ranked second by shipyard S2 (Türkiye—medium sized shipyard) and third by shipyard S5 (Italy—large sized shipyard). Capacity building was ranked equal first by shipyard S5, second by shipyards S1, S3 and S4 and last by shipyard S2.

Governance and corporate social responsibility (CSR) was ranked equal first by shipyard S5 (Italy—large sized shipyard), second by shipyard S2 (Türkiye—medium sized shipyard), third for the shipyards S2 (Türkiye—large sized shipyard) and S4 (Bangladesh—small sized shipyard), and fourth for shipyard S1 (Türkiye—

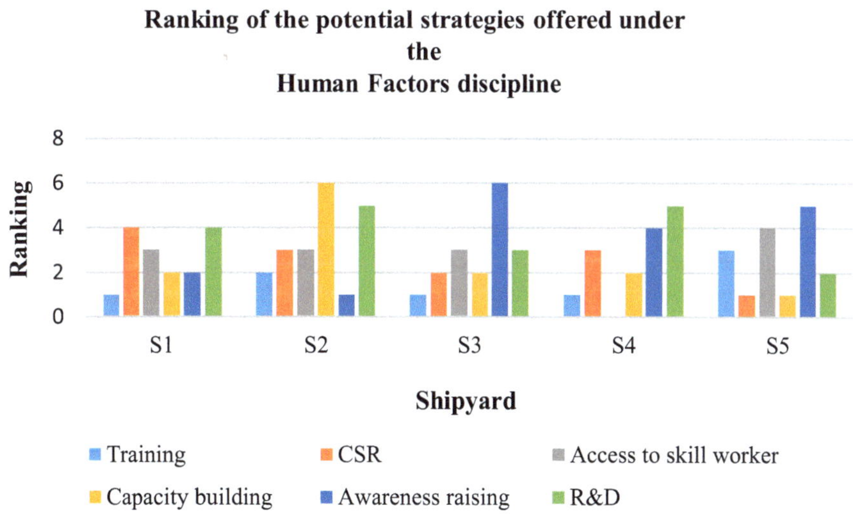

Fig. 2 Ranking of the potential strategies in the human factors discipline

small sized shipyard). Following CSR principles should support profitability, environmental protection, climate adaptation and promote the reputation of shipyards in a competitive market. However, shipyard S5 was the only yard that had a comprehensive CSR report. The shipyards which had CSR in their top priorities appeared to consider the stakeholders' theories within their context and considered their long-term survival in terms of multiple stakeholders rather than just the needs of shareholders.

Access to skilled labour plays a key role in reducing human error in shipyards. It was the third highest priority for all the Turkish shipyards (S1, S2, S3) and the fourth highest priority for S5 (large Italian yard), but of no priority to shipyard S4 (small Bangladeshi shipyard). This reflects the position of the shipbuilding industry in the various countries. While Italy is among the top shipbuilding countries and the industry contributes well to the country's economy, shipbuilding in Bangladesh is a new economic driver and less attention is paid to the skills of the workforce. The Italian shipyard had problems in accessing qualified personnel—hence the higher priority. Obtaining an appropriate workforce in Bangladeshi shipyards is not problematic, particularly since the Bangladeshi shipyard only produces small and relatively simple ship types in comparison to the Italian and Turkish yards.

To move towards zero emissions in shipping (from a life cycle perspective), an energy transition must take place using renewable energy, cleaner alternative fuels, and new technologies (Vakili et al., 2022a, 2023a). Changing shipyard staff behaviour and mind-set has a role to play in how shipyards address climate change and help reduce emissions. In this context, increased awareness (H_5) was ranked highest only by shipyard S2 (Türkiye—medium sized shipyard) and second by shipyard S1 (Türkiye—small sized shipyard). According to the findings, S5 (Italy—large-sized shipyard) and S3 (Türkiye—large-sized shipyard) were perceived to possess adequate and satisfactory awareness programs for their workforce regarding climate change initiatives aimed at promoting sustainability and aligning with the green economy's objectives. Conversely, S4 (Bangladesh—small-sized shipyard) did not give priority to implementing measures that target sustainability and climate change concerns. Notably, in terms of human factors, S4 (Bangladesh—small-sized shipyard) ranked awareness-raising as its sixth priority, while S5 (Italy—large-sized shipyard) and S3 (Türkiye—large-sized shipyard) placed it fourth and fifth on their respective lists of priorities.

Although the largest air emissions are related to the operational phase of ships, the shift to cleaner fuels and renewable energy may increase the ship construction phase as a major contributor to ship pollution (Vakili et al., 2022d). Studies show that in some cases the construction phase can contribute more than 50% of the carbon footprint during the life cycle of a ship (OSK Group, 2022). To achieve zero emissions from a life cycle perspective, shipyards need to focus and do more research on improving energy efficiency and reducing air emissions within processes (Vakili et al., 2021b). Interestingly, in terms of the human factors, shipyards S5 (Italy—large sized shipyard) then S3 (Türkiye—large sized shipyard) were the only yards that considered R&D as one of their higher priorities (second and third priorities, respectively). According to the interview results, shipyards S3 (Türkiye—

large sized shipyard) and S5 (Italy—large sized shipyard) were the only yards that had a short-, medium- and long-term energy strategy plan, in contrast to the other yards, which did not have any. Shipyards S5 (Italy—large sized shipyard) and S3 (Türkiye—large sized shipyard) considered improving energy efficiency as one of the most important topics on their R&D agenda.

Technology and Innovation

Technology and innovation are key to achieving the climate policy goals. As Fig. 3 shows, the strategy of replacing old equipment was the most popular of the options under the Technology and Innovation discipline and can play a major role in accelerating a shipyard's carbon reduction.

Technology and Innovation was ranked as the first priority for shipyards S2 (Türkiye—medium sized shipyard), S3 (Türkiye—large sized shipyard) and S4 (Bangladesh—small sized shipyard) and second priority for shipyard S5 (Italy—large sized shipyard). However, it was only ranked fifth priority for shipyard S1 (Türkiye—small sized shipyard), which specialises in ship repairs requiring less complex technology compared to the shipbuilding yards. Electrification will also play an important role in reducing CO_2 emissions in industry and can accelerate the reduction of CO_2 emissions in shipping. Electrification was the highest priority for shipyard S1 (Türkiye—small sized shipyard), the second highest for shipyards S2 (Türkiye—medium sized shipyard) and S5 (Italy—large sized shipyard), and third priority for shipyards S3 (Türkiye—large sized shipyard) and S4 (Bangladesh—small sized shipyard).

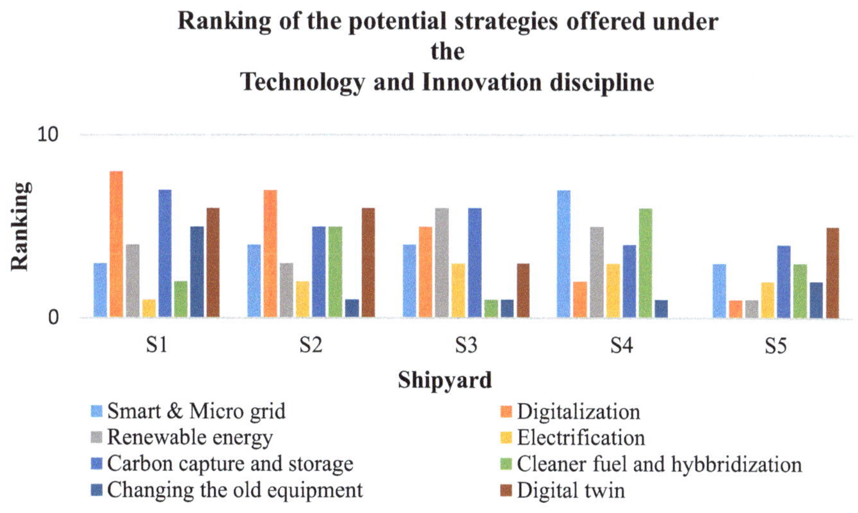

Fig. 3 Ranking of potential strategies under the technology discipline

Zero emission industries cannot be achieved without the use of clean and carbon-free fuels. They will play a crucial role in reducing carbon emissions in the shipbuilding industry (Vakili et al., 2022d). Cleaner fuel and hybridization was ranked first priority for shipyard S3 (Türkiye—large sized shipyard). This was the only yard among the shipyards that had a short-medium term energy strategy, and switching to cleaner fuels was one of its strategies. Cleaner fuel and hybridization was ranked second priority for shipyard S1 (Türkiye—small sized shipyard)—the yard had a plan to expand the use of LNG in its operations. Cleaner fuel and hybridization was ranked third priority for shipyard S5 (Italy—large sized shipyard). Shipyard S5 (Italy—large sized shipyard) had a plan in its long-term energy policy to act as an energy hub in synergy with land-based industry and the maritime industry. Cleaner fuel and hybridization was ranked fifth priority by shipyard S2 (Türkiye—medium sized shipyard). Shipyard S4 (Bangladesh—small sized shipyard), located in Bangladesh, a less developed country, ranked cleaner fuel and hybridization lowest as its sixth priority.

Different levels of digitalization are being used in shipbuilding processes. Digitalization was not a high priority among the Turkish yards. Shipyard S5 (Italy—large sized shipyard), in Italy, had a plan to digitalize to maintain its competitive advantage in the market and ranked Digitalization as its first priority in the Technology and Innovation discipline. It was the second priority for the small Bangladeshi shipyard (S4). This yard had a strategic plan to expand its operations and enter the global market by replacing old equipment with electrification and digitalization.

Green economy theory serves as a driver for using renewable energy in industry (Salvarli and Salvarli, 2020) to promote sustainability and minimise air emissions. Utilising renewable energy was an equal-first priority for shipyard S5 (Italy—large sized shipyard) and third priority for shipyard S2 (Türkiye—medium sized shipyard). Both had a plan to harvest solar energy for their offices and warehouses. Renewable energy was ranked fourth by shipyard S1 (Türkiye—small sized shipyard), fifth by shipyard S4 (Bangladesh—small sized shipyard) and sixth by shipyard S3 (Türkiye—large sized shipyard).

Smart grids and micro grids were the third highest priority for shipyards S1 and S5, and digital twin was third priority for shipyard S3. Shipyard S3's interest in introducing digital twinning was due to the size of the shipyard and its strong commitment to digitalization.

Carbon capture and storage was ranked fourth priority by shipyard S4 (Bangladesh—small sized shipyard) and S5 (Italy—large sized shipyard), it was ranked fifth priority by shipyard S2 (Türkiye—medium sized shipyard), sixth by shipyard S3 (Türkiye—large sized shipyard) and seventh by shipyard S1 (Türkiye—small sized shipyard). Some yards considered that the technology is not appropriate given the size and nature of their business and it is an expensive and immature technology (Roussanaly et al., 2021).

Operations

Operations play a crucial role in increasing productivity, efficiency, reducing costs and reducing GHG emissions from shipyard operations. Figure 4 shows the ranking for each shipyard of the potential strategies offered under the operations discipline. Shipbuilding involves several complex projects facing limited resources, and resource management can play a crucial role in reducing costs, schedule overruns and improving energy efficiency in shipyards (Pinha et al., 2016).

Resource Management was the most popular option in the operations discipline. It was first priority for shipyards S1 (Türkiye—small sized shipyard), S4 (Bangladesh—small sized shipyard) and S5 (Italy—large sized shipyard) and second priority for shipyards S2 (Türkiye—medium sized shipyard) and S3 (Türkiye—large sized shipyard). The second most popular option was Production Planning and Strategy. Production Planning and Strategy was first priority for shipyard S2 and second priority for shipyards S1, S4 and S5. It was third priority for shipyard S3.

Optimising shipyard design was first priority for shipyard S3 (Türkiye—large sized shipyard) and second priority for shipyard S5 (Italy—large sized shipyard). Shipyard design has a significant impact on the improvement of overall productivity and energy productivity in shipyards. Optimising shipyard design was ranked second by shipyard S5 (Italy—large sized shipyard) and third by shipyard S2

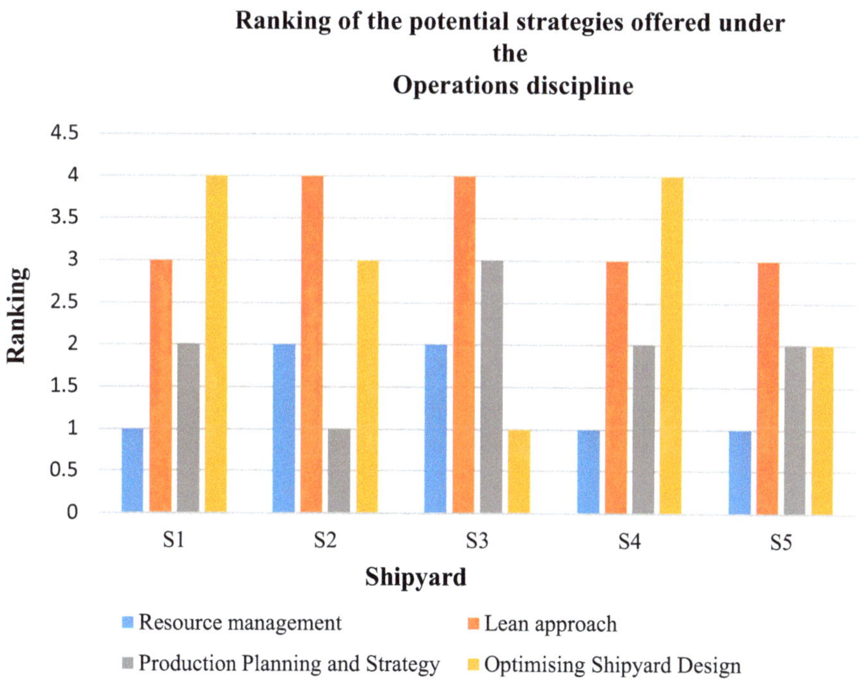

Fig. 4 Ranking of the potential strategies offered in the operations discipline

(Türkiye—medium sized shipyard). Shipyard S5 had a plan to change the design of its yard because the current design creates challenges for transferring blocks and shipyard S2 (Türkiye—medium sized shipyard) had a plan to expand its yard area.

Lean Approach refers to the elimination of waste and non-value-add processes within shipyard operations and the supply chain to improve the customers' satisfaction and increase productivity (Koenig et al., 2002). Implementing a lean approach is an important tool to improving the performance of shipyards (Shahsavar et al., 2021). Lean Approach was not strongly supported by the shipyards. Lean Approach was ranked third out of 4 by shipyards S1 (Türkiye—small sized shipyard), S4 (Bangladesh—small sized shipyard) and S5 (Italy—large sized shipyard) and last priority by shipyards S2 (Türkiye—medium sized shipyard) and S3 (Türkiye—large sized shipyard). Shipyards S2, S3 and S5 reported that they had already followed lean methods in their operations.

Policy and Regulations

The shipbuilding industry is striving to improve its environmental performance, but a more holistic and 'cradle-to-grave' approach involving collaboration with other key stakeholders is required (Vakili et al., 2022d).

Figure 5 shows that from the ten policy and regulatory options suggested to the shipyards, Environmental Management Systems (ISO 14001) was the most popular.

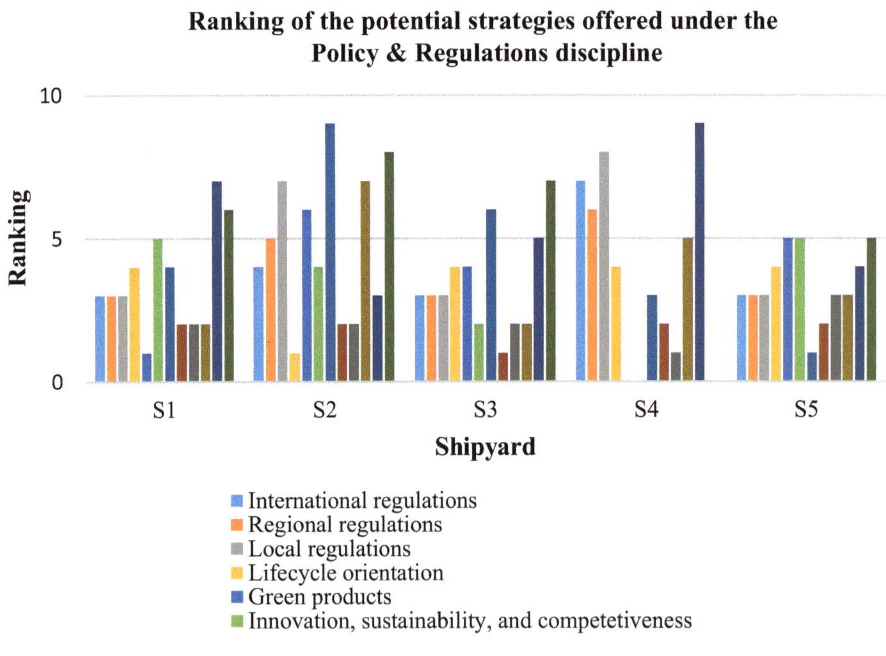

Fig. 5 Ranking of the potential strategies under the policy and regulations discipline

The implementation of environmental management can promote the sustainability of a shipyards' portfolio. This makes sense as all Turkish shipyards and the Italian shipyard held ISO 14001 certification and the Bangladeshi shipyard follows similar national legislation. Although the implementation of Energy Management (ISO 50001), can improve the energy performance of shipyards, it was the top priority only for the Italian shipyard S5 (Italy—large sized shipyard); the yard had a plan to implement it in the next year. Energy Management (ISO 50001) was the third priority for shipyard S4 (Bangladesh—small sized shipyard) and not one of the top priorities for the Turkish shipyards. Shipyards reported that they considered Environmental Management Systems (ISO 14001) is an appropriate measure to manage energy within their portfolio while the implementation of Energy Management (ISO 50001) represents an additional cost for the yards.

Transition to the fourth industrial revolution in the shipbuilding industry increases the importance of cyber security (Vakili et al. 2022d). Cyber Security was the second highest priority within the policy and regulations discipline. Shipyards S1 (Türkiye—small sized shipyard) and S2 (Türkiye—medium sized shipyard) ranked Cyber Security as a first priority, shipyards S3 (Türkiye—large sized shipyard) and S4 (Bangladesh—small sized shipyard) ranked it as second. The Italian shipyard S5 (Italy—large sized shipyard) considered cyber security as its third most important priority in the Policy and Regulations discipline. Noting that the Bangladeshi shipyard had a plan to replace old equipment with modern digital systems, it was concerned about the potential risk of cyber-attacks. The Turkish yards (S1, S2 and S3) already use digitalization in their activities.

The circular economy was ranked second by shipyards S1 (Türkiye—small sized shipyard) and S3 (Türkiye - large sized shipyard) and was third for shipyard S5 (Italy—large sized shipyard). The size and nature of these businesses would explain this. Shipyard S1, due to its role in ship repair and refitting, and shipyards S3 and S5, due to their size, generate significant amounts of waste which allows them to better participate in the circular economy.

A lifecycle perspective can improve and accelerate the maritime industry's reduction of carbon emissions (Vakili et al. 2022d). Lifecycle Orientation was ranked first for shipyard S2 (Türkiye—medium sized shipyard) and green product policy was the top priority for shipyard S1 (Türkiye—small sized shipyard). Shipyard S1 operations emphasised green production by considering its supply chain system and its subcontractors.

Regulations (international, regional and local) played a more important role for the Turkish and Italian yards than for the Bangladeshi shipyard. This may be due to the geographical location of the yards. The Turkish and Italian yards are members of the Community of European Shipbuilders and Ship Repairers Associations and are OECD countries, which means that they have to comply with stricter environmental regulations.

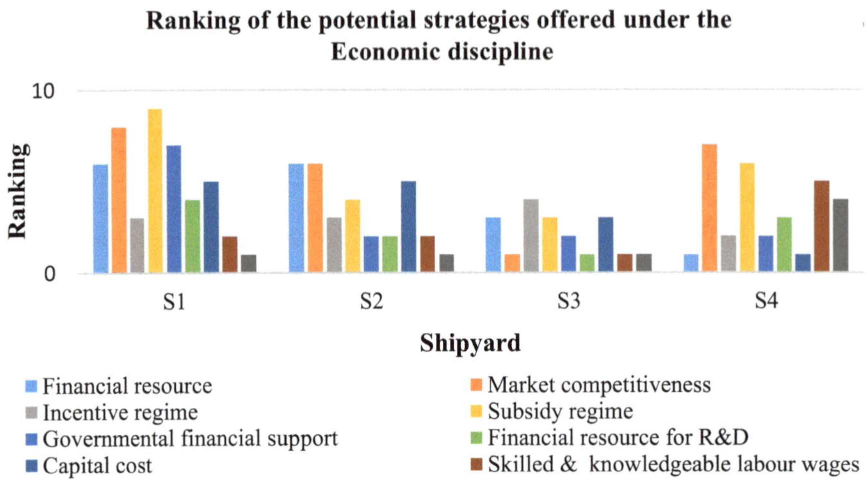

Fig. 6 Ranking of the potential strategies offered under the Economic discipline

Economics

Figure 6 shows that the creation of Pool funds (E_{17}) was the most popular economic option for the Turkish shipyards. This may be a consequence of the total number of shipyards in Türkiye and Türkiye's position among the top shipbuilding nations, which facilitates the formation of such pool funds among shipyards, unlike the situation in Bangladesh. In addition, the economic situations of Türkiye and the Turkish shipyards is much more conducive to the creation of pool funds.

Skilled and knowledgeable labour wages was a first or second ranked priority issue for the Turkish shipyards. However, this was not the most important issue for the Bangladeshi shipyard, as the average wage of Bangladeshi workers is lower than that of Turkish workers.

No data was made available for the Italian shipyard.

Financial resources for R&D and Government financial support packages were other top priorities among shipyards. It is interesting to note that while the small and medium-sized shipyards (S1 (Türkiye—small sized shipyard), S2 (Türkiye—medium sized shipyard) and S4 (Bangladesh—small sized shipyard)) were keen to receive government financial support in the form of incentives, such as money for investments in energy efficiency measures, the large Turkish shipyard (S3) preferred to receive this support in the form of subsidies, such as reduced energy costs and taxes.

Shipyards' priorities regarding sustainability theories.

Table 3 shows the results of the shipyards' preferences with regard to sustainability theories.

The larger shipyards in developed countries were more interested in the sustainable business model (SBM) in the context of corporate sustainability (CS) theories

Table 3 Shipyard priorities regarding sustainability theories

Sustainability theories	Shipyards				
	S1 Türkiye—small sized shipyard	S2 Türkiye—medium sized shipyard	S3 Türkiye—large sized shipyard	S4 Bangladesh—small sized shipyard	S5 Italy—large sized shipyard
CS	BM	BM	SBM	BM	SBM
CSR	–	–	✓	–	✓
Stakeholder theory	Traditional	Traditional	Traditional and non-traditional	Traditional	Traditional and non-traditional
Green economics	–	–	✓	–	✓
Economics pillar	✓	✓	–	✓	–

and corporate social responsibility (CSR) theories. However, the level of corporate social responsibility (CSR) implementation differed between the two major yards. The large Italian Shipyard S5 had a higher level of CSR implementation than the large Turkish shipyard S3. This may be due to the regional regulations in force and the market position of the Italian yard. The Italian yard had to comply with stricter regulations and considered CSR as an important measure to increase their productivity and promote their reputation in a competitive market. In addition, it was taking the needs of both traditional and non-traditional stakeholders into account for long-term sustainability in accordance with the theory of a green economy.

The shipyards in developing and less developed countries focused more on economic pillars of sustainability and prioritised a business model (BM) rather than a sustainable business model (SBM). They did not pay much attention to CSR theory and focused more on the needs of traditional stakeholders.

Another factor that should be considered in the implementation of sustainability theories in shipyards is the ownership and management of the shipyards. The small and medium-sized yards were usually family businesses, where decision-making within their portfolio was more family and/or individual based. They focused more on a business model approach to make money from their own operations. By contrast, the large yards were not owned by one individual or family, rather shareholders were involved in decision-making in various ways.

Closing Remarks

Shipyards are a polluting industry located close to cities threatening the sustainability of cities and society. Although the reduction of air emissions from the operational phase of ships is a priority for the maritime sector, policy makers and active stakeholders cannot turn a blind eye to air emissions from the manufacturing phase of ships (Vakili et al., 2022d). The original aim of the research study was to promote the reduction of air emissions in the maritime industry from a life cycle perspective and to increase the energy efficiency of shipbuilding processes. Although around 96% of GHG emissions occur during the operational phase of the ship and the market trend is towards fuel switching in the shipbuilding industry, the contribution of the shipbuilding phase to GHG emissions is expected to increase in view of the energy transition towards zero emission fuels and the use of renewable energy during the operational phase (Vakili et al., 2022d), and may even exceed 50% in some cases (OSK Group, 2022). To achieve the vision of zero emissions in the maritime industry, one-dimensional thinking needs to be replaced by a systematic, holistic and transdisciplinary approach, and within the framework of a life-cycle approach, taking into account global cooperation among all stakeholders at different levels is essential (Vakili et al., 2022c). In addition, it is important to change the sustainability concepts from a definition of sustainability to the implementation of sustainability theories and consider a more holistic and interdisciplinary approach accordingly (Vakili et al., 2021a).

IMO, as the regulatory body for international shipping, could influence the creation of instruments for measuring, limiting, controlling, and recording air emissions during the shipbuilding phases and could consider and record the amount of air emissions in ship certificates, such as the International Air Pollution Certificate, International Energy Efficiency Certificate and account for it in ships' Energy Efficiency Design Index (EEDI) and Carbon Intensity Indicator (CII) calculations (Vakili et al., 2022d). However, this requires transparency and cooperation on the part of the shipyards and other stakeholders like the International Association of Classification Societies (Vakili et al., 2022c).

The study analysis has shown that safety and security and the reduction of air pollution are more important to shipyards than the reduction of GHG emissions from their processes (Vakili et al., 2021b). National, regional, international regulations and policies, managers' environmental commitments, economic conditions, size, geographical location, ownership, management, and shipyard portfolio were the main factors explaining the attitudes and commitments of decision makers towards reducing air emissions and improving energy efficiency in shipyards (Vakili et al., 2021a).

The study analysis showed that large shipyards in developed countries had a more multidisciplinary approach than small and medium-sized shipyards in developing and less developed countries with respect to reducing air emissions and improving the energy efficiency of their processes. In addition, they had short, medium, and long-term energy visions, which could make them energy hubs by harnessing renewable energy and producing green hydrogen and ammonia (Vakili et al., 2021a, 2023a). This energy policy can bring environmental, social and economic benefits at both micro and macro levels by creating jobs, reducing energy costs, promoting energy security, reducing air emissions and avoiding the effects of climate change, and increasing the sustainability of shipyard-cities (Vakili et al., 2022a).

The study results showed that the definition and meaning of sustainability differs from case to case and from individual yard to individual yard. The larger shipyards were committed to reducing GHG emissions from shipyard operations, while the smaller shipyards and in less developed countries were more interested in economic performance than environmental issues. The larger yards in developed countries in the study were the more interested in the theory of corporate social responsibility and the concepts of green economic theory. They focus on the sustainable business model in the context of corporate sustainability theories as part of ensuring the long-term survival of the yard, considering the needs and desires of various stakeholders. They considered sustainability as a reputation and brand differentiator in a competitive market and used it as a competitive advantage over others. They believed that if they incorporated sustainability into their processes, they could act as a driver for their economic recovery and attract more capital, financial support and investment and a better bargaining position. By investing in more sustainable technologies, the yard could have the opportunity to stimulate its economy by creating green jobs. However, the small and medium-sized yards in the developing or less developed countries focused more on the economic pillar of sustainability and a business model. They were primarily concerned about the needs of traditional stakeholders such as shareholders and their approach was focused on maximising profit for shareholders.

The case studies showed that the shipyards had prioritised the replacement of old equipment and have an aim towards automation, electrification, digitalization, alternative fuels, especially LNG, renewable energy sources, and the promotion of cyber security measures. Green and clean energy sources, economic measures, policies and regulations can accelerate the reduction of air emissions in the industry, but this cannot be achieved overnight (Vakili et al., 2022b). Behavioural changes are required to reduce energy demand, use renewable energy, use lower or zero emission fuels, and promote sustainable aspects of the shipping industry's life-cycle approach, and accept the extra cost of moving to a sustainable lifestyle (Vakili et al., 2022c).

Achieving zero emissions in the maritime industry requires a broader vision and a 'cradle to grave' approach with cooperation between all the stakeholders and policy action is crucial for shipyards to reach their emissions reduction potential. Although reducing airborne emissions from the operational phase of ships is a priority for the maritime sector, policy makers and active stakeholders need to regulate air emissions from the manufacturing phase of ships, too. This can lead to improvements in the sustainability of shipyard-cities.

References

Ballini, F., Vakili, S., Schönborn, A., Ölcer, A., Canepa, M., & Sciutto, D. (2022). Optimal decision making for emissions reduction measures for Italian container terminals. *Proceedings of the Institution of Mechanical Engineers, Part M: Journal of Engineering for the Maritime Environment, 236*(1), 283–300.

Barriball, K. L., & While, A. (1994). Collecting data using a semi-structured interview: A discussion paper. *Journal of Advanced Nursing-Institutional Subscription, 19*(2), 328–335.
Bryman, A. (2016). *Social research methods*. Oxford University Press.
Chang, R. D., Zuo, J., Zhao, Z. Y., Zillante, G., Gan, X. L., & Soebarto, V. (2017). Evolving theories of sustainability and firms: History, future directions and implications for renewable energy research. *Renewable and Sustainable Energy Reviews, 72*, 48–56.
Empson, L. (2018). Elite interviewing in professional organizations. *Journal of Professions and Organization, 5*(1), 58–69.
Grim, B., Gromis, J., & Harmon, A. H. (2006). Focused group interviews as an innovative Quanti-Qualitative Methodology (QQM): Integrating quantitative elements into a qualitative methodology. *The Qualitative Report, 11*(3), 516–537.
Hanlon, W. W. (2018). Skilled immigrants and American industrialization: Lessons from Newport News Shipyard. *Business History Review, 92*(4), 605–632.
International Maritime Organization (IMO). (2023). MEPC\80\WP. 12. IMO STRATEGY ON REDUCTION OF GHG EMISSIONS FROM SHIPS. Retrieved from MEPC 377 80 (imo.org).
Joung, T. H., Kang, S. G., Lee, J. K., & Ahn, J. (2020). The IMO initial strategy for reducing Greenhouse Gas (GHG) emissions, and its follow-up actions towards 2050. *Journal of International Maritime Safety, Environmental Affairs, and Shipping, 4*(1), 1–7.
Kitzinger, J. (1995). Qualitative research: introducing focus groups. *BMJ, 311*(7000), 299–302.
Koenig, P. C., Narita, H., & Baba, K. (2002). Lean production in the Japanese shipbuilding industry? *Journal of Ship Production and Design, 18*(3), 167–174.
Lehmacher, W., & Lind, M. (2022). Partnering on decarbonisation, 29/9-2022. *The Loadstar*. Retrieved from https://theloadstar.com/news-podcast-october-2022
Lind M., Lehmacher W. (2022a). *Positioning partnerships in shipping decarbonization*. Article No. 92. (UNCTAD Transport and Trade Facilitation Newsletter N°95 – Third Quarter 2022). Retrieved from https://unctad.org/news/positioning-partnerships-shipping-decarbonization
Lind, M., & Lehmacher, W. (2022b). *Decarbonizing the maritime sector: Mobilizing coordinated action in the industry using an ecosystems approach*. Article No. 94 (UNCTAD Transport and Trade Facilitation Newsletter N°94 – Second Quarter 2022). Retrieved from https://unctad.org/news/decarbonizing-maritime-sector-mobilizing-coordinated-action-industry-using-ecosystems-approach
Lind, M., Lehmacher, W., De Tremerie, L., Dubielzig, F., Forsström, E., Holthus, P., Morgante, A., Singh, S., & Tenenbaum, L. (2022a). Enablers for Decarbonising the Maritime Industry: Decarbonisation playbook Part 3, 25/9-2022. *The Maritime Executive*. retrieved from https://www.maritime-executive.com/editorials/enablers-for-decarbonizing-the-maritime-industry-part-3
Lind, M., Lehmacher, W., Doepel, T., Heinimaa, J., Hoffmann, J., Laurilehto, M., Lebmeier, M., Petersen, M., Rytkölä, I., Saari, J., Singh, S., Walls, R., & Watson, R. T. (2022b). The benefits of a clusters of value chains perspective in Decarbonising shipping: Decarbonisation Playbook Part 2, 22/8-2022. *The Maritime Executive*. Retrieved from https://maritime-executive.com/editorials/the-three-maritime-value-chains-decarbonization-playbook-part-2
Lind, M., Lehmacher, W., Kuttan, S., Carson-Jackson, J., Cummins, D., van Gogh, M., & Rydbergh, T. (2022c). Partnering Towards Zero Emissions Shipping: Playbook Part 4, 4/11-2022. *The Maritime Executive*. Retrieved from https://www.maritime-executive.com/editorials/partnering-towards-zero-emissions-shipping-playbook-part-4
Lind, M., Lemacher, W., Bentham, J., Kuttan, S., Tikka, K., & Watson, R.T. (2022d). Establish sufficient, transparent, and predictable financing and pricing mechanisms, like a levy on high carbon marine fuels and subsidies for low carbon solutions: Playbook Part 6, 11/12-2022. *The Maritime Executive*. https://www.maritime-executive.com/editorials/four-steps-towards-maritime-decarbonising-actions-playbook-part-6).
OSK Group. (2022). *There is no such thing as a zero-emission ferry!* Retrieved from There is no such thing as a zero-emission ferry! Retrieved from www.osk-group.dk

Parker, A., & Tritter, J. (2006). Focus group method and methodology: Current practice and recent debate. *International Journal of Research & Method in Education, 29*(1), 23–37.

Pinha, D., Ahluwalia, R., & Senna, P. (2016). The combinatorial multi-mode resource constrained multi-project scheduling problem. *International Journal of Supply and Operations Management, 3*(3), 1391–1412.

Roussanaly, S., Berghout, N., Fout, T., Garcia, M., Gardarsdottir, S., Nazir, S. M., et al. (2021). Towards improved cost evaluation of carbon capture and storage from industry. *International Journal of Greenhouse Gas Control, 106*, 103263.

Salvarli, M. S., & Salvarli, H. (2020). For sustainable development: Future trends in renewable energy and enabling technologies. In Renewable energy-resources, challenges and applications. IntechOpen.

Shahsavar, A., Sadeghi, J., Shockley, J., & Ojha, D. (2021). On the relationship between lean scheduling and economic performance in shipbuilding: A proposed model and comparative evaluation. *International Journal of Production Economics, 108202.*

United Nation Conference on Trade and Development (UNCTAD). (2022). *Review of Maritime Transport.* Retrieved from https://unctad.org/publication/review-maritime-transport-2022

Vakili, S. V., Ölçer, A. I., & Schönborn, A. (2021a). Identification of shipyard priorities in a multi-criteria decision-making environment through a transdisciplinary energy management framework: A real case study for a Turkish shipyard. *Journal of Marine Science and Engineering, 9*(10), 1132.

Vakili, S. V., Ölçer, A. I., & Schönborn, A. (2021b). The development of a transdisciplinary framework to overcome energy efficiency barriers in shipbuilding: A case study for an Iranian shipyard. *Journal of Marine Science and Engineering, 9*(10), 1113.

Vakili, S. V., Schönborn, A., & Ölçer, A. I. (2022a). Techno-economic feasibility of photovoltaic, wind and hybrid electrification systems for stand-alone and grid-connected shipyard electrification in Italy. *Journal of Cleaner Production, 366*, 132945.

Vakili, S. V., Schönborn, A., & Ölçer, A. I. (2022b). Application of the transdisciplinary shipyard energy management framework by employing a fuzzy multiple attribute group decision making technique toward a sustainable shipyard: Case study for a Bangladeshi shipyard. *Journal of Shipping and Trade, 7*(1), 1–28.

Vakili, S. V., Ballini, F., Dalaklis, D., & Ölçer, A. I. (2022c). A conceptual transdisciplinary framework to overcome energy efficiency barriers in ship operation cycles to meet IMO's initial Green House gas strategy goals: Case study for an Iranian shipping company. *Energies, 15*(6), 2098.

Vakili, S. V., Ölçer, A. I., Schönborn, A., Ballini, F., & Hoang, A. T. (2022d). Energy-related clean and green framework for shipbuilding community towards zero-emissions: A strategic analysis from concept to case study. *International Journal of Energy Research., 46*, 20624–20649.

Vakili, S., Schönborn, A., & Ölçer, A. I. (2023a). The road to zero emission shipbuilding industry: A systematic and transdisciplinary approach to modern multi-energy shipyards. *Energy Conversion and Management: X, 18*, 100365.

Vakili, S., Ballini, F., Schönborn, A., Christodoulou, A., Dalaklis, D., & Ölçer, A. I. (2023b). Assessing the macroeconomic and social impacts of slow steaming in shipping: A literature review on small Island developing states and least developed countries. *Journal of Shipping and Trade, 8*(1), 2.

Ship Engine, Equipment and Fuel Options for Decarbonization

Matteo Natali and Rui Rego

Target Audience

This chapter has been written to serve private and public organisations in the formulation of their decarbonization strategies, bridging the technology advancements with the latest regulation developments.

It is intended for all management levels. From professionals in the board of management to project managers. Professionals working from strategy development to the different execution stages.

This chapter is also for those that seek a deeper understanding on how to power ships in an energy efficient and zero-emissions way, both now and in the future.

Key Takeaway Messages

Throughout the chapter, we provide fact-based information, to support organisations not only in designing their strategies but also to support them in their decision-making processes. We will elaborate on the decarbonization alternatives available today that may also help them gain a competitive advantage.

The chapter covers:

M. Natali (✉)
Wärtsilä Marine Power, Trieste, Italy
e-mail: matteo.natali@wartsila.com

R. Rego
Wärtsilä Marine Power, Asker, Norway
e-mail: rui.rego@wartsila.com

M. Lind et al. (eds.), *Maritime Decarbonization*,
https://doi.org/10.1007/978-3-031-39936-7_27

- How to apply the Energy Efficiency Existing Ship Index (EEXI) and the (Carbon Intensity Indicator (CII). Different technological drivers for decarbonizing maritime operations.
- The technologies available.
- The shift from mono-fuel to multi-fuel.
- The importance of upgradable fuel flexible technology.
- Green corridors and zero-emission energy distribution.

The IMO GHG Strategy

Shipping, which is not covered by the Paris Accords, is working towards the ambitions set by the IMO (International Maritime Organization) GHG strategy (IMO GHG Strategy, 2023). The IMO's revised strategy aims to reduce well-to-wake emissions from international shipping below 2008 levels. The revised GHG emissions indicative checkpoints are a 20% reduction striving for 30% by 2030 and 70% striving for 80% by 2040, all leading to the ultimate net-zero emissions goals by 2050. The EEXI and CII measure introduced in 2022 remain unchanged, and two mid-term checkpoints have been added: 1) 40% reduction in carbon intensity per transport work by 2030 and 2) 5% uptake striving for 10% of low- and zero-carbon fuels in international shipping by 2030.

The EEXI is focused on design. Simply stated, if you cannot get your vessel below the required EEXI threshold, the vessel will not operate. To meet an initial 2023 deadline, the time for evaluating options and deciding is relatively short. The way the index is calculated—in terms of a specific speed, at a specific power output—leads you to look immediately at two alternatives. Either you reduce the vessel's power and therefore you lose speed, or you improve the efficiency of the vessel, so you use less power to maintain the same speed. The immediate process of achieving compliance is a balancing act of these metrics, and when faced with the sudden need to comply with EEXI, those are the first options to be considered (Decarbonising maritime will take more than technology, 2021). DNV, the world's largest classification society, estimates that a colossal 30,000 vessels will be non-compliant with EEXI should owners decide to take no action (DNV Launches New Digital EEXI Calculator, 2021).

CII quantifies the operational carbon intensity—the real-life annual carbon dioxide (CO_2) produced versus the nautical miles sailed. There is no one-off pass or fail for CII. Compliance is graded A to E with the criteria becoming more stringent over time. If a vessel is the class underachiever, with a D rating 3 years in a row or a single annual E grade, it will be necessary to submit and implement improvement plans. Compared to a binary index like EEXI, the CII has the merit of pushing the industry to look at decarbonization over the longer term. Many options are available, and fuel conversions, of course, will play a significant role and become increasingly common when alternative fuels are available on the market. It is estimated that as early as 2024, only 1 year after CII comes into force, more than half of the world's fleet subject to CII will fall out of compliance and therefore need to submit improvement plans. By 2030, if no action is taken, 81% of bulkers, 80% of container ships and 57% of oil tankers would find themselves at the bottom of the class in category E (Pacini, 2022).

EU Fit for 55

An increasing number of countries have demanded that the IMO increases its green targets and some countries have already introduced their own, more ambitious, decarbonization agenda. For example, alongside the push for global action at the IMO, in July 2021, European Union (EU) legislation has been adopted to deliver the European Green Deal—the 'Fit for 55' package, setting out how it intends to reduce its net greenhouse gas emissions by at least 55% by 2030, compared to 1990 levels (Fit for 55, 2021). This is crucial for Europe to become the world's first climate-neutral continent by 2050.

Since all sectors need to contribute to the EU's climate ambitions, several proposals were made to address maritime transport's climate impact, including the extension of the EU Emissions Trading System to maritime transport, a maximum limit on the greenhouse gas content of energy used by ships calling at European ports, a boost in alternative fuel infrastructure and shore-side electricity supply at ports, and a revision of the existing ETD (Energy Taxation Directive). The EU will also continue supporting research and innovation towards the decarbonization of shipping, in particular, through Horizon Europe, the EU's key funding programme for research and innovation and its Innovation Fund for the demonstration of innovative low-carbon technologies.

Such measures reflect the target to cut greenhouse gas emissions through two complementary angles: the improvement of energy efficiency—using less fuel and the higher use of renewable and low-carbon fuels—using cleaner fuels.

Green Financing

Financing for projects is also changing as lenders factor in the risk of non-environmentally sustainable operations. The EU's Sustainable Finance Strategy (Strategy for financing the transition to a sustainable economy, 2021) and the European Investment Bank's impending energy lending policy set stringent emission limits for fossil-based energy generation.

Meanwhile the Poseidon Principles, launched in 2020, commit signatory banks to investments that reduce emissions in line with the IMO's 2050 emission goals. This means that banks are beginning to offer sustainability-linked loans where interest rates are linked to AER (Annual Efficiency Ratio) or EEOI (Energy Efficiency Operational Indicator) scores (Poseidon Principles: A global framework for responsible ship finance, 2019), Only those players that are better positioned, with more far-sighted plans, will secure funding. It is safe to assume that customers coming out of this journey greener will also be stronger and more competitive and emerge with a larger portion of the market.

Furthermore, more and more shippers have their own roadmap to reduce carbon footprints, and are seeking lower-carbon supply chains and are willing to pay a premium for green services. This means that a fleet owner who begins decarbonizing sooner is also likely to be a more attractive investment partner for banks required to have a green portfolio and more attractive to those seeking to move cargoes.

The Decarbonization Technology Landscape

Whether through regulatory necessity—EEXI and CCI being the most pressing—or pressure from cargo owners wanting to decarbonize their supply chains, or even the first sustainability-linked loans becoming more attractive, everybody is beginning to feel the push or has at least seen the unavoidable direction of travel. Whereas previously there may have been a prevailing 'wait and see' mentality, where owners and operators were doubtful of taking the first-mover risk, these pressures have—or very soon will—necessitate immediate decisions. And to a great extent, the technologies to make them a reality are already available.

In 2020, the IMO's Fourth Greenhouse Gas Study identified 44 currently available GHG abatement technologies (Fourth IMO GHG Study, 2021). These include shaft generators that reduce reliance on auxiliary engines, air lubrications systems that help vessels maintain the same speed with less power, and wind rotors that can generate additional thrust, reducing propulsion power requirements. All these solutions enable compliance with both EEXI and CII while allowing vessels to continue sailing at market speeds, thereby maintaining their attractiveness to charterers and potential buyers.

Deciding how to implement new arrangements is anything but easy. Two elements are needed. First is a clear view of current emission performance and compliance status, along with the ability to model the evolution of compliance in the future. Second is the capability to understand and simulate how various solutions will affect future performance. In general, pinning hopes on a single technology is rarely the optimal solution. A single vessel may need several solutions to ensure compliance, while suitable technologies may vary even across a fleet of similar vessels.

Ensuring Optimal Engine Performance

In the discussion around decarbonization, vessel owners and operators are faced with an array of options in terms of energy-saving hardware and software. But one basic thing is sometimes overlooked: ensuring that the engines themselves are operating as efficiently as possible (Bass, 2021b). The starting point for optimal engine performance—and therefore minimised emissions—is to make sure that the powertrain is set up to match the vessel's operating profile. Engine retrofits and improvements in operating the engines can enable substantial fuel savings, and therefore a significant reduction in emissions. Equally important is to ensure that these assets are properly maintained. Every single component has a part to play; for example, exchanging a filter or cleaning an air cooler at the right time can help to cut fuel consumption. Data collection and expert analysis can be employed to identify the optimal timing for such maintenance interventions.

Future Fuels

While future fuels have a critical role to play in helping the maritime industry to achieve the IMO's targets, the path ahead presents many uncertainties. Liquified natural gas (LNG) is both an established reality in the newbuild market and an excellent option for retrofits; it instantly reduces CO_2 and NOx (nitrogen oxides) emissions, while almost eliminating SOx (sulphur oxides) and particulate emissions. It is well established as a maritime fuel around the world in virtually every vessel segment, with mature legislation frameworks and robust bunkering infrastructure. When it comes to the future, it is difficult to identify clear winners among the many different fuel options, but ammonia and methanol seem the most promising carbon-neutral fuels at present. Although interest in hydrogen is growing, there are barriers to be overcome before it can become a mainstream solution for shipping, such as the high price of clean hydrogen, difficulties in storage and transportation, lack of bunkering infrastructure, and lack of a regulatory framework. Hydrogen, however, will play a key role as a building block in the production of carbon-neutral fuels such as e-ammonia, blue ammonia, and e-methanol.

Engine Power Limitation

For electronically controlled engines, power can be limited directly in the system with the implementation of a software upgrade. For mechanically controlled engines, it is possible to install an EPL (engine power limitation) interface box which includes all the necessary hardware to interface with the engine. The EPL, which operates at all times during normal operations, can be manually overridden via a switch on the bridge to allow for situations where a power reserve above the normal limit is required for the purpose of safely securing the ship, in man overboard situations or other purposes defined by the IMO. Any such override must be recorded and indicated to the relevant classification societies. Both the override function and recording of override events are mandatory features stipulated by IMO MEPC (Marine Environment Protection Committee) guidelines.

Shaft Power Limitation

ShaPoLi (shaft power limitation) systems limit shaft power during normal operation. With this solution a torque measurement system attached to the propeller shaft sends a signal to the propulsion control system to limit the power at the shaft by limiting the pitch and/or shaft revolutions setting in a controlled manner (Bass, 2022a). Systems can be overridden with a switch on the bridge and includes automatic data logging for reporting purposes. One of the biggest advantages of this solution is that it does not limit operational flexibility for vessels with multiple shaft lines or multiple engines per shaft, or those with PTO (power take-off) and/or PTI (power take-in) systems.

EPL and ShaPoLi are both economically attractive, quick-to-implement solutions that enable compliance with EEXI. However, they will only have an impact on CII if the vessel reduces real emissions by sailing slower, thus limiting the operational profile.

Energy Saving Devices

ESDs (energy saving devices) have a direct impact on vessel propulsion efficiency by reducing hull resistance and improving propeller thrust. This can be pre- and post-swirl devices as well as high-performance hull coatings to reduce resistance and fouling. Installing a replacement propeller that is optimised for the vessel's current operational profile also offers significant potential benefits. Depending on the vessel type, energy savings in the region of 5–10% can be achieved by combining ESDs and an optimised propeller (Bass, 2021b). Many newer vessels already have ESDs installed, so the room for improvement is limited. For this reason, alternative ESDs such as air lubrication systems and wind rotors may continue to gain traction in the market.

Air Lubrication

Air lubrication fundamentally changes the interaction between water and a vessel's hull, shearing air from air release units to create a carpet of microbubbles that coat the flat bottom of the vessel. This reduces fuel consumption and associated emissions by decreasing the frictional resistance (Thurman, 2022). Owners can choose whether to maintain normal operational speed and benefit from a reduction in fuel consumption and emissions or opt for higher speeds with the same power requirement. Air lubrication is a clean technology recognised under the IMO's Energy Efficiency Design Index (EEDI) for new builds and EEXI, and the technology also helps vessels to reduce their carbon intensity and meet the requirements of the IMO's operational CII.

Rotor Sails (Flettner Rotors)

Rotor sails, also known as Flettner Rotors, are modern mechanical sails—tall cylinders that, when spinning round, provide extra propulsive power for vessels and thereby reduce the amount of fuel consumed on board. When the wind speed and direction is optimal, rotor sails, which are powered by electric motors, can be switched on automatically. When the wind flow meets the sail, it creates an aerodynamic phenomenon called the Magnus effect, wherein the air in front of the sail accelerates as it is pulled in the direction of the spin. This faster-moving air has a lower pressure while the air behind slows down and increases in pressure. This pressure differential propels the ship forwards. Powering the sails requires limited energy and the gains in propulsive power can be in the order of 10–15 times input (Bass, 2022e).

Electrically Enhanced Propulsion Systems

Diesel-mechanical PTO/PTI or diesel-electric setups often reduce the required installed power and fuel consumption as well as improve a vessel's EEDI. The main benefit of electrically enhanced propulsion lies in its flexibility to adapt to different vessel operating profiles and speeds, as the number of engines running is decoupled from the number of propellers and other energy consumers. While at full load a purely mechanical driveline can have an efficiency advantage, at low speeds electrically enhanced propulsion can easily reduce consumption by 10–25%, as a vessel's entire energy needs can be covered by a single engine running at optimum load (Johannesen & Heine, 2021). Many industry experts still labour under the assumption that electrical losses in these types of systems are as high as 15%, but this is no longer the case with modern technologies (Johannesen & Heine, 2021), (Fig. 1).

For example, the innovative Wärtsilä hybrid-electric concept, combining generator sets and energy storage system, enables engines to run always at their best efficiency and provides flexible power supply modes to adapt to various load demands.

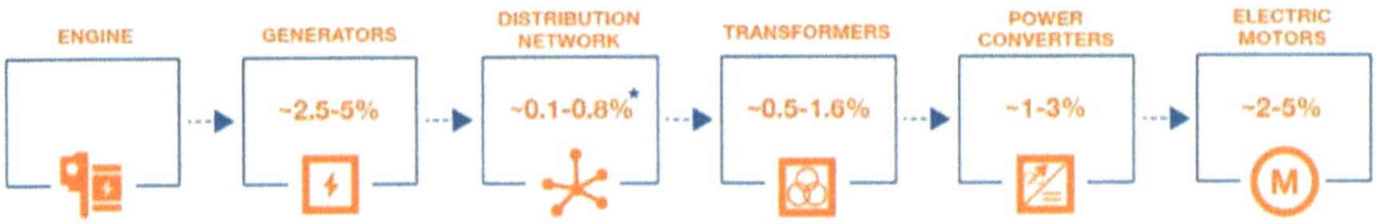

Fig. 1 Typical energy losses at each stage of an electric driveline

Shore Power

Connecting to shore power when in port eliminates the need to use auxiliary engines to generate electricity, reducing emissions and fuel costs as well as lowering operating expenditure. Regulators around the world are taking action to secure a level playing field and many governments are now making it mandatory for ports to install shore power facilities and even co-funding projects as part of their decarbonization efforts. As an example, EU's 'Fit for 55' legislative package, will drive both, the supply and demand sides of shore power. This includes the AFI Directive for port-side infrastructure development and the Fuel EU Maritime Regulation, which mandates certain vessel types to connect to shore-side electricity when at berth. There are hundreds of such projects on both US coasts, throughout Europe and at the large Asian port hubs. As it eliminates vessels' emissions in port, shore power can provide substantial improvement to the CII.

Shaft Generator Systems

Shaft generator systems, which have been around for several decades, aim to cover a vessel's onboard electricity needs during sailing by using the main engine as opposed to the auxiliary engines. With the help of modern converter technologies and software, these systems can produce electricity across a wide engine speed range. Due to their positive impact on a vessel's EEDI they are now standard onboard certain types of vessels, and with the rapidly approaching EEXI deadline there has been a huge increase in demand in the retrofit market. A shaft generator system has the potential to improve a vessel's energy efficiency by 3–5% and cut both fuel and maintenance costs as auxiliary engines running hours are reduced.

Batteries

A hybrid system combines an energy storage system and an internal combustion engine. It is available as both a standard solution for newbuilds and as a retrofit solution for existing vessels. Hybrid systems are not yet in the EEXI formula, and the value proposition is not so strong in ocean-going vessels with stable sailing profiles. However, they have clear advantages in operations with intermittent loads or high load peaks, such as dynamic positioning, where total fuel consumption can be cut by up to 20%.

Full-battery propulsion power systems have seen a recent uptake in coastal shipping. However, batteries have technical limitations including energy density, power density and lifetime, and need a recharging infrastructure in port, which drastically reduces the vessel's operational flexibility in terms of speed and range. Thus, the applicability of full-battery propulsion power for wider commercial shipping is limited.

New Energy Converters

There is growing interest in PEM (proton exchange membrane) and SOFC (solid oxide fuel cell) technologies. Fuel cells, combined with alternative fuels, can efficiently reduce, and even eliminate emissions and noise, while energy efficiency can be higher than for conventional combustion engines. However, fuel cells come with significant disadvantages related to cost, power density, operational flexibility, durability as well as regulatory and market uncertainty, which limit their uptake for the time being.

Carbon capture can also be reduced by applying onboard CCS (carbon capture systems). While originally developed for larger stationary emissions points such as power generation plants, onboard CCS is a potential option for decarbonizing the deep-sea portion of the world fleet. Demonstration or implementation of onboard CCS systems are planned on commercial vessels.

The Shift from Mono-fuel to Multi-fuel

One of the key challenges remains the choice of future fuel and the question of which one will be readily available and widely adopted in years to come. The point is not necessarily to identify a single fuel, but to accept the fact that the landscape of green fuels could vary. It is not just about what the best future fuel for marine is; meaning how well it performs, how much space it requires, how difficult it is to store, transport and so on. Another key aspect is to look at which fuels will be available for different industries and how they will compete for these. The marine industry will not be the sole beneficiary, so it is key to consider how the entire fuel landscape develops, across all sectors, before establishing what will be available for marine, when and why.

Fleet owners are faced with a multitude of options when looking at future-oriented solutions: alternatives such as ammonia, hydrogen, methanol, biofuels, bio-liquid fuels, bio- gases, synthetic fuels to name but a few. The selection is made more complex by varying stages of market readiness and infrastructure availability before any can be considered viable for maritime.

All in all, there is little certainty around the future of fuels in either shipping or energy. Methane will play a role whether fossil, synthetic or from biomass. So too will hydrogen, either as a fuel or a feedstock. Flexibility will be crucial. And for many potential pathways the best solution will be to develop engine and fuel handling solutions that already exist rather than create entirely new concepts.

It is also important to understand the timeline and speed of change in the industry, because if we think of LNG, the maritime transition has been a 20-year process, and today we are at a point where about 1 or 2% of the fleet can run on LNG. Over the next 30 years, we need to transition 60–100% of the entire global fleet to new green fuels. Marine asset lifetime is measured in decades. Therefore, if a fleet owner invests today, the asset in question must be able to return value well into the industry's journey towards complete decarbonization.

LNG

Global availability, greenhouse gas reduction potential, mature legislative frameworks and extensive bunkering infrastructure are driving the uptake of LNG as a transition fuel in most vessel segments.

We have seen a steady rise in LNG's popularity as a fuel option for both newbuilds and vessel retrofits. As of January 2022, LNG vessels comprised 4% of the existing global fleet and 30% of the global newbuild orderbook in gross tonnage. Bunkering infrastructure continues to develop at a rapid pace too, particularly across Asia and the Middle East.

In tank-to-wake terms, it drastically reduces local emissions, emitting virtually no SOx or PM (particulate matter) and less CO_2 (carbon dioxide) and NOx (Bass, 2022b). Overall, LNG can unlock close to a 20% improvement in CII, and similar improvement can be expected for a vessel's EEXI. This comes despite the LNG fuel tank may reduce cargo capacity. The EU acknowledged the key role that LNG has to play by including the fuel in its taxonomy for sustainable activities, provided fossil LNG is gradually replaced by carbon-neutral alternatives by 2035. While vessels' equipment manufacturers' focus is on tank-to-wake, stakeholders further up the LNG supply chain are working to minimise well-to-tank emissions. Producers are investing in cleaning up their part of the chain by using carbon capture in hard-to-abate processes, using renewable energy to decarbonize energy-intensive processes like liquefaction, and closely monitoring pipelines for emissions.

LNG consists mainly of methane. During the energy conversion process, most of the methane is converted into mechanical energy, some of it remains unburned and escapes with the exhaust gases into the atmosphere. This is known as methane slip. Due to the high $CO2\text{-}_{eq}$ (carbon dioxide equivalent) value of methane, equipment manufacturers are working to reduce it. Over the past 25 years, Wärtsilä has slashed by 75% the methane slip in the dual-fuel engines (Bass, 2020).

The emissions from modern LNG fuel engines are 14% lower than its antecessors. Wärtsilä is working on a new combustion concept that will drastically reduce methane slip again. These technological advancements are expected to challenge even the onerous 20-year measure of GHG emissions (GWP_{20}).

Converting to LNG is a concrete step towards decarbonization that vessel owners can take today, and it opens the possibility to use bioLNG and, eventually, synthetic methane. Fuel flexibility can be further enhanced by blending LNG with gases such as VOCs (volatile organic compounds) that can be emitted by certain cargoes. LNG can also be blended with ammonia or hydrogen. For example, Wärtsilä 4-stroke dual-fuel engines are already capable of operating with a blend of up to 15% hydrogen by volume, equating to around 5% by energy, with the remaining energy coming mainly from LNG and some from the pilot fuel.

Methanol

Methanol—a biodegradable alcohol—shows great promise as a future fuel for maritime applications.

Methanol slashes NOx and SOx and particulate emissions, it presents a low risk to the environment because it biodegrades rapidly in water and, as it is liquid at atmospheric pressure, it can be stored in similar tanks as traditional diesel onboard a vessel. Additionally, there are already established storage and handling facilities at or nearby most major ports (methanol is available as a marine fuel at over 120 ports around the world). Thanks to its chemical properties, bunkering requires only minor adaptations to infrastructure, and no cryogenic storage is needed to convert from conventional marine fuel.

Converting a vessel to methanol requires approximately double the volume of fuel tank capacity compared to diesel to maintain the same level of fuel endurance. Also, methanol tanks require additional cofferdams to prevent any potential leaks into machinery spaces. After conversion, a vessel's EEXI value and CII rating is expected to be improved by around 7% when switching from HFO (heavy fuel oil) to methanol, if all consumers are converted (Thurman, 2023). IMO's revised GHG strategy introduces LCA (Lifecycle Assessment) guide-lines for calculating marine fuel emissions on a well-to-wake basis. The LCA includes, among others, preliminary well-to-tank - *for production* - and tank-to-wake - *for use* - emissions factors for the various fuels. The Life Cycle emissions calculation has therefore additional impact on the attained EEXI and CII values, depending on weather the vessel is operated with grey, blue or green methanol. From the perspective of onboard safety, there are well-established rules and regulations pertaining to the use of methanol as a marine fuel in the form of IMO MSC.1-Circ.1621—Interim guidelines for the safety of ships using methylethyl alcohol as fuel.

One of the biggest challenges from the perspective of maritime decarbonization is that most methanol today is produced using natural gas (grey methanol) or coal (brown methanol). Conventional plants that produce methanol from the steam reformation of natural gas can reduce their carbon footprint by recirculating natural gas within the facility, sourcing additional CO_2 from a neighbouring industrial facility or using renewable electricity or green hydrogen in place of processing natural gas. These approaches are used to produce low-carbon methanol, which is known as blue methanol. Methanol can also be produced from other carbon-containing feedstocks like biomass, biogas, waste streams and captured CO_2. When methanol is produced using renewable sources like biomass, and if the power used to produce it comes from renewable energy, it is considered to be green methanol.

Methanol has traditionally been produced and consumed as a chemical feedstock and is relatively new as a marine fuel. However, production may increase as demand from the shipping industry grows, and a growing proportion of the new supply will be renewable methanol. Since the methanol molecule—CH_3OH—is the same whether it is produced from grey, blue or green feedstocks, blending methanol is a viable option to facilitate the transition from conventional to renewable fuels.

Ammonia

Ammonia has traditionally been produced from hydrocarbons, although in the future there is potential for carbon capture to reduce the emission footprint of production (so called 'blue ammonia') or for production from non-carbon renewable energy sources such as wind or solar ('green ammonia'). Independent of how it is produced, ammonia does not contain any carbon molecule, so when it is used in an engine it produces no CO_2 emissions. It is also a known quantity and, although there is currently no infrastructure to support its use as a fuel, it is widely manufactured and traded, primarily for use in the production of fertilisers.

Although using ammonia does not emit CO_2, there does need to be some form of abatement to handle the NOx emissions and possible ammonia gas releases, for example by using a wet scrubber system (Bass, 2021a).

Compared to LNG and hydrogen, ammonia is easier to handle in liquid form as it is stored at around −33 °C, meaning the fuel storage and delivery systems are less complex and therefore less costly. However, it requires stainless steel tanks due to its corrosive properties, as well as special precautions due to its toxicity. LNG is easier in that aspect, as all you need is a material that can withstand cryogenic temperatures, intrinsically safe electrical and a place to ventilate out the evaporated gas. With ammonia, the toxicity adds a new dimension to the handling of leaks, as you cannot simply dump it into the water or ventilate it without looking at the toxicity risks. Ammonia's lower volumetric energy density (around 3 kWh/L, somewhere between LNG and hydrogen in terms of storage volume) means much more storage capacity is required on board. The sacrifices in terms of passenger or cargo capacity need to be weighed up against the benefits of adopting ammonia as a fuel.

Today there are engines that can run 100% on LNG, but at the moment no engine can use ammonia alone as a fuel. The future pathway will likely be a fuel mix involving LNG, diesel or even methanol—different blends are being tested—and this, of course, has implications for the onboard storage and handling systems.

The cost of ammonia-fuelled vessels should become clearer when the fuel is included in the International Code of Safety for Ships using Gases or other Low-flashpoint Fuels (IGF Code), providing more clarity on regulatory requirements. At present, the code only covers LNG and methanol. It can be done by following the alternative design approach of the IGF code, but you need to do a lot more on the safety analysis side and you have less visibility of costs when you start the project because you do not know upfront what the Flag State and classification society will require. This is where LNG-fuelled vessels were more than a decade ago.

Hydrogen

Hydrogen has been used for decades in a variety of different industrial processes, including oil refining, metallurgical processes, production of other future fuels such as ammonia and methanol. But almost all the hydrogen used today is so-called grey hydrogen and is produced using fossil fuels, typically natural gas, in a process known as steam reforming. Moving along the colour spectrum we have black or brown hydrogen, produced using coal. Blue hydrogen is hydrogen that has been produced in a process where the carbon generated during steam reforming is captured and stored, while green hydrogen production uses clean renewable energy to split water into hydrogen and oxygen in a process known as electrolysis. Global hydrogen production was around 70 million tons in 2018. Currently, almost all hydrogen is produced at or very close to where it is needed. However, February 2022 saw the world's first liquefied hydrogen cargo transported between Australia and Japan.

Compared to diesel operation the assumption is that CO_2 tailpipe emissions are non-existent when using hydrogen as a fuel. On the downside, even as a liquid, hydrogen storage takes up significant space compared to marine gas oil. To get the same equivalent energy content requires a tank volume that is almost eight times more than that of marine gas oil, thus limiting vessel endurance (Bass, 2022f). Land-based storage for liquid and compressed hydrogen already exists so there is technology that can eventually be adapted for use in maritime applications.

Hydrogen could be stored onboard either as liquid hydrogen, which gives the biggest storage capacity in the smallest possible space, or possibly as compressed hydrogen in 200 or 700 bar pressurised tanks. Liquid storage, however, brings its own set of challenges due to the extremely low temperatures required. To keep hydrogen in liquid form it needs to be stored below −253 °C, which places huge demands on the storage and supply system in terms of insulation requirements. The extreme cold can lead to oxygen from the air condensing on the pipework, resulting in a risk of explosion. There is boil-off to deal with as well, which means there is a need for an energy-intensive reliquefication solution. Leakages are another important consideration because of the highly explosive nature of hydrogen. In principle, it is possible to use a similar setup as with LNG but with a greater focus on insulation and the prevention of leakages.

From a regulatory perspective the biggest challenge is that there simply are no rules concerning the use of hydrogen as a fuel for shipping. The IGF Code provides high-level requirements for using low-flashpoint fuels like hydrogen in maritime applications but to date it has mostly been applied for projects involving LNG. DNV has published a Handbook for Hydrogen-Fuelled Vessels, which covers the key aspects such as safety and risk mitigation, as well as engineering specifications for systems. As it stands today, new hydrogen applications must follow the Alternative Design approval process, which is a risk-based process for designs that cannot be approved with current regulations.

The Importance of Upgradable Fuel Flexible Technology

If you invest in a vessel today, you can expect it still to be in service in 2050. Therefore, the upgrade pathway should ensure that when new green fuels become viable, ship owners do not have to scrap their ship and invest in a new one but can rely on upgradeability for continued compliance of their asset. And this is not just the concern of those ordering a newbuild vessel. Due to the heightening demands of legislation, and the gathering pressure as the timetable becomes tighter year upon year, the issue also becomes a central one for the existing fleet.

There is consensus about a continued need to improve combustion technologies for fuels that are already widely used. Shipowners or plant operators using natural gas can use their existing dual-fuel or spark-ignited engines to transition to synthetic or biomethane. Diesel engines can easily switch to biodiesels and other liquid fuels. By refining these technologies, engine manufacturers can ensure that their customers retain flexibility in their fuel choices as cost and availability become clearer. New fuels including hydrogen, ammonia and methanol will play an important role in the marine and energy markets.

While the energy transition is in process, assets are unlikely to be operated on the same fuel for their entire lifecycle. Power plant built today may operate on natural gas, then natural gas with hydrogen, before finally running on renewable hydrogen alone. Fuel flexibility and the ability to convert for fuels will be crucial to secure uninterrupted operations independent of fuel availability while ensuring environmental performance.

In most cases, the design of the ship itself is a more important consideration than the extent of the engine conversion: if you have not designed a ship to hold a gas tank from day one it will, in many cases, not be economically viable to add one later. When designing a vessel for gaseous fuels, futureproofing is essential—it might be an LNG tank today, but correctly designed it could hold biogas, synthetic methane or ammonia in the future.

Example: Wärtsilä 2-Stroke Future Fuels Conversion Platform

The Wärtsilä 2-Stroke Future Fuels Conversion Platform is a new retrofit fuel injection technology and combustion concept that combines the benefits of diesel and Otto cycle technology (Bass, 2022d). The platform allows the use of LNG on diesel engines and provides the flexibility to handle methanol or ammonia with only minor modifications.

The solution uses cryogenic LNG at −150 °C, which is supplied directly to the engine at low pressure. This is followed by on-engine amplification before the fuel is injected into the cylinders at medium pressure. Using cryogenic LNG reduces the complexity and energy consumption of the overall fuel gas supply system compared to normal LNG operations, where the fuel is heated to around 40 °C before injection. This eliminates the need for expensive, energy-intensive, and high-maintenance equipment between the fuel tanks and the main engine. As well as reducing complexity, the solution minimises the footprint of the fuel supply system, providing greater flexibility for retrofitting. It also offers redundancy with backup VLSFO (very low sulphur fuel oil) or MDO (marine diesel oil) /MGO (marine gasoil) fuels.

Prefabricated, preassembled engine component modules mean that installation is a simple process where no off-hire is needed beyond the usual dry-docking time. Also, no major changes to the engine are required beyond new cylinder covers and add-on components.

Initiatives to Speed-up Implementation

Green Shipping Corridors

The 2021 UN climate conference COP26 in Glasgow saw a coalition of governments issue the Clydebank Declaration, which seeks to establish green shipping corridors—routes where the economic, logistical and political conditions are favourable to zero-emission shipping and where rapid deployment of solutions can be supported by combined policy and industry action. The 22 signatories committed to establish six such corridors by 2025, with the goal of accelerating the development of fuels, infrastructure, legislation, and regulation.

As argued in the Practical Playbook for Maritime Decarbonization (Lind et al., 2022), cross value-chain cooperation is a basic prerequisite for establishing a corridor, enabling the context to be built for the various members of the value chain to cooperate instead of relying on industry players to create partnerships themselves. This reduces risk and establishes the right conditions to encourage first-movers.

Above all else, ship owners need to be confident that the clean fuel they require will be available on the routes they operate. Green shipping corridors allow the build-up of an ecosystem of producers and consumers, and when owners know they have a secure fuel supply they can invest with confidence in vessel upgrades and newbuilds. The green economy requires a new way of thinking, new business models and close collaboration. The focus is on de-risking across the board for all parties and maintaining an open and transparent dialogue.

The second fundamental element is a viable fuel pathway. What makes green shipping corridors a particularly effective way to tackle decarbonization is the focus on the routes rather than the fuels themselves. Certain fuels make more sense on certain routes while others will be more attractive elsewhere. This makes it easier to gain consensus early on the right fuel to use and simplifies the discussion because everyone is on the same page, focused on one fuel pathway. Action from first-movers who have strategic reasons to drive green shipping forward, for example, to gain market share or reduce their emissions footprint, will help to consolidate fragmented early demand around a given corridor and accelerate collaboration between value-chain players (Bass, 2022c).

Finally, policy and regulations directed to specific corridors will be easier to apply and will play a pivotal role in bridging the fuel cost-gap in the early stages. There is potential for the EU, for example, to build on its Emissions Trading System by recycling tax revenues into green shipping corridors.

Zero Emission Energy Distribution at Sea (ZEEDS)

The Wärtsilä-initiated ZEEDS (Zero-Emission Energy Distribution at Sea) initiative is based on an idea to create an entire ecosystem of offshore clean fuel production and distribution hubs and deploy them in strategic locations across the globe. The ecosystem would be based on existing technology, meaning it is practical and can already be rolled out in pilot projects. The initiative includes Wärtsilä, a leading technology company, Aker Solutions, an offshore engineering company, DFDS, an international shipping and logistics company, Equinor, a multinational energy company, and Grieg Star, an international shipowner. These five companies form the core of the group by contributing with different knowledge and competencies.

The initial infrastructure of the future as imagined by the companies involved in ZEEDS is composed of fuel hubs set up next to offshore wind turbines, built as two-level platforms. The energy produced by the turbines will be used to produce hydrogen from water on the first level of the platform while on the second level, ammonia will be made from hydrogen and nitrogen extracted from the air. Other clean fuels could be produced and stored as well.

The ZEEDS initiative is also collaborating with other stakeholders, including NGOs (non-governmental organisations), politicians at all levels, and local communities who stand to benefit from the initiative's circular approach—for example by reusing waste heat and oxygen from production processes in other commercial activities.

References

Bass, C. (2020). *How to be smarter about methane slip – Right now*. https://www.wartsila.com/insights/article/mind-the-methane-gap

Bass, C. (2021a). *Ammonia – Fuel for thought in our deep-dive Q&A*. https://www.wartsila.com/insights/article/ammonia-fuel-for-thought-in-our-deep-dive

Bass, C. (2021b). *Complying with EEXI – How to speed up decarbonisation without slowing down vessels*. https://www.wartsila.com/insights/article/complying-with-eexi-how-to-speed-up-decarbonisation-without-slowing-down-vessels

Bass, C. (2022a). *Are you geared up to comply with EEXI?* https://www.wartsila.com/insights/article/are-you-geared-up-to-comply-with-eexi

Bass, C. (2022b). *LNG – Fuel for thought in our deep-dive Q&A*. https://www.wartsila.com/insights/article/lng-fuel-for-thought-in-our-deep-dive-q-a

Bass, C. (2022c). *Green corridors – A way to accelerate maritime decarbonisation?* https://www.wartsila.com/insights/article/green-corridors-channelling-efforts-to-scale-up-maritime-decarbonisation

Bass, C. (2022d). *The Wärtsilä 2-stroke future fuels conversion platform*. https://www.wartsila.com/insights/article/the-wartsila-2-stroke-future-fuels-conversion-platform

Bass, C. (2022e). *Are rotor sails the answer to CII and EEXI compliance for ships?* https://www.wartsila.com/insights/article/how-rotor-sail-technology-can-boost-maritime-decarbonisation-efforts

Bass, C. (2022f). *Does hydrogen have what it takes to be a future marine fuel?* https://www.wartsila.com/insights/article/hydrogen-fuel-for-thought-in-our-q-a

Decarbonising maritime will take more than technology. (2021). https://www.wartsila.com/insights/article/decarbonising-maritime-will-take-more-than-technology

DNV launches new digital EEXI Calculator. (2021, June). https://www.dnv.com/news/dnv-launches-new-digital-eexi-calculator-202945

Fit for 55. (2021). https://www.consilium.europa.eu/en/policies/green-deal/fit-for-55-the-eu-plan-for-a-green-transition/

Fourth IMO Greenhouse Gas Study. (2021). *International Maritime Organization*. https://wwwcdn.imo.org/localresources/en/OurWork/Environment/Documents/Fourth%20IMO%20GHG%20Study%202020%20-%20Full%20report%20and%20annexes.pdf

IMO GHG Strategy. (2023). Revised GHG reduction strategy for global shipping adopted (imo.org). https://www.imo.org/en/OurWork/Environment/Pages/2023-IMO-Strategy-on-Reduction-of-GHG-Emissions-from-Ships.aspx?refresh=1

Johannesen, P., & Heine, U. (2021). *Dispelling the myth of high losses in modern electrically enhanced propulsion systems*. https://www.wartsila.com/insights/article/dispelling-the-myth-of-high-losses-in-modern-electrically-enhanced-propulsion-systems

Lind, M., Lemacher, W., Bentham, J., Kuttan, S., Tikka, K., & Watson, R. T. (2022). *Four steps towards maritime decarbonizing actions: Playbook part 5, 11/12-2022*. The Maritime Executive. https://www.maritime-executive.com/editorials/four-steps-towards-maritime-decarbonising-actions-playbook-part-5

Pacini, G. (2022). *Is the global fleet ready for CII?* https://www.wartsila.com/insights/whitepaper/is-the-global-fleet-ready-for-cii

Poseidon Principles: A global framework for responsible ship finance. (2019). *Poseidon principles*. https://www.poseidonprinciples.org/download/Poseidon_Principles.pdf

Strategy for financing the transition to a sustainable economy. (2021). https://finance.ec.europa.eu/publications/strategy-financing-transition-sustainable-economy_en

Thurman, A. (2022). *Busting the most common myths about air lubrication for ships*. https://www.wartsila.com/insights/article/five-common-misconceptions-about-air-lubrication-and-why-they-re-wrong

Thurman, A. (2023). *Methanol as marine fuel – The solution you are looking for?* https://www.wartsila.com/insights/article/methanol-fuel-for-thought-in-our-deep-dive-q-a

Decarbonization Action by Energy Companies

Steve Esau and Jeremy B. Bentham

Target Audience

This chapter has been written for those seeking insights into the experience of energy companies already participating in the ecosystem to reduce emissions in the maritime industry. It is especially relevant for leaders in the private sector who are considering their company's future orientation and both the opportunities and challenges of being a forerunner in decarbonization. It is also relevant for policymakers seeking to encourage private sector activity.

S. Esau (✉)
SEA-LNG, Oxford, UK
e-mail: steve.esau@sea-lng.org

J. B. Bentham
World Energy Council, London, UK

Scenarios Team, Shell International, The Hague, The Netherlands

Mission Possible Partnership, Washington, DC, USA

Boston Consulting Group, Amsterdam, The Netherlands

Transformative Scenarios B.V., The Hague, The Netherlands
e-mail: jbentham@live.com

M. Lind et al. (eds.), *Maritime Decarbonization*,
https://doi.org/10.1007/978-3-031-39936-7_28

Key Takeaway Messages

This chapter highlights:

- Two case-studies of first movers in LNG (liquified natural gas) Bunkering.
- Lessons learned from the LNG experience for the introduction of other low-carbon marine fuels, including:
  - Opportunities and challenges for forerunners.
  - The significance of transformative collaborations between both private- and public-sector actors in the ecosystem.
  - The significance of an Anchor Partner in collaborations.
- Potential paths forward.

Introduction

The major investments by energy companies to date in low and zero-carbon marine fuels have been focused on LNG and biofuels, more specifically bio-oils, namely (fatty acid methyl esters (FAME) and (hydrotreated vegetable oil (HVO) with small investments into hydrogen and methanol for marine purposes.

Regarding LNG, energy suppliers are servicing a rapidly growing LNG-fuelled fleet. Approximately 20% of deadweight tonnage on the shipping new build order book is LNG dual-fuelled and some sectors, such as car carriers, are seeing a remarkably high degree of LNG penetration—with the latest data from Clarksons (Clarksons Research, 2023) showing that 93% of new build orders are LNG dual fuel. Based only on existing orders, DNV (2023) forecasts the number of LNG-fuelled ships, excluding LNG carriers, will reach almost 1,000 by 2030—this compares to only 36 LNG-fuelled vessels in operation a decade ago. Growth has accelerated dramatically over the last 2–3 years, as first movers have secured competitive strongholds and competitive dynamics have kicked in (see also Bentham (2023) for a broader discussion of such dynamics).

Investment in LNG was initially driven by the need to meet local emissions regulations, in particular the introduction of the International Maritime Organization (IMO) global 0.5% sulphur cap in 2020. Increasingly, ship owners recognise the immediate greenhouse gas emissions (GHG) reductions offered by LNG and the pathway it offers to net zero through sustainable bioLNG, derived from sustainable biomass resources, and e-LNG, the electro-fuel equivalent of LNG, produced from renewable electricity.

By the end of 2022, according to Clarksons LNG was available at 185 ports worldwide, with a further 50 facilities planned by 2025. Increasingly, most of the large LNG bunkering companies in northwest Europe are offering bioLNG blends and a number are looking at investments in e-LNG production projects.

There is also a growing interest in methanol and ammonia fuelled ships. At the time of writing there are 27 methanol-fuelled ships in operation. All but four of these are methanol carriers which use grey methanol, produced from natural gas as a fuel. There are 177 methanol-fuelled ships on order, mainly container vessels which should provide a major stimulus to green, or renewable methanol production.

As for ammonia, in the absence of any ammonia-fuelled engines, there are no ammonia fuelled ships in operation or on order, only vessels classified as 'ammonia-ready'. There is effectively no green ammonia production. A number of blue ammonia projects are under consideration by fertilizer companies who are looking to decarbonize their product and at the same time marketing it for use in power generation and maritime.

Finally, with regard to hydrogen, there are a small number of hydrogen-fuelled ships in operation and on order. Because of hydrogen's extremely low density and storage challenges, however, these vessels are currently limited to short sea operations and consist mainly of ferries, tugboats, and very small, specialised cruise ships. Most hydrogen produced at the time of writing is grey hydrogen.

Case Studies: First-Movers in LNG Bunkering

Introduction to the Case Studies

The introduction of LNG as a marine fuel is the first attempt to provide a new solution to the way the international shipping fleet is propelled and fuelled since the replacement of coal by fuel oil in the first half of the last century. Lessons learned from the experience of first mover companies developing LNG as a marine fuel can provide a template for the introduction of other alternative fuels such as methanol, ammonia, hydrogen and indeed the renewable forms of LNG.

Here we present two case studies describing the development of LNG bunkering projects in Europe and the USA in the early 2010s when the use of LNG as a marine fuel began to increase in international shipping.

Case Study 1: Development of Ship-to-Ship LNG Bunkering in the Port of Rotterdam

Background

The commissioning of the LNG bunkering vessel, Cardissa, in September 2017 was the culmination of several years' collaboration between the petrochemical giant Shell, the Port of Rotterdam together with its GATE (Gas Access to Europe) Terminal to develop largescale LNG bunkering infrastructure in the second biggest conventional oil bunkering port in the world.

Shell is one of the first movers in LNG as a marine fuel both in terms of supply and in use of the fuel in its own shipping operations. It has built a global presence in LNG as a marine fuel offering bunkering services in 15 locations in 10 different countries, worldwide (Shell Global, 2023).

The Port of Rotterdam is the largest seaport in Europe and the largest in the world outside East Asia. It is the biggest marine fuel bunkering port in Europe with sales of approximately 9 million tonnes of marine fuels per year. The Port is host to the GATE LNG terminal, one the biggest regasification terminals in Europe, which commenced operations in 2011.

During 2017, Shell concluded a number of major bunker supply deals with customers who would be serviced, at least in part, out of Rotterdam. These included LNG for Siem Car Carriers' new builds exporting Volkswagen vehicles from Europe to North America; Sovcomflot, for the first LNG-fuelled Aframaxes in the Baltic and northern Europe; Carnival, in northwest Europe and the Mediterranean for its LNG-fuelled cruise ships; and Containerships OY, for dual-fuel box ships deployed in northwest Europe.

Aligning Around a New Business Opportunity

The three partners saw the opportunity to build a new business, servicing large sea-going vessels based on leveraging the existing LNG infrastructure in the port.

At the time Shell had a global strategy to develop the market for LNG in transportation, linked to a huge supply portfolio, representing approximately 30% of the global LNG market. As part of this strategy Shell was looking to develop LNG bunkering at existing fuel oil bunkering hubs such as Rotterdam, Singapore, and the Gulf Region.

The Port of Rotterdam saw LNG as one of the strategic pillars of the port's broader energy transition ambitions, having had a target of reducing its carbon dioxide (CO_2) emissions levels by more than 90% by 2050. The port was approaching this step by step, with a strong focus on cleaner fuels. LNG was seen as an important first step in decarbonization and it also addressed local emissions. Rotterdam's goal was to make the port an attractive place for shipping lines to bunker LNG, just as it had done for conventional, oil-based fuels.

The GATE Terminal had been developing facilities to service small scale LNG customers since 2012. It started with exploring how to connect 5000–15,000 m^3 loads to high value markets in Scandinavia where small scale LNG terminals were being built. In 2014, it acted on customer demands for 50, 100 and 200 m^3 loads for short-sea shipping vessels by developing a loading station to supply LNG for truck-to-ship bunkering. This market continued to grow but GATE recognised a gap for 200–5000 m^3 loads for large sea-going vessels which could not be serviced by trucks or bunkering at its two unloading jetties, where LNG bulk carriers have priority.

Bringing Together the Pieces of the Jigsaw

To realise this new business opportunity at the Port of Rotterdam, the three partners needed to work closely together. Shell, taking advantage of the fact that capacity at the GATE Terminal was underutilised, acquired 1 bm^3 (1 billion cubic metres) of RWE Supply & Trading GmbH's capacity in 2015. It worked with the GATE Joint Venture partners, Gasunie and Vopak, providing them with the contractual commitments for loading slots for them to be able to make the investments in a small-scale loading jetty for bunker vessels. And, in parallel, it made the investment in the Cardissa LNG bunkering vessel—a Shell-only venture.

With Shell as the anchor bunkering partner, GATE developed the third jetty, including the LNG loading infrastructure. It worked closely with both Shell, aligning on technical requirements for the bunker vessel, and the Port of Rotterdam which made the necessary investments in the marine facilities—the quay and basin associated with the jetty. Finally, the port introduced incentives to stimulate the uptake of LNG as a marine fuel. These consisted of two elements: the ESI (Environmental Shipping Index)—a points-based system which offered a 10% discount on port dues for the cleanest ships; and a specific LNG bunkering incentive—a further 10% discount was available to shipping lines if they chose to bunker LNG in Rotterdam.

Throughout the development of the project, partners were in constant dialogue with existing and potential customers to understand their needs and their concerns. Their ambition was to ensure that LNG bunkering could take place in the same way as conventional oil-based bunkering and for Rotterdam to become an LNG bunkering hub.

Dealing with Market Uncertainty: Pro-active Risk Management and Building Optionality

Building a large-scale LNG bunkering solution in the early stages of market development meant that the partners needed to take on a significant amount of technical, commercial, and regulatory risk.

When Shell decided to make its investment in the Cardissa, it did not yet have customer demand secured. It would take 2 years to complete the third jetty and two and a half years to build the bunkering vessel. It managed this risk by designing a very flexible vessel as customer requirements were uncertain. Would they have atmospheric or pressurised tanks? Where will the bunker manifold be located? How big will they be? These were questions that came up time and time again. To minimise the technical risks associated with this new vessel type and the potential for delays, Shell chose to work with established OEMs (original equipment manufacturers) with whom it had good relationships.

If the GATE Terminal had taken the safe, 'utility approach' the third jetty would never have been built. However, GATE could not take all the investment risk, so agreed a contractual framework with Shell, where Shell committed to take the majority of the loading slots.

Given the market uncertainty, the jetty was also designed to be flexible with three loading arms. GATE needed to iterate the design with Shell and the rest of the market, informing everyone of what was possible and what were the associated costs. GATE's view was that it was all about creating optionality, for example the basin could accommodate 40,000 m^3 vessels but was at that time only dredged for 20,000 m^3; and GATE had the option to build a fourth jetty.

The other issue that the terminal had to manage was the 'fit' of the third jetty and related operations within the existing GATE set-up. It could not jeopardise what already existed at the terminal. For example, in developing potential solutions to deal with the boil-off gas associated with bunkering operations, GATE had to fit in with the existing customer contracts. GATE also had to fit into existing financial structures and contracts. GATE managed these issues by working with the existing bulk LNG customers and bankers, keeping them informed through a constant dialogue.

The absence of clear regulation, obtaining the required permits, and local community acceptance of LNG bunkering were other key project risks. The Port of Rotterdam had been pro-active in developing LNG bunkering regulations and accreditation, with an eye on the bigger picture of ensuring consistent regulation across ports in Europe and elsewhere. It made a big effort to inform stakeholders such as the local fire brigades and safety authorities and involve them from early in the process. This was also the case for developments on the seaside where the permitting authority is the port harbourmaster. Permits were also needed on the land side from the local authorities and the Port played a major role in communicating with local communities.

Case Study 2: Development of LNG Bunkering at the Port of Jacksonville

Background

The Port of Jacksonville (JAXPORT) is located in northeast Florida. It is a full-service, international trade seaport situated at the crossroads of the south-eastern USA's rail and highway network. The Port is a major gateway for cargo moving between the continental United States and the US territory of Puerto Rico.

In the space of just over 3 years, from 2013, Jacksonville went from a port with limited experience of LNG, no existing infrastructure, and a relatively small market in marine fuel bunkering, to become the leading LNG bunkering operation in the US and one of the first movers globally. This was the consequence of two shipping companies, first Tote Maritime followed by Crowley Maritime, entering into close collaborations, each independently, with energy suppliers to develop their own unique fuel supply chains to service their newbuild LNG-fuelled vessels.

The JAX LNG: Tote Maritime Collaboration

LNG bunkering began in Jacksonville on 9 January 2016 with the fuelling of the Isla Bella, one of two Marlin-class containerships—the world's first LNG-fuelled containerships—owned and operated by Tote Maritime. This was a key milestone for the port where Tote had worked with its supply chain partners JAX LNG, Clean Marine Energy (CME) and other commercial partners and stakeholders in a phased approach to develop LNG bunkering. This early LNG bunkering started with a truck-to-ship program in 2016, progressing to barge-to-ship bunkering in 2018.

The Project

In 2013, the Tote Maritime began planning for the development of their future fleet as part of a strategic approach for sustainable shipping and in anticipation of pending emissions regulations, namely the introduction of the North American and US Caribbean Emission Control Areas (ECAs) in 2012 and 2014 respectively.

Tote took the decision to initiate a newbuild programme to replace existing vessels in the Puerto Rico trade with the world's first LNG dual-fuelled container vessels. In making this decision, Tote recognised the need to establish a new supply chain for LNG bunker fuel in Jacksonville and to work with a variety of industry and regulatory stakeholders to ensure safe, compliant, and effective operations.

The LNG supplier Tote chose to work with was JAX LNG, which was at that time a partnership between Pivotal LNG, a wholly owned subsidiary of Atlanta Gas and Light, and NorthStar Midstream, LLC (a venture of Oaktree Capital).

JAX LNG constructed a state-of the art small-scale liquefaction facility and marine loading jetty at Dames Point, on the St. Johns River. This was North America's first small-scale waterfront LNG facility. The facility included on-road and marine-loading capabilities. In addition to servicing the marine sector the facility was also designed to provide LNG for rail, drilling, mining, trucking, power generation, commercial, and industrial markets through having truck loading capabilities.

JAX LNG's liquefaction facility came online in early 2018. A bunker barge, Clean Jacksonville, was designed and built to deliver LNG from JAX LNG to the Tote Marlin Class containerships weekly. The Clean Jacksonville was constructed by Conrad Shipyard and managed by a subsidiary of Tote Maritime, Tote Services. Prior to the commissioning of the Clean Jacksonville, JAX LNG delivered LNG to the Tote vessels by truck, utilising supply from their network of LNG plants in the southeast United States at Trussville Alabama and Macon Georgia. They conducted bunkering operations using an innovative custom-built skid-mounted cryogenic loading manifold, developed by Applied Cryogenic Technologies (ACT) of Houston, Texas. The skid system allowed four chassis-mounted ISO containers to simultaneously offload LNG to the Marlin Class Ships enabling 25 trailer loads of LNG to be transferred to the ships tanks in 5–6 h.

To develop bunkering infrastructure and the necessary safety management policies for LNG operations in Jacksonville, Tote and its partners committed to work closely with a variety of stakeholders. Early engagement with first responders, the regulators (the United States Coast Guard) and the Jacksonville Port Authority, JAXPORT, was vital as the concept of LNG bunkering while also simultaneously conducting cargo operations was novel. It was through rigorous operational risk analysis that mitigation strategies, safeguards, personnel training, and operational doctrine were established to ensure a safe and secure operation was achieved while maintaining simultaneous container operations.

The business partners, Tote and JAX LNG, spent considerable time building strong relationships with the Jacksonville Fire and Rescue Department to establish LNG handling and safety training, and liaising with local port and community stakeholders. They were joined in these endeavours by Crowley and their LNG partners, Eagle LNG. These strategic partnerships enabled success.

Leadership, Innovation and Communication

Tote's strategic decision to invest in and deploy LNG dual-fuel vessels in the Puerto Rico trade created a major incentive for infrastructure providers and suppliers to establish LNG bunkering in Jacksonville. From the outset, Tote took a leadership role in bringing together experienced suppliers for all aspects of the development from the design and building of the vessels to the creation of an LNG supply chain.

Engagement from senior leadership within the company—the CEO and executive team—was strong, as was the commitment from leadership in partner companies, the port authorities, and regulatory authorities. Strong, supportive leadership enabled innovation to flourish. This was evident in the interim skid loading system developed to speed up truck bunkering of the Tote containerships. It can also be seen in the design of the Clean Jacksonville bunker barge. The barge was built using GTT membrane technology, as opposed to the Type-C tanks that had previously been used in all bunker vessels. Also, it was designed with high levels of automation which resulted in significantly lower operating costs.

Transparency and early and continuous engagement with stakeholders were key in Jacksonville to secure effective collaboration. In the words of one of the partners "Come early, come often".

The Eagle LNG: Crowley Maritime Collaboration

The second LNG bunker supply chain in the Port of Jacksonville was developed by Eagle LNG in collaboration with Crowley Maritime. Crowley Maritime is one of the main providers of supply-chain solutions between the US Mainland and Puerto Rico and is headquartered in Jacksonsville, Florida. Eagle LNG is an energy company which develops fully integrated, small-scale LNG solutions focused on the marine, power generation, export, rail, and mining markets in the Caribbean and Latin America.

The Project

In December 2015, Crowley made the decision to partner with Eagle LNG as the LNG supplier for El Coquí and El Taino, the two new LNG powered, combination container—(ConRo) vessels scheduled to come into service in 2017 and 2018.

The supply chain consisted of two main assets developed by Eagle LNG. The first, the Maxville LNG plant which liquefies natural gas from the local grid in West Jacksonville; the second, an LNG fuel depot located within Crowley's Talleyrand Marine Terminal on the St. Johns River, with two LNG storage tanks. LNG was to be transported to the Talleyrand fuel depot by trucks from the Maxville LNG facility.

The storage tanks, supplied by Chart Industries, were at the time the largest located on a marine terminal (supporting vessel operations) anywhere in the world and represented a first for the maritime industry. They feature an inner shell to hold the product and an outer shell that is insulated and kept under vacuum, to keep the LNG cold. Each could hold 1000 m^3 of LNG. The tanks were fitted with two internal LNG pumps and each tank held sufficient product to fuel Crowley's two LNG powered vessels within an 8-h period.

The design of the Talleyrand LNG fuel depot was developed jointly by Eagle and Crowley's LNG engineers in consultation with JAXPORT, the U.S. Coast Guard and the Jacksonville Fire and Rescue Department. The new bunkering terminal utilised state-of-the art technology to allow safe and efficient transfer operations in a working cargo terminal while minimizing the overall terminal footprint. The LNG bunkering operation is performed by tank-to-ship transfer from the storage tanks and directly onto the vessel.

Partnerships and Risk Allocation

The guiding principle for Eagle's development of a marine supply chain was that LNG needed to end up being easier for the customer than traditional bunker fuel. For that to happen it is important that customers and partners choose experienced operators that are comfortable with all the regulations relating to LNG. Working with the right partners that have the required expertise from the outset meant that things happen on time and on budget.

One of the key challenges in creating LNG bunkering infrastructure was the need for harmonised investments and risk allocation throughout the value chain. Eagle brought to this challenge business models that involved various ranges of risk sharing. Potential market participants and investors are comfortable with the types of risks (pricing, contracts) they are used to. Usually, global LNG infrastructure developers and suppliers favour long term contracts, but that trend has been changing. A shipowner considering LNG or dual fuel engines for an upcoming newbuild does not want their fuel purchasing process to dramatically change. The LNG fuel supplier needs to ensure the fuel price is a transparent and predictable price with a commitment term that suits the needs of the customer. The Eagle LNG integrated business model considers the entire gas value chain with the risks being shared between partners. This approach is vital in the early stages of market development when infrastructure is scarce.

Lessons from LNG for the Introduction of Other Low- and Zero-Carbon Marine Fuels

Attention to LNG as a maritime fuel has taken off in the past decade thanks to local/global emissions concerns with associated regulatory developments and the actions of several trailblazing companies who have built workable commercial alignments. A number of lessons can be drawn from the first-mover experience of developing LNG bunkering which have relevance for other low and zero carbon marine fuels. There are certainly opportunities for forerunners to secure valuable competitive advantages but, in securing new opportunities, several challenges need to be addressed.

First Mover Challenges

The challenges energy suppliers and their partners faced can be broken down into technical, commercial, regulatory, and operational categories. These are discussed in the following sections, together with the potential solutions LNG first-movers used to address them.

Technical Challenges

Challenge	Solution
Delays and cost-overruns associated with new technologies and new value chains.	Work with established original equipment manufacturers (OEMs) with whom you have good relationships. Work with the right business partners who have the relevant experience. Avoid bleeding edge technology and focus on leading edge technologies that have a reasonable risk profile.

Commercial Challenges

Challenge	Solution
Buyer—seller disconnect: ship operators/charterers prefer to buy fuel on a spot basis; fuel suppliers and infrastructure developers look for long term agreements to underpin investments.	Careful risk allocation between project partners. Investors need to understand market differences and adjust their risk profiles. Involvement of anchor customers, typically those operating on liner routes.
Uncertainty in type of customer demand (vessel type) to be serviced.	Build flexibility and optionality into fuel bunkering vessels and associated infrastructure, such as jetties.

Regulatory Challenges

Challenge	Solution
Absence of clear regulations for bunkering of new fuels.	Engage early, transparently, and frequently with port authorities, first responders (fire brigades and safety authorities) and local and national maritime law enforcement agencies, involving them in the project. Take a pro-active approach in influencing the development of bunkering regulations and guidelines.

Operational Challenges

Challenge	Solution
Operational risk, especially relating to simultaneous operations.	Undertake rigorous operational risk analysis to develop mitigation strategies, including safeguards, personnel training, and operational doctrine to ensure safe and secure operations.

Underpinning all this is the need for:

- strategic alignment and close collaboration between energy suppliers, infrastructure providers port authorities and regulators;
- senior leadership commitment in partnership companies which enables innovation to flourish; and
- stakeholder engagement—early, continuous, and transparent engagement with local port and regional communities to address safety concerns relating to the supply and usage of new fuels.

First-Mover Opportunities

For the maritime energy transition to accelerate, more energy suppliers are needed who are prepared to be forerunners. This means companies who understand the associated risk-reward profiles and also policy-makers and regulators who are willing and able to provide long term incentives and stable regulatory frameworks.

Business-school textbooks teach us that front runners, or first movers, typically benefit from the following competitive advantages:

- Strong brand recognition
- Technology leadership
- Control of resources

These competitive advantages typically translate into higher rewards for first movers after an initial period of them accepting higher or less-familiar risks.

Brand Recognition

Early-mover energy suppliers should be able to capture high value, anchor customers—early adopters of low and zero carbon fuels on the shipping side who are also seeking to capture their own early-mover advantages. Early operational experience gained should also position them to establish a reputation for safety and reliability. This is important as many of the new fuels will present significant safety challenges for crews and port communities. All this should help with long term customer growth and retention as and when the market for these new fuels develops.

Related to brand recognition, first movers will be positioned to help set industry standards, shaping bunkering regulations and guidelines.

Technology Leadership

In terms of supplying low- and zero-carbon marine fuels, technology leadership relates primarily to two areas. First, leadership in the end-to-end supply chain for those fuels. This includes production, transportation, and storage technologies for advanced biofuels and for electro-fuels. Second, leadership in complex project integration will be necessary to bring the fuels safely and securely from production sites to delivery at the vessel flange.

Control of Resources

Analysis by UMAS (UMAS and UNCCHLC, 2022) estimates that if shipping is to decarbonize in line with the IMO's Initial GHG Strategy ambitions for 2050, the total additional capital required will be between US$1.0 and $1.4 trillion. The biggest share of these investments, more than 80%, will be needed in the land-based infrastructure and production facilities for low and zero carbon fuels. First movers should be able to gain access to 'scarce resources' such as the best sites for fuel storage and bunkering infrastructure in key bunkering ports; jetty capacity; and also advantaged fuel production sites and transportation routes.

Looking Forward

The Pathway(s)

It is likely that maritime decarbonization will require a basket of fuelling solutions depending on vessel operations, trade routes and the different markets served. This is the case today as different vessels use marine diesel, marine gasoil, heavy fuel oil, low sulphur fuel oils and LNG depending on environmental and commercial factors. LNG makes a valuable contribution to reducing emissions, but the full transition from fossil and fossil-based fuels is likely to start with a scaling up of biofuels (bio-oils and bio-methanol) and biogas (biomethane and, in its liquefied form, bioLNG). The technologies to produce these are generally mature and the costs relatively low, compared with other alternative fuels and, importantly, they can be used as drop-in fuels in existing oil and LNG fuelled vessels. Availability of sustainable biomass is a challenge, but this is often exaggerated, particularly in the case of bioLNG.

Longer term, as renewable electricity production continues, its exponential growth curve and its costs fall, along with the costs of electrolysis, it is likely that electro-fuels, such as e-LNG, e-methanol, e-ammonia and e-hydrogen will become dominant.

The Companies

The companies involved in developing and supplying these low and zero-carbon fuels include the traditional energy companies involved in marine fuel bunkering, for example major integrated oil and gas companies such as CEPSA, CNOOC, Petronas, Repsol, Shell and TotalEnergies and independent bunker suppliers such as Peninsula and World Fuel Services.

LNG has seen the emergence of new entrants into the bunkering business. These include State- and privately-owned gas companies, such as Eagle LNG, Elenger, Gasum, JAX LNG, KOGAS, Pavilion Energy; joint ventures between shipping and energy companies, such as Japan's CLMF and Ecobunker; and new, specialist independent bunker suppliers, for example Titan and ProBunkers.

Many of these companies, and specialist providers such as Titan and GoodFuels have made significant investments in bio-oils and bioLNG which are already commercially available. The growing interest in electro-fuels has resulted in project announcements from power utilities such as EDF Energy and Iberdrola; renewable electricity producers including Vestas and Ørsted; and renewable fuels producers and consortia, for example WasteFuels, SunGas Renewables, Liquid Wind and MarHySafe.

Other new entrants include fertilizer manufacturers such as Yara and Fertiberia who are looking to green their traditional ammonia products and looking to expand into other adjacent markets such as power generation and marine fuels.

The Strategies

Notwithstanding their significant LNG, bio-oil and bioLNG investments, faced with the uncertainties of the ultimate fuel destinations, timing and a host of technology, regulatory and commercial risks, most energy companies have so far generally adopted a cautious, 'wait-and-see' strategy of R&D, participation in industry coalitions and green corridors.

R&D

Some of the larger energy companies, such as Shell and TotalEnergies, are collaborating with industry and academic partners from around the world, to undertake research into a variety of biofuels and electro-fuels including e-LNG, e-methanol, e-ammonia and e-hydrogen. They are also looking closely at other technologies such as carbon capture and storage with a view to ensuring these can develop at pace as market conditions emerge. The application of these fuel solutions will centre on pilots, which are designed to demonstrate the capability of new vessels using these fuels.

Industry Coalitions

A number of major energy companies have been involved in setting up and funding coalitions focused on maritime decarbonization. These enable them to understand

and help shape the overall maritime decarbonization process and offer opportunities to develop strategic partnerships with different companies from across the maritime value chain. These coalitions include:

- The **Getting to Zero Coalition**: an alliance of more than 200 companies and organisations within the maritime, energy, infrastructure, and finance sectors, supported by key governments and inter-governmental organisations (IGOs). The Coalition is committed to getting commercially viable deep sea zero emission vessels powered by zero emission fuels into operation by 2030 leading to full decarbonization by 2050.
- The **Mærsk Mc-Kinney Møller Center for Zero Carbon Shipping**: a not-for-profit, independent research and development centre looking to accelerate the transition towards a net-zero future for the maritime industry.
- The **Global Centre for Maritime Decarbonisation:** a Singaporean based non-profit organisation which supports decarbonization of the maritime industry to meet or exceed the IMO goals for 2030 and 2050.

Green Corridors

Green shipping corridors, specific trade routes between major port hubs where zero-emission solutions are supported, while a relatively new concept, are increasingly viewed as an essential tool to kick-start shipping's transition to zero emissions. Since the signing of the Clydebank Declaration at the 26th United Nations Framework Convention on Climate Change (COP26) in 2021, more than 20 initiatives have emerged around the world (Getting to Zero Coalition and Global Maritime Forum, 2022). It is critical that port authorities, key players in the maritime energy transition, partner with suppliers in these initiatives.

Energy suppliers are involved in the following Green Corridors:

- Antwerp-Montreal North Atlantic green shipping corridor—Greenfield Global
- Clean Tyne Shipping Corridor—EDF Energy
- Decatrip Green Corridor—Kempower
- Gothenburg-Rotterdam Green Corridor—Ørsted and Liquid Wind
- Green Corridors Spain—Fertiberia
- Rotterdam-Algeciras Green Corridor—CEPSA
- Singapore-Rotterdam Green Corridor—BP and Shell

Many of these corridors are in the very early stages of development and it is likely that more energy companies will participate as they mature and discussions progress with shipping operators.

Concluding Remarks

An increasing number of energy supply companies are already becoming active in developing the alternative fuels ecosystems for the maritime industry and working with others to do this. Nevertheless, more first-movers or front runners will be required to accelerate progress in emerging areas, building on the positive experiences and lessons that can be drawn from the LNG arena which is already growing significantly. Some of these experiences and lessons have been described in this chapter, and extra encouragement for shifting from 'wait and see' approaches to 'early-mover' strategies may be found in the competitive value dynamics outlined in Bentham (2023).

References

Bentham, J. B. (2023). How to drive and use scenario thinking (to build business advantages that accelerate decarbonisation). In M. Lind, W. Lehmacher, & R. Ward (Eds.), *Maritime decarbonization – Practical tools, case studies and decarbonization enablers*. Springer.

Clarksons Research. (2023). *World fleet register*. https://www.clarksons.com/research/

DNV. (2023). *Alternative fuels insight (AFI) platform*. https://www.dnv.com/services/alternative-fuels-insight-128171

Getting to Zero Coalition and Global Maritime Forum. (2022). *Annual progress report on green shipping corridors*. https://cms.globalmaritimeforum.org/wp-content/uploads/2022/11/The-2022-Annual-Progress-Report-on-Green-Shipping-Corridors.pdf

Shell Global. (2023). *Energy and innovation, natural gas LNG for transport, LNG for marine*. https://www.shell.com/energy-and-innovation/natural-gas/lng-for-transport/lng-for-marine.html

UMAS and UNCCHLC (UN Climate Change High Level Champions). (2022). *Climate action in shipping, progress towards shipping's 2023 breakthrough*. https://climatechampions.unfccc.int/wp-content/uploads/2022/09/GTZ_ClimateActionInShipping.pdf

Decarbonization Support from Digital Solutions Providers

Pekka Pakkanen and Roberto Vettor

Target Audience

- Shipping companies and charterers: technical and sustainability managers, ship Captains and officers
- Ports: strategy and innovation managers, safety, protection, and environment managers
- Governmental bodies: policymakers

Key Takeaway Messages

- Digital tools support the maritime industry in reducing greenhouse gas (GHG) emissions by enabling: operations monitoring and reporting, voyage optimisation, fleet allocation and schedule optimisation, port call optimisation, energy efficient ship design, and monitoring the cost and supply of alternative fuels.
- International regulations targeting improvements in ship operations (such as the International Maritime Organization (IMO) Carbon Intensity Indicator (CII)) are fostering the adoption of technological solutions and collaborative approaches to the decarbonization challenge.
- While energy efficiency measures and transition to alternative fuels can have a global impact in the long term, operational measures are mandatory to reach the mid-term decarbonization targets

P. Pakkanen (✉) · R. Vettor
NAPA, Helsinki, Finland
e-mail: pekka.pakkanen@napa.fi; roberto.vettor@napa.fi

M. Lind et al. (eds.), *Maritime Decarbonization*,
https://doi.org/10.1007/978-3-031-39936-7_29

- Availability of Automatic Identification System (AIS) data, improved weather forecasting models, and cloud computing have enabled much of the technology required for operational efficiency optimisation, but also business model and process changes are needed to obtain the full benefits.

Introduction

The International Maritime Organization (IMO) has ambitions to reduce CO_2 emissions across international shipping by at least 40% by 2030, pursuing efforts towards 70% by 2050, compared to 2008; and that total annual GHG emissions from international shipping should be reduced by at least 50% by 2050 compared to 2008 (IMO, 2023). This is an ambitious target which requires the reduction of emissions from the existing fleet by improving operational efficiency and adopting new technologies.

The IMO ambitions are, however, still far below what is needed to meet the target agreed in Paris in 2015 at the 21st UN Climate Change Conference (COP21) to limit the global temperature increase to no more than 1.5 °C. The path we should be on requires a net zero ambition by 2050 and a finite emission budget until then. Over 50% of the emissions budget for shipping is expected to be spent in this decade, long before zero fuels become available at any meaningful scale. Thus, today's fleet will be releasing the vast majority of those emissions and it is not enough to consider only CO_2 emissions, but rather all greenhouse gases. So, unless we reduce GHG emissions from today's fleet, there is no hope of meeting the 1.5 °C target. This is indicated in Fig. 1.

There are several key strategies for removing GHG emissions from the existing fleet, including:

- Transitioning to alternative fuels, such as biofuels, ammonia, hydrogen, and methanol, or electrifying ships using battery or fuel cell technology.
- Energy efficiency measures: Improving the energy efficiency of ships through hull design optimisation, engine upgrades, waste heat recovery, and installation of other energy-saving devices.
- Operational optimisation: Reducing emissions through more efficient voyage planning, speed reduction, and improved fleet management.

While there are various options for decarbonization, the industry faces several challenges, including:

- Lack of infrastructure for alternative fuels: Alternative fuels require dedicated infrastructure for production, distribution, and storage, which may not yet exist in many regions.
- High capital costs of energy-saving devices and other retrofits: many decarbonization technologies are still in the early stages of development, and the upfront costs of implementing them can be significant.

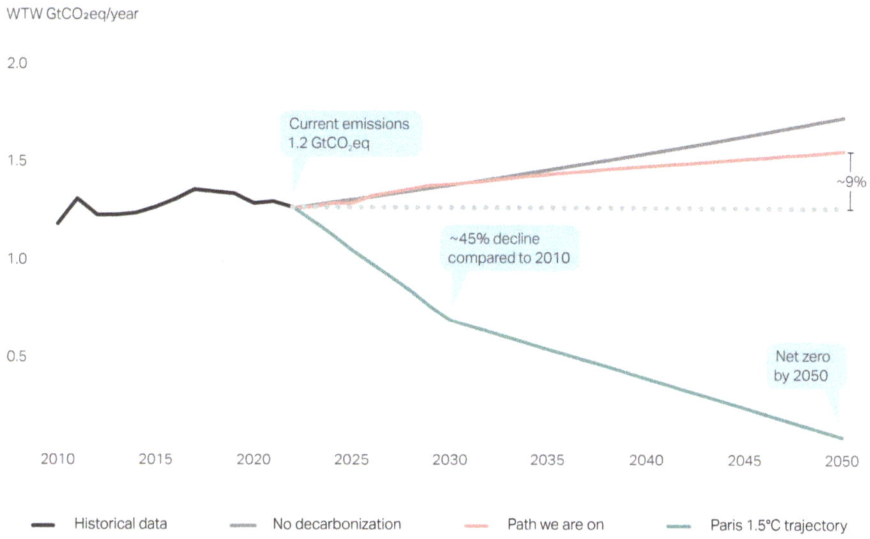

Fig. 1 Historical and predicted emissions between 2010 and 2050 (Source: Mærsk Mc-Kinney Møller Center for Zero Carbon Shipping, 2022)

- The maritime industry is slow in changing the way it operates. Operational optimisation could be supported by digitalisation, but the maritime industry is lagging behind other industries on this. Although the majority of industry professionals have a clear understanding of why digitalisation is needed, why it is a positive thing for the industry, and what the benefits are, there is still resistance to change. A report published by Wärtsilä, a Finnish company which manufactures and services power sources and other equipment in the marine and energy markets, States that almost half of their respondents admitted to having a volatile attitude toward technology and over a third said they are actively resistant to change (Wärtsilä, 2023).

The optimisation of shipping requires changes in processes and training for personnel. This does not require any investment in new fuels, retrofits, or other physical devices. The changes are ultimately undertaken by shipping companies and ships' crews, but many of them can be supported, enhanced or enabled by digitalisation and automations. A report in 2022 by maritime innovation consultancy, Thetius (Kenney & Brunton, 2022) estimates that digital tools for decarbonization offer the best value for money. Decarbonizing maritime transportation is estimated to cost approximately $1.9 trillion. At a small fraction of the cost, the digital optimisation of conventional assets could deliver up to 38% of the GHG emission target by 2050. In addition to being the best value for money, optimising the use of existing assets is vital if the Paris Agreement target of no more than a global 1.5 °C temperature increase is to be achieved.

Improvements in operational efficiency is the most realistic and effective supplement to the needed and urgent GHG reductions.

There are several digital tools on the market that can be used to reduce GHG emissions from maritime shipping. These tools can be broadly divided into six groupings:

- **Monitoring and reporting tools**: tools that allow shipping companies to monitor and track their GHG emissions, as well as report on their progress in reducing emissions. This can help to increase transparency and accountability, as well as identify areas where further emission reductions can be made.
- **Voyage optimisation tools**: these tools use data on vessel performance, fuel consumption, and other factors to help shipping companies optimise their routes and reduce fuel consumption. This can help to reduce greenhouse gas emissions from shipping by reducing the distance travelled and the amount of fuel consumed.
- **Fleet location and schedule optimisation tools**: optimising the location and schedule of fleets can help improve vessel utilisation rates, which means that vessels spend more time carrying cargo and less time waiting for cargo or traveling empty. This can reduce costs and improve overall efficiency. Optimising the schedules of fleets can help to maximise ton-mile and reduce idling times for vessels, which can improve efficiency and reduce costs.
- **Port call optimisation tools**: these tools aim at fighting the inefficient 'sail fast, then wait' practice by orchestrating the traffic heading to the ports and optimising intermodal transportation links. These tools can be driven by port authorities with local scope, or independent entities and collaborative agreements among stakeholders. This can help in reducing average sailing speeds, maintaining an even speed profile along the voyage and minimising waiting time, thus reducing emissions on passage and pollution in the port areas.
- **Ship design tools**: software used to design vessels that are more energy efficient, for example by incorporating features such as energy-efficient lighting and insulation, as well as using materials that are more thermally efficient. The same tools can be used to simulate the benefit of various energy saving devices, and lifecycle analysis of emissions of various designs of new ships.
- **Tools to monitor supply and cost of low carbon marine fuels**: these tools enable vessels equipped with next-generation dual-fuel engines to make the best use of their design, support the development of a sustainable fuel chain, and foster wider adoption of new technologies, thereby supporting the maritime industry towards zero emissions targets.

Maritime software vendors have been providing digital solutions for optimising the designs of ships and the operation of ships for a long time. In the last two decades the availability of computational power, bandwidth, and AIS data from ships has accelerated the possibilities for providing and using such tools. As seen in Fig. 2, since, 2010, the number of companies in this domain has quadrupled.

Although the market has been providing more solutions for the last decade, a large part of dry and wet bulk transportation is still not applying best practices for operational efficiency. Fleet operational optimisation strategies are not widely used, as can be seen in Fig. 3.

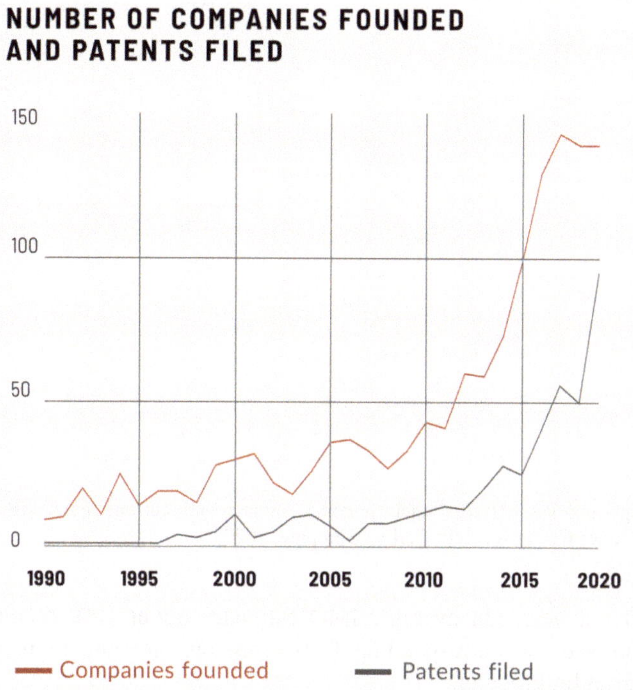

Fig. 2 Number of maritime digital solution companies funded and patent filed in the field (Source: Kenney M. and Brunton L., 2022)

In the following sections, we explore some of the software tools and projects that are available on the market and explore the applicability and impact of these.

Performance Monitoring

Performance monitoring of ships is used to assess the efficiency and emissions performance of a vessel over time. The main purpose of this is to ensure that a vessel performs as intended and to identify optimisation possibilities in the use of the vessel. The performance monitoring activity involves collecting data on a range of operational parameters, such as fuel consumption, speed, cargo load, weather conditions, and engine performance, and analysing this data and producing output that is fit for a specific purpose.

The most significant uncertainty in vessel performance is the fouling and roughness of the hull. The ship's drag resistance might, but does not necessarily, grow at

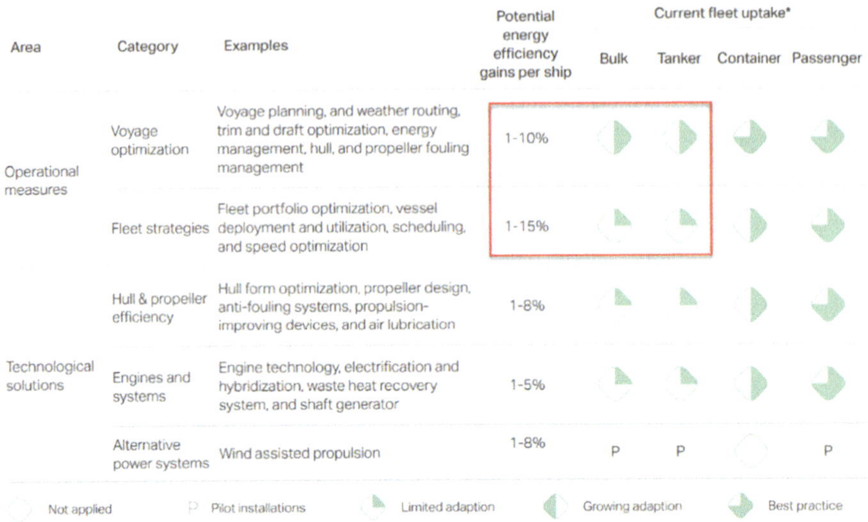

Fig. 3 Energy efficiency levers, their potential impact and current uptake (Source: Mærsk Mc-Kinney Møller Center for Zero Carbon Shipping, 2022)

about 7–10% a year. On average, IMO estimates about 10% of maritime fuel consumption and the corresponding CO_2 emissions are due to increased drag resistance from hull fouling.

Performance monitoring data is also used to identify situations where a vessel is operated in an inefficient manner, for example when unexplained speed changes are made, or when multiple auxiliary engines are running when one engine would be sufficient to produce the required energy.

In addition to achieving cost savings and lower emissions via better use of the vessel and lower fuel consumption, performance monitoring is also used for achieving reporting compliance; performance monitoring can help ensure compliance with regulations and standards related to emissions and efficiency, such as for the IMO Ship Energy Efficiency Management Plan (SEEMP); and the European Union (EU) Monitoring Reporting and Verification (MRV), and the IMO CII reporting schemes; and input to the IMO Data Collection System (DCS).

Regulatory reporting is mandatory for all vessels; sometimes it done with well-collected data, which can then also be also used for analysing the performance of a vessel, but with poorly collected data that is not validated properly, the only use is to fulfill the regulatory requirements—though not very well.

Some shipping companies collect performance data with their own in-house reports and have marine engineers responsible for monitoring the data; other companies use solutions from performance monitoring software vendors such as NAPA, and others.

Overall, performance monitoring of ships is an important tool for improving the sustainability and competitiveness of the shipping industry. It can help vessel

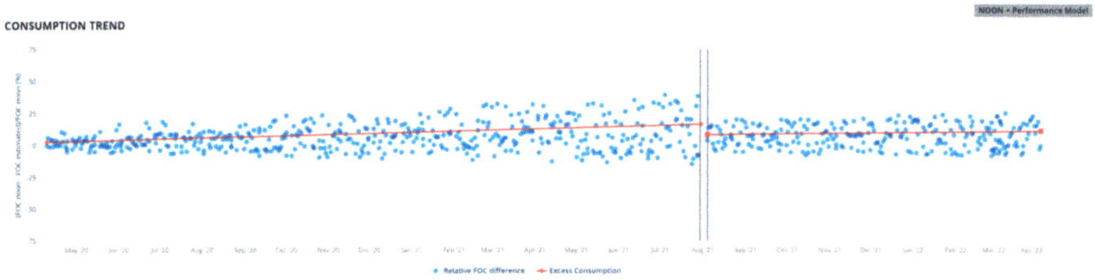

Fig. 4 Hull fouling chart from NAPA Fleet Intelligence (Source: NAPA, 2023)

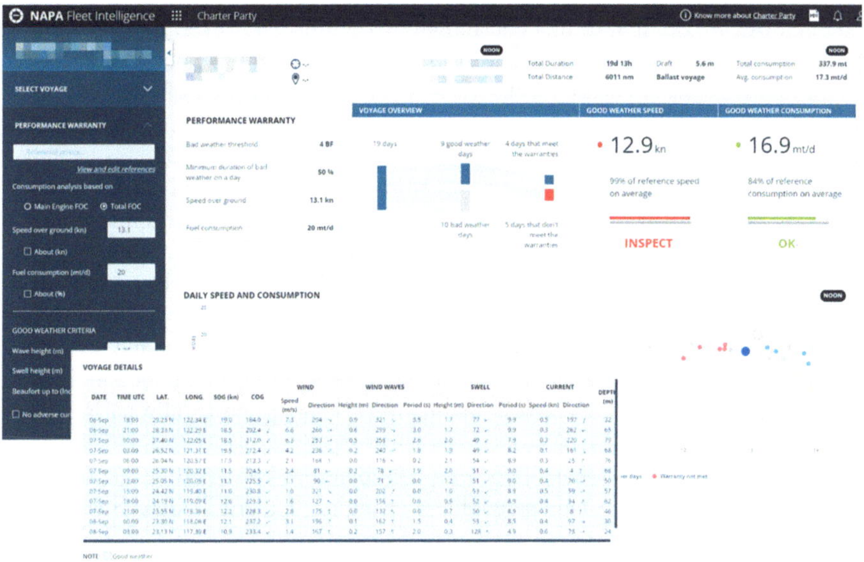

Fig. 5 Example of performance monitoring view from NAPA Fleet Intelligence (Source: NAPA, 2023) used to analyse the fuel consumption against the charter party performance warranties

operators optimise operations, reduce costs, and improve environmental performance, while also supporting compliance with regulations and standards.

Performance monitoring is applicable to all shipping segments. Reporting the data on a voyage level is mandatory, and thus all shipping companies collect the data in at least some form. Many companies are now using that collected data for performance analysis. The performance analysis for shipping companies can mean evaluating the current performance against a technical benchmark, or against the performance warranties of time charter parties. Examples of these are shown in Figs. 4 and 5.

Voyage Optimisation

Since humans started sailing the oceans selecting the most favourable route has been among the greatest challenges before any voyage. For centuries avoiding dangerous conditions and enjoying favourable winds and currents has been crucial for wind-propelled vessels, relying on experience handed down from one generation to another.

Starting with the first industrial revolution, steamships gave greater flexibility to seafarers, and weather routing was mostly limited to storm advice services. In the second half of the twentieth century, the era of automation and computers offered new opportunities to optimise voyages and several algorithms have been developed to minimise arrival time or fuel consumption. Their use, however, remained mostly restricted to shore-based centres and storm avoidance recommendations.

In the twenty-first century, both research and the application of weather routing has experienced increased attention as evidenced by the number of publications on the subject, as shown in Fig. 6.

The research community has developed more complex optimisation processes, such as adopting 3D dynamic programming and genetic algorithms, aimed at identifying the optimal trade-off between competing objectives, such as safety, cost and scheduling, and accounting for uncertainties. Industry seeks to take advantage of the scalability of the latest optimisation software solutions by moving beyond ship safety as the baseline to now also consider cost/fuel reduction and scheduling compliance. Machine Learning techniques are gaining momentum, though the huge amount of information collected in the maritime industry on a daily basis remains largely unexploited.

The shipping industry has often been considered as conservative towards technological improvements. This paradigm is changing. Experienced shipmasters still

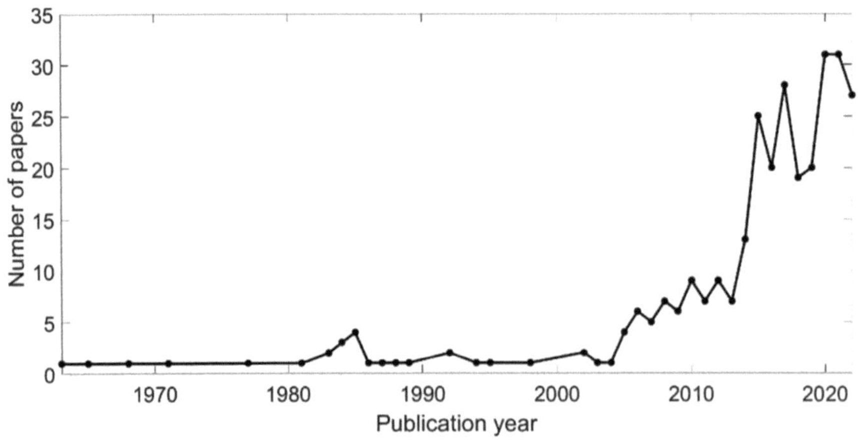

Fig. 6 Publishing trend in the area of ship weather routing and voyage optimisation (Source: Scopus December 2022)

play an irreplaceable role in planning a voyage, but intuitive user interfaces, cloud computing and comparative studies are clearly showing that a comprehensive appreciation of all the available information regarding all weather factors and ship performance in different loading, fouling and environmental conditions, is beyond human effort. Even the most knowledgeable and experienced seafarers can reduce their time spent optimising a route and focus on the other vital tasks for which their attention is regularly required onboard.

Ensuring a positive impact on commercial performance and the environmental footprint places integrated weather routing at the forefront in the green transition. Contrary to other technologies, supporting voyage planning decisions with data driven solutions promises an immediate impact without significant capital investment and is applicable to any vessel, newbuilt or existing, and any fuel type or propulsion system.

Consequently, voyage optimisation has multiple benefits and no envisaged disadvantages. It is an extremely cost-effective way to reduce operating costs, improve safety, control and minimise delays, and meet decarbonization targets. It allows industry to start decarbonizing today, and it will become even more critical with the adoption of alternative fuels, for which any saving is precious as they are often characterised by lower energy densities and higher costs, and are essential for more novel propulsion configurations, such as wind propulsion systems.

An example of a weather-optimised route across the Atlantic is shown in Fig. 7.

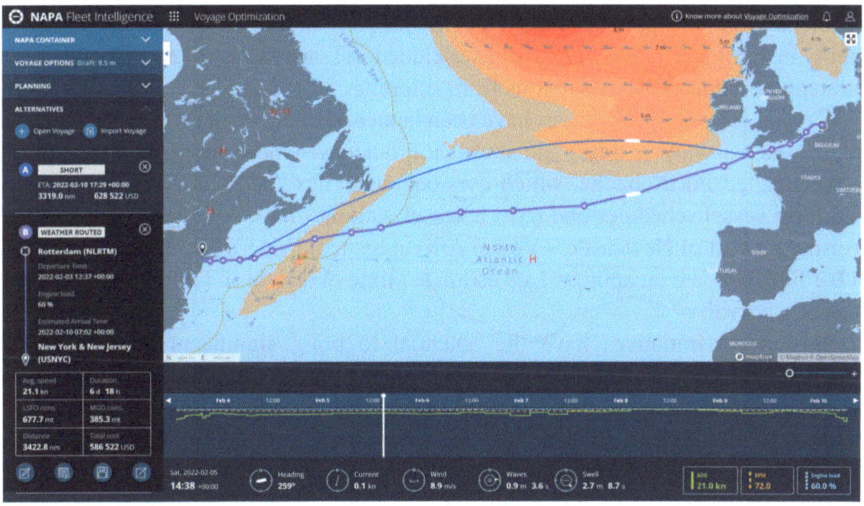

Fig. 7 The difference between the shortest navigable (blue) and a weather optimised route (purple) (Source: NAPA, 2023)

Just-in-Time Arrival, Virtual Arrival, Blue Visby

Currently, most shipping sectors suffer from the lack of coordination for arrival times at ports (Lind et al., 2020), causing ships to wait at an anchorage or loiter offshore (IMO, 2020). In some shipping sectors, this is caused by poor port logistics optimisation and information flow not being automated. In other sectors, contractual incentives discourage coordination and cooperation between competing services. During 2020, ships spent an average of 5–10% of their time waiting for berthing availability. This statistic includes time spent at anchorage, and in the common practice of loitering at very slow speeds in the vicinity of congested ports. Around 70% of shipping is related to wet and dry bulk cargoes (such as, grain, coal, crude oil, coal.). These market sectors also suffer from the longest waiting times, with the average ship spending 8–10% of its time at anchor.

Just-in-time (JIT) arrival is an initiative in the shipping industry that aims to reduce vessel waiting times and optimise vessel speed to achieve more efficient and sustainable operations. There are various studies that indicate that the practice of ships waiting excessive times at an anchorage is the most significant individual operational inefficiency in shipping. JIT arrival involves coordinating vessel schedules and port operations to ensure that vessels arrive at the port just in time to begin loading or unloading, rather than waiting in an anchorage or offshore for extended periods of time.

The JIT arrival concept was first introduced in the early 2000s, but it has gained traction in recent years as a key strategy for reducing emissions and improving efficiency in the shipping industry. The initiative is supported by various organizations, including the IMO, which has included JIT arrival as a key element in its strategy to reduce GHG emissions from shipping.

Several JIT arrival initiatives have been launched in different parts of the world to reduce vessel waiting times and improve efficiency. One example is Rotterdam's project called PortXchange, which uses data analytics and predictive modelling to optimise vessel schedules and reduce vessel waiting times. Another example is the Australian port of Newcastle's Vessel Arrival System (VAS), which assigns vessels a berthing slot and an approximate estimated time of arrival (ETA) 10 days before a vessel's arrival.

JIT arrival initiatives have the potential to bring significant benefits to the shipping industry, including reduced fuel consumption and emissions, improved vessel utilisation, and reduced waiting times and congestion in ports. However, implementation can be challenging, as it requires coordination between multiple stakeholders, including shipping companies, port authorities, and terminal operators. Another obstacle is that the thousands of ports and terminals in the world are all in different phases of their digitalisation, and some might not be ready for optimisation for a long time. Due to these challenges, although just-in-time arrival solutions can be implemented in individual ports, wide implementation is seen as problematic and slow and thus not likely to provide major improvements from a maritime decarbonization perspective for some time.

During 2022, a new collaborative project called Blue Visby Solution was announced. The Blue Visby Solution (BVS) is a technological and contractual platform, which aims to eradicate the practice of ships sailing fast only to wait at anchor. The BVS adopts a collaborative approach, which both alleviates the factors that entrench the practice and tackles many of the barriers faced by other proposed solutions to date. The initiative differs from others by including a collaborative framework and contractual architecture.

Blue Visby combines a contractual framework with state-of-the-art digital technology to help the industry collaborate to optimise and stagger arrival times for groups of vessels travelling to the same port. Taking into consideration parameters such as the performance and characteristics of each vessel, port congestion at the destination, and weather conditions, the Blue Visby algorithm provides an optimal target arrival time for each vessel, while keeping their order of arrival as if they had sailed independently without the solution. This enables vessels to travel more often at optimal speeds, cutting their fuel consumption and emissions, but still "keep their place in the queue" and arrive one after the other, which reduces unnecessary waiting times outside ports.

As opposed to JIT arrivals, Blue Visby does not require ports to develop complex queuing systems and handle communication with vessels. Instead, it solves the problem by enabling vessels to proactively collaborate to stagger their arrivals. While JIT arrivals typically see ships receive notice in the last days of their voyage (typically 24–48 h before arrival) about their expected berth availability, Blue Visby goes beyond that by providing vessels with a recommended arrival time as soon as they start their voyage. The recommended arrival time is updated and refined throughout the journey as more detailed information becomes available. Having a target arrival time early in their journey, while also having the assurance that their place in the queue is kept, enables crews to sail more slowly and optimise their routes to reduce emissions—which is key to unlocking the full benefits of weather routing, for example.

For the shipping industry, Blue Visby is an example of collaboration in practice, showing how the different stakeholders involved in a voyage, but also competitors, can come together to achieve the common goal of reducing GHG emissions from shipping.

Future-Proofing a Ship Design During the Conceptual Design Phase

Over the last century ship design has progressively evolved from an experience-based to a simulation-based process (Nowacki, 2010). This change in approach has been enabled by the advances and integration of computer-based tools that complement the knowledge and skills of the designers. This has enabled ship design to match the fast-paced demand created by new technologies. Innovation is also stimulated, allowing experimentation with different solutions in a parametric optimisation loop.

Future-proofing allows designers to account for the evolving regulatory framework and market needs, and technological progress (DNV, 2022). For example, the international regulation path points towards a decarbonization of the maritime industry and is rapidly integrating design verification standards, such as the Energy Efficiency Design Index (EEDI), with operational indicators, such as the Carbon Intensity Indicator (CII). In this context, the ability to account for the actual weather and operational conditions and to integrate innovative propulsion systems will result in a competitive vessel design that reduces the possibility of incurring penalties or operational restrictions.

Digitalisation and the possibility to effectively handle a large amount of data is the lifeblood of future-proofed design. Integration of different digital services in a coherent design process, including, but not limited to, computer assisted design (CAD), computational fluid dynamics (CFD), finite element method (FEM) design, manufacturing, administrative and lifecycle management tools, led to an increasingly holistic decision-making process. The Holiship ((HOLIstic optimisation of SHIP design and operation for life-cycle) Project, made up of a team of European leaders from the maritime industry, research and academia, is an example (Holiship, 2023). Development cost and time could not be kept in a sustainable range without integrated digital tools; errors and incongruences are promptly detected and resolutions properly tracked.

Digitalisation has also contributed to moving both design practices and regulatory requirements towards a probabilistic approach that accounts for uncertainties and establishes a more realistic basis to define critical design aspects, but it also enabled the more accurate simulation of discrete events, such as flooding simulations (Ruponen et al., 2022).

Holistic and future-proofed ship design accelerates the adoption of innovative technologies such as:

- Advanced and alternative propulsion systems such as hybrid engines, wind assisted propulsion, and solar panels, to reduce dependency on carbon fuels and improve efficiency.
- The use of advanced materials in ship building such as carbon composite and aluminium, to reduce cost and weight and increase resistance and structural life.
- The development of autonomous and unmanned vessels thanks to digital testing of system integration and navigation systems.
- Operational based design optimising hulls for actual operational conditions through simulation in realistic virtual environments.

Collaboration among stakeholders to standardise processes and mutually benefit of design and operational data is unlocking new ways to exploit the potential of digital tools and data-based decisions. In this regards digitisation of design documentation enables a transparent, smooth and flawless process of verification and inspection, increasing maritime safety. The creation of the Open Class 3D Exchange (OCX) standard is an example of this interoperability of modern design data (OCX, 2023).

Several commercial initiatives have been promoted gathering the expertise and interest of different stakeholders including shipbuilding, shipping companies and classification societies, to foster efficiency, safety and sustainability in ship design. Some examples are the Lloyd's Register's Maritime Decarbonization Hub or Wärtsilä's Smart Marine Ecosystem.

The multiple benefits of future-proofed ship design can be summarised in greater control and transparency over a vessel's lifecycle, improved safety and efficiency, reduced environmental impact and increased competitiveness both in the design and in the operational phases.

Closing Remarks

The global maritime industry is facing an urgent need to reduce emissions in order to combat the climate crisis. To achieve this goal, all actors operating in the maritime ecosystem must adopt a multifaceted approach that includes innovative solutions from the time a vessel is conceptualised all the way through its operation, so as to enable the regular and eventually continuous use of the low or no carbon fuels of the future and use them in the most efficient manner.

However, the oceans are used by over 50,000 merchant vessels, most of which are characterised by traditional hull forms and propulsion systems, with still a long-life expectancy. Operational measures such as performance monitoring and voyage optimisation then become fundamental to meeting the decarbonization targets in the transition towards the next generation world fleet, and will maintain their critical role with the advent of alternative fuels due to their higher cost and lower energy densities. Port call optimisation approaches, such as *just-in-time* and *virtual arrival*, has raised great interest in the last decade, however they have so far failed in achieving their promised impact on a global scale, remaining so far confined to a few innovative ports.

The maritime industry is being asked to collaborate and team up to turn operational optimisation initiatives into scalable and impactful actions through smart and mutually favourable cooperation. Technology is ready, and initiatives like Blue Visby show that many stakeholders are eager to play their role when a viable and effective way to improve becomes reality.

Although there are hurdles to overcome, technology and digital solutions are now available, enabling data sharing, transparency, awareness, and decision support in an integrated approach which is the only way to successfully tackle the challenges. Rather than a limitation, the required actions are an opportunity that will enable the players who invest in innovation to contribute towards decarbonization of the industry, gain competitive advantage, and at the same time overcome the traditional maritime market paradigms.

References

DNV. (2022). *Maritime forecast to 2050.* https://www.dnv.com/maritime/publications/maritime-forecast-2022/index.html

Holiship. (2023). http://www.holiship.eu

IMO. (2020). *Just In time arrival guide barriers and potential solutions.* https://greenvoyage2050.imo.org/wp-content/uploads/2021/01/GIA-just-in-time-hires.pdf

IMO. (2023). *Initial IMO GHG strategy.* https://www.imo.org/en/MediaCentre/HotTopics/Pages/Reducing-greenhouse-gas-emissions-from-ships.aspx

Kenney, M., & Brunton, L. (2022). *THE OPTIMAL ROUTE. The why and how of digital decarbonisation in shipping.* https://thetius.com/wp-content/uploads/2022/04/Inmarsat_Thetius_Digital_Decarbonisation_Report_2022.pdf.gc_.pdf

Lind, M., Ward, R., Bergmann, M., Haraldson, S., Zerem, A., & Hoffmann, J. (2020). *Digitalizing the port call process, TRANSPORT AND TRADE FACILITATION, series no 13. 10.13140/RG.2.2.33562.26568.*

Mærsk Mc-Kinney Møller Center for Zero Carbon Shipping. (2022). *Maritime decarbonization strategy 2022.* https://cms.zerocarbonshipping.com/media/uploads/publications/Maritime-Decarbonization-Strategy-2022.pdf

NAPA. (2023). *NAPA fleet intelligence monitoring and analysis modules.* https://www.napa.fi/software-and-services/ship-operations/napa-fleet-intelligence/monitoring-and-analysis-modules/

Nowacki, H. (2010). Five decades of computer-aided ship design. *Computer-Aided Design, 42*(11), 956–969.

OCX. (2023). https://3docx.org/

Ruponen, et al. (2022). International benchmark study on numerical simulation of flooding and motions of a damaged cruise ship. *Applied Ocean Research, 129*, 103403.

Wärtsilä. (2023). *An industry on standstill: Maritime progress at risk over fears of digitalisation.* https://www.wartsila.com/docs/default-source/voyage/wartsilavoyage_myths_of_digital_transformation.pdf

The In-House Production of Biofuel by Shipping Companies: A Case Study

Mia Hytti, Petri Rautanen, Jessica Saari, Minna Suuronen, and Riinu Walls

Target Audience

This chapter has been written for those working on future fuel options in the maritime industry. This includes people in shipping companies, cargo owners, fuel providers and policy makers, and anyone responsible for related strategic development activities.

Key Takeaway Messages

The chapter emphasises:

- Most marine biofuel alternatives can replace fossil distillates.
- Decarbonization requires standardisation. Several liquid biofuel standards and sustainability certification schemes are available at a regional level (for example, European Commission, 2022), however all are not necessarily allowed by the International Maritime Organization (IMO) to be used in marine traffic today.
- The use of recycling-based bio-oil is probably not a global solution, but rather a regional, State-specific solution.
- Biofuel is well-suited for retrofit/multifuel solutions, and it can be a solution for the transition phase towards other alternative fuels.

M. Hytti · J. Saari (✉) · M. Suuronen · R. Walls
Meriaura Ltd, Turku, Finland
e-mail: mia.hytti@meriaura.fi; Jessica.saari@meriaura.fi; minna.suuronen@meriaura.fi; Riinu.walls@meriaura.fi

P. Rautanen
Järnros Oy, Salo, Finland
e-mail: petri.rautanen@jarnros.fi

M. Lind et al. (eds.), *Maritime Decarbonization*,
https://doi.org/10.1007/978-3-031-39936-7_30

- Uncertainties with the price development of different biofuels, especially in comparison with conventional fossil fuels, continues to influence the development of the entire sector.
- Availability issues and competition over sustainable fuels among and between industries are expected to increase.
- It is forecast that by 2050 it could be possible that biofuels account for 27% of the total amount of fuels in the transport industry.

Status of Marine Biofuels

Maturity (Technology/Commercialisation)

Biofuels are by definition derived from the biomass into liquid or gas fuels. Biofuels are divided into two groups; biofuels (for example, ethanol, Fatty Acid Methyl Ester (FAME) to be used as a blending component or in a special design engines) and renewable biofuels (for example, Hydrotreated Vegetable Oil (HVO), so called drop-in fuels, which are fully compatible with fossil fuels) (IEA, 2022). There is still a great diversity in the products and definitions of different product generations. In general, there are only few, if any, alternatives for replacing heavy fossil residual marine fuels. Instead, most marine biofuel alternatives are for replacing fossil distillates. The road transportation sector has an advantage in the form of a broader selection of approved biofuels such as biogas, bioethanol, biodiesel (blend of fossil diesel and mono-alkyd ester, FAME), and renewable diesel (HVO).

There are some commercial technologies which allow the production of true drop-in distillate fuels (renewable diesel) like HVO utilising biomass, animal fats, and biobased waste streams (European Union Technology and Innovation Platform, 2020). HVO fulfills the international diesel standards (ISO, European Standards (EN), and standards organisation ASTM), indicating its similarity to traditional fossil diesel. There are also commercial technologies which provide biodiesel, such as FAME, which can be added in varying concentrations to fossil diesel or similar distillates (typically 10–20%), but the blending ratio is limited and traditionally, biodiesel components (FAME) are not allowed in the residual marine fuels. There are some products available as a residual marine fuel with FAME-like products provided (Uniper Energy DMCC, 2022; ExxonMobil, 2023), but there is no standard at engine site to support this (yet).

Road transportation has been using some biobased alcohols (like methanol and ethanol), but these are rare in marine applications. There is some interest to apply methanol in multi-fuel systems and a similar approach is interesting for other gas phase biofuels like green hydrogen and ammonia. The first vessels are sailing with these light biofuels for demonstration and test purposes, and the future projections indicate strong interest for these light biofuels (DNV, 2022a, b).

Fermentation of biobased material into alcohol and further upgrade processing or simply deconstruction-upgrading (like pyrolysis-hydrotreating) of biobased material are finally yielding similar products as Power-to-X (P2X) technologies. P2X technologies are electricity conversion, energy storage, and reconversion pathways that use surplus electric power, typically during periods where fluctuating renewable energy generation exceeds load. Green hydrogen, ammonia, biogas / methane, even liquid fuels (kerosine, gasoline, diesel) can be achieved with some advanced upgrading technologies. These developments all aim to create fuels which would then be a drop-in substitute for fossil fuels. Several programs are already established to speed up the development of these technologies (IRENA, 2016; IEA, 2022).

The challenge related to biobased feedstock as well as P2X is sustainability. There is competition with the food chain, and land use (wind and solar power). Life cycle assessment (LCA) sustainable wind and solar power materials still requires concrete and construction materials which form hazardous waste after use. Positively, the side and waste streams of potential biomass, algae and lignocellulose are widely recognised as a next potential feedstock to allow sustainable production of biofuels.

Marine liquid biofuels have low maturity, only HVO is gaining global acceptance as it fulfills the global specifications (by being fully interchangeable with fossil diesel). The other marine biofuels are more local and often require modification or refitting of vessels' fuel systems.

Rules and Regulations/Sustainability Criteria and Standardisation

The revised Renewable Energy Directive (EU) 2018/2001 (RED II) establishes an overarching policy for the promotion and use of energy from renewable sources in the European Union (EU). As a proof of sustainability biofuels must fulfil some requirements, for example, the renewable origin of the feedstock of the fuel must be certified according to one of the certification schemes that are accepted by the EU (European Commission, 2022).

Renewable energy in transport could consist of biofuel, renewable fuels of non-biological origin and possibly recycled carbon fuels. At all times, the sustainability requirements should be met. According to the directive, advanced biofuels 'are produced from the feedstock listed in Part A of Annex IX (lignocellulosic energy crops, waste and residues)'. The directive sets advanced biofuel targets of at least 0.2% in 2022, at least 1% in 2025 and at least 3.5% in 2030. The directive also reinforces the sustainability criteria of bioenergy through different provisions, including the negative direct impact that the production of biofuels may have due to indirect land use change (European Commission, 2022).

The IMO's initial GHG strategy was agreed in 2018 and updated in 2023. This includes targets for the reduction of carbon intensity by 30% by 2030 and 80% by 2050 relative to 2008 levels. An IMO Energy Efficiency Existing Ship Index (EEXI) and Carbon Intensity Indicator (CII) requirement entered into force in January 2023

(IMO, 2022). These new regulation introduce mandatory reductions in carbon emissions for both new and existing ships, using energy efficiency indicators to determine these levels. The IMO reference fuel standard ISO 8217 is being updated to include renewable fuels.

New rules (or mainly exceptions to existing rules) are being introduced rapidly and it is challenging to keep up with them. A ship's engines were once made for either marine gasoil (MGO) or heavy fuel oil (HFO). With the introduction of bio-obligations at the same time as biofuels enter the market, engine manufacturer must now incorporate functionalities to enable compatibility with new fuels. The new or revised engines must then be tested either under laboratory conditions or at sea, the relevant classification societies must certify/approve the tests and Flag States must give permission to use the newer fuels. In addition, ship insurers must include a new risk in the insurance, and finally the shipping companies must dare to introduce the newer engines and fuels.

Standardisation is key to the wider use of biofuels in marine traffic. The fuel itself must be of standardised quality, and it must meet the specifications of the engine manufacturer. There are several standardised liquid biofuels available, not all of which are currently allowed by IMO to be used in marine traffic. Standards are available for treated and further processed biofuels, such as FAME and HVO. However, the standards differ depending on the region.

Two major specifications establishing the quality requirements for alkyl ester-based biodiesel fuels such as FAME are ASTM D6751 in the USA and EN 14214 in Europe. There are also other regional guidelines for biodiesel, which differ in content. HVO is a paraffinic diesel fuel and is specified in the standard EN 15940: 2016, which covers hydrotreated HVO and Fischer-Tropsch GTL (gas to liquid) products containing up to 7.0% (V/V) of FAME. HVO also meets diesel fuel standards, such as EN 590 and ASTM D 975 high blending ratios. Biodiesel (FAME) standards are not applicable for HVO. HVO has also been approved to be used as an aviation (bio jet) fuel, based on ASTM D7566-14 (Jääskeläinen, 2009).

Keeping the production chain for biofuel as simple as possible minimises the GHG impact and production costs of the fuel. Raw vegetable oil can be used as marine fuel but there is no standard available for it. This is because it has not been widely used and specific requirements need to be agreed in order for wider use to be successful.

Scalability

It is fair to say that the use of recycling-based bio-oil is probably not a global solution, but rather a regional, State-specific solution or even the choice of individual companies. It can only be scaled up to a limited volume due to the restricted availability of the raw materials. It suits retrofit/multifuel solutions, and might well be a solution for the transition phase on the path towards other alternative fuels. Nevertheless, all waste should be re-used. When the knowledge and the product is in place, then recycling-based bio-oil can be used to power multifuel engines. This recycling-based bio-oil would best be produced in small units locally, to minimise the transport of raw materials, and thereby further minimise emissions. Scalability is possible from a technical point of view.

Meriaura Case: How to Proceed with a Non-standard Fuel

Over the years the Finnish shipping company Meriaura, which seeks to operate an environmentally sustainable fleet, has successfully used recycled bio-oil as fuel in its ships. This fuel is neither hydrogenated or esterised, so there is currently no applicable standard available. In terms of being able to use bio-oil continuously and in the long-term, the fuel needs to be standardised and certified.

Meriaura has been unable to identify a standard or list of test parameters that could be applied to the recycled bio-oil that it is using, such that a classification society and Flag State could provide certification.

The only option has been for Meriaura to develop a specification and ensure that its fuel meets it. A classification society could then update the Supplement of the International Air Pollution Prevention (IAPP) certificate for a ship, by referring to the new specifications. Once done, operating a ship with fuel that conforms to those specifications becomes legal. What complicates things further is if a ship's engine manufacturer does not have a certification for using the specified biofuels. The fact is that few have, especially for older engines.

If nitrogen oxides (NOx) emissions must be below the Tier-2 limit, in accordance with the International Convention for the Prevention of Pollution from Ships (MARPOL) regulations, then the use of selective catalytic reduction (SCR) becomes necessary. There have recently been changes to this requirement, when in 2022 the IMO Marine Environment Protection Committee (MEPC) determined that those fuels with a biofuel content up to 30% fall under the definition of marine fuel oil derived from petroleum refining (MARPOL Regulation 18.3.1) and no further NOx testing is required. However, for fuels that have a biofuel content of more than 30%, there are no changes to the requirement for NOx testing (DNV, 2022a, b), and therefore the need for SCR. In any case, it is Meriaura's aim to generate minimum emissions and the use of SCR is part of that.

Requirements for the Fuel Supplier

To meet MARPOL regulations (MARPOL Appendix V, Annex VI) a fuel supplier must provide an appropriate bunker delivery note to ships. These requirements, in short, mean that:

- the fuel does not cause limit-breaking sulphur emissions,
- the fuel does not cause limit-breaking nitrogen oxide emissions, and

- the fuel does not cause any harm to the operation of the machinery and therefore any danger.

An analysis of the fuel is required to obtain a number of the required values, including:

- Density at 15 °C, (kg/m^3) (ISO 3675:1998 / ISO 12185:1996)
- Sulphur content (%m/m) (ISO 8754:2003)

This analysis involves additional work for a fuel that is currently non-standard and can be a problem area for bio-oil (water, particles).

In practice, a supplier undertakes that its fuel meets the requirements of the standard (for mineral oils it is ISO 8217) for the marine fuel sold under a particular type name (with mineral oils, for example, MGO, DMA (marine distillate fuel), DMB (marine diesel oil)).

The signatory of the bunker delivery note is legally responsible for ensuring that the supplied fuel meets the required specifications, even if a complete certificate of analysis is not required for each batch. For this reason, it is necessary for suppliers to test their fuels on a frequent basis, so that possible quality fluctuations do not cause unintentional rule violations.

The Pros and Cons of Biofuel for Ships

Enablers and Obstacles

Novel fuel sources are at the core of the decarbonization of the global shipping sector and to meet the GHG targets. Biofuels can offer rapid, regional options to speed up a green transition in maritime transportation. They are not only generally more affordable than other alternative fuel options, but also, they do not require costly modification actions from a technical perspective and can therefore be applied to both an existing fleet and newbuild vessels. Despite the high decarbonization potential, several obstacles remain with the short- and long-term implementation efforts of different shipping companies and in different geographical trading areas (Hsieh & Felby, 2017).

A SWOT (strengths, weaknesses, opportunities, threats) analysis is a strategic analytical tool used by many small-to-medium enterprises (SMEs), but it can offer valuable insights to all decision makers regarding internal and external aspects influencing a project or case being studied (Liu et al., 2018).

Figure 1 shows a SWOT analysis for the use of bio-fuel in ships. It is followed by a short discussion on the key topics identified in the analysis.

Fig. 1 SWOT analysis of the use of biofuel in ships

Strengths

Various private sector players, including the shipping company Meriaura, have already gathered experience from trialling biofuel as a potential bunker fuel. In Meriaura's case, the long-term research and development (R&D) efforts started to materialise in the 2010s after the company's first biofuel-compliant newbuilding entered its fleet. The development path has since led to a mature product portfolio with tailored production facilities in Uusikaupunki, Finland. The process from material sourcing to bunkering activities of biofuel is controlled by the in-house expertise team. This reduces dependency on other market players in the world of scarce resources and an intensely competitive market environment. Prominent leading industry players with serious biofuel use goals are, MSC Mediterranean Shipping Company S.A. (MSC, 2023) and Maersk Group (A.P. Moller-Maersk, 2023).

These companies, with ambitious and sustainably-oriented ESG strategies, are beginning to see their efforts paying off (Carvalho et al., 2021).

While long-term agreements with the cargo owners are important to further enhance investment in technological development and general production capacity of any individual company, the existing direct synergies between Meriaura's business divisions are allowing the blue growth process, the long-term strategy to support sustainable growth in the marine and maritime sectors as a whole, to proceed seamlessly on a local scale. This is because of the company's 'double agent' role of having both biofuel production and shipping operations under the same umbrella.

Due to the long development path with biofuel utilisation, the company is not in start-up phase today, unlike many other emerging biomass-based bunker producers and vessel operators. This provides several first mover advantages from both decarbonization and commercial aspects. Fuel analysis and testing ashore and onboard vessels has already occurred, production facilities are running, and the fuel supply infrastructure is being established. This includes biofuel bunkering and storage, as well as ensuring longer-term availability of the fuels. Handling biofuels on board also requires knowledge from both shoreside staff and ship's crew regarding the rules for the safe use of fuels, as well as the operation of new systems designed for biofuels or biofuel blends.

Weaknesses

There are potential sustainability issues with biofuels related to the impact of growing the raw materials on food security, land usage and upstream GHG emissions (Lloyd's Register, 2020).

Even in situations where shipping companies are controlling the biofuel production chain, the supply chain includes various external parties, which influence the profitability and sustainability of the process. The external parties include the raw material suppliers, road-based logistics providers and other possible subcontractors.

There may be routing limitations for a biofuel-compliant fleet in regions where biofuel bunkers are not available.

Smaller shipping companies, such as Meriaura, do not usually have the same bargaining power as larger companies that are targeting the same markets and resources.

Biofuels are seen as a regional asset in the future fuel mix. This introduces some constraints, due to the international nature of maritime trade and the routing and scheduling uncertainties of ships. In general, the supply infrastructure and entire supply chain from the sourcing of raw materials to port bunker facilities would need to be increasingly available to enable economies of scale. Even then, biomass availability and quality will vary in different geographic areas. These are challenges that are not present with existing conventional fuels with mature ecosystems in place. Some drop-in biofuels are compatible with the existing infrastructure, but this alone will not overcome the remaining barriers for feedstock and technology across the entire biofuel segment.

The current lack of standardisation of biofuels is another weakness. Standardisation issues, as well as sustainability-related constraints have already been discussed in some detail earlier in this chapter.

Opportunities

Widely recognised demand drivers, especially the IMO sustainability and decarbonization targets that are being placed on the shipping industry are pushing demand and hence the willingness of regional and global customer groups to pay. The emerging regulatory targets are expected to increase the availability of biofuels beyond the regional areas of the EU and US, and make the technology adoption procedures easier for individual companies as more appropriate guidelines, led by the IMO, are introduced in the near future.

Drop-in and blending possibilities are recognised as a huge opportunity for some biofuels. Certain biofuel-classed products require little to no retrofitting of existing vessels in the market. The advanced second and third generation biofuels can be used with existing onboard technologies (Hsieh & Felby, 2017). Hence, green maritime transition can commence without expensive and time-consuming fleet renewal activities, and with considerably reduced GHG levels—a minimum of 65–70% when the biofuel follows the EU Renewable Energy Directive (RED II).

It is widely recognised by the maritime community, as well as by policymakers, that the future belongs to multifuel set-ups. In future, engine technologies will increasingly support the simultaneous use of a larger fuel family than ever before. The development of other alternative fuels on the side can also open new opportunities for biofuels as a solid part of the most sustainable energy mix.

There are no significant safety issues connected to biofuel use, in contrast to many other promising alternative fuel options, such as hydrogen.

Bunkering infrastructure and easy logistics exist for several biofuels.

The identified biofuel-related challenges and barriers are generally solvable—higher prices can be compensated by suitable policy incentives.

Future generation, advanced biofuels manufactured from non-food biomass are already a reality.

Shipboard technology is in an active testing phase among the industry players.

Threats

Uncertainties over the pricing of the different biofuels, especially in comparison to conventional fossil fuels, continues to influence the development of the entire sector, especially until the shipping industry has a clear pathway and regulations in place in terms of emission reduction schemes regionally and globally. Today, even if recent traditional bunker price fluctuations have made biofuels more attractive from the cost point of view, it is not ideal for long-term innovation and investment plans to be driven by the fossil-fuel market prices. Without authoritative emission-related regulatory schemes, the biofuel providers are too heavily reliant on negative market shocks in conventional fuel prices, together with individual clients' internal decarbonization policies, as the mechanism to increase their share of the fuel provision mix.

Market-based measures for the decarbonization of the global shipping industry and coherent sustainability certification for biofuel as a bunker are still under development. The lack of these measures is potentially reducing the credibility of emission reduction claims and causing challenges for the commercialisation of biofuels on a larger scale (Lloyd's Register, 2020).

Even if the scalability of biofuel is considered to be somewhat limited, it is not in shipping's best interest to leave the biofuel efforts to the private sector and individual local companies, without any overarching international goals and guidance set by policymakers and leading organisations.

Plant-based oils are particularly favoured by the aviation industry as well as being considered by the shipping industry. Many land-based heavy industries are looking at biofuels as the future fuel mix. It may be that would-be energy providers for the maritime sector, like the forest industry and hydrogen-derived production plants will use their generated fuel sources both for their own processes and to service other markets. This could create an intensely competitive environment for biofuels if it is a sustainable but limited resource.

Work on other promising future fuels, mainly the so-called e-fuels, could limit the potential of biofuels, as there may not be enough R&D resources and investment funds available to allow all the transition-compliant fuels to reach their full potential.

In-House Biofuel Case Study: Meriaura

Established in 1986, the Finnish shipping company Meriaura has its main office in Turku, Finland. The Meriaura fleet operates mainly in the Baltic and North Sea areas but can also operate on a more global scale. The company's cargo volume is about 3 million tons or is 3% of the total volume of Finland's foreign sea trade. The company specialises in demanding special and project cargoes as well as bio-, circular economy and agri bulk freight (Meriaura, 2023).

History/Background with Biofuels

The founder of Meriaura, Jussi Mälkiä, made his first bio-oil experiment onboard tugboat Aura in 1992. The test was partially successful: the main engine of the tug worked well but the generators did not.

Meriaura Group started the development of waste-based bio-oil in 2009; raw material used in the first experiments was fish guts, which was soon complemented with other materials for further testing purposes. Used cooking oil has been part of the raw material mix since 2014, and has slowly gained its status as a sole leading energy source over the years. Making second generation bio-oil, which does not compete with the food industry was important from the outset.

The design and building of the open deck cargo carrier, m/v Meri began in 2010. The test use of bio-oil started quite soon after the delivery of m/v Meri in 2012. In 2014 a biogas plant was up and running, feeding energy to the bio-oil production plant. Facilities for producing bio-oil were improved and a production plant was opened in 2015. Sister vessels m/v Eeva VG and m/v Mirva VG were built in 2016 and like m/v Meri, they can run entirely on biofuel or biofuel blended with fossil-fuel oil, if necessary. So far Meriaura has been using their bio-oil only in their own vessels and only in the newest ones, mv Meri, Mirva VG and Eeva VG. Its older vessels have not been retrofitted as yet.

Biofuel Process Description

Used cooking oil (UCO), is defined as waste and is not allowed to be recycled back to food chain. Thus, it provides a sustainable feedstock to biofuel production. Meriaura has a collection system together with selected partners covering the whole of Finland. UCO processing starts with the collection. The first quality screening takes place during the pick-up, followed by a more detailed quality analysis at the processing site in Uusikaupunki. The process itself is an automated two-stage process having several separation and purification steps to finetune the quality of the final product. More than a decade of knowledge of the local UCO market (quality and quantity), test runs on previous biofuels and close cooperation during the process development phase with different equipment and technology vendors has achieved the process, which is able to remove contaminants like salts, food residues and water. The biofuel can be used in the selected vessels described above in blending ratios from 0 to 100%. This provides operational flexibility for the crew and planning. The process uses energy from an adjacent biogas plant, further improving the sustainability of the production/product. A tailored additive package is blended into the product prior to loading. The biofuel, VG MEF (VG Marine EcoFuel) is transported from the processing plant to the ships in the company's own bio-fuelled truck.

Latest Developments

As stated earlier, Meriaura has been actively using biofuels made from recycled oils in its fleet for a dozen years. As a latest milestone, a development project was launched in 2020 with the aim to develop a biofuel product that is more uniform in quality than the previous biofuels and can be standardised for vessels' use. The project included a physical re-configuration of the production line in Uusikaupunki biofuel plant, and investments were also made in the fleet by installing equipment that better enabled the use of the fuel blends onboard. The blending equipment can be used to standardise the blending ratio of bio- and fossil fuel, allowing continuous use of the bio component. The raw material base has been improved by expanding the collection area of UCO to more regions in Finland.

EcoVoy

In 2021 Meriaura launched a carbon neutral sea transport concept called EcoVoy, where its clients can buy almost carbon neutral sea transport by placing their cargoes in those vessels using only bio-oil. This development project plays an important role in meeting both the overall decarbonization goals and the commercialisation targets of the company.

By using 100% waste-based biofuel, emissions are up to 98% lower than using fossil fuels, reducing the company's carbon footprint and enabling cargo owners to decarbonize their logistics chains. A carbon footprint report indicating the CO_2 reduction achieved through an EcoVoy contract is provided to customers together with other supporting documentation. Meriaura's VG Marine EcoFuel and its processing is independently audited and assured by a third party and has ISCC certification.

Meriaura has set a 4% annual emission reduction target for its shipping operations. Together with efficient operations, increasing the use of bio-oil is the most significant means of achieving its decarbonization goals. The potential sustainability constraints presented earlier in this chapter do not apply to Meriaura's biofuel product because it relies on a fully waste-based, second-generation biofuel set-up, making it a true asset for the decarbonization efforts of companies such as Meriaura, as well as for the wider supply chain that takes advantage of this bunker source in their logistics chain.

To boost development even further, the company has a new newbuild ship program in which the biofuel options will be supplemented by green ammonia.

Co-operation Aspects When Using Biofuel

As with any emerging new technologies and operations in the global maritime sector, interdependent value chains and different partnership models are seen as one of the key elements of future success (Lind et al., 2022a, b); the biofuel development path being no exception (Fig. 2). Three interdependent maritime value chains are playing a critical role in decarbonizing shipping: the marine fuel, the shipbuilding and the maritime operations value chains.

When looking at the maritime operational value chain, the key players are ports and vessels, with fuel being an important common factor in this chain. Fuel is

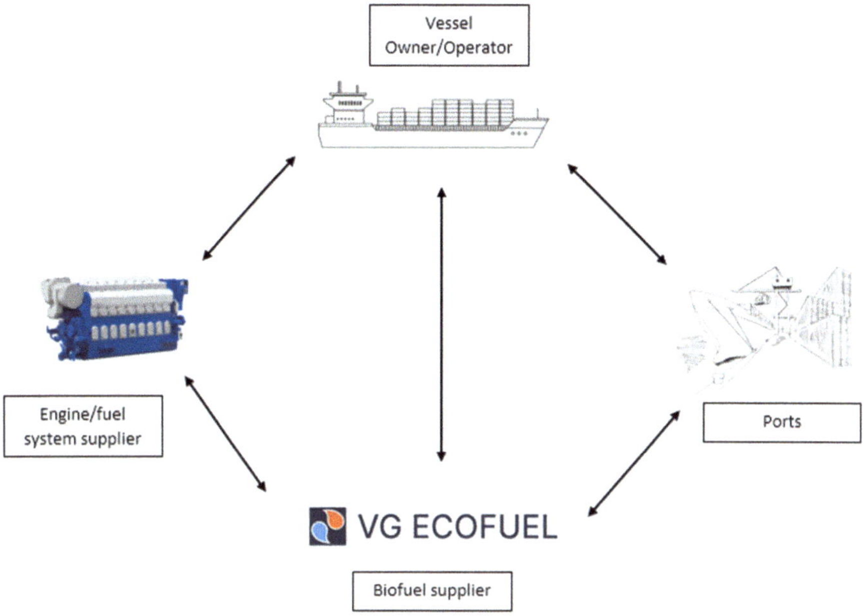

Fig. 2 Key maritime value chains (adapted from Lind et al., 2022a, b)

creating direct interaction with other critical value chains as part of the wider maritime cluster, namely the marine fuel value chain (Lind et al., 2022a, b).

Meriaura has streamlined certain parts of the relatively complex value chains and its overall partnership network, by having both biofuel production and its fleet of vessels under the same company group. Furthermore, biofuel activities, including the sourcing of raw materials, production, distribution and bunkering are all conducted locally. A long and close co-operation with engine/onboard fuel system manufacturers has complemented the process over the years, stretching from joint R&D efforts to practical onboard reconfiguration and system management. The three main value chains, marine fuel, shipbuilding and maritime operations, are therefore all involved in the biofuel development path in a form of close co-operation with the company's long-term partners. While the ports are not key players in the current operations value chain established by Meriaura, in the future they will have a strong influence on the overall infrastructure, regulations, and scalability efforts of the various biofuel options at the international level.

Closing Remarks

Shipping plays a valuable role in the global economy and trade and will continue to be essential. It is estimated that by 2050, fuel consumption by ships will rise by 43.5% even considering the best scenarios (Bilgili, 2021).

Since the maritime industry has been under pressure to decarbonize, interest in liquid biofuels has been increasing. The International Energy Agency has forecasted that in year 2050 it could be possible that biofuels account for 27% of fuels in the transport industry (Serrano & Gameiro da Silva, 2018). That could reduce CO_2 emissions annually by 2.1 gigatonnes.

There is strong interest in using liquid biofuels simply because an existing engine would not require much retrofitting. Another aspect is that the bunkering infrastructure is already in place, as the bunkering procedure is the same as for fossil fuels.

The issues with bio-oil in shipping are the limited availability of feedstock and potential competition with aviation and other likely users. This competition will most likely increase in the future as advanced liquid biofuels appear to be a most promising option for decarbonizing air transport, particularly for long-distance flights (ETIPBIOENERGY, 2022a, b).

Biofuels may be challenging in terms of analysis and standardisation (Fivga & Mayer, 2016), but the standardisation of liquid biofuels is required. As the pace of decarbonization in shipping continues to increase, the need for standardisation grows. Standardisation and testing will help to grow the market, ensure reliability and decrease emissions.

Some stakeholders consider biofuels to be only a short-to-medium term transition solution. Long-term decarbonization alternatives being considered include ammonia, hydrogen fuels and battery-powered shipping. It is an open question as to whether a robust regulatory mechanism for biofuels will eventuate and the full commercialisation potential of biofuels is ever reached. This could depend on whether policymakers and international organisations place most of their focus on future fuels, rather than including today's sustainable and already available biofuel options that require minimal retrofitting action and rely on proven concepts.

References

Bilgili, L. (2021). Life cycle comparison of marine fuels for IMO 2020 Sulphur cap. *Science of the Total Environment, 774*, 145719. https://doi.org/10.1016/j.scitotenv.2021.145719

Carvalho, F., Portugal-Pereira, J., Junginger, M., & Szklo, A. (2021). Biofuels for maritime transportation: A spatial, techno-economic, and logistic analysis in Brazil, Europe, South Africa, and the USA. *Energies, 14*(16), 4980. https://doi.org/10.3390/en14164980

DNV. (2022a). Webpage. *IMO update: Marine Environment Protection Committee (MEPC 78).* Referred 22.12.2022. https://www.dnv.com/news/imo-update-marine-environment-protection-committee-mepc-78%2D%2D226640

DNV. (2022b). https://www.dnv.com/maritime-forecast

ETIPBIOENERGY. (2022a). Webpage. *Biofuels in aviation*. Referred 22.12.2022. https://www.etipbioenergy.eu/value-chains/products-end-use/end-use/air

ETIPBIOENERGY. (2022b). Webpage. *Factsheet HVO*. Referred 22.12.2022. ETIP_B_Factsheet_HVO_feb2020.pdf (etipbioenergy.eu)

European Commission. (2022). *Biofuels, sustainability criteria [An official website of the European Union]*. (https://energy.ec.europa.eu/topics/renewable-energy/bioenergy/biofuels_en).

European Technology and Innovation Platform, Bioenergy Fact sheet. (2020). https://etipbioenergy.eu/images/ETIP_B_Factsheet_HVO_feb2020.pdf

ExxonMobil. (2023). https://www.exxonmobil.com/en/marine/technicalresource/press-releases/marine-bio-fuel-oil

Fivga, A., & Mayer, Z. (2016). *Understanding biofuel standards [Biofuels digest]*. https://www.biofuelsdigest.com/bdigest/2016/10/02/understanding-biofuel-standards/

Hsieh, C. C., & Felby, C. (2017). *Biofuels for the marine shipping sector – An overview and analysis of sector infrastructure, fuel technologies and regulations [IEA bioenergy]*. https://www.ieabioenergy.com/wp-content/uploads/2018/02/Marine-biofuel-report-final-Oct-2017.pdf

IEA. (2022). *Biofuels*. IEA. License: CC BY 4.0. https://www.iea.org/reports/biofuels

IMO. (2022). Webpage. *Press briefings, rules on ship carbon intensity and rating system enter into force*. Referred 21.12.2022. https://www.imo.org/en/MediaCentre/PressBriefings/pages/CII-and-EEXI-entry-into-force.aspx

IRENA. (2016). https://www.irena.org/-/media/Files/IRENA/Agency/Publication/2016/IRENA_Innovation_Outlook_Advanced_Liquid_Biofuels_2016.pdf?rev=b7aa8fbc56254be18fb286066c9d45f7

Jääskeläinen, H. (2009). *Biodiesel standards & properties*. dieselnet.com

Lind, M., Lehmacher, W., Doepel, T., Heinimaa, J., Hoffmann, J., Laurilehto, M., Lebmeier, M., Petersen, M., Rytkölä, I., Saari, J., Singh, S., Walls, R., & Watson, R. T. (2022a). *The benefits of a clusters of value chains perspective in decarbonising shipping: Decarbonisation playbook part 2, 22/8-2022*. The Maritime Executive. https://maritime-executive.com/editorials/the-three-maritime-value-chains-decarbonization-playbook-part-2

Lind, M., Lemacher, W., Bentham, J., Kuttan, S., Tikka, K., & Watson, R. T. (2022b). *Four steps towards maritime decarbonizing actions: Playbook part 5, 11/12-2022*. The Maritime Executive. https://www.maritime-executive.com/editorials/four-steps-towards-maritime-decarbonising-actions-playbook-part-5

Liu, Y., Liu, T., Agyeiwaa, A., & Li, Y. (2018). A SWOT analysis of biodiesel production from waste cooking oil. *IOP Conference Series: Earth and Environmental Science, 170*, 022136. https://iopscience.iop.org/article/10.1088/1755-1315/170/2/022136/pdf

Lloyd's Register. (2020). *Techno-economic assessment of zero-carbon fuels* [Lloyd's register: London, UK; UMAS: London, UK, 2020].

MERIAURA. (2023). Webpage. *In the frontline of developing sustainable shipping*. Referred 27.1.2023. https://meriaura.fi/en/

Moller-Maersk, A. P. (2023). Maersk eco delivery [A.P. Moller-Maersk]. https://www.maersk.com/transportation-services/eco-delivery

MSC. (2023). *Journey to net zero [MSC]*. https://www.msc.com/en/sustainability/enabling-logistics-decarbonisation/journey-to-net-zero?_gl=1*mnryw0*_up*MQ..&gclid=EAIaIQobChMI3fOX8puz_QIVA20YCh1vSQjrEAAYASAAEgImofD_BwE&gclsrc=aw.ds

Serrano, L. M. V., & Gameiro da Silva, M. (2018). *Study about nitrogen oxide emissions and fuel consumption in diesel engines fueled with B20. Biofuels – State of development*. InTech. https://doi.org/10.5772/intechopen.72955

Uniper Energy DMCC. (2022). https://www.uniper.energy/sites/default/files/2022-04/ued_biofuel_brochure_sept._16%20%281%29.pdf

Establishing Green Shipping Corridors to Accelerate the Use of Alternative Fuels

Johan Byskov Svendsen, Elizabeth Petit, Martha Selwyn, and Anne Katrine Bjerregaard

Target Audience

This chapter has been written for senior leaders and strategic thinkers looking to accelerate the decarbonization of the maritime industry, particularly in relation to advancing the use of alternative fuels in shipping through the implementation of so-called *green corridors*.

Key Takeaway Messages

The five key points covered in this chapter are:

- Green shipping corridors aim to bring together stakeholders from across the maritime value chain to promote the early uptake of alternative fuels on specific shipping routes.
- More than 20 green shipping corridor projects have been announced, but many have faced problems moving from announcement to action due to the complexity and costs associated with the value-chain encompassing alternative fuel projects.

J. B. Svendsen (✉) · A. K. Bjerregaard
Mærsk Mc-Kinney Møller Center for Zero Carbon Shipping, Copenhagen, Denmark
e-mail: johan.byskov@zerocarbonshipping.com;
anne.katrine.bjerregaard@zerocarbonshipping.com

E. Petit
The Sustainable Shipping Initiative Limited, Hartley Wintney, UK
e-mail: E.Petit@sustainableshipping.org

M. Selwyn
United Nations Global Compact, New York, NY, USA
e-mail: selwyn@unglobalcompact.org

M. Lind et al. (eds.), *Maritime Decarbonization*,
https://doi.org/10.1007/978-3-031-39936-7_31

- A framework for bringing green shipping corridors from idea to execution is described, particularly the first two phases of the framework: pre-feasibility and feasibility.
- The framework is being used on more advanced green corridors in Chile, East Australia-New Zealand, Gothenburg, and Rotterdam-Singapore, some of which are presented as case studies.
- In addition to emission reductions and accelerating the use of alternative fuels, well-planned green shipping corridor projects can support a just and equitable transition by identifying and maximising social benefits while mitigating risks.

Introduction

Decarbonizing the maritime industry will require transitioning to low- and zero-carbon fuels, such as bio-fuels, e-fuels, and blue fuels. (MMMCZCS, 2022a). In its thousands of years of history, shipping has already gone through several fuel transitions from sailing ships to wood-burning steam ships, then coal-fired steam ships, and eventually to the internal combustion engines fuelled by oil that we all know today. Each of these transitions relied on brave first movers who sparked change and initiated the first steps of the transition when the path ahead was unsure.

Decarbonizing the industry will again rely on first movers, followed by a fast adoption by the rest of the industry. However, if we hope to decarbonize the shipping industry by 2050, as lately stated by IMO, the green transition will need to happen much faster than previous transitions, and zero-emission fuels and vessels will need to be deployed this decade. The shipping industry is varied and complex, and implementing industry-wide decarbonization solutions will be challenging for several reasons. First, alternative fuels are not yet widely available. Furthermore, supplies are expected to be globally scattered and differ in availability, scale, and price in the coming decades (MMMCZCS, 2022a). This leaves stakeholders across the industry unsure about which fuels to invest in. Second, alternative fuel costs are much higher than fossil fuels. We can expect alternative fuel costs to be 2–8 times higher than fossil fuels (MMMCZCS, 2022a). Furthermore, with the demand for green shipping scattered across the industry (BCG, 2021), it may be impossible to recoup these costs. Finally, introducing alternative fuels will require cooperation across the value chain, with fuel producers, ports, and vessel owners/operators working together in a new paradigm for the shipping industry.

The Clydebank Declaration for Green Shipping Corridors (Department of Transport, 2022) aims to catalyse the green transition by the development of green shipping corridors. Green shipping corridors use a network of ports and shipping lanes to create dedicated routes for low- and zero-carbon alternative fuels, where participants share the costs and benefits of using alternative fuels, thereby incentivising their use. In addition to immediately reducing emissions, this can encourage regulatory development and investment in green vessels, infrastructure, and fuel production by providing increased demand certainty. Additionally, once the infrastructure for green shipping corridors is in place, it can also be used on adjacent routes, accelerating decarbonization outside the corridor.

The Clydebank Declaration aims to bring together first movers who want to take the first steps in the transition to alternative fuels and overcome some of the challenges described above. It was agreed at the 26th United Nations (UN) Climate Change Conference of Parties (COP 26) in Clydebank, Scotland in 2021. As of mid-2023, the Declaration has 24 signatories, including Australia, Chile, Denmark, New Zealand, and Singapore. The signatories of the declaration agree to support the establishment of green shipping corridors to accelerate maritime decarbonization. The signatories have committed to establishing at least six corridors by the middle of this decade, with more operational by 2030.

Green shipping corridors have gained momentum following COP26 and the Clydebank Declaration. More than 20 green shipping corridor projects have been officially announced to date, with prominent examples in Latin America, Northern Europe, and North America-Asia. (Global Maritime Forum, 2022). However, several projects have faced challenges moving from announcement to action. The infrastructure and construction of a green shipping corridor is a large, complex, and costly project with no clear commercial incentive, making progress difficult. Furthermore, due to the novelty of the concept, no well-established processes and methodologies exist for green shipping corridor projects, which has further limited progress. The IMO has laid forward the path for the green corridors by aiming for uptake of zero or near-zero GHG emission technologies, fuels and/or energy sources to represent at least 5%, striving for 10%, of the energy used by international shipping by 2030 (IMO, 2023).

In order to tackle this and drive the maturation of green shipping corridors in the pace set by IMO, the Mærsk Mc-Kinney Møller Center for Zero Carbon Shipping (MMMCZCS) and its partners are developing the first processes and methodologies to move green shipping corridors forward. MMMCZCS has various roles in around 15 green shipping corridor projects (some of which have not yet been officially announced) where it is applying its methodologies and providing independent guidance to ensure successful progress. The Center is using the learnings and insights from these projects to further refine and strengthen its methodologies. This chapter outlines the frameworks established by MMMCZCS to take green shipping corridors from idea to reality and details several case studies from green shipping corridor projects so far.

Maturation of a Green Shipping Corridor: From Idea to Emission Reduction

Realising green shipping corridors hinges on leveraging opportunities and competencies across the entire supply chain in a coordinated manner. To ensure a smooth development process for green shipping corridors and to share the costs and risks of decarbonization, stakeholders from fuel producers to cargo owners must form a

Fig. 1 Phases of a green shipping corridor project (MMMCZCS, 2022c)

project group of first movers. Furthermore, green shipping corridor projects require thorough planning as the production, distribution, and use of alternative fuels across multiple ports is a complex process. As a result, green shipping corridor projects require a comprehensive and coherent project framework.

In collaboration with partners, MMMCZCS has developed a six-phase framework to bring green shipping corridors from concept to execution. This is shown in Fig. 1 (MMMCZCS, 2022b, c).

The phases include pre-feasibility, feasibility, selection, definition, execution, and operation. As stakeholders progress through each stage, uncertainty decreases, and stakeholder commitments and investments increase.

The pre-feasibility stage involves screening an area of interest (region, country, province) to identify potential green shipping corridors. This phase builds on publicly available data or data sources, and the commitment from participants at this stage is purely time resources (MMMCZCS, 2022b). In the feasibility stage, work is centred around a specific corridor, which can include dedicated ports, specific vessel segments, cargo types, or alternative fuels. The specificity is higher than in the previous stage, and project participants must be those likely to participate in the project, and they commit time resources required to address all identified risks and their mitigating measures, such as surveys and demonstrators (MMMCZCS, 2022a).

Next comes the selection and definition phases, followed by the final investment decision for a specific green shipping corridor. Then, the execution stage begins. The commitment at this stage is primarily the capital expenditure to construct the project. Finally, the green shipping corridor enters the operation phase, where the primary commitment is operational expenditures to operate the project throughout its lifetime. Time resources are naturally also committed in the project's later stages, but they are low compared to monetary commitments.

Most of the ongoing green shipping corridor projects are currently still in the ideation phase, while a few have progressed to the pre-feasibility or feasibility stages, which are discussed in more detail in the following sections together with several case studies of pre-feasibility and feasibility stages.

The Pre-feasibility Phase

In 2022, MMMCZCS, together with Rocky Mountain Institute, an organisation in the United States dedicated to research, publication, consulting, and lecturing in the field of sustainability, with a focus on profitable innovations for energy and resource efficiency, published the Green Corridor Pre-Feasibility Blueprint (MMMCZCS, 2022b). This provides a detailed step-by-step process for the pre-feasibility phase of a green shipping corridor project. In the blueprint, or framework, the pre-feasibility phase contains three steps: scoping, assessment, and a consortium incubation workshop (MMMCZCS, 2022b). In the scoping phase, project participants define the

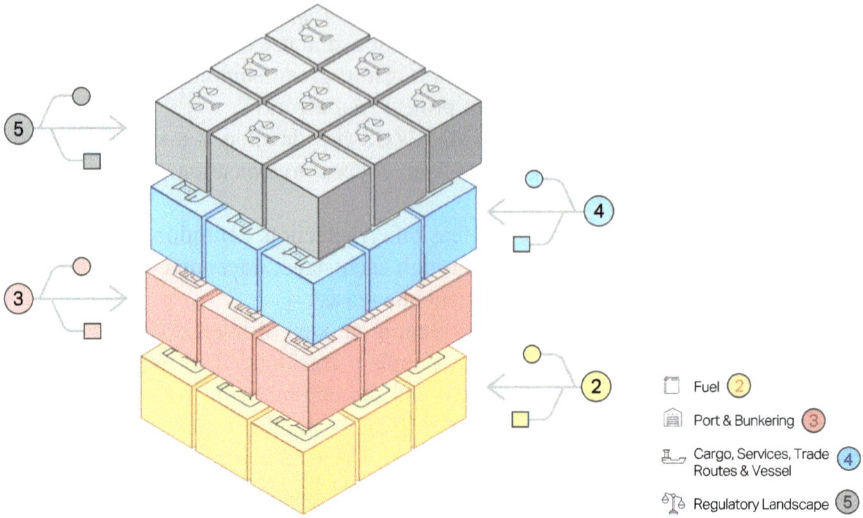

Fig. 2 Data collected in the pre-feasibility assessment phase of a green shipping corridor project forms a multidimensional data cube

project's goal and objectives, agree on the project deliverables and deadlines, outline the project work scope and roles, and assign responsibilities to the project members.

In the assessment phase, project participants gather data about the geographical area covered by the pre-feasibility study, including potential alternative fuel supplies, port and bunkering opportunities, vessel types and routes, and the regulatory landscape. In doing so, the result is a multidimensional data cube. This is illustrated in Fig. 2.

The more complete the data collected during the assessment is, the larger the variety of potential green shipping corridors the project will identify. If there is only data from two ports and container transportation, the only potential is a container corridor. If the data includes insight into the fuels produced in the area of interest, multiple ports, insight into multiple cargo flow, incentive scheme mapping, and political strategic focus areas, a diverse suite of potential corridors can be developed.

Once the assessment is completed, the results are presented at a consortium incubation workshop. In the workshop, stakeholders prioritise potential corridors and partake in a round-table discussion about any barriers to moving on to a feasibility assessment for corridors with the highest interest and the scope of work the assessment will involve. The workshop ensures that the corridors that progress into the feasibility phase are those where commercial companies have a genuine interest (referred to as 'first wave' corridors). This allows the scoping phase of the feasibility assessment (including delegation of roles and responsibilities, and commitment of manhours) to be efficient and ensures momentum in the corridor maturation. For the first wave corridors, a preliminary assessment of the incremental costs of the green shipping corridor and possible emission reductions are also included in pre-feasibility reporting.

The methodologies outlined above have already been used in various green shipping corridor projects led by the MMMCZCS. Two examples are outlined in the following sections as case studies.

The Chile Green Shipping Corridors Pre-feasibility Assessment

Chile has unique geographical conditions making it a prime location for renewable energy production, specifically solar and wind energy. With the Atacama Desert, which boasts one of the world's highest levels of solar radiation, Chile has a technical potential of 1865 GW for solar, wind, and hydropower (IRENA, 2022). Furthermore, the country has set an ambitious goal of converting 70% of its energy consumption to renewables by 2030 and reaching net-zero emissions by 2050 (Government of Chile, 2020a). Chilean authorities and commercial companies are already investigating options for producing green hydrogen and alternative fuels (Government of Chile, 2020b). As a result, Chile is expected to become a global leader in renewable energy production in the coming decades.

Given the potential for producing alternative fuels in the country in the next few decades, Chile is a natural choice for early green shipping corridors. The Chilean authorities have voiced their support for green shipping corridors, with the vision of decarbonizing both domestic maritime transportation and international trade by 2050 through the use of alternative fuel (Government of Chile, 2020a). Chile's unique geographical conditions, ambitious renewable energy goals, and widespread political support for renewables make it a natural leader in green shipping corridors and alternative fuels. By prioritising and investing in green shipping corridors, Chile hopes to continue building on its renewable energy production foundation and pave the way for a more sustainable future.

The pre-feasibility phase of the Chilean green shipping corridor project was initiated at COP26 in 2021, where Chile signed the Clydebank Declaration. The project officially kicked off in March 2022. Partners in this project included the MMMCZCS and the Chilean Ministries of Energy, Transportation and Telecommunication, and Foreign Affairs. The project gathered data about potential alternative fuel supplies, port, and bunkering opportunities, vessel types and routes, and the regulatory landscape (MMMCZCS, 2023).

During the pre-feasibility study, an analysis of over 40 renewable energy projects announced in Chile showed that the vast majority of fuel projects aimed to produce ammonia, as there is a lack of sustainable CO_2 sources in the country. Green ammonia production is expected to reach 12 million tonnes by 2030, highlighting the potential for green shipping corridors fuelled by ammonia. The most promising port regions for green shipping corridors are Mejillones/Angamos and Punta Arenas (including Cabo Negro), which already handle numerous fuels/chemicals and have port facilities that could be adapted for alternative fuels (MMMCZCS, 2023).

Assessments of vessels, cargo, and trade in Chile revealed the importance of shipping in the copper industry, both related to the end products (refined copper and copper concentrate) and the materials and equipment needed for copper production. As a result, shipping of copper could be a commercially interesting green shipping corridor project. Additionally, an emerging market of ammonia exports could develop in the country over the next decade, making ammonia shipping a potential target for green shipping corridors. Finally, the regulatory landscape assessment revealed that the northern and southern extremities of the country have more funding options and incentives than the rest of the country, making these regions more attractive for green shipping corridor projects.

The MMMCZCS pre-feasibility methodology allows project participants to create their own selection criteria for green shipping corridors. In this project, the Chilean ministries provided selection criteria to ensure that potential green shipping corridors were aligned with their national strategies. These criteria included domestic use of ammonia as cargo or fuel, transitioning top CO_2 emission vessels to

Loc.	ID	Short description
D	1	Chilean Powerplant Ammonia
D	2	Chilean Mining Explosives Ammonia
D	3	Austral Ferries
D	4	Austral Cruise
I	5	CuS Corridor
I	6	Copper China Corridor
I	7	Green Cupper Europe
I	8	Car Import from Japan/South Korea
I	9	Agri/Aqua-culture Corridor
I	10	ContainEurope
I	11	CircumSouthAmericas
I	12	Ammonia Exp Japan
I	13	Ammonia Exp Rotterdam
I	14	Ammonia Exp Los Angeles
I	15	Ammonia Exp Singapore
D	16	Austral Fish/Aqua
D	17	Tug/service
D/I	18	H_2SO_4 Carrier for mining

D: Domestic, I: International

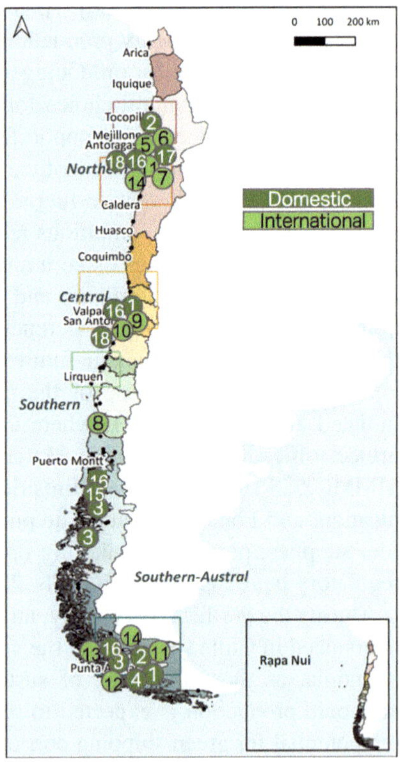

Fig. 3 Potential green shipping corridors identified during the Chile green corridors pre-feasibility assessment (MMMCZCS, 2023)

alternative fuels, and international transport of ammonia to enable it as a future commodity.

As shown in Fig. 3, the assessment resulted in a list of 18 potential green shipping corridors in Chile, half international and half domestic.

These were presented and discussed at the consortium incubation workshop, and from this list, four corridors were identified as the most promising and taken forward to feasibility studies: shipping copper concentrate from Antofagasta Region to Japan/South Korea, sulfuric acid transportation from Chile, Peru, or Southeast Asia to Mejillones, ammonia export from Northern Chile, and tugboats in Chilean ports.

The East Australia-New Zealand Pre-feasibility Assessment

Australia is a country with a high potential for renewable electricity production and is therefore expected to be a net exporter of alternative fuels in the future (IRENA, 2022). With this in mind, an Australia-New Zealand green shipping corridor project has been initiated with the goal of contributing to the development of a green hydrogen economy in Australia and New Zealand, with the ultimate aim of delivering zero-carbon shipping by 2050.

To achieve this goal, a pre-feasibility assessment was initiated in early 2023. The project aims to identify possible green shipping corridors that can operate on alternative fuels either domestically in Australia and New Zealand, between the two countries, or from either country to other countries.

The project team for the East Australia-New Zealand pre-feasibility study includes governmental departments of both regions, companies with a specific interest in Australia or New Zealand, and multinational companies, ensuring regional and international interests are both considered. The involvement of commercial companies across the supply chain at this early stage is a unique feature of this study. It is hoped that this approach will test whether including such companies enables corridors to have a greater probability of fast-track maturation in the next phases.

The first stage of the project was to reach out to relevant companies, institutes, and governmental departments, to define the roles and responsibilities of the study. As of May 2023, the data-gathering phase of the study is ongoing, and the aim is to have the green shipping corridors identified by the end of the year. This will enable the team to proceed with the next phases of the project, which include a feasibility assessment, followed by developing a roadmap for the development and implementation of the green shipping corridors.

The Feasibility Phase

Once promising green shipping corridors have been identified in the pre-feasibility assessments, they must go through feasibility assessments to determine whether they are technically and economically feasible and if there are regulatory barriers to progression. The work done in the feasibility phase is used to determine whether a green shipping corridor project should continue to the next phases—where costs and commitments escalate.

In 2022, MMMCZCS, together with management consulting company McKinsey & Company, published the Green Corridor Feasibility Blueprint (MMMCZCS, 2022c). This provides a detailed step-by-step process for the feasibility phase of a green shipping corridor project. As shown in Fig. 4, the feasibility phase consists of four steps: scoping, assessment, summary, and roadmap (MMMCZCS, 2022c).

The scoping phase uses the insights and knowledge from the pre-feasibility assessment. It involves defining the goal and objectives of the project, agreeing on deliverables and deadlines, outlining the work scope, and determining roles and responsibilities for project members. As the feasibility phase may involve sharing confidential data, a Project Agreement or Project Commitment Letter stating the confidentiality, objectives, deliverables, and deadlines are prepared and signed.

The next step is the feasibility assessment itself, where project participants gather and analyse data about alternative fuel supply chains, port and bunkering infrastructure, vessel decarbonization pathways, and cargo demand dynamics. These studies identify technical and regulatory gaps and the costs of delivering the project, including capital and operational expenditures. This can be seen in Fig. 5.

In the summary section of this phase, the data from the feasibility assessments are gathered and consolidated into summary technical, regulatory, and economic feasibility assessments. The technical feasibility assessment specifies any technical areas that must be addressed and specifies mitigating actions. The regulatory feasibility assessment identifies any required regulatory or policy changes or gaps needed for the green shipping corridor to proceed, identifies regulations and policies that could close cost gaps, and ensures alignment with UN commitments and directions. The economic feasibility assessment assesses cost gaps and the options for covering part of the cost gap within the value chain. The residual cost gap is identified, and opportunities for closing the gap through external sources are assessed and described. Finally, a risk register is developed to identify risks from across all the project aspects, estimate the probability and impact of risks, identify mitigating actions to reduce their probability or impact, and identify the optimal sequence for these actions.

The final section of this phase is the roadmap, in which the participants outline the short-term and midterm actions required to move the green shipping corridor forward to the next stages. This roadmap forms the basis for discussions with regulators, policymakers, and financial institutions around closing the residual cost gap.

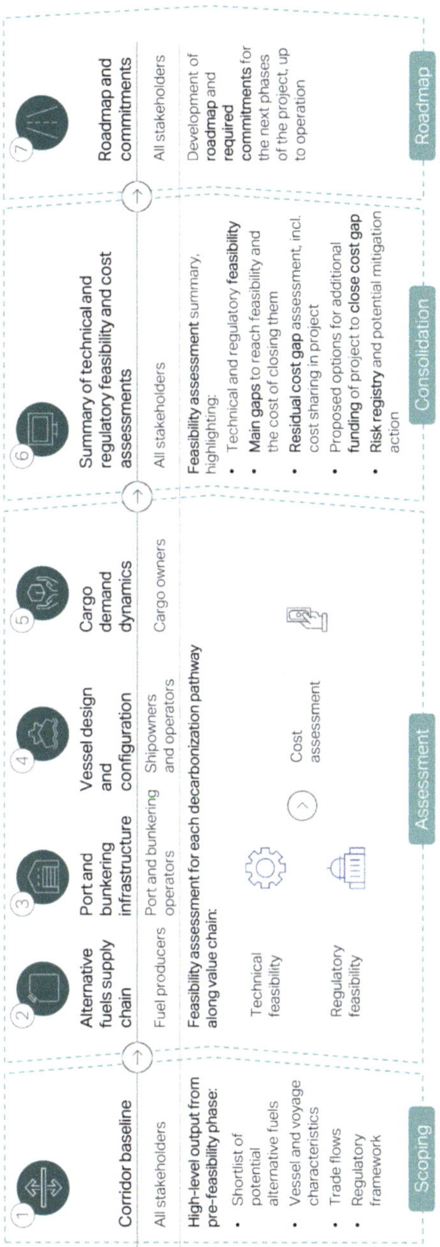

Fig. 4 Structure of the feasibility phase of a green shipping corridor project (MMMCZCS, 2022c)

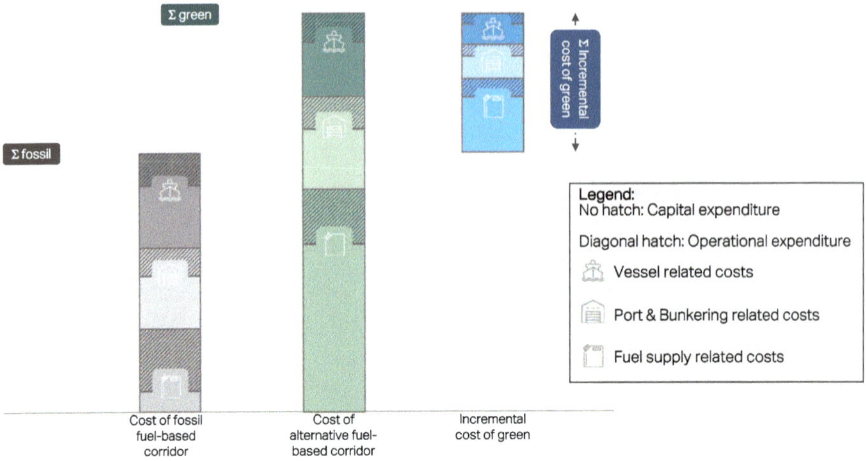

Fig. 5 Cost-gap analysis framework in the feasibility phase of a green shipping corridor project, identifying the capital and operational expenditures associated with fossil-based operation, alternative fuel-based operation, and the incremental cost of green shipping corridors

So far, the majority of the green shipping corridor announcements are still strategic statements only or in the pre-feasibility phase. Only a limited number of green shipping corridor projects in the global portfolio have reached the feasibility stage. The following section describes two promising corridors which are currently in the feasibility phase and are following the MMMCZCS methodology: The Chile Copper Corridor and The Rotterdam-Singapore Corridor.

The Chile Copper Corridor Feasibility Assessment

Copper is used in virtually all electrical products. As a result, it will be a key material in the green transition, and global demand is expected to increase from the current level of around 20–36 million tonnes per year by the end of this decade (McKinsey & Company, 2023; IEA, 2021). Chile currently produces over 20% of the global copper (IEA, 2021), and copper exports from ports in Northern Chile have a total value of around 30 billion USD (OEC, 2023).

As described earlier in this chapter, the Chilean Green Corridor Pre-feasibility study outlined four first-wave corridors, including an ammonia-fuelled copper concentrate corridor from Mejillones/Angamos in the Antofagsta Region to Japan/ Republic of Korea. The Antofagasta Region handles over 20% of the copper concentrate exports from Chile. Furthermore, the port operators in Mejillones/ Angamos have years of experience handling chemicals, including sulphuric acid and ammonia, an ammonia unloading facility, production facilities for explosives, and potential renewable electricity projects close by, making it an ideal candidate for a green shipping corridor.

The feasibility phase of the project kicked off in early 2023 and will be conducted according to the MMMCZCS Green Corridor Feasibility Phase Blueprint. The first phase of the project was the scoping phase. As committed stakeholders were identified in the consortium incubation workshop at the end of the pre-feasibility phase, constructing a project team for the feasibility phase and moving forward with the project has been straightforward. The scoping phase also determined the project's goal, which is to deploy ten ammonia-fuelled supramax vessels from Mejillones in Antofagasta Region to East Asia (Japan, South Korea), bringing up to 2 million tonnes of copper concentrate across the Pacific before 2030, with the first vessels expected in the water in 2028. The project team includes representatives from across the supply chain, including Sumitomo (fuel producers), Interacid (ports and logistics), NYK (vessel owners and operators), MAN Energy (engine technology provider), the MMMCZCS, and the Chilean ministries for Energy, Transportation and Telecommunication, and Foreign Affairs. After agreeing to the goals and objectives of the project, the stakeholders were asked to define their commitment level. This commitment process feeds directly into the project governance structure, which was finalised in May 2023, when the project moved on to the assessment phase, where the economic, technical, and regulatory feasibility will be analysed in detail.

The Rotterdam-Singapore Corridor Feasibility Assessment

The shipment of containers between Asia and Europe is one of the most fuel-demanding routes in the shipping industry. Data from MMMCZCS's partner organizations shows that over 20 million TEU (20-foot equivalent units) are moved along this route annually by more than 150 large container vessels, with an estimated fuel consumption of 3.7 million tonnes of marine fuel oil. A few companies offer eco-delivery on the route, but the vast majority of the vessels are still using fossil fuel. The resulting WTW (well-to-wake) emissions from this shipping route are around 14 million tonnes of CO_2 equivalent each year.

Singapore and Rotterdam are key ports on the Asia-Europe shipping lane and are among the largest bunkering ports in the world. In August 2022, the Port of Rotterdam and the Maritime and Port Authority of Singapore announced the kick-off of the world's longest green shipping corridor (MMMCZCS, 2022d). The objective of the corridor is to 'accelerate decarbonization of the shipping industry by working with stakeholders to provide low or zero carbon fuels and bunkering infrastructure in Singapore and Rotterdam over the next years and deliver solutions at scale by 2030.' The corridor will also be a digital shipping corridor, with the additional goal of creating trade lanes where relevant information and data are shared between stakeholders to ensure more efficient port operations and the flow of goods.

In contrast to the Chile Copper Corridor, no dedicated pre-feasibility study was conducted in advance of this feasibility study, and the project partners were those working closely with the Port of Rotterdam and the Maritime and Port Authority of Singapore. The project partners include industry partners across the supply chain, including bp, CMA CGM, Digital Container Shipping Association, Maersk, MSC, Ocean Network Express, PSA International, Shell, the Global Centre for Maritime Decarbonisation, and the MMMCZCS.

The Rotterdam-Singapore feasibility assessment will follow the MMMCZCS methodology. It will investigate a range of potential alternative fuels for use on the green shipping corridor, including hydrogen, ammonia, methanol, and biofuels. As the vessel and engine technologies, the bunkering experience, and the production cost for the various fuel types are in different stages, the project has been split into a series of sub-projects for each alternative fuel. The project is currently in the scoping phase, with the assessment phase expected to begin in June 2023.

Green Shipping Corridors Support a Just and Equitable Transition

When considering green shipping corridors or any other decarbonization projects, we must ensure that we are developing pathways to decarbonization that are just and equitable for all, with no one left behind (UNCTAD, 2022). The industry has already committed to this cause by setting up the 'Maritime Just Transition Task Force' at COP26. The task force was established to ensure that the decarbonization of the shipping industry is supported by globally established 'just transition' principles (UNGC, 2022). According to the International Labor Organization, a 'just transition' means decarbonizing in a way that is as fair and inclusive as possible, creating decent work opportunities and 'leaving no one behind'. A just transition involves maximising the social and economic opportunities of climate action while minimizing and carefully managing any challenges—including effective social dialogue among all groups impacted and respect for fundamental labour principles and rights (International Labour Organization, 2015). Chapter "Ensuring Seafarers Are at the Heart of Decarbonization Action" in this book covers the Just Transition in greater detail.

Green shipping corridors can play a vital role in supporting a just and equitable energy transition, with potential social opportunities for workers, communities, and countries. For example, green shipping corridors can create decent green jobs in alternative fuel production, distribution, and bunkering and will give workers upgraded capabilities for handling alternative fuels and the associated energy infrastructure. Furthermore, the jobs provided by green shipping corridors offer a chance to build a new, more diverse workforce. Communities can also benefit from green shipping corridors through increased economic activity related to green shipping corridors, health benefits from reducing fossil fuel use, and increased resource availability from, for example, renewable electricity infrastructure. At a national level, green shipping corridors can provide social benefits, including developing entire economies, opportunities for innovation and technology transfer, and increasing participation in international trade. These social opportunities for workers, communities, and countries should be maximised to support a just and equitable transition.

However, to make the most of these benefits, green shipping corridor projects must also be aware of risks threatening a just transition and carefully navigate them in their planning phases. For example, if green shipping corridors rely on foreign workforces instead of upskilling workers and building capacity in domestic workers, the local population will not benefit from the social opportunities of the green shipping corridor. There is also a risk of job misalignment, where jobs are lost in fossil-fuelled related supply chains but are not replaced by jobs in the same location requiring the same or similar skills. This may leave some workers without jobs. There are also community-wide and national risks that must be carefully managed, such as green shipping corridors impacting ecosystems and displacing traditional industries. Furthermore, countries may miss out on the benefits of green shipping corridors if projects require upfront investments that they are unable to fund or if they continue to be disproportionally affected by increased shipping costs.

Closing Remarks and the Way Ahead

Green shipping corridors are innovative value chain projects that seek to promote the adoption of low- or zero-carbon alternative fuels. These projects have gained significant prominence following the signing of the Clydebank Declaration during the COP26 conference, where these signatories pledged to establish and support green shipping corridors by the middle of the decade and a larger number by the end

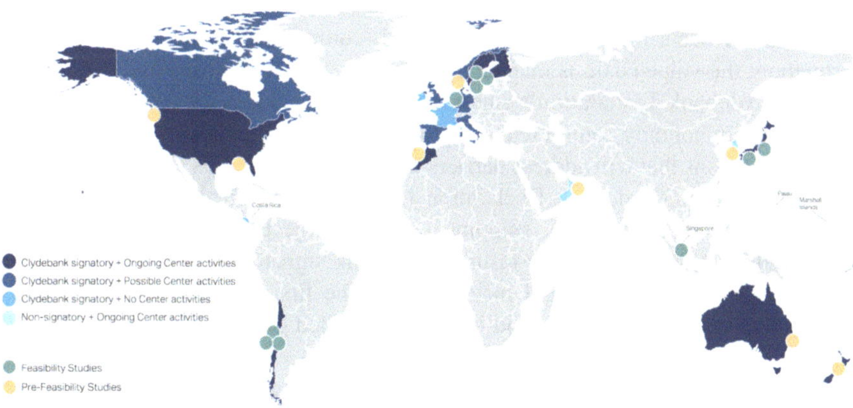

Fig. 6 Map of Clydebank signatories, MMMCZCS activities, and ongoing green shipping corridor projects

of the decade. The disposition of the current signatories, the ongoing projects and the involvement of the MMMCZCS is shown in Fig. 6.

The MMMCZCS has made a firm commitment to support green shipping corridors and expects several corridors to be operationalised in the next few years. To support this, it has developed a comprehensive framework to help green shipping corridors move from announcements to action. The Center believes that its framework can serve as a valuable guide for organisations and governments seeking to establish and implement green shipping corridors while also prioritising the needs of local communities and the environment.

While there have been announcements of several green shipping corridor projects, few have progressed beyond the early stages, and none have reached execution. The importance of these corridors cannot be overemphasised, and the transition from conceptualisation to actualisation of green shipping corridors will be a significant step toward achieving a sustainable future. However, the deployment of new alternative fuels will be significantly more costly than fossil fuel-based alternatives. Bridging the cost gap could be achieved by implementing a substantial global price on CO_2 emissions. But until this is implemented, there is a need to accelerate the initial green shipping corridor projects, gain knowledge, and thereby start the cost-down, the reduction of cost in the supply chain through the review of actual costs and the adoption of new materials, standards, processes or behaviours to reduce cost. This early cost-down will pave the road for bunkering hubs that can support more corridors.

Three activities are required for green shipping corridors to overcome the barriers and become operational. First, regulators and policymakers must recognise that financial incentives and support are necessary. Transportation on green shipping corridors will begin as more costly than fossil-based alternatives, and supplementary public funding will be needed for green shipping corridors to progress. The cost gap for using alternative fuels cannot be closed by customers or commercial companies alone, while the future of carbon or carbon equivalent pricing remains unclear. Second, a stringent and transparent assessment of technical and economic aspects is crucial for securing public funding. Third, commitment from project partners throughout the value chain is mandatory for accurate and qualified assessments.

The Clydebank Declaration's mission statement includes phrases that confirm signatories are not only committed to supporting green shipping corridors but also to exploring actions that will address barriers to their formation. It is imperative that the signatories of the Clydebank Declaration follow through on their commitment to support and incentivise green shipping corridor projects to ensure that they are successfully implemented. As a result, Clydebank signatory countries should provide the necessary support and incentives for the first corridors to enable early deployment of alternative fuels and initiate the needed cost-down.

Acknowledgments The authors would like to thank Emily Nordvang (MMMCZCS) for providing support in writing this chapter. They would also like to thank Torben Nørgaard and Tanja Ebbe Dalgaard for reviewing the chapter drafts and providing valuable feedback. Finally, Taila Senanu and Joe Bettles are thanked for assistance in the graphics.

References

Department of Transport. (2022). *COP 26: Clydebank declaration for green shipping corridors.* https://www.gov.uk/government/publications/cop-26-clydebank-declaration-for-green-shipping-corridors/cop-26-clydebank-declaration-for-green-shipping-corridors

Global Maritime Forum. (2022). *Annual progress report on green shipping corridors.* https://www.globalmaritimeforum.org/publications/annual-progress-report-on-green-shipping-corridors

Government of Chile. (2020a). *Chile's nationally determined contribution.* https://unfccc.int/sites/default/files/NDC/2022-06/Chile%27s_NDC_2020_english.pdf

Government of Chile. (2020b). *National green hydrogen strategy.* https://energia.gob.cl/sites/default/files/national_green_hydrogen_strategy_-_chile.pdf

IEA. (2021). *World energy outlook special report: The role of critical minerals in clean energy transitions.* https://iea.blob.core.windows.net/assets/ffd2a83b-8c30-4e9d-980a-52b6d9a86fdc/TheRoleofCriticalMineralsinCleanEnergyTransitions.pdf

International Labour Organization. (2015). *Guidelines for a just transition towards environmentally sustainable economies and societies for all.* https://www.ilo.org/wcmsp5/groups/public/@ed_emp/@emp_ent/documents/publication/wcms_432859.pdf

International Maritime Organization. (2023). Revised GHG reduction strategy for global shipping adopted. Revised GHG reduction strategy for global shipping adopted (imo.org)

IRENA. (2022). *Global hydrogen trade to meet the 1.5°C climate goal: Trade outlook for 2050 and way forward.* https://www.irena.org/publications/2022/May/Global-hydrogen-trade-Cost

McKinsey & Company. (2023). *Copper-processing technologies: Growing global copper supply.* https://www.mckinsey.com/industries/metals-and-mining/our-insights/bridging-the-copper-supply-gap

MMMCZCS. (2022a). *Maritime decarbonization strategy 2022.* https://www.zerocarbonshipping.com/publications/maritime-decarbonization-strategy/

MMMCZCS. (2022b). *Green corridors pre-feasibility phase blueprint.* https://www.zerocarbonshipping.com/publications/green-corridors-pre-feasibility-phase-blueprint/

MMMCZCS. (2022c). *Green corridors feasibility phase blueprint.* https://www.zerocarbonshipping.com/publications/green-corridors-feasibility-phase-blueprint/

MMMCZCS. (2022d). *Maritime and port authority of Singapore and Port of Rotterdam to establish world's longest green and digital corridor for efficient and sustainable shipping.* https://www.zerocarbonshipping.com/news/maritime-and-port-authority-of-singapore-and-port-of-rotterdam-to-establish-worlds-longest-green-and-digital-corridor-for-efficient-and-sustainable-shipping/

MMMCZCS. (2023). *The Chilean green corridors network pre-feasibility study summary.* https://cms.zerocarbonshipping.com/media/uploads/documents/Chile-Pre-Feasibility-Report-Summary.pdf

OEC. (2023). *Copper ore in Chile.* https://oec.world/en/profile/bilateral-product/copper-ore/reporter/chl

The Boston Consulting Group. (2021). *Global shipping's net-zero transformation challenge.* https://www.bcg.com/publications/2021/global-zero-carbon-shipping-transformation-challenge

UNCTAD. (2022). *Why should we talk about a 'just and equitable' transition for shipping?* https://unctad.org/news/why-should-we-talk-about-just-and-equitable-transition-shipping#:~:text=While%20a%20%E2%80%98just%20and%20equitable%E2%80%99%20transition%20may%20be,fair%2C%20socially%20just%2C%20technologically%20inclusive%20and%20globally%20equitable

UNGC. (2022). *Mapping a just transition for the global maritime workforce.* The Just Transition Task Force.

The Getting to Zero Coalition Story

Mette Asmussen, Randall Krantz, and Ingrid Sidenvall Jegou

Scene Setter: The UN Stage in 2019

It is a sunny Monday in September 2019 when Heads of State and Governments are gathered in the rotunda of the General Assembly in New York at the UN Climate Action Summit. On stage before them, jointly with representatives from other hard-to-abate industries, is a powerful duo from A.P. Moller Maersk and the Port of Antwerp. These two leaders represent an alliance from across the maritime industry, comprising companies from shipping, energy, infrastructure, and finance sectors. They are about to present the newly-formed Getting to Zero Coalition, set up to radically advance shipping decarbonization. Months of work—for some it has been years—have gone into this day, and the press release calls it 'Shipping's moon-shot ambition' (Getting to Zero Coalition, 2019).

The UN Secretary General Antonio Guterres convened the Climate Action Summit asking that countries and sectors showcase action with a focus on the 'how'. Climate activist Greta Thunberg, arriving at this year's UN General Assembly on a zero-emission sailing boat, has called out the World leaders for their lack of action and made it clear, with support from a global youth movement, that there is no time to wait for action. Real transformative action is needed to meet the Paris agreement. On the Summit's main stage are Chief Operating Officer Søren Toft from A.P. Møller Mærsk and Chief Executive Officer Jacques Vandermeiren from the Port of Antwerp-Bruges. They represent a broader group with the shared objective to have commercially viable zero emission vessels operating along

M. Asmussen (✉)
World Economic Forum, Geneva, Switzerland
e-mail: mette.asmussen@weforum.org

R. Krantz · I. S. Jegou
Global Maritime Forum, Copenhagen, Denmark
e-mail: rkr@globalmaritimeforum.org; isj@globalmaritimeforum.org

M. Lind et al. (eds.), *Maritime Decarbonization*,
https://doi.org/10.1007/978-3-031-39936-7_32

deep-sea trade routes by 2030 signed by 74 companies from the maritime sector and members of civil society and endorsed by 11 progressive countries at the time of its launch. At its launch, it was hoped that the Getting to Zero Coalition could be a showcase model for other hard-to-abate sectors (Maersk, 2019).

After the official presentation on the main stage, a press conference was hosted with attendance of the two representatives as well as Jeppe Kofod, Minister for Foreign Affairs of Denmark and Rachel Kyte, CEO of Sustainable Energy for All. The presence of the Danish government emphasised a component that, over the years, was also an inevitable factor for success: namely the collaboration across private and public sectors that drives the ongoing work of the three founding partners of the Getting to Zero Coalition. Søren Skou, then CEO of A.P. Møller Mærsk, was quoted saying, '*To take the next big step change towards decarbonization of shipping, a shift in propulsion technologies or a shift to clean fuels is required which implies close collaboration from all parties. The coalition launched today is a crucial vehicle to make this collaboration happen*,' (Getting to Zero Coalition, 2019).

Shipping had been identified as one of the hard-to-abate sectors a long time before this moment at the UN General Assembly. A little over a year before, the UN International Maritime Organization (IMO) had agreed in April 2018 that international shipping must reduce its greenhouse gas (GHG) emissions by at least 50% compared to 2008 levels by 2050. This level of ambition might not sound impressive from today's point of view, but it was ground-breaking at the time, and the industry was not aligned on what the future could look like and had no roadmap or strategy to get there. '*Starting now is essential because ships built today will stay on the water for decades,*' said Ben van Beurden, CEO of Royal Dutch Shell (Maersk, 2019).

Now an industry-led coalition was setting a 10-year ambition to make that a reality.

How did this come to be? Where would it go?

Backstory: How Did We Get Here?

Climate and Shipping Before 2018

It can be hard to recall where the industry stood with respect to decarbonization before 2018. It is not that conversations on decarbonization were non-existent, but the idea was more abstract, seemingly less urgent, and far from actionable. A big effort had already been made within the IMO, but it had not yet been possible to reach a common agreement on a roadmap for the reduction of GHG emissions from ships.

Participants at the Danish Maritime Forum in 2016 identified 'a clear risk of national or regional regulation if the industry does not act; regulation that will impose a significant burden on companies and undermine the global nature of shipping' (Danish Maritime Forum, 2016). In December 2017, a growing number of countries announced their support for the Tony de Brum declaration on climate and shipping, which called for an IMO deal in 2018 to 'set a level of ambition for the sector that is compatible with that of the Paris Agreement, including a peak on emissions in the short-term and then reducing them to neutrality towards the second half of this century.' (Pacific Island Nations, 2017).

Going into the 2018 IMO negotiations, 44 countries supported the Tony De Brum declaration, yet the IMO's plan was a deal to ensure new ships are 30% more efficient by 2025. However, Brussels-based non-governmental organisation (NGO) Transport & Environment showed that almost three quarters of container ships were already ahead of that low bar (Transport and Environment, 2017). Meanwhile, shipping's largest and most influential industry associations, the International Chamber of Shipping (ICS) and BIMCO, were calling for shipping decarbonization *after* 2050, claiming that the sector could not accept any 'commitment or intention to place a binding cap on either the international shipping sector's total CO_2 emissions or the CO_2 emissions of individual ships' (Adamopoulos, 2017).

Against this backdrop, the achievement of the IMO initial GHG strategy, announced after lengthy negotiations concluding on 19 April 2018, was groundbreaking, mandating a reduction in carbon intensity of international shipping by at least 40% by 2030 compared to 2008 and a reduction in the total annual GHG emissions by at least 50% by 2050 and work towards phasing out GHG emissions from shipping entirely as soon as possible in this century.

A 'Burning Platform' for Climate Action

This unprecedented global agreement created the 'burning platform' for industry, requiring change despite the fear of the unknown consequences. This was exactly what the Global Maritime Forum was looking for at the time, and they entered the shipping decarbonization space with a project to create a collective and encouraging industry reaction to the new IMO policy. Working with a handful of ambitious companies, A.P. Møller Maersk, Cargill, Euronav, Gaslog, Lloyd's Register, and Trafigura, a Call to Action: CEOs and maritime industry leaders in support of decarbonization (2018) was developed. The statement lauded the IMO strategy as 'a step towards achieving GHG emissions reductions consistent with the Paris Agreement temperature goals', and highlighted that 'the shipping industry needs to further improve operational and technical energy efficiency, and must transition to zero carbon fuels and new propulsion systems.' (Global Maritime Forum, 2018a). This statement was signed by 50 Chief Executive Officers (CEOs) from shipping companies and shipping banks, and launched at the Global Maritime Forum's first Annual Summit in Hong Kong in October 2019.

At the same time of this first step, it was clear that the transformation of the shipping industry would require increased attention at a global level, collaboration with other industries, and engagement with stakeholders beyond the maritime sector.

To help fill these gaps, the Global Maritime Forum approached the Friends of Ocean Action, a coalition of ocean leaders fast-tracking solutions to ocean challenges and hosted by the World Economic Forum, to propose a partnership. It was agreed that the three organisations could meaningfully accelerate shipping decarbonization by reframing the alternative fuels conversation among industry leaders, policy makers, and other key stakeholders.

Birth of the Getting to Zero Coalition

In January 2019, a session hosted by the Friends of Ocean Action as part of the first 'Ocean Day' at the World Economic Forum Annual Meeting in Davos brought together industry leaders, NGOs, and experts to explore the question, 'How can we rapidly decarbonize the shipping industry?' The session, 'Shipping emissions: Setting sail toward a carbon-free future,' (World Economic Forum, 2019) built on several advances over the prior months, including new research from the Energy Transitions Commission, which set out a realistic and economically viable pathway for shipping decarbonization (Energy Transitions Commission, 2019). A second advancement was early decarbonization commitments from shipping companies such as Maersk, who led the industry response by committing to decarbonize their shipping operations by 2050.

Ahead of that Ocean Day session, a group of 20 leaders from industry and civil society had met in Davos to explore what an industry-led collaboration to decarbonize shipping might look like. Building on these successes, a core group of eight leading companies representing the full value chain (A.P. Møller Maersk, Cargill, Citigroup, Euronav, Gaslog, Lloyd's Register, Shell, and Trafigura) came together to frame the ambition of an action-oriented coalition for shipping decarbonization. Several key elements guided the ambitions as they were being laid out:

- **Urgency**—Despite hard targets from the IMO focused on 2050, there is a need to act urgently in the 2020s and focus on deliverables by 2030. During the decade up to 2030 the trajectories required for decarbonization in line with the IMO ambition and the Paris Agreement are the same. This can be seen in the figure below (Fig. 1).
- **Ambition**—While there was much debate around what would define a sufficiently ambitious goal for an industry decarbonization coalition, the agreed goal was to get 'commercially viable' zero emission vessels on the water by 2030. Commercial viability went beyond pilots and demonstration projects, and set out to have zero emission vessels being the default choice of a new vessel in 2030.
- **Scope**—From the beginning, the focus of the ambition was on scale and long-term solutions. Efficiency measures were quickly deemed out of scope, as were drop-in solutions such as biofuels, which were neither scalable, nor drivers of the technology and infrastructure investments required for scalable zero emission fuels. Bringing clarity to this scope started out as a 'fuels footnote', and quickly

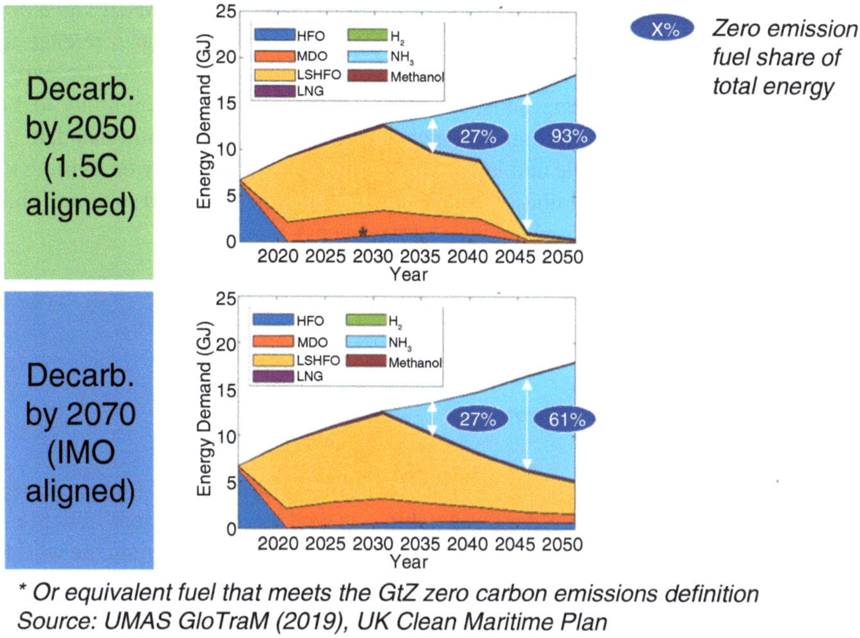

Fig. 1 Comparison of decarbonization trajectories for international shipping

	Biomass derived (biofuel, biogas)	**Hydrogen and synthetic non-carbon fuels** (ammonia)	**Synthetic fossil fuels** (e-methanol, e-methane, etc.)
Carbon and GHG operational emissions	CO_2 and GHG	None	CO_2 and GHG
Zero or net zero	Net zero	Zero	Net zero (depending on source of carbon)
Zero carbon upstream available today	No	No	No
Zero carbon upstream possible in 2030	Not likely at volume	Not likely at volume	Not likely at volume
Zero carbon upstream possible in 2050	Yes	Yes	Yes
Potential for volume/ sustainability constraint	Yes	No	No

Fig. 2 Summary table of getting to zero fuels scope

expanded into a paper (Smith, 2019) longer than the Ambition Statement itself (Fig. 2).

At one level, the resulting Ambition Statement (Getting to Zero Coalition, 2019a) of the Getting to Zero Coalition was deliberately amorphous. It was unquantified, and creatively set ambitions for the industry as a whole rather than for each signatory company. Even the name was a bit of a trojan horse; it was a clear reference to getting zero emission vessels on the water, but also spoke to getting the entire shipping industry to zero emissions, a concept that was far too ambitious to be explicitly included in the ambition statement at the time. However, the mandate of the Coalition was also flexible and led by pioneering companies that were willing to look ahead and ratchet the ambitions that they and their peers would take on. This turned out to be one of the fundamentals of its success.

Process: Partnering to Drive Action

Choosing the Right Partner

These days there are partnerships everywhere: business partnerships, public-private partnerships and multi-stakeholder partnerships, as well as collaborations, alliances, dialogues and many other forms of working together. Every partnership in the world, regardless of its size, specific topic or country of operation, has the same mission statement: to work together more effectively and efficiently to accomplish a common objective through shared resources, shared risk and shared responsibility. Implementing that simple mission, however, can get confusing, and it is very different for driving systems change than it is for a commercial partnership.

The World Economic Forum, the Friends of Ocean Action, and the Global Maritime Forum are all built around similar impact strategies (sometimes called theories of change) in catalysing collective, industry-led action with multi-stakeholder support to drive systems change. In forming the Getting to Zero Coalition, each brought to the table complementary resources and skills—the World Economic Forum has strong industry engagement across multiple industries, access to a broad network of experts from the harder to abate industries, a proven record of building communities for impact and relationships at the highest levels of government, while the Global Maritime Forum has a deep network of leaders from the maritime industry, strong relationships across industry media, and staff with in-depth knowledge of the decarbonization challenge. Last, but not least, Friends of Ocean Action is a unique, informal group of global ocean leaders from a range of sectors who are fast-tracking solutions to the most pressing challenges facing the ocean curated by the World Economic Forum's Ocean Action Agenda and has been highly impactful in creating awareness about the consequences for the health of our oceans.

Foundations for a Successful High Ambition Coalition

Tackling an enormously complex problem such as shipping decarbonization can be intimidating and overwhelming, especially in the face of all those who said (and some who still say) that it cannot be done. Therefore, in addition to finding aligned partners, optimism is a clear prerequisite for addressing such a 'wicked problem'. By building a partnership on the basis of a depth of resources, solid communication and strong interactions between partners, it is possible to shift from a transactional mindset associated with commercial partnerships, into a relational mindset that is required for a social partnership to be successful in the longer term.

From the beginning, the Getting to Zero Coalition was built upon a clear and common ambition embraced by the founding partners, the industry members, and the knowledge partners. As this ambition evolved over time (see below), it continued to have the support of the partners and members. The clarity and simplicity of the vision allowed for it to be translated into a comprehensive theory of change that allowed tracking of progress towards its goal. One challenge with the ambition of the Getting to Zero Coalition has been to ensure that it stays relevant and ahead of the curve as the coalition grows and as the industry advances. It has been important to ensure that the leading players remain engaged, and also that those who are committed observers in the coalition are brought along. One simple metaphor that is sometimes used is that of a Slinky, a spring-like children's toy that can stretch, but not too far that it might break. Balancing the bold ambition of the coalition with its growth—now over 200 members—requires deft agility, especially to avoid the danger of consensus decisions that could drag ambitions down to the lowest common denominator.

Systems Leadership

Shipping has gone through evolutionary steps before, among them the shift from coal to liquid fuels a century ago and the containerisation of the cargo industry 50 years ago. Reducing and eliminating GHG emissions is now one of the most pressing challenges for an industry that moves up to 90% of all goods around the world, facilitating global trade and enabling transportation to more remote locations. To drive such a change, it is important to take a systems leadership view, which drives convergence around three elements: understanding the system more deeply, engaging fellow stakeholders more meaningfully, and taking action in new ways (Senge et al., 2015). The Getting to Zero Coalition set out to achieve all three of these.

From the beginning, the Getting to Zero Coalition aimed to contribute significant, lasting impact on the very complex issue of industry decarbonization by mobilising action among a diverse array of relevant stakeholders. This type of initiative is sometimes defined as a 'Systems Leadership initiative' (Dreier et al., 2019), which engages collaborative leadership, coalition building, and complex systems thinking. The collaborative leadership for such an initiative is the use of 'backbone support', whose role includes both building alignment, securing commitment, and supporting ongoing collaboration, alongside the practical aspects of project management to support initiative activities. The function of coalition building and advocacy serves to develop alignment and mobilise action among stakeholders across the system. This is supported by understanding of the complex systems shaping the decarbonization challenge. Through the staff at the Global Maritime Forum, the Friends of Ocean Action, and the World Economic Forum that have been dedicated to the Coalition, the support went well beyond a typical secretariat.

Timing as a Factor for Success

Finally, while building a coalition follows no exact recipe, timing plays a pivotal role. In the case of shipping decarbonization, a number of disparate companies and organisations had been picking up the issue years before, but there was nothing to bring them together. The momentum to act was created by the combination of the IMO Initial GHG Strategy creating an effective goal post in 2018 and the UN Climate Summit in 2019 providing a stage for launch with shipping as one of the few sectors within the hard-to-abate industries taking a step forward and the leaning in from key well-known companies.

Almost 4 years later, timing is once again a critical factor. This time more how the Coalition jointly with other initiatives in the shipping decarbonization space leverages a unique window of opportunity for policymaking on both international and European levels. The IMO is expected to adopt its Revised GHG Strategy at the 80th meeting of the Marine Environment Protection Committee (MEPC80) in July 2023 and the EU is officially adopting more and more crucial files on shipping within the Fit for 55 Proposal. With the Coalition being rather mature in its work and structure, one of the key instruments the Coalition work has revolved around is empowering industry champions to convey the messages and creating platforms for dialogue and engagement between these industry champions and policymakers.

As It Happened: Ratcheting and Spreading of Ambition

Spreading Ambition

The main stage at the UN General Assembly was not the end of the journey, but the beginning of the real work. As the Getting to Zero Coalition came together, an increasing number of partnerships and parallel pieces of work started to emerge on shipping decarbonization. Many of these initiatives focused on bringing together complementary pieces of the value chain.

Cargo Owners for Zero Emission Vessels (coZEV) was a first-of-its-kind cargo owner-led network to enable maritime freight customers to come together to accelerate maritime shipping decarbonization through a series of actions and projects (Aspen Institute, 2022). By aggregating commitments of beneficial cargo owners, coZEV was able to send a powerful signal to the shipping industry that demand for zero emissions shipping was on its way, and that it would be a decisive factor for freight purchasing decisions.

The Poseidon Principles for Financial Institutions is a global framework for responsible ship finance developed in an effort spearheaded by global shipping banks The Poseidon Principles for Financial Institutions were the first of three initiatives developed by the Global Maritime Forum with the shared aim to decarbonize shipping. Along with their sister initiatives, The Poseidon Principles for Marine Insurance and the Sea Cargo Charter, they are guided by four Principles: assessment of climate alignment, accountability, enforcement, and transparency (Poseidonprinciples.org, 2023). Together, these transparency initiatives brought shipping banks, insurers, and charterers to the decarbonization table.

It was not just the private sector that was pushing on shipping decarbonization, the ecosystem also comprised NGOs and academics that were pulling as well. Many of these came together as part of the UN Climate Change High-Level Champions, a series of government-supported campaigns seeking to rally 'non-State-actors' to support and raise ambitions at the UN Framework Convention on Climate Change

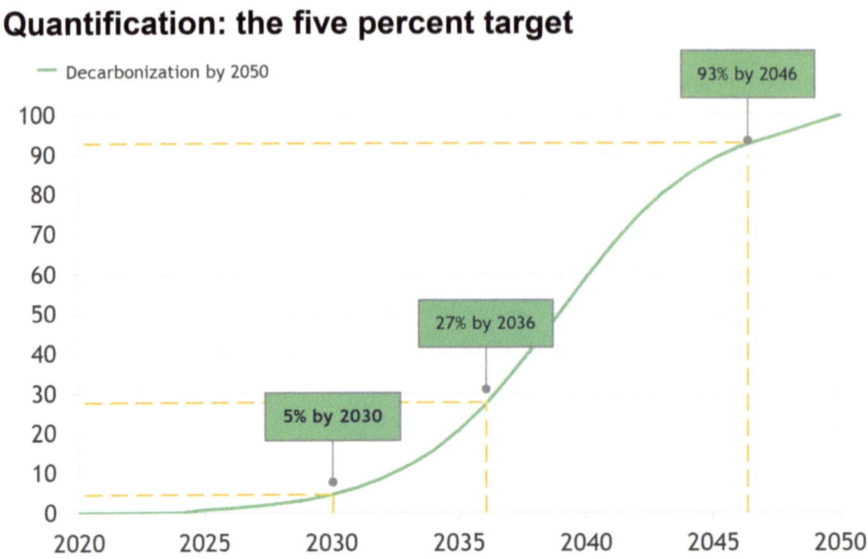

Fig. 3 Zero emission fuel adoption rate for decarbonization by 2050

(UNFCCC) negotiations. The High-Level Champions for COP25 in Madrid and COP26 in Glasgow, Gonzalo Muñoz and Nigel Topping, established the Climate Champions Team to help deliver on their mandate to enhance ambition and strengthen the engagement of non-State actors. In the run up to COP26, a shipping team was assembled and the ambition was similar to that of the Getting to Zero Coalition.

Working closely with the experts at the University College London (UCL) Energy Institute and the secretariat of the Getting to Zero Coalition, they sought to quantify at what degree of adoption zero emission fuels become 'commercially viable'. Analysis suggested that zero emission fuels need to make up 5% of the international shipping fuel mix by 2030 to enable decarbonization in line with Paris goals, as seen in Fig. 3 below. This 5% was seen as a tipping point between the emergence phase of a new technology, in which it is used in pilots, demonstrations and by first movers, and the diffusion phase in which it can rapidly scale up by being cost competitive (including with subsidies and/or market-based mechanisms). This idea was first presented in a Getting to Zero paper in March of 2021 (Osterkamp et al., 2021), which was co-authored by Climate Champions, UCL, and the Getting to Zero Coalition.

Quantification: The Five Percent Target

This target subsequently emerged as a base for targets for many shipping decarbonization initiatives, including the intergovernmental initiative, Mission

Innovation (2021). Effectively creating some of the foundations for a common understanding and goal for stakeholders to aim at. That common understanding among the industry and non-State actors was also influential when the First Movers Coalition was set up by the U.S. Department of State and the World Economic Forum and in which carriers set a target that at least 5% of their deep-sea shipping will be powered by zero-emission fuels by 2030, and cargo owners set a target that at least 10% of the volume of their goods shipped internationally will be on ships using zero-emission fuels by 2030, on the way to 100% by 2040 (World Economic Forum, 2022).

Ratcheting the Ambition to Zero

If one loose end of the Getting to Zero Coalition was quantifying the short-term 2030 goal, the other was raising the ambition to full decarbonization of the industry. While this seemed impossible to the vast majority of members at the Getting to Zero launch in 2019, less than 2 years later, it was already on the cards. Once again, the process started with a drafting group, and in this case, it was to create a text for a Call to Action from industry to call on governments to raise their ambitions as part of the UNFCCC process and at the IMO. Signatories of the Call to Action for Shipping Decarbonization (2021) urged governments to do three things: (1) Commit to decarbonizing international shipping by 2050; (2) Support industrial scale zero emission shipping projects through national action; and (3) Deliver policy measures that will make zero emission shipping the default choice by 2030 (Getting to Zero Coalition, 2021).

The Call to Action for Shipping Decarbonization (2021) had a soft launch at the UN General Assembly in September 2021, with the goal of bringing more signatories in the run up to the UNFCCC COP26 in Glasgow. In the end more than 200 companies signed the Call to Action, making a big impact as one of the more concrete and widely supported industry initiatives in Glasgow. Interestingly, the Call to Action for Shipping Decarbonization (2021) was drafted by the Getting to Zero Coalition, but was not a requirement for Getting to Zero Coalition members to sign up to, nor was it limited to the coalition. This was by design, and served as a way to test how well the ambitions of coalition members aligned with a full decarbonization target by 2050. At the time of its launch in Glasgow, about three quarters of coalition members were signed up to the new ambition.

Following approval by the Getting to Zero Coalition steering committee, the Coalition set about formally raising the bar. Over the coming months, a workshop and one-on-one calls helped engage the broader membership of the Coalition with the new ambition and allowed them to voice any concerns. Ultimately, there were a few companies that were hesitant, but not one backed down from the new commitment. Six months after its Glasgow launch, the ambitions of the Call to Action for Shipping Decarbonization (2021) became the formal ambition of the Getting to Zero Coalition, demonstrating the power of systems leadership and collective action.

Around the same time, the critical mass of industry associations started to migrate their ambitions en masse. The formal changing of positions for industry decarbonization targets has brought an even more consensus across the key industry stakeholders and further emphasised momentum to set formal regulatory ambitions. While different approaches remain and there are supporters of both the net-zero approach and the full zero approach, there is today more convergence than divergence.

From UN Stage to IMO: Ambition Loop and Government Action

At the core of shipping industry decarbonization stands the UN International Maritime Organization (IMO), which has the potential to bring a global level playing field to a truly global industry with assets that move across borders and through regions. In the run up to Glasgow in autumn 2021, the Getting to Zero Coalition launched an Industry Transition Strategy, a comprehensive study of the actions that governments, industry, and international bodies must take to deliver on a transition to zero emissions by 2050 (Smith et al., 2021). This report underlined that the transition to full decarbonization by 2050 is possible, but all actors need to prepare in their own way.

The report pointed out that those countries and companies with potential to support and deploy zero emission shipping this decade must begin to work together on doing so, and all parties should work to enable robust action globally through the IMO. To the dismay of some, the report also described the scenarios in which shipping industry decarbonization would be possible with a laggard IMO, in which case regional governments might step forward with carbon pricing schemes, creating a patchwork of regional regulations. While this would not be an ideal scenario for any global business, it is coming to bear as the EU Emissions Trading System (EU ETS) embraces shipping in its mandate.

Simultaneously—and launched also at COP26—governments were also taking actions outside closed door negotiations and conversation impacting the public conversation and looking towards the critical 80th session of the IMO Marine Environmental Protection Committee (MEPC80) meeting. In Glasgow two statements were presented to further pave the way for the increased ambition level. The *Declaration on Zero Emission Shipping by 2050* stressed the importance of reaching zero emissions by 2050, as well as goals for 2030 and 2040, and the role of IMO as the regulator (Multiple Governments (2021a). In the *Clydebank Declaration for Green Shipping Corridors* signatory States declared their ambition and intent to support the establishment of green shipping corridors, defined as specific shipping routes where the technological, economic and regulatory feasibility of the operation of zero-emission ships is catalysed by a combination of public and private actions (Multiple Governments, 2021b).

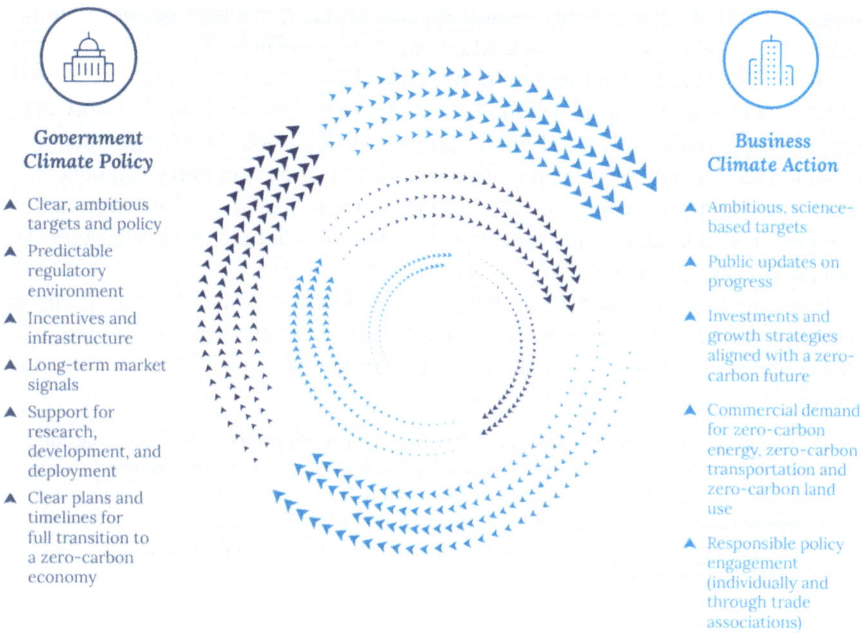

Fig. 4 'Ambition loops' support bolder climate action from business and governments

Influencing policy has always been both a direct and indirect mandate of the Getting to Zero Coalition. This has been done in the global north, and also through partnerships with countries such as Chile, Indonesia, Mexico and South Africa. This government engagement is key to the success of the coalition and critical for the transformation of the industry.

Building on the work of the UN Global Compact and the We Mean Business Coalition, the concept of the ambition loop is a core part of the theory of change of the Getting to Zero Coalition. Business and governments must push each other to accelerate the pace and scale of innovation and investments in low-carbon solutions, requiring a positive feedback loop—an 'ambition loop'—between bold business leadership and bold government policies (Knight, 2018). The 14 Governments that have endorsed the Getting to Zero Coalition is also a testament to this ongoing ambition loop (Fig. 4).

The Coalition's theory of change relates to catalysing and showcasing industry action to facilitate and shape political action to further support international shipping decarbonization at scale. Over the past 3 years, this theory of change has again proven its impact on global shipping. The interaction of high ambition members of the Coalition and the showcasing of the resultant progress that the industry has been making has visibly influenced global confidence in the viability of the transition. Policymakers are increasingly calling for high-ambition targets and frameworks to support the efforts, partly to the testament of the progress that the Coalition members individually and the Coalition as a whole has been showing.

New political statements and frameworks, including the EU's sub target for 2030 and the inclusion of a clear fuel uptake goal by 2030, this work has been pivotal in normalising cross-industry and public-private collaboration. Most importantly, the Coalition has helped create the narrative that the transition is possible and underway, making shipping a leading industry amongst other harder-to-abate sectors. The influence and impact that the Coalition has had on shipping decarbonization and especially policy is undeniable.

While the Getting to Zero Coalition has entered its next phase, the story leaves off where it started: with the UN. Secretary General Antonio Guterres is yet again calling for action, but this time he is calling on the IMO—a UN agency—to take action:

> The maritime sector must accelerate its voyage to decarbonization. Without concerted action, emissions from shipping are projected to grow considerably without action. Governments and private companies need to work together to harness innovative technologies such as digitalization. and automation and foster a just transition that includes developing countries and promotes renewable energy and alternative fuels—Secretary General Antonio Guterres, September 2022.

Epilogue: Where Are We Now?

After 3 years the Getting to Zero Coalition reached maturity and the government model was reviewed and evolved. The Global Maritime Forum assumed the lead, now hosting the Getting to Zero Coalition, with the founding partners assuming contributor roles on the steering group for the Coalition. Whilst continuing to provide input into each other's work, all three founding partners work to advance decarbonization goals through both associated, and distinct projects.

The World Economic Forum continues to initiate partnerships with industry, government, academia and civil society leaders to collaboratively explore and incubate a broad spectrum of accelerative, multi-stakeholder industry transformation initiatives. One such cross sectoral partnership effort is the First Movers Coalition—this initiative aims to harness the purchasing power of the world's leading companies to create guaranteed early markets for advanced technologies.

The First Movers Coalition, co-chaired by the US Special Presidential Envoy for Climate and the World Economic Forum, was launched at COP26 in Glasgow to accelerate the availability of clean technologies across all seven hard-to-abate sectors. Getting to Zero Coalition is one of the many notable initiatives involved that recognises the importance of demand in driving the adoption of green technologies.

By harnessing the procurement power of major brands and companies worldwide, the shipping sector within the First Movers Coalition sends a strong signal of demand for green fuels from shipowners and shipping service providers. Commitments to this demand are made through individual actions, with CEOs confirming their engagement through a letter, however the First Movers Coalition also encourages collective actions and innovative procurement approaches across the companies.

As the text for this chapter was wrapping up the outcome of the revision of the GHG Strategy during IMO negotiations in July 2023 provided a framework that can be a catalyst for change as well as a testament to the power of industry action and the continued bold actions from non-State actors. The political agreement reached in IMO provides many reasons for optimism – and while it remains to be seen how this will be implemented the enhanced ambition of the GHG Strategy between 2018 to 2023 is significant. One observation also being that during that time-period, the industry across the value chain has leaned in and taken a step forward individually and through collective action in a coalition of the willing. Many of the core messages delivered by the Getting to Zero Coalition and the main voices in the Coalition are also reflected in the outcome from the 2023 revision of the GHG Strategy and together with other decarbonization initiatives in the industry Getting to Zero Coalition has played a significant role securing that momentum and remains as relevant in the coming years.

Further Reading

Adamopoulos. (2017). *ICS and BIMCO call for decarbonization after 2050*. Adamopoulos A. Lloyd's list. Accessed September 18, 2017, from https://lloydslist.maritimeintelligence.informa.com/LL111473/ICS-and-BIMCO-call-for-decarbonization-after-2050

Aspen Institute. (2022). *Aspen Institute's shipping decarbonization initiative*. coZEV 2040 ambition statement: Leading cargo.

Danish Maritime Forum. (2016). *The new normal*. https://cms.globalmaritimeforum.org/wp-content/uploads/2018/02/Danish-Maritime-Forum-2016_The-New-Normal.pdf

Dreier, L., Nabarro, D., & Nelson, J. (2019). *Systems leadership for sustainable development: Strategies for achieving systemic change*. Harvard Kennedy School. https://4sd.info/wp-content/uploads/2021/02/Harvard_CRI_System_Leadership_Report_Sept_2019.pdf

Energy Transitions Commission. (2018, November). *Mission possible: Reaching net-zero carbon emissions – ETC*. https://www.energy-transitions.org/publications/mission-possible/

Energy Transitions Commission. (2019). *Mission possible sectoral focus: Shipping | ETC*. Accessed January 2018, from https://www.energy-transitions.org/publications/mission-possible-sectoral-focus-shipping/

Getting to Zero Coalition. (2019). *Maritime shipping's moon-shot ambition announced at UN climate action summit*. https://www.globalmaritimeforum.org/content/2019/09/Maritime-shipping%e2%80%99s-moon-shot-ambition-announced-at-UN-Climate-Action-Summit.pdf

Getting to Zero Coalition. (2019a). *Ambition statement*. https://www.globalmaritimeforum.org/content/2019/09/Getting-to-Zero-Coalition_Ambition-statement_230919.pdf

Getting to Zero Coalition. (2021, October 27). *Launch of getting to zero coalition transition strategy: With concerted collaborative action, full decarbonization of international shipping by 2050 is doable*. https://www.globalmaritimeforum.org/press/launch-of-getting-to-zero-coalition-transition-strategy-with-concerted-collaborative-action-full-decarbonization-of-international-shipping-by-2050-is-doable

Global Maritime Forum. (2018a). *Call to action – CEOs and maritime industry leaders in support of decarbonization*. https://www.globalmaritimeforum.org/content/2018/11/Call-to-action-in-support-of-decarbonization.pdf

Global Maritime Forum. (2018b, April 10). *34 maritime CEOs sign call for action in support of decarbonization*. https://www.globalmaritimeforum.org/press/34-maritime-ceos-sign-call-for-action-in-support-of-decarbonization

Knight. (2018, November 27). *The key to faster, zero-carbon growth? Harness the ambition loop*. We mean business coalition. https://www.wemeanbusinesscoalition.org/blog/the-key-to-faster-zero-carbon-growth-harness-the-ambition-loop/

Krantz, R., Søgaard, K., & Smith, T. (2020). *The scale of investment needed to decarbonize international shipping*. Getting to zero coalition. https://www.globalmaritimeforum.org/content/2020/01/Getting-to-Zero-Coalition_Insight-brief_Scale-of-investment.pdf

Maersk. (2019, September 26). *Søren Toft, COO of Maersk, one of the speakers of the United Nations climate action summit, New York*. https://www.youtube.com/watch?v=n-W2h8JttW8

Mission Innovation. (2021). *Mission statement for zero-emission shipping mission*. http://mission-innovation.net/wp-content/uploads/2021/05/Zero-Emission-Shipping-Joint-Mission-Statement.pdf

Multiple Governments. (2021a, November). *Declaration on zero emission shipping by* 2050. https://eng.em.dk/media/19538/declaration-on-zero-emission-shipping-by-2050-23-05-23.pdf

Multiple Governments. (2021b, November 10). *Clydebank declaration for green shipping corridors*. https://www.gov.uk/government/publications/cop-26-clydebank-declaration-for-green-shipping-corridors/cop-26-clydebank-declaration-for-green-shipping-corridors

Osterkamp, P., Smith, T., & Søgaard, K. (2021). *Five percent zero emission fuels by 2030 needed for Paris-aligned shipping decarbonization*. Getting to zero coalition. https://www.globalmaritimeforum.org/content/2021/03/Getting-to-Zero-Coalition_Five-percent-zero-emission-fuels-by-2030.pdf

Pacific Island Nations (2017). https://www.climatechangenews.com/2017/07/03/pacific-islanders-shipping-mustcomply-paris-climate-goals/

Poseidonprinciples.org. (2023). *Poseidon principles for financial institutions*. https://www.poseidonprinciples.org/finance/

Senge, P., Hamilton, H., & Kania, J. (2015). The dawn of system leadership. *Stanford Social Innovation Review, 13*(1), 27–33. https://networkpeninsula.org/wp-content/uploads/2014/12/The_Dawn_of_System_Leadership-1.pdf

Smith, T. (2019). *Definition of zero-carbon energy sources*. Getting to zero coalition. https://www.globalmaritimeforum.org/content/2019/09/Getting-to-Zero-Coalition_Zero-carbon-energy-sources.pdf

Smith, T., Baresic, D., Fahnestock, J., Galbraith, C., Velandia Perico, C., Rojon, I., & Shaw, E. (2021). *A strategy for the transition to zero-emission shipping*. Getting to zero coalition. https://www.globalmaritimeforum.org/content/2021/10/A-Strategy-for-the-Transition-to-Zero-Emission-Shipping.pdf

Transport and Environment. (2017). *Almost three-quarters of new containerships already meet 2025 energy efficiency requirement*. https://www.transportenvironment.org/discover/almost-three-quarters-new-containerships-already-meet-2025-energy-efficiency-requirement

World Economic Forum. (2019, January). *World economic forum annual meeting – Session: Shipping emissions: Setting sail toward a carbon-free future*. Davos. https://www3.weforum.org/docs/WEF_FOA_Ocean_Day.pdf

World Economic Forum. (2022). *First movers coalition shipping commitment*. https://www3.weforum.org/docs/WEF_First_Movers_Coalition_Shipping_Commitment_2022.pdf

Worthington, B. (2019, September 23). *Shipping commitment shows industry and nations' willingness to step up climate ambition*. Environmental Defense Fund. https://www.edfeurope.org/news/2019/23/09/shipping-commitment-shows-industry-and-nations-willingness-step-climate-ambition

Zero Emission Shipping Mission. (2022). *Industry roadmap for zero-emission shipping*. https://dma.dk/Media/637847381174295461/ZESM%20Roadmap.pdf

Part VI
Concluding Remarks: Calling for a Holistic and Inclusive Approach

Highlights of the Book: A Menu of Possible Actions for Decarbonization Today and Tomorrow

Wolfgang Lehmacher, Mikael Lind, Gavin Allwright, Jeremy B. Bentham, David Cummins, Theo Notteboom, Johan Byskov Svendsen, Kirsi Tikka, and Louise De Tremerie

W. Lehmacher (✉)
Independent Supply Chain Expert, Hong Kong, China
e-mail: w.lehmacher@gmail.com

M. Lind
Research Institutes of Sweden (RISE), Gothenburg, Sweden

Chalmers University of Technology, Gothenburg, Sweden
e-mail: mikael@realsearchers.com

G. Allwright
International Windship Association (IWSA), London, UK
e-mail: secretary@wind-ship.org

J. B. Bentham
World Energy Council, London, UK

Scenarios Team, Shell International, The Hague, The Netherlands

Mission Possible Partnership, Washington, DC, USA

Boston Consulting Group, Amsterdam, The Netherlands

Transformative Scenarios B.V., The Hague, The Netherlands
e-mail: jbentham@live.com

D. Cummins
Blue Sky Maritime Coalition, Houston, TX, USA
e-mail: president@bluesky-maritime.org

T. Notteboom
Ghent University, University of Antwerp and Antwerp Maritime Academy, Ghent, Belgium
e-mail: theo.notteboom@ugent.be

J. B. Svendsen
Mærsk Mc-Kinney Møller Center for Zero Carbon Shipping, Copenhagen, Denmark
e-mail: johan.byskov@zerocarbonshipping.com

M. Lind et al. (eds.), *Maritime Decarbonization*,
https://doi.org/10.1007/978-3-031-39936-7_33

Target Audience

This chapter is an extended summary of the contents of this book. It is intended for all those seeking an overview of possible actions to reduce greenhouse gas (GHG) emissions in the various and diverse sectors of the shipping industry. The recommendations should help policymakers, and executives and project managers in the private sector to make better decisions on actions to take, and should be of value to all stakeholders within the global decarbonization movement. It may also lead to identifying individual chapters to obtain greater knowledge in particular areas of interest.

Key Takeaway Messages

The recommendations, and thus the key take-aways from this extended summary chapter are:

1. Use the 'five decarbonization lever' framework to recognise the full spectrum of levers.
2. Set environmental targets and reflect on concrete outcomes of decarbonization efforts.
3. Understand the global shipping fleet as a key area for decarbonization.
4. Use a four-step model to guide decarbonization efforts.
5. Develop scenarios to build context for decarbonization strategies.
6. Adopt a value-chain focus to tackle decarbonization.
7. Identify and activate relevant decarbonization enablers.
8. Select and contribute to decarbonization partnerships.
9. In respect to outcomes, balance economic with societal value.
10. Place a strong focus on people.
11. Ensure global alignment of regulations related to decarbonization.
12. Leverage circular economy principles as a driver for systemic change.
13. Boost global research in maritime decarbonization.
14. Adjust to finance requirements in a more sustainable age.
15. Be an early-mover: even if you choose not to be a single pioneer, be prepared to be an early adopter.

K. Tikka
Board Member Ardmore Shipping, Pembroke, Bermuda

Board Member Pacific Basin Shipping, Hong Kong, Hong Kong SAR

Board Member Foreship, Helsinki, Finland

L. De Tremerie
European Parliament, Brussels, Belgium
e-mail: louise.detremerie@europarl.europa.eu

Introduction

The following overview of actions with potentially promising outcomes is based on today's knowledge and has been derived from the contents in the chapters in the first half of this book. Complementary perspectives and recommendations have been drawn up in relation to the topics covered in the various chapters. The second half of this book provides case studies and practical examples supporting the recommendations.

We thank the contributors to this book for their inputs. Through sharing their knowledge and insights, they have created a valuable contribution to the public discourse on maritime decarbonization.

Use the 'Five Decarbonization Lever' Framework to Recognise the Full Spectrum of Levers

As outlined in the chapter "Broadening the Scope of Decarbonization in the Maritime Sector" (McKinnon, 2023), the International Maritime Organization (IMO) fourth Greenhouse Gas (GHG) Study predicted that almost two-thirds of carbon reductions in the maritime sector by 2050 will come from the switch to alternative fuels (IMO, 2020), which could include also a wind component such as the use of rigid or soft sails, large kites or wind turbines and rotors on deck. The use of very low carbon fuels is required for the transition and ultimately net zero emission fuels to achieve a net zero shipping future by the middle of the century.

There are two respects in which a pre-occupation with the 'defossilisation' of maritime energy appears to be based on too narrow a view of the subject. First, it under-estimates the carbon-reducing potential of a range of other measures that can be applied more quickly and cheaply to reduce the amount of fossil fuel that needs to be phased-out, sooner rather than later. Second, it is 'voyage-focussed' and fails to fully consider options for decarbonizing the whole supply chain, encompassing ports and hinterland logistics as well as shipping operations (Lind et al., 2023c, d).

It is important to recognise the full spectrum of carbon-reducing initiatives and avoid an over-reliance on a few, much-debated and much-researched options. The decarbonization of all forms of transport will be achieved by the application of many mutually-reinforcing measures rather than a few 'silver bullets'. In the process, it is crucial that the sector avoids locking-in transitional solutions that are mostly fossil-based.

Various classificatory schemes are now being used to assess the potential impact of decarbonization measures systematically by grouping them into several categories. The most commonly referenced is the Avoid-Shift-Improve (ASI) framework, distinguishing measures that reduce the demand for transport, shift it to lower carbon modes and improve their carbon efficiency. The Activity-Shift-Intensity-Fuel (ASIF) taxonomy (Schipper & Marie, 1999), adopted by the Intergovernmental

Panel on Climate Change (IPCC) (Sims et al., 2014), uses different words for two of the three categories and introduces a separate one for the switch to alternative fuels. The so-called 'five decarbonization lever' framework covers five levels:

- freight traffic intensity
- choice of freight transport mode
- capacity utilisation
- energy efficiency
- and switching to low carbon energy.

The framework distinguishes capacity utilisation from energy efficiency in the improve/intensity category, as each can be separately influenced by technology, business practice and public policy (McKinnon, 2018).

We recommend using the 'five decarbonization lever' framework which can expose a set of options for decarbonizing maritime supply chains by testing the various outcomes, for example, when free energy (as in wind propulsion) is inserted into the framework. We need to ensure that the approach to maritime decarbonization remains fact-based and that no single party or industry influences the narrative towards biased outcomes.

Set Environmental Targets and Reflect on Concrete Outcomes of Decarbonization Efforts

The chapter "Decarbonizing the Maritime Industry: Current Environmental Targets and Potential Outcomes" (Raza & Singh, 2023) indicates that, as a general rule, shipowners and operators should set decarbonization targets, prioritise transparency, and use clear and comparable environmental, social, and governance reporting. This can be considered as a recommendation which should be relevant for every actor in the maritime decarbonization ecosystem.

An overarching goal should be to ensure that decarbonization is inclusive. Shipping is a global industry and the transition to a climate net-zero sector is a global challenge. Regional measures and initiatives can take the lead to pressure and influence what happens at the global level, where it is crucial to facilitate the path towards globally addressing GHG emissions from international shipping by both developed and emerging economies. Some of the revenues generated by a levy or market basket measures (MBMs) should be used to support vulnerable countries in their efforts to mitigate and adapt to climate change, with the remainder going towards research and development and administrative costs. Also, those regions may benefit more than others from certain non-fuel decarbonization enablers such as wind propulsion, especially if relatively simple/easy to fabricate systems are available. Small Island Developing States (SIDS) in the South Pacific are ideal for wind assisted and primary wind ships that are supporting business models for long distances, low cargo levels and high fuel costs. Concerns have been raised among a number of least developed countries (LDCs)/SIDs that the MBMs being proposed may be 'neo-colonial' instruments, where they will have to pay a carbon price, but the fuels/technologies will be developed and monetised in the developed world and only some compensation will be delivered to LDCs/SIDs. There are of course some winners with large amounts of renewable energy investment, but many view the current approach to MBMs as a perpetuation of the existing economic order, thus not a just/equitable transition. This needs to be addressed to ensure a just, inclusive and equitable transition.

The accelerated development of effective GHG reduction measures requires regulators, policymakers, financial institutions, and customers to de-risk the investments and activities of first and early movers. All stakeholders should support initiatives that drive collective decarbonization, share costs, benefits, and risks, such as 'green corridors', while ensuring that green corridors do not become an exclusionary exercise. One way towards an inclusive approach could be to also consider 'wind corridors', a concept that would need to be developed further.

Policymakers at regional, national, and local levels should not only set clear targets and provide a clear regulatory framework, but also develop roadmaps that encourage dedicated investments in green energy and fuel infrastructure, as well as engineering capacity, to build these facilities.

The IMO should play a more decisive role in guiding the sector on a global scale towards a net zero future. The organisation should move to the next level of impact and provide clear enforcement mechanisms, tighten compliance levels, and find regulatory solutions to ensure shared responsibility among all parties that influence ship emissions. We may need new institutions that are responsible for areas not covered by the IMO, like ports and commodity trading. In general, the IMO should do everything possible within its powers to drive and accelerate maritime decarbonization. Recent regional developments by the European Union (EU) may trigger responses at the IMO level opening a window of opportunity to speed-up the work on a global market-based measure for maritime shipping emissions.

In line with these recommendations, it is important for the IMO to define more granular interim decarbonization targets consistent with the ambitions set for the far future so that actors in the industry can gauge where they stand at any time and their progress resulting from implementing their decarbonization measures. All stakeholders should support discussions about more ambitious and intermediate targets in shipping. But the focus needs also to be on attainable targets. Many IMO Member States are uncomfortable about stepping up and declaring support for undeliverable targets, just considering, for example, the likelihood of comparatively little zero-emissions fuel being available by 2030. To make the leaps, it is recommended to engage in a collaborative effort to set high ambitions backed by roadmaps and supporting actions that align the targets with the ambitions.

Understand the Global Ship Fleet as a Key Area of Decarbonization

The chapter "The Extent of Decarbonization in the Global Shipping Fleet" (Pålsson & Rydbergh, 2023) deepens the understanding of the state of the global shipping fleet. The industry, and those involved in maritime decarbonization, can see how many ships that are currently trading are due for replacement in the near future and how many could be expected to be trading for several decades more.

The age profile by number of ships and the age profile by tonnage shows that the world fleet is relatively young (an average age of 16 years). Ships which are now more than 20 years old make up 26% of the current fleet by number and most will reach end of use in the next 5 years. But these 13,973 vessels account for only 161 M dwt or only 7% of the total fleet tonnage, given that more modern ships have become increasingly larger.

This is relevant, and important information because it has an impact on how quickly new ships with new propulsion solutions may come into service and when. A slow penetration means that retrofit and operational solutions of the current fleet becomes relatively more important than if the rate of ship replacement was faster.

We cannot afford to wait until ships are old enough before we start to retrofit. This will not get the industry to a zero emissions state. We need new ships with different engines and support systems on board, that use non-fossil-fuel-based energy sources, and we need to start now. Experts have identified relatively easy fixes, such as wind propulsion which, for example, can be installed within days, with many of the systems being able to be reinstalled on other vessels when ships go for breaking and/or moved to different routes. This also represents a flexible option.

It follows that marine equipment manufacturers need more incentives to enable feasible and economically viable retrofitting solutions. Another recommendation is for the building up of capabilities to recycle ships in sustainable ways, and in accordance with agreed standards and processes in support of green recycling. The pending ratification of the Hong Kong International Convention for the Safe and Environmentally Sound Recycling of Ships (IMO) and the existing EU Ship Recycling Regulation are important first steps in that direction.

As resources become scarcer and the ecological boundaries of our planet are being stressed, circular economic thinking plays an important role in changing business models towards those that are closer to following the principles of nature and the planet. Enabling market-based incentives can only encourage marine equipment manufacturers to develop feasible and economically viable retrofitting solutions. As one part of the circular economy, the continuous use and re-use of parts and materials will help to avoid GHG emissions. New ship designs should cater for more modularity for retrofitting, reuse, and re-manufacture, and on construction based on sustainable methods and materials, keeping in mind the specific characteristics of certain alternative fuels like the toxic nature of ammonia, and to a lesser extent methanol, which requires specific safety protocols and investments. We believe that shipping can contribute to transforming the economy into a circular economy that not only excels in value creation but also in value preservation.

Use a Four-Step Model to Guide Decarbonization Efforts

The chapter "Four Steps to Decarbonization" (Lind et al., 2023a) presents four foundational concepts for climate action that underpin a '4-step model' that can drive strategies, business cases, the execution of plans, and decision-making. The four concepts are *scenario analysis* (context), *value chain mapping* (scope), *enabler prioritisation* (focus), and *partnership selection* (synergies). Although there is a natural sequence, the four steps support each other in an iterative symbiotic co-development.

Exceeding the current 2023 IMO GHG Strategy ambitions for carbon-reduction and thereby reach the EU ambitions and the Paris Climate Agreement goals requires a holistic and inclusive approach. The idea behind the four-step model, as a key recommendation from this book, is to support such a holistic approach.

The way the maritime value chain is designed creates inefficiency, through stepwise, sequential bi-lateral negotiations, which lead to a situation that can be described as the *'Tragedy of the Commons'*. We are unlikely to achieve our decarbonization ambitions unless we approach solutions as part of a collective systems-wide optimisation challenge, and therefore change the very nature of how the global value chain operates. Hence, achieving a no/low carbon future requires that we drive a systems approach rather than an aggregate of multiple individual solutions by companies/entities or sub groups of the value chain.

Develop Scenarios to Build Context for Decarbonization Strategies

The chapter "Scenario Thinking and Its Place in Maritime Decarbonization" (Bentham, 2023a) makes clear that maritime decarbonization cannot be seen in isolation and independently from its overall context and that there is therefore an important place for scenario thinking. Powerful influences, transitions and disruptions are shaping our society and economy, indeed our whole world. Every strong influence can also generate others, and you can rarely tell in advance which of these will prove to be the stronger. Therefore, there are inevitably multiple different plausible pathways for our future. Much of this is beyond our direct control, and even our own actions can affect the future in ways that may surprise us.

However, while not predictable in detail, neither is the future completely random. There are constraints imposed by, for example, physics and biology, and features of society that remain relatively stationary for considerable periods, like birth and death rates, human biases, or the time it takes to build major public infrastructures. It is, therefore, possible to explore plausible futures in a systematic way to identify both critical uncertainties and relatively settled trends. This is the art of building scenarios.

Scenario thinking is a means for grappling with uncertainty. It is acknowledged that the human mind and business logic may struggle with such an approach. Nevertheless, it is recommended that stakeholders use scenario analysis as a learning tool to help them to see beyond the horizon of our necessarily limited personal experiences and current circumstances.

Adopt a Value-Chain Focus to Tackle Decarbonization

As related in the chapter "Adopting a Value Chain Focus to Tackle Decarbonization" (Petersen & Renken, 2023), contemporary value creation is often distributed throughout extensive global supply networks. Hence, taking a value chain perspective is critical to understanding and assessing decarbonization enablers and building partnerships beyond industry borders. There are obviously three interrelated value chains across the maritime ecosystem that are playing a critical role in decarbonizing shipping. The three value chains are marine fuel and direct propulsion technologies, shipbuilding, and the maritime operational value chain (Lind et al., 2022).

The asset value of the world fleet stands at USD 1.4 trillion (UNCTAD, 2022). The most commercial value is likely to be concentrated in the operational value chain. A significant decarbonization potential is expected from optimising international trade patterns, driving down the demand for international shipping in the first place (Wang et al., 2021).

Energy-efficient newbuilds and retrofits will be needed to reduce GHG emissions from the existing and future shipping fleet. What ships and engines will be built and used sustainably largely depends upon what fuels will or can be made available and at what cost, but also what is required by regulation. Public sector programmes can support retrofitting and incentivise zero GHG emissions newbuilds. But public programmes are not the silver bullet either and it is stressed that only a collective effort will lead to a climate neutral future.

The green energy transition shifts dependencies from fossil fuel producers to renewable energy and e-fuels providers as the feedstocks shift from petroleum towards green electricity (and biowaste). These shifts may reduce the importance of some regions of the world and bring new opportunities to other locations with possible shifts in geopolitical power as newer feedstocks are likely available throughout the globe. Market structures will also shift. Today, the available quantity of alternative fuels is very limited. A huge challenge and responsibility lies with the energy industry to ramp up and scale up production of renewable energy. Similarly, ports need to provide the bunkering infrastructure for alternative fuels, clean sources of power, like renewable electricity, and onshore power supply solutions (OPS) (Lind et al., 2023c, d).

A worldwide supply for new alternative fuels also leads to the potential for unwanted emissions from pipelines/bunkering of products. Hydrogen for example is not a direct GHG, but interacts with free radicals that break down methane in the atmosphere. Thus, hydrogen can lead to lengthier methane retention in the atmosphere. This kind of scientific finding is not yet completely clear, so it would be prudent to adopt precautionary principles when contemplating systems that do not produce fuels adjacent to their place of use.

As recommended throughout this book, decarbonization should be seen as a joint undertaking of all stakeholders within multiple intertwined value chains within and beyond the maritime industry across the maritime decarbonization ecosystem. There is the additional challenge that other value chains across the wider economy are also competing for currently scarce low-carbon and net-zero emissions fuels and energy sources. The fact that shipping is just one customer for green fuels creates a basket of challenges around supply, competition, fuel price variability, and fuel standardisation, all of which need to be and, in time, will be addressed.

Identify and Activate Relevant Decarbonization Enablers

The chapter "Identifying the Key Decarbonization Enablers" (Tikka & Esau, 2023a) explains that moving towards the current and future global decarbonization targets set by the IMO requires the adoption of multiple enablers with varying GHG reduction impact and different levels of required investment (MEPC.304(72), 2018). The enablers can be categorised within the three value chains: the marine fuel and direct propulsion technologies value chain, the maritime operational value chain, and the shipbuilding value chain. Some of the enablers contribute to only one value chain, whereas others have contributions to two or all the value chains. The categories of enablers identified are as follows.

Shipboard Energy Efficiency Technology

Large parts of the maritime fleet is already taking advantage of the technologies available today to improve both technical and operational efficiency. Energy efficiency of ships can be improved by reducing the power requirements for the main propulsion and for auxiliary energy generators. Energy savings depend on many variables such as the vessel type, routes, weather conditions, and operational practices, but potential savings are typically relatively small—less than 10%. Although the individual savings are small in percentage terms, a combination of measures can offer significant overall fuel and emission savings. Nevertheless, this will not be a simple addition game, but a more complex undertaking that needs to be understood.

Operational and Commercial Practices

Some of the measures can be implemented onboard a vessel, others involve multiple stakeholders and commercial arrangements. According to the *Mærsk Mc-Kinney Møller Center* for Zero Carbon Shipping (MMKMCZCS, 2022) the vessel and fleet specific operational energy efficiency measures offer energy efficiency gains up to 15%. This does not factor in wind propulsion. Wind propulsion is significantly boosted by wind routing, voyage optimisation and speed (MEPC 79 /INF 21, 2022).

Digital Technology

Technology tools for real time data sharing and communication can eliminate bottlenecks in the logistics chain. Digital technology can now provide software tools for design and maintenance, weather routing, energy management, data analytics to transform operational data into information, and commercial platforms and satellite communication for value chain optimisation. Onboard automation, and eventually autonomy, allows more efficient operations. Although digital technology and automation are already widely used in the maritime industry, they are expected to have a greater impact on maritime decarbonization in the future. Standardisation of a digital optimisation platform, and associated machine learning predictive algorithms, will be essential for a systems approach to regional and global efficiency within the maritime value chain as well as across connected value chains. However, cybersecurity programmes also need to be implemented and keep up with concerns over the hacking of digital systems.

Zero-Carbon Fuels and Technology

Since the worldwide large-scale availability of zero-carbon fuels is still several years away, the focus is on the transition from the current use of fossil fuels to low-carbon and eventually net zero-emission fuels, as well as the alternative fuel pathways to produce these net zero-emission fuels. The transition focuses on the use of multi-fuel engines that currently burn fossil fuels but offer an option in the future to burn zero-carbon fuels, or the use of biofuel and fuel oil blends, and in the case of liquefied natural gas (LNG), biomethane and LNG blends, that can be burnt in the existing internal combustion engines without modifications (drop-in fuels). It is crucial not to lock-in these transitional carbon-based technologies and instead move towards the deployment at a large scale of net zero-emission fuels. When considering the fuel pathways, it is important to differentiate between well-to-wake (WTW) and tank-to-wake (TTW) emissions. WTW assessments consider the GHG emissions from the fuel production to the end use onboard a vessel, whereas TTW accounts only for the emission from the onboard use of the fuel. If the TTW assessment is used the fuel choice will not account for the full GHG impact. New innovations in the coming years will continue to advance new fuels types and technologies, making flexibility a critical part of any advancement. For example, ports will need to provide for the bunkering of multiple fuels, and ships will probably need to have propulsion system technologies, such as fuels cells and other advanced technologies that can operate with multiple fuels.

Energy Conversion and Shipbuilding Technology

Ships built today should incorporate the available technology for maximum energy efficiency. However, full maritime decarbonization requires retrofitting and renewal of the fleet to burn zero emission fuels and the use of wind propulsion technologies. Shipbuilding requires large amounts of energy to produce steel and other materials and to construct the ships themselves. Maritime decarbonization will ultimately require green steel produced with zero carbon emissions and designs based on circular economy principles, to enable the re-use of materials when ships reach their end-of-life.

Policies and Regulations

Industry and market driven efforts are necessary for decarbonization, but an effective global regulatory framework could accelerate the worldwide adoption of all the decarbonization enablers available today. Global regulations play a critical role to set the targets for the global fleet to improve energy efficiency and fast track the transition to net zero emission fuels. The IMO has a unique role and mandate to regulate ships globally, including the protection and encouragement of first movers. The short-term measures adopted by the IMO to address the fleet's technical and operational fuel efficiency is a start, but more is required from the global regulatory framework. The IMO GHG-reduction targets should be in line with the findings of the more recent sixth IPCC impact assessment report (IPCC, 2023).

Financing and Incentives

Market based measures (MBMs), such as the fuel levy proposed at the IMO or the recent decision on the inclusion of shipping in the EU Emission Trading Scheme (ETS) starting from January 2024, are needed to accelerate and expand the adoption of low-carbon (transitional) and net zero emission fuels beyond the early movers. Incentives have to be put in place to drive the uptake of alternative fuels. In the past shipping has been burning fuel that no other industry uses, but going forward and transitioning to more sustainable fuels, shipping will compete with other industries for supplies of the new fuels. Therefore, it is critical that the shipping energy demand is considered in global energy production projections and infrastructure planning. MBMs and their impacts should be carefully evaluated, with taxes that return to the industry being fairly distributed as subsidies for research and development and for the installation of green fuels and technology. It is recommended to consider including ships under 5000 gross tonnage (GT) in the ETS as this would help innovation enjoy a fast and strong learning curve for new technologies, as it is in this segment of smaller ships where large numbers of easily/quickly scaled units can be delivered and systems can be optimised further before being scaled-up for larger ships.

Ports will need to fulfill their role as providers of bunkering infrastructure, battery charging stations, and shore-power supply as alternatives for ships alongside. National policies will be important for both energy availability and electricity grid and fuel infrastructure development.

Select and Contribute to Decarbonization Partnerships

The chapters "Four Steps to Decarbonization" (Lind et al., 2023a), "Decarbonizing International Shipping Through Collaborative Partnerships" (Kuttan, 2023) and "Effective Partnerships To Support Maritime Decarbonization" (Lind et al., 2023b) underline that one player can activate some enablers, but collaboration between multiple actors is required to activate the full range of decarbonization enablers. In fact, without collaboration no effective decarbonization of the maritime industry and any other sector will be possible. Collaboration helps to align, accelerate, or intensify efforts. Hence, partnerships are critical to driving decarbonization across the larger ecosystem and need to be inclusive to achieve their maximum impact. Making partnerships work effectively requires strategies grounded in a profound understanding of what collaboration means in meeting needs for all parties and the available collaboration options.

Based on what enablers they require to activate, actors can benefit from selecting specific partnerships to align, close gaps, accelerate, and intensify their decarbonization efforts. It is therefore recommended that actors should:

- Select partnerships to gradually establish a portfolio of collaborations to align and cover unmet needs/capabilities at the company and possibly at the industry and ecosystem level.
- Ensure sufficient partnership management capabilities are developed across the organisation or accessible through partnerships.
- Establish cross-value chain coordination, for example, along zero-emissions corridors.

- Coordinate wider stakeholder engagement and interaction in view of securing social and public support for decarbonization trajectories.

Partnerships in the shipping industry need to be composed of many more stakeholders than it might appear at first. Decarbonization is everybody's business. However, considering the limited resources of the smaller players in terms of capital and talent, it requires the larger actors to take initiative and include them into their efforts. In addition, the public sector or international regulators can support the private sector efforts by crafting conducive policies and programmes to empower the long tail to also accelerate their decarbonization efforts. Furthermore, we suggest that the current partnerships, that mostly consist of larger players in developed countries, should increase their efforts to also bring the myriad of smaller actors on board, and widen their scope to also include less developed countries.

This will make it more likely that the goal, as set by the Paris Agreement, can be achieved (Lind & Lehmacher, 2022). But this requires that the IMO aligns its ambitions with the Paris Climate Accord and that trust is built and the interests of the smaller players and all regions are protected and respected.

In Respect to Outcomes, Balance Economic with Societal Value

In particular in today's western countries, citizens and consumers expect more from companies than just good products. Many stakeholders of the private and public sector expect responsible behaviour. Balancing economic and societal capital creation is the call of the chapter "How to Get Started: CDES—A New Paradigm for Tackling Decarbonization Projects" (Lind & Lehmacher, 2023).

We assert that all industries need to place greater emphasis on the interrelationship between *collaboration* (c) and *digitalization* (d), as this powerful duo impacts *economic* (e) and *societal* (s) success through enhancing human and social capital and preserving and restoring natural capital. A *cdes* mindset can take supply chain management and logistics practices to higher levels of symbiosis.

Collaboration and digitalization are critical drivers of economic and societal value creation. These drivers need to be mutually reinforcing to generate synergistic gains. Digitalisation promotes collaboration through swift and efficient digital information exchange enabling effective coordination. Simultaneously, digitalisation requires collaboration. Otherwise, it is destined to fail or produce suboptimal results. In the biological world, many species have symbiotic relationships, mutual dependencies, with other species to increase their ecological fitness. There is a symbiotic relationship between digitalisation and collaboration. Neither can exist without the other, because they co-determine economic fitness. Successful partnerships co-evolve their collaboration through cooperative digitalisation to contribute to an emerging era of digital symbiosis.

Decarbonization of supply chains thus requires end-to-end, closed-loop, and cradle-to-cradle thinking and particularly digitalisation and collaboration. Decarbonizing shipping is about working together towards an economy in which GHG emissions and waste/excess material are avoided and products and materials are used to the maximum extent possible. This is empowered by new design principles, digitalisation and collaboration which creates and increases economic and societal capital.

The world needs a new paradigm. The *cdes* model, focusing on collaboration and digitalisation for balanced economic and societal value creation, is intended to guide industry action. While currently, incorporating the *cdes* approach might be a voluntary business model shift, new regulations, particularly in Europe and North America, will make this new recommended way of thinking and operating a prerequisite for economic survival.

It is therefore recommended that all actors place greater emphasis on the *cdes* approach. Focusing only on one of both dimensions of each pair, either on collaboration or digitalisation, or on economic or societal value, leads to suboptimal results. A conscious, holistic approach addressing all four components of the cdes formula ensures durable wealth and well-being for humanity. A *cdes* mindset can take decarbonization in the maritime sector to higher levels.

Place a Strong Focus on People

People, and particularly seafarers, are a critical success factor for maritime decarbonization. This is the message of the chapter "Ensuring Seafarers Are at the Heart of Decarbonization Action" (Platten et al., 2023). Without a trained workforce in ships and in ports, the decarbonization movement will struggle. To limit the otherwise devastating impacts of climate change, unprecedented collaboration is needed to facilitate rapid moves away from the use of carbon-intensive fuels to renewable energy sources. It is therefore recommended that governments, employers, workers, and all stakeholder groups work together to create positive change, investing in new fuels, technologies, and infrastructure to enable a green transformation.

The guiding principles of a Just Transition are established in the International Labour Organization (ILO) 'Guidelines for a Just Transition towards environmentally sustainable economies and societies for all' (ILO, 2015). These guidelines are the main globally endorsed framework on Just Transition. They reflect the views and perspectives of governments, employers, and workers' organisations and outline principles and potential policy entry-points to promote and manage a Just Transition; and are relevant for all countries and sectors, including shipping.

In the outcomes of the 27th Conference of the Parties to the United Nations Framework Convention on Climate Change (COP27) at Sharm el-Sheikh, Egypt, and in particular, the Implementation Plan, governments 'emphasised that enhanced effective climate action should be implemented in a manner that is just and inclusive while minimizing negative social or economic impacts that may arise from climate action' (UNFCCC, 2022). They also affirmed 'that sustainable and just solutions to the climate crisis must be founded on meaningful and effective social dialogue and participation of all stakeholders' (UNFCCC, 2022).

The global seafaring workforce will be key to powering shipping through a successful transition. Low-carbon (transitional) and zero emission fuels, technologies and ships are expected to introduce new skillsets and training needs for seafarers, requiring a health-and-safety-first approach. A maritime just transition for seafarers will therefore ensure that those seafarers have the adequate skills, education, training and familiarisation, to operate new technology systems on board and to manage new fuels.

Alongside governments, employers and workers (including in shipping) also have a role to play as social dialogue is key. The effort could entail, for example, ensuring that there is Just Transition planning, as part of wider decarbonization plans. Some companies, including from the energy sector, have also developed Just Transition plans. It is recommended that businesses support a just transition through their own policies and strategies (UN Global Compact, 2022).

Ensure Global Alignment of Regulations Related to Decarbonization

The chapter "Securing Global Alignment in Regulations Related to Decarbonization" (Tikka & Esau, 2023b) makes the point that the adoption of decarbonization enablers has been led by early movers while others are waiting for regulatory mandates. Consequently, the change in carbon dioxide (CO_2) emissions from shipping is not on track with the Paris Climate Accord target of limiting global warming to 1.5 °C. The fluctuations can be attributed to the changes in trade volumes and reductions in ship speed (in other words, slow steaming) rather than decarbonization measures adopted by the maritime industry.

Effective global regulations and climate ambitions play a critical role in achieving steady progress across the global fleet. According to the *Mærsk Mc-Kinney Møller Center* for Zero Carbon Shipping *Maritime Decarbonization Strategy 2022* (MMKMCZCS, 2022), even if the net zero pledges made by shipowners in the tanker, bulk, container, and RoRo/car carrier sectors materialise, they would translate to only a 13% reduction in global emissions from the sector.

The shipping industry has demonstrated in the past that environmental goals can be reached once there is regulatory clarity. Successful past regulatory developments include the introduction of double-hull tankers, which has contributed to the significant reduction in oil spills from tankers (NASEM, 2022). However, past regulations were silo-approached and a more holistic climate regulation, taking into account the various effects and different sorts of emissions and pollution, is recommended.

The International Maritime Organization (IMO) has its unique role and mandate to regulate global shipping. Within the IMO structure the Marine Environment Protection Committee (MEPC 79 /INF 21, 2022) addresses environmental issues. The process within MEPC, and more widely in the IMO, is largely based on finding consensus. Since the GHG regulations will have wide-reaching impact on IMO Member States, finding agreement can be challenging as it requires that the regulations be perceived as fair and equitable by multiple parties in different circumstances.

In 2018, the IMO agreed on an initial GHG strategy (MEPC 304(72), (2018)) with a goal to cut annual GHG emissions from shipping by at least half by 2050 compared with the emissions in 2008, and to work towards zero GHG emissions as soon as possible. The strategy included an ambition to reduce the international shipping carbon intensity by at least 40% by 2030 and 70% by 2050, compared to 2008. As these targets are not in line with the Paris Agreement the strategy has been reviewed in 2023 with the aim to align with the Paris Climate Accord target of limiting global warming to 1.5 °C. There needed to be better alignment with IPCC AR6 (IPCC, 2023) which calls for 50% reduction in GHG emissions across all sectors by 2030. The outcome of the review is a strongly improved 2023 IMO GHG Strategy which significantly increases the pressure to prepare for reducing greenhouse gas (GHG) emissions and the shift away from fossil fuels. With this achievement in combination with further additional IMO action, and wider national, regional and industry measures, a 1.5-aligned GHG reduction pathway is now more clearly in reach than before the meeting of the Marine Environment Protection Committee (MEPC 80) on 7 July 2023.

Recent regional developments in the EU also show that it is possible to opt for ambitious maritime regulations that set a price on shipping emissions and regulate the use of certain fuels on board. After more than two years of negotiation, the European institutions came to an adopted agreement on including maritime shipping emissions, including in ports, in the European Emission Trading System (ETS). The system will be phased in between 2024 and 2026 and starting from 2027 also methane and nitrous oxides (NOx) emissions will come into scope (EU 2023/957). This should not be regarded as a measure with only regional impact. The EU maritime ETS will also have an impact on part of the voyages outside EU waters as it covers voyages between the EU and the rest of the world, where ships docking into an EU port will have to comply. There are also provisions to avoid evasive port calls to nearby non-EU ports However, a mechanism to account for potential developments at IMO level, if they occur and are of equal climate ambition, is built in. In addition, a provisional agreement that sets energy intensity targets of maritime fuels used on board for ships that go to or depart from EU ports is set to be adopted very soon. It is an interesting time ahead in terms of maritime regulatory implementation and the EU is taking a very ambitious stance.

A sound regulatory framework with clear and ambitious targets in place is recommended as this is crucial to providing the industry with the direction it needs to invest in technologies that will advance the decarbonization of the maritime sector and meet the climate change targets set out by the Paris Climate Accord. All those involved in the industry have a part to play. It is recommended that participants should consider:

- Provide input into regulatory development at IMO by engaging directly with the Member Governments, or through NGOs with consultative status at the IMO.
- Provide input to regional regulatory development, such as the EU, by engaging with Governments and NGOs.
- Support a well-to-wake-approach and life cycle assessment (LCA) methodology in emission regulations.
- Adopt a dual-term GHG accounting standard: 20-years global warming potentials (GWPs) alongside the accepted 100-years GWPs as ships are 20–30 years assets and environmental and climate tipping points are likely to be reached within a 20 years scope.
- Call for the removal of subsidies for fossil fuels (direct and indirect).
- Support the use of actual cargo carried in the formulation of the Carbon Intensity Index.

The public and private sector need to support each other by providing transparent information in respect to effective decarbonization and other emissions and pollution reducing (technology) measures. Accordingly, the developed countries should support the LDC governments with capacity building and funding and ensure that they can deal with all the documentation issued and are able to derive effective strategies from it.

Leverage Circular Economy Principles as a Driver for Systemic Change

The chapter "The Implications of Circular Supply Chains and the EU Digital Product Passport in Maritime Decarbonization" (Jensen et al., 2021) explains that without a competitive global circular economy, we will not be able to reach the global climate and environmental goals. The current leading sustainability measures in the maritime sector, as well as in most other industries, focus primarily on electrification and alternative fuels. However, these two paths together only address 55% of emissions. The remaining 45% comes from producing the cars, clothes, food, equipment, and other products we use every day (Ellen Macarthur Foundation, 2021).

Although circular economy business models (for example, re-manufacturing) are widespread among sectors that produce capital-intensive and durable goods (including other transportation sectors such as aircraft, aerospace, automotive and rail), they tend to be underdeveloped in the maritime industry (Wahab et al., 2018; Milios et al., 2019; Sornn-Friese et al., 2021). There are several '*semi-circular business models*' in the existing maritime industry such as sharing equipment in container logistics, chartering, reselling ships, and ship demolition (Jensen et al., 2021). However, an efficient global circular maritime sector is not yet in reach.

Service-based business models such as renting, sharing, and pay-per-use can increase the utilisation (that is, the intensity of use) of maritime products and assets, as well as their lifetime. During ship operation, numerous interventions can be initiated to enable circularity. These include onboard repairs, drydock, retrofit and refurbishing. Implementing modular designs in shipbuilding and standardising ship parts can greatly enhance the ability to refurbish, repair, upgrade, and recover components and resources when ships reach the end of their operational life. Keeping maritime products and components in use at their highest value at all times means their embodied energy is preserved for longer, and the need for new production and end-of-life treatment is reduced.

At the end-of-life phase, recycling activities help avoid even some of the hardest to abate emissions from production and incineration by bypassing the need for new material production and using less energy-intensive facilities compared to the production of virgin materials. One of the key materials in shipbuilding is steel. Steel recycling is already well established, with a largely electrified process. However, current product design, end-of-life dismantling, and scrap handling processes are polluting and degrade the quality of the steel. Increasing recycling rates would therefore require measures to prevent the downgrading of the steel stock (Önal et al., 2021). Okumus et al. (2022) have identified '*that current practices in the ship recycling yards prevent the full utilisation of the industry's recycling potential*'. Increasing recycling rates for plastics can be reached by improving uptake and quality. Key measures include improving recyclability, collection, and sorting processes, as well as reducing contamination of recycling streams and exploring the potential of chemical recycling to maintain or restore virgin quality (Aurisano et al., 2021; UNEP, 2023). There is also an untapped potential through harvesting rare-earth materials in the maritime sector, such as cerium (used for ignition in some engine types), terbium (in lighting systems and navigation equipment), and yttrium (used in such things as compressors, radar systems, and turbochargers).

Full decarbonization requires circular thinking. Whether it is in the area of ship recycling or green steel. The circular economy model has the potential to play a pivotal role in addressing climate change. The maritime industry can extract a lot of value from rethinking how it extracts, produces, consumes, uses, re-uses, upcycles, recycles and ultimately rethinks its attitude towards resources. Circular economy thinking will drive new business models that are in line with nature and climate.

It is thus recommended that the maritime industry embraces circular economy principles to capture an additional critical and extensive source of GHG emissions reduction potential and drive systemic change. Of importance are modularisation and the minimisation of toxicity of materials to be recycled. Product information will be critical and the responsibility for breaking and circularity of ships needs to clarified. Banning of last-minute cash sales of ships heading for breaking may also be part of the mix.

Boost Global Research in Maritime Decarbonization

As outlined in the chapter "Engaging the Global Research Communities in Maritime Decarbonization" (Manderbacka & Forsström, 2023), the global research communities play an important role in the efforts to decarbonize maritime transport by identifying and developing technologies and strategies that can reduce greenhouse gas emissions from shipping. This can include the development of low-carbon (transitional) but more importantly zero emission fuels, and propulsion technologies, as well as the identification of policies and regulatory measures that can encourage the adoption of these technologies. Open source is a way to spread the benefits of these technologies equally across the globe and ensure a more inclusive approach.

The role of research in decarbonizing maritime transport is to identify and develop technologies and strategies that can reduce GHG emissions from the shipping industry, inform the public and policymakers about the potential benefits and challenges of decarbonization, and assess the potential impacts of decarbonization on different stakeholders.

Substantial research and development (R&D) effort is still required and recommended to make the technologies expected to contribute to the lowering of emissions from shipping by 2050, or even better to be market ready before 2040. The technology readiness level (TRL) of the most frequently discussed alternative fuels, such as ammonia, hydrogen, methanol (bio or CCS), falls in the range of TRL 4–7, meaning somewhere between development and prototyping, where fuels are in an earlier stage of development. Reaching TRL 9 (proven in operational environment) still represents a significant leap in maturity and will take from several years to decades, depending on various factors such as availability of funding and level of collaboration. This highlights the need for large-scale testing, and validation in the real environment with full-scale pilot demonstrations. Many of these demonstration projects are run in form of partnerships. In addition, there are many research groups and initiatives focused on maritime decarbonization within universities and research institutes in the developed world. Capacity needs to be built in less developed countries.

In the report 'Mapping of Zero Emission Pilots and Demonstration Projects' (Getting to Zero Coalition, 2022), pilot and demonstration projects are described as the key to accelerate the energy transition within the maritime industry. In the same report, a comprehensive screening of current pilot projects is presented and reviewed. The number of pilot and demonstration projects has grown rapidly during 1 year. At the time of publication in March 2022, 203 projects were identified, compared to 106 projects a year earlier. The acceleration in the number of projects indicates the industry's increased interest and need to decarbonize. While these efforts are highly appreciated, the movement needs to pick up more pace to keep up with the needs of the maritime industry.

Research that covers the full field of decarbonization is needed with a specific focus on next generation technologies like fossil free fuels and other zero GHG technologies and solutions. It is recommended that research, regulation, and experimentation are driven in parallel because it is the trio of academia, governments, and business that form the key pillars of decarbonization.

Adjust to Finance Requirements in a More Sustainable Age

As elaborated in the chapter "Sustainable Finance in the Maritime Sector" (Biermans et al., 2023), sustainable finance is becoming an important factor in the maritime sector. Sustainable finance refers to financial products, services, and activities that demonstrate a positive impact on the environment and/or on societal matters. It encompasses a wide range of financial instruments (such as sustainability-linked bonds, sustainability-linked loans, green bonds, green loans and sustainable bonds) and practices that support the transition to a more sustainable (and in some cases also a more equitable) society.

Over the past decade, integrating Environment, Social and Governance (ESG) factors into investment decisions has become increasingly important. This shift has been driven by regulatory pressure and investor preferences. During that same period sustainable finance became more prevalent in various financial products. A baseline helps to understand the magnitude of such shifts and make assessments more comparable. The designation by the IMO of the year 2008 as the baseline for its emissions reduction targets was fortuitous, since it was one of the worst years for GHG emissions.

Financing the decarbonization of shipping will require a combination of both public and private funding sources. Governments and international governmental organisations, being the public sector, can and already do, play an important role in providing financial incentives, such as through providing subsidies, tax credits and other financial incentives, to encourage investment in low-carbon (transitional) and (net) zero emission technologies. In addition, these institutions, can alter conditions through new policies in ways that can benefit those companies that are quicker to decarbonize. At the same time, the transition towards a low carbon sector will require a lot of private sector investment, particularly from ship owners and operators. In addition, innovative financing models, such as green bonds and more general sustainable finance is recommended to be used broadly to play a bigger role in financing decarbonization efforts in the maritime sector.

Leasing models, pay-as-you-save and other types of financing models have been proven helpful when focused on wind propulsion (free energy) and energy efficiency technologies as these have pay back periods that can be leveraged. A key issue around newbuilds of zero emissions and primary wind vessels (Todd, 2022) is the long-term commitment from charters to give for example guaranteed 5–10 years contracts to unlock finance for those builds.

Although the maritime sector was not necessarily at the forefront of the advance of sustainable finance, various elements of the sector have embraced it all the same. A number of maritime companies have issued Green and Sustainability linked Bonds and/or have taken out sustainability-linked loans with many more considering obtaining them. In the maritime space, sustainable finance has been used to finance a range of projects that promote sustainability. Green bonds have been used to finance the construction of energy-efficient ships and the retrofitting of existing vessels with more sustainable technologies.

The data shows the very large increase in annual capital deployed in the Maritime Sustainable Finance transactions, from slightly above 2 billion USD in 2018 to more than 9.2 billion in 2021. The largest growth has been in the form of sustainability linked loans.

The EU Emissions Trading System and global carbon credit markets will impact the decarbonization of shipping. Shipping will be gradually included in Emissions Trading System (ETS), with full inclusion by 2027, leading to an increase in costs. Given this anticipated cost increase, the ETS is expected to accelerate the demand for cleaner ships and retrofits, speeding up decarbonization in the sector.

The green finance developments only accentuate the need for ship owners to change their current operations if they want to have access to finance and remain competitive in a rapidly changing market. In addition, market-based measures also generate significant revenues which can in their turn be used to speed up the green transition. As an example, part of the EU ETS revenues (around 20 million allowances) will be recycled back to the sector (EU 2023/957). Depending on the emissions allowance price, this amount will range between 1.7 up to 2 billion euros. It will be key to focus these revenues on innovative projects that accelerate the update towards net-zero climate solutions.

Concluding Thought

Be an Early-Mover: Even If You Choose Not to Be a Single Pioneer, Be Prepared to Be an Early Adopter

Decarbonization challenges business models, contractual arrangements, legal and regulatory frameworks, working conditions and current skills. No one can tackle this piecemeal or in isolation. The maritime ecosystem is critical to the global economy, but it can be fragile, as we have witnessed during the SARS-CoV-2 pandemic when fleet capacity and equipment shortages, port congestion and major crew change issues contributed to supply chain disruptions around the world. Decarbonization requires a holistic approach that addresses the challenges from different angles and is based on collaboration and learning from each other. We do not need to wait and hope for the decarbonization *silver bullet* in order to make progress now.

Without pioneers, little may happen in maritime decarbonization. Pioneer protection is therefore critical. The importance for early-movers is emphasised and discussed in the chapter "Scenario Thinking: To Build Business Advantages That Accelerate Decarbonization" (Bentham, 2023b) along with the frequently underestimated economic value of forerunners. Decarbonization also needs a nurturing space where inventors and innovators thrive, with an iterative process of development and learning in place. A space where they can also meet incumbents seeking innovation partnerships. System demonstrators are one form of creating a real-life innovation and adoption space.

We stand at a breakpoint in time in terms of investment choices that will be made by shipping companies. Some will be bold and go beyond the targets that are currently set, leading as industry role models. Others will adopt a rather 'wait and see' approach. However, what we need is to avoid that many wait too long and we collectively miss the boat, literally. The course is altered towards a climate neutral sector. It is time to get as many actors on board as possible to keep our planet liveable in which every sector needs to carry its weight, also the maritime sector.

In his TED talk, Derek Sivers,[1] author of philosophy and entrepreneurship, explained the critical role of the first follower. If we wish decarbonization to turn into a mainstream movement we need early adopters. For this reason, it is the last, but not least call in our list of calls to action and the final recommendation. Be an early-mover: even if you choose not to be a single pioneer, be prepared to be an early adopter or fast-follower.

Pioneers and fast-followers, please reflect on the recommendations and encouragements in this book, learn from the knowledge of the broad range of experts, the projects, case studies, experiences, and the success stories that they have shared. All can fuel you on your journey of transition towards a climate neutral future.

References

Aurisano, N., Weber, R., & Fantke, P. (2021). Enabling a circular economy for chemicals in plastics. *Current Opinion in Green and Sustainable Chemistry, 31*, 100513.

Bentham, J. B. (2023a). Scenario thinking and its place in maritime decarbonization. In M. Lind, W. Lehmacher, & R. Ward (Eds.), *Maritime decarbonization – Practical tools, case studies and decarbonization enablers*. Springer.

Bentham, J. B. (2023b). Scenario thinking – To build business advantages that accelerate decarbonization. In M. Lind, W. Lehmacher, & R. Ward (Eds.), *Maritime decarbonization – Practical tools, case studies and decarbonization enablers*. Springer.

Biermans, M., Bulthuis, W., Holl, T., & van Overbeeke, B. (2023). Sustainable finance in the maritime sector. In M. Lind, W. Lehmacher, & R. Ward (Eds.), *Maritime decarbonization – Practical tools, case studies and decarbonization enablers*. Springer.

Ellen Macarthur Foundation. (2021) Completing the picture – How the circular economy tackles climate change. . https://ellenmacarthurfoundation.org/completing-the-picture.

EU (2023/957). Regulation (EU) 2023/957 of the European Parliament and of the Council of 10 May 2023. Official Journal of the European Union. https://eur-lex.europa.eu/legal-content/EN/TXT/PDF/?uri=CELEX:32023R0957.

Getting to Zero Coalition. (2022). *Mapping of zero emission pilots and demonstration projects* (3rd ed.). Getting to Zero Coalition. https://www.globalmaritimeforum.org/content/2022/03/Mapping-of-zero-emission-pilots-and-demonstration-projects_third-edition.pdf

[1] https://youtu.be/V74AxCqOTvg

ILO. (2015). *Guidelines for a just transition towards environmentally sustainable economies and societies for all.* https://www.ilo.org/wcmsp5/groups/public/@ed_emp/@emp_ent/documents/publication/wcms_432859.pdf

IMO. (2020). *Reduction of GHG emissions from ships. Fourth IMO GHG study 2020 – Final report.* International Maritime Organisation. https://wwwcdn.imo.org/localresources/en/OurWork/Environment/Documents/Fourth%20IMO%20GHG%20Study%202020%20-%20Full%20report%20and%20annexes.pdf

IPCC. (2023). *AR6 synthesis report: Climate change 2023.* The Intergovernmental Panel on Climate Change (IPCC). https://www.ipcc.ch/report/sixth-assessment-report-cycle/

Jensen, H. H., Andersen, M., Dao, A., Lind, M., Pandey, V., Bapuji, G., & Turos, A. (2021). Digitalisation in a maritime circular economy. In M. Lind, M. Michaelides, R. Ward, & R. T. Watson (Eds.), *Maritime informatics – Additional perspectives and applications* (p. 17). Springer.

Kuttan, S. (2023). Decarbonizing international shipping through collaborative partnerships. In M. Lind, W. Lehmacher, & R. Ward (Eds.), *Maritime decarbonization – Practical tools, case studies and decarbonization enablers.* Springer.

Lind, M., & Lehmacher, W. (2022). *Positioning partnerships in shipping decarbonization, Article no. 92.* UNCTAD Transport and Trade Facilitation Newsletter N°95 – Third Quarter 2022. https://unctad.org/news/positioning-partnerships-shipping-decarbonization

Lind, M., & Lehmacher, W. (2023). How to get started – CDES: A new paradigm for navigating decarbonization projects. In M. Lind, W. Lehmacher, & R. Ward (Eds.), *Maritime decarbonization – Practical tools, case studies and decarbonization enablers.* Springer.

Lind, M., Lehmacher, W., Åhlén Björk, S., Haraldson, S., Pålsson, C., Penttilä, R., Tikka, K., & Watson, R. T. (2022). *Decarbonizing the maritime sector: Mobilizing coordinated action in the industry using an ecosystems approach, article no. 89.* UNCTAD Transport and Trade Facilitation Newsletter N°94 – Second Quarter 2022. https://unctad.org/news/decarbonizing-maritime-sector-mobilizing-coordinated-action-industry-using-ecosystems-approach

Lind, M., Lehmacher, W., Bentham, J. B., Kuttan, S., Tikka, K., & Watson, R. T. (2023a). Four steps to decarbonization. In M. Lind, W. Lehmacher, & R. Ward (Eds.), *Maritime decarbonization – Practical tools, case studies and decarbonization enablers.* Springer.

Lind, M., Lehmacher, W., Kuttan, S., Carson-Jackson, J., Cummins, D., van Gogh, M., & Rydbergh, T. (2023b). How to set up and run effective partnerships. In M. Lind, W. Lehmacher, & R. Ward (Eds.), *Maritime decarbonization – Practical tools, case studies and decarbonization enablers.* Springer.

Lind, M., Haraldson, S., Lehmacher, W., Raza, Z., Forsström, E., Astner, L., Bentham, J., Fu, X., Suroto, J., & Zuesongdham, P. (2023c). *Thinking the future energy model nodes of the world – A reflection framework for port development.* UNCTAD Transport and Trade Facilitation Newsletter N°97 – First Quarter 2023 Article No. 103. https://unctad.org/news/transport-newsletter-article-no-103-future-energy-nodes

Lind, M., Haraldson, S., Lehmacher, W., Raza, Z., Forsström, E., Astner, L., Bentham, J., Fu, X., Suroto, J., & Zuesongdham, P. (2023d). Towards ports as energy nodes: Strengthening micro energy systems. In M. Lind, W. Lehmacher, & R. Ward (Eds.), *Maritime decarbonization – Practical tools, case studies and decarbonization enablers.* Springer.

Manderbacka, T., & Forsström, E. (2023). Engaging the global research communities in maritime decarbonization. In M. Lind, W. Lehmacher, & R. Ward (Eds.), *Maritime decarbonization – Practical tools, case studies and decarbonization enablers.* Springer.

McKinnon, A. C. (2018). *Decarbonizing logistics: Distributing goods in a low carbon world.* Kogan Page.

McKinnon, A. (2023). Broadening the scope of decarbonization in the maritime sector. In M. Lind, W. Lehmacher, & R. Ward (Eds.), *Maritime decarbonization – Practical tools, case studies and decarbonization enablers.* Springer.

MEPC 304(72). (2018). *Initial IMO strategy on reduction of GHG emissions from ships.* Resolution MEPC.304(72) Adopted on 13 April 2018. IMO MEPC 72/17/Add.1 Annex 11. https://

wwwcdn.imo.org/localresources/en/KnowledgeCentre/IndexofIMOResolutions/MEPCDocuments/MEPC.304(72).pdf
MEPC 79 /INF 21. (2022, October 7). *Reduction of GHG emissions from ships – Wind propulsion*. Paper submitted to MEPC by Finland, France, Saudi Arabia, Solomon Islands, Spain, Union of Comoros, RINA, International Windship Association. https://www.wind-ship.org/wp-content/uploads/2022/10/MEPC-79-INF.21-Wind-Propulsion-Finland-France-Saudi-Ar....pdf
Milios, L., Beqiri, B., Whalen, K. A., & Jelonek, S. H. (2019). Sailing towards a circular economy: Conditions for increased reuse and remanufacturing in the Scandinavian maritime sector. *Journal of Cleaner Production, 225*, 227–235.
MMKMCZCS. (2022). *Maritime decarbonization strategy 2022 by the Mærsk Mc-Kinney Møller Center for Zero Carbon Shipping*. https://www.zerocarbonshipping.com/publications/maritime-decarbonization-strategy/
National Academies of Sciences, Engineering, and Medicine (NASEM). (2022). *Oil in the sea IV: Inputs, fates, and effects*. https://nap.nationalacademies.org/catalog/26410/oil-in-the-sea-iv-inputs-fates-and-effects
Okumus, D., Gunbeyaz, S. A., Kurt, R. E., & Turan, O. (2022). Towards a circular maritime industry: Identifying strategy and technology solutions. *Journal of Cleaner Production*.
Önal, M., Neşer, G., & Gürsel, K. T. (2021). Environmental impacts of steel ship hulls building and recycling by life cycle assessment (LCA). *Ships and Offshore Structures, 16*(10), 1061–1066.
Pålsson, C., & Rydbergh, T. (2023). The extent of decarbonization in the global shipping fleet. In M. Lind, W. Lehmacher, & R. Ward (Eds.), *Maritime decarbonization – Practical tools, case studies and decarbonization enablers*. Springer.
Petersen, M., & Renken, K. (2023). Adopting a value chain focus to tackle decarbonization. In M. Lind, W. Lehmacher, & R. Ward (Eds.), *Maritime decarbonization – Practical tools, case studies and decarbonization enablers*. Springer.
Platten, G., Selwyn, M., Vicente, H., & Cotton, S. (2023). Ensuring seafarers are at the heart of decarbonization action. In M. Lind, W. Lehmacher, & R. Ward (Eds.), *Maritime decarbonization – Practical tools, case studies and decarbonization enablers*. Springer.
Raza, Z., & Singh, S. (2023). Decarbonizing the maritime industry – Current environmental targets and potential outcomes. In M. Lind, W. Lehmacher, & R. Ward (Eds.), *Maritime decarbonization – Practical tools, case studies and decarbonization enablers*. Springer.
Schipper, L., & Marie, C. (1999). *Transport and CO_2 emissions*. World Bank.
Sims, R., et al. (2014). *Transport in climate change 2014: Mitigation of climate change. Contribution of working group III to the fifth assessment report of the intergovernmental panel on climate change*. Cambridge University Press.
Sornn-Friese, H., Roth, E., Sofev, P., Kaiser, B., Sinding, K., Vágsheyg, H., & Stuer-Lauridsen, F. T. (2021). *Creating circular economy clusters for sustainable ship recycling in Denmark*. CBS Maritime.
Tikka, K., & Esau, S. (2023a). Identifying the key decarbonization enablers. In M. Lind, W. Lehmacher, & R. Ward (Eds.), *Maritime decarbonization - Practical Tools, Case Studies and Decarbonization Enablers*. Springer.
Tikka, K., & Esau, S. (2023b). Securing global alignment in regulations related to decarbonization. In M. Lind, W. Lehmacher, & R. Ward (Eds.), *Maritime decarbonization – Practical tools, case studies and decarbonization enablers*. Springer.
Todd, S. (2022). *French shippers drive development of modern cargo-carrying sailing ships, 5/4-2022*. The Loadstar. https://theloadstar.com/french-shippers-drive-development-of-modern-cargo-carrying-sailing-ships/
UN Global Compact. (2022). *Think Lab business brief on just transition*. https://unglobalcompact.org/take-action/think-labs/just-transition
UNCTAD. (2022). *Review of maritime transport 2022: Navigating stormy waters*. United Nations Publications.
UNEP. (2023). *Chemicals in plastics: A technical report*. United Nations Environment Programme and Secretariat of the Basel, Rotterdam and Stockholm Conventions.

UNFCCC. (2022). *Sharm el-Sheikh implementation plan*. https://unfccc.int/sites/default/files/resource/cop27_auv_2_cover%20decision.pdf

Wahab, A. D., Blanco-Davi, E., Ariffin, A. K., & Wang, J. (2018). A review on the applicability of remanufacturing in extending the life cycle of marine or offshore components and structures. *Ocean Engineering, 169*, 125–133.

Wang, X.-T., Liu, H., Lv, Z.-F., Deng, F.-Y., Xu, H.-L., Qi, L.-J., Shi, M.-S., Zhao, J.-C., Zheng, S.-X., Man, H.-Y., & He, K.-B. (2021). Trade-linked shipping CO_2 emissions. *Nature Climate Change, 11*, 945–951. https://doi.org/10.1038/s41558-021-01176-6

The Destination: A Vision of a Climate Neutral Future

Wolfgang Lehmacher, Mikael Lind, Lars Jensen, and Louise De Tremerie

Target Audience

This is the closing chapter of the Maritime Decarbonization book and is for everyone that wishes to contribute to achieving a climate neutral near future. The chapter provides a glance on the state of decarbonization and green transition today, how we can decarbonize and work towards a zero greenhouse gas (GHG) emissions maritime sector and what it could look like.

Key Takeaway Messages

Key messages from this chapter:

- Setting the goal for a climate neutral maritime sector by mid-century is possible, but it will require the strong will and decisive action by the key actors.

W. Lehmacher (✉)
Independent Supply Chain Expert, Hong Kong, China
e-mail: w.lehmacher@gmail.com

M. Lind
Research Institutes of Sweden (RISE), Gothenburg, Sweden

Chalmers University of Technology, Gothenburg, Sweden
e-mail: mikael@realsearchers.com

L. Jensen
Vespucci Maritime, Copenhagen, Denmark
e-mail: lars.jensen@vespucci-maritime.com

L. De Tremerie
European Parliament, Brussels, Belgium
e-mail: louise.detremerie@europarl.europa.eu

M. Lind et al. (eds.), *Maritime Decarbonization*,
https://doi.org/10.1007/978-3-031-39936-7_34

- Reaching a climate neutral future requires system-thinking, in which the key role of the maritime sector and its significant environmental footprint must be recognised.
- Regulations can be key drivers to steer the market towards a climate neutral future, but the industry will have to deliver on the change.
- Innovation is critical for decarbonization and the green transition towards net zero fuels and technologies.
- Volatility requires flexibility and is something to prepare for with determination.
- Broader and deeper collaboration is paramount.
- Decarbonization and the green transition of the sector must be human-centric with respect to the ecological boundaries that we are stressing currently.

Introduction

A lot of different and sometimes diverging views have been expressed in the collection of essays in this book. Now, some may ask themselves what the climate neutral future that we are building for the middle of the century will look like? It would be too easy to just map out an ideal state. Instead, it appears more helpful to select and discuss some of the specific drivers that are likely to characterise that future state.

That we are in trouble cannot be ignored. Oxford Economics concludes that 2.2 °C of warming by 2050 has the potential to reduce global gross domestic product (GDP) by up to 20% and warming of up to 5 °C by 2100 would lead to economic annihilation, consistent with scientific research on mass extinction thresholds.[1] What has created today's standard of living for many and what has alleviated millions out of poverty has also put the future of humanity as a whole at jeopardy. We have been great in value creation but failed miserably in value preservation and more importantly the preservation of the ecosystem that allows such value creation and us to exist. We take from nature and hardly give back. We damage. We hardly preserve, we sometimes repair. We destroy. We hardly build back. This is not sustainable and we are already in certain risk zones for some of our planetary boundaries which leads to irreversible changes, such as climate change and biodiversity loss, with other boundaries moving towards the zones of increasing risk such as ocean acidification. These planetary boundaries represent a *"safe operating space for humanity"* (Rockström et al., 2009) and human activity is putting us on a path towards overshooting them. We need to put more effort in to protecting nature and the climate and factor the cost into our economic activities. We need to balance economic and societal capital creation in which we need to rethink growth within our planetary boundaries. Rethinking growth will have us rethink our business models, in which it can be challenging to address concepts of profitability in the light of internalising external resource costs and the damage being caused.

[1] https://www.oxfordeconomics.com/resource/the-global-economic-costs-of-climate-inaction/

Fortunately, while this is necessary it is also do-able, as human problem-solving ability seems fairly close to limitless.

We are good in focussed commercial efforts but fall short in managing public goods (Hoffmann, 2022). This, because it is much easier to design processes and products irrespective of their impact on the environment and climate than it is to understand and work through system effects within a world of interrelated, interconnected and interdependent systems. This book calls for and provides examples of a holistic approach to ensuring human wellbeing in the long-term. In this book, we consider societal progress and human well-being as the ultimate purpose of economic progress and capital creation, which is dependent on a healthy and liveable planet. This way of thinking manifests itself, for example, in our *CDES* model which stands for collaboration and digitalisation for economic and societal capital creation (Lind et al., 2022; Lind & Lehmacher, 2023). Societal progress and human wellbeing as the purpose and goal of all human activity within a healthy and liveable planet seems, for us, to be a good start, also for thinking about and planning for decarbonizing and the green transition of the maritime industry. We need technological pioneers but even more so, we need pioneers in responsible behaviour and ultimately many early adopters to create movements for balanced outputs. Such as a climate neutral future. In the following we have identified some properties that we feel should characterise the transition towards a climate neutral maritime sector.

A System-Oriented Transition

The world is a system of interrelated systems; even more so in future. What does, but also what does not happen, within one system can affect some other systems. Systems may be disrupted or actors in other systems may be hindered and unable to execute their plans to deliver on their needs and aspirations. The maritime ecosystem is self-organised and conducted with autonomous actors that align in relation to each other (Lind et al., 2021a). The dependency across marine fuels, ship engines, and ships is a good example. Ships built for engines powered by alternative fuels require that those fuels are available and that the supply matches demand. Which is not the case today. Hence, system-orientation implies coordination and alignment across industries or systems. Driving decarbonization across the maritime industry requires work and collaboration across marine fuel, engine, and shipbuilding supply chains, and shipowners, charterers, and ship operators need to be able to buy and use the resultant clean ships. Ideally, they signal or commit demand upfront as an incentive for the energy sector to make the necessary investments. In a net zero GHG emissions maritime sector, the actors in the decarbonization ecosystem will have established platforms and mechanisms that allow the exchange of plans to ensure that supply matches demand.

Scenario thinking (Bentham, 2023) is a powerful tool to frame a discussion, as it also reveals the interdependencies between subsystems, and develops pathways towards a point far out in our future. This forms the basis for projecting the development of different drivers at waypoints along the timeline, such as the advancement of maturity of technologies. This can help companies and governments to prioritise their actions and their investments.

We all are citizens in a world in which the actions of one community can affect the wellbeing of other communities. System-thinking should come with a collective global responsibility for the actions we undertake or refuse to undertake. Our political leaders should assume this role and responsibility as it requires time and effort to understand the systemic relations across the decarbonization ecosystem and make investments that are challenging for many individuals and smaller organisations to afford. We cannot leave the problem-solving to future generations because the ecological and climate future can only be fixed today. One of the roles of the public sector is to undertake activities that individuals or organisations cannot undertake or which provide public goods for which pure commercial interests would often not, due to its capitalist nature, cater for. The private sector, and in particular global industries like shipping, can build bridges across the globe and explain and raise awareness about, for example, the consequences—positive or negative, of certain decisions in one system for other systems which affects them as global actors.

Smart and Climate Ambitious Regulations for the Transition

Regulations can and should play a key role in setting the maritime sector on a path towards climate neutrality, especially on a global level but also on a regional level. Most regulations are the outcome of long negotiation processes, in which some find the level of climate ambition not going far enough, while for others it may go too far. In the context of climate change, increased regulations are particularly necessary as the sector does not naturally deliver on reducing its GHG emissions. However, the industry plays a key role in steering progress and could move boldly beyond (non)-existing regulations. Progress and regulation should form enforcing catalysts. Regulation should set dedicated targets that give clarity to the sector and can create a conducive environment for innovation and ensure that innovations are not harmful to mankind.

In a net zero GHG emission future, we would see that governments have introduced climate effective and supporting regulations in response to developments that appeared useful or got traction after pioneers took the initiative, for example, in form of decisions resulting in investments in clean products and practices. Regulation has also made action inevitable or more preferable and provided the necessary incentives for action towards decarbonization and the green transition. In setting clear targets, regulation can reduce uncertainty and provide predictability for investments, reducing risks and thus investment costs.

Recently we have seen a number of regulations designed to reduce emissions in shipping. The European Union (EU) has officially adopted and published its new law in May 2023 on the inclusion of the maritime shipping sector in the existing EU

Emissions Trading System (ETS). The EU ETS is a key climate instrument that the EU has had in place since 2005 to reduce GHG emissions in heavy polluting sectors such as the energy and manufacturing industries. It is a regulative mechanism and not a prescriptive instrument and is characterised by a 'cap and trade' system of emission allowances (European Commisison, 2023). In other words, setting a price on carbon emissions. In addition, the EU is close to adopting regulations that will set targets on the energy intensity of the fuels used in maritime vessels as well as alternative fuel mandates at the ports side. The inclusion of the maritime sector in the EU ETS, fuel targets and infrastructure requirements send an important signal to the sector that the EU is moving towards delivering on its climate ambition as set out in its Green Deal (European Commission, 2019).

These regulations are pragmatic, as governments set the framework, but allow specific solutions and innovation to come from industry and should be supported. The role of the public sector, including international organisations such as the International Maritime Organization (IMO), is to introduce clear and climate effective frameworks that incentivise actors to comply or if they do not, make them suffer penalties. Such frameworks are a generative force for innovation and adaptation of technologies, products and practices that will help us move towards a climate neutral future.

Now and in a net zero emissions future, policymakers define the 'what' and leave room for the 'how'; they set ambitious targets but do not determine how these targets should be reached. Finding innovative solutions is by and large the role of the private sector and also research institutions. Of course, there are areas where the public sector prevails, for example, with government-run port authorities or in public procurement. Inclusive governments consult experts in business, research, civil society, etc., and participate in private public partnerships to help fill gaps which the private sector alone cannot close. The public sector can also finance activities that support decarbonization, such as research in fossil-free fuels, generating technological advances as a public good that will benefit all, including private sector players and investors. Consultations and involvement also allow policy-makers to decide where they have to regulate to help accelerate adoption or limit harm (Lind & Lehmacher, 2022).

The continuous monitoring of emission reducing technology developments and regular consultations of national and global experts and stakeholders are a necessity to make appropriate policy decisions or finetune where necessary. In the case of decarbonization solutions that are in their infancy, governments should stay informed through consultations with the relevant stakeholders to understand the level of opportunity and threat residing in the technologies and their application, but also mirroring safety and inclusiveness in policies that drive innovation and adoption. In the case of mature technologies and applications, policy-makers can mitigate risks through policies crafted with the support of relevant stakeholders. Crafting effective national policies requires coordination among stakeholders in the ecosystem.

Meanwhile, for decarbonization solutions emerging outside a nation and for national developments with global reach and implications, governments should seek international involvement and alignment to follow proof-of-concept trials to identify threats and encourage pilot opportunities as a foundation for fast adaptation and adoption, but more importantly to ensure that as many companies as possible can benefit from the decarbonization technology. We should strive for as much collaboration as possible and sharing technology is part of that.

It is important to put climate effective regulations on the table on a global scale, as ill-crafted policies may even hamper effective decarbonization efforts, negatively impact a country's competitive position or exclude nationally developed technologies and applications from participating in the global market where international alignment, standards and compatibility are common prerequisites. It is important to monitor and assess existing (and future) policies, where analysis and consultations with experts and stakeholders are key. Intergovernmental organisations like the IMO or other international organisations are useful spaces for exchange, learning, and collaboration.

Shipping empowers trade but is also restricted by the rules of maritime trade. Maritime trade is a web of complex contractual relationships, which has evolved through a process of gradual adaptation to changing needs, assisted by the flexibility of common (predominantly, English) law and underpinned by the principles of freedom of navigation, freedom of contract and party autonomy. This has been achieved within a very light regulatory framework. Litigation has played a major role in defining and clarifying notions in the process of the evolution of maritime law. It is conceptually possible to re-design maritime trade so that it resembles a regulated industry. However, that will require a wholesale repudiation of the existing contractual architecture, a series of new international conventions, and a new international organisation to regulate commodities trading and port activities, which are currently not subject to international uniformity; this will cause considerable dislocation. (Zografakis et al., 2023).

An Innovation-Driven Transition

Reaching net zero GHG emissions requires technologies that are at their very first development steps or have simply not yet been invented. But that does not mean that we should wait to act. On the contrary, we should accelerate the development of what is needed. While technology is critical, we also need innovative regulation and new business models that make clean shipping work for everyone. Therefore, innovation plays an important role in the climate neutral future. Innovation finds its origin in academia, start-ups and large corporates; the latter often struggle with change and innovation and collaborate with the former parties to achieve their innovation ambitions. A zero emissions future results from a close collaboration across these systems.

Collaboration between traditional industry actors and startups is on the rise and maritime testbeds and accelerators have emerged in the maritime industry (Kuttan, 2023). Inmarsat, Cargotec, Shell, HHLA and Wärtsilä launched the Trade &

Transport Impact Program[2] in search for mature startups. Singapore's shipping company, Eastern Pacific Shipping (EPS), teamed up with investor and accelerator Techstars to create an accelerator space.

Innovation efforts are also picking up in ports. Some examples are port and maritime accelerators, such as PortXL,[3] which originated in the Port of Rotterdam, have also surfaced in the ports of Singapore and Antwerp. New data sharing platforms empowering third-party developers to build new applications associated to ports,[4] connecting local information sharing communities to empower them to better respond to the needs of global supply chains (Lehmacher et al., 2021). In physical LivingLab environments, such as the one in the Port of Singapore,[5] service providers experiment and demonstrate solutions in authentic settings. This development is also empowered by the shipper-driven terminal-centric distributed Virtual Watch Tower (VWT) network initiative (Lind et al., 2023), launched in the beginning of 2023, that places a global focus on the collaborative management of disruptions in end-to-end supply chains.[6] Hackathons, in different setups, have also become more prevalent within the maritime sector during the last 5 years.[7] A hackathon is a popup space, offering a broader, more concentrated and probably more diverse participation in an innovation effort, focused on a number of specific use cases, often framed as challenges. The hackathon model is very effective in driving innovation and adoption because, besides yielding great ideas, networked accelerators help to capitalise on the effort and facilitate longer-term collaboration to truly innovate and produce concrete results and returns for all contributors.

Innovations are enabling simultaneously to reduce costs and the impact of the maritime industry on the environment and climate, as in the case of the joint venture between Hamburger Hafen and Logistik AG (HHLA) with HyperloopTT, a 'crowd-powered' company and innovator by design.[8] The goal of this collaborative innovation (Lind et al., 2021b) is to move containers through a vacuum tube, connecting ports with their hinterland in a new way, reducing time and carbon emissions. In Sweden, there are also initiatives such as I.Hamn focusing on the sustainable port as a network node.[9] For I.Hamn the ambition is to allow more than 50 ports in Sweden to join forces to support each other on their way towards a more sustainable and resilient transport future. Another great example of economic and environmental co-benefits is Cubex Global,[10] a digital marketplace selling unused space in shipping

---

[2] www.wartsila.com/media/news/14-08-2019-wartsila-turns-to-startups-to-help-solve-some-of-the-biggest-problems-in-the-maritime-industry

[3] portxl.org

[4] intelligentcargosystems.com/pco#guides

[5] www.mpa.gov.sg/web/portal/home/maritime-companies/research-development/MPA-Living-Lab

[6] www.virtualwatchtower.org

[7] fathom.world/the-rise-of-the-hackathons/

[8] www.hbs.edu/faculty/Pages/item.aspx?num=52627

[9] www.ri.se/en/our-stories/the-port-a-hub-for-sustainable-transports

[10] www.weforum.org/agenda/2020/03/decarbonizing-shipping-without-spending-billions/

containers, developed in the context of the World Economic Forum's UpLink Innovation Challenge.[11] Considering that every year, 100 million containers cross the ocean almost empty, accounting for 280 million tons of carbon emissions and costing $25 billion a year in lost revenue, this digital solution allows an ocean-friendly model for shipping.

In addition, many opportunities are ahead of us in the development of net zero fuels and supporting infrastructure. Where a ship could be seen not only as a carrier and user of such fuels, but maybe in a further future even as a producer of such fuels.

A Multi-facetted Transition

Expecting that we can harmonise the different approaches across the world and reach a similar stage of development everywhere is fanciful. There is geography, the different business models in shipping, and the type of trade, volumes and length of shipping routes to consider. Each combination will require different decarbonization approaches, solutions, and technologies due to differing circumstances. Scandinavia, a region with a lot of biomass, might leverage biofuels as a transitional fuel for shortsea shipping. But this may be an exception due to its conflict with food production or certification issues as highlighted in the chapter on the use of biofuels. Meanwhile, North Africa is well positioned for using solar energy for green hydrogen production. Multiplicity has emerged as a critical component for decarbonization in shipping: multi-fuels, multi-fuel ship engines, and flexible operational models are core to reconfiguring the fragmented landscape of the maritime industry and the volatile nature of the world. Shipping of wet and dry bulk, ferry and cruise, RoRo and RoPax, container and cars, as well as special cargo are all driven by a different business logic and the more than 5500 ports in the world undertake different roles in these trades whether they are feeder or larger hub ports. In such an environment flexibility turns out to be an important risk mitigator.

In a net zero GHG emissions future of shipping some parts of the maritime ecosystem will have converged to ease operational fragmentation and disruptions. In particular the convergence of fuels and law. The world at some point may have invested heavily in preparations to deal with a diverse set of continuously changing situations introducing a high level of flexibility. In particular, inland waterway and short sea shipping will run on a range of power sources. The maritime industry will need flexible strategies that not only work across the globe but also across different probable futures. Modularity and upgradability are features of next generation solutions. However, we should make sure that our eye remains on the goal of climate neutrality by mid-century and the set of collective measures we employ should steer us in that direction.

[11] uplink.weforum.org/uplink/s/uplink-issue/a002o00000vOm4fAAC/restoring-protecting-and-investing-in-the-ocean

An Incentives-Based Transition

Achieving a net zero emissions future requires the alignment of incentives. Throughout centuries, time and again it has been shown that innovation as well as large-scale structural change usual is intimately linked to financial gains. Political attempts to change structural behaviour often fall short if the effort is misaligned with financial gains. Conversely, if financial gains are aligned with political aims success is almost inevitable. This means that decarbonization needs to generate financial returns; this requires that certain preconditions are fulfilled. However, political aims should not only look at financial gains as societal value and the remediation of our planet are crucial. It is important to also stress that not acting on climate change will result in financial loss in the end.

Regulators should not prescribe specific technological solutions, but instead provide a climate-effective regulatory framework with clear targets and a financially conducive environment. The alignment can, or will, be achieved through measures that take multiple angles.

Firstly, regulators should craft regulations that make high emissions solutions more expensive than non-fossil-fuel-based green alternatives. This will provide a strong incentive. The EU is leading the way in this, where it also partly takes into account emissions discharged in non-EU waters. One challenge is that shipping is a global industry and it is unlikely that all nations will have an aligned approach to such regulation. Misalignment, or ineffective enforcement, will lead to loopholes which will certainly be exploited. Not that such regulation will be ineffective, but it will not be sufficient in itself. It is therefore important to work on a global climate-effective market-based measure that applies across the globe.

A second push will result from government supported innovation facilitating lower-cost green options. This opens up financial advantages for green adoption irrespective of regulations based on a cost-efficiency perspective.

The third critical element lies beyond the maritime sector. It is about the shift away from a fossil fuel-based economy and the necessary production of alternative fuels and sources of power. This is of relevance not only to the maritime sector but all modes of transport and industry. A green future can only be accomplished when conditions favour the production of sufficient quantities of fossil-free fuels. Linking this back to the financial argument, such a development will only get sufficient momentum once it is foreseeable that the cost of such fuels is competitive with the traditional alternatives. Or if an alternative business case can be created.

The fourth pre-requisite is predictability for projects. Decarbonization requires not only investment in ships but also the infrastructure for fossil-free fuels to be provided by ports and terminals. Building such infrastructure will take time. There is possibly something to be learned from China that succeeded in building the world's largest high-speed rail network in about a decade. A significant shift towards the necessary green investments will only occur once financial returns are predictable.

In essence this all means that in order to reach a net zero emission future the alignment of financial incentives is critical. Failure to align with financial incentives will delay, or could prevent, such a future. Alignment, largely achieved through supportive regulation, will leave it to the very effective market forces to drive the necessary investments and changes in the industry and the maritime decarbonization ecosystem to enable the goal to be reached.

A Human-Centric Transition

A climate neutral world comes through us and for us. Despite all the technological development, it is people that drive progress and make things happen. Therefore, a net zero fossil fuel future starts and is only achievable with people that wish to engage in the transition. Decarbonization strategies, roadmaps, and operating plans need to be human-centric, also with an emphasis on fair and safe working conditions for those working in the sector. Decarbonization of shipping involves people, people that represent cargo-owners, forwarders, port authorities, terminal operators, charterers and shipping companies, energy and technology companies, arbitrators, government agencies and international organisations, and others. It is also people that make laws, craft policies, and enforce them. It is people that make decisions on how transport is organised, what vehicles are used and what fuel. It is people that work on or oversee the operation of ships, seafarers, machinists, but also terminals, trucks, trains, and dockers. All these people need to be trained and (re)skilled for the climate net zero future.

Furthermore, people need to be convinced that a low carbon economy for the transition is needed and is feasible and the aim is to move towards a climate neutral sector. That sustainable behaviour and the protection of nature, biodiversity, and climate, which constitutes the ecosystem which we need to exist, is in our own interest. If we cannot make decarbonization mainstream in the maritime decarbonization ecosystem we cannot create a movement, and decarbonization will simply not happen. Governments and companies need to involve and engage people across organisations and along value chains (Petersen & Renken, 2023). People need to be encouraged to support the decarbonization effort, and in turn people in organisations should not stop explaining to the leadership that the world needs a change in course and that we need to embed decarbonization into strategies and operational decision-making. Parents need to teach their children the values and principles of nature and its importance for our survival. Children need to constantly remind their parents that it is they that will live in the world of the future, and that the way we operate today is not sustainable. It is now that we need to act to ensure a liveable future for coming generations.

Capital creation starts with us. Responsible economic capital creation starts with customers and consumers and their push for clean and fairer products. In fact, the decarbonization process could be triggered by demand signals, by the people that make cargo transport procurement decisions.

Although hard to achieve, behavioural change is the very starting point of decarbonization. Changes in behaviour have immediate impact. '[All] the major national and international bodies that focus on decarbonization issues, within and beyond the maritime sector, recognise the critical role of energy efficiency in achieving decarbonization goals. The International Energy Agency (IEA) thus refers to energy efficiency as the *first fuel of all energy transitions*: it is the *fuel you do not have to use—and in terms of supply, it is abundantly available and cheap to extract* (IEA, 2019)' (Vanderbilt, 2023). This may be the lowest-hanging fruit and efficiency is central to economic behaviour and should be part of every business' DNA.

Closing Thoughts

This last chapter has been about visioning. All development on planet Earth has its roots in human creativity and imagination. They are the driver of progress and change. Visioning for decarbonization success might therefore be one of the first logical practical steps in the decarbonization process. A step to be accomplished by every stakeholder in the maritime decarbonization ecosystem. A step informed by a set of scenarios. Such an exercise across the ecosystem will provide direction to the decarbonization movement as this helps to converge views. How does success look like to each stakeholder of the maritime value chain? How should the maritime decarbonization ecosystem and the maritime industry look like once the decarbonization ambition has been reached? Currently we have multiple stakeholders looking at multiple visions which is not conducive to the required system change. Humanity has proven again and again that we can work together and find solutions that work for all. Collaborative capabilities are embedded in our natural social fabric.

The decarbonization movement in the maritime industry has started. There are many examples in this book that provide indicators of a maritime industry in motion aiming for different decarbonization enablers (Tikka & Esau, 2023). We observe that the maritime industry wants to change, and the advances in thinking and the development of enablers allow the actors to accelerate their efforts. This requires that the actors have the necessary courage to open up, and that they network, and engage in partnerships.

Our goal has been that this book becomes a support to those that wish to solve the conundrum of driving economic growth without creating harmful climate and environmental consequences. Time will tell whether our ambition turns into such a future. Many experts think that we are running out of time. Therefore, we reiterate Christiana Figueres' quote which we had placed at the beginning of our book. '*If we wait until nature forces us, the cost will be astronomical.*' Her clear message is that we need to act, and more importantly that we need to act NOW!

References

Bentham, J. B. (2023). Scenario thinking and its place in maritime decarbonization. In M. Lind, W. Lehmacher, & R. Ward (Eds.), *Maritime decarbonization – Practical tools, case studies and decarbonization enablers*. Springer.

European Commisison. (2023). *EU emission trading system (EU ETS)*. https://climate.ec.europa.eu/eu-action/eu-emissions-trading-system-eu-ets_en#documentation

European Commission. (2019). *Communication from the commission: The European green deal, COM(2019) 640 final.*

Hoffmann, J. (2022). *The end of the 2020–2022 supply chain crisis, and what we need to learn for the next one(s)*. LinkedIn article. Accessed May 18, 2023, from https://www.linkedin.com/pulse/end-2020-2022-supply-chain-crisis-what-we-need-learn-next-hoffmann%3FtrackingId=fBkyKls7S3Ky%252BNW5gv8KGA%253D%253D/?trackingId=fBkyKls7S3Ky%2BNW5gv8KGA%3D%3D

IEA. (2019). *Energy efficiency is the first fuel, and demand for it needs to grow*. IEA. https://www.iea.org/commentaries/energy-efficiency-is-the-first-fuel-and-demand-for-it-needs-to-grow

Kuttan, S. (2023). Partnerships in action – Decarbonizing international shipping through collaborative partnerships. In M. Lind, W. Lehmacher, & R. Ward (Eds.), *Maritime decarbonization – Practical tools, case studies and decarbonization enablers*. Springer.

Lehmacher, W., Lind, M., van Gogh, M., Becha, H., Kouwenhoven, N., Lund, E., Mulder, H., Simha, A., Clary, F., Renz, M., & Murphy, N. (2021). Responding to humanitarian and global concerns with digitally enabled supply chain visibility. In M. Lind, M. Michaelides, R. Ward, & R. T. Watson (Eds.), *Maritime informatics: Additional perspectives and applications*. Springer.

Lind, M., & Lehmacher, W. (2022). *TradeTech has huge potential to boost trade – Here's what policy-makers should know*. https://www.weforum.org/agenda/2022/04/4-ways-tradetech-policy-regulation/

Lind, M., & Lehmacher, W. (2023). How to get started – CDES: A new paradigm for navigating decarbonization projects. In M. Lind, W. Lehmacher, & R. Ward (Eds.), *Maritime decarbonization – Practical tools, case studies and decarbonization enablers*. Springer.

Lind, M., Michaelides, M., Ward, R., & Watson, R. T. (Eds.). (2021a). *Maritime informatics*. Springer.

Lind, M., Lehmacher, W., Knäpper, I., van Gogh, M., Maaouni, T., Benhayoun, J., Ashikhmin, D., Lahmar, H., & Sigal, M. (2021b) *Collaborative innovation within the maritime sector: The path to grow back better*. Article no. 73 [UNCTAD transport and trade facilitation newsletter N°89 – First quarter 2021]. https://unctad.org/news/collaborative-innovation-within-maritime-sector-path-grow-back-better

Lind, M., Lehmacher, W., & Watson, R. T. (2022). *Collaboration and digitalization for balanced economic and societal capital creation by shipping*. Article no. 96 [UNCTAD transport and trade facilitation newsletter N°96 – Fourth quarter 2022]. https://unctad.org/news/transport-newsletter-article-no-96-fourth-quarter-2022

Lind, M., Lehmacher, W., Fu, X., Lind, K., Yin, X. F., Bolinder, M., Hagerstrand-Avall, B., Hallam, S., Stenhammar, A., & Suroto, J. (2023). *Managing pain points in end-to-end supply chains – How a new networked solution may revolutionize risk management, 20/4-2023*. The Maritime Executive. https://maritime-executive.com/editorials/managing-pain-points-in-end-to-end-supply-chains

Petersen, M., & Renken, K. (2023). Adopting a value chain focus to tackle decarbonization. In M. Lind, W. Lehmacher, & R. Ward (Eds.), *Maritime decarbonization – Practical tools, case studies and decarbonization enablers*. Springer.

Rockström, J., Steffen, W., Noone, K., Persson, Å., Chapin, F. S., Lambin, E. F., et al. (2009). A safe operating space for humanity. *Nature, 461*(7263), 472–475. https://doi.org/10.1038/461472a

Tikka, K., & Esau, S. (2023). Identifying the key decarbonization enablers. In M. Lind, W. Lehmacher, & R. Ward (Eds.), *Maritime decarbonization – Practical tools, case studies and decarbonization enablers*. Springer.

Vanderbilt. (2023). *Pathways to net-zero 2050 in the North American Marine Shipping Industry: Optimizing technology and operations to achieve emission reductions – A report of the Blue Sky Maritime Coalition prepared for Blue Sky Maritime Coalition, May 2023, Vanderbilt University climate change initiative*. https://www.bluesky-maritime.org/_files/ugd/8ed502_e55355faefbb424f8a17a3889694d947.pdf

Zografakis, H., Henderson, N., Rigden, G. A., Mace-Kokota, D., & Turner, J. (2023). The limited role of the IMO, and why contracts are the lifeblood of international maritime trade. In M. Lind, W. Lehmacher, & R. Ward (Eds.), *Maritime decarbonization – Practical tools, case studies and decarbonization enablers*. Springer.

MIX
Papier aus verantwortungsvollen Quellen
Paper from responsible sources
FSC® C105338

If you have any concerns about our products,
you can contact us on
ProductSafety@springernature.com

In case Publisher is established outside the EU,
the EU authorized representative is:
Springer Nature Customer Service Center GmbH
Europaplatz 3, 69115 Heidelberg, Germany

Printed by Libri Plureos GmbH
in Hamburg, Germany